Municipal Management Series

Managing
Human
Services

International City Management Association

The International City Management Association is the professional and educational organization for chief appointed management executives in local government. The purposes of ICMA are to strengthen the quality of urban government through professional management and to develop and disseminate new approaches to management through training programs, information services, and publications.

Managers, carrying a wide range of titles, serve cities, towns, counties, and councils of governments in all parts of the United States and Canada. These managers serve at the direction of elected councils and governing boards. ICMA serves these managers and local governments through many programs that aim at improving the manager's professional competence and strengthening the quality of all local governments.

The International City Management Association was founded in 1914; adopted its City Management Code of Ethics in 1924; and established its Institute for Training in Municipal Administration in 1934. The Institute, in turn, provided the basis for the Municipal Management Series, generally termed the "ICMA Green Books." ICMA's interests and activities include public management education; standards of ethics for members; the *Municipal Year Book* and other data services; urban research; and newsletters, a monthly magazine, *Public Management,* and other publications. ICMA's efforts for the improvement of local government management—as represented by this book —are offered for all local governments and educational institutions.

Municipal Management Series

Managing Human Services

Editors

Published for the
Institute for Training in
Municipal Administration

Wayne F. Anderson
U.S. Advisory Commission on
Intergovernmental Relations

By the
International
City
Management
Association

Bernard J. Frieden
Massachusetts Institute
of Technology

Michael J. Murphy
International City
Management Association

Municipal Management Series

David S. Arnold Editor

Managing Human Services

Community Health Services

Developing the Municipal Organization

Effective Supervisory Practices

Local Government Personnel Administration

Local Government Police Management

Management Policies in Local Government Finance

Managing Municipal Leisure Services

Managing the Modern City

Municipal Fire Administration

Policy Analysis in Local Government

Principles and Practice of Urban Planning

Public Relations in Local Government

Small Cities Management Training Program

Urban Public Works Administration

Library of Congress Cataloging in Publication Data

Main entry under title:
Managing human services.

   (Municipal management series)
   Bibliography: p.
   Includes index.
   1. Municipal government—United States.
2. Economic assistance, Domestic—United States.
3. United States—Social conditions. I. Anderson,
Wayne F., 1924–   II. Frieden, Bernard J., 1930–
III. Murphy, Michael J., 1934–   IV. Institute for
Training in Municipal Administration.   V. Series.
JS341.M36   352.073   77-2464
ISBN 0-87326-017-1

Printed in the United States of America.

Foreword

With the publication of this book, *Managing Human Services,* the International City Management Association is adding an entirely new title to the familiar list of publications in its "Green Book" Municipal Management Series. We are doing so because many local government practitioners and teachers of management-related courses in colleges and universities have felt the need for an authoritative text in one of the newer areas of administrative activity in cities and counties. The human services field may lack the measurability and tradition associated with, for example, such long-established local government services as those in the public works area. But human services are a major component of managerial life in contemporary local government. They consume a significant portion of the budget. They involve complex organizational relationships with both the private sector and with other levels of government.

While the thrust and composition of human services, and their organizational expression, are still evolving, a considerable body of managerial knowledge and experience has now accumulated in this field. It is the purpose of this book to identify and assess that knowledge and experience and to present it in readable, up-to-date form.

Three points may be made about the Municipal Management Series generally, and with particular application to this book. First, every effort has been made throughout the planning, writing, and editing of *Managing Human Services* to emphasize the managerial perspective. We have striven to illuminate the latest theories and research in the field by linking them to specific managerial examples, and also to widen the horizons of local government practitioners by showing how day-to-day decision making fits into wider theoretical perspectives. This book is neither a theoretical treatise nor a detailed administrative manual: instead, it primarily attempts to identify and discuss the key managerial issues and techniques in this complex and changing field.

Second, the authors of the individual chapters or portions of chapters have been selected on the basis of their expertise (including managerial expertise) in a particular subject area, and their ability to communicate the managerial aspects of that expertise to specialist and nonspecialist alike. They have also been given appropriate latitude to discuss their subjects and express their own policy preferences in terms, and by examples, that they feel appropriate. A lively blend of individual perspectives has emerged, and we feel that the text offers a range of authoritative managerial coverage not available elsewhere.

Third, this book, like others in the Municipal Management Series, has been published for the Institute for Training in Municipal Administration. The institute offers in-service training specifically designed for local government officials whose jobs are to plan, direct, and coordinate the work of others. The institute has been sponsored since 1934 by the International City Management Association, and has prepared a training course to accompany this book.

As part of our long-term publications program, we have made a special effort to invite suggestions from practitioners and scholars during the planning stage of this book. The response, both in attendance at early planning sessions and in bringing appropriate case studies and examples to our attention, has truly been impressive. We owe our sincere thanks to Louis N. Garcia, then Special Projects Director for the League of California Cities, for his assistance in bringing together a group of city managers, human services directors, elected officials, and private agency representatives to meet with ICMA staff in San Francisco in October, 1975, and discuss the broad thrust of the new book. Our thanks go also to the following participants (with the positions held by them at the time) at a conference in Washington, D.C., in January, 1976, at which the first-draft outline for the text was discussed: Stanley Cowle, County Administrator, Hennepin County, Minnesota; Manuel Deese, Assistant City Manager, Richmond, Virginia; Sidney Gardner, consultant, formerly Department of Health, Education, and Welfare; John Gundersdorf, New England Municipal Center, Durham, New Hampshire; Dr. Helen Hackman, Human Services Director, Arlington County, Virginia; Bert Johnson, former County Manager, Arlington County, Virginia; Dr. Lisa Peattie, Massachusetts Institute of Technology; William Privett, Department of Health, Education, and Welfare; Frank Scioli, Project Manager, Division of Advanced Productivity, Research, and Technology, National Science Foundation; Elmer Tropman, United Way of America, Alexandria, Virginia; Clifford Vermilya, Town Manager, Bloomfield, Connecticut; and Wylie Williams, Assistant City Manager, Charlotte, North Carolina. Our thanks, too, to William Privett in his capacity as Project Officer for Project Share, the national clearinghouse for improving the management of human services, for assistance in locating bibliographic references. We are also indebted to the several hundred human services experts in local governments, universities, and private agencies who commented on our draft outlines for the book or sent in details of case studies.

In addition, the book has been exceptionally well-served by its three Editors: Wayne F. Anderson, Executive Director of the U.S. Advisory Commission on Intergovernmental Relations; Bernard J. Frieden, Professor of Urban Studies and Planning at the Massachusetts Institute of Technology; and Michael J. Murphy, Deputy Director, Management Development Center, International City Management Association. Each has provided invaluable assistance in formulating the outline for *Managing Human Services,* selecting authors, and reviewing manuscript drafts.

The Municipal Management Series is the responsibility of David S. Arnold, Director, Publications Center, ICMA. Richard R. Herbert, Senior Editor, had primary responsibility for working with the Editors in bringing this project to fruition. Dorothy R. Caeser, Assistant Editor, also worked closely with the Editors and authors, and was responsible for the final editing of the manuscript and proofs through the production process. Special thanks are due to Drew A. Myers, an intern with ICMA and a student in the Division of Community Development, Pennsylvania State University, for his work in helping the ICMA staff select and prepare the illustrations and bibliography. Our thanks also go to Paul M. Dunbar of Design Associates in Washington, D.C., for handling the preparation of all original line illustrations. The index was prepared by Emily Evershed.

Mark E. Keane
Executive Director

International City
Management Association

Washington, D.C.

Preface

One of the most striking changes in local government during the past fifteen years has been its increasing involvement with human services needs. Some of the impulse for this new thrust came from new federal efforts to "eliminate poverty," starting in the early 1960s with the "New Frontier" programs of then President John F. Kennedy. Many local governments played a part in antipoverty programs, Model Cities programs, public employment projects, and other federally funded programs aimed at the disadvantaged. But the impulse for involvement came even more strongly from societal changes. Powerful social movements gripped the country during this period, dominated by and, for the most part, related to the great civil rights movement of the 1960s. The result was that many local governments were faced squarely with social issues demanding a response.

Managing Human Services is a new text in ICMA's Municipal Management Series, and it is hoped that it will help fill a major gap in the literature on local government administration. For while cities and counties have gained experience in recent years with new approaches to human services planning, management, and evaluation, available knowledge on these subjects has not been drawn together in readily accessible form for students and practitioners of local government. *Managing Human Services* represents a first attempt by ICMA to assemble the best available information on local government human services management at the community level.

Unlike other books in the Municipal Management Series that deal with long-established municipal functions (police management, public works, etc.), this text deals with a recently much-expanded and still developing set of services, particularly from the perspective of cities. In many communities, the pattern has not been settled and confusion remains, even about the proper role of the local government in human services. Therefore, the present state of management practices in this field precluded the compilation of a definitive text of long-enduring utility. This book is more properly represented as a first-effort foundation, to be revised and refined as human services management matures and changes. The authors were asked to emphasize alternative approaches and options available to local government, particularly in areas where there is disagreement in practice. The authors were also requested to use, as much as possible, case studies and illustrations of programs and approaches already "in place" in local governments.

The principal audiences to which the book is directed are practitioners in local government, that is, managers, human services directors, department heads, and elected officials; their counterparts working in private agencies; the many groups of professionals actually delivering services, e.g., social workers, nurses, etc.; and the numerous individuals in communities throughout the country who are apt to be involved, directly or indirectly, in developing services.

The text emphasizes concepts, techniques, and program ideas that are relevant to the practitioner. This stress on practicable management approaches is a unique quality of the Municipal Management Series, and should make the present text of particular interest to teachers and students in public administration schools; schools of urban planning, social welfare, public policy and urban affairs, and political science; and schools of public health. Moreover, in view of the heavy stress throughout the book on coordination with other levels of government and with private agencies, the book should be of use to federal and state officials concerned with human services delivery systems, to United Way agencies, and to other voluntary agencies concerned with human services programs.

This book, like others in the Municipal Management Series, has drawn on the first-hand experience of government administrators, teachers, and researchers. We are indebted to the many city and county managers who have submitted to ICMA diverse material on their human services programs; these have provided excellent sources for illustrating specific management approaches throughout the book.

Of special value in developing this volume have been the contributions of the League of California Cities and the New England Municipal Center. Both of these organizations operate programs to assist local governments in their geographic areas in strengthening their management capabilities in human services, and both have shared freely with ICMA the materials and case studies they have developed.

The Editors are grateful for the diligence and the excellent work of the more than two dozen chapter authors, and for the meticulous work of ICMA's Senior Editor, Richard R. Herbert, who shepherded the book from its early planning stages to its completion and, with unfailing good cheer, somehow managed to keep everyone on schedule. We also wish to thank Dorothy R. Caeser, Assistant Editor, who worked closely with the Editors throughout the preparation of the text, and Drew A. Myers, an intern with ICMA, who assisted in the preparation of the illustrations and bibliography.

Wayne F. Anderson

Bernard J. Frieden

Michael J. Murphy

Washington, D.C.

Contents

Tables

Part one:
The role of local government in human services

Introduction

In the first of the celebrated *Federalist Papers,* Alexander Hamilton approached the task of deliberating on the nature of what was to become the United States Constitution with the following observation:

It has been frequently remarked that it seems to have been reserved to the people of this country, by their conduct and example, to decide the important question, whether societies of men are really capable or not of establishing good government from reflection and choice, or whether they are forever destined to depend for their political constitutions on accident and force.[1]

For the professional urban administrator, "good government," almost by definition, must be in large measure comprised of "reflection and choice." The alternative is indeed the risk of descending into a stressful environment of day-to-day crisis management, where the disposition of scarce resources is fought out with little "reflection" and even less "choice." As the remarks in the Foreword and Preface have indicated, the function of *Managing Human Services* is to try to enhance the possibility of greater "reflection and choice" in the process of local government human services management. Many experts in this field agree that, as of the later 1970s, there is an increasing interest in this area, coupled with an accelerating programmatic involvement and considerable financial outlay. Experience has also shown that there is considerable, if not bewildering, complexity in the way human services are approached at the management level. But the increasing practical experience is now beginning to point the way, if not to definitive managerial solutions, at least to viable managerial options.

These options hold in counties as well as in cities, in small rural jurisdictions where the chief administrator may wear several managerial hats as well as in huge metropolitan agglomerations where the human services or human resources head may oversee budgets larger than those of many municipalities. The options hold, in fact, whether or not the human services field has achieved separate organizational existence. A young police officer answering a call to a domestic imbroglio is, in practice, as much a human services operative as is the professional caseworker, although recognition of this fact may be difficult for both parties.[2]

Because of the novelty and complexity of the human services field, the structure of *Managing Human Services* has been carefully designed to give attention to the general role of human services in the local government and community context as well as to the operational specifics in particular programmatic areas. The function of the three chapters of Part One of this book, therefore, is to take a broad look at the role of local government in human services. Part One sets in context the later parts of the book, which treat the planning function, the overall management function, and the illustrative programmatic components of human services operations.

The author of Chapter 1, writing from extensive and distinguished experience in the human services field, addresses at the outset the question, What are the human services?, with particular attention to the underlying social patterns that help shape our perceptions in this area. His discussion moves on to a consideration of the evolving historical role of local governments in this field, with emphasis on the main antecedents and landmarks, and then squarely addresses the contemporary challenges in human services. The remainder of Chapter 1 takes a look at the basic programmatic components of human services operations, and concludes with an analysis of some trends and issues that will help local government managers to see what lies ahead in this constantly changing area.

A key question for local government managers is the relative weight accorded to human services by the public sector at the local level, by the private sector, and by other levels of government. This question is addressed by the author of Chapter 2, who possesses wide experience in both the public and the private sectors. Chapter 2 explores the impact of federal and state programs on local governments; local government relations with regional planning bodies and special districts; and local government relations with the private sector. City and county interrelationships are also discussed. The emphasis is not so much on the specifics of an ever-changing legislative environment, but on the broad managerial principles and guidelines that appear to have emerged from the interrelationships described.

The author of Chapter 3, the final chapter in Part One, takes a closer look at the changing roles that local governments can play within the structural frameworks outlined in the preceding chapter. He writes from experience ranging from the federal to the local level in human services management. Realistic goals and basic role options are stressed, as are emerging legislative and social trends and their budgetary and organizational implications. The chapter ends with an assessment of the fundamental issues now confronting local government managers.

In sum, therefore, Part One of this book attempts to answer three principal questions. What are the human services and how have they developed? Who are the main public and private sector "actors" involved? and What roles can these actors play in this setting?

---

1 Alexander Hamilton, James Madison, and John Jay, *The Federalist Papers* (New York: New American Library, 1961), p. 33.

2 See, for example, the discussion in William H. Kroes and Joseph J. Hurrell, Jr., eds., *Job Stress and the Police Officer: Identifying Stress Reduction Techniques,* proceedings of a symposium held in Cincinnati, Ohio, 8–9 May 1975 (Washington, D.C.: U.S., Department of Health, Education, and Welfare, Public Health Service, Center for Disease Control, National Institute for Occupational Safety and Health, December 1975), especially pp. 107–16, from which the following quotation is drawn (a police officer is being interviewed): ". . . Family disputes, nine out of ten times, are between husband or wife or common-law husband and wife. I know most policemen, when they get these, have pretty much of an anxiety or fear in the way of is somebody going to shoot them, somebody going to stab them, is somebody going to do something. You have to use a little caution going, but the main thing that I found was they were always mad at each other and they weren't mad at us, and if you just take your time they like to talk to you. You know, everybody wants to talk, and if you get them separated—take the man in one room and the woman in another, the two guys separate them—if you get a partner who likes to talk as much as you do, then you're home free."

The human services function and local government

What are the human services? What is their relevance to contemporary local government management? The addition of this book to the Municipal Management Series indicates that it is now possible to provide at least tentative answers to these questions and, of course, different authors will be addressing those very tasks from particular professional perspectives throughout the volume.

The purpose of this opening chapter is to set these later discussions in context by introducing and analyzing some of the basic themes to be treated in this book. The discussion is focused on five major topics. The first section attempts at the outset to take a close look at the basic question: What are the human services? The second section outlines the important role emerging for local governments in this area. The third section takes a look at some of the major individual components of the human services and their effect on local life: income maintenance; child welfare; health services; mental health and mental retardation; and the aged. The fourth section examines some of the basic trends and issues that currently preoccupy local government managers in this field, including the thorny topics of the coordination and integration of services, and of county, town, and city interrelationships. The fifth section takes a look at what lies ahead for local governments in what all agree is a fast changing field. There is a concluding summary of the discussion.

What are the human services?

The phrase ''human services'' is the latest in a long history of phrases which seek to capture evolving conceptions about the well-being of individuals, the well-being of neighbors, and the well-being of communities. It is important—and realistic—to emphasize at the outset that discussions in this area have deep and often controversial roots in varying concepts of individual and collective responsibility for human well-being, and in differing perceptions of the social and political mechanisms to be used (or not to be used) in achieving or maintaining this status. Indeed, in the broadest sense, these discussions touch upon elements at the heart of our political and historical development. In a complex urban–industrial world, in which people are constantly on the move (at least in the open societies of the Western world), it seems fair to characterize the human services as representing modern efforts to translate basic ethical concepts about human relationships into some realistic form.

Evolving definitions

In the earliest days of our republic, the common terms signaling the existence of discussions in this area were ''looking after the widow and orphan'' and ''charity.'' Significant later expressions were ''the almshouse,'' ''outdoor relief,'' ''public assistance,'' and ''public welfare.'' In recent years, particularly since the early 1960s, there has been an explosion of organized governmental and voluntary effort which has reached beyond the bounds of any single encompassing phrase. The term ''welfare'' has begun to penetrate many fields in modern society and is used in discussions of such diversified topics as mental illness and other ill health, mental retardation, unemployment, and old age. Suddenly, the phrase "public welfare" has become inadequate to describe not only the range of policy dilemmas which have emerged, but also the programs created in an attempt to cope with them.

In its narrowest sense, the term "human services" is anchored to the idea of economic dependency, that is, in practice, to public assistance. Operationally, the narrow definition thus translates into the provision of a variety of services required by persons of limited income in an industrial society who would otherwise succumb at a minimum to starvation or severe distress. It further assumes that those not "on relief" can provide such services for themselves. This narrow usage has, however, proved unworkable. So—at the opposite end of the spectrum—has the broad definition that attempts to include as human services virtually all of the activities of modern society upon which the existence and well-being of citizens depend: a somewhat utopian assemblage, ranging from the creation of jobs through the achievement and maintenance of a clean and pleasant environment to the production of conditions conducive to happiness. What, then, lies between these two extremes?

Current perceptions: a "middle path"

Between these two extremes lies a middle path which more accurately describes the current social perceptions denoted by the term "human services." The ancient hazards of hunger, of illness, of disability, and of lost opportunity to procure the necessities of existence have taken on new shape. Their specters can haunt not only the poorest "outcasts," but also almost anyone in the population. Modern conditions require that the vulnerable be protected, if only to assure the essentially humane nature of mankind. But today, almost anyone can be vulnerable. And if not today, tomorrow. Anyone may be permanently crippled by injury, accident, or devastating illness produced by disease or by our industrial society's disruption of the environment. The wealthiest and strongest families give birth to the severely retarded and the physically damaged. The aberrations and instabilities of the national and international economies can and will convert a community with a strong industry and stable employment into a dismal backwater afflicted with permanent unemployment. The problems of the widow and of the orphan in the past have been joined by the difficulties of divorced mothers, often left to cope with small children. Without making any attribution of cause, it suffices to note that very deep social changes have introduced these and other hazards which can arise abruptly to confront any person and any family.

As a result, the network of programs and services which once expressed our human attempt to deal with these vulnerabilities now becomes a necessity for the well-being of the entire community, and not merely an expression of charity on the part of the safe and secure directed at the occasional victim.

Human services, conceived of in these terms, thus comprise an intricate variety of programs and services which communities require for their own social health; for the expression of the essential humanity of interpersonal and social relationships; and, possibly, to avoid a breakdown in the civil order. The programs and services are addressed to the urgent economic, psychological, health, and physical requirements of vulnerable sections of any urban (or, if appropriate, rural) population. But that vulnerable section, although representing a minority of the total population in any community at any one moment in time, can be drawn from any part of that community—from the strongest to the weakest, the richest to the poorest.

This complex range, therefore, includes at the very minimum the provision of income guarantees, of child welfare services, of mental health and other health services, and of personal counseling and guidance.

Underlying social patterns

The evolution of such human services, their recent explosion if you will, has been fueled by certain fundamental dynamics of modern society. What are these changing conditions? Without entering into a detailed historical analysis, let us take a brief look at a few of these factors: economic dynamism and employee mobility; female entry into the work force; the changing role of the family; the tempo of modern life; the concept of equity; and a belief that science and technology can provide solutions to social problems.

Economic dynamism and employee mobility   As our economy has become fluid, consumer-oriented, and enormously dynamic, its work force has become correspondingly mobile. The attraction of industries (and, with them, employment opportunities) to particular localities depends upon the assurance that their employees, from executives and managers to unskilled laborers, will have in their community at least minimum health services, care in case of severe disability, adequate education, ongoing retraining for new employment demands, and special services to cope with the alleged correlates of modern insecurity—drug and alcohol addiction and mental illness. This economic dynamism is one which produces a substantial amount of insecurity if not instability in living conditions. Protection against these hazards cannot be generated by the individual alone.

Female entry into the work force   Another fundamental trend has been more social in nature and is best exemplified by the enormous flood of women and especially mothers—even those with the smallest children—into the work force. This has brought in its train the demand for services to care for children (and not only those of the poor) during the day. Another trend can be seen in the demand for additional psychological and correctional services to cope with the increase in youth delinquency which may or may not be associated with the increased employment of mothers in the labor force.

The changing role of the family   This explosion of human services has also been made necessary because the condition of the old residual "social service" target, the family, has been modified by these fundamental social changes. Families are smaller. They rear fewer children. This, in turn, means that the number of family members—aunts, cousins, uncles, etc.—is reduced and thus the total family network potentially able to help out in cases of distress is also reduced. Further, the spread of those fewer family members across all parts of our huge country reduces their ability to rise to emergencies and to take care of each other face-to-face as did the larger, neighborhood-centered, extended family. The employment of so many family members—especially women and teen-aged children—is a fundamental dynamic in the economy. It, too, means that there are fewer persons at home capable of providing caring services when these become necessary.

The tempo of modern life   The speed, tension, and tempo of modern life are familiar to all of us. They are reflected on our crowded metropolitan highways in the physiological and psychological stress undergone each day by the commuter driving to and from work in the city as well as in the appalling volume of automobile accident statistics; in the industrial injury rates as well as in the frustration and boredom felt by young workers who see themselves trapped in the monotony of the modern production process; in the pervasive fears about personal safety in a neighborhood, a familiar street, or even in the home—fears shared by all ethnic and economic strata; in the apparently intractable and pervasive incidence of alcohol and other drug abuse; and in a multitude of other facets of our industrial society. Again without drawing firm conclusions about causality, it is entirely possible to correlate some of these modern life patterns with increases in the volume and proportion of severe injuries and illnesses. These are quite capable of permanently incapacitating individuals who then require help for both economic and humane reasons.

The concept of equity   Underlying all these developments has been a constantly growing concept of equity in which the minimum decencies of life are considered essential for all. Quite apart from constitutional rights, the poor are considered to be equally entitled to full medical care as are the wealthy; the severely disabled child is as entitled to a ''normal'' education as is the physically normal child; the severely disabled adult is entitled to an opportunity to move about his or her community rather than being isolated in a room or in an institution.

Technology and science as problem solvers   In recent decades, much of the expanded attention to human services has been sparked by a belief that these and other ''problems'' could be solved by an application of twentieth century technology and science to these very ancient and fundamental human vulnerabilities. This search for problem solution has paralleled the earlier tradition of caring for those in distress. No evidence has been produced to date which indicates that, within the framework of our present society, these fundamental social problems can be ''solved'' or abolished. The impact of dilemma and distress may be minimized, the onset may be delayed, and possibly the incidence of some conditions can be slowly reduced in scale. There is still a hope that unemployment, for example, can be reduced to something like the rate found tolerable in Western Europe without necessitating the adoption of the totalitarian methods associated with claims of its total elimination in Eastern Europe. Starvation has been abolished in most parts of the United States, but it is still found in some pockets. In the cases of mental illness, severe disability, addiction, and the infirmities of old age, there seems to be a growth in number and in proportion rather than any decline. Insofar as crime and delinquency are concerned, there is the hope that this situation can be resolved, but also a recognition that the hope is not yet within realization.

Summary

Such is the scope of the human services. They are not necessarily, or even primarily, governmentally provided. Many services are provided through voluntary, nonprofit service organizations and, more recently, by a very large number of proprietary, profit-making service organizations. These taken together with governmental services touch the lives of most citizens in one form or another. But taken together, they are not subject to the guidance, control, or direct influence of local government or, for that matter, of any one level of government, or of any central guiding authority.

The role of local government

It must be recognized at the outset that we lack any simple clarifying model of local government. In the following discussion, the term is used to apply to city and town governments, to counties, and to townships. All represent the ''bottom line'' of official government closest to the ultimate consumer where he or she lives. It is easy enough to assert that the human services are important for local government because it is that level of general purpose government closest to the people. These services are indeed important to citizens in their local jurisdictions, but—as local government managers are all too aware—it is another question entirely to ask, In what way should local government assume responsibility for the human services, and how? The following discussion therefore takes a look at the basic facts relating to the role of local government in human services; touches on the tensions in our economy and in our constitutional system that those facts reflect; and then proceeds to an outline discussion of the evolution of the local government role and an analysis of the major contemporary challenges that managers face in the human services field.

The basic facts

The basic facts are relatively easy to ascertain. Table 1–1 summarizes the trend line in total state and local government expenditures for the human services as a proportion of all government social welfare expenditures. Table 1–2 identifies aggregate expenditures by local governments only.

Table 1–1   Social welfare expenditures from public funds in relation to total government expenditures. See text for further discussion.

Category	1928–29	1949–50	1969–70	1971–72	1972–73	1973–74
All public social welfare expenditures ($ millions) [1]	3,698	22,741	140,074	184,502	206,591	230,110
Percent of total government expenditures	36.3	37.6	47.8	53.1	55.3	55.9
Federal social welfare expenditures ($ millions)	798	10,541	77,074	106,002	122,291	137,310
Percent of total federal government expenditures	30.9	26.2	40.1	47.4	50.5	52.5
State and local social welfare expenditures ($ millions) [2]	2,900	12,200	63,000	78,500	84,300	92,800
Percent of total state and local government expenditures	38.2	60.1	62.3	63.6	64.2	61.7

Source: *Social Security Bulletin: Annual Statistical Supplement 1974*, Washington, D.C., Government Printing Office, 1974, Table 2, p. 39.
[1] Expenditures from general revenues and from trust funds: excludes workmen's compensation and temporary disability insurance payments made through private carriers and self-insurers. Also excludes government contributions from general revenues to public employee retirement systems that are already reflected in social welfare expenditure data.
[2] From own revenue sources: excludes federal grants-in-aid.

The data are not altogether informative because they conceal wide variations in both the form and content of local government responsibility and expenditure. State and local expenditures represent 61.7 percent of all expenditures in those jurisdictions, while local governments average 16 percent of their budgets for welfare. For example, as late as 1976, New York City was contributing approximately 25 percent of the total cost of public relief expenditures from its local taxation sources whereas, in other states, the total cost had already been absorbed by the state and federal governments. Some cities have developed extensive, publicly administered child welfare programs, placing children in foster care, providing treatment and protective services for the delinquent and the abused, and maintaining children's institutions. Other communities provide no such services under public auspices and still others appropriate local funds to purchase such services from private organizations.

These figures are thus only the tip of the iceberg when seen in proper context. The human services of the later 1970s are in fact a crazy quilt of organizational and jurisdictional responsibilities. There exists an almost infinite variety of categorical and specialized human services programs authorized by the federal government. In order for such programs to become available locally, some administrative initiative and, frequently, some cost sharing between state and local governments is necessary to secure the available federal funds. But the conditions of sharing and the readiness of local communities to share costs vary according to the priorities in each community. Some communities, therefore, have sought to capture every available federal and state dollar and thus to provide a wide variety of local services which, in effect, are mandated and controlled by federal and state legislation and not by local government. Their accessibility to local citizens, however, depends upon some local matching of funds. In the most generous communities, there may be several hundred such programs covering the range of human services outlined earlier in this chapter.

Table 1–2   Local government expenditures according to specific function. Comparison is made between the years 1902 and 1970.

| | Expenditures ($ millions) | | | |
| | 1902 | | 1970 | |
Category	$	% of total	$	% of total
Total	959	100	91,889	100
Human services	84	9	15,360	16
Public welfare	27	3	6,477	7
Hospitals	15	2	3,861	4
Health	13	1	1,019	1
Housing and urban renewal	0	0	2,115	2
Parks and recreation	29	3	1,888	2

Source: Derived from U.S., Department of Commerce, Bureau of the Census, *Historical Statistics*, Series Y817–848, Washington, D.C., Government Printing Office, 1975.

As a result, the position of local government vis-à-vis the human services is, at best, troubled. The trouble, however, can scarcely be avoided. It is not clear whether local government, in view of the complex network of intergovernmental relationships, is a full and equal partner with state and federal government in the setting of priorities, the shaping of program administration, and financing, or whether local government is the hapless "guy in the middle" having to conform to policies and procedures established elsewhere but bearing the burden of disaffection when things go wrong. The same questions can be phrased in other blunt ways. Are local general purpose governments and their officials really the keepers of the common well-being of their citizens? Are they partners? Or are they no more than a kind of janitor trying to sweep up some of the most serious residuals among the problems, yet not really making decisions in the "front office" of the state house or far off beside the Potomac? The change of national administration in 1977 merely highlighted these dilemmas.

Constitutional and economic tensions

The current uncertainty about the role of local government in the matters noted above derives in part from a tension in our constitutional system. Local government is, for the most part, a creature of state government which holds residual powers under our constitutional system. In very few states, however, is there a structure which permits the cities to function simply as the administrative executors of state programs and policies. Instead, local government has taken on a dynamic life of its own and may quite effectively represent the people living within its boundaries. Even without the existence of strong constitutional authority of a sovereign nature, even without a strong statewide administrative structure, local government is often seen by its citizens as their spokesman. They perceive it as the guardian of their rights and liberties and as the direct provider for their essential wants, even though those same governments may have minimal authority and minimal economic wherewithal.

However, the fact that local public officials *are* close to citizens, *are* in the public view, *and* are usually expected to "do something" (even if the problems are not of those officials' making) argues for the conclusion that the responsibilities of local government vis-à-vis the human services will probably grow in the future rather than decline. It is difficult to imagine a situation in which the complex human services needs already described can ever effectively be approached in a flexible and sensitive fashion by the judgment of geographically distant administrators. This issue of remote or local administration can be viewed independently of the strengths and weaknesses of financial arrangements.

Nevertheless, this perception of the position of local government is reinforced by tendencies in the economy. As has been noted, the economic vigor and well-being of a community and of a local jurisdiction depend upon its attractiveness to industry, its capacity to keep industrial complexes, and its ability to adapt to changing industrial technology. While the objective economic constraints of local raw material availability and transportation facilities, and of capital accumulation—not to mention the constraints of national economic growth or decline—may be dominant, there still remains a significant contribution to the local economy which is made by the human services. A well-trained labor force, maintained by retraining and by vocational reeducation, can be a significant factor. The amenities of a community, the attractions of its cultural life, the quality of its schools, the sufficiency of its medical system, and its capacity to handle the consequences of illness and breakdown are all factors influencing the decision made by skilled labor, by executive management, and by capital investors as they contemplate coming to, or remaining in, a jurisdiction. The human services thus become important "bargaining counters" in attempts by local government to create and maintain economic viability while at the same time maintaining humane and socially healthy conditions for their taxpaying citizens.

These constitutional and economic circumstances throw a special spotlight, therefore, on the problem of just how local governments can or should respond, given the position in which they find themselves today concerning the human services. But how did those governments evolve to that position? At this juncture, it is appropriate to address that issue.

The evolution of the local government role

The present status of local government in relation to human services may be placed in fuller perspective when historical factors (including comparisons with the experiences of other nations) are taken into consideration. The following outline discussion therefore considers three such themes: the role of European antecedents and parallel landmarks in the American experience, and contemporary dilemmas.

European antecedents and parallels   Taking a larger perspective, it is important to note that the role of local government—in the United States, in Europe, and elsewhere—has been so closely intertwined with that of national government that the two must both be taken into account in order to obtain any realistic understanding of the current situation. Except for a few small city-states, municipalities are in fact subordinate to the sovereign power of the national state in most parts of the world. The American experience, however, differs from that which prevails, say, in Europe in at least two respects: (1) more social welfare programs are nationally administered and financed in European countries; and (2) the American federal system interposes between nation and city a layer of state government with some sovereign powers which is often lacking elsewhere in the world. These differences do not appear to alter the extent to which municipalities everywhere depend upon national revenues to finance local services, but they do affect the organizational complexities which surround local activities.

In most parts of the world, programs for health protection, health services, income security, the protection of children, or the strengthening of family life through family allowances or by family planning are likely to be nationally financed and administered. Certain other functions (such as recreation, parks, perhaps housing or town planning) often will be left to local governments. In the United States, in contrast, the three levels of government produce a partnership in which each level of government shares in both financing and administering welfare programs. It is this necessity for bringing into congruence the interests of three layers of government that introduces a special degree of complexity into the management of American local human services, although difficulties of varying kinds are encountered everywhere in the world. Two examples—those of the United Kingdom and of Yugoslavia—outline the main differences between the United States and elsewhere.

The example of the United Kingdom   In the United Kingdom (characteristic of much of Western Europe), all income programs are nationally administered and financed in their entirety; all health-related services are nationally financed through the National Health Service; and employment services are a national responsibility. Housing is primarily a local responsibility as regards selection, location, and standards, although the national treasury contributes to the cost of construction. The personal social services for the aged, for children, for the mentally ill, and for the displaced are entirely the responsibility of local governments that decide not only what to offer, but also how much and under what circumstances. Although certain services are mandated by national law, the details are generally left to local government choice. Each local authority must provide for a local department of personal social services, much as if each city in the United States were required to organize a human services department. While there is a certain amount of national agency monitoring of what is done locally, this monitoring is not accompanied by the kind of regulation regarding details of organization which characterizes so much of the American partnership between levels of government.

Despite these differences in system, the national treasury in the United Kingdom finances nearly three-quarters, on the average, of local government costs. But the financial arrangements are less tied than in the United States to categorical programs, each with a different set of requirements and procedures. Instead, for the personal social services, each local government prepares an overall budget about what it proposes to spend, for example, on residential care for the elderly, on child care, etc. It then negotiates with the national government about what an overall national grant-in-aid for all programs will be. The final grant is a general purpose one, not tied to individual programs. The amount is arrived at by a complex formula which takes into account how much the national treasury sets aside for local government grants overall, the financial and demographic makeup of each local jurisdiction, local program plans, and national priorities. Local governments are relatively free to spend the allocated grants as they see fit.[1]

The example of Yugoslavia   A pattern quite different from that of the United Kingdom is found in Yugoslavia. There most services which we would identify as social are the responsibility of local or regional industrial or agricultural complexes or industries. Each economic complex has the authority to set aside some part of its earnings for the provision of social benefits or services for its member workers and their families. The economic unit must earn some profit, but how it spends these earnings is largely a matter of its own choosing. Social benefits, child care, etc. are thus closely geared to what employees of an industry decide they want for themselves and for their fellow members. Medical, educational, and cultural organizations are also treated as largely self-supporting and must negotiate for the sale of their services to other economic units. However, the national government does also allocate some of its funds to consumer groups (as distinguished from producer organizations), funds with which they can purchase social benefits, such as medical care or education. These consumer groups are in the nature of special interest groups or unions, and they help to offset unilateral provider/bureaucratic decision making at the level of local government.

Summary   As may be inferred from these contrasting examples, history, culture, and economy play a major role in determining the character of local government organization for human services delivery. Neither of the above examples confronts the situation in which American cities find themselves: mobile populations, uncontrolled economic changes, vast distances, and a three-tiered constitutional system. In other words, the American situation is quite unique.

Landmarks in the American experience   Contrary to the common belief that the human services are a relatively recent burden cast upon American city government, it is worth remembering that financial support, at a minimum, has been a function of local government in the United States since the earliest days. It has been said that, in the 1700s, over 40 percent of New York City's budget was devoted to maintaining the "poor house." In 1976, 29 percent of all city expenditures ($4 billion) was devoted to social and health services, a rough twentieth century equivalent of the poor house. As a proportion of local government expenditures, the welfare share may not be much more today than it was in earlier times. What *has* changed is the scale and variety and complexity of local government overall, with equivalent shifts in local government's responsibility.

Early roots   In the eighteenth century, expenditures by local government and, therefore, its responsibilities were largely limited to paying strangers to take care of orphans, or making payments to women who were widowed in the rigors of frontier life, or maintaining the poor houses which sheltered the aged without family and the severely disabled and mentally ill. As the nineteenth century progressed, the scope of public payment for these categories increased, especially as the Civil War and epidemics took their toll leaving widows, cripples, and orphans.

   As time went on, cities became more competent and many of them developed public hospitals and public outpatient clinics. Specialized hospitals for the chronically ill and for the provision of birth and delivery services for poor women were established. The construction of special institutions or the creation of foster care programs for children either orphaned or difficult to manage became quite common. Such publicly organized services were intertwined with similar voluntary and nonprofit facilities and services which grew up at the same time.

Twentieth century developments   As far as the national government's involvement with local government goes, the first third of the twentieth century was a period of slowly accumulating special purpose legislation. The nineteenth century saw the federal government's first steps toward a program of health and income security for veterans only and the elaboration of limited public health services. After 1910, the U.S. Children's Bureau was established. Many states set up state level programs of workmen's compensation for industrial injury, mothers' pensions, and pensions for the aged. A national vocational rehabilitation program was created (under the Sheppard–Towner Act) for a short period after World War I. Not until the middle 1930s did the tempo of legislated social provision accelerate. After 1935, all three levels of government became involved in a very rapid accumulation of specialized social programs, beginning with the Social Security Act of 1935. Unemployment insurance; aid to the blind, the aged, the widowed, and dependent children; medical care for the poor and for the aged; hospital construction for all; vocational rehabilitation and training for all injured persons; and maternal and child health protection were all included to some extent.

By the middle twentieth century, local governments were enmeshed in hundreds of such programs, most of them organized independently with sharply limited eligibility requirements, each program serving a selective category of persons. Administration is now frequently in the hands of relatively independent public agencies whose directors are severally accountable to the mayor or to the city council. Many of these categorical and specialized public programs are tightly tied to federal programs, each encumbered with complex limitations, regulations, and qualifications. In such cases, local program directors are preoccupied with conformity to state and federal regulations and with frantic annual and biennial efforts to conform to changes legislated at the national level, in order to secure a steady flow of funds.

Contemporary challenges   By the middle of the twentieth century, it was widely recognized that this intricate complex was literally out of control. The situation continues to plague us in the 1970s. The human problems do not segment themselves neatly into the categories for which the programs were organized. However, differentials in eligibility, in funding, and in staffing are such that it is virtually impossible to consider these hundreds of programs as being articulated into anything which would be called a human services "system."

Lack of a system   It is so difficult for clients and citizens to know what services are available, when and under what circumstances, and so nearly impossible to find access to appropriate services without a tour of scores of offices, that it is necessary to establish special information services to guide citizens to available resources. At the same time, many of the categorical agencies find it necessary to increase their staffs simply to find their own ways through the maze of agencies in order to maintain a decent referral network with complementary programs.

Citizen advocate   Hired specifically to assist Lawndale, California, citizens in finding their way through the maze of government agencies that proliferate in Los Angeles County, the citizen advocate is responsible primarily for resolving complaints, answering questions, and referring citizens to help or further information. The city administrator of Lawndale commented that the advocate plays an important part on the management team by keeping all departments up to date on trends of complaints or inquiries received about city, county, or community services and by providing insight from a citizen's standpoint during brainstorming sessions regarding operating procedures.

The complexity of the system introduced its own pitfalls and even the information services have become specialized, some addressing themselves to the aged, some to children, some to the ill. In 1966, the Model Cities legislation introduced a primitive effort to give to local government some more modern tools with which to seek to weld some order out of this chaos. Despite all of the deficiencies in the Model Cities program, it did provide local officials with an incentive to bring together disparate, categorical programs to achieve a common purpose. Taken together with certain Office of Economic Opportunity (OEO) programs, these brought increasing authority for local government over the flow of economic opportunity funds, and gave to local executive officers and legislators new tools with which to meet the human services needs of their communities on a comprehensive and planned basis rather than on a segmental, categorical, and fragmented one.

Policy planning   Essential to this new direction which emerged in the 1960s, and which is elaborated on throughout this book, is the concept of *policy planning at the level of local government.* By the 1960s it was recognized that the human services, taken in their entirety rather than categorically and segmentally, constitute a major part of local government's activity even though the implications have only recently been recognized. The aggregate of the human services may represent at least a third of all local government operations in some cities; overall, it averages about 16 percent of local budgets. The question posed is whether such relatively large expenditures are best treated as a simple aggregation of small programs, each dealing with segments of problems, or whether it is preferable to see them as a whole. Do the human services taken together represent a potential, an instrumentality, whereby local government officials can adequately discharge the duties expected of them—namely, to shape, create, and maintain local communities which are reasonably healthy in the physical and social senses, and which give pleasure and gratification to their citizens and freedom of opportunity to realize their potential?

It is clear that creating such an idealized environment represents no simple task. It may even be beyond the conscious planned capacity of man's present knowledge and technology. It certainly is not a task which can be achieved solely by local government. As will be pointed out shortly, the role of policy and programs developed by federal and state governments is probably dominant. But even within that limiting framework, it is clear that the substantial array of programs and services in which local government is involved opens up the prospect that local government can use these programs actively to achieve local policies.

The question arises, for the next period of evolution, as to whether local public officials can view the social development of their communities as a fundamental objective, just as they now consider the provision of public safety, fire protection, and road systems a part of the essential expectations of local government. If the answer is yes, then means need to be found by which local governments can examine the social requirements of their populations, can examine the resources of their multiple services, and can devise techniques which will permit them to direct these human services programs to the furtherance or outright achievement of explicitly social policies.

The major challenge   It is this prospect for the future which constitutes the major challenge. It finds expression during a period when local governments are burdened with heavy costs, with limited taxing authority, with limited constitutional authority, and with an inherited tradition of fragmented approaches to local problems. Despite these limitations (which often are a heritage of the past), local governments *are* in fact on the front line confronting the demands of their citizens to realize both the social as well as the economic potential of their country. The city and the county remain the scene wherein this search is conducted. They remain the arenas in which local government can in time shape for itself an important role, using various services to achieve social ends for the common good rather than remaining passive administrators of programs introduced from above.

Local governments have begun to deal with industry and labor on a comprehensive basis in the interests of economic development. They have begun to deal with construction, real estate development, and zoning in a comprehensive fashion to shape and contain and even to create a new physical environment. But equally important as such trends is the creation of a healthy social environment. For this the inescapable conclusion is that a comparable approach to the wide range of human services is called for.

Changes in responsibility   To move in this direction requires a fundamental change in the responsibility and authority which local government will seek to exercise over the human services. Here it is important only to note that the growth of the human services in local government has occurred incrementally without comprehensive design. As a result, directors of public assistance, mental health, mental retardation, child welfare, veterans' affairs, hospitals, health clinics, vocational training programs, and Comprehensive Employment and Training Act (CETA) programs may be appointed and left to do their jobs, subject only to the standards of administrative honesty and efficiency. Since many of these programs are driven dynamically by state and federal programs which provide funds, most of the effort of such administrators has been concentrated on seeking funds for the city or fighting the fires of local complaints.

In recent decades two lessons have been learned about such ad hoc approaches. First, the attempt to administer such specialized programs from the federal or a state capital is not sufficient. Local officials are finding it increasingly necessary to intervene at all levels of federally initiated programs—from policy and priority determination to organization and administration. Local public officials can act either as elected officials, advocating the special requirements of their citizens, or they can acquire a new official role in the shaping of such programs. Second, these specialized programs no longer function segmentally and in isolation from each other, as will be discussed below. Only at the point of applying these services to individuals does it become possible to find out how the various systems work and how the parts fail to mesh with each other, in order to ascertain what is missing in the total complex. Even more, it is at this level of application that it becomes evident how necessary it is to question the purpose of the entire complex—what ends it is intended to achieve and whether it does, in fact, have the potential to achieve them. Local public officials can be at the center of such questions, they can take the first step in the development of more suitable policies, administration, and accounting of services.

The fact that this complex is a hodgepodge of public, voluntary, and proprietary human services need not diminish (rather it increases) the centrality of local government officials as a center from which rationality can be slowly introduced into the present inadequate arrangements. This is made somewhat easier when so many public programs have recently expanded to contract with nonprofit, proprietary agencies for the provision of services which at one time were actually delivered by public administrators. The limits of contracting with private and proprietary interests are many. Nonprofit organizations are not constitutionally guided by government, and proprietary organizations—that is, plain business enterprises—seek to act like other economic enterprises. They try to keep free from too detailed government oversight of their operations. Such questions leave in the hands of local government the choice of whether their efforts should be directed entirely to the attempt to control nonprofit and proprietary service delivery, or whether they should be balanced by the introduction of publicly provided services at strategic points.

Conclusion

Bearing in mind the preceding discussion of contemporary challenges to the local government manager in the human services field and the overall historical context already described, what basic conclusions can be advanced about the role of local government? Perhaps the most vital point to make is that whatever the final mix of human services, the fact is that all forms—public, nonprofit, and proprietary services—are primarily financed by tax funds from all levels of government. But the structure is one in which no one level is in a clear position to control the mix. It becomes all the more opportune, therefore, for local government officials closest to the scene to assume leadership responsibility concerning the way in which the complex mix is actually performing.

This is not to suggest that the task will be an easy one. Quite apart from the differing effects of successive national administrations, the administration of the human services has recently been enormously complicated by the entry of the courts into the human services arena in a much enlarged fashion. There is a rapidly growing body of judicial precedent which is shaping the form and direction of the human services fully as much as do legislation and executive regulation. Recent dramatic examples are seen in the courts' intervention mandating that patients hospitalized for mental illness must be given treatment services or must be released, and in the recent extension of the rights of criminal offenders to certain forms of civil protection and to examination and treatment, especially for juvenile offenders. In the arena of medical care, the rights of the poorest have been increasingly protected by court intervention in the functioning of health delivery systems. In child welfare, many services previously concentrated on select elements of the population have been forced by court action to serve new clienteles. The sum effect of these court interventions is to widely open all human services obligations and to enlarge the scope of responsibilities. In a situation where the funding and other administrative choices are made by executive and legislative branches, it is difficult for any one level of government to be in control of the entire operation. But courts are increasingly saying that the lack of programs, the lack of services, the lack of money is no excuse for public dereliction of duty. When such issues are raised in the human services, it is inevitable that local officials are the first to be considered accountable by their citizens. Uncomfortable as this situation may be for public officials, it also provides them with an opportunity to significantly alter and enhance the role they will perform in the ultimate shaping of human services programs.

It is always easier to arrive at diagnoses of a situation than it is to make effective and useful prescriptions. Before considering specific responses to situations thus outlined, it may be useful to consider in more detail certain examples of major human services which illuminate the situation—the need for localized attention to the entire system rather than to its segments.

Some major human services and their effect on local life

The purpose of the following discussion is not to preempt the more detailed analyses presented later in this book. Rather, the following examples are used to illustrate how the human services just discussed are in fact used by all segments of the populace of a local jurisdiction. The examples also reveal the confused sharing of responsibility among several levels of government, and the existence of multiple, overlapping planning centers. Five examples have been selected for discussion: income maintenance; child welfare; health services; mental health and mental retardation; and the needs of the aged.

Income maintenance

For many decades, the conventional wisdom perceived public relief or public assistance as a rather vague, undifferentiated program simply taking care of people who did not have enough money. Today—that is, as of the later 1970s—the residents of any local jurisdiction are probably provided economic security through one of a number of independently administered federal, state, or local programs.

The seven basic programs   A brief description of the seven most common of these programs follows.

Unemployment compensation   This is intended primarily for those clearly attached to the labor force and temporarily out of work. Attempts to extend unemployment benefits have been partially successful and frequently run a year, but do not touch long-term, multiyear unemployment. This program is state administered with federal sharing.

Workmen's compensation This is intended primarily for those injured in the course of employment, covering medical care for work-related injuries and compensation in case of permanent disability. It is state administered.

Supplementary Security Income (SSI) This program is intended for the aged, the blind, and the permanently disabled—those populations generally considered to be permanently out of the labor force, although many of them do move in and out of it irregularly. It is federally administered with some state participation.

Aid to Families with Dependent Children (AFDC) This is a residual federally financed program with state, and frequently local, matching funds. It is this program which has often been in the hurricane's eye of controversy since it meets the economic needs of able-bodied adults for whom the likelihood of finding employment is minimal: they may be mothers with very small children, or individuals without marketable work skills, or simply those for whom, even with minimum work skills, there are no employment opportunities.

General assistance Between 1940 and 1970, recipients in this program dropped from 3,618,000 to 900,000.[2] The program acts as a "safety net" for individuals not covered by the abovementioned assistance programs, and is funded primarily from local taxation. This program is enlarged when the others are reduced since persons with no income at all have nowhere else to turn. The outlook is for a continuing decline in this program, but it probably cannot wholly disappear since all other assistance programs have eligibility peculiarities which exclude some cases.

Old age, disability, and survivors' benefits This program is the bulwark of income maintenance for persons who have reached retirement age or who become permanently disabled so that they cannot be expected to work again. A little known aspect of this program is that it covers the growing number of children with permanent, severe birth defects who will be classified as permanently unemployable when they reach the age of eighteen. The program is federally administered.

Veterans' compensation This program is primarily comprised of payments to veterans with permanent injuries received in military service and pensions for some unemployable veterans without service-connected disabilities. Many states have complementary veterans' programs.

Voucher-type programs: food stamps, housing, Medicaid, etc. These cash payment programs are complemented by at least three major voucher-type programs. The most substantial is the food stamp program, intended to provide supplementary income to the very poor and the so-called marginal, or working, poor. It has grown rapidly with a set of eligibilities different from all the rest. Its future will be determined by other federal decisions about welfare reform that may be placed in sharper focus by the change of national administration in 1977. For example, an expanded and simplified family assistance plan or negative income tax could lead to a reduction; delay in welfare reform, on the other hand, could lead to some further growth in this popular "relief in kind" program. On a much smaller scale, there are housing vouchers to permit those with very limited incomes to compete in the housing market, and, of course, Medicaid—usually administered by public welfare—which provides essential medical services for those either on assistance or likely to become economically dependent. In addition, a variety of regional or specialized programs can be noted: assistance to Indians, coal miners' benefits, special nutritional programs for children or the elderly, etc.

The interconnectedness of programs: two examples   The interconnectedness of these varying programs, each presumably addressed to a clear-cut category of beneficiaries, is seen in two illustrations. The first concerns use of a social security number. Virtually all eligibility for all programs depends upon the possession of a social security number. Recently, in fact, in Connecticut, a not uncommon case was discovered in which an elderly man, without resources and ill, was found ineligible for any of the multitude of income programs. The reason: his social security number and name were presumably held by another individual who had died, resulting in the anomaly of the living individual with no official "identity" and, therefore, no way to initiate any remedial action.[3]

A second illustration is seen in a study of the Joint Economic Committee of the U.S. Congress.[4] Families and individuals are likely to be entitled to several programs simultaneously. What are the facts regarding this situation? In this study, it was found that, of 1,059 households receiving benefits, there were at least 144 unique combinations of benefit categories and many more combinations of individual benefit programs. Small numbers of recipients are distributed over so many different benefit combinations that consolidation of the programs seems difficult to accomplish without major surgery. Between 60 and 75 percent of income maintenance program beneficiaries receive benefits from more than one source. Between 10 and 25 percent of beneficiary households receive benefits from 5 or more programs. There are gross variations in the level of benefit payments in various parts of the country, reflecting different applications of federal programs, and different eligibility patterns among states and local jurisdictions. The individuals receiving assistance are not permanently on public assistance, and more than 50 percent of the sample studied had earned income during some part of the year, reflecting the instability of the labor market for a significant part of the American population. In at least two of the sites studied, householders receiving 5 or more benefits (10–25 percent of the sample), had total incomes of more than $6,500 a year—a total in excess of the federal poverty standard. All of these findings are based upon standard legal application of existing program operations.

The boundaries of eligibility   Not only do eligibility for and access to these income maintenance programs present a confusing criss-cross of federal, state, and local regulations and interpretations, but the boundaries of eligibility are themselves also not always clear. The key fact is that the conditions of persons needing income supplements change unpredictably. Persons on the margin of the labor force move in and out of work as it becomes available. Once individuals have found employment, it becomes extraordinarily difficult for them to reacquire benefits should that employment be lost. Earnings for this segment of the labor force are virtually never sufficient to permit an accumulation of savings during short periods of employment.

Less recognized, but equally significant, is the fact that individuals who are completely independent economically and would never consider themselves candidates for any public income program find themselves—unpredictably—applicants for benefits. Economic recession throws millions of persons out of work. When business conditions improve, those who are in their forties, fifties, and sixties frequently are not rehired. As their earnings are exhausted and unemployment compensation runs out, they are forced to make relief application which represents a traumatic change in their self-conceptions and their positions in their communities.

Economic and technological changes may throw large numbers of persons permanently out of work. This was demonstrated by the period in the late 1960s when there was suddenly a surplus supply of physicists and engineers, caused by changes in military spending and leaving many of them incapable of finding equivalent substitute employment. In like fashion, there was a surplus of primary school teachers in the mid-1970s when the number of school-age children under ten began to drop. Finally, note must be taken of the devastating effect which the inflation of medical costs has on many otherwise economically independent families. Any severe illness will today pauperize a family even when the head of the household is permanently employed. It is not uncommon to find that medical costs for a chronically ill person may run to $20,000 or more a year, easily consuming all the earnings of a relatively well-paid professional worker.

The outlook   The income maintenance programs, except for General Assistance, remain effectively outside of the control of local government, although local jurisdictions may still contribute up to 25 percent of the cost in the cases of SSI and AFDC.[5]

In the 1970s, a major movement was initiated aimed at the complete federal takeover of all income programs, thus relieving local jurisdictions completely. It is not likely, however, that the search for a simplified, federally administered income maintenance program will remove the necessity for local official engagement with income programs. A simplified, standardized income program for everyone—such as the negative income tax—must, for national administration, be so standardized that millions of persons now not entitled to any income would receive payments, thus enormously escalating the cost. On the other hand, if eligibility for any income program is to be closely controlled, not only for current income but for assets, then large administrative staffs and organizations will be necessary for case-by-case evaluation. In either case, a key problem will be present, that is, that individuals' circumstances change. The delay between a change in a person's situation and a reaction from a computerized system operated at a distance can literally mean the difference between life and death. It seems an inescapable conclusion that localized organization is necessary, either to administer nationally financed programs or to handle the infinite variety of human needs on some type of case basis. Local government can always be expected to be the first object of complaint when income programs fall, when individuals starve, or when unentitled individuals are paid benefits. Just what form local government participation can take in the management and administration of this complex net of income services remains to be developed.

Child welfare

The traditional background   Services for children represent one of the clearest examples in which local government has taken a direct responsibility among the major human services. This responsibility is closely associated with local governments' responsibility for education. Children who are in trouble with the courts, who are difficult to manage, or who are abused and neglected all require attention from some nonfamily organization. Even when the courts intervene and come to some decision about the disposition of young offenders, a resource becomes necessary to which the courts can turn. In the earliest days of the nation, children were frequently removed from families which could not support the children as the family wished, on the assumption that if the children were taken care of, the parents could more effectively manage the basic problems of survival. In the course of time, the needs of children and their families have become more complex. There is a steady, persistent stream of children who have been neglected, abandoned, or abused by their parents as a consequence of broken families, mental illness, and personality and other psychological disorders in adults. Whatever the causes, in 1970, of 53.8 million children to the age of 13, 1,666,000 were not living with either parent and, of these, nearly 200,000 were living in group arrangements of various kinds.[6]

In a few jurisdictions, county governments—and sometimes city governments—have organized child welfare services which provide institutional and foster care and adoption services for this population. In some places, these publicly provided children's services are highly professionalized and represent a community's pride in the protection of their children. In many other parts of the country, these services are provided by private or proprietary child-caring agencies, charging fees paid either by middle income families or by state or local governments when families cannot meet the costs.

Newer trends: day care and juvenile delinquency programs This traditional local responsibility for children, however, has in recent decades been substantially overshadowed by the growth of day care services for children. As indicated in the detailed analysis that appears later in this book (see Chapter 12), this trend was primarily stimulated by the flood of working mothers into the work force. In 1973, of 57 million children to the age of 13, 13 million were in some form of day care arrangement, often with relatives or neighbors, but 2,270,000 of these were cared for in group day care centers or in the homes of strangers.[7] When one limits attention only to working mothers with children under the age of six, 10.5 percent of such children are cared for in an organized day care center. Day care is used by families of all income levels. Some centers are devoted exclusively to low income families whose fees are paid for from some public program; other centers serve children from mixed income levels and are supported by a combination of fees charged to individuals and fees paid by local government.

In addition, the number of children who are in trouble with the law or who present serious behavior problems beyond the control of their families also comes to the attention of the courts which must make disposition. Detention centers, training schools and training centers, and special group homes for children for whom correctional detention is considered undesirable constitute an increasingly

Figure 1–1 Isolation and immobility have been among the stereotypes associated with the role of older people in our society. (Source: From the collection of the Library of Congress.)

troublesome problem for local government. Some of the juvenile programs for this population are funded by local governments, some by states, and some receive supplementation from the federal government.

Issues in child welfare programs   What is clear about the major categories of child welfare services is the fact that they may be used by and on behalf of persons from any social and income class. Programs tend to be categorical and there is no comprehensive guidance which relates these several programs to each other in accordance with a policy for children. Many states have begun to develop coordinating action in an attempt to bring some order into the functioning of many children's services. But these have usually functioned as a meeting ground for the protagonists of various services and agencies, and have seldom exercised significant guiding influence on the evolution of children's services.

When children or their families are in difficulty, or need supplementary day care services as the families search for economic independence, local officials are the first to be under pressure. The assumption that the existing specialized children's services are sufficient for the task has been challenged by recognition that many minorities are effectively excluded from present programs by eligibility definition and by service inadequacies.

These more dramatic child welfare services need to be seen in relation to others concerned with the healthy development of children. Maternal and child health services funded in part by the federal government; special children's nutritional services administered through the schools or through special feeding programs; baby clinics designed to help maintain optimum health for infants and their mothers; and special educational programs for the developmentally disadvantaged (the retarded and those with neurological defects) can be seen as an incremental effort to give all children the healthiest and most substantial start in life that our society is capable of affording them. Unfortunately, these various programs are not well articulated with respect to each other; eligibility differs and programs are not always well-suited to the special requirements of individual local communities, since they have been designed with a coarse grain to apply nationally.

The attempt to look at the needs of children has been enormously complicated in recent years by controversies over racial discrimination and by concern over the phenomenal growth in illegitimacy. Contrary to the common myth that illegitimacy is a function of racial differentiation, the growth of sexual freedom has affected all races and all classes. Certain minorities, less secure economically, find themselves dependent to a disproportionate extent upon public sources of income for support; but the phenomenon of unwed parenthood is as pervasive among white families as it is among black and Puerto Rican ones.

The improvement in contraceptive and family planning education has not resolved the dilemma, an indication that technological advance does not necessarily reduce major social problems. The interrelationship between child and public welfare programs is seen when one considers local management of unwed parenthood. The assertion that this phenomenon is directly related to a breakdown in family life cannot be entirely supported by the evidence. For example, responsible families receiving public assistance have been, until recently, administratively and legally barred from access to family planning clinics, since regulations prohibited their referral. When persons with limited incomes are denied information and access to facilities, it would not be surprising to find that this plays some part in the clustering of young mothers with illegitimate children in the public assistance rolls. However, more deep-seated social trends seem to have led to this relaxation of sexual mores, with the result that many vulnerable young people, denied information and access to preventive means, become parents at a very early age when they lack any marketable employment skills. The combination of child-rearing responsibility, their own youth, and lack of skill tends to lead them to need public assistance.

The question of how child welfare services and income maintenance programs together should be used to deal with a phenomenon which, in large measure, is a consequence of underlying social forces has not yet been resolved. What is clear, however, is that the development of local approaches based upon public support of a policy for children might start the process of dealing with this unexpected social phenomenon.

The outlook In this sense, local government's responsibility or potential for providing leadership in an admittedly thorny and touchy area is clear. It may be that this subject is sufficiently sensitive that local officials prefer that big decisions be made outside of their jurisdiction. In any case, however, the administration of programs in a coordinated fashion would seem to fall upon local officials. Much of the effort in planning in this field at the local level has been relegated either to consultative bodies of children's agencies or to voluntary health and welfare planning councils. These have not been measurably effective in bringing together both public and voluntary services to construct a common approach to a children's policy for the community.

Health services

The background As with the other human services, the treatment of illness and the promotion of health have become major factors in the life of modern governments at all levels. In recent years, the continuing national debate over the development of some form of national health insurance has obscured a long-continuing

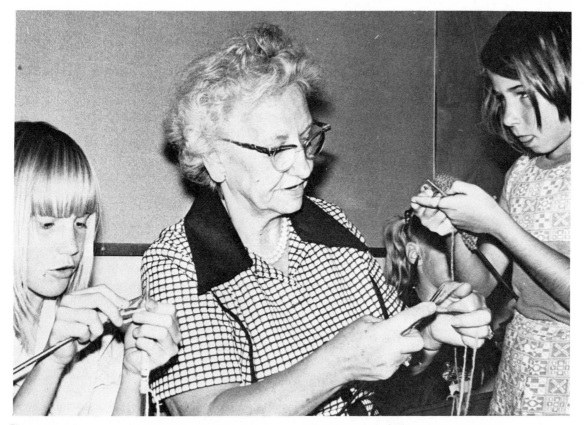

Figure 1–2 Contemporary perceptions of senior citizens often view them as actively involved in community life. This woman was hired through a California city's social services department to teach knitting to youngsters in a local junior high school. (Source: Courtesy of the City of Brea, California.)

engagement of local governments with the health of their residents. This engagement has been difficult to perceive, as the health services—as is pointed out later in this volume—have become more and more entangled with the organization of other human services, especially income maintenance, mental health services, and the needs of children and the elderly.

Until the advent of Medicare and Medicaid, many local jurisdictions were involved in underwriting the delivery of outpatient services and in providing institutional care for the chronically ill. Some times, in major cities, this provision involved the construction and maintenance of very large public hospitals, delivering inpatient and ambulatory care for low income populations.

With the growth of Medicare and Medicaid as mechanisms for financing health care, and the increased demand for equitable distribution of health services, the prominence of the private physician and the nonprofit hospital was challenged. Today a community's decisions regarding Medicaid administration and organization becomes a major factor in the economic viability of most nonprofit general hospitals. Many physicians in private practice derive significant portions of their income from both Medicare and Medicaid payments. At least in the case of Medicaid, such payments are involved in local and state public policies concerning the purposes and distribution of public welfare services since Medicaid is frequently administered by public welfare programs. What is less recognized is that the escalation in the costs of public assistance is frequently accounted for by increased cost in paying for medical care. In many local jurisdictions, one-half of the public budget is expended in payment for medical services.[8] These payments reach not only the persons on relief but a significant proportion of persons with marginal incomes who are in danger of becoming destitute.

The major relocation of urban populations has carried with it a redistribution of physician services so that large segments of major cities have few, if any, physicians available for the normal family practice or for ambulatory care services outside of the hospital. This has led to the development of neighborhood health centers to provide ambulatory services, and originally funded by some combination of OEO, public health, and general revenue funds. These are sometimes very specialized clinics funded by child health and family planning funds; and sometimes they offer comprehensive services providing a full range of ambulatory care for adults as well as children and families.

As populations and professional personnel have been redistributed and as medical costs have inflated, strenuous efforts have been initiated at federal and state levels to contain the costs of medical care. Some of these efforts have concentrated on controlling hospital plants' rate of growth, encouraging the use of lower cost nursing home care, or containing the rapid technological growth in existing medical facilities.

Current issues   Such developments, combined with the increase in the aged population from 4 percent to 10 percent of the total population, have led to an increase in the prevalence of long-term disabling conditions and to an increased utilization of nursing homes as a repository for persons incapable of functioning without the assistance of another individual.[9]

Role of nursing homes   Most nursing homes are under proprietary sponsorship; some are nonprofit or religious. The overall increase in the number of nursing homes has had its effect on local operations. It has required, for instance, zoning variations to permit construction of necessary chronic disease facilities; inspection by public health and fire authorities; and monitoring public expenditures, since these nursing homes depend on tax funds for two-thirds of their total income.[10] These circumstances involve public officials in decisions concerning the location of hospitals and nursing homes and the rate of their growth as part of the attempt to equitably distribute medical resources so that equitable access is available throughout the community's neighborhoods.

Inadequacies of marketplace interactions   In the past it was assumed that local governments could, at the most, provide some payment for treatment of the poor or construct hospitals specifically for that purpose. It has now become apparent that the almost infinite demand for health services and increased costs have created a situation in which adequate health care is not made available if left to the marketplace interaction of health providers. To a large extent, the use of health facilities is determined by the doctors themselves and they do not tend to be responsive to cost constraints. For example, the predominant emphasis of providers is on active treatment, especially in the acute hospital at very high cost. There has been a decline in the attention given by medical authorities to the growing portion of the population with long-term chronic diseases which might be better treated outside of acute hospitals. Also, public health support for preventive measures, in the form of well-baby services, sanitation services, and education concerning diet, has eroded.

Unbalanced priorities have resulted in much attention to the acute episode of illness but leave to chance any attention to problems which follow the acute episode. The result seems to be an unnecessary increase in readmissions and use of the hospital for many conditions which might be cared for through alternative means. In like fashion, the concentration on institutionalization as the primary alternative for partially disabled has led to an increase in costly nursing home care. Twenty-four-hour attention is provided to 25–50 percent of the nursing home population who actually require only part-time attention.[11]

This tendency to use such intermediate institutions has been recently exacerbated by general hospitals' attempts to control costs through early discharge of persons who are not yet ready to return to their own homes. The result has been a vicious circle of institutionalization, resulting in a severe financial drain on government.

The outlook   Meaningful managerial attempts to cope with this complex situation were first attempted by state and local departments of public health. These, however, have had limited authority and support. Between 1966 and 1976, comprehensive health planning agencies were also funded by the federal government and, more recently, health systems agencies have been launched with federal stimulation and incentive in an attempt to plan more satisfactorily for the evolution of health services throughout metropolitan and urban jurisdictions. As of the later 1970s, the effects of these nationally stimulated planning efforts was not yet evident. At best, they have brought together into one organization a variety of health providers and consumer representatives. The operational mechanisms for arriving at agreement among parties with such diverse interests are weak, however, and authority is lacking to implement agreements once made.

The effort to contain and influence the health system is bound to continue. The most tangible example has been the requirement in many local jurisdictions that a certificate of need be secured from some public body before new capital construction or expansion is initiated. Given that the participants in the present planning mechanism represent special interest groups, the role of local, general purpose government officials may become especially significant. In the end, such officials may be the only representatives of the general good of the community who can interpose among the special interests a common objective of the community's interest. Even if local government does not administer a major part of the health services, its budget is affected by expenditures (often in an uncontrolled fashion) of the multitude of service providers. The health of the population is influenced by the extent to which decisions are wisely made regarding both acute and long-term chronic conditions. It is affected also by the adequacy of attention given to preventive health measures which, in the long run, may hold some promise for containing the growth of illness in a local population.

Mental health and mental retardation

The background Health services cover a wide field, and the particular area of mental health and mental retardation is worthy of special note. Services for the mentally ill also cover services for those addicted to either drugs or alcohol. While these indeed come under the general heading of "health services," the evolution of mental health care and specialized personnel, like psychiatrists, psychologists, and social workers, has led to the development of separate service systems for the physically and mentally ill.

For a very long time, local governments were relieved of any responsibility for these populations by the development of state-supported mental hospitals and by reliance on private psychiatric services. Since the 1960s, however, there has been set in motion a strong trend toward deinstitutionalization—returning the mentally ill and mentally retarded to local community life and preventing the initial admission for a large part of this population. In part, this has been a response to changed views in the mental health professions about the most appropriate means of care and, in part, it has been a new response to the civil rights of persons whose behavior is considered deviant or atypical, but who are not threatening to the public safety so as to warrant involuntary institutionalization.

The trend to community care As a result of such shifts, a large part of the population normally identified as mentally ill has either been retained in the local community or has been returned from state hospitals. Unfortunately, this reversal of historic trends has not been accompanied by any systematic effort to provide substitute treatment or support services in the local community for persons identified as mentally ill. As a consequence, the anxieties of neighbors and families have been aroused because of their inability to handle unfamiliar behavior. Many of the mentally ill have historically been isolated from family and other social ties, and have congregated in a variety of boarding houses, nursing homes, and hotels.

Abuses of drugs and alcohol This trend to deinstitutionalize has been, in part, achieved through an enormous increase in the use of drugs to control behavior which has, in turn, permitted faster hospital discharge. It has also fostered the use of drugs in large quantities. The enormous expenditures for drugs have been a factor in the mental health field. More significantly, however, the use of chemotherapy may in time be found to be associated with another long-term behavioral concern—this is, the abuse of both drugs and alcohol. This abuse has now become so widespread that public concern is no longer based on the unsightliness of skid row areas, but on the spread of alcoholism to all parts of the population. In many industries, in fact, this has become a major problem affecting productivity, profitability, and the economy.

The phenomenon of mental retardation Associated with this set of circumstances is the growth of respect for the problem of mental retardation and the evolution of a powerful citizen demand that the mentally retarded no longer be shunted into the back wards of state hospitals but be given an opportunity to join to some extent the mainstream of community life. The provision of special housing and service facilities for the retarded child and adult have imposed new burdens on local services providers most of whom are nonprofit and only partly financed through local, state, and federal taxes.

What is frequently overlooked is the fact that the mentally retarded child now generally survives to adulthood, and a very large number live for decades beyond that. For severely retarded adults without occupational potential and without the ability to care for themselves, the provision of appropriate services (for those whose own families are no longer alive) represent a serious problem for local government.

Problems of the handicapped   A further extension of this problem for local government has been a concern for the physically disabled and the developmentally disadvantaged. The latter group includes conditions which have a neurological origin–cerebral palsy, multiple sclerosis, *spina bifida,* etc. For these, as for the retarded and the mentally ill, the goal is that they be given every opportunity, not only to receive medical treatment, but to live with whatever supportive physical care is necessary in normal community circumstances rather than being isolated in large institutions. Many adults with severe neurological defects are capable of movement with specially designed wheelchairs and the like, but arrangements for their housing require special attention and cost.

The outlook   As in the case of health planning, the attempt to plan systematically for this diverse population has been attempted without notable progress. Planning boards do exist, but are primarily advisory and consultative with little authority.

Even though local governments do not yet directly administer many of these services, they are involved to the extent that some locally supported public health departments have sought to bring some order to the mental health system. Local government is also involved in the income maintenance and child welfare programs which support this population economically, and in the provision of residences. Local government officials can play a major role in the resolution of this housing question: arrangements can be more or less costly and more or less satisfactory for the residents, depending on the integrating intelligence which is brought to bear on the problem. Local government officials, whose position in the community lets them see these problems as part of a larger context, can make a major contribution.

Finally, aberrant behavior in the community and the corresponding deinstitutionalization of populations previously cared for in state hospitals create a new and unprecedented problem for local government which seems to be beyond the sole capacity of private service providers to meet without effective governmental leadership. Since the lives of individuals are infinitely varied, it is doubtful whether effective reaction to this challenge can take place at distant state or national capitals alone.

The needs of the aged

Many of the needs of the aged have been touched upon in previous sections—the need for income support, for health services, and for protective care in case of disability. But the aged are a significant force in most urban communities, their proportion of the total population having grown from 4 percent in 1900 to well over 10 percent in the 1970s. In many local jurisdictions, the percentage of the elderly is as high as 12–15 percent, and is projected to rise as high as 16 percent overall in the next few decades.[12]

Special characteristics of the aged   Aside from the concerns already dealt with, the elderly have, of course, all of the requirements which younger populations have. But they are by and large out of the mainstream of employed activity and generally have fixed incomes. As a result, they have special requirements when it comes to transportation, shopping, housing, and opportunities for leisure. While most of the elderly do have satisfactory family ties, the proportion of those without ties increases as more and more of the elderly live into their seventies and eighties (the fastest growing segment of the American population is that over 75 years). These "old elderly" are likely to have outlived their families and their peers, and will often find themselves with the additional burden of loneliness.

Meeting the needs   To meet these special needs, a bewildering array of small-scale and highly fragmented services have grown up in local communities. Many of them are organized and maintained by religious, proprietary, and other nonprofit organizations, but are sometimes provided directly by departments of public welfare, quasi-public home care corporations, and day care centers. This variety of small-scale organizations may provide transportation, home-delivered or communal meals, special housing, homemaker services, clinical services, legal advice, recreation services, companionship to overcome loneliness, counseling, or advice on a host of personal and legal problems. The number of service-providing organizations has grown exponentially, but the total number served is still only a small part of the aged population in any community. Whether the vast majority requires such additional services or not has never been fully established, but the frontier for growth in these services seems destined to become an increasingly important item in the affairs of local government.

Area offices for the aged have been established with federal stimulation to introduce regional level planning, but, as in the field of health and child welfare, this planning by and large has been consultative in nature and commands limited authority to develop policies for the elderly or to implement those policies through the exceedingly complex variety of existing service-providing agencies.

Summary

Income maintenance, child welfare, health services, mental health and mental retardation, the needs of the aged—all programs in these areas of the human services system can touch the lives of large numbers of local citizens regardless of class and income. At the same time, they are absorbing a large and continuously growing percentage of local government expenditures matched by much larger expenditures derived from state and federal government. In all of these areas, the above discussion has indicated that policies and managerial structures are in a state of flux, with many problems in the way of overlap and other coordination between levels of government, within the same government, and between the public and private sectors. Some of these problems will be dealt with in successive chapters, as will the detailed challenges presented to local government managers by some of the illustrative areas mentioned. It is clear, however, not only that the problems of coordination and changing policies are real, but also that local government, in its role as that level of government closest to the local community, can assume a major responsibility for addressing citizen concerns and needs in these human services functions.

Some trends and issues

Given these circumstances, what responses have local governments, as well as state and federal agencies, come up with? The following discussion, again without attempting to be comprehensive or to anticipate the detailed discussion given later in this book, will take a look at some of the directions in which local governments seem to be moving. The discussion is divided into two parts. The first, and major, part looks at the coordination and integration of services. It touches on the following topics: local government leadership to fill the gaps; the single-entry human resources center; case management; integrated service delivery systems; state level reorganization and planning; de-institutionalization; consumer participation; management techniques; and information and data systems. The second portion briefly addresses the question of county, town, and city relationships.

The coordination and integration of services

One major trend among local governments has been to test out new ways for bringing about either a more effective coordination among the variety of human services, or even to move beyond coordination in order to effect a functional integration of services. With hardly enough time to permit any one intervention to take effect, federally stimulated reorganization of services has been attempted through partnership programs, coordinated service programs (under SITO—Service Integration Targets of Opportunity), capacity building, and the creation of comprehensive human resources and human services agencies which seek to bring under a single administrative umbrella a wide variety of human services. It is helpful in this respect to first concentrate on a relatively limited number of significant efforts in this direction which are rooted in local government before considering the long-term effects of some of the other movements toward coordination. Locally guided, organized, and directed programs can be classified into the major groupings, discussed below, in each of which local public officials have played new and significant roles.

Local government leadership to fill the gaps   All of the human services organizations thus far discussed are incomplete, in the sense that they provide some services and omit others or meet the needs of some populations and ignore those of others. A combination of judicious direction of Model Cities funds, well-conceived use of OEO funds, and vigorous and aggressive acquisition of special categorical funds has sometimes permitted local governments to fill in some of the more obvious gaps. Examples are seen in the development of neighborhood health centers, in the development of day care centers for children and for the aged, and in the slow development of halfway houses and local services to meet the needs of persons discharged from correctional institutions, chronic hospitals, and mental hospitals. This is not to suggest that local governments are single-handedly capable of filling such gaps, but the leadership of local officials has been instrumental in developing resources, with state and federal governments' help, in order to meet the demands of special local constituencies.

The East Cleveland Human Services Department is one of numerous examples. This department is an integral part of the local government with the responsibility which nominally could cover the entire range of human services. It is funded in part by local allocation of general revenue-sharing funds plus special purpose funds secured through negotiation. Since the resources could not possibly be adequate to directly provide all services, the department has sought to radically modify the work of the several score of previously existing agencies. The department has functioned on a flexible basis, sometimes assisting local constituencies with technical aid to help them secure special funding to enable the organization agencies designed to meet the needs of hitherto unserved populations. Sometimes the department has secured funds from categorical programs for its own activities. Sometimes it has used general purpose funds to underwrite activities not otherwise available.

The single-entry human resources center   It has long been an ideal that many public and voluntary services could be housed in a single structure so that applicants would be spared the necessity of travelling to many different geographic sites. A number of communities have more or less consolidated varieties of agencies into a single-site housing, but have maintained the functional independence of each of the agencies. The single-site efforts are found in communities as diverse as Chicago; Brockton, Massachusetts; and Wilkes-Barre, Pennsylvania. The administrators of the single site are nominally in a position to encourage independent agencies to come together where conflicts of interest arise, where there are problems of coordination, and where there are difficulties in securing client access.

However, the dynamics of independent agency functioning mean that major changes in the delivery of human services come about very slowly—if at all—and are governed by the primary commitments of each of the agencies.

Case management   In recent years, case management has assumed special popularity as it has been found difficult to relocate agencies in single-entry sites at a sufficient number of locations to assure uniform access to urban populations. The case management concept permits provider agencies to maintain their geographic as well as functional separation, but provides an individual staff member from an existing agency (or one specially hired for the purpose) to receive applications from diverse clientele. A case plan is worked out by this initial worker, who assumes responsibility for referring clients to other agencies and for procuring—usually through persuasion rather than by administrative ordinance—the effective acceptance of applications by other agencies. Where the services of several agencies are required for the same client, the case manager is in a position to monitor performance of the interlocking services and to see to it that the client is not lost in the maze of interdepartmental eligibility and procedural obstacles. However, the case manager in most places functions without authority and must depend upon persuasive ability.

A substantial improvement over the voluntary case manager exists in some communities where programs are more effectively integrated. For example, in a few communities, agencies agree that an application made to one agency can be treated as an application to another agency without requiring clients to repeat the admission process. Experiments have also been launched to back up the authority of case managers with control over reimbursement to reluctant agencies.

Integrated service delivery systems   A few examples exist in which several human services have been effectively integrated rather than simply coordinated. In communities such as Wilkes-Barre, to name only one, and through the functioning of councils of governments in some western states, something like the following has emerged. A central board is appointed by local governments to represent both consumers and the involved service providers. This board is the channel through which all applications for state and federal grants must be sent for approval and then, when procured, for allocation to the service agencies. Agreements are reached among participating agencies, through the mechanism set up by the board, governing the authority of a case manager, agreements to accept referrals made by participating agencies, and the maintenance of adequate data systems for planning and monitoring purposes. The channelling of external funds is presumably contingent upon satisfactory performance of these obligations.

In some jurisdictions, such as Wilkes-Barre, workers employed under categorical programs are nonetheless expected to accept assignments outside of their category if it is decided to be necessary by the administrator or case manager of the office in which they are working. Thus, while their funding remains rooted in the categorical grant, their responsibilities are diversified. These more integrated programs represent a first step in the creation of a true, publicly financed personal service organization accountable to local government (and to state government as well), but still directly responsible for consolidating separate, fragmented categories of staff in order to deliver more unified services. While no comprehensive evaluation has been completed, these efforts promise a more efficient use of personnel, at the minimum. The more integrated services are generally accountable directly to the chief executive officer of local governments, usually through a board also accountable to the chief executive officer.

State level reorganization and planning   Coordination of services has also proceeded through efforts at more abstract structural changes at the level of state government. The creation of statewide human services departments and restructuring of state government has frequently altered the lines of authority by which categorical local and state agencies submit their budgets, develop their plans, and secure their funding. By and large, this attempt to streamline state government is at a very early stage in which executive officers use concepts of program planning, or planning by objective, to alter the conventional categorical lines of growth which once flowed from a categorical federal program through a state legislative committee to a state categorical program down to the service delivery front with no attempt to correlate the lines of evolution. With budget authority consolidated to work through the funnel of a comprehensive state or local umbrella agency, or through an office of planning and budgeting, it is hoped that in time the most glaring inconsistencies and deficiencies can be identified and strong service agencies can be induced to alter their internal planning to take into account their relationships with other parallel organizations.

The proliferation of "comprehensive" planning entities in several fields has already been noted. The attempts to create new planning organizations in health, children's services, mental health, and for the aging (income maintenance programs lack such planning mechanisms) are primarily coordinative. They bring functionally independent providers and consumers together, but lack authority to influence the direction which the interplay of special interests will take in this planning. But these units have been an important new channel for the introduction of citizen wants through citizen representation. When this trend is viewed alongside the attempt to streamline state and local government by increasing the authority of the executive office and its budgeting procedures, one can discern a wide-ranging series of experiments in American government to try out various devices with the aid of which local and state governments can acquire mastery over the present chaotic complex of independent human services organizations.

De-institutionalization The trend away from institutionalizing difficult population groups has already been noted. In the field of crime, delinquency, mental illness, mental retardation, and chronic diseases, the decade-old attempt continues to return persons, previously incarcerated in large institutions, to more normal community living. But it has been difficult to smooth the transition efficiently: the large state institutions continue to be funded and staffed without much reduction due to civil service, union, and other organizational obstacles. At the same time, the allocation of funds and the creation of services at the local level, to provide what was previously provided in large institutions, has moved very slowly. Progress on this front is complicated by the natural tendency of each governmental jurisdiction to try to pass financial responsibility to another level of government rather than shouldering the cost. Thus state governments seek to pass responsibility back to the budgets of local communities or to Washington, which reciprocate in turn. Nonetheless, this long-term tendency gives to local governments an opportunity to seek the creation of effective service programs at home and in the community for many troubled populations, services which can be guided by local governments and which can be seen as practical achievements of that government on behalf of their populations.

Consumer participation Consumers are increasingly participating in the policy decisions of the human services agencies, supplementing the tradition of having leading citizens serve on advisory boards. Consumers represent new classes of citizens, those more likely to be recipients rather than donors of services. Such participation has made planning more complex by adding to the number and volume of voices introduced into decision making; but, at the same time, it has opened up an awareness of new needs that were not previously perceived. This opening of the participation process also requires a counterresponse in administrative and organizational capacity, to sort out the conflicting voices and to plan how best to meet the increased range of requirements with limited resources. The administrative capacity is not yet strongly provided, but may become an important stimulus as local governments seek to remain responsive to their constituencies.

Management techniques   New techniques to manage human services are being experimented with by local governments. Cash payments to consumers are being supplemented by vouchers to smaller subgroups of the population to purchase special services only. Vouchers plus cash payments spread the access and utilization of the major human services but, at the same time, lend themselves to abuses as the vouchers are used more in the area of discretionary spending instead of being limited to life and death matters such as food.

It is important to note a recent revival of interest in having public agencies *purchase services, through contract, from private providers*. Since 1935, the national tendency had been to avoid subsidizing private social services by tax funds in favor of public administration. Since 1968, a vigorous attempt has been made to diminish public service administration and to exercise government responsibility through the funneling of tax funds to private agencies to meet public needs. A major policy consideration in local government is whether the needs of the local population are best met by such purchase from private and proprietary providers. Such organizations are less directly responsive to overall community needs, concentrating as they must on their own specialized or proprietary interests. On the other hand, comprehensive, direct public service provision is not fully accepted by the restless taxpayer.

While the evidence is thus far contradictory, major attempts at contracting out have not succeeded in effectively dealing with the problems intended. In New York City, massive purchase of child care services from private providers has meant that large segments of the needy population are completely unattended, despite strong governmental controls. In North Carolina, the attempts to contract the administration of Medicaid payments to a private firm collapsed as the costs became uncontrollable by the private mechanism. In Gary, Indiana, the contracting out of special education to a proprietary firm did not produce the expected beneficial results.

The issue is not yet settled, but it is doubtful whether there will be any resolution other than some combination of direct public service provision plus private provision subsidized by tax funds. Purchase of service makes public officials less directly accountable and less vulnerable for failure, but the price of this avoidance of the "hot seat" of public accountability is a relative loss of control which could be exercises through direct public administration of services.

Information and data systems   Information and data systems for monitoring these complex service delivery programs are clearly necessary, but they have proven enormously costly, difficult to manage, and have not provided answers for complex policy questions. They have increasingly become a part of local government and a valuable policy and management tool, but only when managers use them with care.

Just how data systems should be constructed remains a question. Executive officers, through their budget officers, can procure information only if there are accountable direct service units capable of providing reliable data. Valuable as is the data prepared by organizations providing services, it is equally useful to have other sources of information introduced into the data system so that executive officers can arrive at independent judgments without remaining dependent on information produced by the service providers (who may be consciously or unconsciously biased, or limited in their judgments). A comprehensive human resources organization in local government is capable of assembling data more comprehensively for the purposes of local planning. A comprehensive human services agency with competent staff is also capable of tempering the views and information of service specialists with other specialists' perspectives.

County, town, and city relationships

The structure of local government varies so widely in the various states, representing a long historical accumulation of adaptation in local government, that few general propositions can be asserted with confidence. In some states, often those with less dense populations, county government is the major and dominant mechanism for local government and has therefore a dominant influence on the shaping of human services. In other states, the counties have only weak, vestigial functions and major human services responsibilities are located in towns and cities. In still others, responsibilities are divided in ways which defy generalization. These forms of local government are inevitably influenced by recent tendencies to develop substate regions or metropolitan regions in order to consolidate weak, small, and presumably inefficient local jurisdictions into more effective governing units where the relationship between population, tax base, resources, and obligations are in better balance. With few exceptions, however, these attempts at substate regionalization are represented by coordinative bodies with few authoritative powers. They depend for their vitality on the vigor of the basic local governments which make up the region.

One common dilemma lies in the fact that urban concentrations of populations often represent cultural, economic, and social requirements quite different from those in more dispersed rural and agricultural populations. The former have in the past been best served by city-organized human services, and the latter best served by county-organized services. However, the mobility of populations and the restless move from farm to cities and suburbs makes it increasingly necessary for some working arrangements to be developed between these parallel jurisdictions where each has distinctive populations and vigorous governments.

Although no comprehensive nationwide study has been completed of diverse patterns, recent reports of the Advisory Commission on Intergovernmental Relations outline characteristic patterns in various parts of the country.[13]

What lies ahead for local governments

Prediction is, under any circumstances, risky, but it is possible to anticipate certain developments in local government which are especially important and interesting because they involve an evolution in organization where opportunity, accountable responsibility, and limited authority are blended together.

At this writing it seems inevitable that local officials will increasingly be attracted or impelled to view the human services as a cluster of obligations and resources—as tools—with which the life of the city can be improved. At the same time, these tools can be used as a political response to serious problems to which citizens demand immediate attention. The combination of demands and the opportunity to improve the vigorous life of the jurisdiction must be blended with effective, efficient and economical use of always limited resources: this tension between wants and resources represents the arena for local government activity.

To deal with such challenges and pressures, public officials are expected to view all the human services in relation to both the disadvantaged subgroups of the population and the overall well-being of the community. The contradictary pressures require the development of local policies about the best means for dealing with them and local objectives which these policies should seek to realize. Such a policy approach can be expected to increase the demand for an effective planning mechanism at the local government level, which can help elected officials by: 1) assessing needs of various populations groups; 2) generating and evaluating various approaches; and 3) evaluating priorities and the results of funded programs. Such planning will undoubtedly function on a continuous basis as some programs are found wanting and are replaced by new ones and as new gaps are identified which require the creation of facilities and resources to fill them.

Three options can be identified in performing such functions. These options are coordination; activism; and the provision of comprehensive departments.

Coordination

Local government officials can function as the coordinators to assemble information to bring it to the attention of various organizations in the local jurisdiction and to constantly assert the necessity for action by those organizations using persuasion and, sometimes, pressure. In this sense, the function of local government is not merely one of bringing together the parties but also of "keeping their feet to the fire" until acceptable action results.

In performing this function, the elected officials of local government act primarily in conventional political roles. They keep attuned to clues or signs about conditions which are persistently troubling, or about difficulties which are beginning to emerge. When noted, these are publicized through media presentations or are taken up in meetings with other persons or organizations concerned about the life of the city. It is assumed that the basic institutions of the city—voluntary, labor, and business associations— are primarily responsible for initiating detailed actions, which may be limited to the voluntary sector or which may spread to demands made by such groups on city government to act. Permanent agencies of local government are also held accountable by similar prodding action taken by elected officials. Where major responsibility lies with nonlocal government agencies, they too are subjected to the same attention-focusing action by public officials.

In using this option, the leadership of local public officials begins by testifying and acknowledging publicly that a difficulty exists or persists. Sometimes this action produces the public agreement which permits local government to take remedial action; at other times, it defuses the subject by turning action back to less visible voluntary associations.

Activism

Local government managers may go a step further toward activism by using their policy and planning capacities to not only inform public and private officials about the nature of the problem confronting them, but to advocate new approaches to replace those which have not succeeded in the past. They can develop criteria by which new programs can be identified by local government even though the execution of those options may be left to others.

Under this option, locally elected officials assume that the agencies of local and state government have a major responsibility to act in easing human problems. It is not assumed that past regulations, or the constraints imposed by state and federal regulations, must always prevail. The structure of local–state public agency organization is not interfered with: rather, general executive officers use publicity, their appointive powers and their executive planning office to stimulate other executive agencies to explore new ways to operate, given the present structure. Action is seen as lying within the existing agencies, but such federal, state, or local governmental agencies need stimulation and pressure to take into account any distinctive problems which confront a particular local jurisdiction. A variance can be secured in applying a general federal regulation to fit local conditions, extra support can be secured because the population in a given area is especially old or poor or disadvantaged. An agency can be stimulated to alter its staff hiring practices or to change the location of an office. Priorities can be shifted in using agency funds. Decisions about such specific actions originate in the executive office, but execution depends on persuading others to adopt the proposals.

Developing comprehensive departments

Finally, local governments can develop human services departments of a comprehensive nature, as a complement to activities undertaken by voluntary and proprietary agencies. Whatever the combination of public, voluntary, and proprietary services, the needs of all the population must be satisfactorily met according to the criteria which local government fixes.

In this option, local government acts more radically and seeks to bring about a structural change in the way local human services are delivered. It does so by trying out organizational changes which will permit the better execution of major changes in policy. Merging public agency staffs and programs can be seen as a way to accumulate a stronger critical mass of resources under one administration, in order to redirect those resources in accordance with new priorities. With such structural changes to support new policies, one part of the community's population may be especially targeted; or a new emphasis may be given to encouraging citizen groups to propose new ways to deal with their problems; or new techniques may be introduced using government staff. Here, public planning and administration of services are joined into one process to effect public ends as defined by local executives. Voluntary and proprietary organizations continue to function, but are joined by a local government capability as well.

Conclusion

It is not to be expected that local governments, by themselves, will solve the kinds of social problems discussed in this chapter, but they can be at the frontier of caring for these problems since the problems fall, inescapably, into the laps of local officials. In a continuous dynamic evolution, local governments will have at least one choice to make: to develop a public human services program that will deal with some of these problems, linked though it may be to other organizations; or to demand more effective coverage, quality, and coordination from other nongovernmental or nonlocal organizations in the jurisdiction. With either course of action, there is probably no locus more central than local government that is capable of maintaining steady attention to the needs of an entire population in order to consolidate gains and guide further evolution in a situation as complex as that presented by the human services. Whether the evolution involves the creation of a public service system complementary to the voluntary and proprietary systems or depends instead entirely on voluntary organizations, it is inevitable that tax funds from local, state and federal sources will have to be used to programs in either case. Local governments are currently searching for effective ways in which they can influence this evolution.

The quality of life in local governments, especially in cities and towns, has been deteriorating perceptibly. This is not only a function of decaying buildings, inadequate transportation systems, and changing social patterns, but also of constantly moving economies, and increasing unemployment, and neglected pockets of underprivileged persons. These, taken together, produce the decline in urban amenity and quality of life which has been the object of so much attention in recent years. These shifts have endangered not only the oldest but even the newest of cities, not only the old core cities but their newer suburbs. While no simple monolothic form of organization for the human services is likely to succeed by itself in improving local life, organization and services can be introduced to fill the most obvious gaps. All this lies ahead.

Guidance in this complex evolution continues to be in the public interest, guidance which local governments have given and are continuing to give through new forms of organization. In this, they are joined by the efforts of state and federal government, legislatures and, more recently, the courts as well as numerous citizen organizations. But it has already been emphasized that the expression of wants and the identification of needs must be countered by accountable organizational action which will facilitate the choice of structure to meet the wants and to balance these against the available resources in order that the most acceptable blend possible is achieved in the community interest. This is the major role that lies ahead for local government.

1 See Robert Morris, *Toward A Caring Society,* Report of a U.S. Study Team (New York: Columbia University School of Social Work, 1974), pp. 53–55.

2 *Encyclopedia of Social Work,* 16th ed. (New York: National Association of Social Workers, 1971), p. 1593.

3 Personal communication from staff member of Connecticut Human Services Council, June 1976.

4 U.S. Congress, Joint Economic Committee, *Studies in Public Welfare,* Paper no. 6 (Washington, D.C.: Government Printing Office, 1973), pp. 2, 83–95.

5 Federal legislation specifies the portion of AFDC expenditures which the federal government will match. In the original 1935 legislation, the proportions were conventionally: federal, 50 percent; state, 25 percent; local, 25 percent. By the 1970s several states assumed responsibility for the local share. The SSI program has transferred the basic fiscal burden for the aged, blind, and totally disabled to the federal level, with a national standard of payment. Many industrial, northern states previously gave relief allowances above this national average, reflecting higher living costs in those states. These higher allowances continue in most of those states: the additional payment is funded entirely by state and some local governments.

6 U.S., Department of Commerce, Bureau of the Census, *United States Census of Population 1970,* Vol. 2, *Persons by Family Characteristics,* p. 1.

7 U.S., Department of Health, Education, and Welfare, *Federal Programs for Young Children: Review and Recommendations,* by Sheldon White et al., vol.

3 (Washington, D.C.: Government Printing Office, 1973), p. 11.

8 "Public Assistance Vendor Payments for Medical Care by Program, 1954–1974," *Social Security Bulletin,* Annual Statistical Supplement 1974, p. 174. For example, in 1972, assistance dollar payments nationally totaled $11 billion and medical vendor payments totaled an additional $8.4 billion.

9 U.S., Department of Commerce, Bureau of the Census, "Demographic Aspects of Aging and the Older Populations of the United States," *Current Population Reports,* Special Studies no. 59 (Washington, D.C.: Government Printing Office, 1976), p. 8.

10 U.S., Congress, Senate, Special Committee on Aging, Subcommittee on Long Term Care, *Nursing Home Care in the United States: Failure of Public Policy,* Introductory Report (Washington, D.C.: Government Printing Office, 1974), p. 25.

11 See U.S., Congress, Senate, Special Committee on Aging, *Alternatives to Institutional Care: A Proposal,* prepared by the Levinson Policy Institute, Brandeis University (Washington, D.C.: Government Printing Office, 1971), p. 13.

12 U.S., Department of Commerce, Bureau of the Census, "Demographic Aspects of Aging." *Current Population Reports.*

13 See Advisory Commission on Intergovernmental Relations, *Regional Decision Making: New Strategies for Substate Districts,* vol. 1, Case Studies no. A–43; and *Regional Governance: Promises and Performance,* vol. 2, Case Studies no. A–43 (Washington, D.C.: Government Printing Office, 1973).

Relations with other agencies delivering human services

Few problems confronting the human services administrator at the local level are of greater significance than the fragmentation and diversity of the entities that plan, finance, and deliver human services. This lack of unity, and its managerial implications, is recognized at all levels of our system of government, from the highest levels in Washington to city halls and county buildings across the nation. As a Secretary of the Department of Health, Education, and Welfare stated at his swearing-in ceremony:

The hard truth is that we are far from being the sole arbiter of all matters of health, education, and welfare. We are simply one among many—along with the Congress, the other departments of the Executive Branch, and a host of state and local agencies [both public and private] that have a responsibility for these matters. . . . It follows that the strength of the department is necessarily in building partnerships and alliances and bridges.[1]

This Washington perspective is confirmed at the local level, to take an example from an area with which the writer is familiar, by a study of expenditures for human services in Alameda County, California. The study identified 327 different operating agencies providing human services during 1974–75 to the residents of that county. Of the 327 agencies identified, 63 were governmental (2 federal, 5 state, 12 county, and 44 municipal or special district). The remaining 264 agencies were nongovernmental (57 were affiliated with the United Way of the [San Francisco] Bay Area and 207 were independent). Almost all of the nongovernmental agencies were voluntary nonprofit organizations; some were proprietary.

Of the $221 million expended by the 327 operating agencies, however, 96.7 percent came from government sources, 2.1 percent from the United Way of the Bay Area, and 1.2 percent from other nongovernment sources (including foundations). Expenditure of the funds followed a somewhat different pattern: government operating agencies expended 83.0 percent of the funds (4.6 percent by federal; 5.9 percent by state; 31.0 percent by county; and 41.5 percent by municipal and special district). Nongovernmental agencies expended 17.0 percent of the funds (5.4 percent by agencies affiliated with the United Way of the Bay Area and 11.6 percent by independent agencies). The above figures suggest that government has become an increasingly important source of funds for voluntary agencies, primarily through grants and purchase of service arrangements.

The situation in Alameda County is further complicated by the fact that the expenditures by operating agencies amount to only one-third of the total expenditures for human services in that county. If payments made directly to or on behalf of individuals (public assistance, rent supplements, Medicare, etc.) are included, the total expenditure for human services in Alameda County increases by $441.5 million, or a total estimated expenditure of $662.5 million. Of that total, almost all (98.9 percent) of the funds identified come from government sources; 71.7 percent of all funds come from federal sources alone.[2]

This chapter discusses the complexity of the human services delivery system illustrated by the above example, and analyzes its implications for local government decision makers. It focuses on the relationship of local government to federal, state, regional, and special purpose governments and discusses the interface between local government and those segments of the private sector that have an impact on the delivery of human services.

The chapter is divided into four sections. The first section discusses the impact of federal and state government policies and programs on local service delivery mechanisms. It begins by comparing public sector expenditures for human services with each other and with the voluntary sector, and moves on to a discussion of such specific programs as the War on Poverty, Model Cities, Title IV-A of the Social Security Act, the New Federalism, the Short–Doyle Act, and the implications for states of Title XX.

The second section examines the relationships between local government and regional planning bodies and special district governments (notably school districts). The third section assesses local government relationships with the private sector, including voluntary nonprofit agencies, proprietary agencies, health providers, and corporations. The fourth section raises some issues about the specific roles of city and county governments in the provision of human services. There is a brief concluding summary.

The discussion throughout focuses on the decision-making implications of this complex interaction of organizations and governments with each other and (through expenditures of taxpayers' monies and delivery of services) with the citizens of our communities. References throughout are made to the northern California examples familiar to the writer, but it is hoped that they have a wider applicability, if only to hold up a mirror in which local administrators in widely varying communities can view their own specific programs, existing and planned.

Impact of federal and state programs on local government

Nearly every level of government, as well as the private sector, has some role in the funding and delivery of human services in this country. Something of the evolution of these roles has been analyzed in Chapter 1. The key point for the present discussion, however, is that since the Depression of the 1930s the federal government and, to a lesser extent, state governments have had the most extensive impact on human services delivery systems.

The impact of federal and state governments on local service delivery systems will be discussed from two perspectives. The first is a comparison of expenditures for human services by federal, state, and local governments and by the voluntary nonprofit sector; comparability of expenditure figures is somewhat limited, however, by the lack of a universally accepted classification scheme for social services. The second portion of the discussion takes a look at the effect that federal and state programs and regulations have had on local service delivery since the 1960s.

Comparison of human services expenditures

The federal government has been the primary source of funds for public welfare programs since the 1930s. The commitment to such programs developed with the need to provide widespread, sustained public relief during the Depression and was reinforced by the necessity of balancing the unequal responses of the various state and local governments to meeting human needs. The commitment was fostered by the fact that the federal government alone has the tax base and legal authority requisite for creating and implementing human services programs throughout the country.

Human services expenditures by state and local governments and by the voluntary sector are much less extensive than those of the federal government. Much of the money allocated for such services by nonfederal entities is actually federal in origin.

Table 2–1 shows federal expenditures and state and local expenditures for each of seven selected social welfare programs during the fiscal year 1974. During this year, federal expenditures accounted for 57.6 percent of total expenditures for the seven programs. State and local government expenditures exceeded those of the federal government only in the area of education, where 90 percent of total expenditures was from state and local sources.

Table 2–1 1974 social welfare expenditures, by source of funds and by public program.

| | 1974 expenditures ($ millions) | | | | |
| | Total | Federal | | State and local | |
Program	$	$	% of total	$	% of total
All programs	239,303	137,655	57.6	101,648	42.4
Social insurance	98,952	82,829	83.7	16,124	16.3
Public aid	31,997	20,834	65.1	11,163	34.9
Health and medical	14,360	7,130	49.7	7,230	50.3
Veterans	14,112	13,874	98.3	239	1.7
Education	70,150	7,076	10.0	63,073	90.0
Housing	2,554	2,009	78.7	545	21.3
Other social welfare	7,178	3,903	54.4	3,275	45.6

Source: U.S., Department of Commerce, Bureau of the Census, *Statistical Abstract of the United States 1976*, Washington, D.C., Government Printing Office, 1976, p. 293.

Federal government expenditures   The federal government, largely through the Department of Health, Education, and Welfare (HEW) and the Department of Labor (DOL), is the primary source of funds for social welfare programs. By the mid-1970s, approximately $151.5 billion, 47 percent of the total domestic budget, was allocated for these programs.[3] The preponderance of the money, $108.6 billion, was allotted to income maintenance programs. Only $42.9 billion was actually designated for services in areas such as education, manpower, social services, and health. Those funds were dispensed through a variety of federally administered categorical grant programs and through block or revenue sharing grants overseen by state and local governments.

State government expenditures   In general, state allocations for human services are small in relation to allocations for such traditional programs as highway construction, public safety, and corrections. Factors such as population size, mix, and income further influence the relative allocation of funds for human services among the states.

Much of the money allocated by states for human services is derived not from state revenues, but from the federal government. While some state tax revenue is allocated for state administered or initiated human services, much of the money earmarked for such services is utilized as matching funds for federal grants. This trend clearly emerged with state use of federal funds available through Title IV-A of the Social Security Act. It continued in the 1970s with implementation of federal block grant and revenue sharing programs, which permit discretion by the states in the administration and allocation of federal funds. The magnitude of these programs is illustrated by the allocations for social services under Title XX of the Social Security Act. This federal program makes grants, ranging from $3.9 million for Alaska to $245.7 million for California, for the provision of social services to eligible low income residents. In order to receive such funds, however, the states must provide 25 percent of the cost of the services.

Local government expenditures Local government traditionally has not been involved in funding human services, although some local governments have administered general assistance welfare payment programs. The federal government and, to a lesser extent, state governments have provided the real impetus for city and county involvement in social service delivery systems. Through a variety of grant programs, localities have been given the money with which to deliver services. In some cases, such as Title XX, some local funds are required.

Even with the impetus of relatively flexible federal funds to finance social welfare programs, few localities have increased their involvement in supporting those programs. For example, the State and Local Fiscal Assistance Act of 1972 provided approximately $20 billion in general revenue sharing funds to local governments. Only about 3 percent of that money was spent for health and social services for the poor and the aged.

The five-county San Francisco Bay Area provides several illustrations of local utilization of revenue sharing monies. Two counties allocated no money for social services. One county used most of its revenue sharing funds for general assistance payments. The other two counties utilized their general revenue sharing grants to purchase social services from public and private agencies. Of these two counties, one allocated one-third of its $11.9 million grant to community-based social service agencies and organizations.

Put S.P.I.C.E. in your life The city manager of Niagara Falls, Ontario, Canada was instrumental in founding an organization that represents numerous volunteer service groups throughout his city. S.P.I.C.E. (Service People in Community Effort) has been quite successful in encouraging numerous service organizations to work together through common objectives to build recreation and service facilities for the community. Included are such organizations as the Optimists, Kiwanis, and Lions, and volunteer fire associations and Legion branches. S.P.I.C.E. was organized to relate the necessary city recreation projects to individual service associations and to integrate service club expansions within the city's overall recreation plan. Several cooperative projects are under way with many service organizations combining their talents to build an arena, a swimming pool, and playing fields in a newly proposed recreational complex at the southern end of the city.

Local expenditures under the Comprehensive Employment and Training Act (CETA) display a similar pattern. Title I of CETA provides a block grant to units or consortia of local government for the provision of manpower and social services. Nationally, 81 percent of the funds have been used for job training, classroom training, public service employment, and work experience. Less than 20 percent has been expended for social services.

Voluntary sector expenditures The ability of the voluntary nonprofit sector to support human services is more limited by capacity than commitment. As noted in Chapter 1, prior to the advent of major governmental involvement in the field, the voluntary movement played a leadership role in the support of human services. As of the later 1970s, however, the total voluntary sector expenditure for human services, excluding foundation grants, is less than either the federal allocation for

Title XX programs or the total general revenue sharing expenditures of local governments; foundations, while supportive of education and social service programs, award grants primarily for facilities and equipment.

In 1975, for example, the United Way movement in the United States raised a little more than $1 billion to support its affiliated agencies. However, these limited funds have an impact far in excess of their simple dollar value. At the local level, the United Way dollar can be used not only to support existing services but to serve as the local match for state and federal funds.

Federal and state programs, guidelines, and restrictions: impact on local human services delivery systems

As the primary funding sources for human services, the federal and state governments have a direct impact on the components of local service delivery systems and the environments in which they operate. Through priority setting, statutes, and administrative regulations, they influence such concrete aspects of local delivery mechanisms as the services provided, clientele served, procedures utilized for program planning, monitoring, and administration, and level of financing. They also often affect the basic organizational structure of the local government. In addition, the impact of federal and state decisions may extend to the climate in which services are delivered, influencing such factors as community sensitivity to social problems and the degree to which consumers of services are politicized.

The effects that federal and state programs have on local service delivery systems are rarely orderly and comprehensive. While the intent of the programs is to rationalize the delivery of human services, their effect may be just the opposite. In a sense, government—and the federal government in particular—is continually experimenting with new methods and programs to meet human needs. Some are devised from carefully conceived policy decisions and analyses; others are not. The result is the piecemeal development of a grant system whose programs have different goals, services, and clients and differing requirements for eligibility, monitoring, reporting, and administration. One program may be in vogue one year, and another the next, as illustrated by the successive ascendancy and decline of two major federal program thrusts during the 1968–1970 period, one in housing, the other in alleviating hunger. It is also important to note that voluminous reporting requirements, a claimed lack of discretion, and other problems in dealing with a huge federal bureaucracy have been perceived by some state and local administrators as being endemic to major federal programs, although the magnitude of those programs cannot, of course, be denied. Such perceptions, irrespective of the degree to which they are well-founded in any one case, appear the necessary companion of any federal presence.

Federal human services efforts thus have resulted in a hodgepodge of coexisting strategies and programs that never entirely replace one another, that are not necessarily coordinated or complementary, and that continually change. The onset of a change in national administration in 1977 confidently may be predicted to interject a vigorous new perspective into an already complex situation. Be that as it may, for most of the 1970s the local administrator has dealt with a federal government that simultaneously pursues income, voucher, and service strategies to meet human needs through both categorical and block grant programs. Each strategy, each program influences the local service delivery system within which he or she must work.

A review of federal programs in the 1960s and early 1970s illustrates the effects of the federal government on local human service delivery mechanisms. That period was marked by noticeable shifts in federal policies impacting human services, from the War on Poverty to the New Federalism, from categorical to block grants, and from the commitment of funds for social problems to funding retrenchment. The policies and programs especially reflective of this period include the

War on Poverty, Model Cities, Title IV-A of the Social Security Act, and the New Federalism, with its attendant general revenue sharing, special revenue sharing, and Title XX programs.

War on Poverty   The War on Poverty had two major thrusts: one focused on local service delivery mechanisms, the other on the climate in which local government functions. The first involved creation of an alternative local service delivery system, primarily outside government, which was operated by the local Community Action Agency (CAA) with the "maximum feasible" citizen participation. The system was subsequently dismantled with the withering of funds available through the federal Office of Economic Opportunity (OEO). The reasons for its demise are to be found in the ongoing national political debate of the period, and need not be explored here.

The second thrust involved increasing public awareness of and responsiveness to the problems of poverty. The attendant strategies of community organization, politicization of the poor, and advocacy policies had a profound, and often controversial, impact on the climate for service delivery in many cities. In the extreme, these strategies led to confrontation between government and the people involved in the poverty program and to the phenomenon of advocacy law, under which staff of OEO-funded legal services programs sued cities to provide human services.

Model Cities   In some respects, the Model Cities program represented the federal government's retreat from what many perceived as the excesses of the War on Poverty. The basic thrust of the program was to place responsibility for the poverty programs within city government and to mitigate the impact of uncontrolled citizen participation. Model Cities placed city government at the center of a social service delivery system. The Community Development Agency (CDA), responsible to City Hall, had legal responsibility for planning and funding programs, including human services programs. Funds were made available through a flexible block grant from the Department of Housing and Urban Development (HUD). That grant, and particularly Model Cities supplemental funds, enabled cities such as Richmond, California, and Portland, Maine, to finance some nontraditional services, such as a child care network.

The Model Cities program further structured the poverty program by focusing the local service delivery system on specific target areas through the designation of model neighborhoods. In addition, its planned variations component, while implemented in only a few cities, made the local chief executive the focus of the HUD-financed service network.

The program represented a shift in federal policy but did not totally eradicate the strategies of the War on Poverty. Some CDAs did, in fact, create new local service delivery systems rather than tying into those that already existed. Moreover, the program, at least initially, continued to politicize those it affected, since HUD guidelines concerning citizen participation were ambiguous.

The ability of the Model Cities program to influence the local political climate is evident by the evolution of the program in Dayton, Ohio. In that city a variety of social problems, dissatisfaction with the government, and rioting had begun politicizing residents of the model neighborhood. Implementation of the planning phase of the Model Cities program enhanced their political awareness and helped coalesce diverse resident groups into a citizens' organization sufficiently powerful to challenge local officials for control of Model Cities planning and programming.

Title IV-A of the Social Security Act   Title IV-A of the Social Security Act was a major impetus for county involvement in human services programming in those states that took advantage of the grants available under the act. This legislation provided open-ended funding for states to provide a variety of mandated and optional services to clients meeting public assistance eligibility requirements. To receive funds, a state basically had to devise a social services plan acceptable to HEW, and to contribute 25 percent matching funds.

Many states with a system of strong county government delegated responsibility for delivering services financed under Title IV-A to their counties, which were already administering the benefits payment programs to which Title IV-A was allied. The counties, in turn, had to (1) develop services, or linkages with existing service providers; (2) ensure that eligible clients were served; and, in many cases, (3) contribute the 25 percent local share to meet federal matching requirements. Compliance with regulations for implementation of Title IV-A restricted the latitude of counties in shaping the local programs. For example, counties were required to provide a series of social services mandated by the law. In addition, they could elect to provide other services categorized by the regulations as optional services. Similarly, the bulk of the Title IV-A funds had to be used for services to those clients who were classified as current, former, or potential public assistance recipients.

Implementation of Title IV-A programs frequently resulted in changes in the structure, administrative procedures, and service delivery techniques of county governments and in the types of services they provided. It also altered the relationship between county government and other levels of government, and between county government and the private sector. For example, to facilitate Title IV-A programming, counties contracted with public and private agencies for the delivery of services. They fostered the development of third-party umbrella agencies to plan and fund specific services. Finally, they entered into collaborative funding arrangements with voluntary organizations such as the United Way. Under these arrangements, the United Way donated local share funds and, in return, was able to designate the service to be supported with the federal funds and the geographic area in which the service was to be provided. These contracting arrangements, in turn, led to administrative changes within county government so that counties could ensure propriety in fund use. Hence, county social service departments became involved in the development of monitoring and reporting requirements and procedures for use in contract administration.

The Maricopa County, Arizona, experience is illustrative of one county's implementation of the Title IV-A program. In that county, the welfare department decided to delegate responsibility for planning, funding, and coordinating child care services. Child care services and such ancillary services as training and administration were purchased from the Maricopa County Community Council, a United Way planning instrumentality. The purchase of services contract was funded with Title IV-A money secured through a local match from the Maricopa County United Way. The community council used the federal money to create a Child Care Project which served as the conduit through which the welfare department purchased child care services from as many as nineteen different voluntary provider agencies. The Title IV-A funds for those contracts also were secured with United Way matching money. Both the Child Care Project and the service providers were required to submit reports to the county outlining fund use, in accordance with both county and federal monitoring regulations.

The New Federalism   The New Federalism wrought changes in federal programs and policies and in local responses to them. These changes are reflected in the block grant programs created by the New Federalism. Particularly illustrative are programs created by the State and Local Fiscal Assistance Act of 1972, the Housing and Community Development Act of 1974, and Title XX of the Social Security Act.

State and Local Fiscal Assistance Act of 1972   This legislation created the first of the major block grants, the general revenue sharing program. It authorized approximately $30.1 billion over six years in relatively unrestricted grants to state and local governments. Cities, counties, and other general local governments received about two-thirds of that money for expenditures in nine program areas, including health and social services for the poor and aged. The method for allocating the funds, determining the programs to be supported, and evaluating fund use was left to the discretion of the individual communities.

Local response to general revenue sharing varied, and in many localities the program never affected the human service delivery mechanism. With no federal mandate to utilize the money for social services, few localities expended the funds for that purpose. Those that did employed a variety of mechanisms. Some, such as Berkeley, California, allocated the money through the normal budgetary process. Others, such as San Francisco, California, funneled funds to the county departments for disbursement at their discretion. Still others, such as Alameda County, California, distributed the funds to community-based agencies on the basis of proposals reviewed by citizen advisory groups. Several of the localities which used general revenue sharing monies to fund human services programs also developed methods for evaluating those programs. Many did not have an evaluation capacity and either developed an internal evaluation unit or contracted with appropriate agencies for evaluation services.

While general revenue sharing has not yet (as of the later 1970s) dramatically altered the environment in which local government operates, it has mobilized consumer groups and service providers in communities in which funds are disbursed on the basis of competitive proposals. In those communities, local government has become a focus of the social services grant system and is thus subject to some of the same pressures as are placed on the federal and state governments. In Alameda County, for example, voluntary sector agencies and organizations have lobbied for and obtained citizen participation in that part of the general revenue sharing allocation process concerned with funding human services.

Housing and Community Development Act of 1974   The major impact on local human services systems of the Housing and Community Development Act was the elimination of Model Cities as a discrete HUD program. This block grant program consolidated Model Cities and five other HUD programs into a block grant geared primarily toward physical development of the local community. Under the provisions of the act, only 20 percent of funds available to the local community could be used for human services, and those services had to be adjuncts to physical development programs. In addition, communities using HUD funds to provide human services had to demonstrate that funds were not available from other sources. The effect of the block grant, then, was to reduce overall funding for human services and to enable localities that did not want to support such services to allocate the federal monies (including Model Cities) elsewhere.

Title XX of the Social Security Act   Title XX is a modified social services block grant program which replaced Title IV-A in 1974. Like Title IV-A, its major influence at the local level is on county government. While its full impact on county human service delivery systems cannot be ascertained, some effects already are evident. Title XX has effected a change in the amount of funds available for human services. Unlike Title IV-A, which provided for open-ended funding, Title XX limits the total allocation for human services to $2.5 billion nationally. In states such as California, which quickly reached its maximum level of funding, many counties have experienced static or reduced allocations which have led to reductions in services.

Title XX also influences the services provided by counties. The statute does not mandate the provision of any services except family planning, so that localities theoretically can determine the services to be provided locally, as long as those programs are consistent with state requirements. In addition, Title XX increases the population allowed to receive county social services by relating eligibility requirements to the median family income in each state, rather than to public assistance criteria.

The effects of the administrative regulations governing child care services supported by Title XX provide a concrete example of how this program influences, and sometimes complicates, local service delivery. Until enactment of Title XX, governments, and those child care providers with whom they contracted, used net family income as the basis for determining the eligibility of a child for federally subsidized child care. Title XX regulations, however, changed the basis for eligibility determination to gross family income. The result of this change was implementation of an expensive and time-consuming major recertification process which also prohibited previously eligible children from receiving free services.

Impact of state government   State government, while less pervasive and bountiful than the federal government, can also affect local government's management of human resources. The impact of state government results from the development of state human services programs, as well as from the promulgation of state policies and regulations governing the implementation of federal programs administered by the state. The California Short–Doyle Act and the legislation and administrative procedures governing initiation of Title XX in California are examples of that impact.

The Short–Doyle Act   The Short–Doyle Act, through its statutory provisions and grant program, prodded local governments within California to establish a network of community mental health services. The program, enacted in 1957, requires counties with populations of 100,000 or more to provide ten specific services; smaller counties and cities are permitted, but not required, to provide those services. Also specified are the planning and administrative procedures to be followed in program implementation.

Over the years since 1957, program amendments, regulations, and state policies have altered the service network created at the local level by the Short–Doyle Act. For example, during the period 1967–72, Short–Doyle allocations increased steadily, lending impetus to the extension of local service delivery. A funding shift in fiscal year 1972–73 subsequently resulted in nearly static appropriations for several years and a reduction in local programming. Further, in 1973 a decision was made to close fourteen mental hospitals. This action was consistent with the community-based care priorities of the Short–Doyle program, but it was also based on economic factors. As a result of that decision, state hospital patients were returned to their communities for care, compelling local governments to develop a service capacity to meet the needs of those people.

The development in 1969 of the Westside Community Mental Health Center project in San Francisco is one example of the effect of the Short–Doyle program on local mental health delivery systems. That project consists of a consortium of hospitals, community agencies, and other mental health service providers coordinated by an administrative entity, all working together to provide a range of services to clients with mental health problems.

The idea for the center and the initial efforts to create it emanated from a group of psychiatrists who perceived a need for a 24-hour crisis clinic to serve drug users in the Westside area of San Francisco. At the same time, the County Department of Health was considering steps to decentralize its mental health services. This confluence of interest sparked county interest in the Westside project. Passage of two pieces of legislation helped secure county support for the project and funds to implement it. The first was a federal law permitting the National Institute of Mental Health (NIMH) to make staffing grants to community mental health centers. The second was an amendment to the Short–Doyle Act which liberalized the formula for distribution of funds and consequently increased state reimbursement for local mental health programs. As a result, San Francisco obtained the funds necessary for decentralization of mental health services and support of the Westside project.

State regulation of Title XX   Although Title XX is a federal formula grant program, states have latitude in its implementation. The states can formulate laws, regulations, and procedures which directly affect the agencies providing services funded under Title XX. In California, the county social services departments are the local administering entities, and the local service delivery systems reflect both legislative and bureaucratic decisions at the state level.

Over time, the state legislature has enacted several laws governing the provision of federally subsidized social services within the state. These laws primarily mandate the provision of a variety of specific services. The effect of these laws is to leave largely intact the county delivery system developed under Title IV-A, thus undermining the flexibility of programming that Title XX was intended to create. The repeal of these laws could radically alter local service delivery by giving the counties the discretion to develop a service program responsive to their perceptions of community needs. Such discretion might result in the delivery of new and/or expanded services, or in the elimination of existing services.

The California Health and Welfare Agency has made several decisions which particularly affect local planning for implementation of Title XX. In the first two years of the program, that is, during 1975 and 1976, the agency decided not to require counties to undertake a formal needs assessment or to develop a formal structure for citizen participation as part of their planning procedures. These decisions, largely the result of time and funding limitations, left the Title IV-A planning processes essentially intact in many counties. As a result, organizations such as the United Way and the League of California Cities initiated efforts to pressure the state and county governments into involving consumers and service providers in the Title XX planning process. The response to such efforts has been mixed in California.

Local government relations with regional planning bodies and special districts

Regional planning bodies

Regional planning agencies outside the field of human services have been familiar across the country for many years. The emergence of either single-purpose or multipurpose regional planning bodies in human services has, however, been slower. Only recently has government attempted to plan and coordinate the delivery of human services on a regional basis.

Early development of regional planning for human services   The voluntary health and welfare (or social planning) council, usually funded by the United Way, can be viewed as an ancestor to the present regional planning efforts in the field of human services. This is particularly true in some of the highly urbanized areas of the country, where health and welfare councils were established to serve a multicounty area congruent with the area served by the United Way. Representatives of both county and municipal governments traditionally participated actively in council programs, which included interagency coordination.

Such councils differed widely in their programs, their relationships with governmental entities, and their impact on the community. Funding limitations, lack of a mandate to act, and, in some cases, questioning of legitimacy of authority have contributed to the uneven performance of the councils. Many also have struggled with the dilemma between serving as an advocacy organization or adopting the role of an objective third party.

With an increasing proportion of the funding and delivery of human services being borne by government in the 1950s and 1960s, it was perhaps inevitable that health and welfare planning should become a major interest and concern of government at all levels during the later 1960s and 1970s.

A report of a special committee appointed by the board of directors of the Bay Area Social Planning Council (Oakland, California) records the changes in the San Francisco Bay Area during the decade of 1965–1975:

Perhaps the most significant change has been the active entry of all levels of government into planning for health and welfare services at the local level, as evidenced by the emergence in the five-county Bay Area of over twenty-five new citizen-directed planning instrumentalities which are financed in whole or in part by government, including the following: six comprehensive health planning councils; five criminal justice planning boards; five Model City planning boards (with many additional district level boards); seven economic opportunity councils (with numerous neighborhood planning groups); four areawide planning projects for the elderly; and one regional citizens forum—Association of Bay Area Governments (with fourteen citizen task forces or committees).

The new organizations provide citizens with an opportunity to serve on planning boards, commissions, and committees which are concerned with the development of comprehensive plans for health, criminal justice, mental retardation, the environment, and social services. . . . Such organizations have several major advantages over a voluntary planning council, . . . including the power of proposal or project review and a federal, state, or local mandate to develop plans for specified fields of service. In short, governmental participation in planning activities has resulted in a significantly modified situation which has left many . . . frustrated and without a significant role in the community comparable to that available to boards of social planning councils in 1965.[4]

A similar situation is developing in most urban areas of the United States, as the shift continues from human services planning under voluntary auspices to that under governmental auspices.

The single-purpose regional planning body Governmental interest in health and health planning has resulted in several major pieces of federal legislation authorizing and funding new regional planning efforts (voluntary or governmental) at the local level. The Comprehensive Health Planning Agency, the Area Agency on Aging (AAA), and the Regional Criminal Justice Planning Board are particularly illustrative of the single-purpose agency involved in the planning and coordination of human services on a regional basis. Although the impact of each of these agencies has been hampered by funding limitations, diluted coordinative authority, or delimited statutory mandate, their actions exert some influence on local human service delivery systems.

Comprehensive Health Planning Agencies (replaced by Health Systems Agencies, as noted in the following section of this chapter and discussed in Chapter 13 of this book) represented an initial attempt to coordinate the planning and development of health facilities on a regional basis. Through its veto power over proposed plans for development of hospitals, nursing homes, and clinics, the agency could influence the expansion or limitation of additional patient beds or new health facilities. However, the agency had neither final decision-making authority nor direct control over the funding for facility development. Consequently, its veto of a facility proposal could be, and many times was, overturned at the state level.

The Area Agencies on Aging are responsible for planning and coordinating services to the aged at the local and county levels. The scope of the AAA mandate is limited, however, to a predetermined range of existing operating services designated by the federal government. The effect of this policy precludes the agencies from encouraging the development of new services in response to unmet needs.

Regional Criminal Justice Planning Boards set priorities in the field of criminal justice and allocate funds for adult and youth diversion programs. In some communities political infighting over the control of funds has resulted in the delimitation of the agency's area of jurisdiction, in effect reducing or eliminating its regional scope.

The multipurpose regional planning body   A more complex regional planning body is illustrated by the Association of Bay Area Governments (ABAG) in the San Francisco Bay Area of California. ABAG serves as a council of governments (COG) for the area. The impetus for the development of COGs was a desire on the part of federal officials to create a structure for the coordination of programs and funds coming to local governmental jurisdictions from Washington. In its capacity as a COG, ABAG is responsible for carrying out the federal A-95 Project Notification and Review Process under which projects seeking federal funds are reviewed. The A-95 review function not only enables ABAG to keep apprised of developments in the Bay Area but provides the agency with some semblance of control or "clout" over funding.

ABAG was established in 1961 under the state Joint Exercise of Powers Act. Membership of the agency includes eighty-five (of ninety-three) cities and seven (of nine) counties in the San Francisco Bay Area. The purpose of the agency is to deal with regional problems (including development of a regional plan for land use, etc.) through cooperative action of its member cities and counties. ABAG's movement into the field of human services was initiated in the 1970s, primarily through a capacity building project supported by a grant from HEW. That project has been limited to assisting local governments in the development of appropriate human service delivery systems through the provision of technical assistance, information, legislative advocacy, and the encouragement of citizen participation. The impact of ABAG on the human services delivery system depends on the willingness of component agencies to work through or with the regional agency.

Another example of multipurpose regional planning agencies are the Health Systems Agencies (HSAs), which replace the Comprehensive Health Planning Agency. These agencies appear to offer greater promise for effective coordination of human service delivery and for development of clearer roles in relation to local government. Under legal mandate, the HSAs have direct funding authority as well as a review function with regard to federal grants. In addition, states may look to HSAs for recommendations concerning the local distribution of mental health and other state health funds. (More detailed discussion of HSAs and their impact on local governments is found in Chapter 13 of this book.)

Special district government [5]

School districts are the primary special district governmental units that relate to local government in the delivery of human services. City and county governments traditionally have worked jointly with local school districts in the provision of after-school recreation programs and activities for adults and children. Additional coordinated efforts have emerged through the joint funding, planning, and administration of child day care services, food programs, and preschool programs, all of which are largely supported by federal funds. The relationship between local governments and school districts appears to offer continued opportunities in the future for coordinating the delivery of human service programs, not least because of the immense expenditures (over $60 billion annually) channeled through the local government educational sector.

Park and recreation districts represent another important single-purpose special district government. These districts exist on a multicounty basis, or may be established to assist small cities in providing park and recreational services to residents. In some instances, local jurisdictions have developed contractual relationships with regional park and recreation districts. In these cases, the districts have sometimes undertaken the development and operation of recreational facilities and activities that go beyond existing neighborhood playground and park services operated by local city departments.

Local government relations with the private sector

In the human services field, the term "private sector" is used to describe the *nongovernment* entities which provide human services or support and which affect the overall provision of human services in the community. The diverse components of the private sector include voluntary nonprofit agencies and organizations that deliver and/or fund human services, proprietary human services agencies, health institutions, and corporations. The private sector includes important human services resources that should be considered by local government decision makers as they plan and develop comprehensive human service delivery systems.

The voluntary sector

The voluntary sector is comprised of diverse agencies and organizations—secular and sectarian, traditional and grass roots independent and affiliated with a fund-raising or coordinating entity. Their boards of directors and advisory committees are comprised of professional and lay members of the community; their management and, in some cases, their services are undertaken with volunteer help. The Boy Scouts, Big Brothers, Family Service Agency and Red Cross are but a few examples of voluntary agencies.

Voluntary agencies provide a wide variety of services, such as counseling, legal aid, information and referral, child care, health care, vocational rehabilitation, and aid to alcoholics and drug abusers. Several hundred agencies may operate in an urban area (as they do in the San Francisco Bay Area) and may serve a combined total of a million or more persons representing various socioeconomic and ethnic groups.

Most voluntary organizations make their services available to the general public. Some, such as self-help groups like Parents Without Partners, assist only their members. Others concentrate on raising and allocating funds in support of providers of human services. Fund-raising organizations include: service clubs, such as Kiwanis and the Soroptimists, which annually donate money to "worthy causes;" more complex organizations, such as the United Way and Catholic Charities, which raise funds and provide some support services for affiliated provider agencies; and eleemosynary or charitable foundations, which consist of family trusts, community foundations, and corporate foundations that make grants for a variety of purposes and programs.

The United Way and foundations represent the major sources of nongovernmental funds for human services programs. Nationally, local United Way organizations raised and allocated approximately $1 billion in 1975. Foundations, while distributing far less for human services programs, nevertheless play an important role in the delivery system.[6]

Legitimacy of the voluntary sector   Voluntary agencies and organizations comprise and fund only a small portion of the human services delivery system. Government has preempted a field that was created and initially dominated by the private nonprofit sector. With government dominance has come a questioning of the need for, utility of, and cost-effectiveness of services delivered by voluntary entities. This is a complex and often controversial area going to the root of many of our social and political value judgements regarding the role of government and its limitations.

Proponents predicate the importance of the voluntary sector not only on the diversity of services that agencies fund and deliver, but also on its serving as an alternative to government in meeting human needs. Voluntary agencies can provide services that are not available from public agencies and can assist clients not usually eligible for, or receptive to, participation in government programs. The proponents further contend that voluntary agencies are more flexible in their ability to respond to those changing human needs because they are not hampered by established bureaucracies and stringent program regulations. A final argument for the voluntary sector is that the agencies are closest to, and most representative of, consumers and are therefore best able to respond to their needs and to serve as their spokesman.

Development of public–voluntary sector relations   A sustained relationship between the public and voluntary sectors did not fully develop until the 1960s, when government at all levels sought to involve private agencies in the implementation of Title IV-A of the Social Security Act, the Economic Opportunity Act, and the Model Cities program. Agencies, in need of funds, responded to governmental efforts despite fears of loss of autonomy and reliance on an unstable funding source. That relationship continues in the later 1970s, particularly in urban areas, in response to the decentralization policies of the New Federalism. As of the later 1970s, however, voluntary agencies are developing relationships with government at the local level, since the cities and counties are increasingly becoming the source of funds for human services and the focus of local human service delivery systems. (Chapter 8 of this book includes a discussion of existing and potential options for a variety of cooperative relationships between the public and voluntary sectors.)

Impact of the voluntary sector   Although a small component of the funding network, the voluntary sector can have sufficient impact on local service delivery to be of concern and interest to city or county government. At the least, the services provided by voluntary agencies and the allocation patterns of voluntary funding organizations should be considered by government in the development of local human services plans, needs assessments, programs, and budgets. In addition, consideration should be given to two primary resources of the voluntary sector: services provided by the agencies, and funds available from United Way and other funding organizations for use as the local matching share for federal grants. Many communities have made extensive use of these resources in shaping local service delivery mechanisms. For example, in fiscal year 1974–75, Alameda County, California, expended approximately $3.8 million in general revenue sharing monies for the purchase of social services from more than sixty voluntary agencies.

Other voluntary sector resources also might be utilized by government. For example, paid and volunteer staff of agencies may have the expertise needed to develop a comprehensive human service delivery system. These people could be recruited to work with government advisory committees and planning bodies. Some individuals might also have sufficient political influence to affect decisions at the state or national levels.

Confluence of interest   Just as the voluntary sector can affect local government, the reverse is also true. Human services policies developed by local government regarding funding, planning, contract monitoring and evaluation, and citizen participation will have a bearing on the functioning of voluntary agencies and organizations. There is thus some reciprocity of influence between the two sectors. There is also a certain degree of confluence of interest, based on mutual funding and delivery of services, that suggests the validity of some coordination between government and the voluntary sector. Certainly, both are affected by changes at the federal level and both have similar considerations in the provision of human services. Some of these considerations are related to processes both sectors must undertake, such as the planning, delivery, and evaluation of services; others are related to factors, such as citizen participation, capacity building, and the use of volunteers.

Public–voluntary sector collaboration   The value of some type of public–voluntary collaboration in the area of human services appears to be self-evident. Such collaboration has occurred in several localities with varying degrees of formality and in a variety of human services activities. In Baltimore, Maryland, for example, the Department of City Planning and the Health and Welfare Council of Central Maryland, Inc. (the United Way planning instrumentality) jointly developed a social services classification system. The intent of this joint effort was to ensure consistency in the terminology utilized by both the public and voluntary sectors in order to facilitate planning and allocation procedures. Another type of collaborative effort evolved in San Diego, California. The city and county governments pooled the general revenue sharing funds that had been earmarked for social services and, in conjunction with the United Way of San Diego, jointly determined specific allocations to social services projects. While the United Way did not include its contributions in the social services pool, it helped to finance the allocations process.

Finally, in 1975, Alameda County, California, organized a Human Services Council representing the county government, public planning and coordinating bodies, independent voluntary agencies, United Way agencies, foundations, and the community at large. Formation of the Human Services Council followed a feasibility study conducted in 1974. The study concluded that:

1. Improvements are needed in the total human services delivery process, particularly in the areas of coordination of human services delivery and maximization of community-based input.
2. Under the present pattern of federal general and special revenue sharing with local jurisdictions, it is both feasible and necessary for the Alameda County government to take primary responsibility for a long-term program to effect improvement in the total system for the delivery of human services.
3. The establishment of a human services council will provide the framework needed to introduce changes into the system which are acceptable to the community and which, in many instances, will be generated from the community. It is a feasible concept because there already is an acceptance of the need for change which has its own momentum in the community; there is support from federal, state, and regional organizations; initial funding is available for such a structure; and benefits to be obtained by the formation of such a council outweigh potential disadvantages.[7]

The study report went on to suggest a series of goals and objectives for the proposed council. Four goals were identified which included: improving the efficiency and effectiveness of public/private service delivery; assuring maximum opportunity for consumer input to the delivery process; assuring maximum effectiveness of available resources; and working toward a broad understanding of human services delivery by individual citizens, and public and private organizations and institutions. The objectives outlined in the report included: development and maintenance of an up-to-date countywide inventory of providers and services; development of a countywide socioeconomic–demographic data bank; assessment of human needs in the county; establishment of priorities for meeting those needs; determination of gaps and duplications in the system and development of new concepts and structures for delivery of services; application of standards for the evaluation of services and service delivery; development and recommendation of legislative and administrative changes which could effect improvement in the system; and establishment of an information system which can effectively communicate with the general public and all the special subpublics involved in and affected by the implementation of this program. The report recommended that the Alameda County administrator take responsibility for initiating, leading, and monitoring the proposed program.[8]

The merits of the proposed Human Services Council were discussed by the board of supervisors during late 1974. In January 1975, a director was hired with funds made available by the California State Office of Planning and Research for a one-year project designed to promote coordination and more effective planning and delivery of social services. In September 1975, the board of supervisors adopted a resolution authorizing formation of the Human Services Council. The first meeting of the council was held on January 16, 1976. Figure 2–1 shows the composition of the council and its relationship to the county government's structure. The council structure provides for a formalized set of relationships between the public and voluntary sectors of the community. Among the potential areas of activity for the council are the review of proposals for general revenue sharing funds, involvement in the Title XX needs assessment process, and development of a human services classification system.

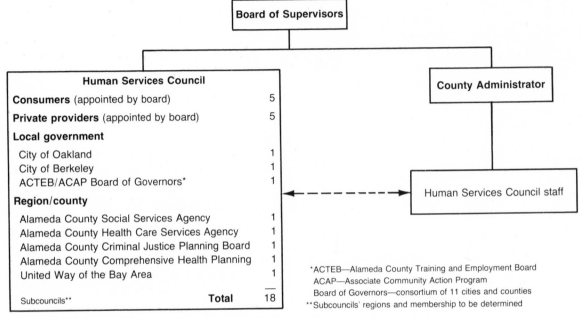

Figure 2–1 Illustrative organization chart shows the composition of the Alameda County Human Services Council and the council's place in the county's administrative structure. (Source: *Alameda County Pilot Project on Human Services Planning, Final Report,* prepared by Arthur Young and Company, Sacramento, California, 1976.)

Proprietary agencies

Proprietary agencies are business firms that provide human services for profit. Such agencies may also be set up as limited profit or limited dividend operations. These agencies may be owned by a single individual or a family or may be part of a chain operated by a large corporation.

Contracting with proprietary agencies can serve to improve the human services delivery system. Involvement of proprietary agencies can contribute to governmental cost economies and facilitate early response to local needs which localities, for various reasons, do not have the capacity to meet. On the other hand, there is often insufficient profit incentive within selected human services to insure effective and efficient service delivery by proprietary agencies. In addition, development of an effective monitoring system, necessary to ensure the provision of a high quality of service, can be difficult and costly.

For the most part, proprietary human services agencies are found in the health field. Nursing homes are typical of the kind of services that are provided through proprietary ownership. This type of facility accounts for significant public and private financial investment. Nationally, 23,000 nursing homes serve a total of

1.2 million people. Public support of the homes amounts to almost $4 billion; private patients provide another $3.5 billion.[9] One of the problems in the nursing home industry has been the unrestrained development of facilities in recent years. The availability of federal construction funds under the Hill–Burton Act resulted in an explosion of nursing homes during the 1960s. In Alameda County, California, for example, the number of nursing homes increased from a scattered few to more than one hundred in about four years. Today, the county has a total of 102 nursing homes, serving 6,400 patients. All but nine facilities, with 502 beds, are proprietary operations.

The profit margin for operation of these homes was so small, however, that land and construction costs were a deterrent to the construction of facilities in areas accessible to the population in need. Moreover, a substantial amount of public money was necessary to hire competent professional staff to provide technical assistance and consultation to nursing home operators in order to insure a high quality of service. Although the state of California still supports the licensing of facilities, it has largely withdrawn from provision of consultative and technical assistance.

Health providers: a special case

Health providers include both proprietary and voluntary service operations. Hospitals and convalescent homes are primary examples (nursing homes, as discussed previously, being largely under proprietary operation). Services rendered by these providers include medical care, counseling, and mental health services. These services may be provided to the public on a fee-for-service basis or under a prepaid plan. Health providers are primarily supported by individual payments or private contributions which comprise a substantial portion of the total expenditures in the field of human services. The total national expenditure on health care in 1974 was estimated to be about $104.2 billion. Of this amount, nearly $63 billion was from private sources, and more than $41 billion was from public sources. Hospital care alone cost Americans $40.9 billion in 1974. Private sector payments, commercial insurance, Blue Cross payments, out-of-pocket philanthropy, and payments by individual patients amounted to $19.3 billion of the total.[10]

Similar to the situation with voluntary agencies, relationships between local government and health providers were developed in the 1960s under the mandate of prominent federally sponsored social programs. In some instances, these cooperative working relationships have been sustained. They offer greater planning opportunities for cities and counties in the 1970s under general and special revenue sharing and other federal block grants.

The task of developing cooperative relationships between health providers and local government can be tedious and time-consuming in spite of legal and funding incentives. Efforts by local government to impose evaluation and monitoring controls over provider performance often become obstacles to cooperative efforts. Nevertheless, health providers, particularly hospitals, offer a reservoir of service capacity, staff competence, financial resources, and physical facilities that should be taken into consideration by local governments in the planning, management, and budgeting of human services systems.

Corporations

Corporations are a source of support to human services agencies, through direct funding or indirect staff assistance. They can also serve as a stimulus for the development of additional human services programs. Clearly, through their employees and their customers, they can have significant impact in communities.

Corporations consider it good business to participate in support of "worthy causes." They do this by contributing funds to the United Way or directly to specific agencies. So great is the demand for contributions that some corporations have developed corporate foundations to handle the problem. Very large corporate foundations—Ford, Rockefeller, Kellogg, and Kaiser, for example—started as family trusts but now have close ties with industry and employ a large staff to control the awarding of grants for community projects. Corporations also may lend time and talent to a cause by assigning an employee, usually at the management level, to provide specific assistance to an agency or group of agencies. Many corporations encourage their employees to serve on boards and commissions, and some allow such activities to be carried out on company time.

In a few communities, informal meetings of corporation executives are held to determine which local enterprises will receive support and how much will be given. A group of business executives in Oakland, California, recently began construction of a youth development center for a deteriorating section of the inner city. The drive was spearheaded by the executive of a large company, and both foundation and corporate support were secured to fund the construction and operation of the center. Clearly, corporations can influence the development and administration of human services through the provision of matching funds to attract federal grants, technical assistance, and citizen involvement.

City–county relations

Patterns of city and county functions across the nation

Patterns of local governmental participation in the provision of human services vary among the states in response to differing government organizational arrangements and laws governing the provision of human services. In the states of Maine and Massachusetts, human services programs are organized at the state level in response to a legislative mandate, and services are delivered on a subdistrict basis through decentralized state offices. The state of Washington also plays the major role in the provision of health and social services. Cities and counties in Washington have never been responsible for administering welfare programs; that has always been a state function. In some states, counties assume a major role in the provision of human services. In California, for example, counties have been given complete responsibility for this. In Illinois, the role of counties is important, but more restricted in scope than in California. County governments in Illinois are responsible for the administration of public assistance and welfare support services.

Federal programs and funds provide the major incentive for involvement of local governments in human services. Many counties that were responsible for the administration of public assistance significantly expanded their involvement in the provision of social services in the 1960s following enactment of Title IV-A. Liberal federal funding assistance for social services was made available under this program, and local needs were directly linked to public assistance eligibility. Federal programs, such as the War on Poverty and Model Cities, increased local pressure for improved human services and placed city government in the center of social services planning and coordination. In major cities this experience often served as the impetus for the establishment of local multipurpose human services departments to organize and manage the delivery of social services. Moreover, these departments generally received a substantial portion of their budgets from the city, rather than from state and federal sources.

The Chicago Department of Human Resources assumed responsibility for youth welfare, correctional services, manpower, family welfare, services for senior citizens, and community relations. Its purpose focused on the coordination and planning of the existing delivery system. New York City's Human Resources Administration consisted of five distinct agencies: departments of social services, manpower and career development, community development, youth services, and addiction services.

Funds available through general revenue sharing, special revenue sharing block grants, and Title XX presently provide opportunities for city and county involvement in the planning, coordination, and delivery of human services. However, the record of activities indicates that cities and counties have been reluctant to exploit these opportunities.

California is illustrative of an increasing recognition by city governments of their responsibility for the planning and delivery of social services. In 1973, the members of the League of California Cities adopted a resolution outlining the social responsibilities of cities. At their option, cities could assume the responsibilities of assessing social needs and insuring the delivery of social services within their boundaries, and of developing a social services element to their general plans.[11] It is important to note that, under this resolution, cities are not bound to accept responsibility for providing social services or for preparing a social element. In fact, only a few California cities have, as of the later 1970s, developed social elements.[12] There has been discussion in the legislative and administrative branches of California government about establishing legal mandates for a social element for local general plans.

The thrust of local governments has not, generally, been on development of a service capacity. Under general revenue sharing, local government often has opted to contract with outside agencies for the delivery of services, while developing the internal capacity for monitoring and evaluation of agency efforts and serving as a conduit for the funding of local service agencies.

Potential role of the city in providing human services

There probably is not one specific role for all cities or all counties to assume in the delivery of human services. Both cities and counties are involved in the human service delivery system. Patterns of involvement and relationships between governmental jurisdictions vary, and there appears to be no standard system of relationships. Where county government has been traditionally influential in the provision of human services, it remains so. Where cities have had to play a major role in local service delivery, they continue to do so.

The separation of the income maintenance function from the provision of social services could have a significant effect on future participation by local government in the human service delivery system. The assumption by the federal government of the income maintenance function would lift a substantial financial burden from county government; in particular, it would allow greater opportunities for generating resources to finance social services.

The role of cities in the planning and delivery of human services will vary, depending on several factors. These include population mix and size, special problems, institutions present in the city, government tradition, experience in dealing with social problems, and ability to finance services. In spite of the myriad of social services available through community voluntary agencies and the county, the city of Berkeley, for example, has attempted to support additional services to deal with the special problems of transients, drug users, "hangers-on" attracted to the city by its reputation, and members of the University of California community. The city council has received community support in this effort.

The executive director of the League of California Cities questions the direct provision of services on the part of most cities. He states:

Because of the slowness in improving the delivery of social services, ... a number of cities in frustration moved rapidly into the "delivery" of social services. Most have since found such action inappropriate for two reasons:

1. an emphasis on services only promotes an activity doomed by limited resources to have

a minimal overall impact. The amount even the most committed cities can allocate to human services is miniscule compared to the funds available to existing county, state, and even private programs; and

2. the trend toward services—once set in motion—threatens to strain already "taxed" city budgetary resources.

Our view is that cities can make their greatest impact—not by services—but by using their political leadership to generate improved service and policy in those agencies already responsible for the solution of social problems *and* by examining and maximizing the social responsiveness of their existing services and programs through legislation, zoning regulations, police policies, and recreation programs which already effect [sic] large numbers of citizens.[13]

The secretary of the California Health and Welfare Agency sees the responsibilities in yet another way. He emphasizes the planning role for local government (in this case, county government), and states:

Local governments, throughout California as in other states, are becoming increasingly involved in the provision of social and human care services needed to ensure a minimum acceptable level of human existence as the federal government continues the administration's policies of placing the responsibility for resolving local problems and the expenditures of available tax dollars on locally elected officials.

Because of this increasing involvement and responsibility at the local level, it is clear that a basic framework for decision making needs to be established to assist elected officials and administrators in determining an optimum allocation of limited resources for human care services, assure citizen access to the decision-making process, and provide continuous and timely communications to the public.

Local governments must place an emphasis on identifying major problems in planning for and delivering human services and develop and refine the tools and processes necessary to improve the state of social planning and service delivery.[14]

Throughout his recommendations he sees a close partnership between city, county, and state staff as they jointly work to plan and improve the delivery of social services at the local level.

Summary

This chapter has treated the relations of local government in the area of human services with the full spectrum of other levels of government—federal, state, regional, and special district—and with agencies in the private sector—voluntary, proprietary, and corporate. Funding for human services programs and expenditures of the monies available were discussed. This was followed by explanations of various state and federal programs which have had significant impact on local service delivery systems since the 1960s. Local government relations with regional planning bodies, special district governments, and private sector agencies were dealt with. The chapter concluded a section on the present and potential roles to be played by both cities and counties in the provision of human services.

Continuation of the federal block grant policy should continue to encourage greater participation by local government in the establishment of human service delivery systems. Although the amount of funding available is reduced, the block grant approach allows local government greater flexibility than was possible under the categorical grant system in determining its own role in the provision of human services. However, in the context of the limited funding capacity of cities and the magnitude of today's social problems, the role of most cities in human services may be limited to providing selected services to meet the unique problems of residents and to fill serious gaps in a delivery system primarily administered by the county with federal and state funds.

1   Statement of David Mathews at his swearing-in ceremony as secretary of the U.S. Department of Health, Education, and Welfare, Washington, D.C., 8 August 1975.

2 Bay Area Social Planning Council, *Expenditures for Human Services in Alameda County During Fiscal Year 1974–75* (Oakland: Bay Area Social Planning Council, 1976), Appendix A.

3 William A. Morrill, "Federal/Local Relations in Human Resource Development," *Public Management,* September 1974, p. 13.

4 Report of a special committee of the board of directors, Bay Area Social Planning Council, Oakland, 1976.

5 Special district governments, and their particular place in local government finance, are treated in depth in a companion volume in the Municipal Management Series. See Seymour Sacks, "User Charges and Special Districts," in *Management Policies in Local Government Finance,* ed. J. Richard Aronson and Eli Schwartz (Washington, D.C.: International City Management Association, 1975), pp. 166–88.

6 For a comprehensive discussion of the contributions of voluntary agencies and foundations, see *Giving in America: Toward a Stronger Voluntary Sector* (n.p.: Commission on Private Philanthropy and Public Needs, 1975).

7 E. Bartlett Kerr, "Alameda County Human Services Council: A Feasibility Study for the Board of Supervisors," Oakland, July 1974, pp. 2–3.

8 Ibid., pp. 5–6.

9 "Dr. Butler Calls for Research Role," *Senior Citizens News,* July 1976, pp. 1, 4.

10 N. L. Worthington, "National Health Expenditures, 1929–1974," *Social Security Bulletin,* February 1975.

11 League of California Cities, "Action Plan for the Social Responsibilities of Cities," Berkeley, 1973.

12 Bay Area Social Planning Council, *Development of a Social Element to the General Plan of Cities in the Bay Area and in California, Part 2* (Oakland: Bay Area Social Planning Council, 1975), pp. 1–15.

13 Don Benninghoven, "An Emerging Role For Mayors and Council Members," *Western City,* April 1976 p. 7.

14 Mario Obledo, "Improving the Delivery of Social Services," *Western City,* April 1976 pp. 10–11.

The changing role of local governments

The basic human services issues confronting local governments in the 1970s lie along a spectrum. The limits of this range of discussion may be represented by the positions of two hypothetical participants in a dialogue. On the one hand, the neighborhood activist may vigorously claim that:

Cities are in the business of serving people, whether they want to be or not. We need to put more money into "people" programs, and not into bricks and mortar or tax cuts.

On the other hand, a city council or budget-conscious official may claim with equal sincerity that:

We simply can't afford an open-ended commitment to trying to solve problems that are caused by economic forces outside this city. We can't meet the service needs we've already taken on, and providing social programs isn't our normal business.

The crux of the matter, as responsible local government managers and community activists alike will be quick to recognize, is that jurisdictions must grapple on a daily basis with the social concerns and pressures described in the first two chapters of this book. These concerns and pressures have given rise to service demands that often seem unlimited and financially impossible to satisfy. These pressures have indeed changed the roles of cities and counties by elevating human services problems to a place on community agendas. They have also resulted in a greater degree of importance being accorded to many other issues that were already on those agendas. These would include, of course, the physical development and maintenance of the city; the feeling of many taxpayers that local taxation has reached its upper limits; and the growing competition among all programs and agencies of governments for a share in budgets that have been rocked by inflation, recession, and wage demands from local government workers themselves attempting to maintain their own standards of living.[1]

The role of American local governments in the provision of human services as of the later 1970s reflects two basic kinds of pluralism. First, there is the pluralism in the human services field itself. Second, there is pluralism in the ways in which communities have chosen to respond to the social concerns of their citizens. The first of these themes is, of course, treated throughout this book. This chapter will address therefore the various approaches implied by the second theme, that is, the approaches to defining appropriate roles for cities and counties in their attempts to deal with human needs. It will set forth and discuss the emerging human services policy themes which seem likely to shape the leadership environment for local government managers in this critical field.

It may be helpful to consider briefly three salient factors which serve to explain, at least in part, the differences among local governments' responses to human services needs and problems. First, there is the novelty of the field of human services itself at the local level. Local government decision makers lack any proven models for the "one best way" to deal with social concerns that vary widely from community to community.

A second, and related, factor is that social problems differ in impact and are perceived differently in different communities. In one city, for example, the health needs of older residents can be of prime concern. In another city, recreation outlets for teenagers may lead the human services agenda. In a third, the human services issue of greatest importance may be the impact of the city's zoning regulations on the establishment of day care centers. The internal and external forces shaping social issues across the nation operate very differently from one community to another. A wide variety of community values results in an equally wide range of reactions to emerging social concerns. Differences among local governmental and political systems also color the various systems' sensitivities to new issues as they are added to the local agendas.

Third, communities differ in their approaches to human services because of the different financial and staff resources available (or not available) to them. Some communities may have the resources to play direct roles in providing services; others may need to establish intergovernmental arrangements or work with nongovernmental organizations in order to provide services to community residents. One community may have a tradition of activism; another may require a manager to struggle with citizens' lack of concern with social issues.

Throughout this chapter, these pluralistic settings are treated as the prevailing framework for decision making in the management of human services at the local government level. While frequent reference is made to "the city" and to "cities," it should be emphasized that the policy issues addressed have applicability to counties as well as to cities, and also to a wide range of communities from rural villages and townships through medium-sized cities to giant metropolitan areas. It should also be pointed out that, while the discussion of indirect service delivery mechanisms is more extensive than that of direct service provision, it is not meant to imply that either of these two forms of service delivery is necessarily the more advantageous. Their relative merits must be determined case by case, based on consideration of factors such as budgetary constraints, personnel availability, and the extent of the need within a given community.

The chapter begins with a discussion of the origins of changes in local government roles in addressing human services needs. It moves on to an item-by-item discussion of emerging trends in human services. This is followed by a discussion of budgetary and organizational implications for the local government decision maker. An outline of the major human services issues at the local level is then presented. An evaluative conclusion summarizes the discussion and focuses on the importance of community values and human services.

Changing roles: the origins

The concluding words of the first chapter in *Managing the Modern City,* though written at the start of the present decade and specifically referring to cities, continue to serve well as an introduction to the topic of changing local government roles in human services:

The city is a key element in society. . . . The city's impact upon society, in turn, places major responsibilities upon the city's government, responsibilities which increasingly must go beyond the caretaker, housekeeping role which city government has played in the past. Now the city's government must also be concerned about the . . . life styles of people within the city, and about opportunities for improving the health, vitality, and happiness of those people. These, then, are the ultimate challenges confronting the developing city.[2]

What are now referred to as human services have, of course, been at least a partial concern of American local governments since the foundation of the Republic, and even in colonial times. A relatively recent perspective in many communities, however, is the conscious concern for the policy role of those jurisdictions in human services. In this more specific context, the search for the proper role for government involvement in human services did not always figure in the initial years of a community's involvement in social programs.

Impact of the 1960s

In many cities, for example, the first steps toward a role in managing human services (referring now, to some extent, to the later 1950s and, more specifically, the 1960s) came with a one-time commitment to respond to a new federal initiative or to cooperate with a private social services agency or county government which already provided some particular service. These first human services ventures (again in the contemporary sense) were the city's responses to social problems which had become serious enough to warrant city attention. The response usually took the form of a human services program which devoted limited funds and staff resources to the needs of a small portion of the city's residents. In both small and large communities, a handful of such programs, supported by matches of local funds with intergovernmental or private resources, often represented the extent of the cities' initial commitments. These programmatic responses multiplied rapidly in many of the larger cities under the stimulus of both federal funds and local pressures from activist groups.

In the 1960s, elected officials and managers in many cities and counties saw the federal government marching behind the banner of its new "Great Society" projects, offering itself as a welcome partner in dealing with the needs and problems of people. The creation of the Office of Economic Opportunity in 1964, the establishment of the Model Cities program in 1966, and the passage of legislation enabling hundreds of new categorical programs throughout the 1960s all represented, to many local officials, a responsive federal government coming to understand the need to support programs aimed at combating social problems at the state and local level.

Government at the grass roots level   Providing a representative from his office to work closely with the staff of the school district, the city administrator of Lakewood, Colorado, was instrumental in the development of a nine-week course on state and local government to be used in the Lakewood school system. The syllabus provides a bibliography of basic and supplementary texts on state and local government, sample visual aids, and a course outline.

As a result cities were reorganized, new staffs were hired, and jurisdictions took on a variety of new commitments to deal with these new federal initiatives. Nonetheless, this initial role remained one of program management. City staffs and local matching funds were used to respond to opportunities that often came from outside the cities themselves, in the form of the new funding sources.

Impact of the 1970s

In the 1970s, however, new pressures on cities and counties came to play a critical role in shaping views of human services. The levels of funding for most of the new intergovernmental human services programs had reached a plateau by the mid-1970s. This reflected both national political trends and growing public and congressional skepticism about the effectiveness of these programs.

It is important to note, however, that federal aid to state and local governments totaled—to take one year as an example—nearly $60 billion in fiscal 1976, with $39 billion flowing into metropolitan areas and nearly 40 percent of that total derived from federal human services programs.[3] For the most part, those programs—such as public assistance and Medicaid—which reflect increased spending by state and local governments have received funding increases. Funding which would reduce the pressure on state and local budgets, however, has not seen a similar increase. Service programs, as opposed to income support programs, have generally declined or, in some cases, remained constant. Service programs for the elderly are one notable exception; in this case, strong national lobbying has brought gradual expansion of programs under the Older Americans Act of 1965.

Increased pressures on local governments

This combination of factors has had the net result of increasing the pressures on local government—the leveling off of program funds, the impact of inflation on existing programs, and concomitant increases in the demand for such programs. Communities are urged to "pick up" and expand these programs under pressure from newly organized constituencies that often include both clients and staff. As local elected officials repeatedly put it, "Federal promises equal local commitments." It should also be noted that state involvement in the same programs has given rise to the statements, "State mandates equal local commitments."

As a result, important changes in the roles of local governments have taken place. In some cities, active participation in the grantsmanship style has been replaced by more passive activity and skeptical views of federal programs. Other cities, however, have gone beyond a negative reaction to the reductions and leveling off of federal funding to a more thoughtful attempt to rationalize human services programs into human services policy. Such policy orientation can serve as a guide for local government decision makers as they confront some basic questions about the local role in providing for human needs. It also provides a basis on which to make decisions regarding more specific matters—whether to request federal funding for a particular program, to cite one example. The first years of uncertain decisions about pickup of federal programs have given way, in many jurisdictions, to more advanced planning and strategic decision making.

Planning strategic choices

In the author's introduction to the League of California Cities' "Handbook on Human Resources Policy Planning," these strategic choices were compared with the investment strategy of a private sector investor:

Political leaders are entrepreneurs—risk-taking investors in an uncertain future—in many ways. One of the most important strategies of a responsible entrepreneur, who is working with funds given him in trust, is the principle of *leveraging,* through which he seeks to use a portion of his own investment to trigger much larger investments by other parties. Rarely do entrepreneurs invest only their own funds in ventures with uncertain results.[4]

The league's other materials stress the same point:

. . . . The key choice lies between employing city resources to *provide* the services directly or working with other agencies to *obtain* the service from outside resources. This decision, which may change for different problems and services, will shape the kinds of activities, resources, strategies and organizational relationships devoted to the particular problem. Cities should explore more fully the potential for obtaining services before they move towards service *providing*. . . . One of the strongest reasons for cities staying out of the business of delivering services directly, or at least separating their basic policy planning activities from any actual service operational efforts, is the fact that the rigors and demands of ongoing services tend to obscure the perspective and detachment necessary for policy planning and decision making. . . .[5]

This latter point might be called Gresham's Law of Policy Planning—"Operations drives out policy." If local officials must meet the increasing implementation demands of their own programs, this viewpoint stresses, it is less likely that they will be able to develop coherent policy for leveraging the full array of human services available to the local residents.

The formal statement of what a city's policy goals will be—and what they are not—is seen by some as an important policy action for local governments. Cities subscribing to this view have been careful, in formulating policy statements, to exclude those programs and policies which are not under the effective control of the city or to place such items in a separate section aimed specifically at policies of other levels of government. In that way, a city may state its goal as "adequate income for all city residents who cannot become financially self-sufficient" while stressing that achievement of this goal depends upon state and federal contributions to income support programs.

This sort of approach seems to give implicit recognition to the human services programs begun in the mid-1960s. Characteristically, the national statement of a goal in universal terms—"full employment," "model cities," "comprehensive employment and training"—has been followed by appropriation of funds adequate to serve only a small portion of the eligible (and needy) population. These gaps between program goal requirements and actual appropriations have been referred to by Elliot Richardson as "unredeemed promissory notes" [6] in pointing to the failure of congressional appropriations committees to carry out the promises of congressional authorizing committees. Richardson's point is no less true if applied to the last several administrations in the federal executive branch.

Local elected executives and legislators are increasingly unwilling to repeat the mistakes of their national counterparts in promising more than they can deliver for new human services programs. As a result, the traditional reluctance of local government to take on new responsibilities has increased, and "overpromising" has assumed new negative connotations, having become one of the harshest criticisms local politicians can level at each other.

Realistic goals and nongoals

The counterbalance to such overpromising, many would hold, is candor about what the city cannot achieve—either with its own resources or perhaps under any circumstances. While there has not been a rush to draft "nongoals statements," development of formal statements of policy, as mentioned previously, has been accorded greater importance and seems to signal a more realistic appraisal of the city's capabilities and potential roles.

The League of California Cities articulated these issues well in 1973 with the development of its "Action Plan for the Social Responsibilities of Cities" and in a variety of subsequent handbooks and guidelines for human services needs assessment and policy planning. [7] In assessing this evolution of the policy-making role of cities, Don Benninghoven, the executive director of the league, made the following statement:

. . . A number of cities in frustration moved rapidly into the "delivery" of social services. Most have since found such action inappropriate for two reasons:
1. an emphasis on services only promotes an activity doomed by limited resources to have a minimal overall impact. The amount even the most committed cities can allocate to human services is miniscule compared to the funds available to existing county, state and even private programs; and
2. the trend toward services—once set in motion—threatens to strain already "taxed" city budgetary resources.

Our view is that cities can make their greatest impact—not by services—but by using their political leadership to generate improved service and policy in those agencies already responsible for the solution of social problems *and* by examining and maximizing the social responsiveness of their existing services and programs through legislation, zoning regulations, police policies and recreation programs which already effect large numbers of citizens. [8]

Eight role options

The League of California Cities has emphasized the distinction between two kinds of roles for local governments: one of *providing* services to residents, the other of *obtaining* services from other sources. The league's "Handbook on Human Resources Policy Planning," drawing on work of both the league and the New England Municipal Center, makes further distinctions among eight different kinds of roles appropriate for local governments in the area of human services.[9] The breakdown that they propose follows.

Interagency liaison As an advocate of human services goals which other providers do not yet accept, a city can use interagency forums to encourage the other providers—counties, state governments, voluntary agencies, local employers, consortia of health and welfare agencies—to change patterns of human services delivery in such a way as to support the city's own goals.

Monitoring and evaluation A city can assess over time the adequacy of other providers' services to residents, as a means of strengthening the city's case in interagency discussions.

Information and referral The city can use its own field workers and central city hall staff to direct residents to other agencies already providing services. A follow-up procedure may be instituted to determine if the other agencies are meeting the residents' needs. Such follow-up, of course, provides another means of monitoring and evaluating others' services.

Program initiation and planning A city can work directly with other providers to help develop programs which fill identified gaps in existing services.

Program demonstration A city can agree to sponsor or operate a new program on a demonstration basis, with an understanding that, if successful, the program will be transferred to another established agency.

Contracting for services On its own or jointly with other agencies, a city can fund noncity agencies by purchasing services on a contractual basis—annual payment, reimbursement per client, or payment based on performance measures developed jointly by the service provider and the city.

Direct service provision A city can accept a direct operational role for a new human services program, placing it in a new agency, operating it jointly with adjacent communities, or fitting it into an existing department of city government.

Nonservice delivery A city can also affect the provision of human services without the development of programs. The city's existing powers of regulation and taxation may be used to encourage private agencies or employers, for example, to include desired services or facilities in their own plans.

Summary: overall advocacy role

In order to determine which or how many of these roles is to be adapted by a local government, the community's decision makers must build a foundation for their policy by considering two important questions. What services does the community need and how much financial support can the local government afford to give to those services? The answers to these questions will shape all future decisions about the community's specific role in human services.

The principal role of decision makers in all areas of activity is as an advocate for the community itself—in a sense, a "spokesman" for the local residents' shared goals. In this respect, the local government as advocate need not "take a side:" options may simply be presented for consideration, as in the eight alternative roles described above. A reduction in services whose cost is borne by local taxpayers can be advocated as easily as an expansion of those same services might be recommended because they benefit the local residents.

Advocacy which encourages fulfillment of the needs of a majority of the community's residents is as valid as advocacy which zeroes in on the unique needs of minority groups. So long as the various perspectives of the entire community are genuine factors in the decision-making processes, there will be a legitimacy to whatever secondary roles are selected.

The local government, through its decision makers, should do more than just react to the goals and programs of other human services providers in the community. Citizens will be better served by program decisions based on the broader consideration of policy and strategy.

Emerging trends in human services

In assessing the continuing changes in the human services roles of cities and counties, it is useful to determine, to whatever extent is possible, the impact of seven emerging trends and developing concerns in human services.

Some of these concerns have emerged as a result of the same demographic changes discussed in the first chapter of this volume and cited as partially responsible for the expanded role of local governments in human services: the "youth bulge," the increased proportion of the elderly in the population, and the growing number of working women were among the changes mentioned. Others of the concerns are products of legal and political changes in American society and the human services function. Still others have arisen from changing patterns in intergovernmental and interorganizational relations.

The items identified for discussion in the following section are: demographic shifts; expanding citizen involvement; legal pressures for equity in services; local links to income programs; federalization and localization; the use of private and third sector delivery mechanisms; and deprofessionalization.

Demographic shifts

Demography determines policy in human services to a considerable extent. The increase in social expenditures for both services and income support to the elderly cannot be understood without reference to the expansion in recent decades of this segment of the American population. Each day in the 1970s, there is a net increase of 1,000 in the population over sixty-five years of age. The elderly in 1970 represented a little more than 10 percent of the nation's population; by 1980 it is estimated that those over sixty-five will account for nearly 12 percent of the population. As of the late 1970s, however, these numbers have exceeded 15 percent in some cities and states. In the 1975 elections, for example, older people were 14.8 percent of the voting age population, but cast 17 percent of the votes.[10] In some local elections, the number of elderly voters exceeds 20 percent of the total. The political impact of the elderly, especially at the local level, is therefore likely to increase in the years ahead. This example highlights the potential impact of demographic change on human services policy.

Similarly, numerous commentators have underlined the importance of the "youth bulge" in the 1960s as a major cause of shifts in social concerns during that decade. Daniel Moynihan, speaking of the age group from 14 to 24, said:

Between 1960 and 1970 the size of this subgroup of the American population grew by an absolutely unprecedented amount, and it will never grow by such an amount again. . . . It grew by 13.8 million persons in the 1960s; it will grow by 600,000 in the 1970s; it will decline in the 1980s. It's all over, it happened once, it will not ever happen again. . . . suddenly a new social class was created in the United States so large in its number that it was fundamentally isolated from the rest of the society, it was isolated in a way in the armed forces . . . It was apart from the rest of society. . . . State and local government went through absolute hell in the 1960s. Why is that? It is because it is traditionally the job of state and local government to look after young people fourteen to twenty-four, to get them through high school and perhaps college; to see that they don't steal cars; if they have children, to provide maternity hospitals for them; to provide new housing, and so on, down a long list.[11]

Others looking at demographic trends have seen the rapidly increasing creation of new households, due in part to the increasing divorce rate, as the single most important trend in the housing market of the 1970s and 1980s, creating new demands for smaller, less expensive forms of homeownership.[12]

Further demographic changes are more difficult to predict. The spatial dimension of demography—where people live—has been among the primary determinants of cities' roles in physical development for over thirty years. In the 1980s, the choices made by Americans about desirable life styles will continue to affect growth and will have an impact upon human services policies as well.

Will the emerging "back to the city" movement of the mid-1970s emerge as dominant, or will the simultaneous migration from metropolitan areas to smaller towns prove to be the most important change? How will rising energy prices and the strength of new techniques for growth management and environmental control affect the pace of continued suburbanization? Is the increasing return of black families to the South likely to continue, or will out-migration from the North by low income families come to a halt as the South catches up with the living costs of the rest of the nation? What are the trends in the in-migration of Hispanic residents from Mexico, Puerto Rico, and Central and Latin America? Will youth seek or shun the cities? Will the elderly continue to move to the Sun Belt?

We can identify key questions such as these, and even project the beginnings of important trends, but it will take more time before we know how the separate decisions of millions of American families add up to patterned changes in the demographic makeup of cities, suburbs, and counties across the country. Understanding the impact of such changes on a jurisdiction's tax base, its political makeup, and its citizens' demand for various kinds of human services represents one of the most important parts of the needs assessment process discussed in Chapter 5 of this volume.

Expanding citizen involvement

One of the most important of the recent trends affecting the roles of cities in human services is the expansion of the forms and targets of citizen involvement in human services programs at the local level. Under the combined impetus in the early and mid-1960s of the civil rights movement and federal support for greater involvement of neighborhood residents in the programs of the Office of Economic Opportunity (OEO), a wide variety of Community Action Agencies (CAA's) developed and gained strength. In the later 1970s, a decade after the federal government ceased its strong support for the concept of "maximum feasible participation," there remained over nine hundred CAA's in cities and rural areas across the country although many may be only organizational shells of their former selves. Some of these groups, in fact, have moved their focus out beyond the programs of OEO (later the Community Services Administration) to other federal, state, and local programs which affect the poor and, in some cases, the middle income residents of American communities.

In the view of some observers, the "welfare rights" organizations of the late 1960s have had a more profound impact upon human services budgets in the ensuing ten years than any governmental program.[13] The legal services centers, sponsored originally by OEO and then funded by the National Legal Services Corporation, have brought suit on numerous occasions to demand increased expenditures by local, state, and federal governments in human services programs, as discussed in the following section.

Of importance also to the evolving local role in human services has been the broadening of citizen involvement pressures in nonminority, middle income, and white working class neighborhoods. The tactics of the antipoverty agencies have been credited by some neighborhood activists as some of their most useful mechanisms in the accomplishment of such activities as blocking highway expansion, demanding changes in neighborhoods schools, and seeking expanded services to senior citizens. The "neighborhood preservation movement," as some have termed the efforts of a variety of loosely connected groups in American cities, has used direct action tactics aimed at real estate agents, bankers, and others engaged in alleged "redlining" and other economic practices which accelerate the decline of urban core and older suburban neighborhoods. Groups from nearly every part of the country that take pride in their national and ethnic origins have sought broader involvement in local decision-making processes. Some of the most skilled managerial leadership in American cities today has been put to use in the 1970s in dealing with these and similar groups whose agendas for neighborhood action grew out of those of the community action agencies of the 1960s.

Increasingly, the targets for human services programs cannot be neatly categorized as either "poor," "near poor," or "middle income" clients. A variety of services have, in fact, been extended to "nonpoor" clients; others have been expanded substantially due to political pressure exerted by the nonpoor group. Some service areas affected by this have been programs for the mobile elderly, drug abuse and alcoholism treatment programs, counseling to ease marital stress and parent–child strains, day care facilities, homemaker services, and home health care programs.[14] Legislative tests of the support for such programs have arisen: organizations, each advocating the special interests of such groups as low income clients, have formed coalitions and made common cause in expanding the legislative bases for child care, services to the elderly, and drug abuse treatment. For instance, the recognition that drug abuse was a suburban as well as an inner-city problem gave new impetus to national efforts to eliminate the sources of illicit drugs in the United States.

Citizen participation in human services programs at the local level presents special challenges to local leadership. The tendency of citizen groups to focus upon their own special interests rather than citywide policy issues is widely noted in the literature on citizen participation. In some cities, this special-interest perspective has taken the form of geographic factionalism. An example of this may be seen in neighborhood-based groups unwilling to accept citywide financial constraints and demanding services expansion in their own neighborhoods without regard for the impact on total budgets.

In addition to the geographic component that sometimes separates the special interests, there are at least two other sources of divisiveness in the area of citizen participation. First, the "human services" label itself masks dozens of special interests, as indicated in the first two chapters of this book. A "human services coalition" as such would be a rare phenomenon. More typically, a coalition focusing on interests related to health, for example, will represent groups whose primary concern may be children's health, maternal health, drug abuse, alcoholism, mental health, or some other relatively narrow category. The participation of such coalitions in the local policy-making arena more often mirrors than coordinates each group's specialized interest.

This is true despite the accepted ideal of a human services system that provides all clients with the full range of services needed for successful treatment and freedom from dependence. Myron Weiner's statement that, "in a client-oriented management system, boundaries are meaningless," serves better to critique the parochialism of existing systems and citizen groups than to describe the status quo in most American cities.[15]

Second, citizen involvement in human services may present local managers with problems which arise from the differences in the interests of those who serve and those who are served. The public and private agencies employing human services professionals and paraprofessionals are rarely outside the local political system; in some communities these agencies are easily the strongest political interests when human services issues are at stake. Professional associations and municipal workers' unions are seen at times as concerned more with the effect of local budgets and reorganizations on their membership than with the importance of meeting the needs of clients as effectively and completely as possible. Conflicts in some jurisdictions between teachers' unions and parent groups over education issues demonstrate well the potential tensions between service providers and service recipients. The local managerial leadership often finds itself caught in the crossfire from such conflicts.

Bright lights The borough of Lambeth in London provides prepaid postcards to all households which have a streetlight out front. When the light malfunctions or goes out, the citizen is encouraged to drop the postcard in the mail to alert the maintenance crew.

A poll of urban administrators which was widely cited in the mid-1970s gives further evidence of the growing importance of active citizen roles. When asked which functions of city government represented the greatest *present* involvement by, and *future* importance to, public management, administrators ranked "citizen participation" last out of twelve functions in present involvement, but first in future importance.[16] This trend will certainly provide continuing challenges to local human services decision makers.

Growing legal pressures for services equity

A complex network of issues which has had a major impact on local roles in human services is manifested in the growing legal pressure on all levels of government to increase funding and access to services. In *The Creative Balance,* Elliot Richardson summarized these issues and the pressures they have created, and traced the origin of the pressures to a 1964 article by Charles Reich. Reich, in arguing that government benefits had come to represent for many a new kind of right, provided a line of reasoning which has been used repeatedly in legal cases over the past decade.[17] In rulings on the rights to treatment of prisoners and mental patients, in court orders requiring hearings for public assistance recipients deprived of their benefits, and in decisions about equalization of financing for education, federal and state courts across the nation have grappled with these intricate issues. Regarding a Supreme Court case cited by Richardson, then Solicitor General Robert H. Bork stated that a patient has "a constitutional right to receive such individual treatment as will give him a reasonable opportunity to be cured or improve his mental condition." [18] Other efforts have been made to extend this to include delinquent children who are deprived of liberty, and to press for the imposition of new forms of taxation in several states as a means of reducing the financing inequities among wealthy and poor school districts.

Dr. Harold A. Hovey has also reviewed these recent judicial interventions in executive and legislative branch decisions at the state level, and concludes:

The judiciary is becoming very interested in making a judicial matter such issues as the level of service that should be provided in various programs. In this process, the judiciary is getting into the business of allocating public resources among competing programs. In the process, the judiciary is invading some territory that I do not believe it should be in. . . . If the courts start to make decisions based upon standards such as the number of psychiatrists per patient, the available nursing care, the existence of special education teachers and the like, the courts will be traveling down a road that has no logical end short of taking over the entire budgeting function.[19]

Many observers of state and local government share Dr. Hovey's view, but others argue that the near abdication of responsibility for equity in taxation and resource allocation by the executive and legislative branches has given the judiciary its justification for questioning current levels of spending which are based upon inequitable patterns of state and local taxation.

Whatever the sources of the pressure, it is likely to be as much a concern at the local level in the years ahead as it is already at the federal and state levels. When legislative and other approaches have been unfruitful or rejected, the prospect for citizen groups of using the courts to press a case for greater equity of resource allocation in human services programs can be an attractive one. Local governments which have been compelled to master the legal subtleties of environmental impact statements and urban renewal relocation law may well need to expand their expertise into human services legislation as well.

Legal action, of course, can be used intergovernmentally as well as by spokesmen for special interest citizen groups. This strategy has been employed, for example, by states seeking to enjoin the federal government from granting offshore oil leases, and by some cities which have taken legal action against surrounding suburban jurisdictions.

Local links to income programs

Another shift in the roles of local governments in human services programs has been occasioned by the expansion of income support programs (in cash transfers) from $7 billion in 1950 to over $120 billion in 1976.[20] For the most part, programs such as public assistance, unemployment compensation, and Supplemental Security Income (SSI) for the elderly, blind, and disabled have long been the responsibility of county, state, and federal agencies. Cities have tended in the past to focus far more on services than on income maintenance programs. This was true in part because cities had no direct role in the latter and, in part, because the tendency was to view such programs as a response to national problems reaching beyond city boundaries. As of the later 1970s, this situation was changing.

The distinction between maintenance programs and "opportunity" programs has gained increasing recognition by city governments. The contemporary view holds that both income support programs and services aimed at ending clients' need for support must be included in a city's human services policy orientation.

As discussed above, many local officials have recognized that other levels of government are more deeply involved than ever before in human services. As such, they have defined the city's paramount role as "policy advocacy" aimed at increasing those levels' responsiveness to the city's problems. The expansion of income support programs is a good illustration of an area where this kind of role has developed. This policy advocacy has generally taken one of two forms.

First, cities have lobbied through national and statewide organizations for more federal support of county and state income maintenance financing, in recognition of the fact that an increase in the amount of money going to counties and states may result in a proportional increase to be shared with the cities themselves.

Second, some cities have deliberately established information and referral offices, "welfare outreach" staffs, or other close links with the income maintenance system as a way of ensuring that eligible city residents are provided with state and federal income support at the earliest possible date. This move stems from cities' recognition that the best possible services programs provided at the local level will not free all families and individuals from some degree of financial dependence. Direct income assistance to city residents, as a supplement to locally provided services, is often included as a stated goal in a city's formal human services policy statements. Some cities have worked especially hard for their elderly populations by providing timely referrals to appropriate county, state or federal offices in order to ensure that eligibility for food stamps, medical assistance, and SSI is not overlooked.

This increasing local concern for income support programs does not mean necessarily that most cities wish to play any more direct role in financing or operating these programs than they do today. They do demonstrate, however, the growing awareness of city human services staffs that exercising entitlements of city residents to ongoing income support programs can be a critical dimension in successfully meeting the city's human services goals. Many believe that the present level of local involvement in these programs is appropriate: the programs meet a basic need for which the city cannot provide directly from its own limited resources, but can legitimately rely upon higher levels of government to provide. Those holding this viewpoint claim that not only are the resources substantially greater than those available to any city, but that the whole issue of income support has a geographic base which is also substantially larger than the city. For example, the migration of low income families from the rural South to the cities of the Northeast and the suburbanization of metropolitan areas across the United States after World War II were not events caused by forces within the city, although they can now be linked to some of the need for income support. The circumstances which gave rise to these two profound demographic changes were national in scope, and it is argued that only national action can now effectively respond to the social changes and costs created by those circumstances.

This perspective on human services is underscored by those who have sought to define the "urban crisis" in recent years. While it has been pointed out that cities vary widely across the nation in their fiscal soundness and the demands placed upon them to deal with human services issues, it cannot be denied that there remains an important and growing number of cities, concentrated in the Northeast but including cities from all parts of the country, that can be compared with New York City in light of the relative magnitude they are attempting to handle in human services areas. For these cities, a particularly relevant analysis has been made by Worth Bateman and Harold M. Hochman of the Urban Institute, in which they state that "perceived distributive injustice, coupled with the urban concentration of those who are most dissatisfied, is what the urban crisis is all about." [21] Others have proceeded to conclude that the most important national policy to aid such cities would not be new categorical programs for urban renewal, neighborhood economic development, or job training, but rather national reform of income support programs which affect large numbers of the low income population residing in cities.

Federalization and localization

There is an inherent and sometimes constructive tension in the development of human services policy at both the national and local levels. Major changes at both levels have been sought in recent years. In the various proposals for welfare reform since the mid-1960s, it has been argued that national standards are necessary in order to rationalize the chaotic situation occasioned by the different welfare systems in each of the states and as a way to use federal funds in responding to genuinely national problems. Further arguments for federal standardization have cited the advantages of creating economies of scale in the administration of programs with millions of recipients through computerization of records and cross-referencing of benefits to prevent fraud on an interstate basis. The case for administrative federalization is strengthened by the existing involvement of the federal government in human services programs—for example, Supplemental Security Income, the effort through Title XX following 1975 to locate nonsupporting parents, and the use of national poverty standards and unemployment data.

At the same time, however, other initiatives in human services policy strengthen the case for localization in human services. Block grants effectively decentralize decision making, encouraging state and local control. The federally inspired effort to increase the integration of human services programs at the "delivery point," as discussed in Chapter 16 of this book, is one goal which cannot be accomplished from the federal base in Washington. Increasing emphasis on deinstitutionalization of both youth offenders and the nonmobile elderly requires services based in the community. Popular support for human services policies which build on the strength of traditional institutions such as the family and the neighborhood seem to require sensitive local design and administration of programs which can respond to the conditions in a particular community.

Thus the federalization of human services, particularly income support programs, and its alternative, localization, proceed as two of the most important trends in human services policy. Cities will be directly affected by decisions at both ends of this spectrum. National minima for income maintenance programs established at the federal level could be a great financial aid to cities and counties. But these apparent financial gains may be counteracted to some extent by decentralized accountability and its attendant responsibilities at the local level. These latter factors could end up placing other, new financial pressures on cities and counties, at the same time that the bulk of income maintenance burdens had been transferred to state and federal levels.

Little red city halls The city of Flint, Michigan, and the Flint Board of Education have been cooperating in running a Neighborhood Service Program through the community schools. As implemented by the city administrator, the program provides for a city hall representative (paid for through CETA) at each participating school to take complaints, provide information, report ordinance violations—such as abandoned cars or scattered garbage in the neighborhood—and help residents organize block clubs. As the person on the spot, the city representative also provides feedback to the administration on effectiveness of city programs at the neighborhood level and on gaps in services.

Three identifiable themes in federal and local policy can be seen to have an impact upon cities' role in human services: first, decentralization of service delivery decisions to local governments through block grant programs; second, decentralization of service delivery *within* cities themselves to neighborhood levels of administration and governance; and, third, deinstitutionalization of services in the case of a variety of human services programs.

Federal decentralization The pressures in favor of local decision making have increased from the 1968 passage of legislation approving the first block grant program to the establishment of general revenue sharing through the attempts since 1969 to institute additional block grant programs. Proposals by President Ford in 1976 for four new block grant programs were concentrated entirely on human services. Although there are strong biases against block grants at the congressional level which will be slow to change, the direction for these programs has been set. As of the mid-1970s, 10 percent of all federal assistance to states and cities came in the form of general revenue sharing, with 15 percent of that devoted to the existing block grant programs in 1975.[22]

Local decentralization In larger cities and some counties, continuing efforts are under way to decentralize some administrative operations to the neighborhood or other subcity level. A goal of human services reform in several jurisdictions has been the coterminality of service districts within the city, county, and state. Others have established ombudsmen positions to assist citizens in working with human services agencies. Cities will continue to be affected by the states' efforts to rationalize their substate districts under different federal programs; it will be of increasing importance for city decision makers and human services staffs to discriminate among and support those substate districting approaches which most favorably reflect their jurisdiction's interest.

Local decentralization has brought new awareness of the accessibility of human services. Alfred Kahn states that "the new breed of program has specialized in the access function. . . . Information and referral, linkages among public and private programs, common intake units, common forms, and training for generalist intake workers have all been featured in programs of the past four or five years.[23]

But Kahn also notes that "access services lead only to frustration if they do not lead to services." He cites Will Sahlein's critique of multiservice centers, including the words of one angry woman in Washington, D.C.: "Now I can find out in fifteen minutes that they can't help me. Before it took three weeks." [24] Again, the problem of overpromising can come into play, with some local officials recognizing that sophisticated referral services can be as disillusioning to residents of the city as were previous operational programs which could not deliver effectively.

Deinstitutionalization   Since at least the beginning of the 1970s, the impact of institutional care on juveniles, adult offenders, and the homebound elderly has been a matter of great concern. In addition to concern regarding the psychological effects on those institutionalized, the rapidly increasing costs of institutional care (in contrast with the costs of community-based and home-based services) has resulted in efforts by state and federal agencies to deinstitutionalize large numbers of those for whose care they were responsible. In Massachusetts and California, for example, such deinstitutionalization has had a direct impact on local human services efforts due to new demands for community facilities such as halfway houses, group homes, homes for the mentally retarded, and home health services for the elderly and disabled.

Whether or not cities must finance such new facilities and services directly, they will still feel the impact of deinstitutionalization. Community reaction to a new group home or halfway house has forced some cities to become involved in zoning disputes. In other cases, cities may be required by the state to assume partial costs for city residents who were formerly housed in state facilities. The potential effects of federal and state deinstitutionalization can be significant enough to require major changes in the local human services role. Cities would, in general, be well-advised to develop strategic policies regarding deinstitutionalization.

The use of private and third sector service delivery mechanisms

Since the mid-1960s, the use of private and third sector organizations has been considered as a means to supplement and, in some cases, replace city agencies delivering human services. Under labels such as "reprivatization" and "nonpublic service delivery," there developed extensive use of service providers outside of the governmental sector, including profit-making, nonprofit, and voluntary agencies.[25] This use of outside providers allows local government involvement in human services without requiring expansion of city organizations themselves. To some extent, external service delivery has had acceptance as a response to criticisms of bureaucratic growth.

In an analysis of these patterns of alternatives to public service delivery, Allen E. Pritchard set forth the generally perceived advantages and disadvantages of such approaches.[26] In a thoughtful summary of these patterns, Pritchard noted that advantages include the capacity to bypass time-consuming, rigid civil service requirements and other "red tape," and the ability to attract innovative staff and devise new organizational structures not possible within city government. A major disadvantage, however, lies in the problem of controlling the accountability of private sector or nonprofit service providers to the city government. Because outside service provision is a relatively new mechanism, many local governments do not have staff skilled in the areas of contract management, purchase of services, and project monitoring.

Observers of private and third sector service provision have noted that the

Defense Department—which has long made extensive use of contract purchasing—has encountered great difficulties in keeping costs down and supervising outside contracts. Nevertheless, it is important to note that cities under new financial pressure are turning with increasing interest to ventures in private and nonprofit service delivery.

Of interest in assessing the potential value of private or nonprofit service provision is the degree of tangibility of the service itself. Pritchard notes that solid waste collection, street cleaning, and other "housekeeping" services are far easier to measure and monitor for efficiency and effectiveness than are human services such as maternal and child health care, counseling services for youth, or recreation services in a particular neighborhood.[27] An experiment by the state of North Carolina in contracting out its entire Medicaid program (with mixed results) suggests that the financial management aspects of human services, rather than the less tangible components, are most likely to lend themselves to private or nonprofit delivery patterns.[28]

Other proponents of the private sector as a source of services argue that the introduction of a greater measure of competition, particularly in large city agencies, could have beneficial aspects in itself. A number of demonstration projects providing home health services has made it possible to compare the provision of services by proprietary, public, and nonprofit voluntary agencies. Since the services provided were virtually interchangeable, the cost per unit of service was compared, allowing future decisions to be made on the basis of relatively concrete data.[29]

In those areas where a mix of service providers does exist, the competitive approach is attractive to local governments seeking the optimal combination of quality and cost-effectiveness.

Deprofessionalization

Critics of the human services profession have claimed that each specialty in this highly pluralistic field has its own profession, a fact which results, they argue, in difficulties in communication and cooperation among professionals in each of the narrow specialties. Some have called for the establishment of new generalist positions at the local delivery point of human services; a number of schools of social work and public administration have developed degree programs in human services administration in response to this.

In part, of course, this simply represents a further professionalization of the field, with the creation of a new group of human services generalists who would be trained on an interdisciplinary basis and who would be able to provide oversight and managerial leadership with an understanding of issues across the various specialized disciplines. There is a separate movement which could more fully deprofessionalize human services, in part by building on the acceptance of paraprofessionals since the 1960s. The increased employment of paraprofessional staff creates many new jobs for neighborhood residents without formal degree training in schools, hospitals, and community-based agencies. Under proposals for new forms of "case managers," "neighborhood counselors," and local ombudsmen, a variety of different sources have proposed the establishment of the "generalist" human services position to maintain close contact with the clients of human services agencies, their neighborhoods, and the public and private agencies who are seeking to serve those residents.[30] With the increasing emphasis on access to services as a means of expanding the effectiveness of human services programs, these proposals for new deprofessionalized workers represent an important trend in staffing human services agencies in the future.

Budgetary and organizational implications

The preceding section has discussed seven emergent trends that have helped shape the contemporary environment within which decision makers in local government must consider the basic policy options outlined earlier in the chapter. This chapter will conclude with an analysis of human services issues that are currently of significance to policymakers and administrators at the local level. At this point, however, it is appropriate to take a brief look at some of the organizational and budgetary implications of the matters already discussed. Since the focus of this chapter is on the broader policy issues involved, the discussion will not be a detailed one. (For details of this kind, the reader is particularly referred to Chapter 7, which presents an analysis of administrative structures for human services programs, and to Chapter 9, which treats management and financial controls. Other, more detailed, discussions of particular programs are presented later in the book.)

For cities experiencing these changes in their roles in human services, therefore, it is important to assess the day-to-day operational impact of these broader changes. The importance for cities' financial conditions of the role taken by the city in providing human services has been discussed at the outset. These budgetary implications are direct and inescapable.

What is less obvious, however, is the extent to which any role adopted by a city will have direct budgetary consequences. The emphasis in this chapter upon city roles other than direct provision of services should not be taken as a perspective that seeks to minimize the role of the city. In many cases, in fact, the least costly and simplest alternative is direct service delivery to a token number of city residents with a small, underfunded project housed in a rent-free site with volunteer staff.

Cost considerations and leverage

The dollar and time costs of a city's efforts to obtain services are also substantial and should be understood in depth at the outset of the city's planning for new human services roles. The following analysis outlines four of the most important cost considerations in a strategy which seeks to leverage other agencies' services.

Liaison Sending informed staff members to the sizable number of interagency and intergovernmental meetings which characterize the human services arena creates its own time cost which can become substantial. In addition to these multilateral contacts with other agencies, direct bilateral contacts are an essential way of coming to understand the perspectives and the resources of other agencies. This, of course, requires staff time which will at times need to be diverted from other responsibilities of a more operational nature.

Evaluation The state of the art of social program evaluation, as discussed in greater depth in Chapter 10, is such that major investments of staff energy are required to compile data, analyze it, and compare agencies' performance with that of other agencies in similar settings. If more than "horseback" judgments are to be made by the city in determining which agencies can best deliver services to city residents, the city must be prepared to devote significant resources to this task.

Internal interagency cooperation Once the city has determined which city agencies are already delivering human services or affecting human services through their own operations—such as the police and building code staff—the task of maintaining good working relations with such agencies is an important and time-consuming task.

The search for funding A city may have decided its role will be restricted to helping another provider seek funding, but the time necessary to successfully seek grants on an intergovernmental basis is substantial, and city staff may need to budget their time in recognition of this. Even if the city's funding role is restricted to reviewing and commenting upon grant applications of other agencies, the city will need to assign staff to work with such agencies if more than a "rubber stamp'' role is desired. When the city does not initially approve the grant application, negotiation to iron out differences will also take time.

Thus the organizational and budgetary implications of the city's decisions about its role in human services are unavoidable, no matter what the role—be it activist, catalytic, or passive. None of these options are free of cost to the city. A wholly passive role in which the city's elected and managerial leadership simply reacts to human services problems by blaming another level of government or seeks to shift all possible costs to other providers will also have its costs. These costs can include less congenial relations with county, state, and private providers; staff time for working with frustrated citizen groups seeking some action by the city; and, in some areas, the worsening of the root causes of social problems with a resulting increase in remedial (rather than preventive) programs which can respond to human needs before they worsen and spread throughout the city. Philip Rutledge's advice that cities calculate ''the costs of doing nothing'' is good advice for all cities, for it is rare that problems will simply disappear.[31]

Organizational considerations

Organizationally, many cities have begun their involvement in human services by establishing a separate office of social planning as an adjunct to an existing recreation department, a human relations commission, or a city planning department. Whichever organizational pattern is chosen at the outset, the important considerations for cities venturing into the human services area include the following:

1. The need for such staff to be placed at a level in city government which enables effective oversight of all human services elements in the government.
2. The capacity of such units to work with private sector as well as public agencies.
3. The importance of avoiding the tendency for such an office to become a self-contained social planning staff, separate from day-to-day operations of departments of recreations, police, and other agencies with direct human services impact on residents of the city.

These issues are discussed further in Chapter 15.

Human services issues at the local level

These budgetary and organizational matters are placed in full perspective when considered in conjunction with the more immediate issues (as opposed to the long-term trends discussed earlier) which are likely to shape the role played by many jurisdictions in the human services field. As these issues can represent important constraints to local government managers, they are discussed below. The four issues identified are: the drive for accountability; growth management, regional governance, and human services; racial and economic segregation; and the quest for community.

The drive for accountability

From the perspective of a city or county's managerial leadership, the world of human services is one of blurred accountability. Countless studies of intergovernmental relations have set out to ''rationalize'' the roles of the various levels of the federal system. They have come to a single, simple conclusion: nearly everyone is involved in nearly everything. It is impossible in most human services programs to fix final accountability for a program's effectiveness on any one level of government. Federally funded services are channeled through state categorical agencies down to local service providers, with new layers of financial responsibility and program requirements added at each stage.

As a result, the answer to the question "Who's in charge here?" can often be "Everyone—and no one." An explicit goal of the New Federalism was to clarify accountability for human services programs: the task of financing income maintenance programs was to be shifted to the federal level, and the role of operating programs to be shifted to state and local levels. Important progress has been made toward these goals—the Supplemental Security Income program, the passage of social services legislation under Title XX, and HEW's four-year-old demonstration programs in state and local "capacity building." But the results, as Chapter 2 makes clear, have not progressed to a point where a single level of government can be held accountable for the operations of most human services programs, and in some areas the problem has become worse.

Effectiveness measurement Accountability of a different sort has also been a new thrust in the human services field, with rising expenditures for both services and income support programs creating a perceived need for new ways of testing the effectiveness of human services programs. New requirements for management information systems, for performance measurement, and for other techniques of assessing the efficiency and effectiveness of human services expenditures have been introduced in human services programs within the past few years. At the local level, special efforts have been made to determine the effectiveness of such programs as Community Action Agencies and Model Cities—funded programs which were once seen as operating outside of city influence, but now are viewed as part of local human services and thus subject to accountability for performance.

New pressures have been placed upon human services providers to specify the goals of their services, and then to develop internal management mechanisms which will enable monitoring their progress against newly specified goals. In some cities, efforts have been made to develop "service units" which could be used to measure and compare the effectiveness of one service with another aimed at a similar target. In Louisville; Portland, Maine; Worcester, Massachusetts; and a number of other cities, various categorizations of human services have been used as a way of accounting for the financial costs and the client impact of such human services programs.

Recurrently, however, these attempts to measure the effectiveness of human services encounter the difficulty of measuring goals which have as their final product a change in an individual's or a family's social functioning. As a series of Urban Institute publications have pointed out, measuring the effectiveness of street cleaning services differs greatly from measuring the effectiveness of a social service program which aims to provide unemployed welfare recipients with the skills they need to secure and maintain a job.[32] As a result, some observers see new support for "hard" services such as transportation and day care rather than less easily measured services such as counseling or training programs.

Services inventory and technology In many communities some of the first steps toward greater accountability in human services have come from the simple question, "Who's doing what?" Whether labeled a services inventory or just a series of inquiries to the most likely sources of information about services, this first step is a common one for local planners and managers.

But the lure of technology is often hard to resist, even at this early stage. A local organization or a federal grant requirement may suggest that the inventory of services be computerized, in a form which would enable local services providers to refer new clients to the most appropriate services and then keep track of the services provided them. This reasonable goal, however, almost invariably requires more time, funding, staff expertise, and interagency cooperation than is recognized at the outset of such a project.

HEW and other organizations have appropriately stressed "technology transfer" in human services planning and management during the past several years, through the HEW capacity building programs and other mechanisms. But the caveats about expense, time, and staffing levels are only recently receiving the emphasis local experience seems to suggest is needed. The intricate planning for performance measurement and the development of common service units among widely differing agencies and programs can be a process requiring long months of effort, as HEW studies of human services information systems have documented. The development of this technology promises in time to provide local managers with greatly needed tools for increasing accountability for services' effectiveness. But cities entering into such processes for the first time would do well to consider the appropriate level of technology for their needs on a cost-effectiveness basis.

There are other caveats in the area of accountability, however. To the extent that the local management official understands these realities of human services accountability, he or she will appreciate the literature of recent years which emphasized management skills of interorganizational consultation. In contrast to hierarchical styles of "command structures," the human services arena demands a willingness to work "horizontally" with equals rather than "vertically" with superiors and subordinates. A city social services program director and a county welfare director who perceive each other as interdependent partners are far more likely to arrive at effective working relations than if either seeks a superior–subordinate relationship.

These observations about interorganizational skills hold true throughout city government, of course, as an ICMA publication on team building and management styles have pointed out.[33] But in the tangled intergovernmental environments of human services, the lessons of new demands for skills of bargaining and consultation are even more relevant. Human services managers may share a goal of moving toward clearer accountability within the intergovernmental system, but progress in that direction is likely to be made only by those who understand fully the new skills demanded by managerial interdependence.

Growth management, regional governance, and human services

In some cities where growth management has become a major preoccupation of local officials, special efforts have been made to link growth controls with the provision of community services of a broad variety. In San Jose, California, for example, the city planning and development staffs have worked to develop criteria requiring new developments to provide for community services and facilities which will be required for new residents of the city. San Diego and other communities have made similar provisions for their community services which new growth demands. These efforts reflect a renewed attempt to bring physical planning and development with social planning and development, through careful consideration of the impact of physical growth on the need for community services.

In other communities, growth may not be an issue, due to a lack of annexation opportunities or the city's status as a big planning part of a metropolitan economy. In such communities, however, human services are affected in direct ways due to the lack of opportunities for physical and economic growth. This occurs through the out-migration of parts of the city's population which represent its former middle income tax base or through loss of major industrial and other firms which made up a part of the commercial tax base for the city.

As a result, in such regions the provision of human services is at times constrained by the lack of revenues which the entire metropolitan area can command, but which are not available to the central city. Some communities in this position have made an effort to expand region-wide organizations to include human services as part of their work program. Some councils of government, some community councils and United Ways, and, sometimes, counties themselves have sought to regionalize the financing of human services as a means of relieving the central city of some of the pressure of such economic burdens.[34] In some areas, intertown health districts, shared dial-a-ride transportation networks for the elderly, and other human services programs are provided on a metropolitan or interjurisdictional basis, as a means of sharing the costs for programs which directly benefit residents of cities other than the central city by itself. The A-95 review powers available to some areawide bodies provide further stimulus for the involvement of such organizations in human services, and cities have an opportunity in such cases to affect the delivery of human services on a regional basis, rather than being restricted to single jurisdictions.

Racial and economic segregation

The role of cities in human services is also affected by the strains in their social fabric. The degree of racial and economic integration or segregation in a community can often be an important determinant of the demand for and the supply of human services. Both in its effect on the tax base for metropolitan cities, and in its effect in creating conditions of isolation from employment and adequate housing, segregation by race or income has the effect of intensifying human services demands.

In many ways, it remains the American city, rather than higher levels of government, which is bearing the brunt of American society's attempt to deal with issues of race which are as old as the nation itself. It is in the American city that ethnic identification is strongest, and it is in the American city that school districts have been under increasing pressure from the courts and from minority groups to achieve greater measures of integration. While many observers of human services issues would place education in a special category of human services—or outside the category entirely—others have pointed out that education remains one of the most important human services which cities provide, either directly or through financial support for school districts. From Pasadena to Boston, cities and their school districts have been grappling with these topics in human services issues: the difficulty of fully integrating schools and educational staffs in systems which previously have been segregated. In some cases, the cities which have prepared for this task with other human services programs such as recreation or youth activities have been those cities which have best met the challenge of educational integration.

The quest for community

A final set of issues which is important is the increasing concern among the American population about the loss of a sense of community. For many Americans, this sense of community is best symbolized in the values of a neighborhood or a small town as remembered in the past. This nostalgic remembrance of a style of living in which people lived and worked in a small area among friends and neighbors is a force which some demographers see as a contributing factor to the out-migration in the early 1970s from large cities to nonmetropolitan areas. Others see it contributing to the interest in "theme parks" such as Disneyland and other conscious attempts to conjure up an image of a bygone era of small towns and identifiable neighborhoods.

Both sociologists and presidential candidates in recent years have stressed the importance of policies at the national and local levels which contribute to strengthening the institutions which embody American tradition—the family, the neighborhood, and the small community. From the growth of block associations in New York City to the wide variety of legislative efforts to strengthen the economics of the family farm, there are indications that grass roots organizations and national policy makers are seeking to develop ways of enhancing this sense of community, and ways of understanding how governmental action can strengthen rather than undermine these vital institutions.

At the local level, the quest for community takes the form of the kinds of decentralization options discussed above. In addition, however, community is sought through citywide goal setting exercises, public hearings, and, during 1976, through Bicentennial programs in cities across the country. What these efforts have in common is their attempt to embody the values shared by the city, as a means of finding themes and programs which unite the residents of the city, as opposed to narrow approaches which serve only a portion of the city's residents and have the effect of dividing it. It is to this effort to deal with the values which underlie human services policy that we now turn.

Community values and human services

In discussing the policy role chosen by the city, it was emphasized above that two sets of factors are critical in making such choices: the views of the city leadership about the service needs of city residents and the perception of the city leadership regarding the willingness of city residents to finance such services. A more basic way of discussing these factors, perhaps, is to stress the importance of the values of a community in setting the limits for its human services policy. In the pluralism which is typical of most American cities, there will be a wide range of attitudes toward human services, ranging from those groups which demand services to those who are rigidly opposed to any expenditures of a city's revenues for such purposes.

Despite the intensity and rigidity of such values in the short run, managerial leadership must recognize the significant shifts which have taken place in community values just within the past two decades. Many of the issues and trends discussed in this chapter, in fact, represent striking shifts in values which would have been hard to predict as recently as the late 1960s, in some cases. Shifts in attitudes toward segregation, toward professional disciplines in human services, and toward the role of local government itself have all made up a part of the base for the changes in role which this chapter discusses.

It is important to appreciate that this change goes on in response to large social and cultural changes in society. It is equally important to recognize that these changes can, to some extent, be guided by skillful leadership. To take a single example, day care remains an issue in many American communities, bringing to the surface profound disagreements about raising children and the role of working women in society. Yet a national consensus has emerged which has been reflected in expanded funding from national sources, as well as major expansions of programs serving both low income and middle income residents of many cities in the country. The provision of these services recognizes this emerging consensus, while permitting continuing discussion and debate around the level of such services and the best way of financing them.

The challenge of building consensus, in the midst of pluralism and dissension, is a challenge which both political and managerial leadership cannot avoid in human services programs. In human services, as in no other field of government, the programs are for people and about people and cannot thus be divorced from the views of local residents. The challenge is a dual one, both in coming to understand what those views are at present and how those views may be likely to change in the future, permitting a new consensus around the community's values in providing those services which may help people to become a greater part of the community.

1　These and related matters are treated extensively in companion volumes in the Municipal Management Series. See especially J. Richard Aronson and Eli Schwartz, eds., *Management Policies in Local Government Finance* (Washington, D.C.: International City Management Association, 1975).

2　James M. Banovetz, ''The Developing City,'' in *Managing the Modern City*, ed. James M. Banovetz (Washington, D.C.: International City Management Association, 1971), p. 17.

3　U.S., Executive Office of the President, Office of Management and Budget, *Special Analyses, Budget of the United States Government, Fiscal Year 1977* (Washington, D.C.: Government Printing Office, 1976).

4 Sidney L. Gardner, "Handbook on Human Resources Policy Planning," draft by the League of California Cities, Berkeley, June 1976, p. 6.

5 League of California Cities, "Assessing Human Needs," draft, September 1974, pp. 155–57, for the following publication: League of California Cities, *Assessing Human Needs* (Berkeley: League of California Cities, 1975). [Not included in final publication.]

6 Elliot L. Richardson, *The Creative Balance* (New York: Holt, Rinehart & Winston, 1976), p. 132.

7 League of California Cities, "Action Plan for the Social Responsibilities of Cities," Berkeley, October 1973.

8 Don Benninghoven, "An Emerging Role for Mayors and Council Members," *Western City*, April 1976, p. 7.

9 Gardner, "Handbook," pp. IV-7–IV-12.

10 U.S., Congress, Senate, *Developments in Aging: 1974 and January–April 1975*, S. Rept. 94-250, 94th Cong., 1st sess., 1975, pp. 17–20.

11 Daniel P. Moynihan, *Coping: Essays on the Practice of Government* (New York: Random House, 1973), pp. 425–27.

12 Rochelle Stanfield, "Federal Help Sought for Urban Housing Woes, *National Journal* 8 (17 July 1976): 1004.

13 Frances Fox Piven, "The Urban Crisis: Who Got What, and Why," in Richard A. Cloward and Frances Fox Piven, *The Politics of Turmoil* (New York: Pantheon Books, 1974), pp. 322–23.

14 Alfred J. Kahn, "Service Delivery at the Neighborhood Level: Experience, Theory, and Fads," paper presented at the Symposium on Neighborhood Service Delivery of the Community Society of New York, New York, October 1974.

15 Myron E. Weiner, "An Emerging Paradigm for the Management of Human Services," draft, University of Connecticut, Institute of Public Service, Storrs, Connecticut, 1976.

16 Graham Watt et al., "Rules of the Urban Administrator," in *Education for Urban Administration*, ed. Frederic Cleaveland (Philadelphia: American Academy of Political and Social Science, 1973), cited by Philip M. Burgess, "Capacity Building and the Elements of Public Management," *Public Administration Review* 35 (December 1975): 715.

17 Charles A. Reich, "The New Property," *Yale Law Journal* 73 (April 1964): 733–787, cited by Richardson, *Creative Balance*, pp. 308–10. The role of the courts in intergovernmental relations is discussed in Joanne L. Doddy and Larry C. Ethridge, "Federalism Before the Court," *Intergovernmental Perspective* 2 (Spring 1976): 6–14.

18 Robert H. Bork, quoted in Richardson, *Creative Balance*, pp. 313–14.

19 Harold A. Hovey, "The Future of State Budgeting," paper presented at an introductory seminar in state budgeting, sponsored by the National Association of State Budget Officers, Asheville, North Carolina, 6 August 1975, pp. 9–10.

20 Edward R. Fried et al., *Setting National Priorities: The 1974 Budget* (Washington, D.C.: Brookings Institution, 1973), p. 69; and U.S., Executive Office of the President, Office of Management and Budget, *Special Analyses, Budget of the United States Government, Fiscal Year 1977*, p. 219.

21 Worth Bateman and Harold M. Hochman, "Social Problems and the Urban Crisis: Can Public Policy Make a Difference?," *The American Economic Review* 61 (May 1971): 346–53.

22 Advisory Commission on Intergovernmental Relations, *ACIR: The Year in Review* 17th Annual Report (Washington, D.C.: Advisory Commission on Intergovernmental Relations, 1976), pp. 20–21.

23 Kahn, "Service Delivery," p. 19.

24 William J. Sahlein, *A Neighborhood Solution to the Social Services Dilemma* (Lexington, Mass.: D.C. Heath & Co., 1973), cited by Kahn, "Service Delivery," p. 22.

25 Peter F. Drucker, *Management: Tasks, Responsibilities, Practices* (New York: Harper & Row, 1974); and Bruce L. R. Smith *The New Political Economy: The Public Use of the Private Sector* (New York: John Wiley & Sons, 1975).

26 Allen E. Pritchard, "Alternatives to Public Service," prepared for the National Urban Policy Roundtable, Columbus, Ohio, 15–16 January 1976.

27 Ibid., p. 14.

28 Nancy Hicks, "Medicaid Contractor Runs Out of Cash in Pioneer Program in North Carolina," *New York Times*, 1 June 1976; and Nancy Hicks, "Carolina Experiments on Medicaid Ended," *New York Times*, 13 August 1976.

29 Community Life Association, *The Community Life Association from 1972–1975: Final Evaluation Report, January 1976* (Hartford: Maverick Corporation, 1976).

30 Mark Yessian and Anthony Broskowski, "Generalists in Human Services Organizations," draft, Boston, February 1976.

31 Philip J. Rutledge, "Policy Analysis and Human Resources Management,"

32 Urban Institute and International City Management Association, *Measuring the Effectiveness of Basic Municipal Services: Initial Report* (Washington, D.C.: Urban Institute and International City Management Association, 1974); and Harry P. Hatry, Richard E. Winnie, and Donald M. Fisk, *Practical Program Evaluation for State and Local Government Officials* (Washington, D.C.: Urban Institute, 1973).

33 Team Associates Corporation, *Team Management in Local Government*, Management Information Service Report, Vol. 5 No. 7 (Washington, D.C.: International City Management Association, July 1973).

34 U.S., Advisory Commission on Intergovernmental Relations, *Pragmatic Federalism: The Reassignment of Functional Responsibility* (Washington, D.C.: Advisory Commission on Intergovernmental Relations, 1976).

Part two:
Planning for the
human services

Introduction

In the Introduction to Part One of this book, Alexander Hamilton was quoted as to the advisability of "reflection and choice" in the circles of government. This was a theme also addressed by James Madison as he, too, pondered on the issues presented by the development of a new Constitution. Madison observed, in words that are not without their contemporary echo:

Complaints are everywhere heard from our most considerate and virtuous citizens, equally the friends of public and private faith and of public and personal liberty, that our governments are too unstable, that the public good is disregarded in the conflicts of rival parties, and that measures are too often decided, not according to the rules of justice and the rights of the minor party, but by the superior force of an interested and overbearing majority.[1]

The planning function in human services management offers one way to bring the "reflection and choice" alluded to by Hamilton into viable administrative operation, and similarly to avoid the instability and disregard of the public good observed by Madison. Planning in and of itself is of course no panacea, especially in the delicate area of social relationships. At worst, planning divorced from operational realities and the local government political environment will result in "apple pie and motherhood" statements, bulky and impressively bound, which will merely gather dust on the already crowded shelves of the administrator. At best, however, planning can play a major and effective role in the establishment and maintenance of the whole spectrum of local government human services. The three chapters in Part Two have been written with this latter end in view.

Chapter 4 takes a thorough look at the evolution, current framework and functional methodology of social planning and policy development in local government. Particular attention is paid to linking these topics to the decision making process in local government, a theme expanded in detail in the latter portion of the chapter. The chapter demonstrates that human services planning in the United States is not a child of the turbulent 1960s, but possesses a history deeply rooted in both the American and the European experience. It also offers a detailed framework based on four levels of planning decisions that will serve to help local government managers place their ongoing administrative experience in a broader theoretical framework. Other contemporary theories of interest to managers, from management information systems to futures forecasting, are also discussed.

Chapter 5 takes up one of the themes introduced in Chapter 4 and develops it further by addressing the managerial challenges presented by problem analysis and needs assessment. It presents an authoritative analysis of not only the relationship between needs assessment and the planning process, but also the various concepts and categories of need. It proceeds to an analysis of the options open to managers seeking to answer the question: Who is in need? This discussion covers not only the types of survey that can be employed, but also some of the basic strengths and weakness of the survey method. The chapter concludes by identifying approaches that can be used for locating concentrations of "high risk" groups that are likely to present more than average demands on human services offered by both private and public sectors in a given community.

Chapter 6, the last chapter in Part Two, plays a key role in linking the two preceding chapters with the more specific discussions found in Part Three and indeed in the remainder of the book. It attempts to link the broad planning and needs assessment process to decisions regarding priorities and specific programs. The approach throughout is practical and addressed to the local government practitioner. After an initial discussion of the fundamental question posed by the author in the form: Which insoluble problem do we tackle first? the chapter takes a look at the whole question of the ranking of social programs within the broad funding process. The chapter goes on to consider effective strategies that may be adopted, and then takes a close look at the separate roles that local governments can play in the human services field, from a residual advocacy position to direct service delivery. Other questions addressed include major design problems encountered during the program implementation process, and the crucial question of forging practical links between human services decision making with city planning operations.

In sum, therefore, the three chapters in Part Two attempt to provide at least some of the answers to the questions: Where are we at in local government social planning and policy development?; What is needs assessment and how does it fit into the human services planning function?; and How do we make these themes operational as we decide on priorities and specific programs?

1   Alexander Hamilton, James Madison, and John Jay,
    The Federalist Papers (New York: The New American Library, 1961), p. 77.

Social planning and policy development in local government

The overall policy development aspects of planning for human services in local government provide the specific focus of this chapter. The concept of planning for human services in local government is not new. As has been repeatedly emphasized in Part One, in colonial, revolutionary, expansionary, and recessionary times alike, the historical record shows that local governments have been concerned with the human welfare of their citizens. Associated with this concern, particularly when it found concrete administrative expression, have been the traditional problems of resource allocation and determination of the manner in which services were to be provided.[1]

Today's world nevertheless differs markedly from this historical development in at least three basic respects: the contemporary philosophy of service delivery is more humane; the demands created by a highly urbanized, technological society are more complex; and the institutional arrangements for delivering social services are more diffuse and fragmented. This background, too, has been analyzed in detail in Part One. The basic function of the present chapter, therefore, is to use this background as a basis for explaining the major dimensions of human services planning as seen in modern perspective and describing their managerial implications for the renewal of an historical role for local government.

This chapter is divided into four main sections. The first recapitulates, from the policy-making perspective, the evolution of human services planning in the United States. The second section outlines and analyzes the basic framework of social planning. It offers a functional division of various levels of decision making, and then outlines technological, organizational, and financial factors influencing the most pertinent components. It concludes with a description of the needs dimension of this framework. The third section offers a summary breakdown of the methodological approaches to social services planning. The fourth and final section brings the preceding discussion into practical focus by noting the managerial specifics molding the operational role of local governments in human services planning. There is also a brief conclusion.

Throughout the discussion, however, the chapter will be guided by three major themes, and it is as well to make these explicit at the outset. The first theme is that social planning in the contemporary world is far more demanding than physical planning. This is not because physical planning is more susceptible to quantification (although this provides part of the explanation), but rather because most physical planning has been naive. It has been largely preoccupied with capital investment decisions and their associated locational sites and buildings. There has been a general failure to address the host of concerns about who uses such facilities and under what auspices. The planning of school, library, park, and hospital-dominated health systems have all suffered from this limited vision. Those who dismiss social services planning as "soft" and opt for the more certain world of physical planning do themselves and their communities a major disservice. The operating problems of communication, funding, programming, and management need to be an integral part of initial planning decisions.

The second major theme is that planning, either for services or for buildings, is comprised of two principal interrelated dimensions. It is both a thinking process and a sociopolitical process. While this factor has been overlooked in physical planning efforts of the past, the growth of social concerns during and since the 1960s indicates that the participatory nature of public policy decision making cannot be overlooked. The arena for social services delivery is crowded, competitive, and not always logical. Those entering it have to be prepared to deal with a difficult and often bewildering environment. Citizen participation in planning is not only an expression of democratic ideology; it is also a necessity for coping with the swirl of private interests associated with social services.

The third basic theme of the chapter is that human services planning must take into account all structural and process elements of service delivery. Social services planning is concerned with competing theories of service delivery, differing criteria for resource allocation, differing concepts of types of service to be offered, complex institutional and cultural frameworks, and the attendant diffused distribution of power and resources. Beyond this, social services planning requires specific recognition of tasks, roles, and skills among those delivering service. Finally, many human services systems have developed complex financing mechanisms that have to be taken into account by key decision makers and their staffs.

The evolution of human services planning in America

The key social forces

The origins of contemporary human services planning in the United States can be closely associated with the same social forces that saw the rise of both the city management and the city planning movements at the turn of the century. It has been suggested that:

It was a time of arrogant and callous trusts, corrupt but sometimes benevolent political bosses, bewildered and exploited immigrants, and embittered farmers. It was also a period in which, at long last, groups were forming in city after city to combat fraudulent elections, institute civil service in municipal government, improve sanitation and water supplies, promote education for citizenship, and force predatory utilities to reduce their rates. Indeed, the spirit of reform had been gathering force ever since the 1870s, and as the cities increased in complexity, their industries multiplying, their slums spreading, and their central areas becoming intolerably congested, this spirit suddenly invested every aspect of urban life, even the least political.[2]

While political reformers attempted to smash the urban machine, and engineers and architects attacked the physical squalor and blight of the American city, those who founded the social work movement focused their sights on the urban slum and the social oppression and deprivation of its inhabitants. From these latter roots have grown today's concern for human services planning.

Between the Civil War and World War I, a crosscurrent of ideological strains swept across the nation. Social Darwinism was a dominant theme. It perceived hardship and poverty as the inevitable result of a "natural selection" process. Writers such as William James and John Dewey enunciated a philosophy of pragmatism—a revolt against the formalism and fixed rules of tradition. This development, coupled with the rise of liberal optimism and a positive view of progress, meant an increasing faith in the power of science to better man's lot. Slightly radical concerns were also developing with the origins of civil rights concepts in the formation of the Socialist Labor Party (one of several offshoots of European socialist ideology) and the National Association for the Advancement of Colored People.[3]

City planning and social planning: congruence and divergence

City planning and social planning had much in common in the United States as the twentieth century began. Most prominent was the concern about slum housing conditions and the heavy congestion of population in the nation's largest cities. The historical perspective lines of both professional groups point back to Jacob Riis' *How the Other Half Lives* as a beginning point for contemporary professional practice.[4]

But the divergence of approach that was to prevail until the Great Society programs of the 1960s was already evident at the turn of the century. The city planning movement reverted to a long-standing focus on physical utopianism. The vision of the great city has occupied the mind of mankind since the ancient civilizations of Babylon, Greece, and Egypt. Each age of ancient history exhibits characteristic principles of city building and city form. The city planners of the turn of the century set about to create the image of the Industrial Age city. Great expositions in Chicago and Paris were preludes to the efforts of Daniel Burnham, Charles McKim, and Frederick Law Olmsted.[5] The means and ends of city planning quickly settled upon the development of broad, long-range visions of the good physical city with modern techniques of architecture and engineering linked to the growing momentum of science and scientific management. City planners distrusted the corrupt city administrations of the nineteenth century, but they nevertheless saw government as the institutional instrument that had the capacity to transform the squalor of the city into the progressive vision of the future.

With the possible exception of the most intense years of the New Deal, social planning in the United States has never enjoyed such a clear-cut philosophical or methodological framework. The years prior to the Great Society programs of the 1960s were, in general, fallow indeed. Social reform through social services proceeded in a fashion almost diametrically opposed to the path taken by the city planner. In the first instance, social planning had little of the visionary imagination of city planning. While the United States was the location of many nineteenth century experiments in utopian living, almost all of these failed and were of limited influence on the social reformers of the turn of the century.[6] Minimal questioning of the expanding industrial order resulted in a human services planning ethos that was largely remedial in character. With the assumption that the market place, the family, and the church could meet most normal human needs, the orientation of social planning was seen as being "residual."[7] Human services were to serve a clientele that, for various reasons, could not function normally. This uniquely American perspective was, of course, in contrast to the mass-based socialist movements of Europe which (especially after the Russian Revolution of 1917) saw a much larger role for the state.

If the goals of American social planners were limited, part of the cause could be seen in the limitation of method. City planners enjoyed the firm methodological base of science and engineering. Human services planners operated from a highly limited knowledge of human behavior and even less understanding of how one might intervene. Thus, much of the activity of social planning at the turn of the century focused on legislation to abolish the worst ills (such as child labor and crowded tenements) and the utilization of charitable good works to uplift the plight of the poor.

Laying the groundwork: the adoption of two British examples

Two approaches to institution building laid the groundwork for human services planning. The first evolved from the idea of charity organization societies, cooperative federations of private charitable groups with coordination as their principal goal. Such a society first appeared in the United States in 1873. (The initial charity organization society was established in England in 1869.)[8] Through the coordination of charitable good works, the society attempted to avoid duplication in the raising of funds and the granting of welfare to the needy. The charity organization societies were in the vanguard of social reform efforts in the late 1800s. Their activities included the fight against slum housing conditions, the organization of health associations, and the provision of children's services. The establishment of juvenile courts and probation procedures can be traced to these groups as well.[9]

The second, and perhaps better known, force for institutional development in social planning—and yet another example of British influence in this field—was found in the settlement movement. The first settlement house was established in London in 1884, and the first in the United States was founded on the lower east side of New York in 1886.[10] The reform orientations of the settlements were more activist than the charity organization societies. Set up directly in the neighborhoods they were designed to serve, the settlements were closer to the interests of the charity recipients. Those in the settlement movement saw themselves as the vehicle for the lower classes to gain access to opportunity and upward mobility. Social reform was the basic thrust of the settlements, and social services were seen as the means by which reform would take place.

The settlement movement grew rapidly. In 1891, there were only six settlements in the United States; by 1910, there were over four hundred. They developed primarily in the heavily urbanized East and Midwest.[11] As reformers, settlement movement advocates strongly supported the city planning movement and efforts to alleviate conditions of squalor in housing. Settlement workers were active politically, particularly in forming the Progressive Party in 1912.[12]

The legacy of early efforts

Contemporary social planning gained in three distinct ways from these early efforts. The first came from the quick adaptation of beginning, and rudimentary, concepts of sociology for use in social reform efforts. The years between 1905 and 1910 saw two major fact-finding efforts that were forerunners of modern social surveys: the Pittsburgh Survey of 1907–1910 (funded by the Russell Sage Foundation) was instigated by the Pittsburgh Charity Organization Society,[13] and the Committee on Congestion of Population in New York conducted a study in that city (actively supported by the New York Charity Organization Society and other similar groups).[14]

Second, the concept of coordination and services integration (discussed, respectively, in more detail in Chapters 8 and 16) developed at this time. Uncoordinated patterns of charitable giving produced a mélange of service delivery agencies. Key contributors to the confusion were the independent donors whose wills and trusts reflected their personal perceptions of need and the paid functionaries who administered such gifts. The charity organization society was the first response to this problem. United Way organizations, community chests, health and welfare councils represent some of the efforts at coordination and services integration that persist today.

The third area that emerged from the earlier efforts outlined above was the importance of citizen participation in the planning process. Originating with the settlement houses, the peak effort in this regard was the Cincinnati Plan of 1921 which attempted house-to-house, block-by-block organization of citizen participants in the planning of social services.[15] Client group roles today range from volunteer labor through involvement for therapeutic or educational purposes to a dominant role in decision making.[16]

Two final influences: Freud and the New Deal

Two final factors strongly influenced the development of human services planning in the United States. The first came from the work of Sigmund Freud and the development of psychoanalysis. The period following World War I saw a significant deflection of the profession of social work toward this method. As the social worker turned toward working with individual clients, the reform zeal of the turn of the century abated and human services planning became largely the province of agency executives and administrators.[17]

The other final factor was the Depression and the renewal of interest in government provision of human services. The Roosevelt administration forcefully argued that unemployment was not a local problem but a grave national concern. The establishment of social security, unemployment compensation, public housing, jobs in public works programs, and other means of providing financial security was the thrust of governmental concern in the 1930s. These in turn set the stage for the current patterns of government involvement in planning for the human services.

Summary: the contemporary milieu

What has just been outlined summarizes the forces that have been most prominent in shaping social welfare planning in the United States since around 1900. A highly diffused pattern of services emerged as a result of these forces. There was a multitude of combinations of public, private, and nonprofit agencies, each offering a wide array of types of services with varying levels of specialization and consumer participation.

In the 1960s, the human services underwent an expansion that verged on the explosive. Spurred on by the civil rights movement, student unrest, and what seemed to be a concentrated national attack on poverty and urban blight, social planning came into its own. City planners and social reformers joined forces once again. Federal grant-in-aid programs proliferated and the attack on urban poverty moved to center stage in the nation's priorities. To take but one index of this expansion, welfare roles mushroomed and total public social welfare expenditures rose from $52 billion in 1960 to $214 billion in 1973.[18] Similarly, the demand for woman services was also fueled by the increasing numbers of women in the labor force, an increasing divorce rate, and the general advent of mass consumption and affluence.[19]

With the full effects of the war in Vietnam and a major economic slowdown, the 1970s have ushered in a new period of conservatism and scarcity. This has been associated with an effort on the part of the federal government to give more responsibility for decision making to local general purpose governments. Thus, the effects of general revenue sharing legislation and community development block grants as well as federal administrative initiatives in local capacity building for human services planning have given local governments an increasing role and responsibility in the planning, coordination, and integration of social welfare provisions. Additionally, as Chapter 3 has indicated, the programs of the 1960s (such as the War on Poverty and the Model Cities programs) have gone through major transformations placing their activities more in the hands of local governments. Until the 1970s, local governments often were required to provide matching funds for various categorical social programs without any real voice in the nature or sponsorship of the program. As of the later 1970s, local government is exercising more and more policy control.

Another dimension of local government interest in social services planning involves a number of emerging review and comment procedures. Local government managers will be aware that these include: the Intergovernmental Cooperation Act of 1968; the 1969 Presidential directive, OMB Circular A-95; the amendments of 1972 to Titles XVIII and XIX of the Social Security Act (which require a "certificate of need" for new health services in order to qualify for Medicare and Medicaid reimbursement); and the Health Planning Act of 1974. Basically, these federal actions have resulted in the assurance that local governments will no longer have programs initiated and implemented in their jurisdictions without their knowledge or without an opportunity to analyze potential impacts on, or relationships to, already existing programs.

Thus, even if social services planning has grown up with a serious fragmentation of responsibility, local governments are now being called upon to provide the means by which the delivery of human services can be more rational, more efficient, more coordinated, and more effective.

The framework of social planning

Given the described background of social planning, contemporary local government administrators are faced with a decision-making arena of high complexity characterized by a series of problems. From the point of view of the recipient, too, the delivery of human services poses an incredible array of activities, organizations, and financial burdens with no special guarantees of quality. The recipient sees a host of problems associated with the availability of and/or access to appropriate services (including eligibility, cultural, and knowledge barriers). He or she may find that needs cannot be fulfilled by a single individual or agency because specialization has subdivided the recipient's problem into several professional jurisdictions or areas of organizational responsibility. Seeking assistance may require an organizational road map that few have the skill or knowledge to draw. Obtaining services from a multiplicity of agencies or professionals may result in conflicting advice or counterproductive treatment. Where a sequence of services is indicated, consumers often find that they are left to their own devices as to a future course of action.

The right social element The city of South El Monte, California, has developed its "social element" and overall plan to integrate identified needs into its resource allocation process. The social element contains a section on statistical assessment of needs, using relevant social indicators, and a section on staff identification and listing of available resources to meet the needs identified. The city has also created a human resources commission as an instrument for residents of the city to voice their opinions and add to the assessment of needs by the human resources department staff. The residents also make recommendations to the city council regarding citizen-defined priorities and valid programs.

The factors just described present problems that the decision maker planning human services provision must face. Further, as local government managers are well aware, the task is compounded by problems of method, definitions, goals, and measurement. The definition of social planning itself has long been a morass of confusion. Some have distinguished "societal" planning (which would approach social planning in a manner similar to the land use comprehensive "master" plan) from "social services" planning (which focuses only on the planning of services). Some have seen social planning as different from physical planning because citizen participation was involved (as though citizen participation were not necessary in physical planning). Another view suggests social planning should be primarily concerned with racial or economic justice. The present discussion focuses on the planning of social services although this can never be undertaken in a vacuum separate and distinct from the social and economic conditions which give rise to the demand for such services.

In this contest, the following section describes two frameworks within which the tasks of human services planning can be viewed and understood. The first framework presents a functional description of the *levels and types of decisions* that must be made in planning for human services delivery. It introduces four levels of decision making, then presents a detailed analysis of technological, organizational, and financing factors influencing the important third level of decision making. The second approach is that of a needs framework, within which the *goals* of social services planning may systematically be viewed by the decision maker, a subject elaborated upon in more detail in Chapter 5.

A functional framework

Concept of the four levels of planning decisions Figure 4–1 suggests the outline of a functional framework for human services planning. It proceeds through a series of decision levels showing the planning dimensions involved in each. It represents an effort to provide a general statement regarding the elements involved in planning any community service—from the traditional services of water supply and transportation to newer programs such as halfway houses for alcoholics or special projects for children with learning disabilities. The first level deals with the vital value aspects of human services planning. The second level addresses the question of the types of services to be supplied and the allocations among services. The third level is, as Figure 4–1 indicates, the most complex level of decision making and the most pertinent for purposes of this discussion. Technological, financial, and organizational factors all intrude at this point as the method of delivering goods and services is considered. Finally, fourth-level decisions concern the design of the specific delivery unit and service setting. Having introduced these four levels, it is now possible to consider each in turn. Because much of the critical area of management decision focuses on the third level, that level will be examined in greater detail.

Level One The first level might appear to be more theoretical than practical at first glance. It asks the question that is fundamental in any political economy: Who gets what? [20] It determines what services are to be provided, and whether they are to be provided by private enterprise or by government. How such decisions are made is extremely complex and involves more than just the issue of whether private enterprise makes a profit (thereby, some would argue, presumably dictating that government refrain from involvement).

Such decisions are not, however, necessarily beyond the scope of the local planner, particularly in human services planning. Because of the variety of historical forces outlined above, local government planners frequently face the necessity of determining whether the community is better served by private or public sponsorship of a particular service. Most local health systems, for example, involve public agencies, nonprofit private agencies, and proprietary firms. One entire segment of the health system—nursing homes—is dominated by private, profit-making firms in many sections of the country.[21]

The basis for making such decisions is thus far from clear-cut and managers will recognize that it depends on the traditions, values, and existing institutions of the community. Even economic efficiency is not a completely dependable criteria. In this field, the conventional wisdom that private organizations are more efficient than public ones does not necessarily hold. Many such decisions are made at the legislative level or are based on certain predispositions in the federal executive branch. For example, both the Partnership for Health Act of 1966 and the Health Planning Act of 1974 tend to favor private, nonprofit agencies for local health planning rather than public agencies. This is in spite of the resultant problems of integration and local sanction that such agencies have experienced. On the other hand, federal acts and agencies tend to favor public agencies in such areas as education and manpower training.[22]

One finds a multitude of variations at the local level. For example, cities such as Jacksonville, Florida, and Cincinnati, Ohio, have a long history of municipal sponsorship of local primary health care clinics.[23] In other communities, this function has been the exclusive province of private physicians or community hospitals. Emergency health services are provided by city government in Boston, but by private funeral parlors in the south and midwest.[24] Home care in one region of upstate New York is provided by both county government and nonprofit organizations. In some instances, this is characterized by cooperation, in others by competition.[25]

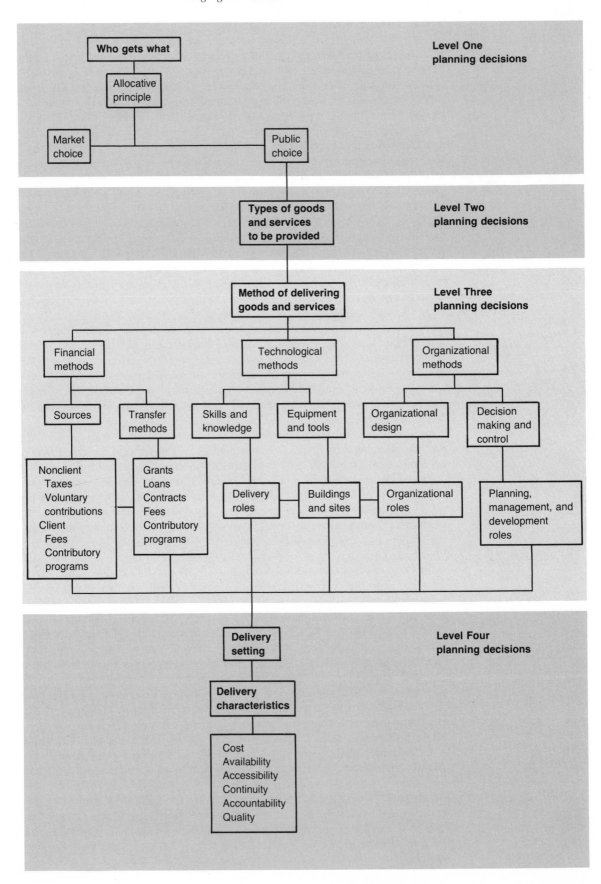

Criteria for such decisions depend heavily on the goals of the individual community. Two extreme models have been developed to highlight the range of possibilities. The first is a monopolistic one which envisions a service network controlled by a central planning and management authority. Each agency in the system performs its subunit tasks in concert with all other agencies. This is a highly interdependent model with centralized authority and decision making; it would feature strong emphasis on public organizations delivering services. The second model might be characterized as a free enterprise, free market model. Here service providers would be private autonomous agencies competing for clientele, with policies and programs determined by the unseen hand of the market. Neither model is likely to be found in pure form in any community. But the dominant values and traditional roles of the community will play a large part in determining which model local officials lean toward in their planning decisions.[26]

Level Two   At the second level of decision making lies the question of the types of services to be supplied and the allocations among services. Decisions such as how resources should be allocated toward education as opposed to health, or mental health versus manpower training, or recreation versus child care programs become key issues for local government managers. In addition, this level is the locus of decisions regarding who should be eligible for services and the design of the various components of the service package based upon concepts of need (again, the reader in referred to Chapter 5 for a fuller discussion of needs assessment). Once again such decisions are frequently made at the legislative level, but, as already pointed out, they are increasingly being left to local governments.

Of key importance at this level is the issue of universality versus selectivity.[27] In other words, should a service be provided to the entire population as a matter of right (such as public education in the United States) or should some services be provided only to a select group of people (such as the mentally retarded or the poor)? Gilbert and Specht, in their *Dimensions of Social Welfare Policy,* have indeed suggested that there is a "continuum of need" which further articulates the issue of universality versus selectivity. They suggest four illustrative classifications of need ranging from the most universal to the most selective as follows:

1. Attributed need—services are provided to all members of the community based on the assumption of a common need, e.g., health care in Great Britain and public education in the United States are viewed in this light. Such determinations of common need are based primarily on the values of the community—be it national or local—involved.
2. Compensatory need—services are provided to compensate people who have suffered unmerited hardship at the hands of the community (e.g., those displaced by urban renewal); who have made some special contribution to the community (veterans' benefits are the prime example of this); or who have contributed in advance for perceived future needs (e.g., unemployment compensation, social security payments, and other forms of prepayment insurance).
3. Diagnostic differentiation—services are provided based on a professional diagnoses of individual cases. Many health and mental health problems are seen in this light, particularly those that focus on acute care. While the concepts of attributed need and compensatory need are strongly rooted in the values and culture of the community, the criteria for diagnostic differentiation are purely technical.
4. Means tested need—services are provided to those unable to purchase goods or services for themselves. This is the most selective end of the continuum and is based on economic criteria of eligibility. This has been a relatively prevalent way of defining need in the United States and can be found in welfare, health, public housing, legal aid, and food distribution programs.[28]

Figure 4–1   A functional framework for human services planning. Planning dimensions and considerations are illustrated for each of the four decision levels. See text for further discussion.

In addition to the concepts of how social services are demanded, the ways in which the producers define their skills and organize their resources for service delivery also impact decision making at this second level. While the technology of service delivery is discussed in more detail below, the historical evolution of some skills (and the resulting professional or trade associations this has produced) is an important determinant of the nature, scope, and organization of services. For example, because of ideological and professional differences, mental health services have grown up operationally separate from general health services and the mental health profession has come to be defined according to a completely different set of ideals.[29] (See Chapter 13 for a fuller discussion of general, mental, and specialized health services.)

In local communities there is a great deal of variation at this level of decision making. The field of alcoholism, for example, is characterized by the operation of two distinct treatment modalities. On the one hand, community hospitals rely to a great degree on physician professionals; on the other hand, private groups such as Alcoholics Anonymous depend exclusively on nonprofessionals in the treatment of the disease. Mental health services rely increasingly on paraprofessional providers while health systems function with rigidly hierarchical professional roles.

From the point of view of local human services planning, this second level of decision making is the key frontier in determining the nature and quality of the services network. Needs assessment surveys, a full understanding of existing community resources, analyses of local and external forces shaping the community environment, and the development of consumer and provider participation are the crucial elements at this level. As Figure 4–1 indicates, subsequent plateaus are increasingly technical in nature and are shaped conclusively by decisions at this level.

Level Three   At the third decision level, one begins to encounter the full range of complexity in human services planning. Figure 4–1 shows three key areas which are involved at this point: technological factors, organizational factors, and financing factors. This level is of sufficient importance to warrant a separate and detailed analysis later in this discussion (see below, following the characterization of Level Four).

Level Four   Decisions concerning the design of the specific delivery unit and service setting constitute the final level of planning decisions. These include such things as the location and quality of land sites; the design, financing, and construction of buildings; the staffing arrangements and positions (including the relationships between practitioners, paraprofessionals, administrators, supervisors, planners, board members, and supporting clerical and maintenance positions); and specific budgetary allocations.

Many of the planning concerns at Level Four are typical of traditional city planning views of the design of public services. One further complication arises in human services planning, however, which has an important impact on this fourth level of planning. Settings in which services are actually delivered may be quite varied and separate from the offices of a human services agency. Guidelines for health systems plans, for example, specify the following six types of settings for the delivery of health services: home; mobile; ambulatory; short-stay (i.e., acute care); long-stay; and freestanding support settings.[30] In addition, human services are rendered in factories, offices, store fronts, and many other locations. Thus, for some services, the location of the agency may be nothing more than the place where the provider has his or her desk and maintains supplies, materials, and client records.

The third level of planning decision: a detailed analysis   Having outlined the implications of a four-level functional framework of planning decisions for human services, it is now possible to return to the crucial third level and examine it in detail. The following analysis therefore takes a look, in turn, at technological, organizational, and financing factors operative at this level.

Technological factors As used in the present discussion, the term "technological factors" refers to the ways in which service is to be delivered. These may vary significantly, and are thus one source of complication and confusion in services planning. In the delivery of water to a community, for example, there is a combination of human skill and capital equipment which comprises what an economist would call the "production function." In systemic terms, water as found in its natural state is fed into a system of purifying treatment plants, storage facilities, and pumping equipment to prepare it for delivery to the consumer. There is then developed a distribution network (in this case, pipes) which conveys the purified water to the consumer at the point of use. Civil engineers and skilled technicians are required to design and build the service system and to monitor its functioning and the quality of its product.

The delivery of human services requires the same conceptual approach. Some are more labor intensive (requiring relatively greater input of human skill) and some are more capital intensive (requiring equipment, machinery, etc.). For human services, the production function can be extremely complex and sophisticated since the goal of any particular service may be an adjustment in client behavior. Much more is known about the technology of water supply than is known about the "technology of behavior." [31] Thus, the goals of a municipal human services program are much more difficult to derive, measure, and evaluate than the goals of a municipal sanitation program. The human services production function does not in every case provide the appropriate direction, therefore, toward the provision of the optimal type of treatment.

For this reason, the technology of human services delivery is constantly changing and evolving. One prime example of this is the mental health field. At the close of World War II, mental illness was seen as entirely analogous to physical illness; that is, it required treatment by a physician specialist trained in psychoanalysis who sought to effect a "cure." Patients were hospitalized and care was administered in a centralized location. Unfortunately, hospitalization often led to no treatment at all, high levels of institutional dependence, and the isolation of patients from their communities and daily lives. In the 1950s, two major changes in "technology" dramatically altered the mental health field. One was the advent of mood-altering drugs (i.e., a physical agent) and the second was the idea of "community mental health" which encouraged the return of patients to a community environment as soon as possible (i.e., a change in the use of human skills). Group and "milieu" therapy emerged along with community mental health centers, halfway houses, sheltered workshops, and other rehabilitative services. The result was the complete transformation of the "technology" of mental health.[32] In the transformation, the governments of local communities have taken on significant new responsibilities.

Similar changes in technology can be documented in a human service traditionally provided by local government—public education. The old image of the classroom and the traditional roles of teacher and pupil reflected a very simple "technology." The teacher's skills were the result of a prescribed training program, and very simple physical agents or tools were employed—books, paper, pencils, etc. But the classroom of today only slightly resembles that outdated image. The technology of education has significantly expanded. New learning theories have produced not only new methods of teaching, but a whole new range of physical tools as well. Television, films, audio cassettes, computer "teaching machines," and computerized libraries are but a few of the highly sophisticated physical agents found in today's schools.[33]

Variability of technology may occur even within the same service. A neighborhood clinic offering primary health care may range from the application of purely human skills (e.g., health education or family planning, nutrition, and child care counseling) to the application of a number of physical agents (e.g., drugs, X rays, minor surgery). When one thinks of a full-scale modern teaching hospital, the technology employed is immediately perceived to be significantly advanced in both human skills (highly sophisticated practitioners in a wide range of specialties) and complex physical agents (linear accelerators, cobalt machines, dialyzers, etc.).

Thus, human services run a gamut from very simple technologies to the most complex. This places an added burden on the human services planner. He or she cannot possibly be knowledgeable in all of the many areas of technology and in their changing characters. The planner then is highly dependent on the collaborative advice and counsel of the specialist providers. City planners who followed traditional paths of training in engineering and architecture have sometimes found themselves with a technical capacity to function in many fields of municipal public works. This is clearly not the case for human services planners, be they specialists or general managers.

Flowing from planning decisions that are influenced by the technology of a service are decisions that relate to the organizational arrangements which will provide for the most effective delivery. Some of these concerns are traditional and well-recognized. Others emerge from the ever-changing nature of the technology of services. Still others stem from the increasing concern of consumer groups around issues of quality assurance and responsiveness of providers.

Traditional concerns include questions of organizing around geography, function, area of specialization, or clientele.[34] Each of these questions will now be addressed in turn with a brief concluding look at other organizing methods.

Organizational factors: geography   One area in which the planning of human services has been significantly deficient has been in the field of location theory and analysis. For private industry, it is currently possible to analyze with some precision the best location for production facilities, the appropriate size of market area, and the most effective means for distributing satellite facilities.[35] In the human services, however, this analysis is replaced by what can only be described as largely guesswork. One frequently hears of a need for developing uniform service areas, but there are as yet few, if any, objective criteria for designing such areas. A typical approach is described by Chu and Trotter in their analysis of the federal government's community mental health center program. In deciding on the service (catchment) area size for a community mental health center, the federal planners intuitively "felt" that a population of fewer than 75,000 individuals was insufficient to justify or support the staff and services being planned in such centers. At the other extreme, it was felt that a population service area much larger than 250,000 would be too large, exceeding the image of a local community service. This, unhappily, was the extent of the analysis for what is recognized in private industry as a key analytical concept in service delivery.[36]

Organizational factors: function   The delivery of human services can also be viewed in terms of functions which organizational arrangements can serve to highlight. There is a substantial literature in this field, but the following are essentially the key functions in social services: *maintenance, service, intake and referral, outreach, treatment, follow-through, record keeping,* and *evaluation.*[37] Human services vary considerably along this dimension both between organizations and within organizations. Some human services organizations perform all eight of the listed functions; others perform only a few. Some localities, for example, have developed centralized intake and referral organizations (such as Chattanooga's neighborhood service centers[38]) which primarily serve to link the client

to other appropriate organizations for treatment. Some health services have devised separate organizations for centralized record keeping or maintenance.

The fragmentation of these functions into separate organizational units has been
the focus of much concern. For many services, follow-through, for example, is
nonexistent because no single organization sees this process as its responsibility.
Where this occurs, the real outcomes of services can never be known or evaluated.
Separating the record-keeping function from treatment may result in errors arising
from inappropriate or inaccurate information. Recent efforts at services integration
and the employment of such techniques as case management or client advocacy
functions have attempted to focus on this problem.[39]

Organizational factors: specialization   Organizations form around professional
specialties quite naturally. This process is most evident in medicine and health,
but can also be seen in other areas of social welfare. A group of individuals with
common professional interest in a given problem or area of need come together for
closer communication and to refine and further develop their skills and interests.
Presumably, such activity also yields better service to the client. That it may result
in too narrow a view of client problems and treatment is one negative dimension
of such arrangements. Needed supporting functions are often overlooked by specialist organizations so that continuity of service is sacrificed for the higher sophistication of the specialist. Thus, the factor of specialization places unique demands
on an organization for close linkages with other agencies that are able to provide
the necessary additional dimensions of a comprehensive treatment program.

Organizational factors: clientele   Since the beginnings of charitable organizations, social services have developed organizationally around specific clients, e.g.,
retarded children, juvenile offenders, the elderly, unwed mothers, the blind, the
handicapped, drug abusers, and alcoholics. Since the 1960s, organizations have
developed which include among their specific client groups minorities and other
uniquely disadvantaged groups. Many such organizations perform a full array of
functions (in many varied geographical settings); others (such as client advocates)
serve only in a limited fashion.

As noted, these factors constitute the traditional ways in which organizations
have developed in human services delivery. They have guided agencies in their internal management decisions and have also served to elucidate organizational development on a communitywide scale. A key difficulty is that none of these factors provide any certain criteria for choice. As was pointed out as long ago as
1948, these factors often conflict with each other and result in a lack of theoretical
or rational guides as to which should prevail.[40] Particularly difficult in human services delivery has been the development of organizations around specific functions
or specialized areas which leads to fragmentation, lack of continuity, and lack of
accountability.

Contemporary views center more on analysis of actual flow processes in services treatment. Borrowing from work in the management sciences and the application of systems analysis to organizational problems, human services planners are
attempting to go beyond the traditional organization design guides. The work of
Forrester, for example, has provided considerable stimulus to the current thinking
of human services planners.[41] His industrial systems model examines the implications of tracing various flows (material, orders, money, people, and information)
through an organization as a means of finding more effective arrangements of
roles, tasks, and functions. Examples of the impact of such an approach can be
seen in current integration efforts based on a client ''pathway'' analysis which
traces the route of a client through a human services system while observing all
who come into contact with the client and the functions and roles they perform. At
a deeper level, the support activities necessary to maintain those with primary

client contact are analyzed, leading to essential control functions such as administration, planning, and development.[42]

Organizational factors: other methods Another contemporary approach to organizational design focuses on the distribution of power and decision-making responsibility in various functions of the organization. Still another approach analyzes in depth the communication function within an organization.[43] Today's organizational analysts, in short, seek to assess many features of the internal functioning of agencies from the point of view of the behavioral sciences. Their work is founded in large part on the basic concepts of Chester Barnard: he posited that an organization consists of a group of people who are willing to work for a common goal and are able to communicate with each other.[44]

Approaches with broader political implications are also noteworthy. A key approach to organizational design involves greater consumer control of provider organizations. This concept is reflected in the fact that consumer representation has been established by statute in many of the federal categorical grant-in-aid programs and in the federal provisions for local planning.[45] The basic idea behind this approach is that, with consumers serving in the key policy oversight role, greater accountability can be realized. Evidence that this is, in fact, so is not yet conclusive, but consumer representation on policy boards of human services agencies is clearly increasing, and can be viewed as a major element in organizational design.[46]

Coping with citizens The city manager of Cincinnati, Ohio, reports that the city is embarking on an ambitious program to achieve more effective communications between citizens and government, and within the government. It is called Project Cope, and is funded jointly by the city and HUD 701 funds. It includes a neighborhood liaison program, with staff from the city manager's office personally handling complaints and requests from citizens' groups. A new citywide citizen participation mechanism has been developed, with strong roots in the neighborhoods: its emphasis is on setting goals and program priorities for the city and on bringing citizens into the budget process. A city-management-by-objectives program will translate goals stated by the citizens into specific actions by city personnel. A program-oriented budget and a comprehensive program evaluation system also will be established as part of the effort.

Yet other approaches include developing review and comment powers for centralized local planning agencies that would guide the flow of public funds to service agencies; dispensing governmental aid contractually to private agencies with specific accountability measures included; granting more powers to local general purpose governments; and awarding federal grants for implementation of experiments in services integration and capacity building.[47]

Financing factors: appropriation to delivery The intricate web of human services delivery involves even greater complication when one examines the factors involved in the financing mechanisms currently in use. (For a more detailed examination of such mechanisms, see the discussion in Chapter 9.) From the simple days of charitable donations, the human services field has evolved into a sector of the national economy of major importance. Current estimates indicate that more than 25 percent of the gross national product (GNP) is spent in the human services field, exclusive of fee-for-service payments. Eleven percent of the GNP is spent on direct services (excluding insurance and pension programs) and about 90 percent of these expenditures come from government.[48] The pathways by way of which these funds move from legislative appropriation (or from charitable gifts) to the actual point of service delivery can be tortuous and complex.

Gilbert and Specht have suggested that this subject can be broken down into two parts: the sources of funding and the transfer arrangements directing funds to the point of service delivery.[49] Figure 4–1 again reflects this analytical distinction. This two-fold division will be adopted in the following discussion.

Financing factors: sources of funding   Funding sources for human services can be summarized in terms of two general points of origin. Funding can be derived from the *clients* themselves or from *nonclient sources.* A traditional mechanism in the health and mental health field has been the fee-for-service practice where the provider directly bills the client for services rendered. This method of funding places the provider in the same position as any private entrepreneur in a market economy (although some providers charging on a fee-for-service basis may be nonprofit or even public). Fees are structured to meet all costs incurred in providing the facilities, equipment, and staff necessary. This, of course, is the simplest funding form. Increasingly, however, it is the least satisfactory in many instances: rapidly escalating costs (particularly in the health and mental health fields) mean that, in many cases, the service is only available to more affluent clients.

Funding through third-party payers has become more prevalent since World War II. This mechanism operates through a prepayment scheme. It is best exemplified by medical insurance, social security, and membership in health maintenance organizations. These contributory programs operate in the form of insurance for the individual consumer but, in the last analysis, it is a consumer-derived payment. In the health field in recent years, approximately two-thirds of health expenditures have been derived from consumers and about 40 percent of this is covered by health insurance.[50]

Nonclient sources of funding include funds derived from charitable gifts and public taxes. In the later 1970s, gifts have accounted for about 10 percent of nonclient funding; about 90 percent has come from governmental sources.[51]

Financing factors: transfer arrangements   Public funds are applied to human needs in a variety of ways. In the simplest method, local government units directly appropriate funds from the tax base which are then applied by a city or county operating department. Such funding is part of the normal local government budgeting function and need not be discussed in detail here. Funding for local services from state or federal sources, however, requires some arrangement which can direct the funds to the point of service delivery. Four such transfer arrangements have developed over the years:

1. Grants-in-aid—grants provide the most common method for transferring funds from one level of government to another. Under housing and urban renewal programs, grants were often made directly from the federal government to the local unit. In social services, however, the traditional procedure has been for the federal government to make grants to state governments which, in turn, make grants to either local governments or local private providers. (In some programs, grants have been made directly to a local private agency by the federal government, particularly for research or experimental efforts.)
2. Loans—funds are advanced as a loan for the development of human services. Use of this method of transfer is most prominent in housing and urban renewal programs, particularly in governmental underwriting of private housing mortgages.
3. Contracts for service—governmental units may enter into contracts with private providers for the delivery of services. This is a feature of public welfare under Title XX of the Social Security Act which permits state governments to enter into such contracts. It has also been used in community action and Model Cities programs.
4. Third-party payments—the Medicare and Medicaid programs have established

the federal government as a major third-party payer. This method for transferring federal tax revenues to local providers preserves the fee-for-service system by reimbursing health providers on the basis of standard bills for services.

These transfer methods of nonclient funds clearly may have significant impact on the stability, size, and operating characteristics of social welfare organizations. They may also pose significant planning problems where numerous combinations of funding sources and transfer arrangements coexist for a single provider as well as for the entire local human services network.

Summary   The preceding discussion has attempted to outline a functional framework for social planning. It has identified four levels of decision making and described some of the characteristics of each, and has taken a closer look at the third level—the key level for the local government manager. As the discussion has indicated, this area can present greater demands than might be realized at first glance by the manager immersed in day-to-day crisis management. But it is also important to note that, while the framework indeed suggests pitfalls and difficulties, it also indicates that the task is not wholly unmanageable. It can be subjected to careful analysis, and eventually brought under rational control. Of course, there will always be difficulties in defining the goals and measuring the achievements of those who would enhance the social welfare. But the framework outlined in the preceding discussion and portrayed in Figure 4–1 can greatly enhance the prospects for successful management and control by local general purpose governments and their officials.

The needs framework

Having taken a look at the functional framework of social planning, it is now possible to move on to a look at the needs framework. The human services system reflects a bewildering array of organizations, professions, and services. At first glance, any systematic generalizations about such diversity seem nearly impossible. Many managers will agree, however, that it is important in developing the human services planning framework to assemble some organizing principles to describe and systematically view the total network. A variety of ways have been devised to do this. Two of the most promising—the concept of human need and the *UWASIS* approach—are presented below.

The concept of human need   The concept of human need is derived from such theoretical formulations as Maslow's "hierarchy of needs" as well as the more developmental concepts of personality growth exemplified by the work of Erikson.[52] The Maslow hierarchy begins with fundamental physiological and survival needs and builds on a pyramid to more sophisticated human demands for love, esteem, and self-actualization. Such needs may be partially satisfied in a variety of social services oriented toward increasing independence, averting isolation, and providing opportunities for human expression.

Erikson, on the other hand, is a leading figure in a school of psychology which sees human needs in a developmental light. This view may be instrumental in clarifying the role of a number of human services geared to very specific target populations. Erikson identifies eight "identity crises" in the maturing process of the human life cycle. A number of human services can be identified that serve people as they pass through these eight critical points in their lives. Four stages of childhood are viewed as influential to later development and many service providers concentrate on serving children in these crucial years. A number of specialized providers focus on people undergoing the stresses of subsequent life transitions as well, such as adolescence, marriage, retirement, and aging.

Many people argue that history suggests that people undergoing these transitions do not require special agencies and services. Indeed, this argument will undoubtedly arise in appropriations debates in city and county councils for some time to come. But the rise of social services described previously suggests that the advent of urbanization and industrialization has induced changes in the social structure such that many of the formerly supporting institutions (e.g., the family or church) are no longer adequate to deal with the stresses and frustrations of contemporary life. Additionally, many human needs may now be better met by trained specialists who are able to provide more sophisticated help, thereby permitting more satisfying levels of social functioning.

Whatever the arguments pro and con, the needs framework of the developmental psychologists can serve as an organizing principle by which social services may be classified and understood. An example of the use of such a framework by the city of Cambridge, Massachusetts, illustrates an application of this model to human services planning in local governments. In conjunction with the social planning component of its community renewal program, the city developed a matrix which correlated six "life stages" (which are generally age-defined) with six basic areas important to individual health and welfare. The life stages included: child, 0–6 years; child, 6–12 years; teen; adult; elderly; and family. Health and welfare needs were allocated according to the following divisions: education, recreation, employment, physical health, mental health, and fiscal health. Each cell of the matrix was then used to list the kind of needs, in line with the established divisions, appropriate to the various life stages. These listings, when coupled with relevant demographic data, were employed by the city to provide estimates of need for services among each group, and to predict related changes in the levels of need.

The two-dimensional needs framework used by Cambridge can be expanded to various scales of geographic organization. Figure 4–2 illustrates a three-dimensional format which permits analysis on neighborhood, community, regional, and/or national scales.

The UWASIS approach A second approach to classifying human services providers was developed by the United Way of America—the United Way of America Services Identification System (*UWASIS*).[53] This system, first developed in 1972 and revised in 1976, was based on the identification of six major goals of social functioning which represent the basic organizing principle of the system. From this, a series of service system objectives to meet the goals could be derived. "Clusters" of service programs designed to fulfill the objectives were then specified.

The published version of the original *UWASIS* included a chart which listed the six goals and, under each, the various objectives and specific programs which applied to them. Although the chart as such does not appear in *UWASIS II,* the 1976 revision, an example from the chart highlights the system's general-to-specific organizing principle and its potential value to key decision makers in local governments. For example, the *UWASIS* goal that is defined as "optimal personal and social adjustment and development" is itself divided into three areas representing different objectives intended, as discussed above, to help the general goal. One objective—an individual and family life services system—is comprised of services devoted to family preservation and strengthening, family substitution, crisis intervention and protection, and support to individuals and families. The specific programs listed for the family preservation and strengthening aspect include counseling, homemaker services, and family growth control and planning assistance.[54]

Although the specifics of this system will not, of course, be susceptible to direct application in all cases, it represents an approach to the definition and classification of human services which all local officials can use as a foundation for the planning and decision-making processes in their own communities. *UWASIS* is designed, in fact, to be a flexible tool which can be tailored to the individual requirements of local needs. As the human services encompass an ever broader spectrum of concerns and as the human services aspects of traditional local functions become more widely recognized, *UWASIS* also provides a means for relating some of the traditional public services to the "newer" human services.

Summary

At this point, a brief recapitulation may be helpful. The discussion so far of the framework of social planning has been divided into two main parts—a functional and a needs framework. Each in turn has been broken down into components: the functional framework into four levels of decision making; the needs framework in terms of two basic approaches, the concept of need and the approach exemplified by *UWASIS*.

It is hoped that this discussion of the framework for social service planning will serve two purposes for the managerial practitioner. First, by showing the theoretical constructs which underlie—or can underlie—managerial practice, the theory will be enriched and the practical tasks will be placed in a clearer overall perspective. Second, it is perhaps worth emphasizing that the idea of a human services "system," though used throughout the discussion, is in fact an elusive and not altogether accurate depiction. The word "system" implies logical connections between the parts of a group of activities and, by inference, a boundary which circumscribes it. At best, the human services system is an open one with shifting boundaries and many variations in relations between the parts. Logical connections are not always obvious, and relations may be intermittent rather than sustained. A more logical term might be "field" or "arena"—that is, a collection of disparate service organizations which may operate competitively or cooperatively. With this framework providing the skeletal structure of the discussion of social services planning, it is now possible to flesh out that structure by analyzing the main methodological approaches to the social planning function.

Methodological approaches to social services planning

An overview: the political and the managerial approaches

Until recent years, self-consciousness about the methods of social services planning has been notably absent. Since the turn of the century, two major strains may be identified: political methods and managerial methods. The first originated in the reform spirit which conceived of solutions to social problems in political terms. These nineteenth century traditions can still be found in the work of Saul Alinsky and like-minded community organizers.[55] Social problems in their view represent a conflict between the haves and the have-nots, and social action is largely a struggle for power and resources. Virtually no structured analysis was undertaken since adherents to this view believed that the ideology "explained" the origin of social problems.[56]

The managerial orientation, on the other hand, has its roots in the charity organization societies and the later health and welfare councils, community chests, and United Way organizations. People's needs had to be met with scarce resources and, therefore, budgeting, merit systems, and efficiency techniques were applied to ensure that those needs were met no more lavishly than necessary. Few substantive analyses of the nature or causes of need were undertaken.

Contrasting these methodologies of social planning with those of city planning points out their respective values. City planning developed as a profession with an apolitical bias. Government was used as an institutional base, but the rules of urban development were structured so that political processes intervened only

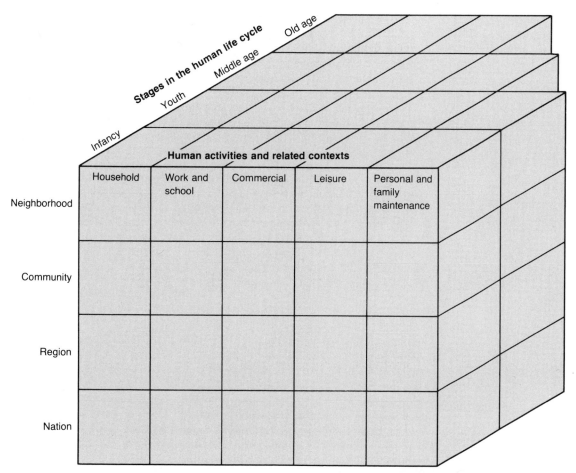

Figure 4–2   A three-dimensional framework for organizing social welfare services. This type of format permits analyses which consider separately and relate to each other the stages in the human life cycle; various human activities and related contexts; and geographic units ranging in scope from the neighborhood to the nation.

minimally. From 1950 to 1967, the focus of city planning was on the adaptation of the social sciences to a better understanding of the complexities of urbanization.[57] City planners saw their role in society to be that of deriving the optimal rational choice for action. If the political system rejected their prescriptions, they blamed it on the hidden, unknowable forces of ''politics.'' In retrospect, the political perspectives of social planning could well have made city planning more effective, just as the scientific perspectives of city planning could probably have improved social planning.

In the 1970s, city planners have generally become much more well-versed in the intricacies of political processes, and social planners have come to accept the fact that social problems and human needs require more complex treatment than simply getting the right committee together or conducting demonstrations in front of city hall. Both groups have come to realize what Webber pointed out some years ago—there is unity between research and action.[58]

An illustration of the orientation of social planning may be noted in a concept of developmental process which was part of the evolution of city planning method. Four stages of methods development can be identified:

1. The practice or craft perspective—practitioners agree upon very simple goals and rely upon experiential judgment;

2. The cognitive, or scientific, perspective—scientific methods are used in an attempt to develop greater understanding, more reliable generalizations, and more certain outcomes from intervention;
3. The policy development perspective—the complexities of the value framework become the focus for increased understanding and enlightened social action; and
4. The policy analysis and program evaluation perspective—the approaches of the cognitive and the policy development perspectives are combined to form the basis for a "sophisticated search for a combination of analysis, design, and process knowledge." [59]

For city planning, these stages evolved slowly, providing opportunities for the growth and maturation of each perspective. Social services planning has not had the same germination of methodological focus. It remained much longer in the "craft" stage of development and then, focusing on values and process, bypassed the cognitive stage. The profession that might have pursued more advanced cognitive development—social work—turned its attention to psychoanalytic methods and working with individuals. Those in "community work" among social workers quickly became (and have remained) a small minority.

Talent bank   Faced with the problem of an increasing number of complex municipal questions that needed study before taking action, the borough of Madison, New Jersey, initiated a "mayor's talent bank." It is a file listing the names, qualifications, and experience of citizens who have volunteered to assist the borough in studying and finding solutions to various questions. The request for volunteers went to 5,300 homes with the borough's water and light bills. Some 156 citizens volunteered their services. One of the first questions faced was the purchase of new billing machines. An ad hoc committee was appointed from the talent bank, including systems experts and individuals knowledgeable in office equipment. Other ad hoc committees were created to study purchasing procedures, cable television, city pension plans, etc. The program has provided expert professional assistance to the community at virtually no cost, and has involved citizens—most of whom would be reluctant to accept long-term committee or board assignments—in local government problems.

Thus, human services planning draws its practitioners from a variety of training and methodological orientations. Emergence from the craft stage began to occur in this field around 1970. With conservatism and scarcity came increased demands for accountability and evaluation of effectiveness. Burgeoning welfare case loads, rising unemployment, increasing complexity and bureaucratization of health care, shifting technologies in mental health, and other factors placed tremendous burdens on human services planners to demonstrate capabilities more focused on the substance of social problems.

In sum, human services planning of the later 1970s may be characterized as weak in the substantive understanding of human need and social problems. Its strengths may be found in skills related to those social action processes which involve both consensus and conflict strategies, and in the appreciation of community values and their role in shaping and forming the need for human services. Because of this combination of strength and weakness, planning in human services tends to be incremental, remedial, and short-term.

Given the above overview, it is now possible to identify the methodological approaches currently being developed in human services planning with the appropriate understanding of their tentative and underdeveloped nature. In the discussion that follows, four key strains of methods development are described. The full range of activity and research cannot be adequately covered within the scope of this chapter but the major highlights and applications of each are provided. The four strains are: management and social control methods; social science methods; systems theory methods; and futures forecasting methods.

Management and social controls

The 1970s have seen a confluence of a number of strands of thought that first appeared in the 1950s and evolved into a variety of applications in the 1960s. The origins can be found in group dynamics research and in the study of industrial human relations.[60] These themes, combined with the discipline of scientific management,[61] produced in the 1970s a highly sophisticated view of social control mechanisms for formal organizations. These views have found their way into human services planning for a variety of reasons, accountability and evaluation of the effectiveness of service providers being the most notable. The following are typical areas where managerial viewpoints and philosophies have become a part of social services planning. Many managers have found these methodological tools a useful—if not integral—part of their working environment.

Human resources management information systems Essential to any planning effort is the availability of adequate information related to the problems at hand. The lack of appropriate data for planning has been a long-standing problem in the provision of social services. The availability of computer technology has done much to ease this problem. Local areas are increasingly developing standardized management information systems (MIS) as a foundation for local planning efforts. One such effort is found in the Chattanooga Human Services Delivery System, the centralized data bank of which contains information about available service programs as well as uniform client records.[62]

The key problem in developing such systems lies in determining the exact nature of the data to be collected. While many studies describing the design of urban services data banks make them appear to be very precise and workable, the actual selection of variables to be included requires a sophisticated understanding of contemporary social theory. The operationalization of such theories into meaningful and appropriate social indicators requires considerable skill and creativity. The task includes decisions about whether to maintain information about resources, processes, or outcomes. Desirable knowledge is often not easily measured or observed, and "proxy" variables have to be devised and substituted. Additionally many technical problems of data accuracy and reliability abound.[63] Finally, there is the major problem of what to do with the deluge of information when it reaches the decision maker's already-crowded desk. Difficulties notwithstanding, many managers have found that the task of developing a useful body of information that can provide the means to monitor and evaluate the delivery of social services is an initial step in developing a truly effective planning process.[64]

Merging of planning and budgeting Development of the planning-programming-budgeting system (PPBS) of management has had an increasingly important influence on human services planning. While some consider PPBS a fad of the Johnson administration, many of its key principles were, in fact, enunciated at the time that Franklin Roosevelt was president.[65] While many have suggested that this method is on the wane, in fact the use of the key ideas of PPBS is actually on the rise in contemporary human services planning.

One of these key ideas is the preparation of budgets in terms of performance goals, or outputs, rather than in terms of inputs (as most municipal budgets traditionally have been prepared). The adoption of goal-oriented budgeting necessarily requires a higher level of precision in planning: the budget is thought of in terms of activities, programs, and services rather than salaries, equipment, and supplies.

Greater attention is also given to the process by which priorities are developed. The techniques of cost-effectiveness determination make explicit the differences in efficacy of alternative programs seeking the same objective.

The application of such methods to planning social services has encountered considerable difficulty. Measuring the qualitative effects of complex service delivery networks in quantitative terms is more often than not unsatisfactory.[66] Used with understanding of its limitations and application, PPBS can be an effective method of planning for human services by local governments. Its key advantage lies in its emphasis on monitoring and evaluating the actual effectiveness of service delivery.

Management by objectives   Management by objectives (MBO) represents a refinement of PPBS which retains many of the latter's key ideas. One of the difficulties of PPBS is that it tends to centralize decision-making responsibilities in a single office or individual. MBO, although it takes the same goal-oriented approach to the budgeting process, explicitly provides mechanisms which make broader-based decision making available. The principal idea of MBO is that goals and objectives are prepared by the people who will be responsible for carrying them out. In theory, this not only allows for those with the greater expertise to design the objectives and related programs, but also makes for greater commitment on the part of those who will be expected to carry out those objectives. Thus, central decision makers can focus more on the standards and guidelines for budget preparation, on the problems of overall resource allocation, and on the monitoring and evaluation function. Program administrators jointly plan and negotiate their own objectives and then carry them out. The other key idea of MBO is an explicit effort to structure programs hierarchically so that problems in service delivery can be identified and directly approached at the appropriate level.

Other major ideas involved in MBO may be summarized as follows, include provision for: operational objectives with clearly defined performance measures; explicit priorities, including the justification for abandoning or deferring activities; and specific targets and timetables, not only for ultimate program outcomes, but also for each step along the way.[67] Advocates of MBO also argue that organizational structure should follow program strategy, an idea derived from Warren Bennis' concept of "organic" organizations built around impermanent task forces.[68]

Integration techniques   From the fields of both community organization and business management have come a number of approaches that attempt to overcome the fragmentation and diffusion of the human services delivery system. These are primarily aimed at the integration and coordination of programs, services, and systems.

The sophistication of such efforts is varied and has not been effective in all cases. The root of the problem has been stated succinctly by Chester Barnard in his *Functions of the Executive:* "Cooperation has no reason for being except as it can do what the individual cannot do." [69] In short, services integration techniques have yet to produce the leverage which stimulates the motivation and desire for cooperative action at all levels. The range of methods runs a full gamut from complete government reorganization to selective and incremental cooperative arrangements on a limited and highly focused basis. For a fuller discussion, the reader is referred to Chapter 16, which addresses the topic of services integration in some detail. Many current integrative techniques have been borrowed from private industry where corporate expansion and diversification have created some of the same problems faced by the human services delivery system. Some, however, are unique to human services agencies. Industry, for instance, does not have to face the problem of integrating completely autonomous units as social services planning frequently does. Human services integration generally requires substantially greater sensitivity to reward and incentive systems for effectiveness.

Community organization and organization development Techniques of social change have been a major focus of two separate disciplines: community organization and organization development. Both attempt to devise specific methods of intervention in social networks in order to foster higher levels of cohesion and effectiveness. Whether they are part of already structured formal organizations; newly emerging citizens groups; or ad hoc, interdisciplinary task forces, proponents of these methods attempt to establish a base for cooperative effort toward social change. Drawing significantly on group dynamics, these methods place heavy emphasis on behavioral approaches to change. One common technique derives from Lewin's "field theory" where the "change agent," together with the client group, analyzes the forces available in support of, and resistant to, change. Such techniques stress awareness of the need for change and the levels of change, methods for developing the goals of change, and overcoming resistance to change.[70]

These techniques clearly require trained and experienced change agents, but many managers have found that the importance of the techniques to the planning of human services cannot be overemphasized. For many communities, the human services delivery system has become so complex that major efforts are needed to bring it under effective control. The achievement of such control requires skill in planned social change; its implementation will significantly impact the existing patterns of rewards, statuses, and roles.[71]

Social science methods

It is beyond the scope of this chapter to review fully the social science theory and methods that are relevant to human services planning. In many respects the social sciences enrich and enlighten human services planning even more than they do physical city planning. This, however, would be difficult to discern from a glance at many human services planning efforts. There is little question that one of the major needs for improvement in human services planning is a more conscious application of social science methodology. Let us therefore take a look at some familiar and less familiar social science techniques.

The use of the social survey began—at least in the United States: there are European antecedents—in 1905 with the Pittsburgh Survey. This tool is now a common technique found in virtually all human services planning efforts. Interview programs among households, service providers, and clients are frequent tools for data collection. They form the basis for needs assessments as well as for evaluation of how well needs are being met by the providers of the community.[72] As always, the problem of unduly raised expectations must be kept in mind.

Other applications of social science techniques, however, are more often implicit. The assumptions about utilization behavior (or help-seeking behavior) and problem behavior are firmly grounded in contemporary knowledge of psychology and other behavioral sciences.[73] Such assumptions are rarely stated explicitly and the human services planner is hard-pressed to keep up with the latest theoretical developments in these disciplines.

Some of the analytical tools common to city planning should perhaps be applied more consciously to social services planning, demography being a particularly apt example. Changing birth rates, longer life spans, increased mobility, changing life styles, and alterations in family composition all have a significant impact on the demand for human services, and the application of advanced techniques of population analysis and forecasting could play a significant role in determining the implications of these issues. This has been recognized in the health and mental health fields, but is seldom applied in other areas of human services planning. Forecasts of economic and social conditions in a community have also been long overlooked. The need for greater cooperation between the human services planners and the city planners of any given locality is clearly evident. This situation poses a particular challenge for administrators.

The mathematical techniques of the social sciences are increasingly being employed in social planning. Such techniques as multiple regression, factor analysis, discriminant analysis, and path analysis are slowly finding their ways into more inventive planning efforts. These mathematical modeling techniques have been most helpful in understanding the complexities of service delivery and in designing more effective modes of operation.

Yes, SIR! Carpenteria, California, is developing "social impact reports" (SIRs) as a means of determining the social effects of development. Social impacts are those events which affect the quality of life and the relationships among human beings within a community. In much the same way that environmental impact reports attempt to anticipate the physical effects of actions prior to their implementation, social impact reports attempt to anticipate the purely social effects so that they can be incorporated into the decision-making process.

The use of social indicators has also become prevalent in human services planning, particularly in the development of data banks and information systems noted above. Such indicators are now required elements in the preparation of federally aided comprehensive health plans. Numerous problems are involved, however. In many circumstances, only so-called input indicators are available (numbers of hospital beds, physicians, or school teachers; pupil–teacher ratios; etc.). Such indicators can reveal very little about the effectiveness of programs or the quality of life in the community. Thus, the major goal is to develop output, or goal, indicators. The data for such indicators, however, is much harder to define and much more difficult to measure. Additionally, indicators of agency or program effectiveness (referred to as process indicators) are useful but equally difficult to develop. Thus, while there is a growing literature of social indicator potentials, there is relatively limited application.[74]

Systems theory

Systems theory has become increasingly prominent in human services planning. Its appeal lies in its "common sense" character; its seeming simplicity (in spite of frequent intricate computer modeling); and its reduction of complex phenomenon into simple, manageable parts.[75]

In elementary terms, a system is comprised of discrete sets of activities which are closely linked together. These linked subsystems exist in an environment that is constantly making demands on the system: in the language of systems theory, these demands are a part of the system's inputs. The linked subsystems deal with the inputs in various ways and transform them into system outputs which are consumed in the environment. This process culminates in evaluation and feedback which may result in changes in the demands on the system from the environment.

This has proven an attractive metaphor in attempting to understand human services systems. Systems models can be developed from a number of points of view. One of the more promising perspectives is the conceptualization of a system along the "client pathway," but other flows—of communication, data, or personnel, for example—can be used with equal effect, depending on the purposes of the analysis. Such views permit a close examination of each subsystem, its linkages, and its support requirements.

Systems analysis is an excellent method for quickly comprehending complexity. It has its limitations, however, as a planning methodology. It assumes a high level of stability in linkages between subsystems and implies an assumption of no technological change. There is disagreement over the question of whether systems theory allows for any significant change. However, the systems depiction of human services networks is proving to be of significant practical value, notwithstanding its theoretical limitations.

Futures forecasting

A final perspective on human services planning methodology lies in the area of futures forecasting (including the Delphi method and technology assessment). The techniques suggested here have not been extensively used in this context. They are mentioned only because they are gaining prominence in other areas of planning and could easily be adapted for social planning purposes.[76]

One such technique is the Delphi method of forecasting. This involves independent consultation with experts in the various aspects of human services delivery with the purpose of developing a list of likely technological changes in human services delivery and estimates of dates for the probable development of such changes.

Another closely related technique is technology assessment, which involves efforts to trace out the impacts of a given technological improvement.[77] It is usually thought of in terms of physical technology (such as the impact of automobiles or television on American society), but can also be applied in human services planning. A thorough assessment of drug therapy and its impact at all levels of the community may have revealed many of the problems now being experienced as state and local governments attempt to deinstitutionalize patients and put them under the care of local community services.

Futures forecasting proper is still another approach to developing innovative and creative concepts in human services planning. The method, as implied by its title, is the preparation of "future scenarios" around a specific set of assumptions. Alternative future scenarios permit planners to trace various possibilities as a basis for decision making. One scenario may well represent a "do nothing" or "drift" situation; others may make an attempt to play out the consequences of specified policy alternatives.[78]

As suggested, these techniques have not been widely adopted in human services planning, but their potential use seems highly promising. Many managers are keeping an eye on these developments.

Summary

The preceding discussion has analyzed the methodological approaches to social services planning. It has been divided into five parts. The first has taken a look at broad aspects of political and managerial approaches. The second has looked at management and social controls, specifically, human resources management information systems, the merging of planning and budgeting, management by objectives, integration techniques, and community organization and organization development. The third part has taken a look at social science methods, and the fourth and fifth have discussed systems theory and futures forecasting.

The role of local government in human services planning

Following from the foregoing description of a framework for human services planning and the brief inventory of its methodology, it is now possible to discuss the potential dimensions of human services planning in local government. Needless to say, there are numerous possibilities and the potential mix of roles, responsibilities, and decision-making arrangements are infinite. In any given community, these will depend very much on the staff resources of the local government and the private service providers, historical patterns of service development, community values, and established patterns of communication. In the discussion below, no prescribed role or combinations of roles are set forth as most desirable. Local factors will be such that the relationship between the local government and already existing service providers must be negotiated on a continuing basis.

Generally, the planning role of the local government will bear close relationship to the kind of service delivery role that the local government assumes. In other words, the more the local government is involved in the provider role, the more demanding and comprehensive will be the planning roles. In addition, any determination of the planning role of local government in the social services field is contingent on at least two factors: how the community perceives its local government's planning role in general and the strength of planning resources already available. Finally, as will be suggested below, the distribution of power among the service providers will be an important determinant of the local government planning role.

Potential local government service delivery roles

The New England Municipal Center has suggested that local governments may potentially play five roles in the delivery of human services. For the purposes of this discussion, these roles are summarized as follows:

1. Provider role—the local government directly provides service. Examples of this are numerous and well known—municipal hospitals, schools, recreation programs, and the like.
2. Regulator role—the local government oversees and regulates other agencies who directly provide services. Examples of this include county governments and councils of governments (COGs) which, under authorization by OMB Circular no. A-95, are given review and comment functions respecting any service provider who operates with federal funds. Similar arrangements are also found in comprehensive health planning.
3. Funder role—the local government, utilizing its own funds (sometimes from federal revenue sharing or community development block grants, both of which authorize funding for social services), enters into contracts with service providers. Local government may exercise a performance control over such contracts through contract monitoring and evaluation, including the power to withhold payment, exact penalties, or terminate for any failure of service.
4. Capacity-builder role—the local government provides advice, consultation, and technical assistance to build up the planning, management, and coordination capacities of other agencies. Local government might, for example, use its tax or grant funds to assist a local citizens council in mental health planning or to build a network of emergency services.
5. Facilitator/coordinator role—the local government may focus on providing the mechanisms by which local service providers, client groups, and others may come together and negotiate goals, policies, programs, and activities.[79]

These roles are by no means exhaustive. Many experienced local officials are familiar with the "passive contributor" role in which a local government is asked to contribute matching funds to a federally financed service, but is given no voice in the nature or policies of that service. The focus in this discussion, however, is on active local government participation as illustrated by the five roles outlined above.

Combinations of these roles represent the most common situation. With the fragmented development of social services, local governments might be simultaneously providers, regulators, and funders of social services. They may also be invited to take on capacity-building or facilitating roles in still other service delivery systems. Many cities, for example, have a dual health system with parallel public and private facilities. In other localities, mental health services may also be provided under a dual system. Some services are shifting in their control configuration with the responsibilities of local government changing correspondingly. Some states, for example, now require that public education opportunities be made available to children with learning disabilities.[80] This means that local governments are required to provide special educational and psychological counseling services formerly offered only by private agencies, in many cases.

In short, the five service roles described above are useful analytical categories, but most local and county governmental units are heavily involved in several of these roles.

Relation of human services planning roles to delivery roles

Each of the roles described above reflects a different degree of "activism" on the part of local governments in the provision of human services. Each has a corresponding degree of planning responsibility associated with it. These variations in planning requirements are spelled out in Figure 4–3, which relates the planning levels depicted in Figure 4–1 to the five service roles described above. As Figure 4–3 suggests, the direct provider role requires a full range of planning responsibility from the broadest policy level to the specific design of delivery settings.

Local government planning responsibilities	Direct provider	Regulator	Funder	Capacity builder	Facilitator/ coordinator
Local government service delivery role					
Level One					
Basic goal and policy development	+	+	+	+	+
Development of priorities	+	+	+	(○)	(○)
Monitoring and evaluation	+	+	+	(○)	(○)
Level Two					
Needs assessment	+	+	+	○	○
Inventory of service providers	+	+	+	○	○
Design of services mix	+	+	+	○	○
Development of eligibility standards	+	+	+	○	○
Development of technical and operating standards	+	+	+	○	○
Level Three					
Service area delineations	+	+	+	○	○
Planning of service technology	+	(○)	(○)	–	–
Planning of organization, coordination, and management arrangements	+	(○)	(○)	–	–
Planning of funding arrangements	+	○	(○)	–	–
Level Four					
Site location and site planning	+	(–)	(–)	–	–
Building and facility planning	+	(–)	(–)	–	–
Staffing and program planning	+	(–)	(–)	–	–
Special setting design planning	+	(–)	(–)	–	–

+ = local government responsibility
○ = may be carried out by local government or others
(○) (–) = carried out by others with local government review
– = carried out by others

Figure 4–3   The extent of local government responsibility for various aspects of planning decisions is related to the local government service delivery role.

Consequently, the direct provider role places the greatest demands on local government planning capabilities.

The regulator and funder roles are somewhat less rigorous. They require the following:

1. The capability to provide guides and standards at the highest level of policy development;
2. An understanding of the needs of the community and how such needs are being met;
3. The ability to develop a vision of what the ideal mix of services should be in the community;
4. The capacity to develop priorities; and
5. The capability to develop criteria for decision making in the regulation and funding of services that can be applied continuously and which have the capacity for evaluating and monitoring performance.

Stated in another fashion, local governments in regulator and funder roles must have a comprehensive planning and policy development capacity. Those who are direct service providers need that same capacity plus the added ability to plan specific projects and programs.

The capacity-builder and facilitator/coordinator roles are less active, placing fewer demands on local government. While local government should be directly involved in basic goal and policy development, these roles would also be compatible with the location of a general comprehensive planning capacity in other agencies (such as a health and welfare council or United Way organization). With a local government in either a capacity-builder or facilitator/coordinator role, specific project and program planning may be carried out directly by the private service provider.

Combination roles: dominant patterns in local government planning

As suggested, it is unlikely that almost any local government at the municipal or county level will be playing only one of the five defined roles. This variability can best be seen by using the example of a hypothetical urban community in the northeastern part of the United States. Figure 4–4 suggests the typical dominant provider roles that one might have found in such a community in the early 1970s. This is charted in Figure 4–4 in relation to the six goals for social welfare services set up in the original *UWASIS* classification scheme (discussed earlier in this chapter). Of four possible service deliverers—local government, state government, federal government, and private—the figure indicates the group most likely to actually deliver services in such a community (as opposed to funding, coordinating, or planning services). The resulting pattern suggests the difficulty of generalizing about local government roles.

Under Goal One—adequate income and economic opportunity—the federal and state governments dominate (although county governments might serve as agents of state government in providing such services). Local governments share in the delivery of special needs in manpower development (often a legacy from the War on Poverty or Model Cities programs), but social insurance, financial aid, and consumer protection services are largely in the hands of higher levels of government. This is not to suggest that such a pattern is static. Many localities particularly hard hit by economic distress have used federal revenue sharing, community development, and anti-poverty funds to develop locally sponsored training and consumer programs.

In contrast, Goal Two—optimal environmental conditions and provision of basic material needs—finds local government playing a dominant role. This is not surprising since the traditional services of protection, transportation, utilities,

Goal One

Adequate income and economic opportunity

	L	S	F	P
Manpower development services		+	+	
Special services for handicapped and disadvantaged	⊞	+	+	+
Social insurance services		+	+	
Financial aid services		+	+	
Consumer protection services		+	+	

Goal Two

Optimal environmental conditions and provision of basic material needs

	L	S	F	P
Food and nutrition services	⊞	+	+	+
Clothing and apparel services				+
Housing and urban renewal services	⊞		+	+
Transportation services	⊞	+	+	
Public protection services	⊞	+	+	
Environmental protection services	⊞	+	+	

Goal Three

Optimal health

	L	S	F	P
Health maintenance and care services	⊞	+		+
Mental health services		+	+	+
Mental retardation services	⊞	+		+
Rehabilitation services		+		+

Goal Four

Adequate knowledge and skills

	L	S	F	P
Preschool services				+
Elementary and secondary services	⊞			
Higher education services			+	+
Informal education services	⊞			+
Special education services	⊞	+		+

Goal Five

Optimal personal and social adjustment and development

	L	S	F	P
Family strengthening services				+
Family substitute services		+		+
Other supportive services				+
Recreational services	⊞	+	+	+
Intergroup relations services	⊞			+
Cultural and arts services				+

Goal Six

Adequately organized social instrumentalities

	L	S	F	P
Community planning services	⊞			+
Community organization services				+
Human services funding services	⊞	+	+	+
Economic development services	⊞	+		
Communications and information services	⊞			+
Equal opportunity promotion	⊞	+	+	+

L = Local government
S = State government
F = Federal government
P = Private (profit and nonprofit)

Figure 4–4 Typical providers of certain services, shown according to *UWASIS* goal classifications. The areas most often handled by local government are indicated by the boxed-in crosses. See text for further discussion.

housing, and urban renewal are represented here. While state and federal governments and some private agencies share in delivery (and other) roles, local government is still the dominant force in meeting this goal.

Goal Three—optimal health—presents a very mixed picture. Local government shares responsibilities with others to a large extent and the dominant service provider emerges in the form of private organizations. Public health services (i.e., sanitation, immunization, screening, and prevention programs) are most commonly associated with local government. The delivery of medical care may be found in local government institutions (city or county hospitals, neighborhood clinics etc.), but such care traditionally has been limited to those unable to purchase normal private services. Additionally, local governments have had very little role in mental health, retardation, and rehabilitation services. This is an area where local government influence is very much on the rise, however. Efforts to reduce the costs of health care and rationalize the proliferation of capital–intensive acute care facilities have created a major interest in comprehensive health planning. The deinstitutionalization of patients in state mental hospitals has placed a new burden on local governments to provide community-based services and facilities. State laws have increasingly mandated the education of the retarded in normal school settings; the responsibility for this has fallen upon the local school system. This third goal, then, is, in the later 1970s, in a state of transition: local governments can be expected to play an important and dominant role in the future in the provision of optimal health.

Goal Four—adequate knowledge and skills—has been a key responsibility of local government since the beginning of the public school movement in the United States in the early nineteenth century. Local government is still the dominant provider in this area. Traditionally, the federal government has taken almost no part in the actual provision of education, although it has provided financial assistance at all levels of learning, particularly since the 1960s.

In the area of Goal Five—optimal personal and social adjustment and development—local government has assumed a minimal role except in recreation. This has also been true of state and federal government roles in these areas with some exceptions. Again, this traditional pattern is changing, particularly in regard to family support and group relations services that are linked to the mental health field.

One exception to the above should be noted—the role of local government in dealing with relationships among racial and ethnic groups. In some communities, court-ordered busing programs to achieve integration in the schools have brought this problem to prominence. But increasingly, all local government units must face up to such problems. Many communities unaffected thus far will find themselves, before the decade is out, with major responsibilities for the advancement of more harmonious racial and ethnic relations.

Finally, Figure 4–4 depicts local government as being very heavily involved in Goal Six—adequately organized social instrumentalities. Local government itself is one of the primary social instrumentalities that ensures the quality of life and the provision of needed services. Many of the services under this goal have shared responsibility, but the key role of local government in general cannot be overlooked. And, of course, one of the major thrusts of the New Federalism of the early 1970s was the further enhancement of the role of local government in the planning, development, and delivery of human services.

The variable pattern which has just been outlined highlights the complexity of the human services planning task in all of its principal dimensions. The total range of factors involved in planning—the richness and diversity of methodology, the variability of roles, and the shared responsibilities with other levels of government and private providers—offers a view of human services planning that should prove useful in assisting managers as they adapt to the changing patterns of local government involvement.

Factors in the establishment of human services planning in local government

As the previous discussion suggests, the establishment of human services planning in local government implies a sensitivity to a broad array of factors, including relationships to existing providers as well as to state and federal agencies and wide variability in roles and patterns of service delivery. For the neophyte, however, additional questions must be considered. There are many similarities between the establishment of a human services planning function and a physical planning function. However, numerous differences do exist because of the potentially broader range of roles. Generally, it is important to review questions centering around: first, organization for human services planning; second, the design of the policy-making process; and, third, the functional scope and role of the human services planning function. As the discussion below will illustrate, these three themes are intertwined. For the purpose of clarity in the following discussion, they will be addressed separately.

Organizing for human services planning   Numerous publications describe the pros and cons of different organizational arrangements for city planning. Early efforts to establish city planning in local government argued for a separate planning function unsullied by the immediate political turmoil and self-interest of public officials.[81] The city planning movement in the early twentieth century was consequently characterized by the establishment of independent planning commissions. A survey of the planning role in American cities in the 1930s argued for a planning effort that was an integral part of the chief executive's office.[82] In this way, policy, planning, and implementation could be more closely integrated. Later it was suggested that the planning sphere rest with the legislative body of the local government.[83]

Citizens' "town hall"   The city manager of Casa Grande, Arizona, reported an interesting approach to citizen involvement in his community. The Casa Grande "Town Hall" was organized as a voluntary association of involved citizens of the city and surrounding areas who meet to discuss community problems, study alternatives, and make recommendations to appropriate legislative and authoritative bodies. The association's board includes the mayor, city manager, chamber of commerce president, president of the city's board of trustees, local college president, and school board president and superintendent, as well as 15 citizen members. Every year the association sponsors a Town Hall conference; voting delegates are appointed by the board to represent the various neighborhoods, ethnic groups, and socioeconomic groups in the community. The conference breaks into discussion groups and develops policy and implementation suggestions for the coming year. It also chooses the citizen members of the association's board for the coming year.

These same issues arise in considering the establishment of human services planning. Capoccia, for example, argued strongly for an independent role for social planning. He felt that the planning function would get "lost" in the demands of everyday crises if merged with the management of actual service delivery.[84] Brooks, on the other hand, believes that planning and implementation have to be combined—"keeping the social planners 'close to the action,' thereby increasing the 'reality content' of their plans and decisions."[85] These, in effect, are contemporary restatements of the long-standing debate in city planning.

Available options   The human services planning picture is more complicated. City planners historically have created their own devices for implementing plans by establishing new organizational entities (zoning, capital budgeting, redevelopment, etc.). Local human services planners, however, face a wide variety of public and private agencies already established and delivering services. The means for plan implementation therefore already exist in many respects. The challenge is to find the organizational structure that will best serve to integrate and coordinate an already existing network of providers and to induce them to participate in the design and development of new services.

Numerous options exist. They include, but are not limited to:

1. Expanding the responsibilities of the existing city planning agency to include human services planning;
2. Creating a new office of human services planning within the office of the mayor or city manager;
3. Through legislative action, referendum, or other mechanism for charter change, creating a new department of social planning; and
4. Developing a new quasi-public entity which would incorporate representation from both public and private service providers within its sphere of authority.

The choice among these options for any given community depends on factors which include the political, technical, and financial resources of the relevant local groups and interests. The first option, for example, appears to be one that is logical and relatively easy to implement. However, experience suggests that city planning agencies have historically concentrated on land use and development issues. They tend to approach human services planning with limited understanding and competence. This has been evident in regional planning agencies with A-95 review powers. On the other hand, some city planning agencies (through previous experience with Model Cities programs) have developed significant competence in human services planning. The Cleveland City Planning Commission, for example, assigned priority to the social problems of the city and engaged in significant planning efforts around manpower, income maintenance, and similar social welfare concerns.[86]

City planning agency expansion   Determination of the ability of the existing city planning agency to assume responsibility for human services planning takes into account more than the technical competence of the staff. The breadth of perspective and capability of the agency's leadership (commission or board members and the director of planning) should be considered of paramount importance. Such leadership should be geared to health and social welfare services rather than to such traditional city planning concerns as engineering or real estate finance and development.

Another consideration is the work load of the city planning agency. In a rapidly growing community, the time of both staff and leadership may be completely consumed by the demands of new development (i.e., zoning variances, map changes, subdivision control, etc.). In such instances, even the most competent agency would be diverted from human services planning.

Finally, of course, the political history of the city planning agency must be addressed—and addressed squarely. A respected and influential agency in the locality's decision-making arena that has previously provided leadership of a broad and comprehensive nature might be the ideal location for the human services planning function. All too often, however, the planning agency's image is highly specialized. In some instances, it may be seen as lacking influence or leadership and consequently could not be expected to provide the most auspicious home for human services planning.

Creation of new human services agencies with planning responsibilities is one path taken by local governments in preference to expansion of the city planning agency. This better acknowledges the complexity and variety of unique planning skills demanded by social services as outlined above. Many such agencies, however, work closely with the city planning agency.

Unit in mayor or manager's office A special unit in the office of the mayor or manager is an option adopted by some cities. This approach has the advantage of placing human services planning at the center of power and decision making, provided there is stability in the executive office. If there is significant instability, however, human services planning could suffer. Constant shifts in priorities could make long-term planning efforts difficult to sustain.

Malden, Massachusetts, is an example of a city whose human services effort emanates from the mayor's office. The arrangement, however, is seen as an experiment operating primarily with federal community development funds. After a period of time, it is expected that the city council will create a new department of human services.[87]

New department Another option would create a new human services department and would include the human services planning function. Many of the larger American cities, i.e., New York, Detroit, and Baltimore, have had such arrangements for many years. The increase of welfare case loads underlined the many links between public welfare functions and private and public social services. Thus, in such cities, there has been a trend toward consolidating welfare and social services into single departments.

In the 1970s, in response to a variety of federal pressures, new human services departments were also established in medium-sized and smaller cities. These have often combined the public welfare function with anti-poverty or Model Cities efforts and signaled a recognition of the growing local concern for health, mental health, and other social problems. Such departments have been created through legislative action by the city or county council or by charter change. Examples of cities which undertook this option include Chattanooga, Tennessee; Norfolk, Virginia; and Newton, Massachusetts. County governments doing so include Contra Costa County, California, and Polk County, Iowa.

The organization of such departments for the human services planning function corresponds with the position of Brooks stated earlier—planning is closer to the action when combined with service delivery. A 1974 evaluation of two cities by the Human Services Institute for Children and Families, Inc., suggests both advantages and disadvantages to such an arrangement. The report suggests that human services planning is limited in Chattanooga to "project and policy" planning.[88] It notes that the Chattanooga experience to that date had focused on the annual budget as the instrument of planning. This would lend credence to the fears expressed by Capoccia, that is, that the planning function is in reality subservient to the operations management function. To overcome this, Chattanooga created in 1974 a Department of Community Development Coordination which oversees policy planning for human services.[89]

The same report, however, noted a different result in Norfolk, Virginia. The Department of Human Resources was created in that city by a merger of the Department of Public Welfare and the City Demonstration Agency (the Model Cities instrument). The human services planning effort is shared by the Norfolk City Planning Department and the Department of Human Resources' Office of Management Planning. The City Planning Department is responsible for long-range policy planning and maintains a data base derived from its citywide neighborhood analyses. This data base is then utilized by the Department of Human Resources in developing an analysis of needs and program evaluation. This analysis yields a "definition of the nature and scope of a problem and resources available for problem resolution" from which "the Office of Management and Planning is responsible for the development of programs and strategies which will meet the problem." [90]

This office is also responsible for project planning and performs the A-95 review process on all applications for federal aid for human services. For Norfolk, this division provided the human services planning effort with a well-developed base of information and problem identification.

Public and private joint planning   Human services planning can also be done through continued public and private cooperation and joint planning. One of the most unusual examples of such an approach, which provides a very sharp regulatory role for the city government, is Woonsocket, Rhode Island. In this case, the city government has contracted with a new nonprofit agency for the planning and delivery of social services which involve government funding either through general revenue sharing, community development, or local funds. The nonprofit agency is responsible for planning and delivery of services and works with the city's planning agency. Schenectady, New York, and Worcester, Massachusetts, have created new private, nonprofit social planning corporations in conjunction with local private agencies.[91] Similar examples may be found in Hartford, Connecticut; Jefferson County, Kentucky; and Lancaster County, Pennsylvania.[92]

This arrangement reflects the predominant reality in many communities that the majority of human services providers are private agencies (despite the fact that the majority of the funding is public). The assumptions underlying this approach are fourfold: private providers will be more responsive to a private social planning corporation; they will be more likely to accept policy directives from such an organization; such a corporation provides an opportunity for more meaningful consumer and provider participation in the planning process; and a private corporation will be less subject to city hall politics. A major disadvantage, of course, is that the local government is unable to control directly an important community planning function. This disposition of the human services planning network still requires a role for planning agencies in data analysis, monitoring, and evaluation. It also requires some means of assuring the political leadership that needs are being met and that tax dollars are being wisely spent.

Regional agencies   Another option for organizational arrangements can be found in the use of regional planning agencies for human services planning. Examples include the metropolitan council of the Twin Cities (Minneapolis–St. Paul) area; the council of governments in San Antonio, Texas; and the council of governments in Decatur, Alabama.[93] These focus on metropolitan or multicounty areas and offer a broader planning base. Regional planning, however, is not a panacea and regional planning agencies are not always appropriate in every locale. They are essential in predominantly rural areas where scarce resources for both planning and service delivery may prevail. Despite numerous federal guidelines and regulations, regional agencies do not always lend themselves adequately to human services planning in highly urbanized areas. Demands for human services can be very concentrated, and varying amounts of effort may be required in central cities as distinct from low density suburbs. A great deal depends on the nature of the service (its technology, the demand for it, and its delivery settings) and the existing distribution of resources and service providers.

The design of the policy-making process   A concern for the dynamics of the policy-making process should also be considered in the establishment of a human services planning capability. Regardless of what organizational arrangements for planning are appropriate in any community, how decisions are made, who makes them, and how they are linked to other policy arenas are primary concerns in building an effective planning process. The establishment of city planning agencies has already stimulated difficulties surrounding such questions which are equally vital in human services planning. Some additional complications must be considered, however.

A significant problem in policy-making and planning lies in a key feature of the human services data base—the basic inventory of information necessary for decision making is very often highly confidential. The records of health and mental health patients, welfare recipients, and others are not available for public inspection in order to protect the privacy and rights of those consumers. Thus, information systems utilized in the planning and policy-making process must be tapped in such a way as to maintain legal rights. This often creates handicaps and difficulties for the planning process. Proper safeguards are vital to the maintenance of individual privacy and constitute a key policy matter in the establishment of human services planning activities in the local community. Almost every effort to develop a centralized information system has had to resolve this problem.

Participation in decision making is another dimension of the policy-making process. Such a process should include the maximum amount of involvement on the part of all relevant community interests. The political leaders of a community, of course, are ultimately accountable to the public for the success of programs under their auspices. A new human services planning capability within local government will therefore necessarily involve a decisive role for such leaders. The establishment of a private social planning corporation, however, requires that the role of local government leaders be given careful scrutiny.

The providers of service are vitally interested in the policy-making process. These agencies and individuals implement policy. Thus, their participation in planning is vital if the process is to succeed. On the other hand, providers can represent narrow special interests (an agency or a professional group), so decision-making mechanisms must balance the relationship of provider interests with those of others.

Quiet citizen participation   Fond du Lac, Wisconsin, took an unusual approach to goal setting for its community development program. The city invited people representing every identifiable segment of the community to meetings held in a school cafeteria. To structure the discussions, a "nominal group process" was used. The process was developed for business firms at the University of Wisconsin's Business School. It is highly structured. After small group discussions, the key is to narrow alternatives and make decisions by individual voting, without interaction. In just six weeks, over 100 citizens identified a whole range of community problems, voted on their importance, and ultimately came up with 13 top priorities for the city council's consideration.

Perhaps the most controversial and most difficult issue in the design of the planning process is in the area of citizen participation—what mechanisms are available to provide for the interests of consumers and their families. Federal law requires their participation for many social services. For example, under the Health Planning Act, local agencies responsible for areawide health planning are required to have governing bodies, 50–60 percent of whose membership includes "consumers of health care . . . broadly representative of the social, economic, linguistic, and racial populations . . . of the health service area." [94] There is no tried and true formula for precisely defining such representation, and any given locality will undoubtedly rely on previous experience with citizen participation as a guide to building it into the human services planning process.

Additionally, formal and/or informal roles must be established with planning agencies involved in other areas of concern, e.g., land use and environmental protection, as well as with regional or state agencies having related planning functions. The involvement of these various interest groups can be achieved in a number of ways. Contra Costa County, California, is the first case in point.

Launched by a Department of Health, Education, and Welfare services integration grant, the Allied Services Board and the Allied Services Commission were created by the county in 1973. Both groups were given responsibility for approving human services plans and projects in the county. This method was termed a "double-green-light decision-making process." Although it is not advocated as a pattern appropriate to every community, it does illustrate a very direct mechanism for strong, decisive involvement of relevant interests and groups.[95]

Citizen participation in Norfolk, Virginia, is organized very simply and traditionally through a fifteen-member citizens advisory body tied to the department of human resources.[96] This has long been a common device to secure citizen participation although the evidence is not clear that it has been successful. Chattanooga, on the other hand, has used techniques derived from the anti-poverty and Model Cities experience. The human services department has a citizens advisory board with elected members. Two citizen members are elected from each of seven district councils, representing both the central city and the surrounding county.[97] In Baltimore, Maryland, two separate advisory groups to the department of social services make for a further distinctive pattern: a city advisory commission *and* a client advisory committee.[98] This structure provides for a separate and explicitly organized participatory role for department clients.

Clearly, the traditional citizen or consumer role has been an advisory one. Few localities have gone so far as Contra Costa County in giving consumer representatives veto power in the planning process. But the general experience of the past few years also indicates that meaningful participation is an important consideration in the development of a successful planning process and requires a great deal of attention and sensitivity. Caution and skepticism should be used in viewing the traditional approaches.

Citizens tear into council   The township council of Scotch Plains, New Jersey, now includes a tear-out response sheet in each of its quarterly newsletters. Citizens are invited to fill them in with their complaints, questions, and recommendations, and each response is answered within ten days of receipt. The town has found the sheet to be an extremely effective method for citizens to communicate directly with the town council.

A final factor in the design of the policy planning process is the relationship of human services planning to other decision areas in the community. Three are of particular importance: physical development planning; codes, ordinances, and regulatory activities; and the budgeting process (both capital and operating). Any new activity must be integrated with these decision areas and human services planning is no exception. Patterns of growth and settlement have a direct bearing on patterns of human services delivery. Thus, close working relationships between a locality's physical and human services planning agencies are vital. Similarly, links to other regulatory processes are crucial. Many community mental health facilities and other social services have foundered in conflicts with zoning laws. Finally, as with all public services, human services must be integrated with the local budgetary process. Federal and state funds are heavily involved; but these often require some measure of matching local funds. Although support from other levels of government can waver and fluctuate with changing political times, local communities might wish to have a particular social service continued even if it required local funding. These, then, are some of the key considerations in establishing the policy dimensions of the human services planning process.

The functional scope and role of human services planning   The third major concern in establishing a human services planning process in a local government is the work program of the human services planning agency. Figure 4–1, earlier in the chapter, outlined the range of planning activities involved in human services planning. Figure 4–3 linked these activities with the nature of the local government service delivery role. Others writing in this field have also suggested typologies of planning activities that are worth considering. Capoccia suggests that seven basic activities comprise the work program of a human services planning agency: needs assessment; development of service patterns; information system building; "cluster" building; technical assistance (helping agencies develop new program directions); fund development; and evaluation and monitoring.[99]

A 1974 study offered a list of six human services planning activities:

a. Developing usage patterns of existing services, facilities, programs, and equipment, including behavioral patterns of use. . . .
b. Identifying gaps between services where problems or demands are likely to occur or may have occurred and the responsive service was not there to meet it.
c. Developing an understanding and general awareness of where the services and programs of one or more agencies overlap with other agencies, or duplicate each other's efforts in some inefficient way.
d. Charting the potential utilization patterns by client citizens of present and future services, using wherever possible alternative models and simulation of client and agency-management behavior to determine alternative policy choices.
e. Ascertaining potential formal and informal linkages and relationships that might be developed among and between agencies that are most capable of complementing each other's activities. [This would be comparable to Capoccia's "cluster building."]
f. Exploration and investigation into new methods and techniques of service delivery.[100]

Another approach suggests that a human services planning agency might undertake its task in three different ways:

Project or Operations Planning: The design of individual and specific projects for the delivery of services and the preparation of an operations plan, including a staffing pattern and line item budget for these projects. The planning may include the establishment of operational standards by which to measure the extent and effectiveness of the actual delivery of services.

Program Planning: The development of program activity information and measures of impact upon individuals from the delivery of services and preparation of supporting human services budgets to finance required service levels to achieve desired impact. . . . Program planning deals with program areas such as "health" and how various health projects relate to each other. It is also concerned with the relationship of a program area such as "health" to another program area such as "social services."

Policy Planning: The application of the planning process to relate human services to physical and economic development plans and implementation actions. The allocation of resources between human services and other public activities is a major policy planning activity for the achievement of comprehensive goals and objectives.[101]

This latter description is not unlike the four levels of planning outlined in Figure 4–1. At issue here is the necessity for establishing priorities for these tasks in order to build a planning capability appropriate to local circumstances.

There are many possible strategies. Chattanooga started at the "project planning" level and, after almost two years, took steps to become involved in program planning, following what may be called "building block" approach. Norfolk, however, began at a more comprehensive level because of their existing relationship with an established city planning department.

It is clear that another key task is to determine the number of human services which can be meaningfully included in a newly developing planning operation. In short, the major functional issue is how comprehensive a human services planning agency can be.

In this regard, much will depend on the already existing pattern of private and public service delivery. Many communities begin by planning only those services which local government is actually delivering. Others, however, start from the premise that funds from revenue sharing and community development activities fill gaps in service delivery. They therefore concentrate on planning those services which will respond to those gaps. Still another option is to create the human services planning capability for the purpose of coordination and integration of existing activities, without necessarily considering future demands or unmet needs.

These are difficult questions and there is no general formula for making choices in every circumstance. The priorities and directions that a new human services planning agency sets for itself will depend upon a host of local factors: money and resources; availability of staff; comparative service delivery roles between public and private providers; consumer and public priorities; the legitimacy and sanction of the human services planning agency that is being established; previous planning activities; data availability; and state and local laws.

In summary, there is no absolute prescription for establishing a human services planning agency in local government. The kinds of factors involved and the choices and options that are important have been identified and described, and experiences in a variety of recent efforts have been presented. The above discussion represents an attempt to formulate a guide (albeit imperfect) to sketching a framework by which to determine the best direction for any given community's establishment of human services planning function.

Conclusion: issues and problems in human services planning

This chapter has explored the terrain of human services planning in most of its myriad dimensions. It has discussed the evolution of human services planning in America; the framework of social planning; methodological approaches to social services planning, and, in the discussion just concluded, the role of local government in human services planning.

In the course of the analysis, a fuller range of planning responsibility has been suggested for all public services. The mandates of the New Federalism of the 1970s and the effort to return power to state and local governments signify the increased planning responsibilities at the community level.

Decisions affecting whether public or private agencies shall deliver services, the types of services to be delivered, and the allocations of resources have been assumed in the past by the federal government, local government having had no voice in these decisions in many years. In addition, local planners have usually faced only limited technical modes of service delivery and simple means of financing (frequently severely constrained by law). Planning responsibilities are being returned to local government at a time when the technology of service delivery is rapidly changing and mechanisms of finance are diverse and complicated. It is only recently that local planners have assumed the responsibility for the design of new service organizations from their inception.

Developing a base of understanding of the wide range of human needs was never considered a major practical concern, especially where the family and the church were the institutions that individuals looked to in times of stress. As the discussion in Chapter 2 emphasized, the breakdown of family units, the search for secular roles by religious bodies, and the increase of knowledge and professionalization in the ''helping'' services are forces which have placed the human services provider near center stage for almost all income, ethnic, and religious groups. Local government is thus taking on rapidly multiplying roles to fill the gaps left by other institutions.

This new climate in social welfare brings local government face-to-face with many issues for the future. The most prominent and immediate difficulties are fivefold, and include: the need to integrate methodological development; the lack of agreement on objectives and priorities; increasing problems of coordinating planning; roles and functions in human services planning; and equity and justice in the delivery of human services.

The need to integrate methodological development

Human services planning, more than any other form of planning, is truly multidisciplinary. The biological sciences, the behavioral sciences, the social sciences, and the management sciences all underlie the planner's needed skills. High levels of specialization make the planner very dependent on the service provider. Yet too great a reliance on the specialist overlooks the very great range of self-interest that the specialist may exert in any given planning situation. Means for accountability and for reflecting the legitimate interests of clients, funders, and others must be sought. While participation opportunities can to some degree help, providers still enjoy a higher level of power and status because of their expertise and skill. In the face of this, the planner has looked to the management sciences for methodological assistance, thereby uncovering again the traditional conflict between expertise and organizational hierarchy noted frequently in the literature of organizational studies.[102]

This multidisciplinary character is a likely instrumental cause in the failure to develop a unified methodology of human services planning. Yet this lack of methodology will continue to offer difficulty until the problem is more prominently identified and dealt with. Previous work in utilization and systems theory models is perhaps an appropriate beginning point in this search for higher levels of skill in planning. In addition, more attention to methods of futures forecasting, scenario development, and impact and assessment techniques should prove beneficial.

The lack of agreement on objectives and priorities

Human services delivery is a highly pluralistic arena. Power and authority is diffuse, interest groups abound, and the competition for resources is high. For many communities, it is extremely difficult to find agreement on the basic goals of the human services system. For the general public, it is an arena of confusion, costliness, and ineffectiveness.

Most goals center around vague concerns with adequate social functioning, optimum independence, and good health. Yet the means to achieve these is seldom clear-cut. Indeed, the ways to observe and measure whether the goals are being achieved by any means are not always available. Since goals are essentially statements of values, they are continually subject to change and adjustment. Goals often conflict with each other. Changing techniques of service delivery or funding create changes in goals and priorities. This turbulence in a very complicated arena is most disconcerting for the planner who faces demands for high levels of perceptiveness and adaptability as well as for effective means of communicating the potential effects of turbulence on policies and plans. So long as the system remains pluralistic and the participants retain high levels of autonomy, this turmoil of values, goals, and priorities will remain a prominent characteristic of human services planning.

Increasing problems of coordinating planning

The last few years have seen planning institutionalized in a variety of settings—largely aided and abetted by federal statutes or guidelines. Planning for human services has, as a result, become almost as disjointed as the delivery system itself. Planning agencies have arisen around a variety of functional service areas at numerous geographical levels. Some planning agencies are private, others public; some are local, others regional; some are intended to be "comprehensive," others are focused on a particular service.

As these substate planning units proliferate, the human services planning scene becomes as pluralistic as that of the providers. There have even been examples of planning agencies competing on the same turf in the same community. (Prior to the Health Planning Act, for example, Philadelphia had two competing health planning agencies.) Increasing attention will clearly have to be given in the near future to coordinating and integrating the planning function.

Roles and functions in human services planning

Another issue of importance in human services planning has been alluded to indirectly. It is a problem that touches on virtually all other problems in the field—the relative roles and statuses of various actors in the human services arena. What should be our expectations of citizens, elected officials, professional service providers, administrators, planners, and others involved in human services policy making? How does the planning process stimulate a delivery system that is responsive to needs, accountable, and comprehensive? How can the participation of all these actors be assured, especially where expectations have been changing drastically in the last few years? These questions of roles and functions in human services planning will continue to be a key issue in the coming years.

Equity and justice in the delivery of human services

A final, and extremely important, issue that will continually press upon human services planners is that of assuring equal access to services of high quality for all members of our society, regardless of race, religion, ethnic background, or sex. The presence of dual systems in such service areas as health and mental health (one for the mainstream of American society, another for the poor or minorities) poses grave issues of distributive justice in our overall concern for national social welfare. These issues are particularly difficult at the local level where fears and prejudices are most sharply felt. Human services planning is inextricably linked to this core issue of our society.

This list highlights only the most important issues that face social services planning in the coming years. Others include problems already referred to: evaluation and accountability, cost containment and cost-effectiveness, and the impacts of new roles. These would include those of the paraprofessional, the advocate, or the case manager.

With this array of complexities, ambiguities, quandaries, and competitive dimensions, one might well ask why local government should become involved. There is no single answer for every local unit. The trend, however, is that fewer and fewer localities have the luxury of making such a decision independently. The answer is increasingly being forced both from above (the New Federalism and new state legislation) and from below (neighborhoods and other local organizations continue to turn to city hall to assume responsibility for all aspects of the "quality of life"). In many respects, local government is being viewed as a last resort in the pursuit of rationalizing a system that is, by and large, not of its own making. Ironically this is occurring in areas of responsibility which were taken away from the local governments many years ago for reasons of lack of professionalism, favoritism, parochialism, and other shortcomings.

Thus, human services have come full cycle and are increasingly again a responsibility of local government. This time there will likely be considerably more interest and help on the part of state and national government. Private providers will increasingly look to city hall for funding and sanction. But the times are very different from those of the last century. The contemporary American community has an entirely new array of needs and a completely new array of providers attempting to meet those needs. City hall is being asked to perform tasks that federal and state governments could not previously handle themselves.

But this is also the promise and hope of the future in human services planning. The return of planning and decision making to the local level can do much to overcome the abstract quality and large gaps of understanding and insensitivity that comes from a planning process too highly centralized. The transfer of decision-making power casts an extremely large shadow of responsibility on local government. But only at the local level can the ordinary citizen really sense that he or she is a vital part of the process and has the power to effectuate change that can meaningfully improve the quality of life.

1   Wayne Vasey, *Government and Social Welfare* (New York: Henry Holt & Co., 1958), pp. 435–36.
2   Mel Scott, *American City Planning* (Berkeley: University of California Press, 1969), p. 2.
3   Fred M. Cox and Charles Garvin, "The Relation of Social Forces to the Emergence of Community Organization Practice: 1865–1968," in *Strategies of Community Organization: A Book of Readings,* ed. Fred M. Cox et al. (Itasca, Illinois: F. E. Peacock Pubs., 1970), pp. 37–44.
4   Scott, *American City Planning,* p. 7; and *Encyclopedia of Social Work,* ed. Robert Morris (New York: National Association of Social Workers, 1971), p. 1137.
5   Scott, *American City Planning,* pp. 31–36.
6   *The Encyclopedia Britannica* (Chicago: William Benton, Pub., 1968), pp. 821–25.
7   Harold Wilensky and Charles N. Lebeaux, *Industrial Society and Social Welfare* (New York: Free Press, 1965), pp. 138–40.
8   Cox and Garvin, "Relation of Social Forces," pp. 40–43.
9   Ibid., p. 41.
10 Ibid.
11 Ibid., p. 43.
12 Ibid., p. 42.
13 Ibid., p. 41; and Scott, *American City Planning,* pp. 93–95.
14 Harvey A. Kantor, "Benjamin Marsh and the Fight Over Population Congestion," *Journal of the American Institute of Planners* 40 (November 1974): 422–29.
15 Arnold Gurin, "Social Planning and Community Organization," in *Encyclopedia of Social Work,* p. 1328; Roy Lubove, *The Professional Altruist: The Emergence of Social Work as a Cause, 1880–1930* (Cambridge: Harvard University Press, 1965), pp. 175–78; and Cox and Garvin, "Relation of Social Forces," p. 47.
16 Edmund Burke, "Citizen Participation Strategies," *Journal of the American Institute of Planners* 34 (September 1968): 287–94.
17 Cox and Garvin, "Relation of Social Forces," p. 44; and Gurin, "Social Planning and Community Organization," p. 1327.
18 U.S., Department of Commerce, Bureau of the Census, *Statistical Abstract of the United States: 1975* (Washington, D.C.: Government Printing Office, 1975), Table 446.
19 One illustration of this burgeoning demand can be seen in the use of mental health facilities. The rate of utilization per thousand population in the United States virtually doubled between 1965 and 1973. See U.S., Department of Commerce, Bureau of the Census, *Statistical Abstract: 1975,* Table 130.
20 Neil Gilbert and Harry Specht, *Dimensions of Social Welfare Policy* (Englewood Cliffs, N.J.: Prentice-Hall, 1974), pp. 28–33.
21 Some problems associated with this were highlighted in a series of articles dealing with New York's nursing homes. See John L. Hess, "Care of Aged Poor a Growing Scandal," *New York Times,* 7 October 1974.
22 As of September 1976, 174 Health Systems Agencies (of 196 organized under the Health Planning and Resources Development Act) were private, nonprofit corporations; 18 were regional governmental planning bodies; and 4 were units of local government. See *Health Resources News* 4 (December 1976): 2.
23 Ronald L. Nuttall and Richard S. Bolan, "The Success of Health Plan Implementation: A Test of the Theory," report prepared for the Department of Health, Education, and Welfare, Health Resources Administration, Division of Comprehensive Health Planning, 1976, vol. 1, chap. 5.
24 Ibid., chap. 2.
25 Ibid., chap. 4.
26 Robert Alford, *Health Care Politics* (Chicago: University of Chicago Press, 1975), chap. 1.
27 Alfred Kahn, *Theory and Practice of Social Planning* (New York: Russell Sage Foundation, 1969), pp. 201–04. See also the discussion of different models of social policy in Richard Titmuss, *Social Policy* (London: George Allen & Unwin, 1974), chap. 2; and Gilbert and Specht, *Dimensions of Social Welfare Policy,* pp. 56–59.
28 Gilbert and Specht, *Dimensions of Social Welfare Policy,* pp. 66–76.
29 Alfred Kahn, *Studies in Policy and Planning* (New York: Russell Sage Foundation, 1969), chap. 6.
30 U.S., Department of Health, Education, and Welfare, Bureau of Health Planning and Resources Development, "Draft Guidelines Concerning the Development of Health Systems and Annual Implementation Plans," memorandum, 18 June 1976, pp. 11–12.
31 B. F. Skinner, *Beyond Freedom and Dignity* (New York: Alfred A. Knopf, 1972), chap. 1.
32 Kahn, *Studies in Policy and Planning,* chap. 6.
33 K. Patricia Cross, *Accent on Learning* (San Francisco: Jossey-Bass, 1976), chaps. 3 and 4.
34 Luther Gulick, "Notes on a Theory of Organization," in *Papers on the Science of Administration* (New York: Columbia University, Institute of Public Administration, 1937), pp. 1–45.
35 For a general coverage of the field of location analysis, see Walter Isard, *Introduction to Regional Science* (Englewood Cliffs, N.J.: Prentice-Hall, 1975).
36 Franklin D. Chu and Sharland Trotter, *The Madness Establishment* (New York: Grossman Pubs., 1974), pp. 73–83.
37 Joan Wright and William Burmeister, *Introduction to Human Services* (Columbus, Ohio: Grid, 1973), pp. 21–23.
38 Tennessee Municipal League, *Chattanooga Human Services Delivery System* (Nashville: Tennessee Municipal League, 1975).
39 The Research Group, Inc. and Marshall Kaplan, Gans and Kahn, "Integration of Human Services in HEW: An Evaluation of Services Integration Projects," 1 (August 1972): 110–13.
40 Herbert A. Simon, *Administrative Behavior,* 2nd ed. (New York: Free Press, 1957), chap. 2.
41 J. W. Forrester, *Industrial Dynamics* (Cambridge: M.I.T. Press, 1961).
42 For two case studies which provide excellent ex-

amples of the concept of client pathway, see Stephen D. Mittenthal, *Human Services Development Programs in Sixteen Allied Services (SITO) Projects* (Wellesley, Mass.: Human Ecology Institute, 1975), Apps. B and M.

43 See Jerald Hage, *Communication and Organization Control: Cybernetics in Health and Welfare Settings* (New York: John Wiley & Sons, 1974); and Wendell L. French and Cecil H. Bell, Jr., *Organization Development: Behavioral Science Interventions for Organization Improvement* (Englewood Cliffs, N.J.: Prentice-Hall, 1973).

44 Chester Barnard, *The Functions of the Executive* (Cambridge: Harvard University Press, 1938), chap. 7.

45 See, for example, Public Law 93-641, Sec. 1512 (3)(C)(i)—the Health Planning and Resources Development Act (1974).

46 For a statement of the rationale for this, see Orion F. White, Jr., "The Dialectical Organization: An Alternative to Bureaucracy," *Public Administration Review* 29 (January/February 1969).

47 Sidney Gardner, "Services Integration in HEW: An Initial Report," report prepared for the Department of Health, Education, and Welfare, February 1971; U.S., Department of Health, Education, and Welfare, "Services Integration—Next Steps," by Elliot L. Richardson, memorandum, 1 June 1971, cited in Douglas Henton, "The Feasibility of Services Integration," evaluation report prepared for the Department of Health, Education, and Welfare's Interagency Services Integration Research and Development Task Force, Berkeley, March 1975, pp. 5–8.

48 Estimates derived from U.S., Department of Commerce, Bureau of the Census, *Statistical Abstract: 1975*.

49 Gilbert and Specht, *Dimensions of Social Welfare Policy*, chaps. 6 and 7.

50 U.S., Department of Commerce, Bureau of the Census, *Statistical Abstract: 1975*.

51 Ibid. Estimates derived by author.

52 Abraham H. Maslow, *Motivation and Personality* (New York: Harper & Row, 1954), chap. 5; and Erik H. Erikson, *Identity, Youth and Crisis* (New York: W. W. Norton, 1968).

53 United Way of America, *UWASIS II: A Taxonomy of Social Goals & Human Service Programs* (Alexandria, Va.: United Way of America, Planning and Allocations Division, 1976). This is the second edition of *UWASIS*—the United Way of America Services Identification System—the first having been published in 1972. Much of the text discussion refers to the original 1972 publication and is cited to that edition as appropriate.

54 United Way of America, *UWASIS* (Alexandria, Va.: United Way of America, 1972), App. A.

55 Saul D. Alinsky, *Reveille for Radicals* (Chicago: University of Chicago Press, 1946). See also Harry Specht, "Disruptive Tactics," in *Readings in Community Organization Practice*, eds. R. M. Kramer and Harry Specht, 2nd ed. (Englewood Cliffs, N.J.: Prentice-Hall, 1975), pp. 336–48.

56 See Amitai Etzioni, *Social Problems* (Englewood Cliffs, N.J.: Prentice-Hall, 1976), pp. 9–15.

57 See Lawrence D. Mann, "Social Science Advances and Planning Applications: 1900–1965," *Journal of the American Institute of Planners* 38 (November 1972): 346–58.

58 Melvin M. Webber, "The Roles of Intelligence Systems in Urban Systems Planning," *Journal of the American Institute of Planners* 31 (November 1965).

59 Michael Tietz, "Toward a Responsive Planning Methodology," in *Planning in America: Learning from Turbulence*, ed. D. R. Godschalk (Washington, D.C.: American Institute of Planners, 1974), pp. 86–110.

60 See F. J. Roethlisberger and W. J. Dickson, *Management and the Worker* (Cambridge: Harvard University Press, 1939); Kurt Lewin, "Group Decision and Social Change," in *Readings in Social Psychology*, ed. G. E. Swanson et al. (New York: Holt, Rinehart & Winston, 1952); and Herbert A. Simon, *Administrative Behavior*, 2nd ed. (New York: Free Press, 1957).

61 The "birth" of scientific management is generally regarded as being represented by F. W. Taylor, *The Principles of Scientific Management* (New York: Harper & Row, 1911).

62 Mittenthal, *Human Services Development Programs*, App. C.

63 Demetrius J. Plessas and Ricca Fein, "An Evaluation of Social Indicators," *Journal of the American Institute of Planners* 38 (January 1972): 43–51.

64 For a discussion of computer applications in local government, and of information and record keeping generally, see Shimon Awerbuch, Robert J. Hoffman, and William A. Wallace, "Computer Applications in Public Works," in *Urban Public Works Administration*, ed. William E. Korbitz (Washington, D.C.: International City Management Association, 1976), pp. 53–85.

65 Allan Schick, "The Road to PPB: The Stages of Budget Reform," *Public Administration Review* 26 (December 1966).

66 Elizabeth B. Drew, "HEW Grapples with PPBS," *The Public Interest* 8 (Summer 1967): 9–24.

67 Peter Drucker, "What Results Should You Expect? A Users Guide to MBO," *Public Administration Review* 36 (January/February 1976): 12–19.

68 Warren G. Bennis and Philip E. Slater, *The Temporary Society* (New York: Harper Colophon Books, 1968).

69 Barnard, *The Functions of the Executive*, chap. 3.

70 See Ronald Lippit, Jeanne Watson, and Bruce Westley, *The Dynamics of Planned Change* (New York: Harcourt, Brace and World, 1958), chaps. 5 and 6; and Bell and French, *Organization Development*, chaps. 9 and 10.

71 Robert R. Mayer, *Social Planning and Social Change* (Englewood Cliffs, N.J.: Prentice-Hall, 1972).

72 Discussion of various forms of survey research can be found in Ray Eldon Hiebert, "Research and the Public Relations Process," in *Public Relations in Local Government*, ed. William H. Gilbert (Washington, D.C.: International City Management Association, 1975), pp. 26–40.

73 For a review of utilization studies, see Nancy W. Veeder, "Health Services Utilization Models for Human Services Planning," *Journal of the American Institute of Planners* 41 (March 1975): 101–09.

74 Plessas and Fein, "Evaluation of Social Indicators."

75 Jack Lapatra, *Applying the Systems Approach to Urban Development* (Stroudsburg, Penn.: Dowden, Hutchinson and Ross, 1973), chap. 1.

76 For a good introductory discussion of this method, see Stuart Sandow, "The Pedagogy of Planning: Defining Sufficient Futures," *Futures* 3 (December 1971): 324–37.

77 For a basic description of technology assessment, see Martin V. Jones, "The Methodology of Technology

Assessment," *The Futurist* (February 1972): 19–26.

78 See Sandow, "Pedagogy of Planning." Examples of the use of future scenarios may be found in Energy Policy Project of the Ford Foundation, *A Time to Choose: America's Energy Future* (Cambridge: Ballinger Pubs., 1974); and Alfred Heller, ed., *The California Tomorrow Plan* (Los Altos, Calif.: William Kaufman, 1971).

79 New England Municipal Center, *Opportunities for Municipal Participation in Human Services* (Durham, N.H.: New England Municipal Center, 1975).

80 One example of such a law is found in General Court of Massachusetts, *Acts of 1972,* chap. 766.

81 See T. J. Kent, *The Urban General Plan* (San Francisco: Chandler Publishing Co., 1964), p. 13; Edward M. Bassett, *The Master Plan* (New York: Russell Sage Foundation, 1938); and U.S., Department of Commerce, Advisory Committee on City Planning and Zoning, *A Standard City Planning Enabling Act* (Washington, D.C.: Government Printing Office, 1928).

82 R. A. Walker, *The Planning Function in Urban Government* (Chicago: University of Chicago Press, 1941).

83 Kent, *Urban General Plan,* pp. 16–18 and chap. 5.

84 Victor A. Capoccia, "Human Services Planning at the Local Level: Some Experience, Some Issues and a Future," paper presented to the Local Human Services Planning Group of the New England Human Services Coalition, Durham, N.H., November 1976, p. 25.

85 Michael Brooks, *Toward a More Effective Social Planning Process* (Chicago: American Society of Planning Officials, 1970), p. 48.

86 Cleveland City Planning Commission, *Policy Planning Report* (Cleveland: City Planning Commission, 1975). See also "The Journal Forum: The Cleveland Policy Planning Report," *Journal of the American Institute of Planners* 41 (September 1975): 298–318.

87 Boston College, Graduate School of Social Work, *Human Services Plan, Malden, Massachusetts: Phase III Report* (Chestnut Hill, Mass.: Boston College, Graduate School of Social Work, 1975), pp. 75–81.

88 Human Services Institute for Children and Families, Inc., *Alternative Approaches to Human Services Planning* (Arlington, Va.: Human Services Institute for Children and Families, Inc., 1974), p. 111.

89 Ibid., p. 117.

90 Ibid., p. 124.

91 Capoccia, "Human Services Planning at the Local Level," p. 13.

92 Human Services Institute, *Alternative Approaches,* pp. 131–39; and Mittenthal, *Human Services Development Programs,* Apps. G and I.

93 Human Services Institute, *Alternative Approaches,* pp. 77–86; and Mittenthal, *Human Services Development Programs,* App. E.

94 Public Law 93-641, sec. 1512 (3)(C)(i).

95 Mittenthal, *Human Services Development Programs,* App. D. The individual members of the Allied Services Board include the following officials: county administrator; director, county human resources agency; police chief of the city of Richmond; county probation officer; Model Cities director; assistant city manager of the city of Richmond; superintendent, Richmond Unified School District; county medical director; county social service director; county health officer; and social security district manager. The members of the Allied Services Commission include the following organizations and agencies: Alameda/Contra Costa Medical Association; American Cancer Society; Area Council, Office of Economic Opportunity; Central Labor Council; Youth Development Program; Cornado Neighborhood Council; Council of Richmond Industries; Food Advocates; Greater Richmond Interfaith Project; Human Relations Commission; Iron Triangle; Las Deltas Tenant Organization; League of Women Voters; Model Neighborhood Community Board; Opportunity Children's Center, Inc.; Parchester Neighborhood Council; Richmond Black Caucus; Richmond Elementary Council, PTA; Richmond Welfare Rights; Senior Citizens Drop-in Center; South Side Council; and United Council of Spanish-Speaking Organizations.

96 Human Services Institute, *Alternative Approaches,* p. 127.

97 Ibid., pp. 117–18.

98 Donald Carroll et al., "An Evaluation of the Effect of Decentralization on the Delivery of Income Maintenance and Social Service," prepared at the University of Maryland, School of Social Work and Community Planning, Baltimore, for the Office of the Secretary, Maryland Department of Employment and Social Services and the Mayor of the city of Baltimore, November 1974, pp. 24–25.

99 Capoccia, "Human Services Planning at the Local Level," pp. 19–20.

100 American Society for Public Administration, *Human Services Integration* (Washington, D.C.: American Society for Public Administration, 1974).

101 Human Services Institute, *Alternative Approaches,* pp. 12–16.

102 Amitai Etzioni, *Modern Organization* (Englewood Cliffs, N.J.: Prentice-Hall, 1964), chap. 8.

Needs assessment for human services

As the preceding chapter has indicated, the planning and policy aspects of human services analyzed in Part Two of this book present significant challenges to local government managers and other decision makers. In that same planning and policy context, this chapter addresses the managerial challenges presented by problem analysis and needs assessment.

Problem analysis and needs assessment can be viewed as the first of a number of related activities that, in sum, comprise the planning process. Such a process, according to this viewpoint, would also include the formulation of a policy framework expressed in goals and objectives; the generation of alternative strategies and of appropriate criteria for choosing among them; the selection and implementation of a particular intervention or program; and the management of monitoring, evaluation, and feedback procedures.

What does such an approach imply? It suggests that planners (and, of necessity, the elected officials and appointed chief executives who direct and monitor the planners' activities) begin by asking: What is the problem? What are its facets and its causes? What are the characteristics of those who can be defined as having the problem? How many people are affected? Can they be located geographically? This approach presumes that needs can only be responded to through the management of resources, programs, and services if—and only if—such questions can be answered.

The approach just outlined appears at first glance to be both rational and fruitful. Local government practice, however, would suggest that, as a managerial strategy, it is either ignored by decision makers or carried out in a perfunctory fashion. Why does this happen?

To address this question is to enter into a discussion of some of the key issues confronting local government managers and planners as they attempt to relate needs assessment to the planning process within their given political and administrative environments. The present chapter therefore begins with such a discussion. This sets the scene for subsequent analysis of the concept of need; the various categories of need; approaches that enable local government decision makers to determine who is in need; and approaches that locate concentrations of "high risk" groups within communities served by local governments. Throughout, emphasis is placed on the qualitative, as well as the quantitative, aspects presented by problem analysis and needs assessment in the human services field. The chapter concludes with an evaluative summary.

Two other points need to be stated at the outset. First, a constant theme of this book is the recognition that there is a wide spectrum of local government communities. Managers of the thousands of smaller communities may feel that they have little in common with their colleagues in the giant metropolitan areas that house such a significant portion of our population and have been a focus of major social challenges. Further, the managerial style in a county or a metropolitan council of governments will necessarily differ from that in a municipality. The discussion in this chapter therefore attempts to bring out issues and managerial principles that are broadly applicable across this demographic and jurisdictional spectrum. It is recognized, however, that a comprehensive analysis must address the naturally more complex environment of the larger communities. This is particularly the case where the full range of administrative options is discussed. It is implicit throughout that not every community will be of a size to make use of each of the administrative options under consideration.

Second, the discussion, for convenience, makes frequent use of the term "planner." In the present context, this should not be limited to the professional planner operating out of the specialized agencies or departments in the units of local government. Chief appointed executives, department heads, and other decision makers are also planners in a broader sense of the term. This chapter attempts to speak to their concerns as well as to those of the operational administrators reporting to them.

Needs assessment and the planning process: the key managerial issues

What actually transpires in local governments to render the rational, sequential planning process of problem analysis and policy formulation more of a hope than an administrative reality? Planners and managers tend to respond to problems under discussion in a number of ways. Three basic issues nevertheless emerge: the tendency to state problems in terms of solutions; the distinction between strategic planning and management planning; and the distinction between planning for services and planning to meet needs.

Stating problems as solutions

Many planning efforts are initiated on the implicit assumption that the problems are fully understood and their solutions known. In fact, the problems are frequently stated in terms of solutions, often qualified by "more," as in "more physicians" (or nurses, social workers, counselors, day care facilities, hospital beds, training slots, etc.). A variety of problems then comes to be viewed as a single, and broader, one: that is, a lack of resources to expand existing efforts. This demonstrates a strong belief that, given sufficient resources, most if not all social problems will be dealt with successfully. And yet, since the early 1960s, social welfare expenditures have grown considerably. A resurgence of the national interest in planning paved the way for comprehensive planning. In spite of these efforts, it is generally recognized that serious social problems have not been eradicated. In a number of instances, in fact, they have been exacerbated.[1] The simplistic suggestion that public and private sector resources have been insufficient is just that—simplistic. A more productive approach to understanding the lack of success would be to examine how the available resources were used, what services were developed, and the planning process that guided the decision making.

On the whole, very little time and effort is currently being given to problem analysis and needs assessment. One reason for this is that most local government efforts concentrate on program design and implementation along lines given implicit encouragement by federal and state funding sources. Program and grant proposal developers often find that even minimal planning is made impossible by the time constraints (not to mention the bureaucratic nightmares of paperwork) imposed on them by those funding sources. A manager may well be confronted with already designed programs and accompanying fund requests, prepared by local government agencies with federal and state aid requirements as principal concerns in their development. Problem analysis and needs assessment considerations are relegated to a secondary status and, too often, the programs which result attack symptoms of problems rather than their causes. Experience suggests that insufficient attention to the critical first steps of a comprehensive planning process has been, at least in part, a determining factor in the failure of these programs to significantly diminish social problems. Planners and managers of the later 1970s would do well to proceed with less certainty and more questioning.

Strategic planning and management planning

Two distinct but interdependent types of planning—*strategic planning* and *management planning*—need to be introduced at this juncture.[2] *Strategic planning* is undertaken to decide on the objectives of organizations; to change objectives; to determine what resources to employ in order to achieve objectives; and to establish policies governing the acquisition, use, and disposition of resources. In the context of human services, strategic planning is concerned with four topics. These are: 1) plan formulation—developing and finalizing both short- and long-range plans; 2) policy formulation for plan implementation—deciding how provision of services will be accomplished, for example, by governmental agencies, through outside contractual arrangements, or by private sector organizations; 3) the establishment of criteria for priority setting and resource allocation—assigning the relative weight to be carried by various factors in making specific service delivery; and 4) monitoring and evaluation—deciding questions related to information storage and retrieval requirements as well as criteria to be used in the process.

Management planning encourages the efficient use of resources, once obtained, to reach the organization's objectives. In the context of human services, it includes the three following procedural concerns: 1) the development of operating rules for public agencies—the regulations controlling such items as service eligibility or the receipt and use of public funds; 2) the development of guidelines to assist public and private agencies in formulating projects and evaluating their impact; and 3) the design and implementation of service delivery systems—the actual programs.

Whereas strategic planning is concerned with setting objectives, establishing priorities, and acquiring resources, management planning—as its name suggests—emphasizes the ongoing management of those resources in light of the strategies previously established. Although strategic and management planning in the human services field should be viewed as interdependent processes, traditionally they have been separated. This pattern can best be understood by recognizing the basic fact that, since the New Deal of the 1930s, the federal government has generally set the objectives and established the priorities in the human services field. Strategic planning was carried out at the federal level and controlled through categorical funding. State and local governments were required to accept these objectives and priorities, to accept the programming emphases of the various federal agencies, and to establish the machinery necessary to fulfill the requirements. There was, and still is, a powerful rationale for this practice: there are legitimate national priorities and there is a need to establish baseline standards of service. Also, control at the national level ensures the provision of certain services—services that probably benefit the recipients—even in the face of individual state or local government objections. For several reasons, therefore, categorical funding and national guidelines represent positive approaches.

In practice, however, they have tended to stifle state and local initiative. Since the late 1960s, state and local governments have been critical of being given what many perceived as only a management task. Pressure was put on the federal government to utilize the flexibility offered by block grants on the grounds that state and local governments were more sensitive to local needs. When federal policy did shift—and, as of the mid-1970s, categorical grants still outweighed block grants—the reactions of many states and local communities were mixed. Those jurisdictions beginning to be affected by the new block grants, though still in a minority, were now required to plan strategically. They had, however, a little experience to fall back on, and some complained that the federal planning requirements were just as stifling to local initiative as the categorical funding mechanisms. Thus the new freedom made available through block grants was seen by some as a two-edged sword: the freedom, welcomed in principle, brought with it new responsibilities.

Planning for services and planning for need

Beyond the issue of strategic and management planning, however, lies another issue—the necessity to distinguish between two somewhat contradictory focuses: *planning for services* and *planning to meet human services need*. Traditionally, planning for social "welfare," broadly conceived, might be characterized as management planning with a focus on services rather than on meeting need. Planning decisions were based on the framework provided by the existing network of human services. Counts of personnel, facilities, and service elements were considered indicative of the relation between supply and demand, or at least suggestive of the potential service capability in the area under study. The needs of the population—the other potential planning focus—remained largely undefined, both qualitatively and quantitatively.

Weaknesses of "planning for services"   The danger with the "planning for services" approach is that these services tend to take on a life of their own, thereby reducing their flexibility and inhibiting efforts to initiate change through experimentation. Emphasis comes to be placed on organizational survival; administrators responsible for the management of specific programs structure their agencies so that the services they provide define the purpose of each agency. Staff members tend to view potential clients in terms of those services the staff is in a position to offer. The elderly, for example, may be defined as "needing" homemaker services, "meals on wheels," or institutional care. The mentally retarded may "require" institutional care, special education, or training. Whatever the system, this labeling has the potential to begin at intake and continue, translated into service responses, throughout a client's contact with an agency. Too often services initially introduced as possible mechanisms to assist people in need, quickly become the only way to do things. Services, once seen as potentially beneficial for certain people with particular needs, become solutions whose benefit is rarely questioned. Emphasis on only the management aspect of planning—which tends to highlight the efficiency of the system—traditionally has been the accepted focus for planning. Rarely have planners and managers even had the opportunity to step back and examine the purposes and values of the services being provided.

This approach served to maintain the status quo. The process generally discouraged experimentation while encouraging greater efficiency in the existing system: change came about in the form of minor modifications rather than through overall evaluation of priorities and underlying assumptions. Since the mid-1960s, however, more and more people have been questioning the value of these minor adjustments. As has been noted, government expenditures on social welfare mushroomed during the 1960s, yet the social problems that these expenditures were to alleviate remain intractable. The persistence of serious problems, despite the monumental financial efforts, has brought renewed pressures for experimentation with new processes and changes in the existing systems.

Need for a new approach   These pressures, in part, have stimulated a growing recognition on the part of local government managers and planners that there must be a better way to approach these problems, that there must be a more rational planning process. The historical need for data to justify predetermined service planning decisions is, as of the later 1970s, being replaced with a need for data which will clearly define social problems and help to identify the most potentially effective directions for planning decisions.

Current decision making is not, and probably will never be, a purely technical process removed from the political environment. It can be argued, however, that decision making should be influenced to some extent by sound technical analysis. At least, attempts should be made to establish a more rational decision-making procedure which takes into account both the political and the more purely technical aspects of planning before final decisions are made. Development of a rational style of decision making would allow for broader statements of options and clearer statements of the pros and cons attendant on each. This, in turn, should encourage agreement among involved parties before initiation of a particular course of action. Once such a course is selected and implemented, this type of decision making permits further planning based on impact analysis and evaluation.

The appropriate first activity then is problem analysis and assessment of need. For local government practitioners, this is an activity that is supportive of strategic planning as well as of management planning. It is one that seeks to stimulate independence from the status quo by focusing on the needs of people rather than on the existing network of human services programs.

Defining problems   A problem that is inadequately defined is not likely to be solved. The converse of this is that a problem that is well-defined may be dealt with successfully, assuming that adequate resources and appropriate delivery mechanisms can be generated. Still, it must be understood that problem analysis is by nature more an art than a science. Purely scientific analyses of a problem, no matter the approach or number of investigators, would result in similar conclusions, based on objective methods. Problem analysis is therefore an art insofar as different planners can assess the same situation and produce quite different findings. Each individual shapes the problem in terms of his or her background, training, experience, and values. This is not meant as a criticism of the extent to which subjective factors influence the decisions of planners or managers. "Scientific" objectivity in the analysis of a community's problems would be, in fact, an unrealistic and possibly undesirable goal.

The long-standing debate on the nation's health care system highlights the role of "individuality" in problem definition. One group of experts evaluates the evidence and concludes that the present fee-for-service market system is essentially healthy and in need of only minor modifications. In their view, the government's role in the system should be minimal, limited to minor regulation or purchase of services. Another group of experts examines the same evidence, disagreeing with the first group and concluding that the present system has failed and needs a complete reorganization. The view of this second group is that this extensive restructuring will require that the government's role be a central one. Each analyst brings to the issue a frame of reference that is shaped both by values and technical training. In addition to influencing the analysis of data, it extends to the data collection process which also tends to be selective.

Even if there are no hard rules, there are some strategies that can assist the planner. Problems should not be defined or labeled prematurely nor should the planner attempt to assume complete responsibility for the task. Those with knowledge of a particular substantive problem—program managers, human services practitioners, or potential consumers—should be involved in the process. In this way, various perspectives on the problem may be introduced, perspectives that might otherwise have been overlooked. One of the planner's responsibilities is to encourage as much of such input as possible.

A number of questions are useful guides in this phase of the planning process.[3] What is the nature of the situation confronting the planner? This involves both facts and impressions. What social values are being threatened or brought under question by the situation? How widely is the situation recognized? This provides some idea of potential community support or resistance. What is the scale of the problem? What are possible causes? Problem analysis, in a planning context, is different from analysis in a traditional research framework. It not only includes who?, what?, and where? issues, but also an analysis of the political environment, an assessment of the community's readiness to deal with the problem and a measure of the resources it is willing to commit to its solution. The most critical part of these guideline questions is their emphasis on the need to identify the causes of the problem, a subject discussed in detail later in this chapter.

Summary: the dimensions of need

Need, then, in a planning framework appropriate to the management of local government human services, has both qualitative and quantitative dimensions. The qualitative statement implicitly requires the labeling of a situation as a problem to be corrected. Quantification, or tabulation, of that problem represents the second dimension of need. Planners and other decision makers assume an ability to identify similarities among groups of people who have problems, similarities that can be translated into services, budgets, and appropriate delivery mechanisms. Planners and managers, however, cannot develop policies and programs for an undifferentiated general population. The important differences among individuals cannot be ignored and should influence the specific services each will receive. In this context, the ability to group the general population into target groups is a crucial managerial skill.

The rest of the present chapter will therefore be developed around three major approaches: those useful for determining *what* the need is; others useful for determining *who* is in need; and still others useful for determining *where* high concentrations of people in need are found.

Emphasis will be on the present (i.e., later 1970s) state of the art for needs assessment, and specific methodologies and techniques will be discussed in terms of their contributions and limitations. The focus will be on the practical rather than on the identification of what an ideal system might include. Such a system, built on the use of a highly sophisticated computerized information system and continuous social surveys, would be prohibitively expensive for most governmental units.

The concept of need

As defined in most social legislation, ''need'' is a vague concept. It is often buried in phrases so global that it has little value for placing boundaries on the planning task. Alternatively, it is employed so narrowly that specific services are mandated. The term is used frequently by planners and researchers as well as by executives, but it is rarely operationalized. All too often the professional assumes that it will be understood and therefore requires little elaboration.

Need as a normative concept

In spite of this vagueness, there are some aspects of need that are clear. It should be viewed as a normative concept, shaped by the social environment and involving values and judgments. For example, an assessment is made that an individual, or a group of individuals, has a problem or requires some services. It may be viewed as a need for better housing (e.g., because existing criteria for overcrowding, insufficient plumbing, etc. indicate the existing housing stock is substandard). Yet not many years ago, this ''substandard'' housing would have been considered more than adequate. Even today it would be viewed as desirable in many western countries. There may seem to be a need for greater employment opportunities (based, for example, on society's assumption that jobs are necessary for an individual's economic, psychological, and social well-being). It is conceivable, however, that in the postindustrial society envisaged for some western nations, a person's role and status will no longer be primarily related to his or her employment. Full-time employment may be dramatically less than forty hours, and earlier retirement, too, may become the accepted pattern. A final example might be an apparent need for certain accepted norms regarding health care needs (e.g., that pregnant women should receive comprehensive prenatal care and deliver their babies in hospitals).

Theories of Ponsioen and Maslow

In determining that an individual or group has a need, society—or, more strictly, the segment of society with decision-making power—is establishing standards against which it evaluates existing conditions. In sum, these standards implicitly define the concept of the "quality of life." Unfortunately, this latter concept has been the subject of so much debate that it has become all but meaningless for the planning purposes under discussion. Two theorists—Ponsioen and Maslow—have nevertheless offered a number of useful insights.

Ponsioen [4] suggests that a society's first responsibility is to meet the basic survival needs of its members, including biological, social, emotional, and spiritual components. Each society, or the dominant group in each society, will identify a level below which no individual or group should fall. These levels will, of course, change over time. Within this framework, social need exists when some groups in the society or community do not have access to these "necessary" goods and services while others do. Need, in this sense, is a relative term; the related policy and planning issues become ones of distribution and redistribution.

Maslow [5] takes a slightly different view and proposes the existence of a hierarchy of need. Accordingly, man becomes aware of his needs in a prescribed order—from the bottom up—and only when lower needs are satisfied can higher ones be attended to. Specifically, until his physiological survival needs (e.g., food and shelter) are met, man cannot be overly concerned with his safety and security. Achievement of this second level of need then allows attention to the highest level—the need for love and self-actualization.

While the preceding discussion of concepts may seem far removed from the practical problems of planning in the human services field, it does underscore a number of critical points. Especially significant is the idea of need as a *normative concept* that is *subject to temporal shifts*.

Factors influencing the definition of need

There are a number of factors that influence how need is defined. Three of these factors—the standard of living; the sociopolitical environment; and the availability of resources and existence of technology—will be analyzed in the following discussion.

The standard of living   The first and most obvious factor is the standard of living. It has already been pointed out that some housing considered to be adequate in the past would be classified as substandard today. The housing itself did not change. Expectations about housing did. An example of a similar shift is the official definition of poverty used in the United States. In the 1960s, the Social Security Administration developed a series of poverty profiles. These were based on particular standards which made allowances for the various needs of families with different numbers of adults and children. [6] In all, 124 different types of families were identified. The poverty line was tied to the amount of money a family was thought to require to obtain basic necessities. While even the Social Security Administration agreed that the criteria used are stringent, the standard was changed continuously over the ensuing decade. As the cost of living has increased, the poverty line had to be raised.

The sociopolitical environment   A second factor influencing the definition of need is the sociopolitical environment. Public attitudes and expectations shift constantly. A generation ago, for example, the notion of universal day care would have been rejected out of hand. It was expected that mothers would remain in the home to raise the children, entering the labor market only when this function was completed. Mothers who worked were to do so out of necessity, and many believed that this had a negative impact on family life. By the 1970s, attitudes had changed significantly. Little, if any, stigma is attached today to placing a child in a day care center, and there are many who now believe that such an arrangement affects the family in a positive way.

Resources and technology   A third factor influencing the definition of need is the availability of resources and the existence of technology. If people do not believe that the resources available are adequate to meet social need, it remains unlikely that they will follow through on their concerns to take any significant action. An example of this is the "discovery" in the 1960s of poverty in the United States, stimulated, in part, by Michael Harrington's work.[7] Once the existing poverty had been documented and public consciousness aroused, a massive governmental effort was initiated. Interestingly, a greater percentage of the population was poor during the first half of this century than during the 1960s. With the exception of the Depression years, however, little public action had been taken to alleviate the situation.

Only when expectations changed (based in this case on the willingness of the federal government to allocate a greater portion of its resources to social need) did the alleviation of poverty became a viable policy issue. Furthermore, in conformance with Ponsioen's framework discussed earlier, the poor in previous decades accepted their status more readily insofar as poverty was more widespread. In more recent years, however, the poor were aware that most Americans enjoyed a much higher standard of living than they did. Their expectations changed, and they began to demand more of the resources.

Attitudes toward the elderly have also shifted. From 1935 to 1960, income maintenance programs represented the principal national effort for this group. More recently, elected officials, managers, and human services professionals have begun to support and develop programs whose purpose is to meet the social needs of the elderly. Examples of such programs are provided by day centers, foster grandparent programs, and special employment opportunities as well as by programs catering to the physical needs of the elderly, as in the cases of meals on wheels, home care and homemaker services, and comprehensive health maintenance. The elderly have equal rights with the rest of the population, including the right to live in comfort and with dignity. What is needed in the way of services to ensure their basic rights has not changed; as in other areas of concern, it has been expectations regarding the ability to meet this need that have altered.

The elasticity of need

Need is also an "elastic" concept. If it were absolute (assuming a constant state), the planning task under discussion would be relatively straightforward. Having defined the need and quantified its scope, the primary tasks would be to acquire sufficient resources and to develop a plan for services and programs to meet the defined need. Experience shows, of course, that needs assessment, at best, assists the planner in estimating what needs are thought to exist at that time and in predicting what they might be at some point in the future if attitudes, expectations, and values do not change dramatically.

One example of these limitations in planning for the future may be found in the food stamp program. Careful analysis was used to generate projections of the extent of the need for this program, and the unfortunate result was that these projections were grossly underestimated. And the examples need not be limited to the United States. The British are facing this problem of lack of predictability in almost all areas of the social services. In the United Kingdom, planning targets for specific services were developed, based on national surveys of the elderly. For example, the target for places in residential care facilities (approximating the United States' nursing homes) is, as of the late 1970s, 25 places per 1,000 elderly. In 1952, the existing coverage was 18 places per 1,000; in 1973, 21 places per 1,000. The planners are now faced with major uncertainties. Once the goal of 25 places per 1,000 is reached, will demand level off? If it continues to increase, how can the rate of increase be predicted? It has been found that expansion of services is generally followed by greater demand. It would appear that, at least to some extent, people in need tend to seek services only when they feel that there is a real possibility that the services will actually be provided. Planners—and indeed all local government managers—must therefore begin with the assumption that need is elastic—likely to change over time—and that this elasticity extends also to demand—likely to increase with service provision. The influence of this elasticity can have unintended consequences. To take a somewhat extreme example, it is possible that the allocation of a greater share of resources to institutional services at the expense of community services could result in the institutionalization of people who could function in the community.[8]

Summary

Need, therefore, is a concept deserving of careful analysis by all those responsible for responding to community concerns. As has been indicated, vague or implicit usage of the term can lead to perilous managerial situations fraught with the possibility of misunderstanding, ill-conceived programs, or inaccurate predictions about programs. Essentially, it is important to remember that need is a normative concept; that it is susceptible to theoretical analysis that, in turn, has considerable practical import; and that it possesses an elasticity commensurate with changing social perceptions and social circumstances. A clear perception of the concept of need can enormously aid the managerial process. Bearing this context in mind, it is now possible to move on to a consideration of the categories of need, that is, the *what* of need mentioned earlier.

Categories of need

Conceptually, four distinct categories of need can be identified: these are normative need, perceived need, expressed need, and relative need.[9] They will now be discussed in turn, followed by an analysis of their overall managerial utility.

Normative need

Operating under a normative definition of need, and utilizing professional judgment and surveys of target populations, the decision makers involved propose such desirable standards as the number of nursing home beds, home "helps," meals on wheels, or the amount of human services manpower for a given population. These standards, usually expressed in ratios, are then compared to actual ratios. If an individual or group falls short of a particular standard, it is labeled as being "in need." This approach is basically the type of analysis described earlier with reference to the United Kingdom. Its strength lies in its ability to provide objective targets. Its limitation is that, as has been indicated, overall need will change as knowledge, technology, and values change in a community, or in society as a whole.

Perceived need

Need can also be defined in terms of what people perceive their needs to be. While the idea of felt need is important, people's expectations are susceptible to change and may, in fact, be defined partly by their knowledge of the availability of services. The planner and the manager must be sensitive to what the consumer states and, of equal importance, be able to translate these need statements into appropriate services. A fine line has to be maintained to balance the professional's judgment of client need with the potential consumers' perceptions of what their needs are (possibly leading the provider to focus only on symptoms rather than unrecognized causes). An advantage to the provider in assessing perceived need is that it furnishes information that is useful when designing optimally responsive services. Its major drawback is that, in actively soliciting the consumer's impression of what the need is, professionals are likely to raise expectations. If the planners and administrators then do not make the "expected" services available, they will have frustrated those in need. This raises an ethical question: do professionals have a moral obligation to ignore perceived need if, from the outset, they know that additional human services resources are unlikely to be found and that existing resources are inadequate?

Expressed need

Need can also be defined as the number of people who seek a service. Unmet need is represented by that proportion of such seekers who are unsuccessful. This method of definition implies a reliance on individuals' demands on the system. The legitimate needs of those who seek services should not be underrated. The basic limitation of expressed need is its lack of concern for overall community need.

Relative need

This definition does not assume that there are any "most desirable" levels of service that should be achieved. Need, as established by this approach, is a measurement of the gap between services existing in different geographical areas, weighted to account for the differences in population and social pathology. Unlike normative need, which provides a desirable standard to be worked toward, relative need is concerned with equity of services. Given scarce resources, how are criteria best developed that prioritize population groups and geographic areas? To take one example, even if all counties are below the established standard in a particular service, some are, undoubtedly, in a relatively better position than others.

Need categories and the management process

As the above outline has indicated, need cannot be measured adequately by selecting any one of these approaches. Since each has its limitations, a serious exploration in this area ideally should encompass all four of the dimensions described. A needs assessment survey, to be effective, of course requires an extensive commitment from administrators and their staffs. There are a number of factors which combine to make the process a difficult undertaking: as the previous discussion has shown, need tends to be conceptually ambiguous, elastic, and subject to shifts in scale over time. The generally heavy case loads of human services agencies and the potential frustration—personal and political—to be had from uncovering previously unrecognized need also serve to discourage even the most conscientious chief executives and human services administrators from making the necessary commitment.

There are, however, clear and compelling reasons for utilizing the needs assessment process. In practice, managers must constantly review what money and resources are available to them and employ techniques that make best use of this information. If they do not make the best use of the process offered by needs assessment, they are more likely than not to end up not knowing what the needs of their communities really are. The needs assessment process can feed a well-organized and pertinent flow of information into the overall management decision process. It can show what the actual and potential demand is and can be on human services agencies. It can provide useful information as long-term community goals and capital budget programs are reviewed. Further, needs assessment can provide a useful early warning system regarding potential changes in demand for a jurisdiction's services.

Without this information, managers are likely to find scarce resources being squandered on programs that may well serve, as indicated earlier in this chapter, to further the bureaucratic status quo rather than to speak to the concerns of the community. Finally, it is necessary to recognize that today's overall local government manager must balance out resources among a number of competing agencies. The human services function is but one of those competing functional areas. The needs assessment process helps the manager better assess his or her own executive needs as these competing demands are considered in the budget process and elsewhere. It helps the staff of the human services agency function more effectively in the overall local government decision-making process.

Client analysis

The process known as client analysis illustrates the managerial utility of these approaches.[10] For example, in 1968, planners in one northeastern state were interested in estimating the number of people who were eligible for their Medicaid program. At that time, 10 percent of the state's population had been certified as eligible. Total expenditures had reached $250 million. Using the existing eligibility criteria and analyzing available data bases (e.g., updated census figures), they were able to estimate that 19 percent of the population were, in fact, eligible.

At least two courses of action were then open to the decision makers concerned. The first was to present the results of the analysis to the state legislature and request sizable budget increases. This strategy was rejected. The executives concerned were mindful of the experiences in California and New York, where the legislators closed similar gaps by redefining eligibility according to more stringent criteria. Instead, the data were used selectively to argue that the state should allow for experimentation in providing medical care services to the eligible population. Specific suggestions included proposals to buy into prepaid group practices and health centers. From a managerial viewpoint, therefore, it is important to note that, although the state was confronted with a potentially serious future problem (the negative result of the analysis), it was also given a series of alternatives for the use of existing resources (a positive counterposition.)

This client analysis approach begins with a review of legislation, regulations, and guidelines, and an attempt to calculate the size of the potential consumer population. Actual utilization is then estimated. The resources necessary to close the gap are costed out and future targets are developed. Client analysis becomes a powerful planning tool. It alerts departmental and agency executives, general managers, and elected officials to possible future problems. It can become the means for sensitizing people in the local government political process to necessary policy shifts as well as becoming a method for building up a commitment for additional support.

Summary

As the preceding discussion has indicated, planning, in the broadest sense, is concerned with the short-term decisions of the operating budget cycle and with longer-term projects often linked to capital budget proposals. The "actors" in this process include the staffs of agencies and also the key decision makers in the local government political process—the other competing agencies, the appointed chief executive, and elected officials. At any point in time, agencies and the jurisdictions of which they are a part have a specific set of resources. Both individual agencies and the community as a whole need to think about appropriate allocations as a prelude to the intensive negotiations that are usually focused on the budgetary process.

Whatever the perspective involved, whether it be that of the chief executive or of an agency head, criteria for allocations are in some way linked to perceived hierarchies of needs and of priority setting. Given limited resources, is it possible to make an objective identification of populations or geographical areas with greater need? Quite apart from the pressure generated in the political process, what objective criteria can be developed to determine which group of competing potential clients for human services should receive priority? Long-range planning enables all the "actors" involved in the local government process to project or to estimate what level of resources would be necessary to meet the perceived need. It also allows them to identify, from their particular perspectives, the constraints that operate for and against their acquisition. The political process then balances out resources against expressed or perceived needs in the community. Needs analysis, in both its qualitative and quantitative aspects, can play an important role in the decision-making process. Initial problem analysis can provide managers at all levels with an idea of what might be done and the probable size of target groups. Within the political process, needs can then be translated into measurable objectives, resources, and criteria necessary for program evaluation. This process is more than an abstract theoretical discussion. It can be integrated into effective management practical and its lack can cause an unnecessary waste of scarce resources.

Determining who is in need

The concept of "at risk" populations is essential to any discussion of needs assessment. This concept is explored in the following discussion which attempts to outline answers to the question: *Who* is in need? This section will analyze some of the general problems in this area, then proceed to discuss the following individual methods: existing surveys and expert judgment; service statistics; resource inventories; social surveys; and public hearings.

An overview

The concept of "at risk" populations has been inherent to such programs as Model Cities, maternal and infant care projects, services for school children and preschoolers, manpower, and the wide range of antipoverty programs. Those activities and efforts in the social services field [11] are based on the principle of channeling resources to "high risk" areas in which there are large concentrations of high risk families and individuals.

The reality of multidimensional needs Intrinsic to this approach is a focus on the needs of individuals, families, and groups. This may appear to be an obvious starting point, but it is, in fact, a major departure from common practice. Although evidence since the early 1960s has clearly demonstrated that the needs of people are usually multiple, the focus in human services has been along discrete functional lines. While large numbers of people experience some combination of problems related to health, employment, income, and social functioning, the identification and subsequent treatment of each "need" is usually handled by separate agencies. Services that are fragmented force the consumers to fragment their problems. From a service delivery perspective, it has been almost impossible to meet the comprehensive needs of consumers. Even if one agency is, from a professional viewpoint, able to provide necessary services, success is often minimized because the other problems are ignored. Planners, for the most part, appear to have accepted the inevitability of fragmentation and have undertaken needs assessment along these same categorical lines. Beginning with their own subsystem, they attempt to determine the number of people who may require specific, predetermined services. Instead of asking questions about high risk populations (e.g., the elderly, the mentally retarded, single-parent families), they try to find out how many need day care, counseling, rehabilitation, ambulatory or institutional care, job training, or some other service. The former approach accepts the reality of multidimensional needs and encourages integration of resources; the latter encourages further fragmentation.

It should be emphasized that to label a group of people "high risk" is not to suggest that all members of that group have similar problems or, for that matter, problems at all. The identification of such a group simply indicates a high statistical correlation between that group and specific types of problems. The incidence of cancer and heart disease is significantly higher among cigarette smokers than nonsmokers, but not all cigarette smokers are struck by these diseases. Children from low income families who attend inner-city schools are more likely to drop out or perform poorly on certain achievement tests, but many go to universities and pursue highly skilled professional careers.

To show a high correlation between advanced age and poverty, chronic illness, or social isolation is not to indicate that every person over sixty-five years of age is poor, ill, or socially dysfunctional. What is indicated is that an aged person is more likely to have these problems. As an identifiable subpopulation, the elderly have to be seen as a high risk group when compared to other population groups. While the elderly make up 9.6 percent of the total population, they account for almost 20 percent of the poor. In 1970, 13.6 percent of the total population were identified as poor, but 27.3 percent of the elderly were living in poverty.[12] The incidence of one or more chronic conditions is 85 percent in the population over sixty-four years of age; this compares to 22 percent of those under seventeen years; 54 percent between seventeen and forty-four years; and 71 percent between forty-five and sixty-four years.[13] As many as 25 percent of the elderly live alone.[14]

Similarly, to identify a geographic area or neighborhood as "high risk" does not mean that all residents have the same level of need or even similar needs. Rather, it refers to spatial concentrations of families and individuals likely to be living in substandard housing, or possibly experiencing higher rates of unemployment or higher prevalence of illness in one combination or another.

Two major problems: reliability of estimates and data availability   There are two major problems in conducting a needs assessment over and above the critical issue discussed above. The first is that current methods are only useful for deriving estimates. Decision makers, of course, prefer greater certainty. They have to be informed that such expectations are perhaps both unrealistic and unnecessary for the planning of human services. It is rarely possible to generate precise needs statements. Estimates are nevertheless of value in that they provide targets and mechanisms that allow the decision maker to think beyond an ad hoc approach. Although estimates, by definition, have their limitations, these limitations are not so severe as to make them useless, by any means. Also, any alternative to estimates usually involves either prohibitive costs or too much time.

A health planning issue provides an example. Physicians and hospital administrators might present data showing long waiting lists for elective surgery, high occupancy rates, and general population projections. The hospital in question might be viewed as only one of a number of subsystems that affect and are influenced by such other subsystems as nursing homes and community agencies.[15] Information can be collected on the average daily census of existing hospitals, nursing homes, and other related institutions for each of the past ten years; on inappropriate utilization of each (by means of a sample patient review); on the utilization of existing community care services; and finally, on a detailed population forecast. The data might be fed into a regression model and predictions made of the number of hospital beds the community is likely to need. Such a prediction, however, would still be an estimate in spite of the wealth of hard data generated. For example, it might be estimated that a particular area would require an additional two hundred beds over the next ten years. The actual prediction (taking into account the standard deviation and the confidence interval) might be two hundred plus or minus fifty beds, that is, a range of 150–250 beds. While the data analysts might be comfortable with such an estimate, decision makers would likely be unsatisfied with both the estimate and the error margin. The former are looking for a target to establish parameters; the latter are seeking material to aid in the development and negotiation of budget requests.

Within the context of social services, a planner might estimate that 10 percent of a state's elderly population of 100,000—that is, 10,000 people—need homemaker services. The actual number may range from 9,000–11,000. With the introduction of various standards and criteria, the number of elderly eligible for this service may be reduced to 6,000–7,000. Often, exact numbers cannot be determined. Targets, however, can be established and should be set up so that they can be modified as additional data become available. The second problem is data availability. The analysis described above to estimate the number of hospital beds required considerable data, data that in many cases would be difficult to retrieve or too costly to collect. The patient survey—the only reliable means for assessment of appropriate utilization—would need to be carried out by highly trained medical personnel. The strengths and limitations of surveys will be discussed later, but it is sufficient to point out at this juncture that the administration of such surveys is very costly and is time-consuming. Other parts of the assessment could rely on existing data collected on a routine basis by the relevant institutions and agencies. This information, however, is often not readily usable as it is often in "hard copy" form and not machine readable. Furthermore, existing data bases may not be specific to the particular planning issue insofar as the information may have been collected for other purposes. While this problem may not be severe in hospital utilization studies, it can be so in other aspects of human services. The task may be to estimate the numbers of families in need of day care or mental health services. If a survey cannot be undertaken, the planners may be forced to rely on existing data sources and attempt to identify surrogate measures of these needs. The percentage of working mothers with children under six years of age, single-parent families, and families with incomes below the poverty line have been used as indicators of day care need. Suicide and divorce rates, school dropout rates, and the rates of alcoholism and drug addiction have been identified as indirect measures of mental illness. Although it is reasonable to assume that these variables are highly correlated with day care need and mental illness, they do not directly measure these needs. The problem is twofold: to identify appropriate surrogates (the theoretical requirement) and to develop the best possible argument that they are valid (the political requirement).

Managerial responses In spite of these overall difficulties, it is important to point out that, from the managerial perspective, alternatives are limited and usually counterproductive. One response is to delay the needs assessment until more appropriate data are available. Another is to continue business as usual, making decisions based on intuition. It is unlikely, however, that entirely appropriate data will ever become available, and experience has demonstrated that personal judgments can be very idiosyncratic.

Managers will also recognize that they can accept limitations of the type described and make creative use of existing data sources which, although imperfect, can nevertheless be used to generate targets and reduce some of the uncertainty.

Further, managers have more positive options. While they may desire closer estimates, they do have ways to hedge uncertainties. For example, they may start small operating programs, letting the programs find their proper levels in later years as true needs reveal themselves. Second, they can construct fewer or more expandable buildings and facilities. Third, they have to be completely candid about future uncertainties in their budget projections. The determination of who is in need is a realistic and necessary task, and the limitations of data are not crippling compared to the benefits brought to the managerial process by the generation of even approximate targets.

It is now possible to move on to a discussion of a number of methods for answering the "Who is in need?" question. No hierarchy is implied, nor are the methods mutually exclusive. Experienced managers will be aware that each taps a certain dimension of need and is usually used in combination with one of the others.

Existing surveys and expert judgment

In the context of the four categories of need identified earlier, the method of utilizing existing surveys and expert judgment addresses normative need where standards are proposed and compared to existing standards.

For example, the National Center for Health Statistics (NCHS) is one of four general purpose statistical agencies of the federal government which are charged with collecting, compiling, analyzing, and publishing data for general use.[16] Within the NCHS, the Health Interview Survey (HIS) is one of three major survey programs, the other two being the Health Examination Survey (HES) and the Health Records Survey (HRS). These surveys provide estimates of the prevalence of specific diseases and disability in the United States.

There are also special topic surveys covering various areas such as child abuse,[17] children,[18] the elderly,[19] the mentally retarded,[20] delinquency,[21] and mental illness.[22] These specialized reports provide prevalence rates for given conditions that can, of course, serve as benchmarks against which proposed standards or targets can be measured.

It is helpful to place these reports in context by regarding them as epidemiological studies. Epidemiology is an applied discipline concerned with the study of disease distribution (descriptive epidemiology) and the search for the determinants of the noted distribution (analytic epidemiology).[23] It has proved to be of value in the area of communicable diseases (e.g., in the classic case of the cholera outbreak in nineteenth-century London where the outbreak was traced to the users of a single water pump) and is often applied to contemporary social problems. Its attractiveness is that it posits the existence of causal chains and assumes that if a link in that chain is altered or broken, the problem can be dealt with successfully. In the context of human services surveys, descriptive epidemiology, describing the distribution of problems in terms of age, sex, race, spatial location, etc., might be considered an extension of the discipline of geography to include social conditions. The special contribution of analytic epidemiology, however, is the interpretation of those distributions in terms of possible causal factors.

Managers familiar with the strengths and weaknesses of this approach will, however, point to two important qualifications. First, it must be noted that data from these surveys are not specific to the geographic area of concern. Before the prevalence rates can be applied, it is necessary to compare the population characteristics of the survey with the population characteristics of the area under consideration. For example, most prevalence rates are age- and sex-specific, that is, with different rates for each grouping. Functional status and ability is highly correlated with age. The elderly, for instance, are much more likely to be physically handicapped; yet, an overall rate for the total population of sixty-five years of age or older can be misleading. Managers will be aware that it is necessary to apply those age-specific rates that are available for the "frail elderly" (those over eighty-four), for those between seventy-five and eighty-four years of age, and for those between sixty-five and seventy-five. This refinement will generate more sensitive and precise estimates. When necessary, weights will have to be applied to these epidemiological surveys. If social class is related to some condition or problem, e.g., delinquent acts, school performance, premature births, etc., and the social class distribution for the area under consideration is skewed, statistical adjustments are required.

The second caveat is concerned with the conceptual approach underpinning the survey and the way in which the problem or condition was operationally defined. For example, two national surveys on the needs of the elderly carried out in the 1960s suggested different rates of "impairment." [24] The first survey reported that 62 percent of the elderly seventy-five years of age and older were limited in their normal activities, while the second found that 30 percent were limited. Two factors appear to explain this variation. While both used the terms "impairment," "capacity," and "limitations," the latter study actually used much stricter measurements. Furthermore, the second study tested actual ability while the first only asked the respondents if they were able to carry out certain functions. The elderly were apparently able to do more than they thought they could or than they were willing to admit.

Another example of this problem is the wide range of estimates of mental illness reported by four leading experts in the field: Srole; Jaco; Leighton; and Hollingshead. [25] Each defined mental health and mental illness differently—some more rigorously, some more clinically. On a theoretical level, none is technically more correct than any other: the planner or manager must choose the study using definitions that are most meaningful for actual programmatic development.

Given these constraints, managers and department heads will recognize the utility of having a staff with a broad knowledge of various substantive fields, or at least with access to other research and planning organizations that have this capability. Traditionally in the human services field, this has meant a university, and usually one offering programs in public health, social work, city and regional planning, and education. The unit involved will require an in-house capacity for data analysis and interpretation, especially if the survey data have to be weighted to account for local differences.

A complementary approach to the above also addresses the category of normative need and is based on professional or expert judgment. Given targets for various subpopulation groups, consultants are brought in to translate these into resources, services, and patterns of delivery. Their expertise is not in planning or administration, but in such specific substantive areas as those concerned with the elderly, the mentally retarded, low income housing, and alcoholism. These specialists are likely to be most familiar with existing surveys and relevant research in the area, and they are usually in a position to propose specific strategies and suggest reasonable levels of service provision.

The strengths of this approach are numerous. Costs are likely to be reasonably low and the time involved relatively short. The planning effort benefits in that parameters of need are established by recognized experts and the credibility of subsequent budgetary requests will be fairly high.

While the limitations are considerable, they tend to be subtle. Professionals, even experts, are sometimes biased and have been charged with viewing problems through a form of tunnel vision. In fact, the very successes that gained them recognition can limit their problem-solving abilities should they take on the attitude that experience has provided the "solutions" before any new analyses are undertaken. To counter this possibility, such consultation should be initiated only after a basic strategy has been outlined, e.g., community support services for the elderly, hostels or half-way houses for the retarded or mentally ill. The consultant is thus relied upon to assist in his or her area of substantive expertise, e.g., estimating numbers at risk, establishing feasible targets, and programmatic development.

Service statistics

The service statistics approach utilizes the concept of expressed need and is based on the periodic accumulation of service reports from direct service agencies. These reports can provide a rough measure of the agency effort expended and are valuable in maintaining support activities and establishing monitoring procedures. The obvious advantage of this approach is the availability and accessibility of the data, assuming the issue of confidentiality can be resolved. It is clearly more economical in terms of resources and time to rely on existing data than on special survey data. Needs assessment using available data can be described as a "low profile" activity, minimizing the potential problem, already discussed, caused by increased expectations among recipients or potential recipients. Furthermore, agencies will have these data available over extended periods of time, allowing planners and managers to identify trends and to make comparisons.

However, this approach will not provide data about the prevalence of unmet need which, as pointed out earlier, is essential for strategic or policy planning. Managers will be aware that there is a danger, when planning for the needs of the total population, in relying on data that is descriptive of service utilizers, those who have been placed on waiting lists, or those who have attempted unsuccessfully to receive services. These sorts of data reflect demand and measure only the tip of the iceberg as far as need is concerned. The population that comes into contact with human services agencies is probably different from the nonuser population, and it is conceivable that these very differences determine service utilization. Waiting lists, on the other hand, are affected by actual service provision. For example, in one instance, waiting lists for residential care places had remained fairly constant over a ten-year period.[26] Although there had been significant increases in the number of places, these facilities were always close to full capacity. As more places became available, they were filled from existing waiting lists; as people moved to the facilities, they were replaced on the list by others. The factors associated with this situation are complex, but one reason may be that increases in service provision raised expectations and this, in turn, was translated into demand. If it is known that there are limited resources and that waiting lists are lengthy, many will see no value in even applying for help. If, on the other hand, people find that additional services are available, they are more likely to apply.

Service statistics do, however, have value for managers and their staffs. Utilization data can identify the characteristics of that subpopulation in contact with the human services agencies: who they are, who benefits, where they are located, and the type of services they receive. These data can be used to assess the capacity of agencies to deliver services and, if increased demand is anticipated, the expansion requirements.

Such information can produce census lists, admission and discharge statistics, and other types of population reports useful for planning and policy formulation. Special analyses of needs and characteristics of the current population or case load might also be generated for managerial review. It would then be possible to extract information indicating trends in case loads, patient characteristics, and program needs for forecasting and research activities.

It can also provide the basis for examining the treatment process. As information on individuals and families is accumulated, it becomes possible to identify service needs for total populations and potential case loads for various programs. It is also possible to determine cost patterns incurred in providing services to recipient groups with common problems or needs and, as a result, to offer a more rational basis for adjusting priorities and program plans.

An interesting use of service statistics is the development of profiles of user populations through clustering techniques. The statistical profiles are related to a set of services likely to be needed by an individual or family who can be placed in a cluster. This approach becomes quite useful when integrated with other categories of need, e.g., perceived, normative, and relative need. Utilization data combined with need estimate data offers the planner or manager the capability of moving from needs to resources.

Resource inventories

The use of resource inventories is complementary to that of service statistics and relates to the concept of normative need. Beginning with such identifiable high risk population groups as the elderly, single-parent families, the mentally retarded, and alcoholics, this method attempts to identify all agencies, public and private, offering services to these groups. The inventory, while beginning with existing directories, moves considerably beyond these listings. Optimally, the planner serves a useful managerial function by being able to spend time in developing discrete and meaningful service categories so that they can be grouped across program and agency lines by function and purpose. The planner also analyzes the eligibility criteria used by the agencies and generates standardized formats, and explores the agencies' perceptions of their overall capacities to meet greater demand. The critical problems are in the area of standardization and in developing mechanisms to reduce definitional disagreements.

Given these data as well as the data gathered through the service statistics analysis the planner is in a position to serve management by evaluating whether the existing system is functioning to capacity, whether specific agencies are capable of serving more people, and whether there is an overlap of services. This assessment may result in the conclusion that there is a need for growth and expansion or, just as likely, that resources are misutilized (in a systems framework) and that more effective coordination could be sufficient to meet increased demand.

It is useful to include a survey of service providers under the heading of resource inventories. Asking service providers to identify the problems or needs of "at risk" groups is quite different from asking people themselves what their needs are or from analyzing utilization data and drawing inferences as to an agency's capability to expand. The first approach, a survey of providers, generates statements of normative need—what the providers judge to be the problem or need—based on their day-to-day practice. The inventory itself is usually normative in that the assessment is shaped by some expectations of what is possible given certain resource mixes. The other approach—the consumer (or potential consumer) survey—represents perceived need via the personal statement of the person in need, and utilization data is descriptive of the actual system.

Since the providers are likely to be involved in any attempts to meet need, the planner is seeking more than their opinions. Indirectly, the provider is invited to become a member of the planning team, a strategy that could aid management by facilitating the implementation of new activities. A resource inventory may provide formal information on the system, the provider survey might give insight into the real capability of the system to change.

All this information is vitally necessary if human services management is to be productive and effective. Experienced managers will note, however, that there are considerable difficulties involved in these activities. The methodological requirements already listed are mainly conceptual and time-consuming. Beyond these are the all-important sociopolitical constraints. The planner—and the decision makers to whom the planner reports—must convince program managers and administrators, both inside and outside the agency, that their data should be made available and that some common format should be used. One strategy to minimize a possible "domain" problem is to involve these agencies in the planning of the inventory and to make available to the informants the results of the analysis.

Furthermore, as with utilization data, service providers are likely to make recommendations based on their knowledge of consumers and not necessarily of the nonuser population. Their perspective is on demand and not usually on need. Providers also, of course, tend to have a commitment to the services they already provide and a vested interest in the existing service network. The planner has to recognize that the information received will be biased (in a nonpejorative sense), but that the information can nevertheless be extremely useful for needs assessment leading to the development of human services.

Social surveys

The use of social surveys relates to the category of perceived need in that surveys attempt to determine what people want or perceive their needs to be. Leaving aside considerations of cost, the social survey is probably the single most powerful method of all the approaches to need assessment. It can provide original data tailored to the specific needs of a geographic area and can be sharply focused on a particular problem. The previous approaches rely either on secondary data from which inferences of need are drawn or on the inherently subjective judgment and experience of professionals. Furthermore, the survey offers the one strategy that can generate information on the attitudes of consumers and potential consumers of human services.

The survey usually has two focuses: the *identification of needs* and the *determination of knowledge about existing services*. Both are important for planning. The first provides information useful in the delineation of targets; the second may identify barriers to utilization, be they financial, physical, or attitudinal. Knowledge of these barriers might indicate a need not only for a particular service, but also for various supportive services (e.g., outreach, advocacy, education) that could be instrumental in achieving program success.

The purpose of a survey is to provide a valid description of a situation—a description that will be of use when fed into the managerial and decision-making process. The staff involved begin by defining the problem in conceptual and operational terms. They go on to construct appropriate data collection instruments, draw a sample, conduct interviews, analyze the data, and finally produce planning recommendations.

Beyond the descriptive function, a survey can also provide other benefits. Initially, it was believed that information would produce change.

Most community surveys were initiated in the hope that, once the facts were compiled and artfully presented, the local leadership would be inspired to act. This was the rationale for the "expert survey," in which an outside researcher typically was brought in to recruit a team, gather data, and present his conclusions in the inventive style developed by Kellogg, Philip Klein, and others. Experience in this country, alas, was that knowledge of needs did not guarantee incentive to meet them. Therefore, the emphasis is shifted to marshalling motivation.[27]

In spite of this belief, the social survey has a number of planning benefits. If a survey identifies shortages or barriers to utilization, it can act to legitimize change. In this sense, it becomes a tool for action and a stimulus for support. As a process tool, it can heighten the awareness of a community and serve an educational purpose. To achieve this, the notion of the expert survey has to give way to the concept of a community survey involving agency representatives, community leaders, and actual and potential consumers in the planning and implementation of the survey itself. Involvement of this kind hopefully will produce support for the recommendations that follow. Finally, although most surveys offer a static description of a community at one point in time (continuous surveys are the exception), they can serve to establish baseline data and reference points for monitoring and evaluation that will be of significant use to local government decision makers.

Usually the amount of time and effort likely to be involved in the initial phases of a survey are underestimated. Many planners and administrators equate the survey work with the actual field work—the interviewing of respondents—and allow insufficient time for the design of the survey. A result is that data items are included with minimal thought having been given to their usefulness for the planning task. A typical justification for including a large number of data items is that they may prove to be of value later in the analysis phase. The analysis process, however, begins when design considerations are being discussed and not after the data has been collected. Before any item is included, the planner should know why the information is being sought (the conceptual issue) and how it fits into the analysis strategy (the methodological issue). Without this preparation the analysis may become a fishing expedition with planners and analysts wading through a morass of information. Costs, too, will escalate.

Community surveys utilize random or nonrandom sampling techniques to enumerate either a general cross section of the community or of various subgroups. All too often, surveys are based on methodological and statistically inadequate samples. The size of the sample can range from 100 to well over 1,000 individuals or families. Since sample size is a direct function of the number of variables to be surveyed and analyzed, the required number can be relatively large. Sample size is also directly related to costs. Social survey organizations put the cost per interview between $60 and $75. This cost includes the actual interview as well as training and supervision of the interviewers, related travel expenses, and prorated costs for coding and analysis. A sample of 1,000 would therefore cost as much as $60,000 to $75,000. It is sufficient to suggest the potential value of consultation with a sampling expert in the course of developing appropriate strategy. Without confidence in the final sample, it is impossible to justify any generalization to the total target population—a factor essential for effective human services planning.

A final concern is the time involved in the design and implementation of a survey. Six to nine months from design through analysis represents a conservative estimate. And yet the findings may have a rapid rate of obsolescence because such data can show only the need situation at a particular point in time. Given these limitations, planners ought to at least consider exhausting all available data sources before finally deciding to proceed with the survey. Managers and elected officials will be quick to pose such questions as: Is it really necessary? Are the time and financial costs (as well as the potential danger of raising expectations that might not be met) outweighed by the benefits to be derived?

Public hearings

The public hearing approach to needs assessment usually takes the form of an open meeting to which the general public is invited and welcome to give testimony. Quite apart from political or community relations aspects, such meeting may be required by law. Since the 1960s, such hearings have been conducted through neighborhood meetings first encouraged by OEO-organized Community Action Agencies, later stimulated by programs such as Model Cities and revenue sharing (especially community development programs), and, since the mid-1970s, organized through the Title XX amendments to the Social Security Act.

Ideally, those attending the meetings are able to articulate their own needs, to represent the concerns of their neighbors, and in some instances to speak for an organized constituency. Needs and priorities are then determined by a consensus of those involved in the process or through tabulation of articulated concerns to be prioritized at a later time. Public meetings have the advantages of their compatibility with democratic decision making, greater economy than surveys in terms of costs and time, and their implicit encouragement of clarification and cross-fertilization through open discussion.

As managers who have experienced such meetings will be well aware, the major problem in this approach to determining need is the issue of representation. Do the elderly who attend a meeting represent their individual needs or those of their group? Do all interested groups generally attend or are some self-excluded because of perceived stigma attached to their needs (such as welfare recipients)? Is it possible that those with the greatest need feel uncomfortable or embarrassed in attempting to articulate their concerns? Experience to date suggests that attendees usually are not representative, that certain groups are much more aggressive than others and familiar with lobbying strategies, and that differing communication patterns are sometimes a barrier.

The staffs and managers involved should anticipate these problems before deciding whether or not to hold these meetings. First, they need to recognize there is no guarantee that a cross section of the community will attend these meetings. Further, use of the media might not be successful. Resources should therefore be allocated to help reach important target groups, resources that include outreach and community organization activities. Assuming that attendance per se will not necessarily result in equal and effective participation by all present, process techniques that attempt to structure participation should be introduced. One such method is the "nominal group process" in which internal exchange can be sequenced and all participants given an equal voice whether they are verbal or not.[28]

Summary

It should be apparent that none of the approaches just described are necessarily better than the others. Furthermore, they are not mutually exclusive and, by choosing one, the manager does not necessarily reject others. The use of some combination of the techniques discussed—expert opinion, existing surveys, service statistics, resource inventories and provider surveys, community surveys, or public meetings—can contribute distinct information to the local government decision-making process. Given a specific situation, managers and elected officials might want to authorize and utilize some combination of the above. What is important is an assessment of the available resources and the operating constraints, and then the implementation of what is managerially, politically, and financially feasible.

Where?—approaches for locating concentrations of high risk groups

The primary focus in the preceding discussion was on the determination in terms of needs of the "who?" of high risk target populations for human services delivery. For human services management, the emphasis was on aggregating people with similar needs by determining the characteristics and number of such specific groups as the handicapped or the elderly. An additional task, however, is to *locate* concentrations of high risk groups by carrying out a spatial, or geographic, analysis. The following discussion therefore addresses, from a managerial perspective, this question of "where?"

An overview

How do such locational analyses fit into the overall management picture? Clearly, managers are expected to formulate plans, develop policies for plan implementation, formulate criteria for priority setting and resource allocation, and establish a monitoring system or closely supervise the activities of those who carry out such tasks. These are all aspects of strategic planning. Needs assessment, while related to all of these activities, is a major input to priority setting and resource allocation considerations in the local government decision-making process.

This context requires that, in general, given scarce resources, the decision maker is interested in identifying concentrations of subpopulations with need and, furthermore, assumes a commitment to channeling resources in such a way that areas with greater need will receive larger amounts of resources. Managers therefore require effective indicators sensitive enough to delineate these areas of need.

An example

County-based indicators, to take one example, though useful for state planning activities, have proven to be inadequate for this sensitive spatial analysis. A county may rank relatively high when compared to other counties yet still have geographic pockets of high need. County indicators are usually made up of statistical averages, and more often than not, these averages mask subcounty conditions. For example, in a study of five southern counties, various health and social indicators suggested that their status was similar to the overall state average.[29] After the neighborhoods in these counties were delineated, however, it was found that, in some neighborhoods, mortality rates were almost twice as high as in others (a range of 13.9 per 1,000 population to 35.0 per 1,000); that crude death rates were almost three times higher (3.9 per 1,000 to 10.5 per 1,000); that out-of-wedlock pregnancies were almost ten times higher (3 percent of all live births to 34 percent); that residential fires per month were three times higher (4.3 per 1,000 to 18.3 per 1,000); and that arrests were six times higher (1.6 per 1,000 to 11.8 per 1,000). This example clearly illustrates the basic managerial problem presented by the fact that human problems and social need are not uniformly distributed in geographic space. One critical planning task is to find these variations among geographic units and use this information, when specific sets of programs are ready for implementation, to determine the appropriate location for these services.

Spatial analysis defined

As used in the context of this chapter, spatial analysis refers to the use of social indicators to classify geographic areas into typologies. These typologies are important in helping managers determine the extent of need. Such analyses have generally been carried out in metropolitan areas, though some efforts have explored their application to rural and semirural areas.[30] In deriving social indicators, small area analysis does not establish baseline indicators of quality of life or levels of absolute need but rather attempts to compare relative need by area and population group.

The construction of these indicators usually involves the combination of more than one variable and the formulation of a theoretical construct that measures some phenomenon. For management purposes, this process can be viewed as a device helping managers and others to assess the status of a community, to establish general priorities, to measure program impact, and to document change over time. The underlying assumption of indicator construction is that no one variable by itself is capable of tapping into complex social phenomena. Rather, what is needed is a construct that is able to summarize large amounts of data that are a part of those phenomena. In this sense, a health status indicator might include a combination of such factors as mortality rates, morbidity rates, and accessibility of medical care. An indicator of social equality might include measures of access to educational resources, employment, housing availability, and community participation in decision making.[31]

Planners and the managers to whom they report are faced with multiple data bases and literally hundreds of variables that may or may not prove important in determining need levels and in developing programs to meet those needs. It is inefficient, if not impossible, to obtain a coherent picture of the character of a geographic area by dealing separately with these variables and their permutations. Quite apart from the issue of efficiency is the concern for clarity and comprehension. Nonplanners faced with a deluge of information will have considerable difficulty in selecting for consideration those items of greatest relevance; a succinct presentation of carefully selected information is more likely to have an impact on managerial deliberations.

Factor analysis is a statistical technique which can be used to take a large number of variables and reduce these to a smaller number of constructs or indicators. The basis for factor analysis is the notion that if a large number of variables are intercorrelated, these interrelationships may be due to the presence of one or more underlying factors. According to this technique, those variables which are most highly correlated with the underlying factor should be highly related to each other. Clearly, this process can be of utility in undertaking spatial analyses. However, it needs to be emphasized that if the factors cannot be interpreted, that is, if the related variables do not make conceptual sense, factor analysis is of little value to the planner.[32]

Although the antecedents of small area analysis can be traced to the sociologist Park and the geographical approach of the human ecologists of the "Chicago School" of the 1920s, its major developments began in the early 1950s with the work of Shevky and Williams,[33] later modified by Shevky and Bell.[34] Since that time, a sizable body of information has begun to emerge, initially in developing approaches to classifying cities and gaining knowledge of political behavior[35] and later as a support methodology for the planning of human services.[36] The basic units of analysis are the census tracts which tend to be relatively small geographic areas (averaging 4,000–5,000 population) and which are subject to regular collection through the decennial census. In some cases, the analysis is complemented by the examination of smaller spatial units such as blocks or block groupings.[37]

Human services applications

It was only in the late 1960s that the factor analysis approach was used for human services planning. Wallace and her colleagues[38] reported on a study in San Francisco that utilized both factor analysis of census data and expert judgment based on available health and social data that attempted to identify the high risk areas in that city. Five analysts independently reviewed the indicators, and if an index was judged "useful" by at least four of the five, it was retained. The data were then subjected to a factor analysis, and the researchers worked on the assumption that the factor with the highest "loadings" for the largest number of social indexes represented a high risk factor. A single factor accounted for more than 43 percent of the indexes. The results of the two approaches (expert judgment and factor analysis) were found to be supportive in judging the usefulness of the variables. Of the twenty-nine health and social variables, nine were determined to be of significance: six social indexes—income, education, employment, overcrowding, family status, and illegitimacy—and three health indexes—prenatal care, prematurity, and the incidence of tuberculosis.

In 1967, a dress rehearsal of the 1970 census was carried out in New Haven, Connecticut.[39] Census data were combined with other information to develop a health information system which, in turn, was used to construct social indicators describing the health and social status at the census tract and block group level. The purpose of the effort was (1) to demonstrate how spatial analysis of related health and socioeconomic characteristics might identify high risk populations; (2) to establish a system by which related data could be made retrievable and analyzable by computers; and (3) to produce information which would point out health and social problems and needs as a basis for planning.

Using factor analysis, the researchers were able to identify one strong factor, labeled socioeconomic status, that was highly correlated with the prevalence of a number of human services problems. Following this, the five variables (income, education, occupation, family organization, and overcrowded housing) with the highest factor loadings were pulled out and combined to make up the indicator. Each census tract was ranked on each variable. The ranks were then added and averaged to arrive at a composite score.

This approach, with various modifications, has been used in the studies already cited [40] and each resulted in similar conclusions. To refine the specific types of human services needs, additional data are usually collected from various agencies, e.g., departments of health, social services, mental health, education, police, and housing. The major requirement is that these data be census tract-based. [41]

The sources for these analyses are the decennial census findings and data collected on an ongoing basis by various state and county agencies. (The census data are available on tapes and found in most major universities.)

It is evident that this approach is not a cure-all; as with any survey, it generates a static description of an area. It has value for planning, however, in that it establishes baseline data which help to estimate need levels, to develop priorities, to allocate resources and, eventually, to measure program impact.

A particular disadvantage of census data is its relatively infrequent updating, only every ten years. The Census Use Study of the Bureau of the Census has attempted to develop and maintain a system of social, health, and resource indicators that do not have the usual spatial and temporal limitations. [42] Based on a methodology common to urban planning—the housing unit procedure—1960 census data were analyzed to arrive at a figure for the average number of persons per dwelling unit. Each year from 1960 to 1970 these data were adjusted based on an inventory of building permits and demolitions. The tract population for each year was then derived by multiplying the estimated number of occupied dwelling units and the calculated residency factor. The results were later compared to the 1970 census and error ratios were calculated. Population projections for each tract between 1970 and 1980 were then calculated on the basis of 1960–1970 growth performance.

Summary

It is important to emphasize that the locational analyses and techniques described in this section are of real managerial significance when properly integrated into the local government decision-making and political process. Correct and timely identification of high risk populations by geographical area, when coupled with the proper use of other techniques for needs assessment, promotes both managerial control and a more efficient use of limited resources. The information produced by needs assessment surveys must, of course, be fed into the overall—and intensely political—local government decision-making environment. There, it may be used for different purposes by different levels of management and administration. Overall, however, the decision-making process is enhanced by the presence of such techniques. Their absence, conversely, can lead to less efficient disposition of resources, to the perpetuation of ineffective programs, and to inadequate anticipation of future trends.

Conclusion

The above comments fit into some wider remarks than can be made in conclusion concerning the analysis presented in this chapter. The position outlined, in essence, is that needs assessment has both qualitative and quantitative dimensions. It involves more than measurement of need, and attention must be given to what is to be measured. Needs assessment, in this context, begins with problem analysis;

only after this is completed can the quantitative aspect be addressed. The second major phase of any planning process—the formulation of goals and objectives—is directly influenced by the needs assessment task. Insofar as objectives have to be stated in measurable, timebound terms, needs assessment provides target data. Finally, need estimates become the basis for the evaluation of program adequacy, that is, the impact of the program in relation to the numbers of persons in the target population. All of these processes have clear managerial significance.

A major issue—the concept of need—has also been explored. It was suggested that need is elastic and changes over time. Noted also was the influence on need of service delivery patterns and the indications that need is likely to increase along with the increase of service provision. In spite of this, it was argued that planners and managers should generate targets for both short-term and long-term planning requirements, targets that can be linked to resources and budget estimates. These budget estimates can then be used to inform the general public and to marshal support from other decision makers and elected officials.

Four ways of looking at need were also outlined: the normative; the perceived; the expressed; and the relative. The uniqueness of each approach and the complementary perspectives they provide to planners and managers were discussed. Later, a number of methodologies were explored that are useful for determining levels of need. These methods are interdependent in that none, by itself, provides a total assessment and each can be classified under one of four categories. Strengths and limitations for each approach were identified, and it was argued that time and resource constraints are the critical factors that determine which of these will best serve in a given situation.

1 Robert Mayer, Robert Moroney, and Robert Morris, *Centrally Planned Change: A Reexamination of Theory and Experience* (Urbana: University of Illinois Press, 1974), pp. 1–16.

2 Robert N. Anthony, *Planning and Control Systems* (Cambridge: Harvard University Press, 1965).

3 Robert Morris and Frank Zweig, "The Social Planning Design Guide: Process and Proposal," *Social Work* 11 (April 1966): 13–21; and Nathan Cohen, *Social Work and Social Problems* (New York: National Association of Social Workers, 1964), pp. 362–91.

4 J. A. Ponsioen, *Social Welfare Policy: Contributions to Theory,* Publications of the Institute of Social Studies, Series Maior, vol. 3 (The Hague: Mouton & Co., 1962).

5 Abraham Maslow, *Motivation and Personality* (New York: Harper & Row, 1954), pp. 80–106.

6 Mollie Orshansky, "Counting the Poor: Another Look at the Poverty Profile," *Social Security Bulletin* 28 (January 1965): 3–29; Mollie Orshansky, "Who's Who Among the Poor: A Demographic View of Poverty," *Social Security Bulletin* 28 (July 1965): 3–32; and Mollie Orshansky, "Measuring Poverty," in *The Social Welfare Forum* (New York: Columbia University Press, 1965), pp. 211–23.

7 Michael Harrington, *The Other America: Poverty in the United States* (New York: Macmillan Co., 1962).

8 Robert Moroney, *The Family and the State: Consideration for Social Policy* (London: Longmans, 1976); Brandeis University, Levinson Gerontological Policy Institute, *Alternatives to Nursing Home Care: A Proposal,* prepared for the U.S. Senate, Special Committee on Aging (Washington, D.C.: Government Printing Office, 1971); and Eva Kahana and Rodney Coe, "Alternatives in Long-Term Care," in *Long-Term Care: A Handbook for Researchers, Planners, and Providers,* ed. Sylvia Sherwood (Holliswood, N.Y.: Spectrum Pubns., 1975), pp. 511–72.

9 This delineation is based on the work discussed in Jonathan Bradshaw, "The Concept of Social Need," *New Society,* 30 March 1972, pp. 640–43.

10 Janet Reiner, Everett Reiner, and Thomas Reiner, "Client Analysis and the Planning of Public Programs," *Journal of the American Institute of Planners* 29 (November 1963): 270–82.

11 The Title XX amendments (1975) to the Social Security Act replaced the existing Titles IV-A and VI, and require states to develop comprehensive social service systems to meet the needs of their populations.

12 U.S., Department of Commerce, Bureau of the Census, *United States Census of Population: 1970,* Report no. PC(2)-9A, *Low Income Population.*

13 Lawrence Riley and Saad Nagi, eds., *Disability in the United States: A Compendium of Data and Prevalence and Programs* (Columbus, Ohio: Ohio State University, College of Medicine, Dept. of Physical Medicine, 1970).

14 U.S., Department of Commerce, Bureau of the Census, *United States Census of Population and Housing: 1970.*

15 Although the example is hypothetical, there are a number of examples available of applications of this approach. See Booz, Allen and Hamilton, Inc., "A Methodology for Projecting and Evaluating Health Facility and Service Needs," prepared for the North Carolina Office of Comprehensive Health Planning, Washington, D.C., 27 April 1971; and Metropolitan Atlanta Council for Health, "Assessment of the

Availability of Hospital Beds within the Atlanta Metropolitan Planning Region," Atlanta, 14 October 1971. These studies are examples of a large number of efforts to go beyond the more traditional methodology emerging from the Hill-Burton program where need was viewed as a function of population alone.

16 The four agencies are the National Center for Health Statistics, the Bureau of Labor Statistics, the Bureau of the Census, and the Department of Agriculture's Reporting Service.

17 See, for example, David Gil, *Violence Against Children* (Cambridge: Harvard University Press, 1970).

18 See, for example, Learning Institute of North Carolina, *Who Cares for Children? A Survey of Needs* (Raleigh, N. Car.: North Carolina Department of Human Resources, 1972); and Nicholas Hobbs, ed., *The Futures of Children* (San Francisco: Jossey-Bass, 1975).

19 See, for example, Ethel Shanas et al., *Old People in Three Industrial Societies* (London: Routledge and Kegan Paul, 1968); and Amelia Harris, *Social Welfare for the Elderly* (London: Her Majesty's Stationery Office, 1968).

20 See, for example, Jack Tizard, "Epidemiology of Mental Retardation," in *Early Malnutrition and Mental Development,* ed. J. Cravioto (Uppsala: Almquist & Wiksell, 1974), pp. 27–38; and A. Kushlick, "The Prevalence of Recognized Mental Subnormality of IQ Under 50 Among Children in the South of England with Reference to the Demand for Residential Care," in *Proceedings of the International Copenhagen Congress on the Study of Mental Retardation,* eds. J. Ostler and H. V. Sletved, vol. 2, n.p., August 1964, p. 550.

21 See, for example, The President's Commission on Law Enforcement and Administration of Justice, Task Force on Juvenile Delinquency, *Juvenile Delinquency and Youth Crime,* (Washington, D.C.: Government Printing Office, 1967).

22 See, for example, G. Gurin et al., *Americans View Their Mental Health* (New York: Basic Books, 1960); August B. Hollingshead and Frederick C. Redlich, *Social Class and Mental Illness* (New York: John Wiley & Sons, 1958); E. Gartley Jaco, *The Social Epidemiology of Mental Disorders—A Psychiatric Survey of Texas* (New York: Russell Sage Foundation, 1962); Leo Srole et al., *Mental Health in the Metropolis: The Midtown Manhattan Study* (New York: McGraw-Hill, 1962); and Alexander Leighton, *My Name Is Legion* (New York: Basic Books, 1959).

23 For one example of a general text on epidemiology, see Brian MacMahan, Thomas Pugh, and Johannes Ipsen, *Epidemiological Methods* (Boston: Little, Brown & Co., 1960).

24 The two studies cited are Ethel Shanas et al., *Old People in Three Industrial Societies;* and Amelia Harris, *Social Welfare for the Elderly.*

25 See Leo Srole et al., *Mental Health in the Metropolis;* E. Gartley Jaco, *The Social Epidemiology of Mental Disorders;* Alexander Leighton, *My Name Is Legion;* and August B. Hollingshead and Frederick C. Redlich, *Social Class and Mental Illness.*

26 Robert Moroney, *The Family and the State.*

27 Norman Polansky, "Social Research," in *Encyclopedia of Social Work,* 16th ed., vol. 2 (New York: National Association of Social Workers, 1971), pp. 1102–03.

28 Andre Delbecq et al., *Group Techniques for Program Planning: A Guide to Nominal Group and Delphi Processes* (Glenview, Ill.: Scott, Foresman & Co., 1975).

29 Robert Moroney, "Utilization of Small Area Data Analysis for Evaluation," in *Evaluation in Health Services Delivery,* eds. Richard Yaffe and David Zalkind, proceedings of an Engineering Foundation conference (n.p.: Engineering Foundation, 1973), pp. 246–57.

30 U.S., Department of Commerce, Bureau of the Census, *Social and Health Indicators System: Parts I, II—Rural,* Census Use Study (Washington, D.C.: Government Printing Office, 1973).

31 For a discussion of the conceptual and methodological issues related to social indicators, see Raymond Bauer, ed., *Social Indicators* (Cambridge: M.I.T. Press, 1966); and Jan Drewnowski, *Studies in the Measurement of Levels of Living and Welfare,* report no. 73 (Geneva: United Nations Research Institute for Social Development, 1970).

32 For a comprehensive discussion of factor analysis, see Harry Harmon, *Modern Factor Analysis,* 2nd ed. (Chicago: University of Chicago Press, 1967).

33 Eshref Shevky and Marilyn Williams, *The Social Areas of Los Angeles: Analysis and Typology* (Berkeley: University of California Press, 1949).

34 Eshref Shevky and Wendell Bell, *Social Area Analysis* (Stanford, Calif.: Stanford University Press, 1955).

35 For a compilation of these activities, see Brian Berry, ed., *City Classification Handbook: Methods and Applications* (New York: John Wiley & Sons, 1972).

36 In the area of health, see Helen Wallace et al., "Availability and Usefulness of Selected Health and Socio-Economic Data for Community Planning," *American Journal of Public Health* 57 (May 1967): 762–71; U.S., Department of Commerce, Bureau of the Census, *Health Information System: Part II,* Census Use Study, report no. 12 (Washington, D.C.: Government Printing Office, 1971); U.S., Department of Commerce, Bureau of the Census, *Social and Health Indicators,* Census Use Study (Washington, D.C.: Government Printing Office, 1973); and Robert Moroney et al., "The Uses of Small Area Analysis in Community Health Planning," *Inquiry* 13 (June 1976): 145–51.

In the area of mental health, see Richard Redich and Harold Goldsmith, *1970 Census Data Used to Indicate Areas with Different Potentials for Mental Health and Related Problems,* Department of Health, Education, and Welfare Publication no. (HSM) 72-9051 (Washington, D.C.: Government Printing Office, 1971); and Samuel Korper, *Utilization of Community Mental Health Services: An Approach to Measurement and Factor Identification* (New Haven, Conn.: Yale University, School of Medicine, 1976).

In the area of deviant behavior, see Clifford Shaw and Henry McKay, *Juvenile Delinquency and Urban Areas* (Chicago: University of Chicago Press, 1942); Harold Pfautz and Robert Hyde, "The Ecology of Alcohol in the Local Community," *Quarterly Journal of Studies on Alcohol* 21 (September 1960): 447–56; and Austin Potterfield, "Suicide and Crime in the Social Structure of an Urban Setting," *American Sociological Review* 17 (June 1952): 341–49.

37 For example, the Census Use Study for New Haven, Connecticut, showed that tract data masked heterogeneity. By using block group data (500–1,600 pop-

ulation), more meaningful geographic lines were determined.

38   Helen Wallace et al., "Availability and Usefulness of Selected Health and Socio-Economic Data."

39   U.S., Department of Commerce, Bureau of the Census, *Health Information System: Part II.*

40   Helen Wallace et al., "Availability and Usefulness of Selected Health and Socio-Economic Data."

41   For various approaches to this issue, see U.S., Department of Commerce, Bureau of the Census, *The DIME Geocoding System,* Census Use Study (Washington, D.C.: Government Printing Office, 1970); and U.S., Department of Commerce, Bureau of the Census, *ADMATCH Users Manual,* Census Use Study (Washington, D.C.: Government Printing Office, 1970).

42   U.S., Department of Commerce, Bureau of the Census, *Social and Health Indicators.*

Deciding on priorities and specific programs

Demystifying the process of determining, designing, and managing human services and human resources programs and problem-solving efforts represents one of the central themes of this book. Nowhere is this more appropriate than in the process by which local governments actually design and fund specific human services efforts—the topic of this chapter. Too often the rhetoric of social concern—"war on poverty," "wiping out drug abuse," "ending discrimination forever"—together with the lack of established social planning principles and techniques lead to well-meant but ill-considered and unsuccessful program choices. This chapter therefore outlines a series of decisions and steps that local governments and their managers may take to ensure that they are using a maximum of common sense and clear thinking, together with the best of what we already know about planning and designing social-problem-solving efforts. It thus adds an additional, specific emphasis to the two preceding chapters in Part Two, and provides a "bridge" to the management chapters of Part Three.

Based largely upon municipal experiences in California [1] (the authors are affiliated with the League of California Cities' efforts to help its member cities respond to social problems of the 1970s), this chapter is divided into six major sections. The first four outline the following basic steps: identifying priority problems and goals; adopting effective solution strategies; choosing appropriate local government roles; and developing implementation plans. In addition, the chapter will describe some organizational considerations for integrating this process with the existing city planning and policy-making process, and will conclude by pointing to some resources that might be available for use in this effort. The emphasis throughout the discussion will be practical, and directed at local government decision makers.

The underlying assumptions of the chapter should perhaps be stated at the outset. They may be summarized as follows:

1. Local government funding resources for the delivery of social programs may be very limited.
2. The local government is the most appropriate entity for determining local needs.
3. The local government is concerned enough with the social needs of its citizens to take steps to see that these needs are met.
4. Policy-making involvement—by both elected and appointed officials—is essential to the success of any effort to solve social problems.
5. All resources will be considered—for example, city and noncity, county and noncounty, public and private— in designing solutions.
6. All local government departments, commissions, and members of the council and administration, together with citizens, community groups, service providers and professionals, and business and industry representatives can be involved in this process in one way or another.
7. Any problem affecting community residents—regardless of location or mandated responsibility—may be considered for action by the local government.

These basic assumptions lead to the development of several themes which weave through the chapter:

1. That local governments best explore and exploit the "obtainer" role in their problem-solving strategies since most other agencies have more money and experience in providing direct services.
2. That local governments expand the capacity to relate social problems and their solutions to their ongoing public safety, physical planning, and legislative responsibilities. The development of nonservice solutions to problems is essential, given the limitations on all sources of service funds.
3. That local governments see themselves in a social policy leadership role, regardless of the extent to which they deliver services. As the "Action Plan for the Social Responsibilities of Cities," adopted by California cities in 1973, puts it: "Each city should assume responsibility for identifying all community social needs, and for planning, coordinating, and evaluating programs to alleviate social problems within its boundaries. Cities should ensure the delivery of all essential social services either by serving as an advocate or catalyst to ensure the most effective delivery of service by the appropriate public and/or private agencies or by delivering such services themselves." [2]

The major theme of this chapter is priority setting. The term is used here to mean "effective choice" rather than "absolute value." In any field of endeavor, it is essential that priorities be set and the most efficient, effective, and promising approaches be adopted. We are not discussing whether child care is more important to Americans than programs to alleviate the problems of drug abuse; nor if the remedies for unemployment are more important than those for ill health; nor ways in which cities or counties can make such decisions. Rather we are interested in exploring the specific techniques of problem analysis, program design, and local government activity that will lead to the most effective local government decisions. We hope to describe ways to make "effective choices" about problems, techniques, and approaches.

Identifying priority problems and goals

Some basic considerations:
or, Which insoluble problem do we tackle first?

The most important concept for local government managers to remember is that social planning is an art, not a science. Until it becomes one, decision makers' best tools are plain ordinary information, common sense, and even intuition. (A little luck comes in handy, too.) Most likely, all of a city or county's decision making in the human resources arena can be boiled down to six sets of questions that managers can ask themselves:

1. Does this problem represent a *crying need* in my city or county? Is it clear and understandable to all in the community that this is a problem? Is it a matter of controversy that it is a problem? Or is it something that many can agree is a serious problem?
2. Can my city or county government really have an *impact* on this problem? Where can you be most effective? Is the solution something that the city or county is capable of effecting? For example, many people may agree that the education level of the current school population is not what it should be, or that the administration of welfare is inefficient, or that too many people in town are unemployed. To what extent can the community's resources, political clout, and skill cause or facilitate significant change?
3. Is there a *constituency* of concerned or affected citizens associated with this problem? It is quite possible that some problems in the community have an

identifiable, visible, and vocal constituency. Mental health problems and community recreation issues, for example, frequently have quasi-formal interest groups designed to advance and support their particular concerns. These constituencies, however, can cut two ways: they can provide support for particular local government policy initiatives and programs which may be a plus in initiating their human resources efforts. At the same time, they may solidify as a permanent interest group which may fight future changes that the local government may wish to make. In other words, once you create the program, you also build in a constituency which may limit options in the future.

4. Are this problem and the solutions associated with it very *controversial* in my city? This may be an area to stay away from or, conversely, to use to build credibility for the local government's problem-solving capability. In one California city, for example, serious controversies over drug abuse in the schools led to city involvement in a series of drug abuse programs which, in turn, became the foundation for wide-scale needs assessment and long-range social planning efforts on the part of the city. Its ability to deal with a very controversial and significant problem strengthens its credibility for moving into other areas. On the other hand, it is also possible that controversial issues in the community such as busing—to pick an extreme example—may be ones to stay completely away from. If the local government has little chance to provide constructive efforts on a particular problem, it may be best not to tackle it, especially in your initial human services efforts.

5. What *other public and private agencies* are involved in this problem and are they interested? As mentioned above, sometimes the most effective way for communities to work on social problems is through the services and programs of other agencies, rather than their own. Consequently, if cities are faced with the problem of dealing with educational, health, or transportation problems, the best way to determine which to deal with may be on the basis of the ability of the city to influence the school district, county, or transportation agency responsible for dealing with that particular area. Which agency can you work with? Which not? Which agency is legally responsible for dealing with the problem?

6. Are there any *unique circumstances or opportunities* of which our local government can take advantage in connection with this problem? Are funds available? Has capacity been built in a particular problem area? Are facilities becoming available, such as school buildings? Will a small local outlay of funds leverage significant response from the county, state, or federal governments or from private agencies?

Funding social programs: can social problems be ranked?

Anyone who has ever been faced with the prospect of deciding upon a variety of social services funding proposals knows the impossibility of being totally logical or rational about choosing between a child care program or a drug abuse service, between a park and a hospital. Who is to say which is more important? At the same time, anyone who has participated in a formal ranking process knows that efforts to decide questions of priority and primacy before the allocation decision are also likely to be fraught with elements of irrationality, imprecision, and subjectivity. Furthermore, there is never an ironclad guarantee that the priority-ranking process will be followed to the letter in the allocation process.

The key issue   The key issue for local governments—especially those just entering the human resources arena—is whether to base funding decisions upon prior efforts to define issues and set goals and, if so, whether to establish a formal rank order of services and issues or to set more general priority principles and policies with which to guide funding and allocation decisions.

Many cities and counties simply don't bother at all with such advance planning. They set aside a percentage of revenue sharing or community development block grant funds, invite proposals, and fund the best ones. One California city, for example, assumes that all social program funding proposals reflect substantially legitimate needs. Consequently no effort is made to set priorities among areas of need. Instead, fund allocation is based on two criteria, merits and cost. The advantage of this approach is its simplicity. The problem is its "hit or miss" quality. The proposals funded may not be dealing with the problems the city or county is best equipped to tackle, or they may be in areas in which the prospects for success are limited. There is no assurance that the most severe problems are being addressed. In short, the long-range impact of such an approach is questionable.

Overcoming the ad hoc approach   A great many cities are beginning to overcome this ad hoc approach to social problem solving by making a more substantial effort to define and describe important community problems and to set goals before making funding decisions. Pasadena, for example, compares the purposes of the proposals it receives with the goals established in its general plan and elsewhere. The city of Hayward, which has had a very effective human services department and program of support for community-based service providers, has developed an elaborate and sensitive needs assessment process to guide its funding and programming decisions. Garden Grove, San Leandro, Brea, and others are developing background and issue papers in a variety of problem areas to assist policy makers in resolving human resources issues.

How to fund community agencies without really crying   One problem that has brought anguish to many administrators is that of providing funds to community agencies for programs of interest to the city, without going willy-nilly out of control. In Pasadena, California, the city board of directors adopted a "resource allocation process" to evaluate requests for revenue sharing funds. Its first use will be in allocating CETA funds for manpower programs. Here's how it works. Community agencies are invited to submit program proposals to meet objectives defined by the city. Through its review process, the city selects that combination of proposals which seems best suited to confront the problems. The selection is based on the recommendations of a special task force established by the city board of directors and the city manager. In light of comparative scores, the task force will recommend a comprehensive "action plan" (funding package) to the city manager, who will present it to the board of directors along with his own recommendations.

United Way agencies, whose major function is the allocation of funds to social programs, have a long history of working with priority-setting processes and techniques. They have not settled upon a simple, agreed-upon method for measuring or ranking one set of problems, neighborhoods, target groups, or services against another in any formal, rational fashion. However, they have developed a comprehensive set of tools, techniques, and systems that make social program planning and evaluating a more feasible enterprise. A United Way of America publication suggests two approaches to priority setting—the establishment of guiding policy statements, and the creation of a formal ranking and measurement process. The report concludes that "a simple policy statement approach is intrinsically as valid as a more complex ranking approach." [3]

The ranking approach   The ranking approach most frequently orders specific services, although it could address needs and goals, geographical areas, agencies, or population groups. However, in spite of the possible use of rating scales and like methods, it is still a judgment, not a measurement process. The key to its success is the degree of consensus, support, and involvement in the design of the process which encompasses five elements: (1) what will be ranked (agencies, services, etc.)? ; (2) what criteria will be used? ; (3) what method will be used to apply criteria (a panel, a rating scale)? ; (4) how will the ranking be measured (continuum, groups)? ; and (5) how will the priorities be built into the actual ongoing allocation process? [4]

The Albuquerque Community Council,[5] a United Way planning agency, conducted a priority-setting effort that utilized a group of over 300 community leaders representing such various interests as Model Cities, citizens' boards, city and county governments, the state legislature, United Community Fund, and various ethnic and cultural groups. Their task was to rank the various services present in the community in order of importance to reveal those problem areas deemed most significant. They were also asked to rank the *adequacy of services*. In addition, the professionals were asked to estimate whether the quantity of services was sufficient to meet the needs. This was a rough estimate of the number of people being served versus the number of people estimated to be in need of the services. Thus, a broad-based citizen process was employed to identify priority needs as well as the types of problems most in need of attention.

Formal studies of private-sector ranking processes carried out during the 1960s suggest that, although there were innumerable benefits derived from them, they lacked the precision they appeared to possess and—even more important—they were not as effective in determining allocation decisions as the work that went into them warranted.[6] The efforts did produce invaluable collections of social problem data that were well organized and laid out. The involvement of laymen and professionals provided significant community education and support for social-problem-solving efforts. They did produce generally agreed-upon goals which served as a cohesive, unifying force as well as a jumping-off point for future discussions and plans.

Establishment of priority policies These benefits could probably be obtained from the second United Way approach to priority development: the establishment of priority policies. This technique is much closer to the traditional city use of the general plan to spell out some long-range goals in a number of different areas. The actual decision of how much emphasis to place upon the achievement of each goal is to be taken up in the day-to-day decision-making and strategy-setting processes of the organization. The policies give direction and reflect a broadly based decision-making process, but do not have the apparent finality and rigidity of a rank order priority-setting process. For example, the Columbus, Ohio, United Community Council articulated a set of priorities policies as follows:

The Priority Plan recommends five policies to United Appeal for use in allocating resources to meet the goals of the 70s.
1. Only those services which compare favorably with specific criteria in regard to relevancy and quality should be funded by United Appeal.
2. United Appeal should consider support of core services for their agencies.
3. United Appeal should support selective purchase of services from the agency or agencies best able to supply clearly specified services.
4. United Appeal should support selective evaluation on a regular basis of purchased services provided by agencies.
5. Agencies should be encouraged to find sources of funds other than, but in addition to, United Appeal funds.[7]

Summary In conclusion, therefore, unless cities and counties are committed to the funding of significant numbers of community services and agencies, and are facing community pressure to justify these funding decisions, it seems likely that the general priority policies, needs analyses, and goal-setting efforts will be adequate.

In fact, many communities are utilizing these processes to improve their overall decision-making mechanisms.

Needs assessment analysis and community goal setting:
tools for long-range action and community decision making

Increasingly, cities and counties are developing sophisticated processes for charting paths to long-range problem areas, regardless of funding opportunities. City officials in Hayward, to take an example, expect that the city's needs assessment process will ultimately be built into its annual policy budgeting process to offer a "social dimension" to all of its decision-making efforts. Hayward's effort is an extremely sensitive, multifaceted process for defining community problems. Designed initially for guidance in allocating revenue sharing funds, current expectation is that it will become part of the council's ongoing information and decision-making process. It includes: reviewing key census data, agency service records, and police, health, mental health, and other statistical sources; developing key social indicators in social problem areas; conducting neighborhood meetings in all city census tracts; developing and updating a services inventory; holding citywide conferences for providers and clients to identify problems; meeting with specific community special interest groups; administering a written questionnaire to a representative sample of community residents; conducting in-depth interviews with key service providers and policy makers; and holding public hearings and meetings on design of the needs assessment.

Many communities approach this problem from the point of view of goals, frequently developed in a citizen-oriented goals study process. More and more human resources issues—senior citizens, child care, education—are raised in these endeavors. A goal-setting process in Alameda, California, took a whole year and involved substantial efforts of citizen task forces which produced long-range goal statements in crime prevention, economic development, education, housing and physical planning, human services, planned growth, recreation and cultural facilities, and transportation. (See Figure 6–1.)

To provide a baseline of citizen attitudes and to develop goals for the city's future, the city of Alameda, California, carried out an extensive citizen participation process. Several different techniques were used in the process, including a mail questionnaire, citywide meetings, task forces, and an interview survey. The results of the study were ratified by the city council and used for revising the city's general plan.

The process was initiated in October, 1973, when the city council approved a prospectus for the goals study. Partial funding was obtained through the Department of Housing and Urban Development's (HUD) "701" Planning Assistance Program. The council assigned responsibility for overseeing the process to the goals study steering committee, consisting of two city council members, two members of the planning board, and two citizens appointed by the council. In August, 1974, the firm of Urban Management Consultants of San Francisco, Inc., was engaged to assist the steering committee and to facilitate the process by conducting certain of the more technical aspects of the study, including two surveys.

To determine the problem areas that should be addressed by the study, mail questionnaires were sent to each of Alameda's 27,000 households in October, 1974. Residents were asked to comment on a wide range of community issues: community services, appearance, housing, schools and education, recreational facilities, shopping facilities, city taxes and services, and major problem areas. The response rate to the mail questionnaire was unusually high with 23 percent of the city responding.

The preliminary results of this survey were presented to the community at the first citywide congress, held in January, 1975. The purpose of this general community meeting was to organize citizen task forces around the crucial issues

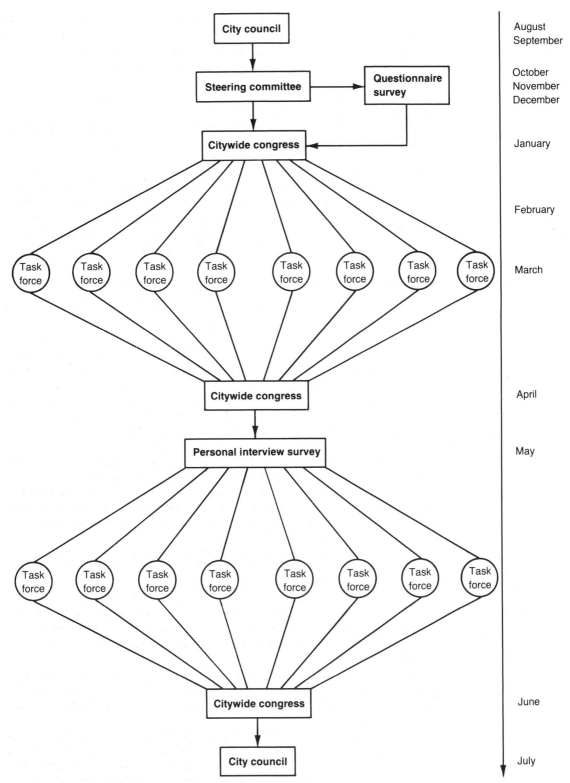

Figure 6–1 Goals study process undertaken by the City of Alameda, California.

revealed through the questionnaire. The congress was attended by nearly 1,300 residents, and over 400 signed up to participate on task forces in the areas of crime prevention, economic development, education, housing and physical planning, human services, planned growth, recreation and cultural facilities, and transportation.

The task forces met at least weekly for the next three months to consider in detail the problems facing the city in their respective areas, and to develop a series of preliminary goal statements. Graduate students in urban planning were hired to provide staff support to the task forces. The preliminary goals were presented in the second meeting of the citywide congress in April.

To validate the task force goals with a cross-section of citizen opinions and to set priorities among the goals, personal interviews were conducted with 1,000 randomly selected residents. This "validation survey" was completed in May, 1975. Each task force used the results of this survey to refine and modify their work, and to prepare a final report. These reports were consolidated into a single document, "Goals for Alameda," which was adopted by the city council.

Three techniques: generating consensus in priority setting

The biggest problem in setting priorities in human resources stems from the fact that the issues are often so controversial and hard to "measure" that broad community agreement is hard to get. Citizens, agencies, city or county staff, and elected officials all have their individual agendas that can be counted on to emerge as "nonnegotiable" at any time. There are no magic formulas that will automatically overcome this problem. The success of any effort depends upon the chemistry of each situation—the insight, patience, imagination, luck, and the courage to make a decision that city or county officials can bring to bear. However, a number of techniques have proven useful in assisting such an effort.

The "nominal group process" The "nominal group process" brings together small groups of diverse individuals.[8] This technique was developed at the University of Wisconsin specifically for problem identification and program planning. It has been used in Hayward's needs assessment process and in a number of other communities. It is uniquely designed to bring together groups and individuals not familiar with one another.

The process begins by dividing participants into small groups of eight to ten. Each subgroup has a trained leader. Citizen volunteers, commissioners, members of the city's needs assessment committee, and, in some cases, city staff have served as leaders. Participants are asked to write down their needs. These individual lists are combined into a single list for each group. After clarification and discussion of each of the needs listed, group members write down their top five priority items. The leader tallies these votes and prepares a list of the group's top five priorities.

The list of each of the groups is posted on a wall where all the participants may review them. Reporters explain briefly each item and then all vote on the top five priority items from each of the group lists. Votes are tallied and reported as the consensus of the group.

The strengths of this approach are that it facilitates innovation and creativity in generating ideas. As distinct from a brainstorming approach, the process is highly structured, and the most verbal participants are not allowed to dominate. This model can be used with groups brought together for the first time or with established groups. It is broadly applicable in situations where creative thinking is needed to identify and rank problems, needs, service strategies, etc.

The process can be used for a large gathering of people as long as there are enough trained leaders to help facilitate the small groups which are created. It is most effective for bringing diverse groups and individuals together where no previous interaction mechanisms had existed. The small groups and the structured discussion process enable all to have an equal chance to participate and, consequently, gain a feeling of involvement and "ownership" in the outcome. The success of the effort in a communitywide needs assessment or goal-setting process depends to a large degree on the representativeness of the group participating and on its willingness to "trust" the process established by the community. The process can be used on a neighborhood basis, or among community groups and service providers.

The Delphi process   The Delphi process was designed to obtain input from a wide variety of knowledgeable people in a formal, systematic fashion, without ever having to bring them together. In fact, by organizing the input process like the spokes and hub of a wheel, the local government staff (at the hub) can control the flow and frequency of the input. The process, carried out by mail over a significant period of time, is capable of obtaining the considered thought of a wide variety of important people at very little expense. There are a number of stages involved.

The process begins with a question. For example, "What do you believe are the ten most important problems confronting our community? Describe them, indicating why you feel they are important." A group of leading professional, technical, and political leaders actively involved in the field are selected and asked to respond in writing. Their responses are compiled and sent out again to all participants with the request that they consider the responses of the others, then answer the question again. Thus, each has the opportunity to see the aggregate set of priorities that resulted from the first round, together with definitions and reasons, before responding again. The tendency is for this exposure to generate movement toward consensus. This step can be repeated several times until the organizers see that individuals are no longer changing their responses. The process is therefore simple and flexible to operate.

Orange County, California, utilized this process as one of the tools to guide the allocation of its social revenue sharing program in the early 1970s. Its base of experts included "participants professionally or otherwise actively engaged in a given area or concern in the delivery of services." Participants were not known to one another. The process went through three stages and produced a list of twenty-two priority human services, together with a list of service descriptions. Significantly, the priority list was supplemented by the board of supervisors in their allocation decisions with statistical analyses, the value of individual proposals, and the existence of alternative methods of funding. The process, however, clearly gave their decisions a "legitimate" public base together with a "consensus" against which discussion and future direction could be measured. It was thus a useful managerial tool.

Simple ranking   Often, the problem is how to generate some direction within an already existing group specifically assigned to make some priority decisions. A human services commission, a task force of city staff from different departments, or a group of human services administrators and professionals that cuts across city and agency lines may have difficulty charting a direction for itself. One way to set some parameters and generate consensus is to present the group with a very comprehensive list of problems and possible issues for its attention. Members can then rank them according to some degree of importance, with those ranking among the highest to be the key areas for the group. In San Leandro, California, for example, members of the human services commission take a series of problem statements and rank them in order of importance on a five-point scale. These rankings are compiled and a composite score reached. All of those with a score of "very important" or above are considered by the city for further analysis to develop specific implementation efforts.

Adopting effective strategies

For many cities, the major difference between the human resources arena and the more traditional domains of physical planning, recreation, zoning, etc. is the fact that cities are already burdened with many programmatic and legislative responsibilities in these areas. Human resources represents a unique opportunity for them to adopt a role and strategy in which they can have specialized and effective impact. The most important asset in local government human resources action planning is the ability to analyze and understand a problem and to discern the most effective community role in resolving it.

Analyzing the situation: or, How come this problem seems insoluble?

Human resources program planning and design begin with the local government manager's ability to analyze and understand the following six factors:

Severity and extent   It is always possible to make some numerical estimation or measurement of a problem. Too often we go overboard with elaborate charts, statistics, and correlations that overwhelm us with more than we need to know. But it is essential that action be predicated on some understanding of such questions as: How many people are affected? How severely? How widespread or concentrated are they? What is the trend?

For example, it will make a big difference in the type of action your community will undertake if a drug abuse problem is concentrated among 14–17-year-olds attending one particular high school than if it is citywide among a broader age group. Similarly, child care needs may differ among varying neighborhoods, and socioeconomic and cultural groups. Most important, if a problem is skyrocketing in incidence compared with previous years, it might merit special attention.

Interrelationships   If they can be discovered, it is useful to understand the connections between problems in one area and those in another. As soft a "science" and as controversial a topic as human resources is, decision makers too often wait for scientific proof before they act on observed connections that ought obviously to be taken into consideration. High incidences of some problems among certain groups or neighborhoods are frequently experienced by those suffering from other problems as well. Poverty, drug abuse, educational problems, and health difficulties frequently go together. It is possible to consider unified or integrated approaches to these problems. Such understanding suggests the possibility of using an existing problem solving vehicle (school counseling, for example) to help with other problems (drug abuse, crime).

For example, it is fairly well-known that burglary and drug abuse often are related to one another. Similarly, ethnically segregated neighborhoods are often sites of higher than normal incidences of housing deterioration, street crime, unemployment, and educational problems. It is also a fact that a number of cities have developed statistical and interviewing techniques to track problems by neighborhood, ethnic groups and by race, sex and age.

Underlying causes   While it is not necessary to find the complete explanation of such age-old problems as poverty, alienation, race prejudice, and social apathy, it is useful to understand how these national patterns operate in your own community. Your own efforts then can be aimed as closely as possible at "root causes." Furthermore, if the deeper causes are understood and solutions voiced from the city level, a basis can be laid for national and state action. There is no magic formula for establishing these understandings and connections. In some cases, common sense, sensitivity, and a willingness to explore these factors will get you on the right road. In others, the dynamics of a problem may be more complex and will require a more thorough analysis.

For example, it is useful to know if your city's unemployment rate is in line with the national rate or if it is higher, owing to local economic problems. Further, significant health problems may be related to particular age groups, such as senior citizens, or to certain subpopulations, such as those associated with military bases. Financial institution lending policies may affect housing starts and/or rehabilitations. State or national regulations or programs may be needed to make improvements.

Barriers to solution   There are a variety of factors that stand in the way of solving the problem. If there weren't, chances are someone else would have already figured out what was wrong and moved ahead. Lack of funds, organizational competition and turf protecting, personality clashes, political rivalries, political trade-offs, public misunderstanding or ignorance, and structural problems will have a serious impact on any step—even the most carefully thought out—that may be tried. It is well to bring an understanding of these realities as a "test" for any of the alternative approaches that are to be considered.

For example, if there are no funds available, some solutions will clearly have to be scrapped or curtailed, or substantial efforts put into fund-raising. Further, if the organizations charged with dealing with a problem are fragmented and uncooperative, a coordinated solution may be hard to accomplish.

Previous efforts   As cities and counties begin to move into new areas of concern, there is a tendency not only to "reinvent the wheel," but to feel that "we discovered the territory." Serious efforts must be made to find out from county and city officials, citizen groups, agency professionals, and others what experience has taught them. Over the years different approaches and strategies have been applied. Previous efforts to provide facilities, to develop new programs, to coordinate services, and to reach new populations hold lessons—both positive and negative—for current strategists. They also provide a key to understanding the motivations and approaches of the other actors on the human resources scene. For example, in the 1960s and early 1970s, numerous efforts through Community Action Agencies, Model Cities, and local "alternative" agencies tried numerous solutions to human resources problems. The accomplishments and problems of these efforts are valuable keys to understanding the roles, potential, and position of current agencies, personalities, and programs.

Current situation   Developing an awareness of current conditions requires knowledge of more than just problem data themselves. Significant elements to be aware of include: evidence of public concern, availability of new or terminated funds, rapid population shifts, evidence of serious program failures or gaps. For example, grand jury reports, newspaper articles, new state or federal guidelines or funding decisions, management problems, or a dramatic human interest event can have a significant impact on the timing, success, and acceptability of human resources initiatives.

Considering alternative approaches:
or, We ought to be able to try something!

There are a wide variety of alternatives to solving problems. Most approaches to social problem solving may be found in the following seven categories: education, prevention, individual treatment, rehabilitation, enforcement, management support, and institutional change. The determination of the most effective solution to the problem should be clearly separated from the decision as to the local government's role in bringing about such a solution. If it is determined that a new service is needed, it should not automatically be assumed that the city or county is the one to build and operate such a facility.

For example, if it were judged that a necessary "intervention" to an unemployment problem was an increase in child care facilities and programs, the role of the community might be completely separate from the actual provision of such services. It might be instead to convene a meeting of city, county, private agency, Community Action Agency, and citizen groups to pool their ideas and resources to develop a plan for such services.

The basic intervention approaches would be:

1. The mounting of *educational* efforts to convince or teach people to avoid the problem or to take steps to cure it—such as drug or VD education programs.
2. Adopting a *preventive* approach to ensure that the problem does not grow worse or, if possible, even exist at all—such as smallpox inoculation programs, well-baby clinics, youth recreation and rap groups (including schools and clinics in local development plans, and police officers trained in alcoholism, drug abuse, and family disturbance prevention techniques).
3. Providing *individual treatment services* to assist people in recovering from or overcoming difficulties—such as detoxification centers, welfare programs, remedial reading classes, meals-on-wheels programs.
4. Offering *rehabilitation* programs designed to assist people in regaining their basic capabilities and skills—such as physical and psychotherapy, halfway houses, and other services designed to help people reenter "unsupported" activities.
5. *Enforcing* regulations that would prevent or overcome problems—such as building codes, drug abuse laws, health laws, etc.
6. Taking steps to *support* and *strengthen* existing or new programs and services—such as the provision of technical and management assistance; the fostering of coordination and cooperation; the integration of physical, public safety, and legislative decision making with human resources planning.
7. Generating *institutional change* activities that relate to questions of equity and access and call for fundamental policy reorientations directed at such issues as income redistribution, access to services, and opportunity—such as affirmative action programs.

Choosing an appropriate local government role

Clearly, local governments should not try to adopt, provide, or manage all of the services and programs needed to solve local social problems. But they can seek to understand and influence development of these efforts. In fact, given the overlapping and fragmented nature of the pattern of agencies, services, and programs, cities and counties with little experience in this area might best play a role that would have a rationalizing and integrative effect on the overall picture rather than trying to provide new services.

While counties are legally mandated to provide human services in most states, cities and counties without such mandates have greater flexibility in determining their responses to social problems. A jurisdiction that recognizes the need for a particular service can choose to provide it directly or obtain it from some other source. The discussion below illustrates a variety of "obtainer" roles that are most specifically applicable to cities and other jurisdictions without strong provider requirements, but should prove useful to any general purpose local government seeking to strengthen the effectiveness of its human resources efforts. In fact, these roles are not mutually exclusive. Consequently, jurisdictions with strong provider commitments can use the obtainer roles to supplement and strengthen their existing efforts.

The ten separate roles

Following is a discussion of ten separate roles illustrating possible approaches to social issues and problems.[9] The various roles are in fact on a continuum, the first being those least connected with the delivery of services, leading on to those closest to service delivery in terms of staff time, skills, and management requirements. It should be emphasized that each of these roles should be adopted based upon information gathered and decisions made according to the kind of process described above, and should be followed up by an evaluation effort. One of the strongest reasons for a jurisdiction's staying out of the business of delivering services directly (or at least separating its basic planning and analysis activities from any actual service operational efforts) is the fact that the rigors and demands of on-going services tend to obscure the perspective and detachment necessary for policy planning and decision making. The various roles involved in the approach to social issues will now be described.

Advocacy   The advocacy function represents all efforts of the local government to encourage, cajole, convince, threaten, or otherwise motivate service providers and others to meet the needs identified. It implies and requires a firm commitment on the part of the jurisdiction to concern itself with any and all problems and service gaps. It imposes a much milder administrative burden than does the actual delivery of services, but it confronts local decision makers with the different responsibility for developing an effective multipronged approach to the complex array of human services planners, funders, and providers. The local officials must establish close working links with other human resources decision makers. This involves the careful documentation of citizen problems and service needs, the marshaling of political support, and the ability to negotiate effectively among various jurisdictions for services and resources.

The advocacy approach should prove useful for smaller cities with fewer resources and larger cities with little experience in providing services. This type of role will probably lead to city involvement in some of the other functions such as coordination or resource providing. For example, once cities have identified and sought to influence county planning processes for alcoholism, health, welfare, etc., their participation will hopefully become normalized and ongoing. And regular participation in a variety of intrajurisdictional efforts is in essence the third role—coordination—described below. Similarly, participation in the advocacy negotiation process may ultimately result in a series of compromises and trade-offs whereby cities begin to offer the resources they are most able to provide. (E.g., "Our city requires a well-baby clinic. The newest county facility is 15 miles away." "Fine. We will budget staff and equipment. Can your city provide the facility?") This then transforms their participation to the fourth role, that of resource provision.

Information and referral   The information and referral ("I and R") function, which can be performed in conjunction with or without the advocacy role, simply commits the city or county to translating the results of needs assessment activities into an information source for its residents. It involves minimal resources including a public desk and answering service and the printing of materials—preferably a comprehensive directory of services and service organizations. Some local governments have decided to go further and provide referral services which necessitates funding for more skilled interviewing and "intake counselor" type staff. Others support 24-hour hotlines. Costs for this function can sometimes be offset by volunteer staffing. In some respects, this represents a type of service delivery. It is included here since it is an appropriate step for beginning involvement in human resources and is in fact a good way for local governments to build capacity and understanding before tackling more complex problems.[10]

Coordination The coordination function, which includes the advocacy role (although not necessarily information and referral), is based upon regular participation in intergovernmental planning processes. The basic difference between advocacy and coordination is that the latter implies long-term, systematic approaches not only to the delivery of needed services, but to the improvement and rationalization of the existing patchwork, fragmented "planning system." At its simplest level, the coordination function is the collection of information regarding the various services available and seeing to it that the community is aware of them. At its more complex level, the coordination role calls for an effort to get the various and fragmented providers to synchronize their services: by dividing the area among agencies to reach more people; by opening on different days or times to expand service accessibility; by sharing facilities to maximize service resources—in short, to encourage among service providers the spirit and practice of cooperation. In a great many cases, cities which have not attempted to provide social services on a large scale before, may enter the discussion with greater objectivity, credibility, and acceptance. Other service agencies may be more receptive to suggestions coming from a more neutral city organization. At little expense effective coordination efforts can produce significant services improvement.

Resource provision Short of expending funds for the actual delivery of services, a jurisdiction can maximize the impact of limited funds by attracting needed services from others with their own less scarce resources. Cities have often used this approach to attract service delivery agencies by providing space, telephone switchboard facilities, reception services, or even intake functions. Some cities, such as Santa Fe Springs, have constructed and now operate centers whose services are provided not by the city but by a variety of county, state, and private agencies. This approach, particularly if the community has identifiable needs and sufficiently attractive resources, may be employed by any size jurisdiction and in conjunction with most other functions. The successful operation of a resource center, such as the one run by Santa Fe Springs, is dependent primarily upon an accurate assessment of needs and a correct inventory and analysis of resources and services. Is the population in the center's immediate area needful and aware of the services that might be offered there? Are the services which would meet community needs likely to locate in the center? It is essential that the provision of a center or other resources be based upon a clear, complete, and accurate assessment of needs.

Coordination and leadership If the resource function involves the operation of a service center in conjunction with other functions such as active advocacy, or information and referral, the local government may find itself playing an ever-increasing role among human resources agencies. By being a single, consumer-oriented agency dealing with a number of service bodies, jurisdictions may find they have both the need and the opportunity to play a leadership role in the planning, allocating and evaluation of services. This role is not one that intrinsically belongs to cities or one they should necessarily seek, but continued fragmentation in the delivery system necessitates initiative from any concerned and capable source. Given city proximity to the majority of service recipients, their concerns can be effectively articulated. This is especially true if cities have founded their position on an effectively performed needs assessment. Cities, by virtue of their closer association with service users and their efforts to take a close look at their needs, may be compelled by circumstances to provide substantial input in identifying the services needed within their boundaries.

Cities playing such a role should be prepared to devote some resources to:

1. Additional needs assessment activities in particular priority area
2. Analysis of service patterns and agencies

3. Analysis of intergovernmental relationships
4. Relationships with various service providers and planners
5. Establishment of, or participation in, particular local and regional bodies.

To summarize, a leadership coordination role is distinguished from the simple coordination role by virtue of the greater weight carried by the city or the county in the intergovernmental process and also because of the additional planning resources required.

Regulation   The city or county makes numerous rules and regulations which can affect the success of particular services efforts, or improve or exacerbate an existing problem. It can consciously structure zoning regulations, physical plans, capitol improvements budgets, and public safety programs with an eye to meeting specified social goals and assisting in the provision of social services. For example, zoning regulations can be structured so as to encourage halfway houses, integrated housing, and child care facilities. Law enforcement programs relating to family disturbances, juvenile crime, and drug abuse can be complementary to programs providing family services, youth activities and counseling, and drug abuse assistance.

Costs for community services such as transportation, water, and garbage removal may be adjusted for low income residents. The jurisdiction's ability to set license fees, grant franchises, and set tax policies can be used to encourage and direct private sector institutions, such as banks, businesses, and industries to cooperate in achieving community-set goals in housing, health care, environmental quality, and employment opportunity.

The use of this power is less expensive than the establishment of program services and their attendant "bureaucratic" structures. Frequently, they generate the kind of change that minimizes the necessity for certain programs. This particular role requires the ability to study and understand the relationships between traditional local government powers and social conditions. As we have noted, this is an uncertain but open-minded commitment of top policy makers to experiment in these often controversial areas.

Technical assistant and catalyst   City hall (or the county courthouse) is often the first place to which citizens with problems come. A local government may find it useful to provide, in addition to individualized ombudsman and information and referral services, assistance to citizens in understanding the overall human resources "system" and in using their own resources to generate changes and programs. This would mean specifically helping citizen groups define their needs, develop proposals, and design programs.

Because of the particularly fragmented nature of human services planning at both the regional, subregional, and even the county level, it is argued that only at the city level is it possible to get a comprehensive view of all the problems impacting on clients and neighborhoods. Consequently, some cities may feel that their best role is to assist citizens and community groups to define problems, identify resources and programs, and develop grant and advocacy strategies that will enable them to obtain needed services. This role can also include management assistance to local human resources programs and agencies.

The benefits of this role are that city officials relate primarily to their own constituents providing them assistance. The city itself is not necessarily responsible for acting directly with other agencies. This is particularly appropriate for smaller cities with limited resources which can work with citizens to have them do staff work activities that save time and money. The risks inherent in this approach is the lack of control by the city and its apparent endorsement of activities conducted by local groups and citizens that may not be welcomed by other levels of government and agencies.

Program initiation and demonstration The remaining three functions differ from those above in that they involve direct local government responsibility for the administration and operation of service programs. The program initiating function calls upon local governments to demonstrate the need for a particular service by providing it. Such demonstration programs may be funded by the jurisdiction or with grant funds. They may properly fall within the province of existing programs or they may be in an unexplored service area. This function is characterized by the fact that each program is operated with the intention of convincing another provider that the service is needed, viable and appropriate. At the end of the demonstration period, administration of the program is turned over to a regular service agency. This process need not require direct local government operation. The function could be performed through city grant/contract agreements with new or on-going service entities or through a joint venture between a jurisdiction and a provider agency.

This approach is appropriate where specific service gaps have been clearly defined and charted, and where there is good reason to believe that another agency is *ready and willing to pick up the service* if the demonstration proves successful. It is also appropriate in jurisdictions which have received sufficient funds—such as those from general revenue sharing—to provide the service but in which the uncertainty of continued operational commitments may be considered too risky.

It is essential in adopting this approach to develop political support and awareness for the experiment and gain the greatest degree of interest and cooperation from *more than one* potential permanent provider. Although this approach has its risks and calls for a certain amount of sophistication in intergovernmental relations as well as in program operations, it is also a good way for cities, in particular, to gain needed experience in services delivery without making permanent administrative and funding commitments.

Although it is not a hard and fast rule, the difficulties and complexities involved in initiating new programs and in arranging a successful intergovernmental transfer suggest that only those local governments whose budget and political support permit margin for error attempt this approach. If the experiment is done through a contract with an established experienced agency by a jurisdiction experienced in this field, then the margin for error may be lessened considerably.

Program administration and service contracting Program administration does not necessarily mean the local government delivery of services. It can mean that the jurisdiction contracts with a more experienced agency to actually provide the service under its administrative guidance. This approach has a number of benefits over direct program service provision. First, it continues to keep elected officials and staff free of operational demands. It allows them to continue "policy planning" as opposed to "operations planning." It also permits the actual costs and responsibilities of program operation to fall upon a potentially more experienced, efficient organization already geared up for the task. Community based agencies are more flexible, less bound by civil service and other regulations, incur lower staff costs, and make good use of volunteers.

This role, however, absolutely requires the development of strong local government planning capabilities. Not only must such ventures be based upon firm needs assessment and priority setting activities but supported as well by firm contracting, monitoring and evaluation capabilities. Sufficient resources must be allocated to these functions. If not, locally administered programs will suffer the same defects—poor planning, unresponsive and inflexibility—that have characterized the previous federal, categorical social program system.

Direct service delivery From a city's perspective, the municipal delivery of social services may be seen as a last resort. This is not generally the case for counties, except in particular service areas that have not traditionally been their responsibility. If a service is absolutely necessary and no other agency can or will provide it, local governments will need to consider its provision.

There are a number of important benefits to the service delivery role. First, direct provision of service can demonstrate to the public and citizen groups the city's sincerity and capability in this area. Second, this experience will equip city staff to understand and deal more effectively with the problems of other service providing agencies as well as clients. Thus, by having direct control and first-hand experience with the program, city staff can translate the lessons of the program into future policy direction.

Direct service delivery involves more intensive, long-term staff commitment than the other roles. Staff, facilities, equipment, and procedures all need to be carefully identified and designed. The relationship of the new services to existing city departments will have to be defined. The way it will relate to other agencies must be developed. Its progress will have to be carefully monitored and analyzed. It is possible to minimize the first problem by placing the program in an existing, experienced service-providing department, such as recreation or the library; the second by having other providers in on the planning of the service; and the third by having a strong management and policy planning capacity—separate from the management of the particular service.

Applying the analysis process: some innovative examples

A great many cities throughout the country are developing their own human service programs and providing direct services to their citizens. As federal programs have been reduced and local interest groups such as ethnic minorities, senior citizens, youth groups and neighborhood associations have developed communication channels to city hall, it has become imperative that cities respond to unmet needs. These new muncipal services are well documented in the chapters which follow. A corresponding, but less dramatic, trend has been for cities to apply the analytical steps described above to devise less expensive, nonservice delivery solutions to these problems. Even when nonservice "answers" are not forthcoming, the process is helpful in identifying additional, nontraditional resources if a nonservice approach cannot be found.

Los Angeles For example, the City of Los Angeles felt a strong commitment to help increase child care services. A number of community organizations were insistent in their demands for an increase in these services. A survey of the needs was conducted identifying numbers of single parent households, unemployment figures and service requests for existing facilities. Professionals and recipients were contacted. The need was definitely established.

The city also reviewed previous efforts to establish such services, the barriers that had been encountered, and the ways in which existing city agencies were involved. Discovered was the fact that municipal fire and safety codes and zoning requirements were fundamental barriers to the creation of low cost neighborhood child care services. Zoning restrictions and stringent fire codes—aimed at large facility child care centers—made the difference. Thus, the city embarked upon a program of reviewing and revising child care facility fire regulations to be more realistic and of creating more permissive zoning regulations. The new ordinances provided for: an increase in the number of children allowed in a residential, nonprofit child care center, from three to six; waiver of the $500 fee charged to nonprofit groups seeking conditional use permits to allow additional children in residential day care centers; establishment of day care centers in industrial and manufacturing zones; and creation of an intermediate category of facilities serving seven to twenty children, with attendant fire and safety codes. Thus, the city "provided" child care services by not "providing" them, but by making it possible for them to exist.

Campbell, California   In Campbell, California, a study of housing conditions and needs revealed the need to increase and maintain low and moderate income housing, to prevent deterioration and to prevent discrimination.[11] The recommendations developed in response were not to build middle income housing but to use the city's regulator role by altering its zoning density mix to spur additional housing, to advocate/educate citizens on the need for housing conservation, and to act as a provider through rehabilitation services and funds under the Housing and Community Development Act.

Chicago   In Chicago, the Mayor's Office for Senior Citizens (MOSC) found that only 4.1 percent of the city's senior citizens reported wages as a source of income.[12] The city's Manpower Planning Council's direct response was to allocate 20 percent of all CETA employment and training slots to seniors. But the MOSC looked beyond this immediate action to other efforts, existing resources and additional senior citizen needs. As a result, a much broader program involving additional funds from the Older Americans Act, the Community Services Administration, and the Department of Commerce as well as from city sources was created. A series of nutrition, transportation, education, nursing visits, occupational crafts facilities, and other direct community services emerged. In many instances, the seniors who are given jobs were providing needed services to other seniors thereby maximizing the impact of the program. City funds for administration were frequently the key to matching and releasing much larger amounts of federal funds.

Seattle   In Seattle, the city identified a senior citizen population with significant health, income, housing and facilities problems. The city embarked upon a series of efforts to ameliorate the situation utilizing the prestige and resources directly at its command. The Mayor was able to encourage small businesses to give discounts and special senior citizen arrangements such as drug discounts, free checking accounts and even free hearing aid and eye glass services. The city-owned electric company not only gave significant rate reductions to seniors but provided free repairs and parts for necessary appliances.

Implementation: designing specific manageable action

Implementation is used in this context to describe the process which translates general goals and specific policy directions into concrete action alternatives and final program decisions. It describes the process of putting a program in place and determining the specific actions which will accomplish this. The process is complete when a program or service is fully operational. In this section, implementation will refer to the design of specific services as well as the creation of coordinative, regulatory or advocacy actions as well.

This area is one in which local government managers have many questions and, also, few answers.

Indeed, the study of implementation carries us into social science's weakest area— dynamics. The determination of whether or not a social program or policy can be implemented cannot be based on a static checklist. Rather, it must involve analysis of whether technical, bureaucratic, staff, and institutional/political elements can be blended into a viable process. Implementation analysis must ask whether the organization can do what is desired in technical terms, whether it can function well in a bureaucratic sense (which involves micro-organizational issues), and whether it can operate successfully in its larger environment (macro-organizational/political issues).[13]

Unfortunately, the area is probably also the most significant. In the 1960s great strides were made in the articulation of human resources and human services policy. The poverty and manpower programs reflected new directions in social intention. Although the shift to block grants and revenue sharing was viewed by some as a lessening of those policies, they can be seen equally as means to sharpen and strengthen the effectiveness of those efforts. There is painfully little research about how implementation decisions get made and how effective they are. Now that considerable responsibility for both policy direction and implementation are placed in local hands, the tools for implementation analysis are only just emerging.

It should be comforting to public administrators—who may be somewhat intimidated by the technical mythology and vocabulary of the social program arena—to note that the major problems will most likely be political and bureaucratic rather than technical. Not that all the technical problems are solved—not by a long shot—but they will "often seem almost trivial when compared to such issues as whether or not political jurisdictions will cooperate or whether a . . . union will be in favor of implementing a new idea." [14] Furthermore, the absence of a science or technology of social program planning should not impede efforts. Even though we do not know enough about what techniques and services work best, our biggest mistakes come from failing to think things through sufficiently. Too often we act as if a "good" policy will automatically produce good programs. Needed is a common sense analysis of the potential technical, organizational and acceptance problems in the designs to be. Policies must be given careful review for their programmatic implications.

The process of implementation involves two basic steps: first, examining the new policy for clarity, rationality and general feasibility. Does it in fact make some sense from the organizational and technical point of view? Secondly there is the step involving the designing of specific organizational, staff and technical activities. In other words, what in fact does it mean we should really do?

The first step can occur before the policy direction and general approach are set, although it rarely does. It would be useful if policy makers in determining direction could get some sense of the relative "reality" and "feasibility" factors of the policy determinations.

The second step fleshes out the actual implementation steps from first initiation to having the program in place. It focuses on the following six questions:

1. What is to be done? Describe the actual steps in the activity.
2. How is it to be done? Create guidelines for carrying out the steps.
3. What organizational changes are needed? Describe the current organizational structures or processes that must be changed.
4. What technical or methodological innovations are involved? Identify and discover the particular treatment, service, or innovation to be carried out.
5. What strategies of acceptance must be adopted? How will cooperation and ownership by staff, clients, and other agencies be obtained?
6. Define specific, measurable objectives for implementation. What are the concrete organizational "outputs" in terms of behavior changes or program modifications that are expected to help reach the articulated social goals?

For example, let us hypothesize it has been determined that the city will pay priority attention to drug abuse, and that the key role of the city shall be to generate greater coordination among existing drug abuse efforts in the community. Then the design issues are what steps can be taken to promote coordination, how these can be taken, and what organizational capacity must exist for this to be done. Some of the possible designs might include:

1. Working with existing community-based drug abuse program directors, county mental health and health officials, and school counselors to form a drug abuse coordinating council. This might involve from one-quarter to one person-year, someone with a knowledge of drug abuse programs, services, and conditions.
2. Working to increase coordination through a city-sponsored and city-operated pilot drug abuse program—for counseling, referrals, and/or detoxification. The

program would be the basis for city involvement with, and leadership in, a coordination effort. This would require one to two professional staff, plus facilities, equipment, and medical skills.
3. Operating a drug abuse hotline, or information and referral center, which would assist in information dissemination and provide the basis for future long-range coordination of drug abuse programs. This would involve one person-year with volunteer and part-time assistance, plus office space and telephones.

In all cases, it would be necessary to devise strategies for obtaining the cooperation of the drug abuse agencies, county officials and individual city staff who would be affected or involved. The measurable objectives for the implementation effort would be the successful operation of the program (i.e., number of people served, measures of increased cooperation, etc.) while the overall policy evaluation would be an assessment of whether or not overall pattern of drug abuse had been positively affected by the coordination effort. The importance of measuring the implementation success is that it will help shed light on the more complex policy evaluation. For example: if it can be shown that the implementation effort succeeded in bringing about coordination but that no change in drug abuse incidence occurred, then we know that coordination or coordination alone is not the answer. If the implementation effort failed, then we know that nothing can be proven about coordination as a strategy for solving the problem since it was not "put in place."

It is beyond the scope of this chapter to define individual program design issues. However, below are described a number of major design problems faced by most human resource programs followed with some brief suggestions about how to overcome them.[15]

Three major design problems

Bureaucratization   Since the emergence of the massive social programs of the 1960s, the institutionalization of welfare, of health services, etc., the delivery of social services has found itself bound up in a myriad of complex, intricate regulations and rules. Concern with abuse, with quality control and rising costs have resulted in overorganization, overprofessionalization and overregulation. Huge sums of money, time and staff go into unwieldy systems that are not effective or efficient. It is essential that these problems be addressed in program design. Cities can develop programs that are more responsive to individuals and local conditions. Programs operated with general funds, revenue sharing—and started at the city's own initiative—need not be burdened by the federal and state strictures that apply to the "traditional" health and welfare programs. In addition, cities can develop programs that assist individuals to "travel" the complex systems of state, county and private services.

Isolation and alienation of particular groups and individuals   In essence this problem is the opposite side of the bureaucratization coin. A key design issue for any service is access. Will people be able to make use of the service? There are numerous well meaning efforts which have failed because they were poorly designed for the groups they were supposed to reach: programs have failed to reach Spanish speaking with English language information bulletins, staff and regulations, office have been located in places where people can not or will not go make use of them. Efforts have been made to reach ethnic groups or neighborhoods that ignored previous problems and attitudes. Service facilities have failed to open at times working people can come in. Failures to provide child care services or to identify costs to service user have caused people to be alienated.

In addition, there is a need to assist the numerous groups of people—the poor, the handicapped, those in need of remedial education—and training to understand ways to obtain the services they need. Many groups—community, ethnic, neighborhood—have coalesced around particular issues and problems but know little of how to make their needs and influence felt.

Fragmentation of programs and services   Policy makers and administrators—as well as the American citizenry—tolerate the most inefficient, uncoordinated patchwork of planning and services efforts in the human resources field. This stems less from the defects of the organization and personnel within the human resources "nonsystem" than it does from the fact that we do not as a society attach to social goals the importance they require. In fact, we do not acknowledge at all as a national problem the existence of human resources problems. The agencies struggle as best they can with the resources and "system" at hand; while society at large hopes those in need will pull themselves up by their bootstraps and the problem will go away.

Nonetheless, the system is there. And we must design our efforts to deal with the disjointed pattern of plans, services and agencies that exist—to minimize the fragmentation and discontinuities of such a disjointed system from within.

The problem manifests itself in the multiplicity of agencies, services, programs, agencies and departments all offering services under different guidelines, auspices, eligibility requirements. Frequently, there is duplication—but more often the service recipient is confronted with a fragmented pattern of community workers, intake counselors, clerks and social workers none of whom have the least interest in or concern with the programs and diagnoses of one another.

Some of the approaches that should be considered to overcome these problems will now be discussed.

Using alternatives   Utilization of alternative and community-based agencies and organizations is a useful way to overcome the pattern of overly rigid and bureaucratic services. The poverty programs of the 1970s and alternative lifestyle groups of the 1970s have produced a plethora of organizations, staff and constituencies with significant problem solving and service delivery skills. Their unique role in the community often gives more effective access to citizens and service users. Their "quasi-professional" status makes them less overburdened with civil service minutiae on the one hand and much more flexible and innovative on the other. As one county executive put it bluntly, "I would just as soon put all my revenue sharing money into these alternative agencies than my overorganized and rigid departments. They are inventive, innovative and enthusiastic. And they reach people. You get far more bang for the buck from these folks."

Ombudsman and community education programs   Be sure that there is a place within the city structure where new groups of citizens—those that would benefit from the social programs being designed can get the hearing, attention and assistance they need. Naturally, such a function could be utilized for all city services. The important thing is that if you are just starting out with your human resources efforts, it is essential to have a method for getting quick feedback to see what problems and difficulties people are having. This function can be particularly useful in helping citizens to obtain attention and new programs from existing service agencies. It helps them to define problems, write proposals and operate programs.

Decentralization   Decentralize operations to reflect conditions among different neighborhoods, ethnic groups, and circumstances. Within a context of overall direction and city hall accountability, staffing, hours, emphasis, activity selection, eligibility can be made as flexible as possible. Recreation departments are good models here. They design new efforts regularly based upon consumer usage and demand. They utilize volunteers, part-time staff which reflect the enthusiasm and needs of particular program areas. They plan for individual community and neigh-borhood centers.

Joint ventures   Joint ventures and coordinating activities are ways in which the inherent fragmentary nature of the human resources system can be overcome or at least moderated. Of course the fragmented nature of the system will not be elimin-ated until the federal government alters its regulations and guidelines and state and local governments develop effective joint planning mechanisms. Locally much can be done in the initial needs assessments and problem analyses which determine the specific strategies and roles to be adopted. It is at this level—the policy develop-ment level—that the issues of fragmentation should be carefully considered so as to avoid adding to the cacophony already on stage. But once the decision has been made to begin a service that will require interface and working relationships with other agencies, programs and services, the question of specifying with clear detail the nature of the interaction and relationships is essential. The design issues here are:

1. Identify the specific skills and resources needed from other agencies given the specific goals and objectives you have.
2. Identify potential resources that could assist in the achievement of objectives.
3. Identify the specific costs and potential risks inherent in a joint venture.
4. Design specific steps that can be taken to minimize risks and costs.
5. Involve top policy makers and key individuals on both sides.
6. Be aware of all federal and state guidelines involved.
7. Write workable plans that include operating details, definitions of success, service standards, time requirements, and staff roles and responsibilities.
8. Before, during, and after operations are in place, continue to be sensitive to feelings and issues of "turf."

Other key design issues

There are a number of other key design issues to consider in the mounting of any social program. Five of them—eligibility, fees, location, staffing, and technique—will now be discussed.

Eligibility   In some respects, target group identification in the needs assessment process determines the target group. But once a program is in operation many peo-ple may feel the need for it. It is essential to think through the issue of how people can qualify for the service. What are the legal implications here?

Fees   Some services by definition should not have fees. Employment programs presume lack of resources on the part of recipients. But transportation services, meals programs, child care are all needed services that may be used by those who can afford them. It is essential that a mechanism be devised whereby a fee struc-ture does not screen out those most in need on the one hand or, that a sliding scale or target group exclusion is not so complicated or embarrassing as to drive people away.

Location   While it may be more economical to use a city office for a service, such a location may foreclose access of those you want to reach. In other circum-stances, the gathering of a number of service programs in one central location may assist access questions. Location can be best determined from the needs assess-ment and problem analysis processes. The nature of the problem, the position and attitudes of those affected by it, and the history of the issue will help. The impor-tant point is to avoid the frequent pattern in which some very sensitive analysis and effective community organization work go into the creation and design of a program only to have its location selected in the most arbitrary and irrelevant fashion.

Staffing   The most important step cities can take in beginning to develop human services programs is to get away from the credentialism that tends to mark public employment. The key issue in which this question surfaces is "professionals vs. community people" as staff. The important point here, as in the location issue above, is to get the staff who can reach the service population, provide the services—in short, get the job done. Much important innovation in the delivery of human services has come from the use of paraprofessionals—many of them women, minorities, the poor (i.e., members of the service population)—who are skilled at reaching individuals and surfacing problems that traditionally trained white professionals did not do. The approach to take is to identify as specifically as possible the concrete tasks that will be performed; the skills, knowledge, and abilities these tasks will require; and the population groups and individuals most likely to possess these skills.

Technique   Use common sense in developing service and intervention techniques and methods. At the same time, keep up with the literature of human resources planning and service delivery. Such periodicals as *Social Work, Transaction,* and *Psychology Today* all report on important innovations. State municipal leagues, notably in California, Texas, and New England, are developing human resources capabilities and can serve as resources for up-to-date program techniques.

Linking human services decision making with city planning

The poverty programs of the 1960s taught local government managers many important lessons: the importance of involving citizens in the solution of their own problems; the significance of community based programs and services, the need to make governmental program planning more flexible and responsive; the importance of understanding causes as opposed to symptoms. There is one question for a new decade and a new generation of public officials to answer, this time at the local level: the question how to destroy the barrier between urban and social planning—a question already addressed in Chapter 4. Meeting social needs and solving social problems has been left a federal, soft money, issue for too long. Too many jurisdictions give it attention fundamentally different than that afforded the land use, public safety and other traditionally "central" functions of city government. As the description of the priority setting and analysis process makes clear: unless all segments and levels of city government are involved it will not be maximally effective.

This integration can be encouraged in the development of social planning tools (general plan and social impact analysis), social planning structures (staffing, departments, citizen bodies) and in rejuvenating the city's overall policy making and management process.

Tools for integrating human services planning

Technically, local governments should begin to give human resource planning the same attention and incorporate it into the same processes as physical, fiscal, and policy planning. There is no magic formula for this. In fact there is little for any administrator to go on save for random experiences of individuals with vision and imagination who were able to take advantage of developing opportunities and circumstances to bring off an unprecedented scheme.

The social element in the general plan   A good first step is to work toward the development of a social element to the general plan. The "Action Plan" produced by California Cities calls for the creation of such an element:

The action plan proposes that . . . all cities prepare and adopt a social element to its general plan, treating it like the other general plan elements and as part of the overall planning process. This element would help to determine city goals and objectives and establish standards and priorities to meet community social needs. The inclusion of the social element in the general plan enables social planning to be coordinated with physical, economic and environmental planning efforts.[16]

The creation of such an element provides the opportunity for the city to marshall staff, citizens and planning techniques in a broad scale process; planners, department heads, citizens and others all have the opportunity to consider social goals in the light of other more traditional city targets and programs. The "revolutionary" theme here is that social concerns are not viewed as ancillary to physical plans but that they are looked at in relation to one another.

Thus, municipal growth and industrial programs can be related to the nature of manpower, health and education concerns of the city. A city with a clear understanding of the nature of its work force, the type of people on unemployment, will have a better idea of the industry it should attract. Similarly, cities with concentrations of elderly with inadequately met health needs should make further increases in elderly housing, contingent upon the development of additional health facilities. Social goals—whether incorporated into the general plan or not—should be developed in conjunction with existing city priorities and processes. A well developed, well articulated social element in one California city was stymied because it was not consistent with the existing process for developing general plan elements.

Social impact analysis   A second major instrument of building human resource planning processes into the mainstream of city government is the social impact analysis (SIA). An outgrowth of the National Environmental Policy Act of 1969, SIAs have associated primarily with land use planning and development. Its purpose is to help identify ways in which a proposed program, development or project will affect the community. Given particular community goals and policies, social impact statements are designed to measure—as far as the state of the art makes this possible—the anticipated direct and indirect results against the kind of community conditions being sought. In San Jose, for example, the city has been developing a formal capacity for measuring the social, fiscal, environmental and economic effects of all its policies and programs. The city's net benefit analysis process, designed in response to a 1972 ballot measure requiring the city to review all new development for impact on existing institutions, is designed as an integral part of the city's policy making process to project impact on city population groups and institutions. The city is currently developing ways to apply the process to the impact of social programs as well.

Most physical developments have significant impact upon the manpower, transportation, social and health conditions of the community. A social impact statement can assist in making a decision on supporting, modifying, or later evaluating the success of the effort.

The social impact analysis may contain several basic elements:

1. A socioeconomic community profile, to get a look at the conditions that may be affected;
2. An in-depth look at the target populations immediately or potentially affected by the project or program;
3. A review of the organizations and institutions affected by the project or program;

4. A description of the intended direct and ancillary impact of the project upon the community;
5. An analysis of problems, benefits, and options.

The state of the art of SIAs is only beginning to emerge. Consequently, there is considerable imprecision in the measurement and qualification of "social impacts." Considerable experimentation is currently being carried out in many parts of the country. It will be some time however, before it reaches the level of even environmental impact reporting—which in itself reflects considerable debate and controversy. Nonetheless, the value of the SIA lies in the nature of the thought processes it stimulates. Too long, we have plunged ahead with projects—possessing excellent internal design and purpose—without giving any thought to unexpected or secondary results or to their impact upon other programs and institutions. The SIA engenders an important broad scale, integrated approach to planning and problem solving. The SIA helps us to bridge the gap—at the staff and research level—between physical and social planners. The process can be used to help representatives of these disciplines match their skills in a common effort.

Structural considerations for integration

Although the issue of organizational structure for the management of human services programs is the specific province of the following chapter, a number of observations that pertain particularly to the importance of integrating the process social analysis described above—can be made. The major criteria for placing the human services policy planning capability in the city structure should be: to utilize that unit or entity closest to the actual locus of city decision making authority without abandoning it to those with little or no interest, capacity or sensitivity in this area. Do not automatically assume that a new department or commission is essential if other departments or commissions are able. Do not assume, further, that such departments will remain forever unable, if they lack capacity now. Too often promising social innovations have been left withered on the vine because "mainstream" city processes passed them by.

The manager's office   It may be that the city manager's office is the best location to ensure that human services concerns and issues are kept in the mainstream of city decision making. In this manner, central staff can trace the development of social programs, human services planning, the activities of their human services actors, and relate them to on-going city actions and policies. By placing the human services policy planning function in the manager's office, larger cities which may be operating a number of human service programs, can keep that function away from the day to day program pressures and needs that tend to obscure longer range policy considerations. Cities, both large and small, just beginning human services activities may find that the manager's office is essential to give the new effort credibility and support.

Planning departments   These represent the logical place to design human service programs and policies except for two overriding factors: many of today's city planners do not have the training or experience to deal with social issues. Secondly, too often the planning department is not a planning department but a zoning variance office, and its work ignored by those in the city with real authority. In those cities in which the work of the planning department is in fact utilized by administrators, department heads and elected officials in making their decisions, the responsibility for some social planning could well be best located here.

Recreation departments These can probably best make a contribution to the city's human services effort through the delivery of programs. Their long history of responsive program based upon local interest dovetails well with the need to put together varied and changing programs in response to changing social needs and techniques. They often have neighborhood facilities which are good vehicles for social programs and have made extensive use of volunteers and part time staff. They do not, however, have the broad based social analysis and planning experience described above. These departments could be represented on a city staff task force or social planning council with the broad goal setting responsibility. Their chief strength seems to be in the area of operating those programs determined to be necessary and feasible by the city.

A number of cities in California, however, have placed social planning responsibilities in recreation departments with successful and innovative results. The life enrichment department in Davis is the location of a wide variety of social programs as well as the basis for the development of a new element to the city's general plan. The Culver City recreation department also provides a series of social program services and in addition has responsibility for the coordination, brokering and advocacy of social services. In the mid-1970s the city was considering placing full and complete responsibility for social planning in that department.

Human resources commissions The development of human resources commissions seems to be the single most frequent technique for the organization of citizen input to the social planning process. A survey conducted by the League of California Cities showed that 20 percent of those responding had developed such public bodies. It is essential such commissions work closely with other entities, such as the planning commission, recreation commission, human relations commission. It is, of course, possible and often desirable to use existing citizen's groups. The city of Hayward developed a broad based needs assessment committee, based in its human relations commission, which is developing a citywide social needs assessment process. The committee contained members of other commissions which have utilized the data assembled by the committee in their own deliberations. Most notably, the citizens advisory commission is responsible for recommending the use of Housing and Community Development funds as well as the social development commission which makes recommendations for the disbursement of "social" general revenue sharing funds.

Human services departments Similarly, the development of human services departments requires special efforts to ensure that their work is understood by other departments and that issues of public safety, land use, municipal growth, etc. are shared with those responsible for social programs. At the same time, it is essential that the responsibilities of such departments include the capacity to make long range social policy judgments and understand the social implications of other aspects of city endeavor. If the department's first and only task is the direct delivery of services, then the capacity for social planning should be located elsewhere. If the human services department does perform planning and policy making processes via departmental communication and coordination, task force meetings and joint meetings of commissions and joint presentations to council. It is essential that the manager's office or someone close to it be given lead, coordinating responsibility.

The office of policy analysis In larger cities there may be opportunity for the creation of an office of policy analysis. Such an office would be responsible for ensuring the program development and legislation was done consistent with long range city goals and strategies. Acting as a catalyst and planner—rather than as a watchdog—the office would perform in support of the chief executive, mayor or council. The office would be the locus for the activities necessary to ensure that social planning, public safety, environmental and fiscal decision programs are co-ordinated and consistent and well thought out and effective. Such an office could provide: policy planning support for the council; internal program development and liaison with departments; and external liaison with United Way agencies, counties, COGS, etc. They can also play an instrumental role in ensuring that local manpower, economic development and community development programs strengthen and augment existing local programs.[17]

A policy development approach to municipal human services planning

In California, since the inception of its "Action Plan," the League of California cities has been involved in a number of projects affecting the policy making processes of cities, particularly the design and development of social problem solving efforts. The several projects were designed to focus upon specific areas of municipal concern—community development, human resources, personnel, and affirmative action—but each started with attention to the policy development process and capacities of target sites. The purpose of these projects was to strengthen local performance in these areas by "revitalizing the comprehensive planning process in each jurisdiction." [18]

A look at local government policy making In this work, the league reports several very important lessons about the nature of local government policy making that have significant implications for municipal human services efforts. In the first place, the vast majority of elected officials do not view the general plan as representing the true, active priorities of the community. Secondly, the real planning in most communities in which the project worked, is not accomplished by the professional planning staff but rather by the city council and the top cadre of department heads and the city manager. Thirdly, city government officials generally are frustrated by their inability to do comprehensive policy planning in such a manner as to affect the priorities of the physical, social economic and environmental development of the community. Consequently, city staff and advisory boards are often frustrated by the lack of specific policy directions from council. Policy-making roles of staff, advisory boards and council are frequently unclear, confused and misunderstood. The ability to analyze proposals and legislation from a policy point of view is usually undeveloped. Finally, even in circumstances in which cities have established a goal setting process, frequently there are no mechanisms to connect these goals and objectives to budgeting and day to day programs.

There are no villains in this tale, only the ever burgeoning demands and responsibilities confronting local government coupled with the "part time" nature of the local elected official. Local government professionals look to councils for leadership on incredibly complex diverse issues. Council persons—many newly elected—represent diverse interests, capacities, personalities, and experiences. Working part time under intense public scrutiny and often acrimony, it is very difficult to develop effective, long-lasting cooperative processes.

Needed, therefore, is a process by which elected officials, taking the lead, can work more effectively with staff and citizens to establish priorities and follow through mechanisms to ensure that the business of the city is accomplished. The process should permit the identification of key issues and problems, the design and implementation of working strategies to be applied and the opportunity at an agreed upon time to return to the issue to review progress, take new steps or move on to new priorities.

Policy planning and management capacity building The California projects have taken the first steps in developing such a process which shows signs of usefulness and success in the places where it has been tried.

The on-site efforts involved three major phases: the development of a planning and management profile, the growth of city leadership and team building assistance for improved policy planning processes, and finally the steps leading to the development of an improved comprehensive policy planning and management process and procedure.

The project team began to analyze the existing policy making processes in the target cities. Council members, managers, department heads and citizens were interviewed. Such basic city documents as budgets, procedures, and the charter were studied. The resulting profile described and analyzed the roles and relationships of council, commissions, and staff in setting direction for the city. It described the planning and management tools and showed how they were used and linked to one another. The profiling process—almost as important as the report itself—ensured that those interviewed were able to review and comment on the contents. It was essential that the team have an accurate picture of the process and that the city officials accepted the information as their own. In fact, the process of assembling and agreeing upon the profile was a first step by which city officials took steps together to develop an improved planning and decision-making process.

Based upon the "reality" described in the profiles, recommendations were prepared for the improvement of policy planning and management. Like the profile, the recommendations were submitted in conjunction with a series of seminars, workshops and illustrative materials designed to maximize understanding and consensus about future directions for the city.

A new approach: third-party team building, the policy team, a policy calendar
As a result of the profiles and the recommendations process, a process of "team building" among their elected and top appointed officials was suggested. The process began with their involvement in responding to the profiling and improvement activities and crystalized in the discussion and analysis of the recommendations. As council persons, the manager, key department heads and commission members sat together, with project support and facilitation, discussing potential future direction the first steps in a comprehensive policy making process were taking place. The training strategy employed by the project—commonly referred to as *team building*—is designed to strengthen interpersonal relationships and collaboration among elected and appointed officials by providing increased opportunities for communication outside the normal, rather rigid role and authority patterns of office and council meeting. The team building strategy is to capture the sense of direction obtained thereby and help participants plan ways to incorporate it into the regular processes of government. In a policy team, council members and staff work as peers with equality assured in the interaction. This initial team building process generally produced the concensus that a more formal, systematic comprehensive planning process was needed.

A key unique ingredient of the process is the *policy team*—generally consisting of elected officials, the manager and key department heads—although often a key committee or commission member is involved.

The role of the policy team—whether concerned with overall city issues or with a specific area such as human resources—is to identify the key problems confronting the city, the particular issues that require attention, and to assess the various options and alternatives open. This discussion, conducted as it is by various participants, ensures that the various concerns—particularly those of implementation—are incorporated into the process at an early date. The policy team, working in conjunction with others, helps to establish the various roles, responsibilities, and time frames for the new policy-making process. Significantly, the policy team's actions do not substitute for council, commission, or management authority but help to energize and coordinate it. Nothing about the team's action is final.

The third most significant aspect of the project is the *policy calendar*. Numerous jurisdictions have determined to set policies more rationally but have failed to institutionalize the process or have gotten burned out on one step. The policy calendar spells out the specific steps of the process including products, events, and meetings. It links these elements with elections, budget preparation, and other significant facets of municipal life. This ensures in advance that there is agreement about what will happen and when. It also serves to remind participants that the process is on-going and recurring—that decisions which are made in one year will be reviewed in another. This process, if supported with third party team building assistance, should help jurisdictions avoid the polarization and fragmentation so frequently characterizing council relationships—particularly in the human resources area.

Summary: a policy approach[19]   Based upon the need for a more comprehensive approach to policy making, together with the team building, policy team, and policy calendar approach, the project developed a model policy planning and management model that included five fundamental elements:

1. The opportunity for policy makers to agree upon basic policies at a given time, with periodic opportunities for reviewing and improving them.
2. The opportunity to select, from among alternatives, particular approaches to carrying out policies, and to review periodically their success and need for revision.
3. A process for coordinating available resources, adopted policies, and alternatives.
4. A mechanism for coordinating physical, social, and economic planning and decision making.
5. The opportunity to evaluate on a regular basis the success of various alternatives and policies.

Many of these elements exist in varying stages of development in many cities. The league's model is designed to pull these pieces together as part of a cohesive process. Cities employing the model outlined below can use it with varying degrees of sophistication and complexity, depending upon city resource experience and technical capacity:

1. *Policy leadership*—The process of organizing a team of policy officials to identify, develop, coordinate, and implement city policy.
2. *Needs assessment*—The process of collecting and reporting data relevant to city needs, problems, and resources. Citizen involvement is important in this phase.
3. *Policy agreement*—The process of formal recognition, understanding, and acceptance of recommended policy by the policy team. In cities, city councils have central responsibility for achieving agreement concerning policy.
4. *Policy analysis and interpretation*—The process of assessment and consideration of alternative approaches for carrying out council policy in a comprehensive and coordinated manner. Citizen involvement is important in this phase.
5. *Policy implementation*—The processes necessary to ensure resource allocation and planning consistency with policies. Organization development, intergovernmental relations, and coordination with the private sector are important in this phase.
6. *Policy evaluation*—The process of measuring the effect of government programs and activities toward implementing policy and meeting community needs.[20]

Although this approach is still in its infancy, it offers a way of ensuring the inclusion of human resources concerns in the center of city policy making. The development of expert techniques—needs assessment, social indicators and social impact analyses—will be wasted if these tools are not servants of elected officials and management committed to and engaged in human resources policy planning.

Even the provision of specific social services—regardless of how many or how well they serve—is no substitute for the capacity for local government to analyze and solve social problems.

The process can be applied specifically to human resources and human services concerns by focusing upon a specific human resources policy making process incorporating the development of needs statements, goals and alternatives, and policies as the mechanism for planning human resources activities and programs. Or alternatively, human resources concerns can be included in an overall municipal policy making process. In either case, the application of such a process will ensure that chief decision makers will be involved in the formulation of basic social policies for the city.

Conclusion: finding and maximizing resources for human services

There is no question that the overwhelming need is for increased funding for social programs and services. At the same time, it should be clear that given the present limits on public social services funding, cities and counties will have to use imagination and creativity in manufacturing the wherewithal to make a significant human resources contribution. Planning funds, other agencies, emerging federal and state legislation, published materials, staff resources, and innovative human resources program techniques all represent opportunities and resources.

Federal funding trends

The rapid changes in federal legislation—and the even more mercurial revisions of their guidelines—preclude any detailed discussion of federal funding programs. Local government managers will be aware that their state municipal leagues, the National League of Cities, the National Association of Counties, or their congressman's office can keep them up-to-date on current legislation. The general trend, however, is for programs to be developed that involve increasing access for local governments and others to the planning process. General revenue sharing, the Housing and Community Development Act, and the Comprehensive Employment and Training Act are all examples of this trend—with direct city involvement. Each of these can be utilized to support social planning and programs. Most human resources programs, however, such as the Older Americans Act or the National Health Planning and Resources Development Act, together with Title XX of the Social Security Act, do not go directly through cities. But they too, are increasingly subject to regulations broadening the planning processes to include cities, private sector agencies, citizens, and others not directly responsible for administering the program allocation process. The Department of Health, Education, and Welfare, for example, has proposed regulations [21] allowing for waivers of HEW regulations that hinder state and local efforts to improve the planning, coordination, and management of human services.

There is no indication that this trend—which began in the late 1960s—will be discontinued through the late 1970s. The significant lesson here is that cities will find their greatest opportunity—to obtain services for their citizens in their ability to influence these broad planning and allocation processes—not in their direct ability to receive direct federal or other service-related grants.

The trend toward broader local participation in planning and allocation processes make it imperative that cities strenghten their capacity to plan as well as deliver services. If cities can approach their regional health, senior citizens, and social services planning bodies with needs assessments which document the problems and requirements of their own neighborhoods and citizens, they will have to be taken seriously. For example, a group of five managers from cities in Rockingham County, New Hampshire, met on a regular basis to develop a method for responding to the growing demands for local human services programs. Supported by an HEW partnership grant they developed a number of needs assessment and other human services management techniques and formed a countywide evaluation and planning council which will ultimately do the Title XX plan for the county.[22]

The "701" planning program of the Department of Housing and Urban Development can be used for the development of social planning tools, such as needs assessment, evaluation, the development of social elements to municipal general plans, and the development of social impact analyses. The requirements of the Housing and Community Development Act permit the utilization of funds for community assessments and planning activities. The Department of Health, Education, and Welfare has also granted "partnership" funds to state and local governments to develop important human resources tools and relationships. This small but significant program has supported a number of innovative efforts to assist cities in California, Texas, New England, and elsewhere to develop important human resources policy making capabilities and mechanisms. Finally, public service employment positions can as easily be allocated to planning functions as to service delivery functions.

It is significant to note that cities do not rely entirely upon federal funds for the human resources activities. A survey conducted by the League of California Cities in 1976 found that, of the 167 cities in the state responding to the questionnaire, over 33 percent used general fund monies for either human resources planning or programming. Fourteen percent used general revenue sharing funds, 25 percent used CETA resources, and 32 percent employed HCDA funds. Only 4 percent cited Community Services Administration funds; 1 percent, LEAA money; and 1 percent, Older Americans Act funds.

Using the resources of other agencies

For the imaginative and skillful city organization, the biggest resource is the existence of other agencies which possess service and planning capabilities. With respect to the delivery of services, county, state, United Way, and Community Action Agencies provide many times the human resources dollars available to citizens than those available to cities. Next to understanding the human needs of their own citizens, nothing is more significant than coming to grips with the planning, allocation, and service activities of these agencies. In all probability, no matter what the problem an angry, disappointed, or unserved citizen brings to city hall, one of these agencies has some sort of program responsibility that would cover it. Chances are that it was only issues of limited resources, miscommunication, transportation, or eligibility difficulties that have created the problem.

Fortunately, these agencies are gradually recognizing the importance of joint planning and are taking steps to work more closely with one another and with the cities within whose boundaries most human resources problems exist. In California, for example, a number of urban counties such as Alameda have taken the lead in establishing broad-based human services councils designed to identify and bring together all the major actors in a common planning process. Private, community-based agencies, cities, Community Action Agencies, regional bodies, and individual county departments are all represented on a human services council in Alameda County that has taken the first steps in identifying priority human services needs and goals for the area. There are growing instances in which cities and counties are collaborating in the granting and administering of funds to local human services agencies and in which counties such as Orange rely heavily on city needs determinations and/or provide detailed human services computerized data to city human resources planning activities. There are many important issues to be ironed out at both the federal and local level, but the potential for city–county collaboration is there.

United Way agencies also have demonstrated an important commitment to work jointly with local governments. Local elected officials have always been important members of local United Way organizations, allocation and planning groups. In California, in recent years United Way staff in San Diego, Orange County, and the Bay Area have shown increasing interest in merging—or at least coordinating—their own allocation processes with that of the city. In San Diego, for example, the United Way agency was an important participant in a joint city and county–private sector allocation process. Community Action Agencies, while continuing to fund services in the community, are making significant contributions to local government human resources planning by making their social planning, community organization and programming experience and expertise available to cities. Community Action Agencies in both Santa Clara and Alameda Counties have developed "partnership" programs designed to assist cities develop important social planning tools. Increasingly people associated with the Community Services Agency (formerly OEO) see this as a major role for their organization. Finally, at the state level, there are efforts underway to strengthen both city and county social planning capabilities. In recognition that the emphasis on categorical program planning must be balanced by comprehensive policy planning capabilities, the California legislature recently passed a bill intended to help state and local governments assess the social impact of planning decisions and to assist in the allocation of resources to the areas of greatest need. The bill, administered by the Office of Planning and Research, will enable the state to explore the feasibility of developing social profiles by census tract for each county, thereby useable by cities. It also provides for the development of common social planning definitions and classification systems. Also under consideration is state legislation permitting cities to make their planning process and state-mandated general plan more flexible, thereby facilitating the integration of social, physical, and economic planning processes.

Materials and associations

There are numerous publications and materials produced in this field although—as has been pointed out—the literature pertaining to social program design and development is painfully inadequate. One of the most valuable resources to emerge in the 1970s is Project Share, the HEW-funded clearinghouse of human services information described in the Bibliography of this book. Useful materials have also been developed by a number of municipal leagues which have unique access to the activities of their members. The Kansas and California Leagues together with the New England Municipal Center have produced worthwhile materials. Similarly the International City Management Association—in addition to publishing this book—publishes significant materials on human resources programs, planning, and decision making in its Management Information Service Reports and elsewhere. Developments in the publications of the American Society for Public Administration, the National Association of Social Workers, the American Society of Planning Officials, the National Recreation and Park Association, and other professional associations are worth following both in terms of the political and policy developments they represent as well as for program methodological ideas.

Colleges and universities offer many potential resources if local government managers can figure out how to tap them. Departments of urban planning, social work, public administration, and sociology are likely places to start. In addition to expertise, staff support may also be found. Many programs require or encourage student internships. With a small investment it may be possible to hire a well qualified student through a work/study program. In addition to people, a manager may be able to make use of some of a school's computer time, an invaluable resource if there is a need to process survey data. Many schools have special opinion research or survey centers which may be willing to help.

Staff and innovative techniques

Among the least expensive resources available are talented staff and innovative techniques. The problem of identifying competent human resources staff is no different than that of picking personnel for any task. Existing city staff frequently can bring solid administrative skills so necessary to this "soft" field. But frequently, they lack the background and sensitivity in dealing with social issues. One of the most fertile fields for human resources managers and professionals is the old community action and Model Cities programs. Many of the young, enthusiastic staffers were tested and tempered in the stuggles of the 1960s and emerged with unusual problem-solving, conflict management, and political skills. They gained invaluable experience leveraging grants with matching funds, working with established social agencies, and creating inventive alliances and linkages. Many returned to school for public administration and other related degrees, and possess unique combinations of traditional management and social program skills.

There are a number of mechanisms for maximizing the impact of municipal human services outlays. Many services bring results limited primarily to the people targeted to receive the services. Others are often able to generate significant ancillary benefits to the city and/or additional services. For example, information and referral services cut across program lines and can serve outreach and screen functions that assist many services and agencies. In addition, an information and referral service can provide the city planning capacity with solid indications of demands for particular services, citizen attitudes and clues to program evaluation judgments. This information can be utilized in coordination, advocacy, and policy-setting activities designed to build cooperation and common direction among various provider agencies.

A human services center—especially if it is in an existing city facility, or one donated or cheaply obtained—is a particularly economical way to see to it that citizens are served. Like the information and referral function it facilitates firsthand contact with clients and program feedback without actual city involvement in the expensive delivery side. More significant, however, its operation of the center provides a mechanism by which influence can be brought to bear on hours of access, issues requiring coordination and the transmission of developing city human services policy. The cities of Santa Fe Springs, Westminister, and Santa Barbara all operate human services centers which bring together under one roof a variety of needed services and provide the opportunity for them to act effectively in the human resources arena.

Finally, the decision to fund community-based—rather than city-administered—service agencies can prove to be a very economical one. Not only do they traditionally make better use of volunteers than do cities, but they involve cost factors generally lower than city services and costs. In addition, they represent a more flexible investment—one that can be altered or discontinued much more easily than an "established" city service. Sparked by enthusiasm and commitment the staffs of these agencies frequently are far more productive and creative than traditional civil service employees.

1   The authors would like to give special thanks to Louis Garcia, former Assistant Director of the League of California Cities, for his contributions to this chapter.

2   League of California Cities, "Action Plan for the Social Responsibilities of Cities," Berkeley, October 1973, p. 2. The "Action Plan" is the basic policy statement of California municipalities on the subject of human resources. It was developed by the cities through the California League, during late 1972 and 1973, culminating in its official acceptance at the annual conference of the league in October, 1973.

3   United Way of America, *The Painful Necessity of Choice* (Alexandria, Va.: United Way of America, 1974), p. 26.

4   Ibid., p. 15.

5   Albuquerque Community Council, "Need and Resources," Albuquerque, 1973.

6   B. Harold Chetkow, "Some Factors Influencing the Utilization and Impact of Priority Recommendations in Community Planning," *Social Service Review* 41 (September 1967): 271–82; Samuel Mencher, "Current Priority Planning," *Social Work* 9 (July 1964): 27–35, and James J. Callahan, Jr., "Some Latent

Functions of Priority Planning," *Community* 43 (November/December 1967): 23–24.

7 United Way of America, *The Painful Necessity of Choice,* pp. 5–6.

8 Andre L. Delbecq and Andres H. Van De Ven, "A Group Process Model for Problem Identification and Program Planning," *The Journal of Applied Behavioral Science* 7 (July/August 1971): 466–92.

9 As part of its excellent Human Services Series of publications, the New England Municipal Center has issued the following comprehensive description of various city roles in human services activities: New England Municipal Center, *Opportunities for Municipal Participation in Human Services* (Durham, N.H.: New England Municipal Center, 1975).

10 For a discussion of the role of information and referral services, as well as of the importance of a broad spectrum of city strategies to obtain services, see Keith F. Mulrooney, *A Guide to Human Resources Development in Small Cities,* Management Information Service Report, Vol. 5 No. 10 (Washington, D.C.: International City Management Association, October 1973).

11 City of Campbell, California, "Social Services Study Committee Final Report," draft report, May/June 1975.

12 U.S. Conference of Mayors, Task Force on Aging, *Serving the Urban Elderly—Strategies for Mayors* (Washington, D.C.: U.S. Conference of Mayors, 1976), pp. 32–33.

13 Walter Williams, "Implementation Analysis and Assessment," in *Social Program Implementation,* ed. Walter Williams and Richard F. Elmore (New York: Academic Press, 1976), p. 271.

14 Ibid, p. 280.

15 Alfred J. Kahn, *Theory and Practice of Social Planning* (New York: Russell Sage Foundation, 1969), pp. 262–305.

16 League of California Cities, "Guidelines for Preparing a Social Element to the General Plan," draft, Berkeley, 1974, p. 4.

17 Stanford Research Institute, "Garbage In, Garbage Out," prepared for the Human Resources Institute of the League of California Cities, Menlo Park, California, July 1975.

18 Louis Garcia, "Improving the Governing Ability of City Councils," *Western City Magazine,* September 1976, pp. 11 ff. For a discussion of local government planning issues, see Steven A. Waldhorn and Edward J. Blakely, "Picket Fence Planning in California: A Study of Local Government Planning," report to the California Assembly, Special Subcommittee on Community Development, Sacramento, November 1976.

19 This approach is described in detail in William R. Raap, "Getting Serious About the Future of the Urban Problem," *Western City Magazine,* May 1976.

20 Ibid., p. 9.

21 U.S., Department of Health, Education, and Welfare, Office of the Secretary, "Waiver of Departmental Requirements Impeding Improvement of Human Service Delivery by State and Local Governments, Proposed Rulemaking," *Federal Register* 41, no. 235, 6 December 1976, 53412–15.

22 New England Municipal Center, *Human Services Consortium: A Combined Municipal Effort in Human Services Management* (Durham, N.H.: New England Municipal Center, 1976).

Part three: Management of human services programs

Introduction

Part Three of this book discusses broad aspects of the management of human services programs. The root of the word "management" is in the Latin *manus*, meaning "hand," [1] and the thrust of Part Three is indeed to lend a helping hand to local government decision makers as they contemplate four basic areas of overall humans services operation: administrative structures; coordination with other public, and private, sector agencies; management and fiscal controls specific to the human services area; and, not least, the question of evaluation.

In Chapter 7, a close and practical look is taken at the varying administrative structures that a community can choose to adopt (or not to adopt) according to its particular circumstances. The strengths and weaknesses of human services departments, of lead agencies, of human services coordinators, of contracting mechanisms and of intergovernmental approaches are all discussed. The chapter then moves on to the theme of organizational techniques at the service delivery level and the all-important implementation details that can make or break a program. A special emphasis is placed on illustrative case studies throughout the chapter.

In Chapter 8, two senior executives take their respective looks at coordination with public agencies, and coordination with private agencies, analyses based in each case on their own experiences in the public and private sectors. In the case of relations with other public agencies, emphasis is placed on the setting and the actors—from the service deliverer to the elected official—and also on the specific techniques of coordination. For relations with private agencies, emphasis is placed on answers to the question: To coordinate or not to coordinate? and also on the differences (and the similarities) between public and private agencies. Types of coordination are then analyzed, with case study examples, and some concluding remarks offered on points to watch for and the political environment of coordination.

Managerial and particularly financial controls are clearly central to any local government service delivery area, and the new and growing field of human services is no exception. Chapter 9 offers an extensive and practical analysis of these topics. It sets the scene by taking a realistic look at the basic problems in this area, then takes a step-by-step look at financial reporting (with particular emphasis on accounting standards), at the allocation of local government funds to human services programs, and at various budget formats.

Chapter 10 takes a thorough look at the growing art and science of evaluation. The early portion of the chapter sets the scene by examining the historical development and current status of evaluation, a process that has bequeathed a number of definitions to today's manager. Those definitions are then reviewed and analyzed, the purposes of evaluation discussed, and the audiences for evaluation summarized. The chapter proceeds to a discussion of the mechanics of the various kinds of evaluation: effort, outcome, efficiency, and impact. It moves on to an analysis of evaluation procedures and the implementation and administration of evaluation, and concludes with a realistic assessment of the utilization of the results of evaluations.

In sum, therefore, Part Three sharpens the focus of this book by concentrating on management issues specific to most or all human services programs by providing some answers to the questions: How do we organize our local government for human services?; Who do we work with outside our own organization?; How can we apply managerial and financial controls to this area?; and How do we assess what we are and have been doing in the most effective fashion? Part Three therefore rounds off the discussion of general principles, planning methods, and managerial structures and operations that have been the main focus of this book up to this point. It helps to set the stage for the detailed discussion of various functional programs that is to be found in Part Four. Practical examples and illustrations will nevertheless be found throughout Part Three.

1 *Webster's New Collegiate Dictionary,* 1974 edition,
   s.v. ''manage.''

7 Organizational approaches for human services programs

An idea of how some local governments are organized—if that is the word—for human services may be given by considering the fate of the following telephone call coming into a city hall switchboard:

Switchboard: City Hall, can I help you?

Caller: My daughter is handicapped and needs special transportation to her therapist. Who can I speak to in the city about this?

Switchboard (after a pause): I think the Office of Aging handles things like that. Let me connect you.

Office of Aging: Good morning, Office of Aging, can you hold please? (Several minutes later.) Sorry to keep you waiting; can I help you?

Caller: My daughter is handicapped and needs special transportation to her therapist. The switchboard said you could help. Usually someone in the family helps out, but it's not always . . .

Office of Aging: How old is your daughter?

Caller: She's only a teenager, but the switchboard . . .

Office of Aging: I'm sorry, but your daughter isn't eligible. Our program is only for senior citizens. Ask the switchboard to connect you to the Youth Bureau. I'll connect you back. (There are several clicks and the connection is lost. The caller dials the main city hall number again.)

Switchboard: City Hall, can I help you?

Caller: The Youth Bureau, please.

Switchboard: Do you want the Delinquency Program or the Recreation Program?

Caller: I think it must be the Recreation Program. It's my daughter. I called earlier and was cut off, but I don't think I talked to you. I just wanted to . . .

Youth Bureau: Youth Bureau, Recreation, can I help you?

Caller: I hope so. My daughter is handicapped and needs special transportation to her therapist. I was wondering if you . . .

Youth Bureau: I'm sorry; we don't have information on that kind of program. You might try the Office of Aging . . .

Caller: But I . . .

Youth Bureau: . . . or the School Board. Their number is. . . .

This unhappy experience, though hypothetical, is probably a fairly typical example of what would happen to such a call in most local governments a few years ago. The underlying reasons are not difficult to understand. Most human services activities of local governments have grown up in an irregular, ad hoc fashion, as responses to a crisis centered on a particular problem or to a mandate handed down from a higher level of government or to the actions of a demanding group of citizens. The end result in most local governments, as has been mentioned repeatedly in this book, has not been an organized human services program, but a "bag of projects." This is still the case in many local governments as of the later 1970s.

But a more positive attitude has also been in evidence as many local governments have attempted to move beyond such ad hoc approaches to develop a more comprehensive approach to human services. Since the burgeoning federally sponsored social programs of the 1960s—when local government involvement in this area increased strikingly—cities and counties alike have developed a variety of organizational approaches designed to help them get a better managerial "handle" on their human services responsibilities.

The chapters in Part One of this book have outlined and discussed the different roles that a local government can take in human services. The organizational structure adopted by a city or county can complement the role it has selected for itself in the human services delivery system. Some organizational structures are more suited for the direct provider role; others for carrying out a coordinating, or broker, role. There are many other considerations shaping the precise organizational approach adopted by a particular locality. The size of a community is of major significance. An organizational structure that is appropriate to the needs of a large city or county may be totally unworkable in a small city, and vice versa. Demographic, socioeconomic, and ethnic factors can play a major role, as well as fiscal status. Political factors are also important in determining what is viable in a particular community. If a particular organizational strategy makes good sense from a technical and management viewpoint, but has no chance of gaining support from local elected officials, an alternative approach will have to be taken.

Most of the attempts to move away from an ad hoc or crisis management approach to more comprehensive organizational strategies have evolved from the late 1960s to the later 1970s. A great deal of further experimentation and refinement of existing structures can be expected in the coming years, perhaps as a result of new federal initiatives. The 1980s, too, will no doubt bring their crop of new organizational structures and techniques that will provide additional—and possibly better—alternatives for local governments and their managers seeking to meet human services responsibilities.

It is now possible, however, to make at least a tentative overall examination of the varieties of human services organizational approaches that can be used by local governments, and that is the task of the present chapter. The discussion is organized under three main heads. The first section takes a look at alternative organizational approaches at the city or county level. Five different organizational approaches—human services departments; lead agencies; human services coordinators; contracting mechanisms; and intergovernmental and regional approaches—are identified and analyzed, and the question of the best approach is also discussed.

The second section takes a look at innovative organizational approaches at the delivery level, and covers such topics as information and referral systems; multipurpose centers; management information systems; and outreach programs. The third section takes a look at the ''nuts and bolts'' aspects of the implementation of service delivery—an area of management concern that can make or break a program. There is a brief evaluative conclusion.

Throughout, the method adopted is empirical rather than theoretical. That is, the discussion is based on examples of existing organizational approaches developed by local governments, some of them based on the writer's own experience. It is also important to note that the services that a city or county directly controls in the human services area will frequently be less than 10 percent of the total human services available in the community. The ''leverage'' effect of that 10 percent, and how it is organized, can, however, be substantial.

Alternative organizational approaches at the city or county level

There seems to be an almost infinite variety of ways to organize a human services program. The diversity and sheer number of services that are offered in a community of any size (in 1975, the Department of Health, Education, and Welfare [HEW] reported over 1,300 different social services funded under various HEW support programs [1]) plus the large number of different actors involved in the delivery of services mean that there are all kinds of combinations possible in organizing a local government human services function.

As of the later 1970s, there appear to be at least five basic organizational approaches that cities and counties have used in putting together structures to deal with their human services efforts, including human services departments, lead agencies, human services coordinators, contracting mechanisms, and intergovernmental and regional approaches.

Several of the above options can be combined or modified, and there are all kinds of variations. One consultant who has studied the organization of local departments engaged in human services delivery found almost as many approaches as there were departments. Notwithstanding this, for local governments contemplating what their alternatives are as they organize, it should be helpful to take a look at what other communities have done and at the essential differences among the organizational approaches that other communities have developed.

Human services departments

The first approach to be discussed involves integrating into a single department various local government agencies dealing with human services issues. Normally the human services department will be responsible for administering programs that are operated directly by the local government; developing contracts for human services that are purchased by the locality from third-party providers; coordinating with other human services agencies in the community; and doing at least some comprehensive planning for future human services needs.

Local government human services departments differ from one another in how they were initiated, in the number and kinds of services they offer, and even in basic policy roles they play on behalf of the local government. They differ also in organizational form: some departments are more like a collection of semiautonomous agencies than an integral department. The following concrete experiences of a select group of cities and counties illustrate some of these variations.

How they got started　One notable difference among local human services departments is the circumstances of their geneses, that is, how they came to be organized in the first place.

In the state of California, over forty local governments have organized human services departments since the early 1970s. This appears to be a more rapid turnaround in organizational approach than in any other state during the same period. Probably a good deal of this movement in California is due to the efforts of the League of California Cities which has encouraged cities to develop a social element as part of their general plan. Cities have set up human services departments to carry out the planning process and to assist in implementation of the goals set in the new social elements of their general plans.

The example of Marin County　It is interesting to note, however, that different communities in California came to the establishment of human services departments from very different directions. Some made such a reorganization as a result of rational considerations of improved efficiency and effectiveness. For example, in the county of Marin in 1973, the board of supervisors mandated the consideration of improved coordination of the departments of public social services, mental health, and probation, and directed the staff to look into decentralization of human services. The county administrator analyzed various alternative strategies and recommended the consolidation of existing departments into a new unified department of health and human services in order to meet the following objectives: (1) reduction of duplicative activities and functions; (2) reduction of the number of agencies and/or contact points for the citizen in need of help; (3) greater accessibility of human services to constituents through a decentralized coordinated system. The manager's recommendations were accepted, and the new department created.[2]

The example of Pasadena The city of Pasadena in southern California established a new department of human services for somewhat different reasons. A major influence in this city was the federal government's redirection of funds, so that general and special revenue sharing monies and block grants became available to the city to fund social services programs. The city was also concerned about the fragmentation of social services that existed throughout the community and the need for comprehensive planning. But Pasadena's new department came into being, in large part, because of the availability of flexible new federal funds, which enabled the city to take a leadership role in dealing with problems in the fragmented service delivery system.[3]

The example of Gardena The city of Gardena, located in the southern portion of metropolitan Los Angeles, developed a human services department gradually over a period of years. The precipitating event that started off the process in Gardena was the death of eleven youths in 1969 from drug overdoses and drug-related suicides. In trying to confront this crisis, the city council concluded that no existing unit of local government could deal with the drug problem and related youth problems. Therefore, it created a new two-person staff unit to provide services for youths in trouble.

The initial effort in Gardena included a youth employment program, a hot line, rap groups, and ties with other youth agencies. But in order to deal with youth problems, overall community issues had to be confronted as well. Staff came into contact with families and adults as well as young people. The success of the youth program and the gradual increase of support services to other groups culminated in city council action organizing a human services department to include three separate programming units: youth services, family services, and a senior citizens service bureau. A later effort of this department was the establishment of an interagency task force composed of representatives of thirty-four social services organizations in the area—brought together to assess needs, coordinate, and plan for unmet needs.[4]

The benefits of incrementalism The incremental process by which the department gradually evolved in Gardena, from initial efforts to meet a crisis to an agency encompassing a larger range of human services issues, seems to be more common in local governments than is major organizational change entered into for the purpose of rationalizing the system and achieving better management. The creation of a major new department almost inevitably brings with it all kinds of fears. It is a threat to staff working in existing programs that are being folded into the new department. It may appear as a specter to elected officials and many of their constituents, who may fear that a new department—whose responsibilities seem to include problems and needs far outside the scope of what the local government was ever involved in before—will give rise to unpredictable new financial obligations haunting them somewhere down the road. And so it is very understandable that, in many cases, major organizational change will come about only over a long period of time and in an incremental way.

How many services? What services should a human services department provide? Two examples, one comprehensive and the other more selective, illustrate the range of possibilities.

The example of Fort Worth One approach is exemplified by the human resources department in the city of Fort Worth, Texas, which is very comprehensive in this respect. The department started in 1972. After a period of stress in the community, the mayor appointed a special committee to come up with a program for developing fully the city's human resources, in the same way that the city already had planning and development activities to maximize its physical resources. Given such a broad mandate, the committee proposed a reorganization to bring together in one unit all functions within city government associated with human resources; it charged this department with responsibility for developing plans and approaches for the whole range of community human needs. To achieve these goals, the department includes the following functions: human resources administration, community affairs, community centers, consumer protection, manpower planning, mayor's council on youth opportunity, human relations, equal employment opportunity, housing and community development, and an office of human development. Figure 7–1 shows an organization chart of the Fort Worth department.

As already noted, Fort Worth has a very inclusive agency, extending to a number of functions that operate more or less autonomously in most cities. Particularly significant is the fact that housing and community development, a program with close to $2 million in federal funds in Fort Worth, is under the human resources department and not vice versa, as is the case in many cities.

The department operates two community multipurpose centers providing a broad range of social services and recreational and cultural opportunities for residents of the surrounding neighborhoods. As a result of the success of these two centers, two more are on the drawing boards as of the later 1970s. The department also runs minority-awareness seminars for all city employees—from top management to line staff—and it has developed pilot projects to improve the city's interfacing with social services agencies and coordination of services by the various providers in the community.[5]

The example of Cleveland Heights Unlike the inclusive approach of Fort Worth, the city of Cleveland Heights, Ohio, has elected to take on relatively few functions through its human services department. The department focuses on key community problems, including racial integration, a high concentration (21 percent) of elderly people, and home maintenance and improvement. Other human services issues deliberately have been left to the network of private and county agencies serving the community.

While Cleveland Heights' approach is more focused, its department of human services includes several programs not traditionally defined as "social services;" for example, a counseling and assistance program for home owners having difficulty meeting housing code requirements, and a comprehensive real estate program aimed at changing practices within the housing delivery system and ending "white flight." [6]

Human services departments and the nonprovider role There are some fairly obvious advantages to forming a human services department when a local government is directly operating a number of social programs. But such departments have been organized in many communities where the approach is not for the local government to provide services directly, but for it to *obtain* services from outside agencies. This is particularly evident in California, where, as mentioned, there has been so much recent growth in city human services departments. The League of California Cities has stated:

Without exception, the social elements of California cities do not recommend that cities become providers of human services. In fact, the adopted general policy of many cities is that the city will provide direct services only when it is possible for other community agencies to do so. The concern of some that the preparation of a social element might encourage a wholesale rush of cities into providing human services is not verified by experience.[7]

The city of Dallas, Texas, also puts a great deal of emphasis on obtaining services from community agencies. Its human services agency is called the Office of Human Development. This office has an annual budget in excess of $6 million, and operates major manpower, elderly services, and youth programs. The manpower component—its largest single program—uses a community-based strategy by contracting for manpower services from community organizations such as the Dallas Urban League, Dallas Opportunities Industrialization Center, Dallas Jobs for Progress, Dallas County Community Action Committee, and Dallas Independent School District Manpower Skill Center.

In addition to these components, the Dallas agency administers a human development fund to provide financial assistance to nonprofit community-based organizations in the city. The bulk of this fund comes from federal revenue sharing funds. As part of its planning process in putting together a human services delivery plan, the Office of Human Development prepared a report on gaps in the existing delivery system and recommended priority areas for the fund: this was used to give guidance to agencies in presenting their proposals. Maximum funding for a single grant was limited to $75,000. When a proposal is accepted for funding, the office enters into a contract for service with the provider agency and arranges for regular audits on contract performance.[8]

It is clear, then, that a human services department can be used not only to bring together social programs directly administered by a local government, but also to provide a central point for contact with community agencies and obtaining services from them.

Organizational form   Another difference among local government human services departments is in organizational structure itself. In many cities and counties, the human services department is primarily a vehicle for coordinating the human services activities of separate programs, with the specialized agencies delivering the services remaining intact. Some local governments, however, have opted for a

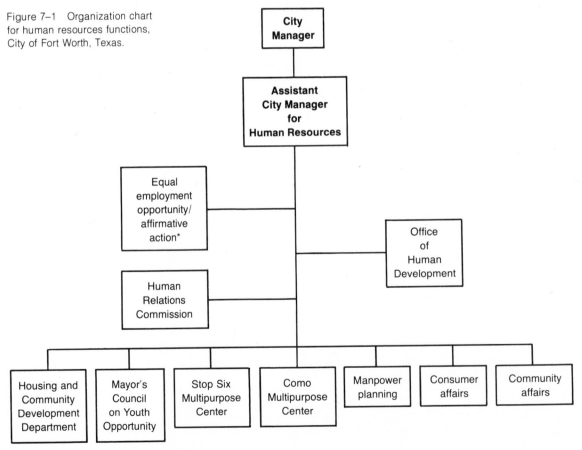

Figure 7–1   Organization chart for human resources functions, City of Fort Worth, Texas.

*Transferred to the Personnel Department in 1975.

more thoroughgoing consolidation of the agencies that existed before the reorganization, so that the resulting department has a better chance of breaking through the highly specialized traditional channels of delivering services. The health and human services department of the county of Marin, California, cited earlier is such a case.

The Marin County reorganization The following are excerpts from a letter from the administrator of Marin County to the board of supervisors. The letter was written in response to the board's request for recommendations on improved coordination among three departments: social services, mental health, and probation.

The factors that led to my conclusion that consolidation is an essential step toward coordination are:

1. The three departments together represent a gross budget of about $20,000,000 and a work force of approximately 600. Salaries and fringe benefits account for about $8,000,000.
2. Certain of the departmental activities represent clear and distinct specialties or specialty functions.
3. Certain of the functions performed in each department are duplicative, such as:
    a. Professional activities involved in intake—identification of the person and problem, and assessment and plan of attack to resolve the problem—and in some continuing services.
    b. Data collection and recording relating to "a" above, resulting, at the present time, in the person having to furnish repetitively such information as name, address, telephone number, social security number, and why he [sic] is addressing the department(s).
    c. Eligibility determinations—a review of income, assets, and other conditions that let a person into the system or exclude him.
    d. Support systems maintained separately for each department—typing and clerical services, records and files, accounting and fiscal management, claiming and payment systems, financial and statistical reporting, communications.
4. As separate entities, the three departments have different departmental and professional orientations, which presents major barriers to a successful coordination of function and elimination of duplication.

A paper restructuring, put together in an organization chart, will not accomplish the fact of a working system to which all people involved are committed. A great deal of detailed work must be done in the areas of job functional analysis and realignment; fiscal systems and management to assure charge-back capability to appropriate state/federal funding sources; administrative systems development in the areas of record keeping, central support services, such as supplies, typing and transcription, communication, payment systems; work management and monitoring systems; staff training to work with the redesigned system; a resolution of legal impediments, including securing state and/or federal waivers to depart from the traditional and proceed with restructuring without loss of outside money.[9]

The above recommendations emphasize the need for a consolidated department to eliminate duplications and make for a more efficient system. But the central objective of the whole reorganization in Marin County was to make human services more accessible to people needing the services, through a well-integrated decentralized system. Getting social workers and medical personnel to work as a team in a program run out of three multipurpose centers was no easy task, as shall be seen in more detail below in the discussion of such centers. It was the conviction of the staff involved in the Marin County reorganization that consolidation was the only path to getting programs really unified at the delivery level.

Confederated, consolidated, and integrated departments As a way of categorizing organizational structures of different human services departments, the Council of State Governments distinguishes three kinds of departments: confederated, consolidated, and integrated.[10] This classification comes out of the examination of human services agencies at the state level in twenty different states, but it would seem to be applicable also for analyzing different kinds of local government departments of human services. A *confederated* human services agency brings together under one department a number of specialized agencies, but allows the agencies to retain most of their administrative and program authority. The delivery of services tends to continue along traditional specialized lines, usually with a tight professional group in charge of the program of each of the component agencies. Each agency has its own planning and administrative staffs.

A *consolidated* department does not leave intact the administrative functions in each of the specialist agencies. Rather, it consolidates for the whole department functions such as planning, evaluation, personnel, purchasing, contracting, and other administrative services. But while a consolidated department pulls together and consolidates such central management functions, the delivery of services continues to be provided through the specialist agencies. For example, the health department will continue to provide screening clinics for the elderly, well-baby clinics, and other such medical programs; staff delivery of these services continues to be under the supervision of the health department.

An *integrated* department is like a consolidated department in that administrative support services are consolidated for the entire human services department. But in an integrated department, the specialist agencies do not retain total control over field operations and day-to-day administration of programs. Rather, the human services department plans and develops programs along functional lines. For example, it may develop a program for the elderly combining a transportation system, food service, health clinic, employment service, and counseling and referral services under a single program staff. Under a consolidated department, in order to put such a program together, the department would have to negotiate with the various specialized agencies to get each to put some of its resources into this elderly program: for example, the manpower agency might provide employment services; the health agency, medical services; etc. Under an integrated department, the staff who actually deliver the services are supervised by generalist program managers, and do not report to specialized agencies. There is thus in the integrated department a great deal more flexibility in designing programs, putting staff together from a number of different disciplines and specializations, and integrating activities into a unified program.

Usually, integrated departments will deliver services in a decentralized way, through multipurpose centers located either in the neighborhoods of those the program is designed to serve or in a central place readily accessible to residents. This is not the only possible mode of service delivery, however. An integrated department can function without multipurpose service centers, but, in that case, it will at least need to operate a central intake and referral system, so that residents looking for services can come to a single entry point and avoid having to go from agency to agency in search of assistance.

Types of departments compared   Clearly there are extensive differences among the three types of human services departments described above. The confederated department brings a number of separate human services agencies together under the umbrella of a single department with a single director. The director in such a system, however, is more a coordinator than a manager of the various agencies, since the planning and management staffs for these programs are retained by the respective agencies. This kind of arrangement can be very good in bringing about better coordination among previously independent agencies, but it represents a surface reorganization rather than a real change in structure. It is not likely that such a department will be able to effect major shifts in program priorities, resource allocations, or service delivery approaches out in the neighborhoods.

The consolidated department, however, is more than a surface reorganization. With virtually all of the planning, personnel, and administrative staff and resources under his or her direct authority, the director of such a department will generally have a much greater capacity to set the directions for the entire human services department, decide new priorities, affect resource allocations, and evaluate program results. The department will usually be somewhat limited, however, in its ability to reduce the fragmentation of service delivery that is such a common problem, since the individual agencies with their specialized professionals will continue to be in charge of actual service delivery.

An integrated department has some of the advantages of a consolidated department in its ability to have an impact on priorities, resource allocations, and overall program direction. Additionally, it has the potential for designing and operating a more integrated service delivery system. The "bottom line" of any reorganization is seen in the changes that take place in day-to-day operations, and in the effectiveness with which services are delivered to the consumer. Since an integrated organization does not have the problem of negotiating with the individual interests of specialist agencies, chances are better that it will be able to have a major impact on the delivery of services. This is not to say that such changes cannot come about through the other two types of departments: it appears, however, that an integrated department possesses a greater likelihood of accomplishing significant changes in service delivery.

In point of fact, there are very few local government departments that could be classified as "integrated." The concept of integrated service delivery is a fairly new one and the resistance of established agencies to it is substantial. Therefore, there are risks attached to moving into an organizational pattern that means such a break with the traditional system. It appears to this author that the move to a fully integrated department will probably have to be a gradual one in most local governments, at least partly because of the degree of built-in resistance. In terms of its ability to bring about needed change in the human services system at the delivery point, the integrated department will, in many cases, best serve the needs of management and consumer alike.

Pros and cons   There are some distinct advantages for a city or county already involved in a variety of human services activities to put them all together into a department of human services. There tends to be a great deal of overlap in the activities of different human services programs—particularly in the clients they serve. Usually, programs are strengthened by close coordination with complementary programs; a human services department has the authority to bring about such coordination among the various programs administered by a local government. Moreover, when a local government has become able to control its own wide range of programs, it is able to more strongly confront the wider problem of fragmentation of services throughout the community. From a public relations viewpoint also, the organization of a human services department can give greater prominence to a local government's role in this field, thus enabling it to have greater leverage with the various provider agencies.

Another advantage, perhaps not quite so obvious, is the greater financial stability that can be given to individual human services programs: by combining funds from different sources, a department is given at least some opportunity to carry a program that suffers a funding lapse from one source. There are opportunities for consolidating some functions, such as intake, record keeping, and outreach, and this too can improve service efficiency. This does not mean, however, that there will necessarily be cost savings, since the reorganization itself occasions new costs. Perhaps most significantly, the human services department provides a chance for a local government to go beyond crisis responses in ad hoc situations to the development of a more comprehensive approach for dealing with social issues.

On the other hand, the organization of such a department is no panacea. A county administrator in Maryland makes the point strongly that a human services department can be a form of tokenism. The services that a city or county directly controls in the human services area are only a small percentage of the total human services available in the community. There is the danger in setting up such a department that the local officials will feel that, by so doing, they are fully carrying out the local government's responsibilities in meeting social needs. The result can be the neglect of the still necessary advocacy role with other service providers.

A major problem in organizing a human services department is the fact that such a reorganization is frequently resisted by the staff of the several specialized agencies that are being consolidated. Human services agencies' staffs are notorious for being protective of their turf and fearful of any intrusions by others outside their particular professional discipline. For this reason, a thorough reorganization can be a very costly process politically. If the reorganization is to succeed, it is important to do groundwork, both with the staff and the general public, in order to give an understanding of the need to use resources better and to improve services.

Resistance to change does not come only from within the existing staff. Frequently, the most powerful obstacles to improved organization are the regulations and bureaucratic constraints coming down from the federal and state agencies that provide the funding guidelines, set the standards, conduct the audits, and otherwise regulate local human services agencies. For some programs, the requirements set by these higher levels of government are so detailed and rigid that there is virtually no flexibility left for deciding at the local level how the program can best be implemented.

Finally, another potential problem with human services departments is that they can become enormously large and powerful, sometimes to the point of being almost unmanageable. Washington, D.C., for example, has a human resources department which is by far the largest governmental entity in the city, with one-third of the city's employees and 20 percent of the population of the District of Columbia under its care. As of this writing, strong efforts are being made to detach municipal hospitals and several other services from control of the Department of Human Resources.[11] New York City ran into similar problems with its human services superagency some years ago.

Despite such perils and obstacles, it appears that a growing number of local governments are organizing human services departments. With the proliferation and fragmentation of social services agencies that has become such a problem in virtually every American community, it is likely that many more localities will undertake similar reorganizations in the interest of creating a tool with which to make at least some improvements in the human services delivery system.

The lead agency and its role

A second organizational approach that can be adopted by a local government is to use an existing department and expand the responsibilities of that department so that, in effect, it will play the lead role for the locality in responding to human services needs. The existing department may be a traditional municipal department such as a welfare, health, or recreation and parks department, or it might be an agency such as a Model Cities agency established through federal funding to meet the needs of a particular target group or neighborhood.

Building on the Model Cities foundation The Model Cities program initiated in the 1960s was a major federal initiative to organize new approaches to deal with neighborhood problems (both physical and social) in 150 cities. For many of the participating cities, it was the deepest experience they had yet undertaken in dealing with human services issues. It was therefore natural that, as the program was phased down in the early 1970s, many cities made use of the organizational structures and staff from the Model Cities program to set up a communitywide human services agency.

With the availability of community development block grants, a large number of jurisdictions have established community development departments to implement the block grant program, and have then used this department to take the lead in human services. For example, the city of Toledo established a division of human resources within its department of community development in 1975. This division continues a number of the city's past Model Cities efforts, and has undertaken responsibility for programs for the elderly, day care services, youth programs, and drug abuse and alcoholism programs.[12] The city of Richmond, California, also carries out its human services activities through its community development department.[13]

From recreation to people services Examples of the use of recreation departments as lead agencies—in two cities in California—follow.

The example of Westminster The city of Westminster, California, found in connection with hearings regarding priorities for the city's new housing and community development program, that there was a strongly felt need among Westminster residents for a community center. The city council decided to move ahead and establish the community center, taking advantage of the availability of an elementary school that was just being closed down. To implement the new community center program, the city combined two existing city departments—recreation and community programs—into a single new department called the Department of Community Services. This new department continued to provide recreation opportunities for people of all ages at parks, playgrounds, and community buildings. In addition, through the new community center, it began to coordinate and provide a wide range of social services to the entire community with an emphasis on the needs of senior citizens, youth, and minorities. Nine different agencies set up shop in the center, with programs ranging from health maintenance and child care to employment assistance and debt counseling.

Westminster's approach was a highly incremental one. The city took advantage of the new community center program to make a relatively minor reorganization; it thereby created a lead agency with greater capability for developing the city's role in human services. In a sense, this is a ''back door'' method of getting a new structure—and a relatively painless one at that.[14]

The example of Garden Grove Another city that has used its recreation department as a lead agency is Garden Grove, California. It was the conviction of city officials in Garden Grove that the traditional functions of recreation should be expanded into the area of people-related services to better meet the needs of the entire community. The city manager wanted to avoid creating a new department, and the recreation and parks department looked like the best available agency to take the lead in human services.

This reorganization did not occur without some difficulties. There was apprehension among recreation department staff who were concerned that the recreation and park functions might be downgraded, with a lesser role for themselves. But the reorganization went ahead, the new human services department was christened, and, in addition to park and recreation activities, it took on responsibility for cultural arts and social programming. The department took the lead in conducting a needs assessment and preparing the social element for the city's general plan. It moved into specific social services areas, including an information and referral service, rent subsidy program, drug diversion program, and senior citizen meals program. In time, the apprehensions of staff of the old department disappeared. This was because, rather than finding their own functions downgraded, they found themselves with more visibility in the context of the human services department than they had had before as a separate department.[15] Some of the difficulties of reorganization thus diminish over the long term.

Pros and cons   The use of a lead agency is a less drastic method of organizing for human services than the organization of a new human services department. Reorganization costs are small, both in terms of money to be spent and risks to be taken. There is relatively little threat to existing agencies and departments.

A lead agency approach appears to be a good way for local governments to test the waters without drowning in the process. A locality can use an existing department to experiment with a new nontraditional program, and see how well it is implemented by the staff and how acceptable it is to the community—before sticking its neck out with a more comprehensive approach. In many communities, it simply would be politically impossible to take a comprehensive approach, and using a lead agency might be the only viable option of the two. In smaller communities, particularly those with relatively few disadvantaged people, it may be the optimal approach.

There are some disadvantages, however, to this approach. It is difficult for a department with a relatively narrow focus to expand its perspective enough to take a truly comprehensive approach to human services. For a local government to move away from an ad hoc approach and have a positive effect on the whole human services delivery system in its area, a comprehensive viewpoint would seem to be rather critical. But it is a lot to ask of a recreation department, community development agency, or any other department, to move so far beyond its original focus so as to take on a really broad-beamed approach to human services. To make this point more concrete, it should be noted that the community development program in most communities is charged with developing social services as an adjunct to, and in support of, physical development activities; for example, if a day care center will enhance a new building complex, that fits the thrust of community development clearly. To put the community development agency in charge of all human services for a city is almost necessarily going to end up with a reduced role for that community in human services.

Looking at the other side of the coin, there is also a problem for the lead agency in seeing that its own former program is not diluted or diminished. The concern of the recreation staff in Garden Grove was a valid one; unless there is a great deal of care, the enlarged mission of the department can undercut some of its ongoing activities.

Role of the human services coordinator

Another approach open to a local government is to hire a staff person as human services coordinator to develop human services programs and activities and to interface on behalf of the locality with other social services agencies. This approach emphasizes the indirect, or "broker," role of the local government in the human services field. It frequently involves the creation of a human services council or task force that includes representatives of major provider agencies as well as of client groups. Whatever specific title the position has, the "coordinator" is essentially a staff position, without direct authority over line operations.

The example of Monroe County   In Monroe County, New York, a human resources council was established by the county manager in 1973. It included representatives of the departments of health, social services, manpower, mental health, and probation, the veteran services agency, the office of aging, the youth board, the community hospital, the United Community Chest, and the dean of the faculty of human services at the local university. The council was aimed at bringing a degree of coordination into the fragmented human services programs then existing in the county. It was charged with the task of centralizing the planning of human services; with encouraging greater administrative control over the allocation of resources to these programs; and with broadening citizen participation.

A year later, Monroe County created the position of director of human resources in the office of the county manager to chair and provide staff services to the human resources council. This staff person is also responsible for providing support to county human services agencies in the area of planning, budgeting, and program review. This is a good example of a human services coordinator position.[16]

The example of Skokie In the village of Skokie, Illinois, the village manager has two human services coordinators attached to his office: a human resources director and the director of the office on aging. The human resources director provides staff assistance to the village's youth commission and human relations commission, and oversees the village's programs for youth, fair housing, and employment. The director of the office on aging plays a prominent role in coordinating services provided by other agencies in the area for older adults, and provides a broad range of information and referral services for the elderly. Both offices are attached to the village manager's office. This arrangement stemmed from the need for close coordination between these two offices and other municipal departments. Without the close cooperation of a large number of village personnel, the offices could not function properly. Linking them to the manager's office gives them the top management support and direction needed for success.[17]

The example of Arlington Heights The village of Arlington Heights, Illinois, established a new position of human services coordinator. Unlike the cases just cited, the job is not situated in the manager's office, but in the health services department. The job description for the Arlington Heights human services coordinator serves well to illustrate the overall functions of such a position, no matter where within the organization it is located. The following is excerpted from that job description:

Distinguishing features of the class: . . . Evaluates, plans, and recommends human service programs and activities. Initiates, organizes, promotes, and supervises approved programs. Stimulates and coordinates human service programs with other public and private agencies. Recruits, trains, and evaluates efforts of volunteers. Assists in development of annual program budget. Insures safe and efficient operation of human service programs. Provides liaison from village manager to youth council and senior citizens commission.

Examples of work (illustrative only): Recommend goals and evaluation criteria for all human service programs. . . . Actively develop cooperative efforts with other . . . agencies. . . . Develop bulletins, brochures . . . for programs. . . . Recommend development of new programs and policies. . . . Attend meetings of service and civic groups . . . to explain and promote human service activities.[18]

Pros and cons A limitation of this approach is that, without line authority over any agencies or programs, the human services coordinator may lack the power to effectively pull together the locality's human services efforts. This can be offset somewhat by locating the coordinator in the chief administrator's office, as was done in Skokie, so that the coordinator will be regarded by the staff of the individual departments as having the authority of the manager's office as a base. Without such leverage, it will probably be very difficult for the coordinator to have any significant impact on the delivery system.

Apart from the question of authority, there is also a limitation on how much can be accomplished by a single individual, since the human services coordinator position usually falls on the shoulders of a single professional staff person. If that staff person is exceptionally talented and creative, and comes equipped with highly developed diplomatic skills, then he or she may be able to accomplish a good deal toward unifying human services activities of the local government and interfacing with community social services agencies. But the human services field is a vast and complex one, and it will be difficult for a single staff person to do an adequate job on policy development, needs assessment and planning, fostering innovative approaches, integration of efforts at the delivery level, evaluation of ongoing programs, etc. This limitation, too, can be overcome by recruiting staff of the various human services agencies to work with the coordinator on these tasks.

There are some advantages that the coordinator approach has over the lead agency approach. The coordinator can be charged from the outset with developing a comprehensive strategy for the local government in the human services field, and is not saddled with the constraints of having to go through a step-by-step process to reach this broad viewpoint, as is a recreation department, for example, that moves bit by bit into larger responsibilities in the human services area. Also, depending on where in the organization the human services coordinator is placed, there is an opportunity to give a higher profile to the local government's interest and concern for human services. All things being equal, for an assistant city manager who is serving as human services coordinator, it will probably be easier for him or her to have an impact on social services providers in the community than it would be for the director of a recreation program or a community development department.

Finally, one strong point in favor of the human services coordinator approach is that it is relatively inexpensive and easy to institute. It does not require the establishment of a new department, or the internal reorganization of an existing department. It does require the appropriation of funds for a new staff position, or the reassignment of an existing staff member. For many communities, it is probably the quickest way to go beyond ad hoc human services projects to get involved in the larger human services delivery system. For many small communities, it may be the only way.

Contracting mechanisms

Some local governments have elected to conduct their human services effort primarily through providing funds and support to existing community agencies in meeting social problems. To carry out this approach effectively entails some modification in the organizational structure—either by designating an existing agency, or creating a new one, to develop and monitor contracts with the provider agencies.

For many cities and counties, the business of contracting with social services agencies is a new one. Much of the stimulus for contracting out these services came from the availability of general revenue sharing funds, as well as community development and Title XX funds.

The "pinata game" Terry Novak, city manager of Columbia, Missouri, describes the rather confusing situation that developed in the early 1970s:

OEO [the Office of Economic Opportunity] died here at roughly the same time as federal revenue sharing began. Revenue sharing was of course allocated by local city councils and, a few years later, community development funds were also allocated by local city councils. The agencies looking for matching monies changed their orientation from OEO to the local city councils.

The first year distribution of general revenue sharing began what I call "the pinata game." You take a pile of money and put it in a pinata. Everyone lines up and hits it with a stick and sees what falls out. That may be overstated, but from the point of view of professional budgeting, that is the allocation system.[19]

In order to get away from this "pinata game" and develop a more controlled allocation system, the city of Columbia joined with Boone County in creating a new agency, the Boone County Community Services Council. The council was composed of eleven volunteer members representing the community, and a small full-time staff funded by the city and county. Approximately half of Columbia's revenue sharing funds were set aside for allocation advice from this council.

Public hearings were held by committees of the council, made up of local volunteer consultants in areas such as health care, criminal justice, and recreation, who heard arguments supporting various proposals. The council not only provided advice to the city and county on how to allocate funds among competing proposals, but also took up the task of reviewing the agencies in a performance audit fashion, trying to assist them whenever possible with management problems.[20]

The examples of Santa Barbara and Santa Monica The city of Santa Barbara, California, has used a similar process, but made use of a preexisting citizens group instead of creating a new one. The city council transformed a citizen–provider committee which prepared the social services plan for the city into an ongoing social services planning board which oversaw implementation of the plan. One of the functions of the social services planning board is to establish priorities for services needed to carry out the social services plan, using a hearing process. This then enables the city to solicit proposals from community agencies to address priority objectives identified by the board (approximately 25 percent of its general revenue sharing funds were allocated to fund such social services programs on a contract basis).[21]

An interesting new wrinkle was added by the city of Santa Monica, California. Santa Monica made use of an existing department of environmental services, and established a new division, known as "grants and community services," to rationalize the allocation process. One responsibility of this new division was to develop guidelines for community agencies submitting proposals and rating criteria, both designed to provide objective assessments acceptable both to the provider agencies and to the city council (the ultimate decision maker). But the division also undertook responsibility for providing technical assistance to community agencies in identifying funding sources outside the city, and provided grantsmanship help to help those agencies secure funds for the provision of essential social services.[22]

The example of Indianapolis One other approach worth noting is a cooperative effort in Indianapolis, where the city made use of a private agency, the Central Indiana Council on Aging, to improve its system for allocating funds to social services agencies to meet the needs of senior citizens. In order to change the previous system whereby proposals came into the city based primarily on the initiative of the social services agencies, the city and the council on aging agreed on an eight-step procedure designed to give the city a more proactive role:

1. Based upon data from the Council on Aging and other sources, the city states the needs of its senior citizens, ranks them by priority, and states the goals that will address the needs. Asks the Council to draft service specifications.
2. The Council defines service objectives, specifications, and service unit allocations based upon estimated level of need and historical user rates.
3. The city reviews the specifications submitted by the Council on Aging. Revises wherever necessary. Asks the Council to submit a proposal based upon the specifications.
4. The Council invites proposals from all potential providers. Each proposal must meet minimum specifications. Unit costs for each service must be determined.
5. The Council reviews proposals, determines compliance with specifications, chooses providers with whom it wishes to enter into contracts.
6. Based upon proposals selected, the Council submits comprehensive proposal to the city. The Mayor's office and the City Council decide how much money they want to see appropriated for senior citizen services. If their appropriation is less than that required to provide the services according to specifications, they decide what services to eliminate or cut back.
7. The City and Council on Aging execute the prime contract based upon the total appropriation by the city–county council.
8. The Council on Aging executes subcontracts with providers. Reimbursement is based upon service units provided times the agreed-upon unit cost. If services are not provided, there is no reimbursement.[23]

What the city of Indianapolis is doing through a private agency, many cities and counties are now doing through their own departments. Priorities are set, and specifications drawn up looking for specific proposals from community agencies. Contracts are then drawn up between the local government and provider agencies under a purchase of services arrangement, so that the local government pays only for services received. (More detail on various contracting procedures open to local governments can be found in Chapter 9.)

Pros and cons Contracting out for all or most human services activities of a local government is a viable strategy, and for many communities it is probably a much better choice than operating programs directly. When this is the basic strategy of a locality, it is important to have a strong mechanism for making decisions on allocation of funds, and also for monitoring performance of the contracts that are let.

If the contracting mechanism stands alone and represents the entire effort of a local government in the human services field, however, the local government will probably have a rather limited role in making improvements in the overall service delivery system. Where the contracting mechanism is tied into an agency with a broader approach to human services, such as the social services planning board in Santa Barbara, the chances are probably better that the locality will be able to have an impact on the overall human services system serving the community.

Intergovernmental and regional approaches

A growing number of cities and counties, particularly small communities, have found that their efforts in the human services field can be more fruitful by combining with other local governments in a unified program.

The example of Rockingham County An example is a human services consortium of five municipalities in Rockingham County, New Hampshire, with populations ranging from 8,000 to 28,000. The municipalities are Derry, Exeter, Hampton, Portsmouth, and Salem. The managers of these communities were faced with significantly increased funding requests from human services agencies; they joined together in an effort to build their planning and management capabilities in the human services field, and to acquire joint staff so that they would be in a position to compete more effectively for federal funds. The consortium received a partnership grant from HEW to support their efforts and engaged a joint staff. The consortium effort produced a needs assessment and a resource inventory for each of the five municipalities, and also developed management tools tailored to each muncipality's program. A countywide human services coordinating council was established, consisting of local elected officials, service providers, consumers, and community leaders. This council is geared toward providing information and referral services, eliminating duplication, and mobilizing voluntary resources.[24]

Two California examples Two cities in Orange County, California (Brea and La Habra), opted for even closer collaboration. The two cities are contiguous and are faced with very similar social problems. Cooperative relations began when managers of the two communities opted to do a joint needs assessment and prepare a cooperative social services plan. Following this, the cities submitted a joint application to the Orange County Board of Supervisors for a $750,000 grant to fund specific social services programs. A number of the programs that resulted were designed so as to serve residents of both cities; for example, a dial-a-ride transportation system, a meals-on-wheels program for senior citizens, and a health and dental outreach program located in La Habra, but serving residents of the two communities. These arrangements have been worked out between the two cities without a formal agreement; there is a monthly meeting of the two communities' social services delivery organizations to coordinate programming and planning decisions.[25]

Alameda County, California, set up a more formalized arrangement, under a joint powers agreement among seven municipalities, to assess needs and the capabilities of existing social services in that area.[26]

The examples of Kansas and Texas Quite a different approach was taken in Kansas under the auspices of the League of Kansas Municipalities. Through an HEW grant, a "circuit rider" program was set up for three small cities (Hayes, Dodge City, and Liberal) to provide management assistance in building up the capacity of these cities to plan and implement a human services program. The circuit rider is technically an employee of the League of Kansas Municipalities, but he spends most of his time working with local officials in the three cities and takes administrative direction from the three city managers. He has assisted the cities in data gathering, needs assessment, inventory of resources, and priority setting. This circuit rider approach seems to have a lot to offer to muncipalites too small to hire a full-time human services specialist.[27]

In recent years, regional planning agencies and councils of governments have become more active in the human services area. An example is the North Central Texas Council of Governments, which provides services to Dallas, Forth Worth, and the surrounding area. This agency has a human resources department which does regionwide planning for the aging, for manpower programs, and for programs dealing with alcohol abuse. It is working with local governments in the region to eliminate duplication, interrelate planning between jurisdictions, and establish referral agreements where needed.[28]

Pros and cons The various intergovernmental approaches mentioned above appear to have much promise for the future. For many small communities that do not have the resources to hire trained human services professionals and set up their own organizations, a cooperative approach with other local governments seems to be a very good alternative. It is also a truism that social problems are not confined to the political boundaries of a city or county. So it may make a great deal of sense for adjacent communities dealing with essentially the same social issue to combine forces in order to deal with it more effectively. Certain types of programs (e.g., a highly specialized mental health program for retarded children) may require such a large population to make the service economically feasible that the service simply could not be provided without cooperation among several jurisdictions. For all these reasons, an intergovernmental approach frequently makes very good sense.

Which is the best approach?

There is no single best approach that a local government can use in human services. There are just too many differences between local governments to make possible a clear hierarchy of organizational structures in terms of which is the best alternative, which is second best, and so on. Four of the major differences can be noted.

Differences between cities and counties First, there are major differences between the kinds of human services programs operated by cities and by counties. In most parts of the country, counties play a much larger role in direct delivery of human services than do cities, particularly in welfare and health services. A good organizational structure for a county might be altogether inappropriate for a city with a similar size population just a few miles away.

Differences in size of communities   A second big difference is in the size of communities. A large city may find the only effective organizational approach it can take to deal effectively with a very complicated human services delivery system is a fully consolidated department of human services. A small city with relatively scarce funding resources might be much better advised to go the route of a human services coordinator operating out of the manager's office (and indeed, this might even be the city manager).

Differences in level of political acceptance   The level of political acceptance for human services goals is a third, and extremely important, factor in determining what is the most viable organizational structure for human services. Where the local governing body or the public at large have a great deal of reluctance and hesitate to move outside traditional municipal services and get involved with ''tricky'' human services problems, it could be disastrous to push for a comprehensive human services department, even if, from a technical viewpoint, this would be the soundest approach for coping with that community's problems. For many local governments, the political climate is such that the local government is able to take on only very gradually and by small steps a more significant role in meeting the human services needs of its residents.

Differences in effectiveness of the present system   A fourth consideration is the tradition that exists in a given community for meeting human services needs, and the effectiveness of the present human services system. If the system is in fairly good shape overall with a tradition of strong nonprofit agencies providing the services, then a deliberately low profile may make sense for a local government with the emphasis on filling in the gaps by contracting out with the existing social agencies. If there are major deficiencies in the service system, and relatively weak service providers, the local government may be much better advised to create new programs and possibly to run them directly. The key question for a local government in this context is, What is the most important step (or steps) that the jurisdiction can take to improve human services for its citizens within the context of the existing system?

The best option?   Having presented all these caveats on the difficulties of prescribing one organizational option as superior to others, it nonetheless appears to this author that the first alternative (that of the human services department and, specifically, the integrated or consolidated department) holds the greatest potential for most local governments in developing fully their capabilities for dealing with human needs. The reasoning behind this is that in most communities of any sizable population, the delivery system is such a complicated morass of competing agencies and entrenched interests that, in order to have any kind of impact, the local government's effort should have at least departmental status. If the human services function is attached to another department, or downgraded in any way as a less significant function than traditional departments such as public works, police, fire, etc., it could end up adding a few more social programs to the already large number that exist—possibly contributing to the rampant confusion that exists rather than helping to straighten it out.

Having stated this personal bias, it should be hastily added that no organizational structure is a panacea. A good deal more goes into making a program work than its central administrative structure. There are, no doubt, illustrations that can be given of both successes and failures for every type of organizational alternative that has been discussed above. The overall organizational structure is only one element in an effective program. Of equal or greater importance is what happens at the service delivery level—the management approaches used there, the involvement of the community, and above all, the competence and sensitivity of program staff.

Innovative organizational approaches at the delivery level

Organizational changes at the central administrative level can be extremely important in putting a local government into a position to be able to do something about the service delivery system, but this is not the same as doing it. Unless a locality's organizational efforts percolate down and extend out to the people using social services, then administrative rearrangements are like shifting furniture around the living room. It may look prettier, but nothing has really changed.

As the example cited at the opening of this chapter indicated, in most communities having a typically fragmented service delivery system, the average person faces a monumental task in trying to find—amid the myriad of agencies and eligibility rules—the right agency to deal with his or her problem. Individuals with multiple problems may have to go to a number of different locations, some far removed from their own neighborhood, in order to get help. Coming in for the first time to an agency to get assistance can be a nightmare of filling out application forms, establishing eligibility, reviewing finances—particularly when the process has to be repeated at several agencies. Worse still is the revolving door treatment, where clients are referred from one agency to another, and then to another until they finally connect with the right agencies almost by happenstance—or give up the search in frustration.

To deal with this kind of problem, local governments in recent years have developed a whole variety of new techniques out at the neighborhood or service delivery level to eliminate some of the confusion, make services more accessible to clients, and to service more effectively the multiple-problem individual or family. Several of these techniques—information and referral systems; multipurpose centers; management information systems; and outreach—that are most commonly used by local governments are discussed below. Chapter 16 lists and describes many additional techniques, not covered here, that can be used to bring about integration of services at the delivery level.

Information and referral systems

An information and referral (I and R) system is an organized program to direct people looking for assistance to the agency or agencies that can best meet their needs. It may be aimed at a particular target population, e.g., senior citizens, or it may encompass all human services agencies in a given community.

The principal value of an I and R system is to assist people in getting prompt service from the right agency, thereby saving the waste, frustration, and inefficiency that results from a merry-go-round cycle where a client is passed from one agency to another until finally making the right contact. Beyond this direct people-serving purpose, it can also have an impact on human services planning. When adequately organized, an I and R unit can provide data that is otherwise very hard to come by, on human services delivery patterns and gaps in service. When this data-generating potential of an I and R system is fully exploited, the system can be a valuable tool for increasing the accountability of social services agencies, and for the future planning and programming efforts of a local government.

The example of Wilkes-Barre The city of Wilkes-Barre, Pennsylvania, has such a system. The city's information system serves a dual purpose: to assist residents in finding assistance to meet both emergency and long term needs, and to gather data for planning and program development. The way the system works from a resident's viewpoint is as follows. A resident in need of assistance can call the Wilkes-Barre Information System, a central communications office. The staff person, an information and referral specialist having casework in-service training, assesses the need of the resident and helps choose the best agency for meeting that need. The staff person will then, through the central communications system, contact the designated agency and establish a three-way conference call between the resident, the agency, and the information–referral specialist. After explaining the problem to the appropriate agency staff person, the specialist monitors the call, at the consent of the resident, in order to aid in any manner possible. If the resident makes an appointment with the agency, the specialist notes this so that the follow-up staff may remind the resident of the appointment a few days in advance of the date. The specialist also completes an information form for each resident's request in order to make a letter service evaluation. If the staff specialist finds that a resident did not receive the needed service, or was displeased with the service, an inquiry is made as to the reasons and action taken to remedy the situation. Information gathered on the data forms is used subsequently to analyze needs and service gaps in a continuing program development process.[29]

The "directory of services" An agency directory or "directory of services" is an important element in an information and referral system. Such a directory should contain information in a succinct, easily accessed format on the agencies providing human services in a community, services offered, eligibility requirements, area or target population served, size of budget and staff, contact point for new clients, etc.

There are many ways of putting together such a directory of services. It is possible to do this on a very limited budget, by following a process such as taken by an interagency council in Sussex County, Delaware. There a voluntary committee was assigned the task of compiling the directory. Individual provider agencies contributed information on a standardized form about their agency's activities. Each agency reproduced 200 copies of their information sheet and this was put together into a booklet. The directory was sold to interested organizations at $1.00 per copy.[30] There are, of course, much more sophisticated ways of producing a service directory, but this example from Delaware shows it can be done on a shoestring budget if necessary.

A Vermont example In recent years, information and referral programs have developed in many different communities. Four of the six New England states have taken a coordinated approach to developing I and R systems. In commenting on developments in Vermont, an official of the human services agency of the state of Vermont stated:

Three years ago, no visible, distinct, general purpose information and referral programs were operating in Vermont. However, through the initiative of community groups, most of the population is now served by I and R systems.

All of the I and R centers in Vermont have been created by local community groups with little or no financial or program assistance from state or local governments. Community support continues in several ways, most notably by providing a volunteer staff. In addition, the community involvement in I and R has had a catalytic effect on all segments of the community, mobilizing people who had not previously been involved in human services. The end result is not only an effective I and R program, but the creation of a large group of persons knowledgeable and concerned about the human services delivery system and trained in basic human service skills. . . .

In Vermont, some financial support for I and R has come from such diverse sources as OEO, Title XX, Older Americans Act (Title III), community development, town government, United Way, local donations and, most important, CETA.

An I and R program has many advantages over other human service programs. It has high visibility to the public, low political risk, and a potentially wide clientele. It often has low start up and operating costs, partly because of its use of volunteers.[31]

It would seem from Vermont's experience that an information and referral program is a relatively inexpensive approach available to localities for making improvements in the human services system.

Multipurpose centers

A multipurpose center is a facility that brings together under one roof several human services agencies. This is a relatively new approach, and the principal idea is to bring needed services directly to areas where people live, thereby making services more accessible to those who need them most. A second aim is to bring about better coordination among the cooperating agencies working out of the center.

The multiservice center is a particularly useful setting for dealing with the problems of the great numbers of social services clients who have multiple problems. For example, a person in need of job training may also need counseling, financial assistance for his family, help in dealing with a drug or alcohol problem or with a health problem, etc. The service center offers some chance of dealing with the whole person in a coordinated way.

The Division of State Service Centers of the state of Delaware offers a graphic picture of the goals of its service center program in the following description:

Scores of barriers separate people from the services they need—barriers of misunderstanding and confusion, of fear and frustration, of social and geographic distance. Sometimes a person does not know that the service is available. Sometimes he [sic] does not know where to get it or how to make use of it. He may be confused by agency policy; he may not understand eligibility requirements, he may not know how to fill out the forms required by the various agencies. There may be the less tangible barriers of being discouraged, of having failed in past efforts, or of no longer believing that anyone wants to or can help. The removal of these barriers is the target of the service center program.[32]

Figure 7–2   Photograph of a model of the Crossroads Community Center, City of Dallas, Texas. (Source: Courtesy of the City of Dallas, Texas.)

The example of Dallas   A multipurpose center that has become widely recognized as something of a model for this kind of program is the Crossroads Community Center in Dallas. This center is operated by the city of Dallas, and is housed in five buildings in a campus style arrangement: core services, medical, library, recreation, and day care. The city does more than provide a building for the various federal, state, and local social services agencies working out of the Crossroads Center. The city employs a center manager who is responsible for developing coordination and team work between the various agencies at the center, and for administering central intake and record-keeping procedures. Other notable features of the program are team diagnosis of social and health problems, a prescribed plan for dealing with those problems, and a greatly simplified system of payment.

The Crossroads Center is located in south Dallas, and has had a discernible influence on the neighborhood. Evaluation studies of the center have noted the favorable impact it has had on that neighborhood, and particularly its contribution to development of new leadership in the community as a result of participation by neighborhood residents in the activities of the Crossroads Center.[33]

The example of Titusville   Another multiservice center that appears to have had a major impact on its environment is the Social Service Center in Titusville, Florida. In 1969, prior to the creation of this center, a Titusville resident with a social service need frequently had to travel 15 to 40 miles to make contact with the appropriate agency. Evidently many persons did not try in the first place or did not know enough about the "system" to find the agency that was needed. Since the creation of the Social Service Center in 1970, the number of residents served by social agencies in Titusville has grown from 200 to 3,000 per month. The Titusville center is administered by the city department of social services, and includes over 45 public and private agencies that operate out of the center. With the dearth of social services in Titusville, the city used a "supermarket" concept with the aim of bringing as many service agencies as possible into the center so that no client would have to leave the city for a social service. The center has a central intake and referral system, and a computerized reporting system. Another feature of the center is client advocacy; that is, center staff are available to represent client interests to agencies where problems occur. Clients also participate in the decision making on center activity through an advisory board.[34]

Role of the center manager   One of the difficult organizational issues in operating a multiservice center is the role of the center manager. If the agencies operating out of the center are completely autonomous and work in isolation from one another, then a great deal of the potential effectiveness of the program is lost. So it is important that the center manager have some authority to coordinate services of the various agencies located in the center. In the county of Marin, California, as the county decentralization program moved from a single human services center to three, the director of the county Department of Health and Human Services issued a directive in an attempt to define the role of the center manager vis-à-vis the directors of the several branches (e.g., social services, public health, mental health) which had staff and programs operating out of the centers. Excerpts from this memorandum may serve to highlight this issue:

The fundamental organizational issue concerns the relative roles and responsibilities of the branch chiefs and the service center managers. A number of alternatives have been considered:

1. At one extreme, all branch chiefs would retain full program and supervisory responsibility for the staff coming to each center from the respective branches. Such personnel would be outstationed and would be expected to work cooperatively with one another toward common objectives. In this configuration, the service center manager would have administrative and coordinative duties mainly concerning the work environment and would interface with the local community.
2. At the other extreme, service center managers would be cross-trained in all programs for which the center has responsibility and would be expected to carry out those programs through supervised staff and external arrangements, representing the department in the local community. In this alternative, branch chiefs would relate to service centers in much the same way as they relate to third party contractors who perform work which helps achieve their program objectives, subject to contract monitoring.
3. Between the two extremes are various arrangements which bring both the branch chiefs and the service center managers into overseeing relationships regarding the functioning of the center. Any model of counterpart management presents the difficulty of dual bosses, and therefore requires further refinement of roles.[35]

In Marin County, the third alternative was chosen, and a very careful attempt was made to work out what is clearly a ticklish relationship.

Current status The multipurpose center concept has caught on in many different states and, like information and referral systems, seems to be a growing phenomenon. In the state of Delaware, a whole network of service centers has been established since 1970, under the leadership of a new state agency, the Division of State Service Centers.[36] The concept has also taken root in Canada. For example, the city of Halifax established a multiservice development office in 1974 to undertake a systematic effort toward decentralization of human services and the organization of multiservice facilities.[37]

Management information systems

Many county and city human services agencies use a computerized record-keeping system to keep information on clients served, services provided, and payments made. But a few localities have gone beyond this record-keeping function and have used the computer as a tool in the service delivery system. A good example of this is the city of Chattanooga's Urban Management Information System. This system emphasizes the capability to review and follow up an individual's progress in making his or her way through the maze of diversified services. It is a combination of an information and referral system and a computerized client tracking technique.

In the Chattanooga system, most intake is performed through three neighborhood service centers. On first entering the center, a client provides basic information such as name, address, social security number, and so on in order to establish eligibility for services. This information is obtained on a family profile–intake form with the help of an intake worker. The data from this form are entered into the system via an IBM display terminal. To simplify data entry, the screen is displayed with the format of the data that are required. The client is on hand to make sure that the data entered are accurate, and the operator has a chance to correct any errors when a review of all data appears on the screen for a final check. Once this information is entered into the system, a record is created and the system generates a client identification number. At this point the client is given an identification card, which is filled out manually by the intake worker. This card is then used as identification at any of the participating human services agencies. Following this intake process, the client is interviewed by a counselor to establish a service plan. Immediate needs are diagnosed, and the client and counselor agree on an appropriate plan of action. Using the display terminal, the teleprocessor then enters the plan into the system by keying in the service codes. As a result of this entry, a printout of the service plan is prepared. The service plan comes in three parts. One copy remains with the community center, and the other two copies are given to the client with the address of the agency to be visited. If the client needs transportation to the agency, this is arranged through a car dispatched from a central transportation pool.

When the client arrives at the agency, the agency performs the requested services. These may vary somewhat from those initially suggested. In any case, the actual services provided are entered by code onto the service plan, along with a worker code. The agency may include comments on the client's condition or medications prescribed, etc. on the open portion of the form. One copy is retained by the agency, and the other is returned to the intake center where the data is entered into the client's record.

When the first service to a client is recorded on a system, an outreach request form is generated. In order to complete the outreach request form, the counselor must make personal contact with the client. The form can be used to record client comments on the services that were received, or the reason why no service was received. The counselor also uses the outreach request form to indicate whether the client is progressing toward his or her goal, has decided to drop out of the service process, or has reached the goal.

A second outreach request form is generated from the system when a client is referred to another agency for additional services. This ensures the client of continuing support from the counselor, and provides a system of feedback on the client's progress.[38]

The Chattanooga system gives to social services personnel an extraordinary capability to follow up clients, so that they do not get lost in the process of being referred from one agency to another. It is a relatively sophisticated system, which at this point is not in common usage by local governments.

Outreach

Another technique for making social services more accessible to those they are intended to serve is called outreach. Outreach is any organized program to actively recruit clients for the services of an agency. Usually an outreach program has community workers or other staff who specialize in going out into the community, although this function in some programs is handled by volunteers.

Genesis of outreach   During the 1960s, with the growth of antipoverty programs, such as Community Action Agencies and Model Cities, outreach became much more widely used. It was recognized in these programs that one of the great problems with traditional specialized social services agencies is that frequently the people most in need of their services are either too isolated or too alienated to come in the front door and make use of them. For example, cultural and recreational programs for the elderly often failed to touch in any way the invalid elderly who are shut off from human contact in boarding houses near the business district. Manpower programs often did not reach the hard-core unemployed in the inner city, who had been so turned off by repeated failures to find or hold jobs that they had just about given up. To deal with this kind of problem, most antipoverty agencies built an outreach function into their overall program whereby workers would go out into the community in an effort to find the people most in need of help, and to encourage them to take advantage of available services.

Roles of outreach staff   Most multiservice centers make use of outreach staff. Usually there is a strong effort to hire people who live in and understand the neighborhood to serve as outreach workers. The Delaware Service Center program, for example, has on the staff of each service center outreach personnel who are recruited from the neighborhood in which a center is located. Some are hired on a temporary basis, while others become permanent government employees with merit system classification. Specialized training is provided to every outreach worker before they are sent out to make contacts with the public; all carry out their tasks under professional supervision; and there is a continuous program of on-the-job training for outreach workers.

Among the specific tasks performed by outreach workers in the Delaware system are finding people in need of services, overcoming their hesitations and encouraging them to come to the center, helping in the process of reception–intake and evaluation, making sure the person gets to the right source of service, arranging for meetings with groups of community residents and participating in such meetings, making home visits for the purpose of keeping professional staff informed on how a client is progressing, and generally keeping in touch with neighborhood problems and concerns by contacts not only on the job, but also in churches, community organizations, stores, and streets. The outreach worker in effect serves as an ambassador in the community, helping to bridge the gap between professional human services staff and the neighborhood people:

To the center's clients this means their needs are met, their questions answered, their confusions clarified by people who speak their language both literally and figuratively—who know them, understand them, share their life styles, their expectations, and their aspirations.[39]

The above may sound like a rather idealized picture of the outreach worker's job, and no doubt it is. In practice, there are a great many problems in providing adequate supervision, training, and support to outreach workers so that they can know clearly what is expected of them and play a genuinely useful role. It is also difficult to get paraprofessional neighborhood people working in a team approach with professionals; jealousies, rivalries, misunderstandings occur all too easily between the two groups.

Bridging the cultural gap   But whatever the difficulties, the problem with which the outreach function is trying to deal is a very imposing one in the human services field, and particularly affects services that are targeted at low income neighborhoods and disadvantaged people. All too often such services either do not reach, or have little impact on, the people for whom they were set up in the first place. A "cultural gap" prevails between the middle class professional and the unskilled; the person behind the desk versus the applicant; the giver of help and the one looking for help; the white person from outside the neighborhood and the minority person; the government agency versus disadvantaged people. Unless the gap can somehow be bridged, the helping power of a human services program is going to be much reduced.

The growing recognition of such sociocultural barriers that stand in the way of success for so many human services activities, has brought the use of outreach workers into common practice by social agencies in recent years. Not only antipoverty programs but health clinics, elderly programs, alcoholism and addiction programs, and many others are frequently incorporating an outreach function in their organization approach. In some communities, even library services have used this approach.

Beyond the "cultural gap," there are other reasons why social programs frequently fail to reach the most needy people. For example, a phenomenon often found in human services programs is "creaming," that is, selecting less needy clients who are more likely to use the service successfully. To take a concrete case, a job training program is indulging in "creaming" if its staff leans towards selecting semiskilled applicants rather than the hard-core unemployed because the former have a better chance of completing the job training successfully and getting hired. Underlying this practice is the natural preference program administrators have for a record of success, as well as a tendency by program staff to work with clients who give them a feeling of accomplishment. When an agency is strongly oriented towards such a "success image," an outreach function may have little chance of extending its services to those in need.

Use of volunteers   An outreach activity does not necessarily require full-time or even part-time staff. Many agencies have made use of volunteers to undertake some outreach activities—although it is difficult with volunteers to have sustained contact with a client from recruitment out in the community to shepherding through the intake and follow up processes. Nonetheless, volunteers can be used in outreach and can be particularly helpful in identifying people in need of services.

An innovative approach in this direction was taken by the Office for the Aging in Westchester County, New York. When the local National Association for the Advancement of Colored People (NAACP) was conducting a voter registration drive covering several Westchester County communities, the Office for the Aging made arrangements to tie in with the NAACP's program in order to do some outreach work. The NAACP agreed that interviewers conducting the voter registration drive would, in the process of canvassing neighborhoods and homes, register the names, addresses, and number of households containing elderly residents.

The senior citizens would be asked whether or not they carried the Westchester County Office for the Aging senior citizen identification card, giving access to a range of services. Those who did not would be contacted later with information on how to obtain the card.[40] In this way, at a very modest cost, the Office for the Aging was able to reach many senior citizens who had not been contacted before. This looks like a technique that can be used by many human services agencies when there is an organization doing door-to-door canvassing.

Current status   Outreach is at bottom a very simple concept—getting out into the community rather than waiting for people to walk in the front door. Depending on the size of an agency and budget constraints, it can be done in a very systematic, highly organized fashion, or very modest fashion. Of course, simply sending people out to look for clients will not solve deep-rooted social problems, but outreach certainly seems a technique worth considering for any human services program targeted at low income residents. As with any human services programs designed to seek out as yet unmet needs, outreach programs do, however, run the familiar risk of raising expectations—perhaps beyond the capacity of existing services to meet them. The perils of such an effect should not be underestimated, particularly in times of local government fiscal crisis.

Implementation: the nuts and bolts of service delivery

What are the key elements that make a human services program successful in its day-to-day operation? What nitty-gritty management details have to be taken care of to keep a program on a straight course towards its objectives, and avoid floundering? These are the questions that are taken up in the following discussion.

Many of the observations contained in this section are taken from the writer's experience with the Model Cities program in the city of Binghamton, New York. Binghamton is a city of 60,000 population in upstate New York. The Model Cities program began in that city in 1968, concentrating on a very old neighborhood adjacent to the downtown business district with a high concentration of elderly, almost all of the city's black population, and a large number of Italian ethnic residents. The Binghamton Model Cities program focused on dealing with housing problems, high unemployment, substandard education, and the special problems of the elderly population. The following is not a case study of the Binghamton program, but rather reflections drawn from experiences in that program on the subject of key elements in the implementation of a human services program. In other words, how do you make it work?

Key role of program staff

There is no question that the most important single factor in making a program work is the program staff. We found in Binghamton that one of the programs that was most carefully designed, with clear objectives and what we thought was an excellent structure and adequate funding, was continually floundering when it came to implementation because of the ineptness of its program staff. Another program, an elderly services project, was rather loosely put together in a rush to meet the deadline for filing the Model Cities grant application, and probably was underfunded for all of the activities proposed. Despite these difficulties, a very creative project director and staff turned this program into a highly innovative and responsive program that not only reached, but surpassed its goals.

The choice of program manager was undoubtedly the single largest factor that made for the radically different performance of the two projects. The weak project was led by a director who came directly from a management position in a private firm. Despite his management background and the goodwill he brought into the program, he ended up alienating many of the neighborhood residents at whom the program was directed, and frustrating both himself and the staff with the slender results of the project. The successful project had as its director a former social work supervisor who was not a specialist in elderly services, but who brought to the program a familiarity with social programming and very strong management skills. This project involved elderly residents heavily in its program planning, and before long blossomed into a highly productive program.

The three essential ingredients

It is difficult to come up with the precise mix of skills that makes for a successful administrator of a human services project. However, there seem to be at least three essential ingredients. First, and perhaps most important, are the personal qualities and attitudes, including sensitivity to other people and ability to listen; willingness to share power; interest and commitment to working with people in solving their problems. Second are general public management skills: the ability to design and operate a service agency; establish coordinating mechanisms with other agencies; operate public education and public relations programs; develop evaluation systems; undertake management planning and grant writing; etc. Finally, there are some skills that are specific to the human services area. These include a basic understanding of the origin and treatment of social problems, community structures, minority relations, community involvement strategies, resource agencies that can be tied into, and workable methods of service delivery.[41]

Into the fishbowl

Many colleagues have shared my observation that it is a tough transition for a person to come out of private business management and take on management of a human services program. Most business managers are not used to working in the fishbowl of publicity, with demands for citizen participation and with the many uncertainties they will face in a typical human services program. The constraints that exist in public agencies on the hiring and firing of staff, and on compensation packages for staff, create added difficulties for business managers accustomed to greater flexibility.

On the other hand, management skills that are important for the successful implementation of a human services project are frequently in very light supply among human services specialists. Program planning, development of alternative strategies, mobilizing public opinion, training nonprofessionals, establishing working relations with other agencies and with local governing bodies—such administrative and ''political'' activities

. . . are not familiar to many psychiatrists, psychologists, nurses, social workers, rehabilitation counselors, special education teachers, etc., and many reject them as outside their area of expertise, or regard engaging in such activities as a negation of years of training, knowledge, experience and client trust. Yet many of the agencies and programs under discussion are presently administered by such types.[42]

In recognition of the need to combine public management skills and social services skills in the formation of competent human services managers, a number of universities in recent years have established departments or schools of human services administration. Schools of public administration also appear to show some movement toward providing special training for those going into human services administration.

A balanced staff

One of the strongest concerns of any human services agency worth its salt is to have on its staff the mix of people that is most likely to respond to the needs of the client group. Unlike many professions, one of the problems in human services is the lack of males in the field. In a number of antipoverty agencies, virtually the entire outreach and field staff were women. As a result, the community organizations they helped put together frequently turned out to be without any significant male representation. In many inner-city and ethnic neighborhoods, it is just out of the question for male neighborhood leaders to attach themselves to organizations that are predominantly female. This may be the unfortunate result of a prevailing "machismo," but whatever it is, it is a fact of life. And for many antipoverty agencies, it has resulted in a relatively weak and unrepresentative community organizational structure in the neighborhoods.

Perhaps an even more important consideration is to have on the staff people who can relate easily with the client group being served. Obviously it is not easy for a manpower program in a Hispanic neighborhood to function well if there are no Hispanics on staff. Neither is it likely that an elderly outreach program will function well if all of its staff are young people.

Getting the proper balance on staff, however, is not an easy thing. Anyone who has had experience in trying to make an affirmative action program work knows this. To take an illustration from the Binghamton experience, the elderly project was recruiting a staff person to make home-to-home visitations in the neighborhood and provide personal services to shut-ins. In terms of getting doors opened and overcoming the fears of elderly shut-ins about a stranger coming to their door, the best choice seemed to be a middle-aged woman. Staff made no secret of what their preference was in finding a staff person for this job, and as a consequence were successfully sued by a young black woman who applied for the job and felt she was being discriminated against.

To take another case, the city manager of Hutchinson, Kansas, was faced with a dilemma in appointing the city's human relations director some years ago. There were three candidates acceptable to the human relations commission—a black, a Chicano, and a white—and the manager had the responsibility to choose one of them. The manager describes his thought processes as follows:

I theorized that a black should be appointed to show good faith with those who had been instrumental in establishing the position. A black director would be most likely to hold the trust of the black community. He would understand and represent the views of the victims of racism. On the other hand a white director would be more acceptable to the "gatekeepers" of the "establishment" (the personnel directors, the realtors, the religious rationalizers). Since the tenets of racism are implemented by the establishment, the efforts to overcome the effects of racism require working to change the attitudes and overcoming the excuses of the "gatekeepers." The establishment is white. Effective racism in our society is that of whites. To overcome racism, we must work on the white establishment; therefore a white director acceptable to whites.

These were the rationalizations. Finally I settled upon a new theory. I would appoint the best person for the job regardless of race or ethnic origin. A Chicano was appointed. He subsequently went on to better things—working for the state of Kansas—where his office investigated a charge of discrimination brought against me stating that I had discriminated against a white applicant when I had appointed him.[43]

Such dilemmas face almost every human services agency setting up shop in an inner-city neighborhood. To make the program work well, the agency will have to find a competent staff, well-balanced and with people who can relate easily to neighborhood residents. It is no easy trick to pull off.

Paraprofessionals

One way of dealing with this dilemma is to give priority to the hiring of neighborhood residents to work either as outreach workers or in other paraprofessional positions. This has frequently been done in multiservice centers, as was discussed earlier in this chapter. There is enormous potential for employment of paraprofessionals in many of the staff-intensive services such as day care, health clinics, special education programs, recreation programs. One community school program in Binghamton had so many different types of paraprofessional aides (teacher aides, lunchroom aides, playground aides) that a wag suggested an aide be assigned to the band and called a "band aide."

The use of paraprofessionals has not only created new and interesting employment opportunities for residents of disadvantaged neighborhoods, but has also brought a healthy infusion of neighborhood viewpoints into the staff of human services agencies. This approach was encouraged under the Model Cities program which gave a strong priority to neighborhood residents in filling staff positions for which they were qualified. In many cities it worked very well.

In some Model Cities programs, however, the emphasis on the use of neighborhood paraprofessionals became so heavy that the countervailing need for competent professional staff was neglected. This was done sometimes with very good intentions, so that neighborhood residents would not be "typed" as having to work at lower level positions while outsiders were imported for the top management jobs. But in trying to prove this ideological point, some programs came apart at the seams because there was not enough experienced management and supervisory staff to give needed guidance and support to paraprofessionals. The moral: use paraprofessionals by all means, but don't put them in positions for which they really have not got the needed skills to do a successful job.

Another difficulty with paraprofessionals is that they sometimes tend to be unemployable in the larger job market. The Model Cities program and similar programs have been somewhat precarious in their funding prospects and such programs can disappear from the scene entirely in a few years. If paraprofessionals working in these programs are to benefit significantly from their work experience, it is important to build in adequate training and also develop career ladders that will put them in a position to move into related jobs in the public or private sector should the special program go out of business.

There is another pitfall that bears pointing out in developing a staff position for a paraprofessional. It is critically important that the paraprofessional have a well-defined job that has clear benefits to a program. If the job is created as "make work," primarily to bring a resident onto the staff of a program, or if the resident perceives the job in this way, the result will probably be a demoralizing experience both for the paraprofessional and for related staff. For example, in the case of a community worker, it is of the highest importance that the community worker and supervisor agree on certain precise tasks, a schedule of activities, a reporting and feedback system, and regular consultation so that the community worker will get any necessary guidance from the supervisor. It appears to me that the more open-ended and flexible the job is, the greater is the need for such attempts to identify concrete work tasks and provide constant feedback from management.

Role of staff training

Staff training is important for an effective human services program. The same can be said about virtually any kind of program, but it seems particularly true for programs dealing with changing human needs where an openness to change is vital.

Like any other organization, a human services agency has a tendency to carve out its own special turf, build little walls around that turf to guard against intruders, and build a bureaucratic structure to protect the interests of those on top—both staff and policy board. It was astonishing to me to observe an antipoverty agency that started out by shaking everyone's apple cart and pressing for radical changes in services provided to poor people, within a few years being so locked into its own specific programs that it was as defensive and close-minded as any other agency in town. Being in business for a while seems to have its perils.

Someone defined a "liberal" as a "radical with two children"—and human services agencies are not exempt from the phenomenon that this represents.

One of the best ways for an agency to keep fresh and open to change is through an ongoing staff training program. There are all kinds of training programs that can be used, ranging from the nuts and bolts of budgeting practices to team management and organizational development training. In most states there are municipal leagues or university-connected training agencies which specialize in providing staff training programs for local government employees. Many of these training agencies are able to provide training for human services personnel. For example, the Action Training Service of the Kansas Municipal League offers a variety of training programs geared toward the human services. The League of California Cities and the Massachusetts League of Cities and Towns operate special support programs for local human services departments. The New England Municipal Center has run specialized workshops for human services administrators in many different locations throughout New England.

As emphasized in the Foreword to this book, a readily accessible training program for local governments is a correspondence course in human services management offered by the Institute for Training in Municipal Administration (ITMA) of the International City Management Association. This course offers college credits, and makes use of this volume (published for ITMA) and other materials, as well as of a number of instructors-by-correspondence who are knowledgeable practitioners in the field.

Many community colleges have set up special training programs for paraprofessional workers in recent years, and these can be used to great advantage by human services agencies. In most places, training opportunities are not lacking. It falls to the director of a human services program to make sure that these opportunities are not missed and that there are sufficient funds budgeted to provide the different kinds of training that staff will need to develop their skills and keep the program resilient, responsive, and open to change.

Using volunteers

Through the use of volunteers, human services, agencies can get a great deal more mileage out of limited resources. There is a strong voluntary tradition in the United States. One estimate has it that volunteers number approximately 40 million nationally.

Human services is a field where the use of volunteers is particularly attractive, both to the volunteer and to the agency. Volunteers have been used in community outreach efforts, information and referral programs, housing programs, elderly services, Head Start and day care centers, mental retardation programs, and drug abuse programs. They have served on planning boards, conducted fund raising drives, answered hot lines, tutored in schools, driven patients to clinics, delivered meals to invalids, and cheered up mental patients. The possibilities for volunteer jobs in human services appear to be limited only by the imaginations of those directing the program.[44]

Private agencies by and large have made more extensive use of volunteers than public agencies. Indeed, one of the major advantages frequently offered to a local government in contracting with a private agency is the capability of that agency to mobilize volunteers and thereby provide more service for the dollar.

The use of volunteers, however, is not without its problems. Sometimes program administrators are reluctant to place any degree of confidence in volunteers, since they have no economic leverage over them. Line workers also may have hesitations about volunteers, and even fear that their own jobs may be replaced eventually by unpaid workers. A volunteer coming into an agency that has this kind of mixed reception may be taken aback and lose enthusiasm for the program.

It is therefore important for the success of volunteer programs that the top administrator actively support the program and work for its acceptance with workers down the line. The volunteers should be given a well-defined role and not appear to be like other general purpose employees. And the work assignment must be of real value; work that otherwise would not be done, or that is of low priority, will not sustain the interest or commitment of volunteers. This is very similar to the situation already discussed about work tasks for paraprofessional staff.

Another limitation of volunteers is that they can best undertake jobs that have a clear beginning and end, and do not extend over a long time frame. It is too much to expect that volunteers will follow through with all details on a complex program. Even when the volunteers are full-time, there can be limitations in this regard. For example, the city of Newton, Massachusetts, employed full-time ACTION volunteers under a federal grant in a city-sponsored street worker program. The ACTION volunteers accepted a one-year assignment on this job. But it took about six months for the street workers to become fully accepted by the youngsters they were trying to reach, leaving only a few months of working at full effectiveness before it was time to wind down the job.[45]

While it is clear that the use of volunteers has its limitations when compared to full-time staff, they can be used to very good effect in working with staff to greatly enlarge the impact of a program. They also can bring strong side benefits in terms of the public image of the agency. Human services agencies often have many problems caused by a lack of public understanding and support. No public relations program can explain a program as completely as having citizens actually working side-by-side with agency staff in making the program work. Those who get involved as volunteers build a stake in the success of the program, and their concerns get shared with friends and neighbors. Volunteers can be a marvelous way of getting understanding and credibility with the public.

Oh no, not citizen participation!

What more can be said that has not yet been said elsewhere about citizen involvement in social programs? It has been one of the juiciest aspects of antipoverty and Model Cities programs for journalists, authors, and voyeurs of the American scene. The comments have varied from lyrical descriptions of fresh winds of change blowing through the country bringing increased political participation and power to the people, all the way to sardonic commentaries on "maximum feasible misunderstanding" and a magnificently funny portrayal of harassment techniques used by citizen groups in Tom Wolfe's *Radical Chic & Mau-Mauing the Flak Catchers.*

Extreme viewpoints on citizen participation have not only been taken by authors, but in some cases by program managers. One Model Cities agency in a burst of populism established a board of directors containing more than 100 members, most of them elected from the neighborhood. At the other extreme, some Model Cities agencies kept a tight rein on citizen involvement and their citizen structure; programs were planned and facilities designed by professional staff and/or consultants, with the citizen board there only to give its final approval so that an application could go on to the Department of Housing and Urban Development (HUD).

It seems to me that both extremes are full of pitfalls. In the earlier days of the Binghamton Model Cities program, the staff made prodigious efforts to keep neighborhood residents involved in every step of the planning process. Staff met with resident committees three or four nights a week, probably thereby contributing to a decline in the neighborhood's birth rate. After a while, the staff was getting worn down with the number of meetings, but we did not want to diminish the opportunities for citizens to get involved. Finally one perceptive young outreach worker cut through our cloudy thinking with the observation that we were starting to "abuse the folks." Sure enough, the citizens were getting as tired of this dreary round of planning meetings as we were. So we cut it down, did a lot more staff preparation, and were able to get more accomplished with fewer meetings.

The other extreme is perhaps even worse; that is, where a citizens group is "set-up" primarily to give its blessing to what the professionals intend to do in any case. This kind of game does not go down very long before neighborhood residents sense that they are being used. As a result, they tend to either drop out and abandon the program, or get mad and go after the program director. Many a Model Cities director's head rolled over this very issue.

So the two extremes of total involvement of citizens in every aspect of the program vs. token involvement of citizens with no real influence on decisions are neither very fruitful. What then is a sound approach to citizen participation? The following, it seems to me, are some of the *key elements for building a successful citizen participation mechanism:*

1. Clearly define the role of the citizen group and its relationship to the administrative staff.
2. Make sure the role of the citizen group is a significant one, of value to the program and capable of influencing the direction of the program. It may be an advisory role, but the advice of the group should carry some weight on program decisions; otherwise it is better not to have the citizen group at all.
3. Don't "abuse the folks," as my outreach worker advised. There is no need for citizens to get into all the administrative or technical details of a program; these tend to be boring and that is why staff are paid to do them.
4. Give close attention in the selection of the citizen group to the group's being representative of the neighborhood or constituency being served by the program. If it involves an election procedure, make sure when the election districts are drawn up that the boundaries will not tend to exclude representatives from any of the various ethnic or age groups in the community or neighborhood. If the local governing body or mayor selects the citizen group, it makes sense to sound out community organizations and neighborhood groups in advance to see who they would like to have representing their viewpoints.
5. The citizen group ought to have some stability. It is disruptive to a program if the entire citizen board leaves office at the same time. A better system is overlapping terms so there will be some continuity from one year to the next.
6. Provide good information to the citizen group so it will be in a position to make intelligent decisions on the issues in front of it. Good information does not mean tons of documents; an oversupply of information can be as effective a way of keeping citizens in the dark as not giving enough information. Clear and succinct briefing papers on the program issues they are considering are most important if the citizen group is to carry out its mission.
7. Orientation and training sessions for citizen groups, particularly when new members first take their seats, can be very helpful in developing a good working citizen structure and creative relationships with staff.

The seven points listed above are, of course, oversimplified prescriptions for dealing with what is often a very complex and highly emotional issue. I am not sure which precept would have been most useful to a colleague of mine who went to his first urban renewal citizen advisory meeting to find residents standing on top of the meeting tables shaking their fists at him—this before the meeting had even been called to order.

There is no question that a poorly organized citizen participation component can create tremendous problems for a human services program, and can in some cases kill the program. But the best approach for a program manager to take is not to shun citizen involvement, but rather to take great care in organizing it. For a well-functioning citizen participation mechanism can add immeasurably to the impact of a human services agency. The citizen group can serve as an excellent feedback mechanism, to convey to program staff the kind of image the agency has out in the community. It can provide reassurance to the staff that they are on target with a given program, or suggest some redirection of another program that is not as well-received by residents. For the people serving on the citizen board, if they are given a meaningful role and their views are heard with respect and responsiveness, the whole experience of serving with the citizen group can help overcome the mistrust and alienation that are so common toward programs "laid on" the neighborhood by outsiders.

Overcoming mistrust can have some very practical effects on a program's performance—and not just in terms of how popular it is with residents. For example, the urban renewal agency in Binghamton rammed through a major new demolition and land acquisition project in one neighborhood in the space of a couple of months, with minimal input from residents. Professional staff on the renewal agency looked with disdain at the slow, ponderous process being used by the Model Cities agency in discussing a renewal proposal for the model neighborhood—explaining it, arguing it, and finally building a consensus. As it turned out, the first neighborhood where the citizens were not involved mobilized public opinion and killed the project, while the Model Cities renewal project moved ahead, once neighborhood consensus was established, for final approvals by the city council and HUD.

The business of building trust of an agency's intentions among the people being served by that agency can have an enormous influence on an agency's ultimate success. If people mistrust an agency, or feel it is trying to play games with them, they will in turn play games with the agency; this simply is not a healthy climate in which to run a human services program. For this reason above all, it seems to me that, despite all the difficulties in making citizen participation work well, it is worth the effort.

Political skills: a must

It doesn't hurt to be a politician. Certain skills that are not much discussed in considering what makes for a good human services administrator are political skills. And yet these are of major significance in making a program work. Most Model Cities directors found that more than 50 percent of their working time was spent not on technical issues, but on building political support and viability for their programs with the city council, the press, community groups, funding agencies, and key interest groups in the community.

In Binghamton there was a great deal of difficulty during the first year or two of the new Model Cities program in winning acceptance by the city council. The council had a strong conservative strain to begin with; but probably the biggest block was simply the newness of the program. Council members were used to traditional city functions such as police, fire, public works, and parks and recreation. For the city now to move beyond all this into special housing programs for a declining neighborhood, job programs for the unemployed, a transportation system for elderly, university scholarships for disadvantaged youngsters, and even a civil rights program was something that went far beyond their experience and seemed somehow foreboding. After a year's planning effort and many meetings between Model Cities officials and the city council, the first-year plan was approved and sent to HUD for funding by the narrow margin of only one council vote. This despite the fact that, in the total funding package of about 3 million dollars, the city share was only 1 percent

What happened in Binghamton was not unique. Many other social programs encounter a great deal of hesitation and reluctance when they first come on the scene. It was interesting to me to find that what overcame many of these hesitations was simply the fact of being around for awhile. After a couple of years of getting used to the idea, even though the conservative make-up of the city council had not changed to any extent, there was no longer any real chance of having the program jettisoned by the council because, by then, everyone had become accustomed to thinking of it as a city program. I suppose this would be called "credibility by force of habit."

Other local government human services programs usually rely much more heavily than did Model Cities on budgetary allocations from the local governing body, and so there is an even stronger need for keeping the governing body informed. This can be done directly through formal briefings and informal contacts between council members and program staff or board members. Another excellent way of getting the message through to the governing body is by building a favorable image with the media. Local elected officials tend to be keenly sensitive to what is reported in the local press, and if an agency has "good press," its chances for winning their support are greatly enhanced.

One reason why many human services programs run into political difficulties is that they do not take the trouble to cultivate local government officials and the media. Many such programs are directed by human services specialists (social workers, psychologists, etc.) with a disdain for what they regard as such political activities.

One does not successfully operate a major human service program by being a purist. In fact it can be argued that a human services administrator who holds back from getting involved in such "political" activities is not doing a full professional job in developing the program. For a vital ingredient in human services programming is to forge links in many directions—with the neighborhood residents of clients using the service; with other human services agencies providing complementary services; with funding sources; and with local government leaders and the public generally. The technical jargon for these activities is "coordination," but there is no question that carrying them out is a job requiring political skills. If an agency regards this as of no importance or beyond its scope, it will almost inevitably isolate itself. This is not a very smart situation for a human services agency to be in; it is a little like a deep-sea diver going below without oxygen.

To put it more positively, human services agencies have a much better chance of gaining credibility and support from community leaders and the general public when their managers go out of their way to promote understanding with local officials and the media.

Conclusion

This chapter has considered some of the basic alternative organizational strategies that are open to a city or county government in organizing a central administrative structure to carry out its human services function. The alternatives have been described not as theoretical concepts, but rather as approaches which are in fairly common usage by local governments. The chapter has also described in some detail four organizational techniques that can be used by local governments at the service delivery level to make social services programs more accessible to citizens: information and referral systems, multipurpose centers, MIS systems, and outreach programs. Again the stress is not on theory, but on techniques which are being used by local governments. The final section considered some of the nuts-and-bolts elements that go into the implementation of a successful human services program.

A continuing dilemma in organizing a human services program, whether it is at the central administrative level or out at the field delivery level, is the need to achieve stability, control, and continuity—and at the same time responsiveness, freshness, and innovativeness in meeting changing needs. It is a dilemma that will not go away very easily. Most human services efforts are aimed at problems with deep roots and complex sociocultural causes. In order to have an impact, a program has to endure and keep working on the problem; and so, the need for stability. However, considering the difficulties of defining what is at the root of social problems and the evasiveness of the solutions, human services programs must avoid settling into a bureaucratic mold, and keep pushing for new approaches and better solutions. And so any organizational structure a local government chooses should combine these somewhat contrary requirements: stability and openness to change.

At present, local governments are still relative newcomers in the human services field. Many of the organizational structures described in this chapter are also relatively new and have not stood the test of time. In the coming decade, if local governments around the country continue to take on increasing responsibilities to meet human services needs of their citizens, it may well be that some of the organizational approaches described herein will be left in the dust by fresh new approaches found to be more powerful in meeting community human needs.

1 U.S., Department of Health, Education, and Welfare, Social and Rehabilitation Service, "Statistics Replace Educated Guesses," *Social and Rehabilitation Record* 3 (October 1976): 8–10.

2 John F. Barrows, Marin County Administrator, to Board of Supervisors of the county of Marin, 5 April 1973, California.

3 Gabriel J. Rodriguez, "Human Resources," *Western City,* June 1975, p. 15.

4 "Human Services Department Description," city of Gardena, California, 1976.

5 "Human Resources, 1974–1975 Annual Report," city of Fort Worth, Texas.

6 Mark M. Levin, Assistant to the City Manager/Director of Human Services, city of Cleveland Heights, Ohio, to the International City Management Association, Washington, D.C., 13 December 1976.

7 League of California Cities, Sacramento, California.

8 "Work Program Strategy for Office of Human Development," city of Dallas, Texas, January 1975.

9 John F. Barrows to Board of Supervisors of the county of Marin.

10 Council of State Governments, *Human Services Integration: State Functions in Implementation* (Lexington, Ky.: Council of State Governments, 1974), pp. 23–35.

11 "Reorganizing the City's DHR," *Washington Post,* 1 January 1977.

12 National League of Cities/U.S. Conference of Mayors, *Local Participation in Social Services* (Washington, D.C.: National League of Cities/U.S. Conference of Mayors, 1976), pp. 28–29.

13 Ibid., pp. 15–16.

14 "Nomination of Dr. Robert J. Huntley, City Administrator, Westminster, California, for Management Innovation Award in Human Services Category," prepared for the International City Management Association, Annual Awards Program, 1976.

15 Michael F. Fenderson, "The Role of the Recreation and Park Profession in the Delivery of Human Service Programs," prepared for presentation at the 1975 Park and Recreation Administrators Institute, Pacific Grove, California.

16 New York State Association of Counties, "Monroe County Human Resources Delivery—A Model," *County Conversationalist,* June 1976, p. 4.

17 John Matzer, Jr., Village Manager, village of Skokie, Illinois, to the International City Management Association, Washington, D.C., 14 December 1976.

18 George L. Weinland, Administrative Assistant, village of Arlington Heights, Illinois, to the International City Management Association, Washington, D.C., 14 July 1976.

19 Edited transcript of presentation made to the Boone County Community Services Council by Terry L. Novak, City Manager, city of Columbia, Missouri, 1976.

20 Terry L. Novak, City Manager, city of Columbia, Missouri, to the International City Management Association, Washington, D.C., 26 November 1976.

21 League of California Cities, "City of Santa Barbara Adopts Social Services Plan," *Human Resources Newsletter,* August 1976, pp. 1–2.

22 "Nomination of James D. Williams, City Manager, city of Santa Monica, California for Management Innovation Award," prepared for the International City Management Association, Annual Awards Program, 1976.

23 John W. Riggle, Executive Director, Central Indiana Council on Aging, Inc., to the International City Management Association, Washington, D.C., 21 July 1976.

24 New England Municipal Center, *Human Services Consortium: A Combined Municipal Effort in Human Services Management* (Durham, N.H.: New England Municipal Center, 1975).

25 Fred S. Knight, "Human Resources: A Multi-City Approach," Municipal Management Innovations Series, vol. 1, no. 3 (Washington, D.C.: International City Management Association, August 1975).

26 Keith F. Mulrooney, "Human Resource Programs for Cities with Limited Budgets: How to Pay for Them and How to Start Them," *Public Management,* September 1974, p. 9.

27 League of Kansas Municipalities, "Circuit Rider Assisting Cities," *Kansas Government Journal,* July 1976, pp. 260–61.

28 North Central Texas Council of Governments, "Human Services Planning and Coordination in the North Central Texas Council of Governments," 1976.

29 "Development and Operation: Wilkes-Barre Information System," city of Wilkes-Barre, Pennsylvania, August 1976.

30 Daniel S. Kuennen, "The Sussex County Inter-Agency Council, Inc.," Cooperative Extension Service, University of Delaware, Wilmington, Delaware, 1973.

31 New England Municipal Center, *Opportunities,* April 1976, p. 4.

32 State of Delaware, Division of State Service Centers, "Service Center Program," p. 2.

33 Frank Breedlove, "The Crossroads Community Services Center Concept and Relationships," in *Human Services Integration* (Washington, D.C.: American Society for Public Administration, 1974), pp. 69–71.

34 Mel Hinton, "Titusville's Social Services Center," *Florida Municipal Record,* January 1973, pp. 10–11.

35 Ronald L. Usher, Director, Department of Health and Human Services, county of Marin, to branch chiefs, assistant directors, and service center managers, memorandum, California, 23 March 1976.

36 State of Delaware, Division of State Service Centers, "Service Center Program."

37 "Towards the Development of a Multi-Service System for Mainland South," city of Halifax, Nova Scotia, July 1975.

38 American Society for Public Administration, *Human Services Integration*, pp. 27–28.

39 State of Delaware, Division of State Service Centers, "Service Center Program," p. 8.

40 Orial A. Redd, Assistant to the County Executive for Human Development, Westchester County, New York, to the International City Management Association, Washington, D.C., 10 November 1976.

41 Robert Agranoff, "Human Services Administration: Service Delivery, Service Integration, and Training," in *Human Services Integration*, pp. 42–51.

42 Ibid., pp. 48–49.

43 League of Kansas Municipalities, "A City Manager's View of Human Relations," *Kansas Government Journal*, December 1973, p. 528.

44 New England Municipal Center, *Opportunities*, October 1976.

45 Ibid., p. 4.

Coordination with intergovernmental and private agencies

How does the local government human services manager coordinate relationships with other public and private agencies working in the community? How does this coordination process fit into the wider public sector decision-making process? The answers to these questions are often of crucial importance in the real world of human services delivery systems at the local level. In addressing this topic, the present chapter therefore carries a stage further the treatment presented earlier in this book. Chapter 2 has outlined the main public and private sector participants in human services delivery at the local level, and given an indication of the range of relationships possible in this complex and shifting field. Chapter 7 has outlined the administrative structures for human services programs in local governments. The present chapter will both sharpen the focus on the managerial aspects of coordination and introduce discussion of some of the practical and dynamic aspects of the topic.

The chapter is divided into two parts dealing, respectively, with coordination with public agencies and coordination with private agencies. The authors of both parts address their subjects from the perspective of experienced executives in public and private management. The first portion of the chapter describes some of the difficulties facing local government chief executives as they survey a bewildering public sector fragmentation in the management of human services delivery systems. It emphasizes that the dynamics of this fragmentation, that is, the roles of the actors involved, and their competitive and conflicting interactions must be perceived and understood before any attempts at coordination can be made. The author warns that the path to a rational system of coordination between public agencies and between levels of government may well be strewn with obstacles— political, legal, bureaucratic, and psychological—and that the local government decision maker may well find that ad hoc approaches alone are workable.

The second portion of the chapter focuses in like fashion on the range of options open to local governments in their relations with the private sector. It begins by addressing the basic question of whether cooperation should or should not in fact take place at all, and moves on to an analysis of the similarities and differences between private and public agencies. It concludes with a detailed analysis of the type of options available and a survey of some of the key managerial issues involved in coordination.

Both portions of the chapter offer specific examples, address practical issues, and offer pertinent comments on the areas of conflict and controversy which are an inescapable part of real world human services management.

Coordination with public agencies

Coordination of human services programs at the local level is an extremely difficult, if not impossible, task for the urban government administrator. This realistic, if unpalatable, observation applies in large and small jurisdictions, in multifunctional agencies, and in communities offering only the most basic services to their citizens. It is a theme that is emphasized in varying degree throughout this book, and one that is confirmed by the experience of many decision makers. It is a fact of managerial life that administrators with human services interests who attempt to replace confusion with order, inefficiency with productivity, and programmatic obfuscation with service to clients run the risk of encountering such frustration that they lose their initial enthusiasm and lapse into that peaceful inertia that can appear much more attractive than an active leadership role.

It is also a fact of day-to-day life at the client's end of human services administration that the citizen in need who attempts to resolve a particular problem can often only do so with great difficulty. If he or she is clever enough, however, the system can be made to work to that citizen's advantage. If intelligence is coupled with unscrupulousness, then the client's advantage can also be the disadvantage of both the system and those who are paying for it. Indeed, energetic clients probably accomplish more interagency cooperation through their personal efforts than agency executives achieve as a sophisticated management process. The multiproblem family, in particular, finds it a severe challenge to cope with conflicting programs; obscure, ever-changing, and duplicative regulations; and even the very identification of programs that are supposed to have been designed to assist quite specific needs.

These unhappy facts confront client and administrator alike. They must be acknowledged, and the circumstances leading to their generation understood, before the specific topic of coordination with other public agencies delivering human services can be addressed. The following discussion therefore identifies and describes the universe within which administrators and clients operate, and the actors in that process. The factors in that universe mitigating against coordination must be identified before any realistic attempts at coordination can be outlined. Only then is it possible to illustrate how urban government managers can attempt to bring rational coordination into otherwise irrationally operating structures and processes. Even then, the basic thrust of the discussion will be that the coordination process is one that must be pragmatic, that is, designed to fit a particular locality's unique organization, programs, legal requirements, bureaucratic attitudes, and political preferences. It seems that such ad hoc approaches provide the only viable managerial option unless and until a more rational and more comprehensive human services delivery system is established at the national, state, regional, and local levels.

The following discussion of the local government setting and the actors within it is presented from the perspective of chief administrators of general units of local governments. These managers have direct administrative accountability for provision of services at the local level. Their elected leaders are the politicians most immediately accountable to the electorate for the action and the inaction of government—whether legal responsibility is vested in them or not. The second portion of the discussion focuses on techniques of coordination, using practical illustrations wherever possible and emphasizing the key decision-making factors involved.

The setting and the actors

The mitigating factors   The most significant, indeed overriding, factor mitigating against coordination of human services between public agencies is that no single government unit—be it national, state, county, municipal, or regional entity—has primary responsibility for the provision of all human resources programs, or even of a majority of them, within a local area. Furthermore, among the states there is no single organizational pattern for the dispersion of such responsibility. Indeed, within some states, different delivery system structures exist for the same programs at the local level.

Dispersed responsibility: some examples   Some examples pinpoint this situation. In one state (and the specifics of time and place need not be cited for present purposes), the health department was, since its inception, a locally controlled operation, with assistance and some guidance from the state health department. In recent years, the state desired to bring these programs under its control in order to equalize service and coordinate program operations. An affiliation program was therefore initiated using the "carrot" of state funding. Concurrently, however, mental health and mental retardation services were provided by local divisions of another state department. This latter agency, on the other hand, became converted to the gospel espousing more local control. It set up a program of disaffiliation at the option of the local government. The net result has been that, whereas health department personnel were once local and are now state employees, the mental health employees were once state and are now local employees in certain of the jurisdictions.

In an adjoining state, health and mental health services are provided through one state agency (with health predominant). County health departments are considered to be the local division serving under the joint policy guidance of the local governing body and the state. The local health director is appointed locally and serves, ex officio, as an assistant director of the state department. The local director is able to operate autonomously because, while everyone is legally responsible, no one is actually accountable. A skillful director can play one off against the other and maintain independence. In such circumstances—and the examples could be multiplied—it is no wonder that the urban administrator finds it almost impossible to force coordination.

The federal government has chosen to bring a number of public assistance grant programs directly into the Social Security Administration and to leave service provision to state and local welfare agencies. How does the urban government administrator achieve coordination with a local welfare or social services agency when that agency's programs are funded mostly by the federal government, guided by federal and state regulations, and managed by a superintendent reporting to a locally appointed citizen administrative board?

Further, the administrative arrangements such as those just described are enormously complicated by the great variety found in human services programs. The familiar labels—education, recreation, employment, manpower, vocational rehabilitation, housing, community development, aging, rural poverty, handicapped, hospitals, police, courts, corrections, parole—illustrate the span of the services provided. Given this background, one can appreciate the problems of managers interested in bringing coordinated services to their citizens.

The real role of the political process A collateral mitigating factor is that some agencies are so distant from the elective political process that the staffs tend to be unresponsive to local needs and priorities. This seems to be particularly true with local divisions of state agencies. It becomes very easy for these divisions to snub attempts at coordination and there is often little that the local administrator, governing body, or elected official can do to force responsiveness.

Conversely, experience also shows that the decision-making process and the roles of the effective decision makers may not be structured in the same manner as the formal organizational structure would suggest. Federal and state legislators and political party leaders may be the de facto policy and priority determiners. For example, in some areas a local division of an agency will make exceptions to regulations only when a call is received from the appropriate legislative official. Such political intervention often becomes critical when individual crises occur and an agency staff takes a rigid position when asked to respond. In others, responsiveness is, in reality, a form of patronage and rewards built into the informal system.

In most cases, of course, no venality is intended. On the contrary, legislators become frustrated with nonresponsive bureaucracies and establish informal mechanisms to achieve results. Most congressional offices have caseworkers on their staffs whose sole function it is to smooth the road for constituents seeking assistance from programs directly administered by agencies such as the Veterans Administration, the Social Security Administration, and the Department of Housing and Urban Development (HUD). Frequently, their cases involve problems with state and local agencies; the caseworkers develop direct communication links with local program managers and, if nonresponsiveness is encountered, with state and local elected officials.

Sometimes the results are not entirely happy. For example, a certain group of constituents receiving public assistance and housing grants became the innocent victims of a housing policy change at the local level combined with muddled federal agency involvement. The congressman in question summoned appropriate federal and local staff members to a meeting with the constituents and personally "coordinated" a solution by forcing rule-bending by the program administrators. It is unlikely that an urban government administrator could have achieved similarly coordinated results in this particular instance. The example illustrates the weakness of a management process in which a legislator must play an executive/administrative role in order to achieve a goal.

Conflicting agency goals: who resolves the differences?   Organizational fragmentation frequently results in conflicting agency goals. These conflicts surface in action programs at the local level and the urban government manager can spend a great deal of time attempting to resolve the differences in order to lessen impacts on the jurisdiction and its citizens. The following example illustrates the type of problems that can emerge.

National housing policy requires the provision of homes for poverty-level families and individuals as well as the protection of the federal government's financial interests in federally assisted projects. In one region, a particular locality had been overburdened with low income housing while other jurisdictions had very little. All localities came together in a regional forum and agreed on a "fair share" formula for allocation of federal low income housing funds; the federal agency concurred in the formula. Because the federal agency was faced with mortgage defaults in some assisted moderate income development, the decision was made to protect the loan and raise the amount of direct federal assistance. Rents were covered so as to fill the units with low income tenants who could qualify for the lower rents. The ad hoc federal policy was thus in direct conflict with regional and local policies. The locality balked, court action was threatened, and the federal government backed off. During the crisis, the manager spent much time in fact-finding, coordinating with the regional council of governments, and contacting federal officials in an attempt to protect the flanks of the jurisdiction.

The phenomenon of competing bureaucracies   A jurisdiction has an unemployment problem. The manager attempts to develop a comprehensive, coordinated retraining and placement program. But the manager is immediately faced with fragmentation among the organizations dealing with employment—the Comprehensive Employment and Training Act (CETA), the state employment service, the Work Incentive (WIN) program in the welfare agency, the state vocational rehabilitation agency, and the public schools' adult vocational education programs. The sheer number of agencies involved in and of itself, of course, presents coordination problems, and yet another mitigating factor results: the phenomenon of competing bureaucracies.

Each independent agency has its own chain of command and staffing dynamic. Agency personnel are naturally protective of their own programs and jobs. An "us against them" attitude develops, particularly when there are overlapping functions among organizations or when one agency threatens to take over another in order to achieve coordination. This is perhaps the most difficult factor for the urban manager to overcome because resistance to coordination becomes a personal rather than an organizational issue. When the process is carried to the extreme— an occurrence that is not all that unusual—agency heads refuse to talk to one another and communicate only through precisely written memorandums. An ancillary problem that may result is the "hoarding" of service recipients: an agency attempts to build its own client base and "neglects" to make referrals to other agencies.

The fostering of competitiveness is an accepted and useful management technique—as long as it is directed toward a common goal. Competitiveness amid conflicting goals can only be counterproductive. Regrettably, such counterproductive imbroglios are a frequent occurrence among human services programs.

What problems are in fact presented by the sheer size and number of human services agencies? Basically, coordination is further inhibited. Effective coordination must include more than interaction among the "big three" departments of health, social services, and mental heealth. However, few localities which have direct responsibility for the first-line administration of these primary agencies have effectively been able to consolidate efforts among them. Given the overall matrix embracing the multiplicity of agencies, both public and private, then coordination becomes a monumental task. The unfortunate chief executive may find that even the relatively simple task of arranging "coordinating" meetings becomes comparable to an exercise in international diplomacy.

Further, there is an imbalance in the strength of agencies to compete successfully for funding, or even for attention. For example, public health agencies historically have been powerful and well-funded; mental health agencies frequently have been underfunded. The imbalance creates a dynamic which tends to mitigate against meaningful program coordination. Inter- and intraprofessional rivalries and "pecking orders" also create roadblocks for the would-be coordinator. Certain elitisms are not unknown. For example, social workers in mental health agencies may feel superior to professional compatriots working in welfare agencies. Public health physicians may feel superior to mental health agency psychiatrists. Specialized professionals question the qualifications of generalist administrators to manage functional agencies or to make policy decisions affecting the agencies.

The issue of confidentiality   Confidentiality is another factor which has become a significant roadblock to coordination in some jurisdictions. Historically, citizens receiving assistance from human services agencies have been protected from public view by statutes and regulations establishing confidentiality of records. Current emphasis on the right to privacy has resulted in some public agencies refusing to share case records with other public agencies. The sharing of information is crucial to the success of referral programs which, in turn, are a key element in providing full services to multiproblem clients. Agencies which are committed to cooperation seem to be able to find means to share records without prejudicing the privacy rights of citizens. For agencies attempting to avoid cooperation, however, confidentiality can become a convenient way to say "no." Claims of confidentiality must be scrutinized carefully for legitimacy and legality.

A demonstrable lack of interest   All the mitigating factors just cited may have less impact on human services coordination in a community than would a demonstrable lack of interest by local government governing bodies and managers. The urban administrator who advanced because of engineering and public works credentials—and such persons still play a major role in the profession [1]—may not comprehend, or be interested in comprehending, the need for coordinated human services delivery systems. The city manager who had been a finance director may not be willing to guide his locality into program areas which have a reputation for being costly.

And costly they can be. Coordination bespeaks efficiency. Clients in need then become less frustrated when seeking services and do not hesitate to make inquiries. The familiar specter of raised expectations described in many places in this book makes an appearance. For example, a county was certain that a number of citizens in a local community needed services and were not getting them because transportation to agency offices was not available and because the various agencies were located in scattered facilities. An integrated services center with central intake was then established in the community and case loads increased dramatically—far above the separate agencies' budgeted ability to provide services. Significant additional appropriations were required the following year, but services were provided in the manner intended by the programs. Traditionally, it is not surprising that human services program emphasis has not been on reaching out, but rather on reacting to clients who walk in. And in the climate of fiscal crisis that frequently envelops many jurisdictions, it is realistic to note that the disinterest in the human services area shown by many managers and elected officials can have an extremely practical foundation.

Yes, Virginia, there is cooperation   In the city of Virginia Beach, Virginia, the spirit of cooperation among the departments of social service, mental health, mental retardation, and public health has been advanced since the institution of interagency workshops. Department heads meet with the understanding that each department has its own individual goals and that, to achieve or implement these goals, each department has a number of supporting objectives. Where a commonality of objectives exists, the departments may collaborate. Each department retains its identity, and at the same time responds to the citizens' needs with a coordinated team approach. A cost savings benefit has been achieved and jealousy over "turf" is conspicuous by its absence. The departments consider the process of collaboration to be a continuous one.

Summary   The mitigating factors just described all play a role in structuring the setting within which any attempts at coordination within the human services must take place. All of these factors—dispersed responsibility; the actual role of the political process; conflicting agency goals; the elaborate rituals of competing bureaucracies; the issue of confidentiality; the tendency of some officials to recoil from the very notion of local government involvement in human services—will influence local government decision makers as they weigh the managerial implications of an enhanced, diminished, or otherwise changed role for human services in their jurisdictions. Coordination decisions will loom large in that process.

The participants   Having outlined something of the setting of human services coordination, it is now possible to move on to an assessment of the persons and institutions who act out their roles against this setting. People are, of course, the key to the entire process. Coordination of human services programs requires the interaction of the people involved in the system. If those persons cannot or will not interact to achieve the desired coordination, the entire effort will be rendered futile. Experienced urban government managers would therefore stress that the chief decision makers' initial efforts must be directed toward identifying the participants and the role each participant plays in the decision-making process. A full understanding and appreciation of these participants' roles and the dynamics of the interpersonal relationships among them is imperative to successful communication and successful coordination. In the real world, coordination must be achieved among and between organizational apples and oranges. No set pattern exists. Each agency has its own unique chain of command, formal and informal power structure, and system of cybernetic relationships. The following discussion outlines the following main actors in this interaction: the service deliverer; the local unit supervisors; top-level agency management; the regional coordinator; citizen advisory committees; the urban government administrator; and the elected official.

The service deliverer   The only organizational common denominator found in each human services agency is the actual service deliverer. These individuals are most important to, and the key to the success of, the coordinating process. They have primary responsibility for assuring that every client is made aware of the services offered by the particular agency and other agencies. Yet they are typically the farthest away from the agency decision-making process, and their input is seldom sought when upper-level coordinating efforts are attempted. Who are they? They include the social worker, the public health nurse, the mental health clinician, the teacher, the police officer, the recreation worker, the congressional office caseworker, the probation officer, and many others. Each of these participants is professionally competent in his or her functional area, but is seldom cross-trained in, or even informed about, the programs of other agencies.

The local unit supervisors   Each local agency has a supervisory bureaucracy, the size and responsibility of which varies widely depending on the character, structure, and responsibility of the agency. Included would be the police precinct captain, the area casework supervisor, the mental health clinic director, the fire department battalion chief, and the day care center director. While each of these supervisory participants has direct responsibility for agency services within a geographical area, the area boundaries are seldom coterminous. Some of these supervisors may, in fact, be located in the state capital. Each supervisor then must coordinate with many different supervisors, the exact number depending upon organizational variables. Realism dictates that it be noted that this factor alone may be sufficient to discourage meaningful coordination.

Top-level agency management   Organizational variations have their most significant impact when the attempt is made to identify top-level management participators. The responsible agency head may be the commissioner of a state department located in the state capital, a city or county department head, a state agency division chief, a federal agency regional administrator, and so on. Departments may be organized functionally at the agency level and more generally at the local level. Coordination could then involve the local chief administrator as well as the program director in a particular department, thus increasing the number of participants. Further, some localities have created "superdepartments" which encompass several major program agencies and consolidate support service and financial functions. Programmatic coordination would then involve management of these broader departments as well as of specific program agencies.

The regional coordinator   In many metropolitan areas, councils of governments have been established to enhance coordination between units of local government and their program agencies. Many of these councils have personnel who are involved in human services programs. The effective roles of these staff members vary widely; at minimum, they process metropolitan reviews of federally assisted programs. While the regional councils usually do not participate in intragovernmental coordination attempts, they have on occasion become convenient catalysts for interagency communication that otherwise might not occur. As of the later 1970s, the federal government and some states were requiring a regional planning effort before funds were granted. The "region" might not necessarily be the same as the metropolitan area but could be instead a subregion within it. The planning unit, such as might be found in health facilities or facilities for the aging, could have its own staff and citizen board which acted independently of the individual units of government and actually hindered coordination.

Citizen advisory committees   Many human services programs have citizen advisory committees mandated by federal, state, and/or local law. Some are essentially powerless and are thus not part of any attempts to coordinate programs; others are extremely powerful politically and are therefore full particpants in the decision-making process.

The urban government administrator   The city manager, town manager, or county administrator can have a leading role to play in human services coordination depending on the size and functional responsibilities of the governmental unit. As has been noted in earlier chapters in this book, counties usually have had greater authority than cities over the traditional human services activities of health, welfare, mental health, and the courts. Cities, on the other hand, have been more involved with police, fire, community development and redevelopment, and, frequently, housing.

What is the situation as of the later 1970s? Some general comments can be made. With new federal programs, distinctive jurisdictional roles are becoming less clear with municipalities and counties having overlapping and sometimes conflicting responsibilities. Counties are becoming more aggressive in program initiation as they develop better forms of governance and more efficient management.[2] Because of their larger geographic size, counties are often, in effect, regional governments and are taking the primary local government role away from the smaller municipalities. The municipal–county conflict can have a detrimental effect on coordination, however. Suspicion and protectionism by chief administrators and program directors may result, and attempts at coordination be thwarted. As generalist local administrators, the managers are nevertheless key participants in the coordinating process. Frequently, their actual authority is greater than their legal responsibility, and their leadership role can be significant.

The elected official   Throughout the matrix of participants are the elected officials. Included among these key policy makers are governors, federal and state legislators, county supervisors or commissioners, and city council members. Depending on the state and locality, strong administrative and political roles may be played by mayors and elected county executives. Political leaders may be able to apply the glue that binds disparate organizational structures together. Political party mechanisms may provide the only means to effect coordination. However, party involvement can become a mitigating factor if the various levels of government are controlled by different parties or factions within the party.

The lobbies of state houses and council chambers are the traditional places where the political interchange occurs. Political lobbying is not restricted to elected officials or party leaders but involves the complete participant matrix. Disparate viewpoints will be expressed regardless of professional, jurisdictional, or political loyalties, or restrictions established by chains of command.

A city council may authorize the mayor to lobby for a particular piece of state legislation. At the capital, the mayor may encounter opposition by fellow council members, county commissioners, and the local department head who is serving as a spokesman for the state professional association. Formal public positions are likely to be relatively controlled and disciplined; informal exchanges are not, and are frequently the most effective.

The techniques

Having outlined something of the setting within which local government human services coordination must take place, and also noting the actors within that setting, it is now possible to discuss the techniques available to the local government manager attempting to enhance the coordination process.

Ideally, all agencies should fully and spontaneously coordinate with each other as part of a normal, dependable management process. As noted throughout this book, however, human services administration is not an ideal management process. Far from it. Managers thus have to develop techniques that will bring together agencies that may not wish to be brought together.

Kissimmee quick A remarkably successful innovation in Kissimmee, Florida, is its new Service and Information Center. The center receives and screens telephone calls and walk-in traffic at the city administration building and sorts inquiries for handling. The two staff members of the center handle an average of 130 calls a day. Routine questions are handled directly with the citizen by the center staff, thus freeing operating departments from some of the time-consuming chores involved. Problems indicating a need for action are processed through the use of an "action order" form, which is forwarded to the appropriate department. The center keeps track of all requests for services until the department has indicated that action has been taken. Later, random postcard questionnaires are mailed to the citizens who requested service to see how well their problems were handled. An amazing 67 percent of the postcard questionnaires have been returned and almost 100 percent have indicated citizen satisfaction with the service received. Organizing the operation required the addition of only one staff person.

The urban government manager will have to develop these coordinating techniques according to the problems at hand. Certain approaches can be identified, but the specific approach must be pragmatically designed and the manager must be flexible in implementation. Further, approaches will differ depending on whether the issue is solving an immediate localized crisis or structuring a continuing coordinative process. These qualifications should be borne in mind throughout the following discussion, which outlines the bilateral and multilateral techniques of coordination; the role of the human services department in the structuring of coordination; colocation; information and referral; and the use of nongovernmental forces and nonprofit corporations.

Bilateral coordination Most human services agencies have developed bilateral mechanisms for coordinating specific programs which are common to two agencies and which do not pose interorganizational threats. For example, local health departments historically have provided public health services to boards of education, even to the extent of funding nurses in the schools for school health programs. There are cooperative efforts between health departments and public schools in programs for the mentally retarded and handicapped. In fact, some jurisdictions have developed fully coordinated programs for the retarded which also incorporate summer day camp programs that are provided by the local recreation department.

Other jurisdictions have not been as successful. In one pertinent example, the school health program in a jurisdiction was provided directly by the school board. The nurses were employees of the board and worked during the nine-month school year. They successfully fought all efforts to develop cooperative programs with the local health department because of real fears that they would have to become twelve-month employees. Cooperative mental retardation programs were not established and the children were not served to the fullest. In another community, the mental health department provides family therapy services for the juvenile court. Historically, the court had contracted with psychiatrists and psychologists at a higher rate than that charged by the mental health agency. Even though both are state agencies, the city manager was able to persuade the court to contract with mental health with the result that a higher level of service was provided with fewer administrative overhead and other costs.

Multilateral coordination   It is axiomatic that the greater the number of agencies that become involved with a human services problem, the more difficult it is to achieve coordination. In addition, an external force is probably necessary to stimulate coordinative efforts. It may be useful to examine a specific problem—that of sexual assault—in order to illustrate the variety of agencies that can become involved. It is an area in which no one unit of government has the administrative or political sanctions necessary to enforce coordination. Many communities are concerned about the proper treatment of victims of sexual assault, but, historically, such victims have been poorly treated by the various governmental and private agencies. Frequently, victims have come to feel more victimized by the system than by their assailants.

Which may be the participant agencies in this case? The city police department may be the first on the scene. A uniformed beat officer takes information for the initial report, followed by an investigator who usually meets the victim at the hospital. Second, the city fire department's rescue squad transports the victim to the hospital and provides first aid treatment, if required. Third, the community hospital's emergency room treats the victim medically. And fourth, the elected county prosecutor discusses the case with the victim after the assailant is apprehended.

Many localities have taken the initiative to coordinate agency efforts to improve the physical, mental, and legal treatment of the victim. Multiagency training programs have been established. Special police investigative teams have been developed with personnel who are trained to deal with victims during a period of personal crisis. Hospitals have counselors on duty who can provide advice and comfort for the victim. The mental health agency remains on call to assist the victim if deep psychological trauma is involved. Frequently, a telephone "hot line" is established to give the victim immediate access to the system without having to personally call the police. The staff then initiates the process and involves all agencies on the victim's behalf. Because sexual assault is a crime as well as a medical and psychological matter, the various participants may find themselves in conflict. The police and prosecutor want to close the case and must be concerned about due process and other civil liberties. The medical profession wants to prevent disease and unwanted pregnancy, and the psychologist or psychiatrist must protect the mental health of the victim.

In this example, multilateral coordination probably was not initiated by the agencies themselves, or any one of them. External pressure most likely stimulated governmental action—possibly emanating from an activist group such as a local women's advocacy commission. Furthermore, the process will probably require external monitoring to assure continuance.

Structuring coordination: the human services department   The preceding chapter has reviewed local government attempts to coordinate human services agencies and programs through the establishment of an umbrella agency. As noted, the authority of local government to effect such consolidation is limited and might not include one or all of the "big three" departments: health, mental health, and welfare. Depending on the state–local organizational matrix, the local umbrella agency might be limited to aging and manpower programs as well as some local "add-ons" such as youth services, handicapped services, and rural poverty programs, for example. In any event, it will not be totally comprehensive in its program responsibility. Police, fire, juvenile court services, and probation and parole are seldom included so that a mechanism will still need to be established if these functional areas are to be coordinated. The manager could assign this function to the head of the umbrella agency, but there is a major disadvantage to this: it is often extremely difficult for an agency head to effect coordination among his or her peers. Alternatively, the manager could create an assistant city managership with the responsibility for supervising and coordinating human services agencies. This technique can also cause problems: the manager can easily become removed from direct contact with key agency heads unless he or she is willing to violate the chain of command. Further, it may well be politically unfeasible to assign an assistant manager to the police and fire departments. There are benefits to be gained, however, from creation of a superagency or from establishment of an assistant's position. The principal one could be the implicit signal that the manager is providing to the community, indicating that the administration is interested in "people" programs. Too often, however, the signal is without substance and the local department of human services has no effective portfolio—perhaps just a group of frustrated staff members.

Colocation   Recognizing that creation of a comprehensive umbrella agency is effectively impossible, some state and local governments have moved toward placing service deliverers from many agencies in a single facility with a common reception area and, sometimes, a common intake process. State, local, federal, and private agency personnel housed together can more easily coordinate cases; programs can be included on a flexible basis depending on the specific needs of the community; service levels can vary, as appropriate according to circumstances; and agency chains of command can be respected since there will normally be no facility supervisory structure. If the facility is leased (which further enhances flexibility), maintenance will be the problem of the landlord rather than that of any of the participating agencies.

Information and referral (I and R)   A central community information and referral service can provide some coordination of services. The multiplicity of public and private services is confusing to the client and to the service agencies. Establishment of an I and R unit has the side benefit of a disciplined identification of all services in the community. Public identification may result in attempts to establish more logical organization. The urban government manager may see this as a constructive first step toward greater coordination. However, duplication of I and R units and crisis "hot lines" has been a recent trend. In one county of over 500,000 population, there are over ten such agencies providing either I and R and/or crisis intervention services: a small city's hot line; a county-funded, private, general hot line; an I and R and crisis service for the aging; a women's crisis hot line; a rape crisis hot line; an Air Force base hot line for youth; a child abuse hot line; an emergency psychiatric service; the county police department dispatchers; the county fire department dispatchers; and the county public library. Small municipalities wishing to add a human services orientation to the government may establish an I and R center. While there may be political advantage and real utility to such a unit, the damage is that it may be duplicative of an existing county or private service. Further, citizen expectations may be stimulated to a higher level than current services can meet, raising frustration at yet another level.

Use of nongovernmental forces   When the manager of a jurisdiction attempts, to no avail, to coordinate certain human services activities, the use of outside forces may be required to bring pressure on the agencies. Immediate recognition must be given to the fact that this is not a controllable management technique and may result in actions other than those desired. Three avenues are available: through political leadership, through stimulation of citizen activists, and through the media.

Political leadership   Managers have a direct link to their governing bodies and may use this relationship to bring problems to the politicians. This is a normal relationship. It is less normal and more problematical for the manager to bring matters directly to the attention of elected officials who are not his or her immediate supervisors, such as legislators, county commissioners, congressmen, and so on. Each manager has to determine the degree of flexibility he or she has to deal independently in the political world. It is a method that is frequently used informally, and is often the most effective means to achieve results. The manager or agency heads may be directed by the council to lobby directly for state legislation. Political protocol frequently discourages lobbying by administrators; in a few states, it is encouraged, however, often at the expense of some of the more traditional political processes.

Citizen activists There are probably no human services programs that do not have an active cadre of citizens overseeing, probing, and lobbying for the interests of the endeavor. The manager must work with these citizen activists continually and may find them more successful politically than many of the elected officials. When coordination problems occur among agencies over which they do not have direct supervisory control, managers may find it more practical to go to the citizen activist groups, discuss the problem, and, in effect, let them play the "up front" roles in the matter.

For example, one manager met regularly and informally with key members of the local chapter of the League of Women Voters. The conversations were strictly "off the record" and gave the manager an effective sounding board for the testing of innovative human services concepts. Of course, managers must take care not to become forgetful of council policies or to become identified with citizen activist groups.

The media The manager must be very certain of his or her relationship with media representatives before attempting to push coordination through news stories. In effect, the manager is pointing to a lack of program coordination among agencies not under his or her control and is willing to stimulate a potentially embarrassing news story which will force the agencies to change. The approach the manager should take is to informally "leak" the problem to a reporter who will investigate the matter and may do a story. The agencies will be queried and the problem will be aired publicly (if there is just cause to do so) in a manner over which the manager has little control.

Use of a nonprofit corporation A rural New England county government was concerned about the need for coordination of human services activities provided by the county, the towns, and private agencies. This concern was coupled with an equal desire to avoid unnecessary increases in the county's bureaucracy. A nonprofit human services corporation was established, with county funding assistance, with the responsibility for coordinating the operations of the several agencies. The corporation was also assigned to develop programs to make citizens aware of available services; gather data for the use of the agencies; undertake program planning and grantsmanship; and, finally, provide information and referral. The board of directors of the corporation consists of agency representatives, citizens, and service recipients.

The nonprofit corporation approach may be an effective substitute for the human services umbrella agency. Localities which are concerned about increases in the number of government employees may wish to consider it. A second advantage would be the potential benefit to be gained from joint participation by agency personnel and service recipients. A disadvantage to be considered is that government agency personnel might resist coordination by an agency outside the government.

A county's experience

A short case study may be useful to show how one county manager significantly improved coordination among human services agencies. Reviewing a county's experience rather than a city's is important because counties historically have had more direct human services responsibility.

The illustrative county is large in area, suburban in character, and has over 500,000 residents. There are few municipalities so that problems of fragmentation are not a factor; the county is the primary provider of local services. Citizen participation is high. A county manager administers the county for a nine-member governing body. Figure 8–1 lists the major human services functions and indicates the responsible unit of government, the individual in charge, and the appointing authority for each.

Many specialized programs typically found in independent agencies were located as subunits of the line agencies, which substantially assisted coordination. All the agencies, even those of the state, had service areas essentially coterminous with the county's boundary, thus reducing the number of localities participating. The county manager did not have legal management authority, however, over many of the key agencies, such as health and social services.

The state was cognizant of the need to coordinate human services at the local level and also realized that, to be effective, coordination required full and active participation by the local governments. Further, the state recognized that no one organizational methodology could be imposed from the capital, but that the localities and state agencies together must develop their own techniques. The state effectively said, Leave them alone. Each state agency can operate independently at the local level, but must follow the limitations imposed by federal and state program and funding restrictions. Latitude was given vis-à-vis program emphasis, coordination with other agencies, purchase of service, avoidance of redundancies, and so forth.

With this in mind, the county manager convened a meeting of all agency heads and suggested that there were many problems of interagency coordination occurring in the ranks as well as at the top policy levels. A method was proposed for identifying these problems and their solutions. In the opinion of the manager, there needed to be full participation on the part of all levels of the bureaucracy, that is, problem identification as well as solutions needed to emanate from the bottom as well as the top. The technique that was used to encourage interaction involved a consultant "facilitator." Each agency designated three employees from all levels who would participate. The designees were realigned into three groups with each agency represented in each group. The groups were charged with the task of independently defining the interagency problems with which they and their service recipients were confronted, and then with developing methods and/or organizational structures to deal with them. The groups reported their findings and recommendations in a plenary session to the county manager and the agency heads.

The groups independently arrived at the same conclusions. They emphasized the need for case coordination (particularly when a multiproblem family was involved) and the establishment of formal mechanisms for assuring such coordination. The need to establish a single, dynamic information and referral system was identified, together with colocation of the agencies' field units, field-level supervisor "cabinets," central intake, and common forms. Most notable, however, was the demand by the groups (and echoed by the agency heads) that the county manager take a firm leadership role in the area of human services, even though it was recognized that he had no legal authority to do so. In effect, each agency head stated that he or she would follow the direction of the county manager in spite of the formal chain of command that already existed at the state, regional, and county levels. This meant that the manager was expected to treat each department as if it were his own. The process was quiet and informal, but highly effective in coordinating services and setting priorities.

An outgrowth of the process was the establishment by the manager of a "human services cabinet" which included the heads of each of the agencies noted. Numerous substantive program problems were noted, and the cabinet became a high-level forum for arriving at solutions. The manager formed task forces with one agency head serving as chairman; staffing was provided by the participating agencies. The chairman was not always from an agency that had a predominant role in the problem area under consideration. As the cabinet became more institutionalized, it became necessary for the manager to designate a middle-level administrative assistant as "human services coordinator." The assistant made certain that the agenda and issue papers for the cabinet were prepared and, most importantly, served as a clearinghouse for information between the agencies, much of which was written up for the cabinet meetings.

Agency	Responsible governmental unit	Supervisor	Supervisor appointed by
Health	State	Director	State health commissioner, confirmed by county
Social Services	County	Administrative board and director	Local administrative board, confirmed by county
Mental health/mental retardation	County	Administrative board and director	Local administrative board, confirmed by county
Community hospital	Hospital association (community-based)	Director	Hospital board of trustees
Juvenile court services	State	Director	Juvenile court judges
Vocational rehabilitation	State	Regional director	State vocational rehabilitation commissioner
Manpower	County	Director	County manager
Aging services	County	Coordinator	County manager
Information and referral	County	Coordinator	County manager
Recreation	County	Director	County manager
Libraries	County	Director	Local administrative board
Police	County	Chief	County manager
Fire	County	Chief	County manager

Figure 8–1   Units of government and individuals responsible for one county's human services functions.

The elected governing board of the county was pressuring the manager to establish a department of human services and to designate a high-level assistant as the line manager/coordinator. The county manager resisted this pressure, believing that more effective coordination and control would occur if he retained a direct link with each of the agency heads, unencumbered by an intermediate line manager. The designated assistant served as the manager's informal spokesman as well as a sounding board for the agency heads, yet did not stand between the agency heads and the manager—an essential element when dealing with the informal management structures as established in this jurisdiction. The assistant facilitated the cybernetic processes necessary for the manager to control and direct.

The management "structure" was pragmatic, participatory, and effective. Its success, however, was largely dependent on the personalities involved and the mutual trusts that were developed. The structure could not be easily transferred to another county manager or to another set of departmental players; hence, its weakness. But, given managers who can work together with confidence and trust, the informal structure is potentially as strong as the more usual, and formalized, structure with its controls and sanctions.

Conclusion

This portion of the chapter has been devoted to discussion of the elements which relate to coordination efforts among public agencies. The local government setting and certain factors which sometimes hold back the coordinative process were discussed. An outline of the seven major participants in the process was then presented; a number of possible coordination techniques, and some of their unique advantages and disadvantages, were discussed—including bilateral and multilateral coordination, colocation, information and referral services, and use of nongovernmental forces and private, nonprofit corporations. The section concluded with a case study of a county's experience with interagency coordination.

The ability to coordinate the "uncoordinatable" is one of the arts of management. Human services agencies present extreme difficulties for managers because of the various organizational frameworks which have developed in the United States. The difficulties can be tempered and even controlled if the generalist urban administrator asserts a leadership role and develops the necessary concomitant political backing. Managers cannot allow themselves to become frustrated by the lack of a rational organizational and management structure. A dynamic, informal, ad hoc "nonstructure" must in some cases be tolerated and, perhaps, even enjoyed. The manager must be results-oriented, must believe in sequential achievement, and must have a good sense of humor. Given these conditions, coordination of programs is not by any means an impossible goal.

Coordination with private agencies

This portion of the chapter attempts to gather together the managerial lessons that can be drawn from the experiences of public officials and of private sector workers and policy setters, with regard to the field of public–private coordination and cooperation in the human services area. It is hoped that this overview will help public officials to recall and assess the kinds of problems that seem to develop, and the solutions that appear to have worked. In this sense, the following analysis takes a step away from the press of day-to-day decisions. It attempts to note some of the characteristics of private and public agencies (the reader is referred to Chapter 2 of this book for additional information on the composition of private agencies), and to take a look at some of the implications for local government of decisions to coordinate or not to coordinate. It also investigates the range of options open, from total noncooperation to joint staffing with private agencies.

The object of the discussion, then, is to cover some facets of public–private relationships in the human services field and to arrange them in such a way that the reader can keep in mind the possibilities and limitations of relating the public and voluntary sectors to each other. One basic point should be kept in mind to begin with: the exercise of thinking about coordination is not an academic one. Many local government managers would agree that relations with the private sector are an extremely important, necessary, and integral part of a public official's public life.

Experience indicates that, just as a good official cannot possibly do his or her planning and executing without full regard for the people in the community, so he or she cannot disregard the private agencies. This is primarily so because, in American society, people are invariably organized into subfederations, subgroups, subcultures, and other sociological clusterings. Perhaps more than any other nation or culture, Americans have a quite unique drive to organize themselves into groups for various purposes. This phenomenon was remarked upon by Alexis de Tocqueville in his travels through the new country almost a hundred and fifty years ago.[3] The net effect for contemporary public officials is that they find themselves thinking about the people in their communities in organizational terms—as participants in defined and established organizations, all of them private, all of them highly individualistic, and all of them consisting of members with fierce pride in their respective organizations. Such groups include churches, union locals, alumni associations, professional societies, hospital boards, bowling leagues, country clubs, library associations, and symphony societies—to say nothing of a multitude of charities and philanthropies, each of them someone's favorite. Moreover, public officials may say to themselves, "I'm not really interested in all of that. I only want to know about coordinating with private agencies *in the human services field.* They will soon find, however, that the interlocking of board members and the closeness of interests among private human services agencies and private educational institutions, cultural organizations, and the like, inevitably draw them into other orbits than those normally thought of as human services. In other words, as is frequently emphasized in this book, the human services terrain is a much wider one than is sometimes perceived in narrower perspective, i.e., as encompassing income maintenance, housing, health care, and family counseling.

In sum, therefore, it is suggested in this section of this chapter that readers keep a wide perspective on the field and "walk through" the following discussion, keeping in mind the kind of role they, as managers, have to play in a highly complicated, highly convoluted, and extremely sensitive area.

The discussion is organized as follows: it begins with a view of the "to coordinate or not to coordinate" question, and goes on to take a look at the essential nature of private agencies and the similarities between public and private agencies. It then takes a close look at the managerial options involved in various "mixes" of public–private coordination. It concludes by pointing to three areas which managers have found to be particularly sensitive: the demand for accountability; other points to watch out for; and, last but not least, some notes on the political environment of coordination. There is a brief conclusion.

To coordinate or not to coordinate

In most communities of growing size and complexity, the options for action on any given problem, or for a direction to take with respect to any given objective, are multiplied. Obviously, as prudent managers will recognize, this requires some talent for planning ahead. Coordination with the private sector is a given evil to those who would rather not have to do it, and a golden opportunity for those who like to do it. In either case, it is a fact of life. There are endless variations in the ways in which such coordination can be approached, however. Each circumstance has its own set of conditions and decision-making bases from the public official's point of view. Thinking ahead about those conditions—about the consequences of whatever decision is made—is a crucial managerial task. Let us therefore take a look at three such options.

Option one Perhaps the manager has a problem that needs a solution, and, for purposes of this first example, it is assumed that only help from the private sector will make a workable solution possible. The question then becomes a matter of whom to ask for help. If one group or element in the community is asked, another may take offense. On the other hand, it may be the wrong approach to bring some individuals or groups together, even though, separately, they may have the requisite helping power. Who has the "clout"? Who, on the other hand, has follow-through capabilities? It may sometimes be better to solve a particular problem on a nonofficial, nongovernmental basis. Solving it that way, however, may create future problems, such as accusations of abrogating public responsibility or of having chosen the wrong private group to deal with it in the first place. Thus this brief illustration shows that, even on a fairly simple matter of solving a particular problem, care must be exercised in thinking through all the possible consequences of any given course of action.

Option two Let us look at a second example. It may be that, in certain circumstances, it would be better to have some programs or services run on an experimental or demonstration basis and, furthermore, that such programs ought to be offered temporarily rather than permanently, at least as far as the public announcement is concerned. This is where it may be of advantage to purchase such services from a private agency, even in a situation in which there may be a public department capable of providing those same services. Here, of course, there arises the problem of interagency friction, the problem of hurting the feelings of the public official's own department heads. Finally, there is the risk that the private agency will do a good job and will thereby create future problems with respect to the service itself—making it impossible for *anyone* to provide the service properly. Again, a dilemma of choice faces the local government decision maker.

Option three Let us take the example of a third option. It may be that it would be to the general public's interest, as well as an aid to the public official's discharge of his or her public responsibilities, to have a mechanism in existence which is outside of any direct public or private interest. Here is the situation where many communities in the 1960s developed so-called urban coalitions, consisting of representatives from public and private interests. The object was to deal, on a concerted and nonconflict basis, with a variety of community problems, both emergent and long-standing.

Summary Essentially, then, it is a matter of deciding whether a given decision to coordinate with a private agency is worth the risks. Often, it may seem terribly time-consuming and unnecessary. It may, indeed, be more efficient, in a given instance, to go ahead and set up a program and get the job done. On the other hand, the *fact* of entering into a coordinating process may reap many benefits—including public support and acceptance instead of constant sniping from various interest groups. In any event, the experience of many officials indicates that the decision to coordinate or not should not be taken lightly, and, whatever the decision, the public official should move into it with forethought and foresight.

The nature of private agencies

In considering the question of coordination between public and private agencies, an early step is, of course, to try to pinpoint the distinctions between them. The following discussion outlines five major characteristics of private agencies which distinguish them from their public counterparts.

Tax-exempt status Private agencies may enjoy a tax-exempt status as provided for by an Internal Revenue Service regulation [Section 501(c)3]. This regulation not only absolves the agency from paying taxes, but also entitles it to receive contributions which are deductible from the donors' taxes. In return for this status, there are some limitations, among them the stricture that no substantial part of the agency's program may be engaged in any lobbying efforts.

Board of directors The private agency has an independent board of directors which functions as an autonomous, self-perpetuating body. The membership of the board is usually staggered over time, with turnover approximately every three years. All members are unpaid, and great care is taken to avoid conflict of interest. Traditionally, there is heavy stress on representation from business, industry, and labor—in short, from the community power structure. While many boards which are undergoing reorganization try to achieve broader representation from ethnic and racial groups, most private agencies continue to have their major strength in volunteers from business, industry, and labor. Indeed, there is a growing awareness on the part of major national corporations of the importance of what has been labeled "corporate social responsibility" (CSR). One of the more popular means of exercising CSR is through participation in policy-making boards of directors of private agencies.

Historical roots The historical development of the private agency usually covers a longer period of time than that of almost any public agency. Many of the major private agencies got their starts long before the turn of the century. Many of the traditions of American philanthropy came out of England—the settlement houses, the Salvation Army, charity organization societies, and the like. A consequence of this historical lineage is that the private agencies are steeped in tradition and have an image of stability and longevity which many public agencies are unable to achieve. In any given community, the YMCA, the YWCA, the Boy Scouts, the Catholic Charities, and the Jewish Federations hold a charisma which is extremely attractive to the general public, including potential donors. This is true whether or not a given private agency is doing a good job, and is a "given" of political life.

Target group specialization Private agencies enjoy the luxury of specializing by target groups. Counterpart public agencies are generally unable to enjoy this freedom of choice of clientele—by sex, race, ethnic group, or particular problem. A given private agency, therefore, can be—or can appear to be—relatively exclusive as compared with corresponding public agencies, e.g., providing a service designed only for boys, subject, of course, to constitutional and judicial guidelines and restraints.

Supportive role The services provided by the private agency are generally supportive of, or ancillary to, the major public services provided through tax funds. Private agencies generally fill the gaps. This characteristic applies to almost every human services operation, with the possible exception of hospitals. Most community hospitals are still operated under private auspices. With that exception, the mainstream of human services is under public auspices; the private agency comes into play to supplement such major survival services as income maintenance, housing, health, and education.

Summary The consequence of the five characteristics just outlined is, basically, that the private agency jealously tends to guard its independence and its autonomy. It is able to be fairly successful in protecting such autonomy because of the "clout" it has in its volunteer leadership. Finally, it is important to note that programs and services can be shifted fairly quickly—perhaps more so than is true in the public sector—because the decision-making power is in a relatively small group and because the impact of such changes is not as massive as it would be in the public sector.

Similarities between public and private agencies

At the same time, it is important to note that there are also some fundamental similarities between public and private agencies. Let us note four of the most significant.

Common expertise The professional practitioners—the staffs—of public and private agencies possess a common expertise. They generally come from the academic disciplines of public administration, public health, law, business administration, social work, or urban studies. These professionals exercise their expertise in much the same way, irrespective of the public or private auspices of the agency for which they work. There is also a great deal of cross-fertilization, with an increasing tendency for professionals in the human services field to move back and forth across public and private sector lines. This is a phenomenon growing out of the tremendous infusion of federal resources into human services during the 1960s. This trend will probably continue, resulting in a decrease in the distinctiveness of private and public agency staffs.

Lack of management capability The major deficiency in *both* sectors appears to rest in a lack of management capability. It is generally recognized that the greatest current need in the field—whether public or private—is to develop better management capability.

Money shortage The third and most common problem is money shortage, as local government and private agency managers alike are all too well aware. Both the public and private agencies face continuing fiscal problems. Moreover, the shortage is not equitably spread, particularly in the private sector. While certain ''popular'' appeals may be supported far beyond their current need, other services may be suffering from inadequate funds for reasons unrelated to the merits of the services provided or the needs of the potential consumers.

''Faddism'' Both sectors are subject to the same phenomenon of ''faddism,'' whereby certain major programs are deemed to be most needed at a given time—whether or not there has been any real evidence or scientifically validated basis for assuming such need. Examples from the 1960s and 1970s would include community switchboards, methadone clinics, drug abuse centers, halfway houses, and the like.

Types of coordination between public and private agencies

Coordination can be achieved between public and private agencies in a great variety of ways. There can, for example, be a financial joint venture: this usually involves matching large tax funds with small, or even token, private funds. There can be a purchase of service arrangement: a public agency buys services from a private agency which the former is not equipped to provide. There can be the formation of a coalition: policies covering both sectors are set to apply on a general basis. There can be coordinating councils: representatives of public and private agencies engage in debate over various community problems. Whatever the form, there seems to be a common basis for a felt need to coordinate: someone has to want it or some event has to occur which compels it. Space does not permit an exhaustive examination of all such options in the present discussion. The method adopted, therefore, is to take four practical examples—of total multilevel coordination; an example of one man's vision; an illustrative use of an available force; and a blending of staffs situation—and describe actual occurrences, followed by a brief commentary on each.

Total multilevel coordination Shortly after the Vietnamese refugee problem burst into the front pages of American newspapers in the spring of 1975, the governor of Pennsylvania was informed that Indiantown Gap would be the location of one of the Vietnamese refugee relocation centers. He hastily formed a statewide committee, consisting of representatives of as many of the major public and private agencies and organizations as possible in order to consider the problems of relocation. One of the organizations he invited was the Health and Welfare Planning Association (HWPA) of Allegheny County. The HWPA, armed with the blessings of the governor's committee, organized a local committee of representatives of thirty-five public and private health, welfare, religious, and educational agencies. This local committee went to work developing a program over the ensuing twelve months.

The result: 1,000 Vietnamese refugees were resettled in western Pennsylvania. Only twelve of these have had to go on public assistance; the others are employed and moving toward self-sufficiency. The University of Pittsburgh sponsored a special training program for teachers to learn techniques of teaching English as a second language. The communications media cooperated with public services information on the progress of resettlement and the condition of the refugees. A fellowship association was organized to sponsor Vietnamese cultural activities. A Vietnamese newspaper was started. Adult education courses were offered in the public schools, and private classes were organized for those unable to attend formal classes. At least two Vietnamese cultural days have been held in Pittsburgh—celebrated by the total community.

Comment   What this example illustrates is that a major national programmatic thrust, i.e., resolving the question of what to do about our national responsibility for Vietnamese refugees, was translated into a statewide response. This, in turn, was dealt with by a particular county in the state through the cooperation of all the relevant major public and private agencies in the region.

Most important of all as a "lesson" in this illustration is the fact that there was an organization in place which could do the job. The organization did not provide a direct service and was therefore not in competition with any public or private direct service agency. It was under private auspices and, as a consequence, the governor's selection did not slight any of the multitude of public departments. The organization had no legislative or regulatory mandate, and no cooperating agency could feel that it was *forced* to do anything; it had the avowed function of planning, coordinating and research; it had top volunteer leadership in its board of directors; and, finally, it had the sanction and financial backing of the local United Way fund raising organization, although it remained wholly independent and autonomous as a not-for-profit charitable corporation. The status of HWPA—and the fact of its existence in Pittsburgh for nearly half a century—made it precisely the kind of vehicle to do the job. The fact that HWPA did a good job was a total plus. Nevertheless, even if the job had not been done as well as it was, it was still a matter of fortuitous convenience for the governor of Pennsylvania to have such an organization in place and to be able to turn to it when it was needed.

One man's vision   In the early 1970s, the city of Cincinnati had a moribund transit system which was charging among the highest fares in the United States. The city manager took the lead in doing something about this situation. In the 1972–75 period, the manager, with the approval of the city council, turned the entire mass transit system around on a permanent basis. This required the enlistment of a substantial array of community organization support, which was accomplished through the formation of the Tri-State Transportation Committee—an ad hoc coalition of transportation-related organizations. A major element in this committee was the planning division of the local United Way organization, which acted as the secretariat for the committee. The result of this effort was that new tax earnings, together with available federal assistance, enabled the city to take over the entire transit system and, concomitantly, to both lower the fares and provide more efficient and responsive service.

Comment   The vision of the city manager about the solution to a concrete city problem, using a private instrumentality to create public understanding of the issues in a relatively short time, solved a long-standing community problem.

It took considerable courage for the city manager to make a move calling for increased taxes and the takeover of the private venture, especially since the venture being taken over was, in the minds of the citizens, a total "loser." It was remarkable, therefore, that the entire process worked as well as it did. Perhaps this illustration points up two things: first, the potential value of a strong city manager—strong in character *and* in the form of government within which he operates. Second, it points up an inherent aspect of coalitions—in this case, the very specific focus of the committee. It was deliberately ad hoc. It was understood from the beginning that, once the specific job objective was met, it would go out of business. Therefore, no one was under any illusion about its place in the permanent bureaucracy.

An available force   In 1972, it was found that the school health program in Detroit was inadequate. (In bureaucratic language, only one-half of one person was assigned to health education and health problems in the entire Detroit school system.) The cause of the problem was identified as jurisdictional, that is, as between the city's health department and the board of education. Under the leadership of the mayor, who enlisted the support of New Detroit (the city's urban coalition), the impasse between the two city departments was broken. The mayor gave priority to its needs for Comprehensive Educational Training Act (CETA) funds, the schools contributed administrative staff, and New Detroit provided funds for training of health staff. New Detroit also approached the state of Michigan for additional funding of the program. The result: the first health staff entered the Detroit school system in September, 1976.

Comment   What does this example indicate? An available private community organization with communitywide credibility broke an impasse between two public departments in order to achieve something that everyone had long recognized as necessary.

New Detroit had come into being in the 1960s as the community leadership's response to the race riots in Detroit. It consisted of the most powerful leaders in the community, representing both management and labor. For a community like Detroit, with its relatively monolithic oligarchy of auto executives and union leaders, New Detroit was an ideal organization to be brought into play in order to bring opposing forces together for the community good—around either public or private resources.

A number of other communities have such organizations playing the same kinds of roles, although their creation came about for other reasons and their forms of operation may differ. Such organizations seem to be most effective in those communities which have fairly strict hierarchies of power and which have as their economic base the heavy industries of manufacturing and building, as distinguished from finance and services. A notable example of this phenomenon is the Allegheny Conference on Community Development, which was formed immediately after World War II and was responsible for Pittsburgh's renaissance—transforming the smoke-infested, grimy downtown into what Pittsburghers now justifiably refer to as "the golden triangle."

Blending of staffs   For a period of three years, a remarkable cooperative program existed between the Boston Parks and Recreation Department and the traditional private youth agencies, such as the Boy Scouts, Girl Scouts, Camp Fire Girls, YMCA, and YWCA. This cooperative effort consisted of blending of staffs of the public and private agencies in order to keep many of the recreation centers open for longer hours in some of the more needy areas. Before that time, department personnel worked from nine to five. As a consequence, most of the centers were closed for the evenings and on weekends, regardless of the time of year. Under the cooperative program, however, private agency personnel took over when public department personnel left, and many of the centers were thereby able to operate on a full-time, full-week basis. This whole arrangement came about, at least in part, as a result of the imagination of the Parks and Recreation Department's commissioner. He had, in fact, been recruited by the mayor with the help of the United Community Planning Corporation, a private research and evaluation organization that had enjoyed a long-standing, high reputation in the community.

Comment   There seems to be nothing more influential to anyone than having participated in getting him or her hired. Thus, commercial "head hunters," as well as community organizations that provide advice and lists of candidates to heads of local general purpose government, have a tremendous influence on the ensuing policies and actions of public agency directors.

The above illustration is perhaps exceptional because the blending of staff is probably the single most difficult form of coordination and cooperation. While such arrangements may look good on paper, the jurisdictional disputes and the philosophical differences create work-related problems that are often insurmountable. There is also, of course, the constant risk of antagonizing the advocates of civil service when private agency staffs are brought into the picture. The fact that it worked in Boston for three years is a credit to the idea, in the first place, but also to the workers themselves and to the commissioner. Unfortunately, after three years of this relatively unique experience, the commissioner left to take another job elsewhere; the program died and has never been revived. This appears to illustrate another point: things can only happen to the extent that the top decision maker is willing to *make* them happen.

The demand for accountability

Of particular importance today for both the public and private sector is the public's demand for accountability. The post-Watergate national ambience of skepticism about the probity of government affects attitudes toward *all* social institutions—churches and charities not excepted. Full and fair disclosure, therefore, of all financial information is the order of the day. Moreover, the demand for accountability itself extends beyond fiscal matters to program results—the logical ultimate extension of this is the insistence on knowing precisely what concrete good all the intentions and "worthy efforts" of human services programs actually did for the people served.

This two-pronged public demand for fiscal integrity and program effectiveness clearly requires a major shift in the way public and private agencies continue to conduct their business. *Both* sectors are in the *same* limelight and, as far as the public is concerned, the same standards and criteria should apply to both. Within the last few years, therefore, attempts have been made to provide guidelines and tools for responding to these public demands. Unfortunately, most of these attempts have been hampered by the complexities of multilevel governmental jurisdictions, the size and proliferation of programs, the waffling on public social policy at the federal level, and the natural reluctance of established institutions to change.

Nevertheless, such attempts will continue to occupy the minds of most planners and implementers in the public and private human services systems. The time will never return when we can rely on a blindly trusting public to accept without question anything but fully and fairly disclosed facts. Three notable examples of attempts to develop tools for accounting—*UWASIS,* AICPA, and the "Standards"—are worth mentioning here. All three came out of the private sector, but the impact of all three tools has been pervasive throughout the country and among all political jurisdictions. For a more detailed discussion of the issues of management and financial control, readers are referred to Chapter 9 of this book.

Role of UWASIS   The first tool is *UWASIS*—an acronym for United Way of America Services Identification System.[4] Conceived in 1970 and first published in 1972, *UWASIS* is the only comprehensive taxonomy in the human services field. Since its publication, some 5,000 organizations and state and local jurisdictions across the country have used it. Its definitions and classification scheme are being followed with remarkable consistency, confirming the 1972 edition's inscription on the cover, "People and Programs Need Uniform and Comparable Definitions.'' *UWASIS* (and *UWASIS II,* the updated edition published in 1976) is a major contribution to the foundation for all coordination, that is, a classification scheme employing a common language.

Role of AICPA   The second tool is *Audits of Voluntary Health and Welfare Organizations,*[5] an industry audit guide published by the American Institute of Certified Public Accountants (AICPA). While this guide confines itself to the private sector, the generally accepted accounting principles promulgated by the AICPA for the first time in this ''industry'' had an instant effect on all human services accounting.

Role of the ''Standards''   The third tool is ''Standards of Accounting and Financial Reporting for Voluntary Health and Welfare Organizations.''[6] The ''Standards,'' originally put out in 1964 and revised in 1974 (to conform to the above-mentioned AICPA audit guide) are now an accepted basis for financial reporting, not only in the private sector but in a number of governmental jurisdictions. The United States Civil Service Commission requires conformity with the ''Standards'' for receipt of annual combined federal campaign funds raised from federal employees throughout the world. The state of Pennsylvania requires conformity with the ''Standards'' as a condition for legal acceptance as a not-for-profit charitable corporation. A major innovation in the original ''Standards'' was the identification of all program services and the differences between them and so-called support services (fund raising and management), thereby establishing the principle of functional accounting.

Summary   These three tools—and, again, the reader is referred to Chapter 9 for more extensive treatment—represent basic first attempts in responding to the increasing public demand for program and fiscal accountability. They also represent sound bases for starting with a common language in interpreting precisely what services are provided and how much they cost—certainly an essential element of coordination.

What to watch for: some benchmarks

Any public official who wants to enter into a coordinative or cooperative relationship with one or more private agencies should examine some benchmarks in looking at a private agency. Four such benchmarks are outlined below.

The executive director's capacity   Of paramount importance is the capability of the agency's executive director. He or she can possess excellent academic credentials, but, without the sophistication and imagination embodied in the word ''smarts,'' it is not likely that a lasting coordinating relationship can be achieved. One good index of the executive's capabilities is the kind of staff he or she has hired. The initiative, imagination, and quality of the staff will often reflect those same qualities in the executive.

Composition of the board of directors   The composition of the board of directors of the agency is important. Does it have an active board with sufficient strength among the individual members to represent a force in the community? Is it merely a ''paper'' board of top leaders who never attend, or a large board of representatives whose primary interests are debate and discussion rather than policy setting and action? The nature of the board leadership, in this respect, is an extremely significant index of the agency's capacity.

Two ways of looking at an agency's programs   Many managers will find it helpful to take a twin look at the agency's programs. First they may want to inquire as to what program or service changes have been instituted in the past ten years. No changes at all or too many capricious changes, are both indicators of uncertain and confused administration. Secondly, they may wish to ask: What about the clientele, the membership, the users? The number and the type should be checked. The agency ought to be serving that number that it can realistically handle in terms of the services it purports to provide. Thus, mass recreation can carry a large number of participants, whereas mental health counseling should have a much smaller clientele.

Sources of funding   The manager may want to take a look at the sources of funding of the private agency. How dependent is it on a given source, such as endowment fund interest, or local United Way campaign funds, or even federal grants? To the extent possible, it should have a respectable and widespread portfolio of funding sources. An examination of the agency's year-end financial statement, properly prepared and audited, can be a fruitful basis for judging its capabilities.

The politics of coordination

As the preceding discussion has hopefully conveyed to the reader, there is really not that much difference between the private agency world and the public agency world. The major difference may largely be because we think there is a difference. In any event, there is just as much "politics" in the private sector as there is in the public. It would seem, however, that politics in the public sector is a relatively straightforward, simple thing—the two determining factors being party and ideology. In the public sector, there is a bottom-line consequence for any given action, namely, that the actor is either in or out of office by election or by appointment. Moreover, he or she has straight-line power—by legislation, by regulation, by patronage, or by the application of legal sanctions.

"Perpetuation" politics?   "Politics" in the private sector, on the other hand, has many strange twists and turns. There is no obvious reward or punishment. At best there is something called "perpetuation." There is something felt to be a matter of prestige or status. There is, however, no concrete reward. Yet the benefits of leadership in the private sector are deemed to be of such value that men and women will strive mightily to preserve a status, develop a prestige, and do all in their power to ensure that their particular arena is preserved in perpetuity. At the same time, all of this must be done without any obvious *effort* to achieve. One does not electioneer to become an officer of a board of directors; one does not send out pamphlets extolling one's virtues to be chosen as a solicitor for charitable contributions. In short, the most one can do is to be known as cooperative and willing to help; and that quality is demonstrated through an ongoing participation in the volunteer's respective interest groups—a church, a social agency, a private school, a museum board, etc.

Avoiding controversy?   One common denominator obtains in such organizational lives: controversy must be avoided at all costs. Communitywide controversy, interorganizational controversy, and, certainly, intraorganizational controversy is as fire is to a crowded theater. Organization after organization, group after group, has gone into panic and destroyed itself when it has moved into controversy. This does not, of course, apply to those organizations whose purported objective is to be controversial. However, in the case of those institutions that avowedly operate as burrs in society's saddle, e.g., Nader's Raiders, Common Cause, Right to Life, and the like, the astute manager will doubtless have noted that they are not, to put it gently, in comfortable association with so-called human services organizations and agencies.

A particular platform?   Having made such a point about the noncontroversial nature of private agencies, however, it is important to recognize, too, the fact that there is no question that each subsector stands on a particular platform. Some have special interests, such as health interests, cultural interests, or educational interests. Others are universal, such as the local United Ways. Moreover, many agencies have particular interest group constituencies deriving their power from certain segments of society. Organized labor is closely involved in a variety of human services activities. Management, through its employing power, is much coveted by community organizations. There are interest groups formed around racial and ethnic backgrounds, and religious beliefs.

Managers have found it helpful to keep in mind not so much the truism that there is great variety among private organizations and their power bases, but the fact that each interest has its own particular set of "politics." For example, in the health arena, the following kinds of possible conflicts arise. The difference in ideology among county medical societies, public health officials, and young "dissident" practitioners may interfere with intergroup cooperation. The increasing growth of health maintenance organizations are sometimes thought to be antithetical to the concept of private medical practice and the community hospital. There are competing fund raising efforts of the various causes based on the parts of the body or types of diseases—cancer, heart, congenital defects, lung, myasthenia gravis, muscular dystrophy, and the like. Then there are such subtle differences of feeling as those between advocates and supporters of services for the mentally retarded and the mentally ill. Alcoholics, in turn, would prefer not to be thought of as drug abusers. And so it goes with other bases for differences.

In any event, in recognizing the politics of coordination, one should—following on the point made by the author of the first portion of this chapter—try to keep track of the players. One should at least know what the characteristics and bases for differences are among the "sides" of any given issue. One should know the backgrounds of the players. For example, a woman who is president of the United Way and presides over a universal operation in the name of charity, may be the wife of a surgeon who has very decided ideas on "socialized medicine." On some occasions, one may indeed bring the Episcopalian and Roman Catholic bishops together. On other occasions, they had better not be seen in the same room.

Another point for public officials to ponder is that, whatever their respective private proclivities and preferences may be, it would be wise not to take sides in the highly complicated and sometimes confusing "politics" of private agencies. Also, they should not assume that, because an agency is private, there will be no public repercussions when controversies erupt. There can indeed be repercussions. A sound axiom to follow is: Avoid any kind of controversy, and assume that all participants, like Caesar's wife, are above reproach.

Conclusion

A major message about coordination with private agencies is that it is worth it. Coordination is of value politically, administratively, and, certainly, to the community. But such coordination needs to be effected with care, with foresight and understanding. It is curious that, despite the proliferation of organizations in our society, despite the political sophistication of most citizens, and despite "town hall" traditions, there are so many of us who spend all of our lives in one or another sector—public or private.

As indicated earlier, there is much greater cross-fertilization among the newer practicing professionals in both public and private agencies. But, among the older decision makers and among many of the more established practitioners, there is a division of experience as between the public and private sectors. This means that there are many prejudices to be overcome. On the parts of public agency workers there could be too great an inferiority complex vis-à-vis private agency workers, on the one hand, or too much indifference about any sector other than the public sector. Likewise, in the private agency world, there can be an incredible amount of misconception about the public sector. It behooves the public official, therefore, to take some leadership in accepting this fact of life and in moving both sides toward each other—by attitude and by action.

In our local community life, Americans are highly individualistic, and a way of American life is organizational pluralism—we live and let live. We would rather have ten useless organizations in existence than feel that one organization was not permitted to operate. Sooner or later, therefore, public officials generally have no choice but to cooperate with some private group or other, no choice but to coordinate with something or other. The one choice they have—and an important choice it is—is *how* they do it, and the timing of it. And on that decision—how they go about it, what they use as their knowledge and attitude base for it, and how they time it in relation to the public good—may rest the success or failure of a given administration. Indeed, the ambience of an entire community may rest on the choice of ways to go about coordinating *all* parties at interest.

1   For a full statistical profile, including educational background, of municipal managers and chief administrative officers, see Laurie S. Frankel and Carol A. Pigeon, *Municipal Managers and Chief Administrative Officers: A Statistical Profile,* Urban Data Service Reports, vol. 7, no. 2 (Washington, D.C.: International City Management Association, February 1975).

2   A comprehensive source of information on various aspects of management in county governments is *The County Year Book* (Washington, D.C.: National Association of Counties and International City Management Association, annually).

3   Alexis de Tocqueville, *Democracy in America,* ed.

J. P. Mayer, trans. George Lawrence (New York: Doubleday, 1969).

4   *UWASIS II: A Taxonomy of Social Goals & Human Service Programs,* 2nd ed. (Alexandria, Va.: United Way of America, 1976).

5   *Audits of Voluntary Health and Welfare Organizations* (New York: American Institute of Certified Public Accountants, 1974).

6   *Standards of Accounting and Financial Reporting for Voluntary Health and Welfare Organizations,* 2nd ed. (New York: National Health Council, National Assembly of National Voluntary Health and Social Welfare Organizations, and United Way of America, 1974).

Management and financial controls

In the human services field, as in other public management systems, it is during the budgetary cycle that the administrative and legislative processes meet, and planning and policy become operational. As Jesse Burkhead noted, "Budgeting is and must remain a political process." [1] It is the point where decisions are made about who gets what.

Eventually all important proposals and ideas relating to human services must be translated into monetary terms. From the selectmen of the smallest New England village to the manager and council members of the largest cities, concern about the expenditure of tax dollars is universal. It is expressed in such questions as: Am I getting the most for my dollar?; What are the hidden costs in the program?; Where can we save a few dollars?

When we remove much of the jargon from the process, we find that the human services budgeting process involves four major steps: (1) planning and evaluation, (2) decision making, (3) allocations, and (4) reporting. This chapter will examine various reporting, allocation, and budgetary methodologies. In addition, it will indicate how the budgetary process can be integrated into planning and evaluation systems to help public decision makers—elected officials, managers, human services directors, fiscal officers, and other interested parties—better implement effective human services programs.

The method adopted is to begin the discussion with an overview of the basic problems in this area. The following section presents a detailed analysis of financial reporting—the concepts of standards and the implementation of standards. Next, there is a discussion of allocation of local government funds to human services programs. Then the various formats of a budget are described and analyzed. The following section describes a "mixed bag" containing such concepts as zero-based budgeting, the performance audit, and requests for proposals.

As the fiscal function permeates the human services processes described in detail elsewhere in this book, the reader will find it helpful to refer to specific human services areas covered in other chapters as appropriate. The present chapter also helps round out the discussion contained in Chapter 7, which deals with administrative structures for municipal human services programs, and Chapter 10, which covers evaluative mechanisms in detail.

Two major points will be repeatedly stressed throughout this chapter, and it is as well to make them explicit at the outset. *First, the budget process is a management information system which, when properly utilized by government managers, can lead to better programming and increased accountability.* However, sophisticated budget systems cost time, expertise, and money. *Second,* therefore, managers have come to recognize that *no local general purpose government should reform its systems until it has investigated both the benefits and costs of a more sophisticated process.* Decision makers and their staffs in too many communities have discovered that implementation of complex fiscal reporting and management information systems was a waste of their time and effort, owing to a lack of willingness and ability to use the processes.

Finally, it is important that the goals identified in budgeting for human services should conform to those of any good public budgeting system. Three basic goals may be summarized as follows:

1. To ensure that local tax revenues are used in the best interest of the community, and especially to ensure that services receiving funding support are effective and directed toward the most important local problems and situations;
2. To ensure that organizations or government departments spending local tax revenues do so in a responsible manner and operate in the most economically efficient way possible; and
3. To provide an equitable and fair means for allocating municipal, county, or other local government funds.

The basic problems: an overview

Management and fiscal control systems for human services expenditures have presented special problems for local government officials. Some of the reasons for this difficulty are obvious; others are more subtle. The obvious stem from such considerations as the facts that the field of human services is a new and fast-developing one; that human services often lack the quantifiability of more established services; and, as the discussion in Chapter 1 pointed out, that they often touch on matters that go to the heart of our ongoing debate about the role of government in our society. The more subtle reasons are directly linked to inadequate human services planning capacity, lack of practical evaluation tools, and the difficulty of many local governments in articulating their responsibility for delivering and funding human services. Few local governments have developed adequate planning mechanisms to provide decision makers with information to help guide them during the budget process. Likewise, local officials often fail to develop policy relating to the funding of human services programs.

Why a reactive posture?

The situation reveals itself by the fact that local officials often take a reactive, rather than a proactive, posture toward the funding of programs. The reactive process can bluntly be characterized as the "who can yell loudest" syndrome, whereby many programs are funded simply to appease vociferous or powerful special interest groups. Questions regarding the benefits of programs, accountability for the funds expended, and the efficiency of operations are too rarely asked. Most local governments in the United States still use a grant system of funding human services programs with little or no financial reporting required. Very few communities require audits of human services organizations receiving local funding.

It is not unusual for quite special emotional and personal factors to come into play when questions are raised regarding the improvement of financial management systems for human services. Efforts to upgrade financial reporting practices have often been met with the rejoinder that "meeting these requirements costs money, and we'd rather be helping people." When considering reform, local officials are, or should be, sensitive to this situation. Many have also come to recognize, however, that too often graphic images of human suffering and need have served as a facade for inefficient services and abusive expenditures of taxpayers' dollars.

The case for improved fiscal management

William Aramony, national executive of the United Way of America, states the case for improved fiscal management systems in words that are applicable to the public as well as to the private sector:

American philanthropy has come of age in recognizing the importance of *full disclosure*, of *public reporting*, and of *honest self-evaluation* based on sound records. Some people have felt that charity should be from the heart [and] not from the head, that helping one's fellow man meant abandoning "businesslike" practices. In short, doing good—or do-goodism—became synonymous with fuzzy reporting and even fuzzier accounting. . . . It is no longer enough to talk about the worthiness of causes. To the degree possible, we now have to measure how much our causes are worth to the people who need service.[2]

For the professional local government manager or the elected official, the same issue can be stated in different ways. As Calvin Canney, the city manager of Portsmouth, New Hampshire, said, "It makes no difference whether it is the city of Portsmouth, New Hampshire, giving $25,000 to the District Nursing Association or the town of Epping providing $200 to their day care center. Both municipalities should have some way of determining how these activities fit into a total program, who is funding the program, how efficiently the services are being provided, and whether it is worth continuing."[3]

The issue of accountability

The underlying question regarding fiscal and budgetary systems is ultimately one of accountability. Robert Fulton, Administrator for Social and Rehabilitative Services of the Department of Health, Education, and Welfare, addressed the issue of accountability:

In the private business world, it is clear that managers are accountable to owners for achieving sufficient profits to enable the enterprise to sustain itself and grow. The profit and loss statement and the balance sheet report the results of the managers' efforts.

Accountability is a far more complex issue in the public sector. In the first place, there is often no clear agreement on the question of to whom accountability is owed. Is it to the taxpayers? To those whom the program is intended to benefit? To the legislators who created the programs? To the administrators at higher levels? To all of these?[4]

At the heart of all questions relating to accountability are a number of issues directly linked to fiscal reporting and budgetary systems. Local officials have discovered a number of "nuts-and-bolts" difficulties in making human services programs more accountable. These include:

1. The fact that local governments have been asked to fund services provided by both internal departments and local nonprofit voluntary organizations;
2. The lack of standardization of terms and budgeting formats;
3. A lack of knowledge and awareness by most local government officials of the accepted standards of fiscal accountability for human services organizations; and
4. Difficulty in linking funds expended to service delivery.

The problem of fragmentation

Of these structural problems, the most frustrating and confusing is the fragmented nature of local human services delivery systems. A bewildering mixture of public and private organizations is involved in the delivery of human services programs. Depending on the community, the same service may be delivered by the local government, a community action agency, the school system, a voluntary organization, a comprehensive multiservice agency, or a proprietary organization. Funding for services may come from the federal government, state, county, city, United Way, fees, foundations, community trusts, or private contributions. Usually, it is from several sources. A recent report by the Hartford, Connecticut, Urban Research Committee described the human services delivery system in that city as "one of seeming chaos and fragmentation. The human services system or nonsystem is an agglomerate of public and private agencies, community organizations, and civic groups that number 600 in the capital region. A mixture of public and private funds from a variety of sources [is] dispensed with no apparent plan or system of priorities."[5]

Lack of a clear-cut funding policy

In contrast to other major human services funding organizations, there is no clear-cut policy as to what the local government's role in the funding and delivery of human services should be. Federal funding policy is established by Congress, within the federal administrative structures. State policy evolves from federal policy and from each state's legislature. Voluntary funding policy is generally the result of years of tradition in each community. Too often municipal involvement in human services funding has been as a reaction to the other major funders. Little if any attention has been placed on human services fiscal management systems used by local government. Few municipalities have seriously considered the development of financial accounting formats, budgeting forms, and allocation methods to meet their needs. The result has been a serious lack of accountability both in fiscal and program terms.

Levelheaded budgets   The city of Walnut Creek, California, uses a budgeting and management control system which identifies a certain level of service for each program area and bases the budget and work program on that level. This technique provides an effective guide for department management control, and has also made the budget more comprehensible to the public.

Lack of standardized reporting formats

The lack of standardization of budgeting and fiscal reporting formats has substantial program implications. Few attempts have been made to coordinate the use of budgeting formats by neighboring municipalities. In fact, few communities have attempted to utilize existing budget formats used by the local United Ways or major state agencies. The following realities of the funding situation for human services providers are at the heart of this issue: one, many human services programs, including ones operated by local governments, receive funding from several sources (i.e., the federal and state governments, United Way, foundations, and the local government); and two, many human services organizations provide services on a regional basis.

The lack of compatibility between the budgeting formats and reporting methods required by different funders has been a primary cause for the growing administrative costs of human services providers. In addition, many human services providers have been able to use this lack of standardization to avoid full disclosure of their financial situation. Serious abuses have occurred as a result.

In 1974, the American Institute of Certified Public Accountants (AICPA) published their industry audit guide, *Audits of Voluntary Health and Welfare Organizations*.[6] As Marvin Gross, a partner in Price Waterhouse, stated at the time, "The accounting profession has laid down some very specific rules for the three most important sectors of the broad category referred to as nonprofit organizations."[7] These standards of fiscal reporting and accountability are specific, reasonable, and fair. Especially important is the fact that they provide the local government manager with a uniform approach to financial control. Unfortunately, many managers, human services directors, and fiscal officers are not aware of these standards and how to relate them to local governments' financial systems.

Summary

The problem areas noted above—the lack of a proactive posture; the need for improved fiscal management; the issue of accountability; the problem of fragmentation; the lack of a clear-cut funding policy; and the lack of standardized reporting formats—combine to present substantial challenges to local government managers in the human services area. Essentially, their problems are a facet of what is probably the most perplexing problem facing local government today: how to link funds expended with services provided. The ability to link the expenditure of funds to the provision of human services requires adequate accounting procedures and a clear definition of program goals and purposes. Too often, these essential management tools and procedures are not in evidence. Further, it would be unrealistic not to note that any reform, but particularly budgetary reform, is frustrating to attempt and difficult to achieve within the public sector. If human services management in the public sector is to come of age, however, this challenge must be met at all levels.

Financial reporting

A number of recent developments have been significant in the area of accounting and reporting for public and private organizations. One observer takes a dim view of historic practices (or nonpractices) in this area. " 'Anything goes!' That seems to have been the rule for nonprofit organizations in the past. Due to rules set down by the accounting profession, however, human services organizations suddenly have found themselves catapulted from the era of permissiveness to an era where the accounting and reporting requirements are spelled out in great detail." [8]

For years the accounting profession paid relatively little attention to the question of fiscal accountability for human services organizations. Although the line-item budget was first introduced in the New York City Health Department in the very early 1900s to control abusive and corruptive practices, no uniform system of reporting was recommended until 1964. In that year a group of larger human services and voluntary organizations jointly published *Standards of Accounting and Financial Reporting for Voluntary Health and Welfare Organizations.* [9] The guidelines set forth in that publication were the first to be widely recognized and accepted by major human services and governmental organizations.

The 1974 AICPA audit guide mentioned above is designed to provide direction to AICPA members—virtually all certified public accountants (CPAs)—in conducting audits and recommending accounting principles. Any CPA who deviates from this guide may be required to justify his or her actions.

In 1974, the United Way of America published *Accounting and Financial Reporting.* [10] This "how to" book expands on and elaborates many of the principles set forth by the AICPA guide. It translates the sometimes confusing jargon of the accountant into language usable by administrators, managers, and other government officials.

The buck passes here In an effort to provide a sound social services delivery system, the city of Santa Monica, California, has established a division of grants and community services. The purpose of this division is to provide technical assistance to community agencies to help them to secure funds for their much-needed services. The unreliability of social services funds and the heavy reliance which private social services agencies have come to have upon municipal support prompted the development of this new dimension of city grantsmanship.

These recent developments relating to accounting and reporting practices are relevant to local government officials for two reasons. First, private, nonprofit organizations delivering human services are more frequently turning to local government for financial support. The standards of fiscal accountability provide the local official with guidelines regarding what information should be required to ensure proper expenditure of local tax revenues. The standards are recognized guidelines which can help local officials assess the fiscal responsibility and effectiveness of not-for-profit organizations. Second, the standards are fully developed concepts which can be used to improve the management of internal local government departments. Government officials can compare their present management practices to these standards and consider methods to improve the management capabilities of their departments and organizations. The following discussion therefore first analyzes the concepts of the standards, and then goes on to describe procedures for implementing the standards.

Concepts of the standards

Traditionally, accounting and reporting procedures for human services organizations have been based on the stewardship concept of accountability for revenues received and funds dispersed. This is often referred to as "fund accounting." Marvin Gross explains that, "unfortunately, fund accounting can get very complicated—not because the underlying principles are complicated but because of the dozens of different 'funds' some organizations tend to set up. Typically each fund is accounted for as a separate entity. As a result, it is usually hard to get an overall picture of an organization's activities." [11] This situation has been encouraged in part by different funding sources requiring different reporting procedures. It can also result, however, in substantial abuse by organizations who desire to withhold from the public information on their gross worth or the real cost of services. Separate funds may be created to hide certain assets, liabilities, expenditures, or incomes from the general public.

Another practice has been for human services organizations to apply operating surpluses to endowment or special building funds. This widespread practice of applying surplus revenues to special funds is considered abusive and can cost a nonprofit organization its tax-exempt status. Unfortunately, multiple funds have caused many organizations to obscure the real cost of delivering services. Typically, one functional area or program of an organization is financed by several funds. This has resulted in unusually high program costs which can escape the attention of the most diligent board of directors or funder. In other words, bad management and inefficient programming can avoid detection through the manipulation of these "funds."

The new standards mentioned earlier will help curb these practices by requiring: the *fair and full disclosure* of all financial activity of the organization; a *single reporting statement* for all activities undertaken with unrestricted income and revenue; and an increased emphasis on the *relationships between programs and expenditures*. Let us now take a look at each of these three elements in turn.

Fair and full disclosure
Fair disclosure implies an ethical goal of providing equal treatment for all potential readers of financial statements. Full disclosure means the presentation of all relevant information regarding an organization's financial position and operations. In other words, any person reading a financial statement should have all the facts regarding the organization's financial operations, and the information should be presented in such a way that it will not tend to deceive the reader.

Inherent in the fair and full disclosure concept is the principle of materiality. All facts which could influence the judgment of a reader should be disclosed. This principle has too often been ignored by human services organizations who rely heavily on volunteers and piecemeal funding to support program delivery. The rule of thumb regarding the reporting of donated personal services (voluntary services) is simple: all donated personal services which are considered specialized in nature, and would otherwise have to be purchased to maintain a prescribed level of service, should be reported at their market value. For example, when a doctor donates his time to a community health center for two hours a week to operate a special night clinic, the value of his time should be treated as both income and expense, and so disclosed in the organization's statements. If the time were not donated, the health center would have to pay for the same services. On the other hand, voluntary services such as participation on a board of directors, fund raising, or paraprofessional services need not be reported.

To achieve fair and full disclosure, the standards also call for the *accrual method* of accounting: revenues and expenditures are related to, and identified with, those specific units of time (a month, a year, etc.) when the revenues are earned and the commitments to expend are incurred. In contrast to the accrual method is the *cash method* where funds are accounted for at the time that they are received or paid out. The cash basis often presents a distorted view of an organization's financial picture. For example, a human services organization with substantial receivables could be operationally and financially sound even though its statements report an operating deficit and cash-poor condition. Health organizations which receive large third-party reimbursements from Medicaid and other sources could easily be in this situation.

Summarizing all activity on one statement   The standards provide for three different reporting formats which summarize all the financial activities of the organization—balance sheets; statements of support, revenue, and expenses and changes in fund balances; and statements of functional expenses. Especially important is that the first two of these formats provide for the recording of all unrestricted contributions in one single income statement. Figure 9–1 shows sample sheets for a hypothetical agency.

Instead of the multiple funds of the past, the standards allow for only four major types of funds, each well-defined. These include current funds, unrestricted, and current funds, restricted (the two types of operating revenues); a land, building, and equipment fund; and an endowment fund (donor-endowed only).

Current funds, unrestricted include all income which is not specifically restricted by the donor. This category includes income from fees for services, donations from government that are not designated for specific programs, general contributions, unrestricted bequests, and other undesignated income.

Current funds, restricted account for funds to be used in the operating budget, but expendable only for purposes specified by the donor. This category might include federal and state grants, foundation grants, and income from endowments and other sources where the donor restricted its use to either a programmatic or operating purpose.

Land, building, and equipment funds represent those monies used for the purpose of acquiring or replacing land, buildings, or equipment. Assets, mortgages, and other liabilities are also included.

Endowment funds represent gifts and bequests accepted with a donor stipulation that the principal be placed in the endowment fund. Only income specifically restricted by the donor may be placed in the organization's endowment fund. Board-designated endowments are not allowed; all other contributions must be reported as restricted or unrestricted current funds.

Linking programs to the expenditures   Perhaps the most significant contribution of the standards is to link the programs of the organization to its expenditures. Equally important is that the cost of administering an organization is recognized and accounted for. Traditionally, human services organizations have reported expenditures by object—salaries, rent, supplies, travel, etc. The standards now require a statement of functional expenditures which correlates these expenditures with the costs of program and supporting services, including fund raising. As Figure 9–2 shows, objects of expenditures (salaries, rent, etc.) are directly linked to particular program and management activities.

FAMILY SERVICE AGENCY OF UTOPIA, INC.
Balance Sheets
December 31, 19X2 and 19X1

CURRENT FUNDS — UNRESTRICTED

ASSETS	19X2	19X1
Cash	$ 45,747	$ 52,667
Short-term investments—at cost which is approximately market value	20,000	10,000
Accounts receivable less allowance for uncollectibles of $130 and $186	2,165	3,087
Pledges receivable less allowance for uncollectibles of $249 and $197	4,968	3,724
Supplies for use, at cost or market, whichever is lower	22,875	14,925
Prepaid expenses and deferred charges	3,516	3,769
Board-designated long-term investments (Note 2)	15,000	15,000
	$114,271	$103,172

LIABILITIES AND FUND BALANCES	19X2	19X1
Accounts payable and accrued expenses	$ 24,611	$ 18,702
Support and revenue designated for future periods	5,215	4,190
Total liabilities and deferred revenues	$ 29,826	$ 22,892
Fund balances:		
Designated by the governing board for—		
Long-term investments	15,000	15,000
Purchases of new equipment	8,300	10,000
Special Outreach Project (Note 3)	25,000	—
Undesignated, available for general activities	36,145	55,280
Total fund balances	$ 84,445	$ 80,280
	$114,271	$103,172

RESTRICTED

ASSETS	19X2	19X1
Cash	$ 3,200	$ 2,300

LIABILITIES AND FUND BALANCES	19X2	19X1
Fund balance:		
Professional education	$ 3,200	$ 2,300

LAND, BUILDING AND EQUIPMENT FUND

ASSETS	19X2	19X1
Cash	$ 1,123	$ 700
Short-term investments—at cost which is approximately market value	15,000	—
Pledges receivable less allowance for uncollectibles of $336 and $638	11,203	21,250
Land, building and equipment at cost less accumulated depreciation of $12,565 and $8,365 (Note 4)	94,644	97,144
	$121,970	$119,094

LIABILITIES AND FUND BALANCES	19X2	19X1
8-1/4% mortgage payable, due 19Z5	$ 52,370	$ 54,194
Fund balances—		
Expended	$ 42,274	$ 42,950
Unexpended-restricted	27,326	21,950
Total fund balance	$ 69,600	$ 64,900
	$121,970	$119,094

ENDOWMENT FUND

ASSETS	19X2	19X1
Cash	$ 300	$ 700
Investments (Note 2)	202,000	201,000
	$202,300	$201,700

LIABILITIES AND FUND BALANCES	19X2	19X1
Fund balance	$202,300	$201,700

Two general types of functions are recognized: program services and supporting services. Program services include those activities for which the organization was originally chartered. Some organizations have only one identifiable program; others have several. Generally speaking, each program service should be adequately described to clearly show its purpose and each should be mutually exclusive. A multiservice family assistance organization might provide the following programs, for example: adoption, family counseling, and foster home care. As pointed out in *Accounting and Financial Reporting,* "One of the most difficult and vexing problems confronting not-for-profit human service organizations . . . is that of identifying and defining program categories in a logical and consistent manner and on a mutually exclusive basis." [12] Care should be taken not to confuse activities such as intake and referral in a family counseling center with the broader programs of the organization.

Supporting services are much less difficult to define and are divided into two subcategories—management and general, and fund raising. Often referred to as "administrative overhead," supporting services are those costs which are necessary for the maintenance of the organization. These costs include expenditures for overall direction of the organization, general record keeping, business management, budgeting, general board activities, and related purposes. All organizations, whether commercial, governmental, or not-for-profit, conduct a variety of activities which are not identifiable with any one function, but which are nevertheless indispensable to the conduct of all programmatic functions and to the organization's very existence. In large organizations, this might involve the full-time services of an executive director, financial manager, planner, and several administrative personnel. In a small organization, only a portion of the time of the director might be involved. In all cases, the "management and general" expenses should be recognized as necessary and therefore recorded.

Fund-raising costs encompass all expenditures incurred in soliciting contributions, including the costs of public appeals campaigns (e.g., mailing, media, etc.) and the salaries of personnel connected with such campaigns. In order to discourage abuses, many contributors have insisted that the cost of fund raising for human services organizations be a matter of public record. In some states this is enforced by state law and/or local ordinances. [13]

Implementing the standards

Clearly the standards just outlined represent a major step forward in achieving uniform financial accountability among human services organizations. Since their adoption, they have been quietly gaining acceptance in the 1970s by funding and providing organizations alike. As Manser and Cass observed:

Not only were the standards acceptable to the voluntary health and welfare fields and the accounting industry, they were even endorsed by the United States Civil Service Commission in its administration of the Combined Federal Campaign Plan; they were incorporated into the regulations of several state and local regulatory agencies, and used by the U.S. Department of Health, Education, and Welfare for developing indirect cost rates for voluntary health and welfare agencies receiving grants and contracts. . . . Conformity a decade ago by all organizations might have reduced later demands for excessive regulation arising from public disclosure of a few cases of excessive fund-raising or administrative costs. [14]

Conformity a decade ago might have eliminated also much of the confusion concerning the management and financial control of human services.

For the local governmental official, the principles and reporting techniques incorporated in the standards offer a substantial opportunity to improve human ser-

Figure 9–1   Sample balance sheets for a hypothetical family service agency. See text for further discussion. (Source: *Accounting and Financial Reporting,* Alexandria, Virginia, United Way of America, 1974.)

FAMILY SERVICE AGENCY OF UTOPIA, INC.

Statement of Functional Expenses
Year Ended December 31, 19X2
With Comparative Totals for 19X1

	Program Services				Supporting Services			Total Program and Supporting Services Expenses	
	Counseling	Adoption	Foster-home care	Total	Management and General	Fund-Raising	Total	19X2	19X1
1. Salaries	$ 86,068	$ 33,776	$ 77,306	$192,150	$ 32,517	$ 7,503	$ 40,020	$232,170	$223,086
2. Employee benefits	16,625	6,846	15,453	38,924	6,591	1,520	8,111	47,035	44,360
3. Payroll taxes, etc.	4,283	1,657	3,497	9,437	1,595	368	1,963	11,400	10,768
4. Total salaries and related expenses	$106,976	$ 42,279	$ 91,256	$240,511	$ 40,703	$ 9,391	$ 50,094	$290,605	$278,214
5. Professional fees	29,105	9,905	12,090	51,100	3,500	—	3,500	54,600	50,459
6. Supplies	3,391	1,281	2,864	7,536	758	206	964	8,500	8,006
7. Telephone	3,965	1,498	3,349	8,812	565	233	798	9,610	9,065
8. Postage and shipping	2,701	1,020	2,282	6,003	583	164	747	6,750	7,350
9. Occupancy	9,658	3,649	8,155	21,462	2,540	598	3,138	24,600	23,192
10. Rental and maintenance of equipment	3,937	1,488	3,325	8,750	—	—	—	8,750	9,237
11. Printing and publications	2,563	1,245	1,291	5,099	850	1,251	2,101	7,200	6,903
12. Travel	11,301	2,015	10,504	23,820	180	—	180	24,000	22,640
13. Conferences, conventions, meetings	7,447	755	5,178	13,380	320	—	320	13,700	12,930
14. Specific assistance to individuals	9,371	1,000	18,129	28,500	—	—	—	28,500	21,573
15. Membership dues	300	202	100	602	75	—	75	677	677
16. Awards and grants—to National Headquarters	—	5,000	—	5,000	—	—	—	5,000	5,000
17. Miscellaneous	2,285	863	1,931	5,079	121	—	121	5,200	4,923
18. Total before depreciation	$193,000	$ 72,200	$160,454	$425,654	$ 50,195	$ 11,843	$ 62,038	$487,692	$460,169
19. Depreciation of buildings and equipment	1,630	620	1,410	3,660	420	120	540	4,200	3,400
20. Total expenses	$194,630	$ 72,820	$161,864	$429,314	$ 50,615	$ 11,963	$ 62,578	$491,892	$463,569

vices management systems. To a great extent these reporting methods have been the missing link in efforts to improve the way we allocate funds, make budgetary decisions, and plan and evaluate the delivery of human services programs. The following are examples of how the standards can be used to improve the management of human services.

Evaluation The functional basis of accounting provides certain necessary ingredients to evaluate the general management and efficiency of human services organizations in the manner described in Chapter 10. It allows for easy determination of an organization's administrative costs and facilitates the development of unit service costs. With an increased emphasis on program and performance evaluation, this information is critical.

Allocation methods Many local government organizations have been experimenting with different allocation methods such as purchase of service contracts and deficit financing arrangements. (These two methods are discussed in detail later in this chapter.) They demand complementary and uniform reporting procedures. The concepts outlined in the standards should complement and assist virtually any funding arrangement established by a local government. This would also include methods for funding internal departments and agencies.

Fiscal planning and budget development The functional basis of accounting provides the opportunity and support for sophisticated methods of financial planning, including performance and program budgeting.

Internal management reform Many concepts endorsed by the standards can be used to improve internal organizational management. The standards should facilitate reorganization efforts to better conform with program and organizational objectives; improved staffing arrangements; personal accountability for performance; reallocation of staff resources; a greater understanding by volunteer boards and advisory groups of an organization's management; improved program planning; and internal fiscal planning and control. A few organizations have complained that the standards have been a burden and an unnecessary expense for their organizations. However, most responsible administrators have found the concepts helpful in providing accurate management information for their own use, and for their boards and funders.

Indirect costs The management and general function of the standards is very similar to the definition of indirect cost developed by the U.S. General Services Administration. Organizations which have adopted the accounting procedures outlined in the standards and are recipients of federal funds should be able to verify indirect cost expenditures which are reimbursable as a percentage of their federal grants and contracts. This procedure can be used by both not-for-profit organizations and local government agencies and departments.

Summary

The gist of the preceding discussion is that local government officials involved in funding and providing human services should be familiar with the standards of fiscal accountability and their implementation. These concepts provide a highly pragmatic, commonsense approach to fiscal reporting procedures. Functional reporting, displaying all incomes on a single statement, and fair and full disclosure are

Figure 9–2 Sample statement of functional expenses for hypothetical family service agency. See text for further discussion. (Source: *Accounting and Financial Reporting*, Alexandria, Virginia, United Way of America, 1974.)

as relevant to internal local government departments as they are to voluntary human services organizations. The uniformity and adaptability of these standards should offer some relief to the harried local government decision maker who is facing a complex human services delivery system, with potential providers ranging from public agencies to private organizations.

Allocating local government funds to human services programs

The method of allocating funds to human services providers can be an effective tool to support local governments' program objectives. Most local governments have yet to take innovative steps in the manner by which they fund both internal departments and local, not-for-profit organizations. Funding involves the local government's allocation of its financial resources to providing organizations, and is an important part of the total budgetary process which also includes fiscal planning, decision making, and fiscal reporting.

Neighborhood reps   Using Comprehensive Employment and Training Act (CETA) funds, Flint, Michigan, hired twenty neighborhood service representatives, who are located in elementary schools throughout the city. The representatives are trained to locating resources available from different agencies in the city, and they service and follow up on all citizen complaints from their neighborhoods. The service representatives report to the city manager's office. CETA funds are available for an experimental two-year period.

At the local government level, most human services allocations are distributed as an outright grant with few or no strings attached. This is especially true in the thousands of smaller municipalities across the country that provide financial support for a variety of local human services including visiting nurses, day care, family planning, community action programs, and the like.

Faced with a rising demand by taxpayers for increased accountability, local governments officials need to understand and consider other approaches to allocating funds to human services activities. This is not to suggest that the grant mechanism is totally inappropriate. Like most management methods, however, it should be limited to those situations where it represents the best of several options.

In addition to direct grants, other methods of funding include purchase of service arrangements, deficit financing, and various combinations of these methods. Each will now be discussed in turn. Overall, it is important to note that—properly implemented—a creative approach to allocating funds can help foster increased accountability and can encourage management innovation by human services providers.

Direct grant

The direct grant is a direct local government appropriation for a human services organization or government agency with few, if any, restrictions. For example, a local visiting nurses association may annually request and receive an appropriation from a town at the rate of five cents per resident. The association may be asked to justify the grant in terms of service to the town and to report on its line-item expenditures. The allocation would be made in a lump sum payment to the organization.

Although this type of allocation method is still the most frequently used to support human services programs, it has several obvious drawbacks. First, fiscal controls are extremely inadequate, with a high potential for abuse by the organization. Second, direct grants are commonly associated with inadequate or nonexistent arrangements for evaluating the organization's management of local funds and for determining the efficiency of its programs and internal operations. Finally, grants of this nature tend to be self-perpetuating. If an organization receives $20,000 from a municipality in one year, chances are that at least that amount will be asked for and received the next year. Without controls, it is extremely difficult to determine whether the organization needs the appropriation, whether it has in past years managed responsibly, and for what exact purpose the funds have been spent.

```
                        Office of the City Manager
                               Utopia, USA




        Mr. David W. Williams, President
        Capital City Boys Club
        Utopia, USA

        Dear Mr. Williams:

        The Utopia City Council is pleased to inform you that it has
        approved your request for a $1,000 grant to implement a
        summer counseling program for underprivileged youth.  This
        grant is based on the following conditions:

                a.   The Capital City Boys Club also appropriates
                     $1,000 for this program.

                b.   The funds be used for a ten-week program to
                     provide counseling services to underprivileged
                     youth in your neighborhood.

                c.   The funds be used to hire an experienced school
                     counselor for this ten-week period and pay for
                     administrative expenses.

        Please understand that Utopia cannot make any commitment to
        support this program in future years.  Police and recreation
        department officials are available to assist you in this demon-
        stration program.  If my office can be of assistance, please do
        not hesitate to contact me.

                                          Sincerely yours,




                                          John Smith
                                          City Manager
```

Figure 9–3 Sample letter awarding a direct grant. See text for further discussion.

The direct grant mechanism does, however, possess a few advantages. It is the simplest method of handling requests—especially small ones—and it does not require extensive paperwork. Perhaps most important is that it tends to encourage innovation by the providing organization. Free of detailed restriction on the use of funds and onerous reporting requirements, the human services organization can concentrate on program delivery and has the flexibility to make improvements. Direct grants seem to have been most successful, in fact, when used to fund small requests or new and innovative projects. Therefore, local governments would generally be well-advised to limit use of the direct grant mechanism to the following situations: (1) when the amount to be allocated is small—for example, when the local veterans' organization requests $500 to support a Veteran's Day parade; and (2) when the money is to be used for new, innovative, or demonstration programs. The sample letter shown in Figure 9–3 awards a grant which meets both of these criteria. It is also an example of the kinds of conditions which might be applied to a grant of this nature.

Purchase of service contract

The purchase of service arrangement as a means of financing human services programs has grown in popularity with local, state, and federal agencies. While these arrangements vary from one-page memorandums of understanding to lengthy formal contracts, all have several common characteristics. Specific services are usually purchased on a per-unit basis; a maximum level of funding is made available for a specific time period; certain standards of service are delineated; and payment is provided on a reimbursable basis.

The benefits of this funding method are numerous. It provides the local government with a relatively easy method for allocating its funds with excellent fiscal and program controls. Since the local government actually buys a specific service, local officials can be assured that tax revenues are dispersed in an accountable manner. The purchase of service contracts can be implemented quickly to meet community priorities. In other words, almost as soon as a community becomes aware of specific social problems, programs can be planned and purchase of service contracts arranged. Likewise, existing contracts which do not prove to be effective can be terminated relatively easily. This suggests that the local government can play a much more significant role in developing and planning for human services programs under purchase of service arrangements.

Finally, it may be noted that it is easier to evaluate programs funded by purchase of service contracts. If the local government officials are precise at the outset about what they are buying and why, they should find it relatively simple to judge the effectiveness (as compared to original goals) of services they are purchasing.

There are some serious disadvantages to purchase of service arrangements which can cause potentially critical fiscal problems for human services organizations. Too often, payment on a reimbursable basis results in serious cash-flow difficulties. Many not-for-profit organizations simply do not have sufficient cash reserves to permit this arrangement. These difficulties can usually be overcome, however, through working capital advances and controlled prepayment programs. A more serious problem occurs when purchase of service agreements fail to account for fluctuations in demand for services. A municipality might engage in a contract with a local counseling agency to provide certain services. The agency would then hire staff to provide those services, only to find, perhaps, that referrals were not forthcoming as anticipated. The contractual arrangement thus may place the providing organization in a position in which it might be required to take more of a risk than it is able to afford.

In addition, because purchase of service arrangements are associated with a centralized capacity to plan for programs and to set priorities and because they are highly structured, they tend to deemphasize the volunteer elements in our human services delivery systems. The traditional control of volunteer boards and local citizens over human services organizations tends to be ignored when purchase of service contracts are executed.

In executing purchase of service funding arrangements, local officials should therefore be aware that they can cause serious financial difficulty to the providing organizations and can tend to disrupt the orientation of traditional community volunteer organizations. See Figure 9–4 for an example of a formal—but still simple and straightforward—purchase of service contract.

Deficit financing

An allocation method which is much more attractive to human services providers, but still provides adequate controls, is known as deficit financing. Under this arrangement, the local government agrees to fund a local organization based on the projected difference between the cost for maintaining a certain level of service and projected income. If the organization's deficit does not materialize, then no funds need to be expended. Usually some type of maximum limit is set.

Deficit financing is the allocation method traditionally used by United Way agencies. It is especially advantageous in a decentralized setting where the provider is expected to plan, develop, and implement programs. Once the ground rules are established, this funding arrangement does provide good fiscal controls if the funding organization possesses the required accounting expertise. Monthly and quarterly statements should be closely reviewed to determine if the projected deficit is likely to materialize. Occasionally, some funds may be returned to the funder.

Because this funding method complements decentralized decision making, it encourages provider innovation. Typically under this method, organizations rather than programs are funded. As with the other methods discussed, the potential disadvantages are several. First, it is often difficult to link local government planning and management priorities to the programs provided by the organization. Second, funding tends all too often to be self-perpetuating.

A common example of this method occurs in the public funding of municipal hospitals. Usually the hospital bases its annual request on the expected deficit of specific operations, e.g., emergency room or ambulance services. Negotiations usually focus on line-item expenditures and projected revenues.

Combinations

The three primary funding methods—direct grants; purchase of service contracts; and deficit financing—are not mutually exclusive. Frequently some combination of the three methods is used to meet the accountability demands and information

---

PURCHASE OF SERVICE CONTRACT
Between
THE CITY OF UTOPIA
and
FAMILY COUNSELING CENTER, INC.

Utopia hereby agrees to reimburse Family Counseling Center, Inc. up to $15.00 per hour for counseling services and up to $50.00 for psychiatric testing for youths, age 11 to 18, and their families living in city-managed public housing units. Total expenditures may not exceed $10,000 for the calendar year 1977, and all clients must be referred by the Housing Authority Director of Social Services.

The Family Counseling Center, Inc. agrees to accept all Housing Authority referrals up to 40 hours of counseling a week. In addition, the Family Counseling Center agrees that all counseling services purchased under this contract will meet standards set by the Family Service Association of America.

_____   _____
City of Utopia   Date

_____   _____
Family Counseling Center, Inc.   Date

Figure 9–4 Sample purchase of service contract. See text for further discussion.

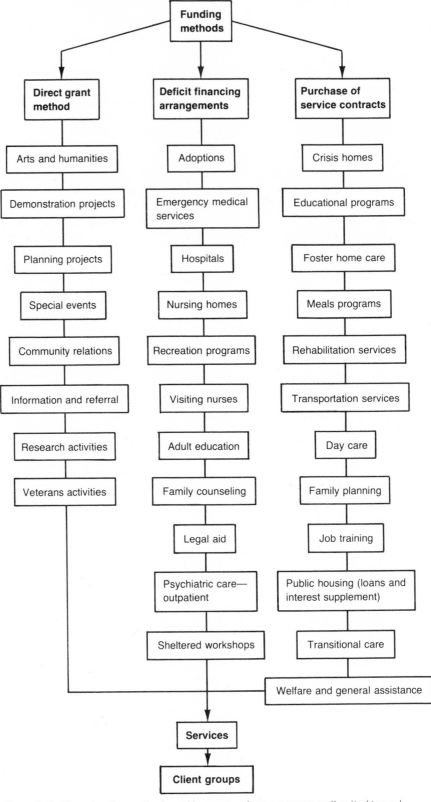

Figure 9–5   Three funding methods and human services programs well-suited to each method.

needs of specific local administrators. Outside factors are often important influences in such decisions. The most common of these is the matching funding arrangement used when federal grants are involved. In this situation, the local government is asked to provide local funds needed to generate additional state and federal funds. In fact, the system is a combination of a deficit financing arrangement for the local government funder and a purchase of service arrangement for the human services provider.

While this arrangement is a productive use of local government revenue and is extremely easy to administer, it does present three serious drawbacks. First, the federal or state programs may not adequately address the local community's needs. Second, there is often a lack of program continuity with federal funding sources, resulting in radical changes every few years. Finally, since these programs are usually administered as purchase of service arrangements by federal and state agencies, they often impose undue administrative hardships upon providing organizations.

Many local governments have begun experimenting with other combinations of funding arrangements. Recognizing the trade-off between fiscal controls and agency needs, some municipalities have combined direct grants with purchase of service arrangements. Other counties and cities are implementing "request for proposal" (RFP) systems as the means for financing human services programs in their communities. This process is described later in this chapter.

The creative approaches that many local governments have taken toward funding human services programs are a healthy and positive sign. The method of allocation can either help strengthen the management of human services or administratively cripple the ability of human services providers to deliver needed programs. Funding organizations should recognize there is usually some trade-off between accountability and delivery. Therefore, it is important that the local funder attempt to work closely with the providing organization to ensure the best arrangement possible.

Budgeting formats

The development of the annual fiscal plan is the focal point of decision making for local government officials. Decisions are made regarding who gets what; programs are evaluated; hard questions are asked; and policy is eventually established. Rarely are there enough resources to support every deserving program and meet every request for funds. As Aaron Wildavsky has stated, "In its most general definition, budgeting is concerned with the translation of financial resources into human purposes." [15] Unfortunately, this definition is sometimes forgotten due to complexities and problems relating to the fiscal management of human services programs. It is therefore crucially important to emphasize that the budgetary systems for human services, as for all public services, are management information systems for decision makers. A significant role in the final decision will be played by the following: what information that decision maker sees; how the information is displayed; and the credibility of the information source.

An overview

There are four basic budgetary systems used by municipal governments with regard to human services commitments: the nonbudget system; the line-item budget; the functional, or performance, budget; and the program budget. Each system will be described below. Some initial overall comments also appear appropriate.

Generally, the choice of format is determined by the local government officials' information needs and the time, money, and expertise available. Putting it another way, each budget format ranging from the nonbudget to the program budget generates increasingly complex and sophisticated information. Additionally, proper implementation of each requires increasing amounts of time, money, staff resources, expertise, and experience.

Allen Schick has noted that all budgetary systems are comprised of planning, management, and control processes:

> In the context of budgeting, *planning* involves the determination of objectives, the evaluation of alternative courses of action, and the authorization of select programs. . . . *Management* involves the programming of approved goals into specific projects and activities, the design of organizational units to carry out approved programs, and the staffing of these units and the procurement of necessary resources. . . . *Control* refers to the process of binding operating officials to the policies and plans set by their superiors. . . . Very rarely are planning, management, and control given equal attention in the operation of budget systems.[16]

Each structured budgetary format—line-item, functional, and program—emphasizes management information directly related to one of these three administrative processes. The line-item format with its emphasis on comparative information regarding objects of expenditures is most closely tied to the control process. Information on the efficiency of the organization and how well it manages its resources is the focus of the functional, or performance, budget. Finally, planning issues which focus on multiyear objectives are best articulated in the program budget.

In practice, the management information focus is not so neat and simple. Owing to the relatively undeveloped state of human services planning and management, local governments have experienced special difficulties in implementing program and functional budget formats. For example, it is extremely difficult to compare the relative merits and impact of specific human services programs, such as day care and transportation for the elderly.

Each budget format requires different personnel expertise and abilities. The line-item format requires accounting expertise; the functional requires management skills; and the program requires planning abilities. Before advancing from a line-item to a functional budget, local government must have confidence in the ability of the providing organization to control its expenditures. With so many human services provided by nongovernmental organizations, a satisfactory "confidence level" often takes years to develop. Likewise, before adopting a program budget format, the local government must demonstrate an ability to effectively manage its human services programs based on sound planning decisions. Given the complexities of the human services delivery network, this is no easy task.

The selection of an appropriate budget format for use by local government is a difficult, but important, task. Often two or more of the formats may be combined, as is the case when line-item detail is presented in a functional budget. However, the basic criteria of selection should be: (1) the information needs of local decision makers, which can be determined by their ability to make funding decisions based on the information available and by their ability to use the information for planning, control, and evaluation purposes; and (2) the funds, time, and staff expertise which the local government is willing and able to commit to this management function. Given this background, it is now possible to discuss the various budgeting formats.

Nonbudget format

The nonbudget format occurs when the local government has no set procedures for funding human services programs. It is characterized by a lack of reporting requirements and common budget request forms, and by lump sum appropriations to the service agencies. Sometimes this informality is compensated for by close personal relationships between providing organizations and local government decision makers. More often, however, it is explained by the fact that the amounts involved are small or the unit's budgeting is generally unsophisticated.

This situation characterizes the budgeting process in many smaller communities. Organizations such as a visiting nurses' association may approach a town by letter or in person seeking to be included for an amount in the annual budget. Depending on the political climate, they may or may not be successful in their request. In a similar manner, a local government agency—such as a municipally sponsored community action program—may seek an annual appropriation by letter request. While the method is the simplest means for handling small requests, it has several weaknesses. Informal relationships often develop and increase the chance for abuse and mismanagement. It is impossible to relate funding decisions to community goals and priorities, and this can result in a lack of accountability to both funder and taxpayers. Usually no formal budgetary review or evaluation occurs. Direct grants are the only allocation method for which the nonbudget format can conceivably be appropriate.

Line-item budget

The line-item budget is a fiscal plan which details objects of expenditures (salaries, fringe benefits, travel, printing, etc.). This information is usually displayed on a comparative basis—describing actual expenditures for several preceding fiscal years, the current operating budget, estimated expenditures for the current fiscal year, and projected expenditures for the upcoming fiscal year.

As noted earlier, the line-item budget in human services dates back to the early 1900s when it was introduced in the city of New York's Health Department to control graft and other abuses. Fiscal control and accountability are the primary focuses of this format. It does not, however, relate expenditures to the organization's activities, to community goals and objectives, or to relevant planning information. Nor does it provide the funding organization with information concerning organizational and program performance.

The following comments made by Roderick K. Macleod, regarding a mental health organization of which he was a volunteer trustee, point up some of these very limitations:

Customarily, about once a year the financial or accounting staff looked at the institution's expenses for heat, light, telephone, professional dues, and so on, and guessed how much these might increase next year. . . . I wonder how many of the trustees have shared my experience of masking feelings of impotence and ignorance as I solemnly reviewed the lists of figures. . . . As soon as the budget was in balance, I approved it, without any real reason for knowing that the year could or should come out that way.[17]

Successful implementation of the line-item budget depends on applying uniform definitions to object expense categories (the line items). One model classification of line items and their definitions can be found in the manual *Budgeting: A Guide for United Ways and Not-For-Profit Human Service Organizations.*[18] These definitions are widely accepted by both the accounting industry and human services organizations.

Clearly, the line-item budget is an important first step in the development of sound financial management tools. Its value is limited, however, because it draws attention away from programs and management questions to issues regarding incremental increases in line-item expenditures. When used in conjunction with an evaluation process, it is helpful primarily in determining an organization's level of responsibility in preparing and following a fiscal plan.

Since the purchase of service arrangement requires performance information and some ability to determine unit costs of services (as mentioned earlier in this chapter's discussion of funding methods), line-item budgets and accounts do not provide all the information that is required, so supplementary cost accounting is needed.

Functional (performance) budget

During the 1930s and 1940s, the idea of functional, or performance, budgeting became popular. In 1949, in fact, the Hoover Commission recommended that changes be made in the federal budget based upon activities and projects.[19] The function of this format is to pinpoint the cost of activities and to relate funds spent to activities and work units performed.

It was not until 1964 that these functional accounting and budgeting principles were applied to human services management. The publication of *Standards of Accounting and Financial Reporting for Voluntary Health and Welfare Organizations* acted as a catalyst, and the functional principles it sets forth became the basis for the reporting procedures outlined in the more recent standards of fiscal accountability.

In the functional budget, line items are related to the activities of the organization. These activities are separated into program services and supporting services: output, or work unit, indicators are developed for each specific program (e.g., round trips for transportation programs or "child days" for day care) and unit costs are displayed where possible. This budget format closely resembles the statement of functional expenses required by the audit guidelines of the American Institute of Certified Public Accountants and illustrated in Figure 9–2. Before these guidelines were established, many funding organizations found it difficult to implement functional budgeting systems. Accounting and financial reporting, of course, are based on and follow the functional format of the budget.

The benefits to be gained from functional budgeting are numerous. It can be used to develop unit cost measurements and benchmarks to aid funders and managers; it relates expenditures to program activities; it provides the fiscal basis for improved program planning; it facilitates alternative funding arrangements, including purchase of service contracts; and it provides program managers with increased management flexibility. It also offers excellent information on organizational and program efficiency during the evaluation process.

If functional budgeting is to be implemented properly, however, it does require extensive management and financial expertise. The human services provider must be able, for example, to adequately define his or her functional programs and related output measures. Funding organizations must be able to interpret performance indicators and analyze cost information. Additionally, the functional budget format does not necessarily relate functional information to community goals and objectives. No attempt is made to measure the level of need for a particular program or to define the benefits of the program as compared to alternative courses of action.

Program budget

Program budgeting is an attempt to address the failure of the functional budget to relate activities to community need. Its orientation is toward planning. It has been said that "the emphasis of program budgeting is on what is being proposed, why it has been proposed, and the effect of these activities on the general public welfare."[20] In program budgeting, the goal or objective is primary; the organizational structure, secondary. Programs are often administered across departmental lines.

The program budgeting format is a proactive one, as opposed to the line-item and functional budgeting formats which are reactive. In a program budgeting system, the funder independently sets his or her goals and objectives, and then weighs program alternatives to meet these objectives. In the case of human services budgeting, the diverse and decentralized nature of the delivery system poses a special problem to the implementation of this proactive system. In addition, the lack of sound planning and evaluation tools poses a serious difficulty to program budgeting.

Essentially, the program budget is a multiyear fiscal plan that articulates community goals and objectives, and designates programs and funds to meet these objectives. The budget generally includes data on operating expenditures, capital outlays, and projected program outputs. Obviously, this type of format requires sophisticated planning expertise of local government officials, and extensive management expertise on the part of department and agency heads. An additional requisite for all officials is a commitment to coordinate and integrate program delivery. Unfortunately, such levels of planning and management expertise and of commitment have not been the norm in human services operations.

A manual published by the United Way of America describes the basic steps necessary for program budgeting:

1. *Preplanning*—the initial activities needed to get organized, or "gear up," for the formal program-planning process.
2. *Launching the process*—defining (or, if defined, clarifying) the organization's broad goals and missions, and stating tentative objectives.
3. *Data gathering and analysis*—needed for the decision making in the next phase of the process; and includes needs and problem, resource availability, and assumptions and constraints data.
4. *Objective setting*—the design of specific statements about what is to be achieved in a given program area.
5. *Programming the objectives*—the effective use of resources by the manager to accomplish the objectives established in the preceding stage.
6. *Preparing and testing the budget*—the core of budgeting, that is, putting figures to words, filling out forms, schedules, worksheets, etc.
7. *Program/budget modification*—changes made depending on funds available and willingness to fund proposed programs.
8. *Adoption of a balanced budget*—the culmination of the program-planning and budgeting cycle.[21]

This budgeting process illustrates several important elements of the program budget. Particularly noteworthy is the fact that budgetary decisions are based on planning and policy decisions made during the fourth and fifth steps. This format clearly requires considerable planning expertise and policy development capacity.

Mixed bag

Since the 1960s, a number of fiscal and management concepts with possible application to human services management have been developed. Many of these are combinations or adaptations of the concepts previously discussed in this chapter. Five of these concepts, however, merit additional attention. They are: zero-based budgeting; planning-programming-budgeting systems (PPBS); program performance budgeting; performance audits; and requests for proposals (RFPs). Each is now discussed in turn.

Zero-based budgeting

More a technique than a system, zero-based budgeting includes any method that requires decision makers to allocate resources without consideration of past budgeting decisions. Numerous governmental units are, as of early 1977, considering the use of zero-based budgeting; this is due, at least in part, to the Carter administration's plan to institute the technique for the federal budget. Under this technique, each potential recipient of resources, in effect, begins the fiscal year with a clean slate. Past allocations decisions theoretically play no role in the decision-making process. Under some zero-based budgeting systems, spending agencies are required to prepare alternative budgets at, say, 75, 85, 95, and 110 percent of their current year budgets. Several states, including Georgia (where President Carter, as governor, employed it in the early 1970s), New Mexico, and Rhode Island;

a number of cities and counties; and many voluntary human services organizations have experimented with zero-based budgeting techniques.[22]

Planning-programming-budgeting system (PPBS)

During the 1960s significant attention was focused on a public management concept known as the planning-programming-budgeting system (PPBS). PPBS was an economic effort to integrate the three functional areas of management—planning, programming, and budgeting—into one process. The concept was put into practice by numerous public and governmental organizations. One effort, the 5–5–5 Project, involved five states, five counties, and five cities: it produced several reports of interest to local government officials.[23]

PPBS also attracted the attention of those interested in human services funding and management. In 1972, the United Way of America published a manual on implementing PPBS.[24] But, like many other management systems, PPBS made many promises which it could not keep, and only three years after it published its PPBS manual, another United Way handbook stated:

Is PPBS feasible and recommended for human service organizations? No . . . First, PPBS concentrates too much on *ends* without adequate regard to the *means*. Second, its orientation to, and overdependence on, *economic rationality* underestimates the fact that decision making on goals and objectives with regard to what should be funded is essentially a *political process* and is rooted in the consensus politics and not in scientific methods. Third, PPBS relies heavily on its requirement of centralization, coordination and comprehensiveness in the decision-making process of resource allocation—which is antithetical to our democratic traditions and the polyarchical nature of our society.[25]

PPBS, however, is not dead. Many of its principles are found in the program budget format and the standards of fiscal accountability. However, its practical relevance remains limited due to the decentralized nature of the human services delivery system.

Program performance budgeting

A number of communities have attempted to combine functional and program budgeting concepts in an integrated approach sometimes known as program performance budgeting. Usually this is a combination of functional budgeting data and work measurement information with a goals-oriented framework. It differs from the program approach in that planning is decentralized and limited. Multiyear fiscal plans usually are not included in this approach.

The city of Lakewood, Colorado, implemented such a system. The system includes a goal-oriented program structure, needs statements, work measurements, and a line-item budget for each of the eighty-seven programs. Under the major service area category of "human resources," for example, senior citizen activities are defined as a program. A general program description and program objectives are then defined. The following measurements are also included in the budget statement: *demand*—members of the population of sixty-five years of age or older; *workload*—persons served by program, and classes and activities offered; *productivity*—cost per person served, and *effectiveness*—percentage of senior citizens served by program. For each measurement, estimates for the year in progress and projections for the following year were given. During the two-year period in question, the budget for senior citizen activities was projected to increase dramatically from $10,840 to $79,347, and the line-item information supported these figures.[26]

As a special bulletin issued by the Municipal Finance Officers Association concluded, "Program performance budgeting is an evolutionary development in governmental budgeting. It synthesizes the most useful elements of existing budgeting systems while avoiding the pitfalls of 'by-the-book' application of theoretical models.'' [27]

Performance audit

In company with the U.S. General Accounting Office and numerous states, some communities and human services organizations have begun to experiment with audit methods beyond the simple disclosure of fiscal information. These range from periodic checks on the volume of program service to detailed follow-up studies with human services program recipients. The performance audit is an attempt to combine the quantitative information of the fiscal audit with program audit data.

A sophisticated form of the performance audit is being attempted, as of the later 1970s, during a five-year period by the Brockton Multi-Service Center of Brockton, Massachusetts, in conjunction with the Human Ecology Institute of Wellesley, Massachusetts. They describe the audit as "a means for assessing system effects; that is, the audit is the means for determining what impact the system is having on those human problems for which the system may be held accountable." [28] The Brockton audit combines extensive needs assessment information (including an in-person survey and socioeconomic data) to determine what effect, if any, the many programs of the human services center are having upon the target population.

The performance audit goes beyond the basic quantitative determination of whether an organization spent public funds appropriately to provide proper services. Here the audit is testing whether the programs and services are having a desirable effect on the community and target population.

Requests for proposals (RFPs)

Requests for proposals, or RFPs, long a popular technique with federal agencies to fund research and development activities, can be used by local governments as a method for funding human services activities. The RFP method of funding is a proactive, as opposed to reactive, funding method. The local government, through its planning and policy process, decides to provide funds for certain programs and activities. After the initial funding is approved, proposals are requested from appropriate organizations to initiate the activity. Contracts are awarded on the basis of cost and performance bids. The RFP method requires both a substantial planning capacity to define program needs and a willingness by local officials to initiate a bidding process for contracts to deliver human services. Both these criteria are unusual in local government.

Recently the city of Malden, Massachusetts, implemented an RFP process using community development funds. However, prior to implementing the process, local officials and the Boston College School of Social Work engaged in a lengthy and comprehensive planning effort to identify community human services needs and designed RFPs to meet these needs. [29]

Conclusion: a question of reform

The standards of fiscal accountability, alternate funding methodologies, and choice of budgetary systems offer the local government manager creative opportunities to improve human services fiscal management. These management techniques can help human services providers increase accountability to the taxpayer and assist local government managers in initiating needed reform. Reform implies change, and almost any local government anticipating reform of their fiscal management systems for human services can expect substantial resistance to such change.

Sources of resistance to fiscal management reform should therefore be anticipated, identified, and properly addressed. Generally, biases against change will be either political or technical in nature. Since the human services delivery system is usually decentralized, autonomous in purpose, and generates high emotion around specific service programs and organizations, local government officials can expect political resistance. Organizations who have been successful in securing local government funds may see fiscal reform as a threat to their continued funding. Local decision makers who have become accustomed to a specific budgeting format and reporting system may be wary of any proposed changes. It is quite reasonable to expect that a variety of interested individuals and organizations will be generally suspicious of attempted fiscal reform.

Sources of technical resistance are usually easier to identify and alleviate. Generally, local government managers should assume that human services providers have a limited technical capacity to easily accept major fiscal changes. Management and fiscal support staff will have to understand new budgeting and reporting systems, and know how to integrate them into the management of the organization. Local government officials and voluntary boards of directors must learn how to use information produced by new budgetary and accounting systems, and local government human services professionals will have to become adept at working with providing organizations. A good rule of thumb is that it takes two to three years to initiate and implement any major budgetary reform. It is not until the second and third years that the providing and funding organizations are able to operate under the new budgetary system with adequate fiscal reports to substantiate budget planning data.

Many local governments have recognized the need to institute fiscal and management reform in funding human services. A few simple rules should help local officials overcome resistance to change. These are: (1) inform all parties involved—including local government decision makers, human services providers, and necessary staff—of the need for reform and expected benefits; (2) solicit input, before the fact, from those who will be affected; (3) ensure that technical expertise is available; and (4) do not expect immediate results.

1   Jesse Burkhead, "The Budget and Democratic Government," in *Public Administration and Democracy*, ed. Roscoe C. Martin (Syracuse, N.Y.: Syracuse University Press, 1965), p. 99.

2   William Aramony, in United Way of America, *Accounting and Financial Reporting* (Alexandria, Va.: United Way of America, 1974), p. i.

3   Calvin A. Canney, "Perspectives on Accountability," *Opportunities—Sharing Information on Human Services in New England*, February 1976, p. 3.

4   Robert Fulton, "Accountability: What, How and To Whom?," *Opportunities—Sharing Information on Human Services in New England*, February 1976, p. 1.

5   Urban Research Committee, *Report on Human Services to the Hartford City Council* (Hartford, Conn.: Urban Research Committee, 1976), p. i.

6   *Audits of Voluntary Health and Welfare Organizations* (New York: American Institute of Certified Public Accountants, 1974).

7   Marvin J. Gross, "Nonprofit Accounting: A Revolution in Process," *Price Waterhouse Review* (Fall 1974): 1.

8   Ibid., p. 1.

9   *Standards of Accounting and Financial Reporting for Voluntary Health and Welfare Organizations* (New York: National Health Council, National Assembly of National Voluntary Health and Social Welfare Organizations, and United Way of America, 1964).

10 United Way of America, *Accounting and Financial Reporting* (Alexandria, Va.: United Way of America, 1974).

11 Gross, "Nonprofit Accounting," p. 3.

12 United Way of America, *Accounting and Financial Reporting*, p. 18.

13 As of the later 1970s, New York and Illinois require full disclosure of fund-raising costs for nonprofit organizations operating in their states. Several cities including Fort Worth, Texas, and Memphis, Tennessee, have adopted ordinances prohibiting organizations with high fund-raising costs from soliciting contributions within their municipalities.

14 Gordon Manser and Rosemary Higgins Cass, *Voluntarism at the Crossroads* (New York: Family Service Association of America, 1976), p. 96.

15 Aaron Wildavsky, *The Politics of the Budgetary Process* (Boston: Little, Brown & Co., 1964), p. 1.

16 Allen Schick, "The Road to PPB: The Stages of Budget Reform," *Public Administration Review* 26 (December 1966): 244.

17 Roderick K. Macleod, "Program Budgeting Works in Non-Profit Institutions," *Harvard Business Review* 49 (September–October 1971): 49.

18 United Way of America, *Budgeting: A Guide for United Ways and Not-for-Profit Human Service Organizations* (Alexandria, Va.: United Way of America, 1975).

19 See U.S., Commission on Organization of the Executive Branch of the Government (Hoover Commission), *Budget and Accounting* (Washington, D.C.: Government Printing Office, 1949).

20 League of California Cities, *A Guide to Program Budgeting* (Sacramento: League of California Cities, 1974), p. 4.

21 United Way of America, *Budgeting* (Alexandria, Va.: United Way of America, 1975), pp. 10–14.

22 See John LaFaver, ''Zero-Base Budgeting in New Mexico,'' *State Government* 47 (Spring 1974).

23 See Selma J. Mushkin, *Planning–Programming–Budgeting for City, State, County Objectives: Notes 1–12* (Washington, D.C.: George Washington University, 1967–71).

24 See United Way of America, *A PPBS Approach to Budgeting Human Service Programs for United Ways* (Alexandria, Va.: United Way of America, 1972).

25 United Way of America, *Budgeting*, p. 8.

26 *Lakewood, Colorado Budget Plan for 1976 FY* (Lakewood, Colo.: City of Lakewood, 1975), pp. 130–31.

27 Bill Henderson and Randy Young, *Program Performance Budgeting: An Effective Public Management System for Evaluating Municipal Services,* Special Bulletin no. 1976A (Chicago: Municipal Finance Officers Association, 1976), p. 10.

28 Michael Baker and Amy Ramm, *The Brockton Multi-Service Center Community Audit for 1975* (Brockton, Mass.: Brockton Area Human Resources Group, Inc., 1975), p. 2.

29 See Bradley Googins and Victor Capoccia, *Phase I Report to the City Council, Malden, Massachusetts* (Boston: Graduate School of Social Work, Boston College, 1975).

Program evaluation and the management of organizations

Evaluation, whether of self or of a social organization, is a delicate process. It touches on such emotion-fraught issues as worth, goals, performance, self-image, power, advancement, and responsibility. The local government decision maker approaching the topic may therefore do so gingerly, at least intuitively appreciative of the pitfalls involved and perhaps fully aware of the contemporary ramifications for the urban manager of the biblical injunction to "judge not, least ye shall be judged." Evaluation, however, is a fact of life. It is a growing discipline and it increasingly is a "given" in the managerial environment. The human services field is no exception. Many local government managers have grappled with some of the pertinent questions about evaluation listed by Wildavsky:

Why don't organizations evaluate their own activities? Why do they not appear to manifest rudimentary self-awareness? How long can people work in organizations without discovering their objectives or determining the extent to which they have been carried out? . . .

Who will evaluate and who will administer? How will power be divided among these functionaries? Which ones will bear the costs of change? Can evaluators create sufficient stability to carry on their own work in the midst of a turbulent environment? Can authority be allocated to evaluators and blame apportioned among administrators? How to convince administrators to collect information that might help others but can only harm them? How can support be obtained on behalf of recommendations that anger sponsors? . . . Can knowledge and power be joined? [1]

The purpose of this chapter is therefore to provide a comprehensive overview of the program evaluation field. The intent is to assist local government officials and administrators in making practical decisions regarding the implementation and utilization of evaluation systems. The method adopted is to begin by outlining something of the development, current meaning, and potential human services applications of evaluation. This initial step is necessary because of the proliferation of literature regarding evaluation in recent years, and because of the variety of possible interpretations of the term. Secondly, the chapter attempts to ground this theoretical material in the real world of local government administration by considering some of the problems associated with the implementation of evaluation systems and the most efficient use of evaluation-generated information by managers. It is hoped that this dual approach will enrich and enlarge the perceptions of the working manager, on the one hand, by indicating something of the theoretical bases of evaluation, and, on the other hand, will emphasize the practical implications for local government human services management of those theoretical principles.

Because of the particular professional experience of the authors, many of the examples cited are taken from the field of health programs, including mental health programs. The principles discussed, however, have a wider application to the entire spectrum of human services provided by local governments and private agencies, although the applications will, of course, differ in specific areas of specialization, as indeed they will from community to community.

The chapter is divided into five parts. The first section briefly traces the historical development of evaluation from its roots in both social and management sciences, and outlines its status as of the later 1970s. The second section assesses evaluation as a general concept, with particular reference to the purposes of evaluation and the needs of the potential recipients of evaluation research. The third section describes the kinds of evaluation relevant to the management of human services programs, and reviews associated technical procedures. That is, it describes the concepts of effort evaluation, outcome evaluation, efficiency evaluation, and impact evaluation, and also discusses procedural constraints and research design as well as providing a checklist of the stages of evaluation. The fourth section shows how evaluation systems can be implemented, with emphasis on the political and administrative challenges involved. The fifth section takes an equally realistic look at the obstacles to effective use of evaluation information, and explores some of the mechanisms whereby managers can mitigate the situation. There is a brief conclusion.

Development and current status of evaluation

Notwithstanding its relatively recent emergence in the human services, evaluation has quite well-established roots and is not a recent innovation. As Osgood, Succi, and Tannenbaum have noted, judgment of worth and quality is a fundamental human activity, providing a foundation for the formal study of ethics and aesthetics, and for much of daily life as well.[2] Indeed, the very process of learning involves alteration of patterns of behavior according to what could be called "evaluation" feedback. As the term is employed in the human services, however, evaluation implies more than judgment of worth; it represents the founding of such judgments on information gathered in a systematic and scientific fashion. This more formal use of evaluation, sometimes called "evaluative research," has its genesis in the parallel developments of the modern social sciences and modern management theory.[3]

Historical development

The social sciences   Among the earliest attempts in the United States to link social sciences with the evaluation of service programs are Ward's recommendation that sociology use scientific principles in the planning and implementation of social legislation, and Chapin's assertion that human knowledge has reached a point permitting actual experimentation regarding solutions to social problems.[4] In Europe, of course, social legislation and the ongoing debate over measuring the effectiveness of social programs can be traced back to Victorian England, the Germany of Bismarck, and the massive Soviet public sector plans. Excepting some early work in education, however, the potential in this beginning was only actualized in this country years later during the New Deal. Under the stimulus of the Roosevelt administration, Chapin investigated the efficacy of public housing projects and work relief programs, Tyler initiated evaluations of progressive education programs, Lewin studied the impact of strategies to alter attitudes toward minorities, and Powers and Witmer assessed the quality of juvenile delinquency prevention programs.[5] By mid-century, academe was extensively involved in evaluation research, providing a laboratory to test principles and a training ground to develop a vast reservoir of future program evaluators.

The management sciences   Concurrent with the development of evaluation in the social and behavioral disciplines was the progressive utilization of scientific procedures in the management of business enterprises. Taylor's early work, *Scientific Management*,[6] was a watershed in this regard, and although his recommendations seem crude by contemporary standards, they represent the beginnings of a movement to rationalize work through an emphasis on feedback and accountability. Tempering Taylor's focus on raw efficiency with a concern for job satisfaction, Mayo assisted the growth of evaluation as a management function through his experiments into the relationship between morale and productivity.[7] In the process, Mayo provided the basis for a new school of management science, based on the study of human relations. Evaluation based on assessment of goal attainment became a prominent management function with the promulgation of management by objectives, one of the first management-oriented evaluation techniques to make a serious inroad in the human services.[8] The implementation of formal large-scale evaluation systems in the public sector, however, is most often associated with McNamara's term as Secretary of Defense during the Kennedy and Johnson administrations. First with the program evaluation and review technique (PERT), subsequently with the planning–programming–budgeting system (PPBS), the Department of Defense implemented procedures that forged formal links among planning, management, and evaluation.[9] Variants of these procedures are being tested and modified in human services settings today, along with such innovations as zero-based budgeting and other fiscal techniques with a strong evaluative component.

Despite the depth and diversity of this background, as recently as the late 1950s, evaluation was still largely the province of academic researchers and management specialists, and was not yet a substantive element of the human services vocabulary. Program evaluation was not listed independently in the literature indexes, was infrequently the subject of formal publication, was not typically discussed in academic courses and training programs, and was rarely a significant agenda item at conferences and workshops. More importantly, formal evaluation was rarely a requirement for funding, and the role of evaluators was not accorded independent recognition by the human services at large.

Current status

As of the later 1970s, however, there are many signs that evaluation is being accepted as an important aspect of the human services enterprise. Books, journals, and magazines are being published: the National Institute of Mental Health (NIMH), for example, sponsors a magazine entitled *Evaluation* that has an estimated readership of over 40,000. A multiplicity of conferences and workshops are being held, and academic courses and professional training programs are being developed: some universities are initiating programs that lead to a bachelor's degree in "program evaluation." Formal institutes of program evaluation have come into existence: one such institute, the Program Evaluation Resource Center, operates in Minneapolis, Minnesota; another, the Databank of Program Evaluation, operates in Los Angeles, California. Professional organizations for evaluators are being organized: an "evaluation network" has been organized by Phi Delta Kappa, and an "evaluation research society," encompassing all of the disciplines related to evaluation, has been formed at Harvard. Perhaps most important, evaluation is now required by many funding agencies, and is becoming a routine function at all levels of government: NIMH has developed guidelines that call for 2 percent of the funds allocated to community mental health centers to be devoted to program evaluation, and Chadwin has reported at length about the activities of newly created state evaluation units.[10] These developments have clear implications for the urban manager.

The emergence of evaluation in the human services is the product of a confluence of various forces—a basic need for information; a hard-won sociopolitical realism; an increased social activism; and a rapid growth in the social and behavioral sciences.

Need for information   A basic need for information has been paramount. The size of government has steadily increased over recent years, and all levels of authority are assuming broad new powers. With these powers comes the corresponding responsibility to determine the effectiveness of newly undertaken programs. Information is needed for planning and policy making. Information is needed for service programs to rationalize allocation of resources. Information is needed by service providers to monitor treatment progress and to provide corrective feedback.

Sociopolitical realism Facilitating the emergence of evaluation has been a hard-won sociopolitical realism. An aftermath of the massive social programs of the New Deal and Great Society has been an apparent decline in the belief that government-sponsored social reforms can easily bring about positive change. The visible failure of such endeavors as Head Start, and the generally marginal performance of other human services projects, has nurtured a growing conviction that even the most attractive reforms have a responsibility to demonstrate achievement of a reasonable standard of success.[11] This conviction is reinforced by perception of what Lynn and Salasin call the "human services shortfall": the gap extant between the nation's social needs and the resources necessary to meet them.[12] There seems to be a growing awareness that limited resources, multiple and intransigent problems, and technologies of limited efficacy require that social priorities be established based on systematic data gathering.

Increased social activism Also fostering the evolution of evaluation has been an increase in social activism. A rise in consumerism, together with a decline in the implicit respect accorded to professionals, means that service recipients no longer passively accept whatever is offered to them. Demands for inside information are being made, and evaluation is being used as a means to open power structures to input from outsiders. Ralph Nader's study group, for example, has already turned a somewhat critical eye toward the "mental health establishment" for failing to elicit or respond adequately to consumer and community opinions.[13]

Growth of social and behavioral sciences Another influence in the development of evaluation has been the rapid growth of the social and behavioral sciences. In recent years, social researchers have been able to supplement the methods offered by the physical sciences with procedures and devices uniquely suited to the study of social processes. Webb and his colleagues, for example, have shown how the validity of social measurement can be increased through the use of unobtrusive measures, and Stanley and Campbell have developed a catalogue of practical research designs for use in the chaotic world of nonlaboratory research.[14] These and other breakthroughs have greatly increased the flexibility and applicability of the tools available to evaluators, with the result that evaluation findings have greater meaning for decision makers. A related factor in the emergence of evaluation has been the accessibility of efficient and inexpensive automated data processing equipment. Even relatively modest evaluation systems can generate an impressive volume of data, and the availability of facilities to process and store this information can greatly ease the inconvenience of evaluation and increase its utility.

In a nutshell, therefore, evaluation is a fast-growing field that is here to stay in local government. But what, specifically, does it mean? And whom can it serve? These questions will now be addressed.

The concept of evaluation

Review of definitions

Since it is a new and developing field, evaluation does not enjoy a uniform technical vocabulary. Indeed, many jargon-weary managers will have noted that an unfortunate characteristic that evaluators seem to share with other social scientists is a disinclination to use each other's definitions. The purpose of this section is to review a sample of definitions from the field and try to derive from these a composite picture of the essentials of the evaluation process that will be of use to managers.

[Evaluation is] . . . the determination (whether based on opinions, records, subjective or objective data) of the results (whether desirable or undesirable; transient or permanent; immediate or delayed) attained by some activity (whether a program, a part of a program, a drug or a therapy, an ongoing or one-shot approach) designed to accomplish some valued goal or objective (whether ultimate, intermediate, or immediate; effort or performance; long- or short-range).[15]

. . . Evaluation establishes clear and specific criteria for success. It collects evidence systematically from a representative sample of the units of concern. It usually translates the evidence into quantitative terms . . . and compares it with the criteria that were set. It then draws conclusions about the effectiveness, the merit, the success of the phenomenon under study.[16]

Evaluation is the process of ascertaining the decision areas of concern, selecting appropriate information, collecting and analyzing information in order to report summary data useful to decision makers in selecting among alternatives.[17]

Evaluation is essentially an effort to determine what changes occurred as the result of a planned program by comparing actual changes (results) with desired changes (stated goals) and identifying the degree to which the activity (program) is responsible for the changes.[18]

Evaluation is the measurement of the desirability and undesirability of an action that has been undertaken in order to forward some good that we value.[19]

[Evaluation is] . . . the process of determining the results of programs and analyzing the extent to which they have accomplished predetermined goals and objectives.[20]

Essentials of definitions

Although there is much variation in the definitions just cited, taken as a whole they describe an approach to evaluation that incorporates three components: (1) formation of criteria, (2) assessment of attainment of the criteria, and (3) utilization of results.

Formation of criteria   The initial step in evaluation is formation or designation of the criteria that will be used to assess the success of the entity under evaluation. In outcome evaluation (described in detail later in this discussion), such criteria are usually goals, derived either from a needs assessment of the type discussed in Chapter 5 or from a statement of the values that a program is intended to serve. Perhaps because the social sciences have struggled for so long to exclude value judgments, there are few systematic ways to incorporate values into evaluation measurement. Some efforts regarding the operationalization of values have been made in economics, and Guttentag has proposed a model that includes quantification of decision makers' values as a link between planning and evaluation.[21] Generally, however, values are simply declared. In the public sector, they emerge as part of the political process.

Assessment of attainment   The second step in evaluation is the use of systematic, disciplined inquiry to determine how well the criteria have been met. Such inquiry may entail experimental, quasi-experimental, field study, case study, or *ex post facto* ("after the fact") designs, and may involve qualitative as well as quantitative measurement schemes. Qualitative judgments become part of the managerial and political process. For example, if a human services program runs into problems, the department head concerned may be fired by a city manager. If the problems are severe, the city manager too may be out of a job, and the council members that appointed the manager may find themselves voted out of office by disgruntled electors. Be that as it may, Glaser and Backer have advocated a "clinical approach" to evaluation assessment, and Parlett and Hamilton have proposed that anthropological and ethnological procedures be used to supplement more objective methods.[22] Some attempt should be made to examine unintended as well as intended consequences of a program. As the astute local government manager will recognize, the political and administrative process demands such realistic assessments, the more so in times of fiscal crises.

Utilization of results   Actual use of feedback in decision making is not logically intrinsic to the process of evaluation, but substantial experience has confirmed the intuitive assessment of many managers that unless a direct attempt is made to link evaluation data to the decision-making process, the impact of findings will be minimal and delayed.[23] At the present time, extensive research is underway to determine how research and evaluation data are diffused. It is hoped that in the near future practical dissemination strategies will be developed to help bridge the gap between the "two solitudes" of research and practice.[24] The tendency of some cost-conscious budget makers to "ax" research funds at the first sign of fiscal difficulties in local government is a further imperative urging better cross-fertilization between research and ongoing budget administration.

Purposes of evaluation

What are the purposes of evaluation? And what is the difference between "summative" and "formative" evaluation? According to Scriven, evaluation may be perceived from two perspectives. The *method* of evaluation is essentially the same in all settings, consisting "simply in the gathering and combining of performance data with a weighted set of goal scales to yield either comparative or numerical ratings." The *role* of evaluation, however, varies according to the purpose to which the information will be put. From the perspective of role, Scriven distinguishes two paramount forms of evaluation: summative and formative.[25]

Summative evaluation   In summative evaluation, assessment of effectiveness occurs *once,* after the program under scrutiny has been concluded. Summative evaluations are usually intended to form the basis for a definitive judgment as to the ultimate worth of a program, typically so that it can be decided whether it should be implemented in other settings. Such decisions are easiest to make when the confounding influence of feedback to the program has been minimized. In regard to summative evaluations, Rossi argues that two considerations are important: the "impact" of the program, and the "coverage" of the impact. Impact is defined as the program's "ability to produce changes in each situation to which it is applied," and coverage is "its ability to be applied in a large number of cases." Rossi warns that a narrow focus on impact may lead to discontinuation of programs that couple modest impact with broad coverage, thus producing a significant cumulative effect.[26]

Formative evaluation   In formative evaluation, assessment occurs *periodically,* and feedback is used to improve performance. Such information can be used both at the program level for organizational development, and as "knowledge of results" data for service providers. Walker and Baxter have shown, for example, that providing staff with feedback in mental health programs is associated with subsequent increases in attainment of client goals.[27] Turner has capitalized on the feedback effect to develop a formative evaluation system wherein staff not only receive information on performance, but are sanctioned according to the degree to which results are positive or negative.[28] Such a system seems to have led to a striking level of efficiency and effectiveness, but there are some questions as to its long-term impact on staff morale.

Audiences of evaluation

Evaluations can serve the information needs of a variety of "audiences" in the human services: service providers, administrators, policy makers, and community and client representatives. How do their needs differ? What types of information produce enthusiasm, and what types generate nothing but boredom, in each audience?

Service providers   Clinical feedback on the quality and quantity of services can provide practitioners with a useful tool for personal and professional growth. As Stelmachers has observed, most clinicians want to learn about the outcomes of their clients when treatment is concluded, but lack the material and technological resources to do so.[29] A formal evaluation system can provide clinical staff with this information, giving them an opportunity to identify weak aspects of their practice, to build on strengths, and to experiment with new procedures. Also, of course, immediate feedback can be used to monitor the progress of a client still in treatment.

Administrators   For managers of human services programs, and indeed local government managers generally, evaluation can serve as a means for efficient allocation of resources, and as a stimulus for constructive organizational change. For example, if a manager of a mental health program receives reliable evaluation information that group counseling and individual psychotherapy are equally effective in reducing client distress, he or she can increase the number of clients served by placing greater emphasis on group therapy while freeing resources for other program activities. Competent evaluation can facilitate organizational change not only by identifying areas of weakness, but by providing empirical rather than personal bases for debating change. Evaluation also can be useful, of course, to managers as a means to call the attention of higher authorities to a successful project.

Policy makers   For policy makers and planners, evaluation can serve to ground the formulation of priorities and objectives in empirical research. At least since the 1960s, Congress has been moving toward a system for development of social policy based on politically acceptable national goals and priorities.[30] Meaningful accomplishment of this task will require that the patchwork of human services programs currently in existence (and frequently noted as such throughout this book) be transformed into a coherent network of compatible activities. Evaluation will be a central aspect of this process, more in assessing the efficacy of broadly aimed social action programs than of specific agencies. The comprehensive evaluation of the negative income tax experiment in New Jersey is an example of how the focus of evaluation can be expanded from isolated service facilities to large-scale policy endeavors.[31] The new national administration that came to power in 1977 confidently can be predicted to enhance the status of evaluation in the public sector generally.

Consumers and community   For the recipients and ultimate funders of a social program, evaluation is a means to ensure that their commitment is utilized appropriately. Community representatives and consumer advocates compose an increasing portion of the governing boards of human services organizations, and recommended National Institute of Mental Health (NIMH) guidelines—to say nothing of the "sunshine laws" in various states—call for public disclosure of evaluation findings. With formal positions of authority and accurate information on efficacy and efficiency, it seems likely that nonprofessionals concerned with the human services will be able to take a more active hand in their development. The implications for the local government general manager are clear.

Summary

Thus far, our discussion has characterized the growth of evaluation and taken an initial look at the key elements in its definition: the formation of criteria; the assessment of attainment; and the utilization of results. The distinction has also been made between summative evaluation—where assessment of effectiveness occurs only once, after the program under examination has ended—and formative evaluation—where assessment is a periodic, ongoing process, and feedback is used to improve performance. A brief look has also been taken at the service providers, administrators, policy makers, and community and client representatives whose information needs provide the audience for evaluation. The needs of this audience will be considered later in this chapter in more detail, when the implementation and utilization aspects of evaluation are assessed. But before managers can make decisions as to the implementation of evaluation procedures, they need to know something of the weaponry in the arsenal of evaluation, that is, of the kinds of evaluation, of evaluation procedures, and of evaluation research design. These topics are now discussed.

Mechanics of evaluation

What kinds of evaluation are available? What are the meanings of such terms as "effort evaluation," "outcome evaluation," "efficiency evaluation," and "impact evaluation"? What are the essential procedural constraints shaping an evaluation project? What alternatives do the experimental or the observational approaches, among others, offer to the manager contemplating the design of an evaluation? And can the evaluation process be reduced to a number of relatively clearcut components or stages? The following discussion focuses on answers to these questions.

Kinds of evaluation

As managers who have browsed through the literature will be aware, evaluation encompasses a great variety of strategies and methods. Suchman distinguishes four major types of evaluation: effort, outcome, efficiency, and impact.[32] Each is capable of subdivision (see Figure 10–1), and will now be discussed in turn.

Effort evaluation Evaluation of effort involves *assessment of the quality and quantity of activities devoted to attaining program goals.* Effort evaluations provide a basic description of a program at work, including, for example, service utilization rates, demographic characteristics of clients, and staffing patterns. Such information can be used for reviewing program priorities and for making budget and staff allocations.

Program monitoring One approach to effort evaluation is program monitoring, that is, the continuous assessment of program functioning to detect deviations from goals, plans, and procedures. In complex organizations, creation and maintenance of the necessary data base is accomplished through a computerized management information system (MIS), which is "a network of component data parts designed to automatically take certain management actions and to provide a flow of key information to decision makers for other managerial actions." [33] The information contained in an MIS system is usually derived from routinely collected forms and records.

A showcase human services management information system has been implemented at the Hennepin County Mental Health Service in Minneapolis, Minnesota.[34] The system is composed of a network of automated subsystems designed to perform certain management tasks. The largest subsystem is the "active caseload tracking system": the system uses "transaction records" for each client that are filled out at each scheduled treatment session, and thus allows staff to monitor the progress of a client through the mental health service. (See Figure 10–2 which shows a sample of the direct clinical transaction record.) The system employs a standardized terminology developed by the Southern Regional Educational Board to answer the questions of *who* did *what* for *whom, where, when,* and *to what extent.*[35] Together with billing information, the system generates monthly activities reports for each service component. Special reports may be requested at any time by unit directors.

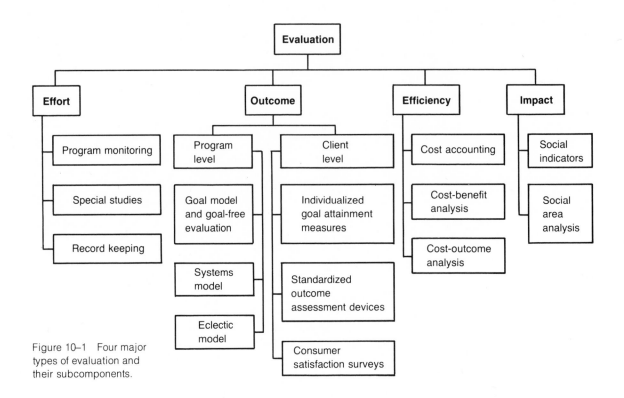

Figure 10–1   Four major types of evaluation and their subcomponents.

Special studies   Even when a program does not have a formal MIS capacity, it is possible to conduct an effort-oriented evaluation through special studies. Tripoldi, Fellin, and Epstein have identified three kinds of special studies: the "accountability audit," the "administrative audit," and the "time-and-motion study."

In the accountability audit, program records are reviewed for consistency and accuracy in relation to allocation of resources and appropriate processing of clients. Accountability audits are typically undertaken to meet the needs of funders, monitoring governmental agencies or community boards. The administrative audit is an analysis of work patterns designed to determine the congruency of staff performance with established program standards.[36]

The third form of special effort-oriented evaluation is the time-and-motion study. The purpose of this endeavor—which tends to conjure up somewhat negative images of white-coated industrial engineers equipped with stopwatches and clipboards—is, in fact, simply to determine the amount of time devoted by staff to particular program activities. Many time-and-motion studies require staff to report activities at randomly selected times during the work day. Williams and Sherman followed this procedure at the Hennepin County Mental Health Service by calling staff aperiodically and asking those who could be reached what they were doing at that moment. In aggregate form, these data provide an accurate and reliable picture of the organization at work. Other time-and-motion studies require regular reporting by staff according to a predetermined format. Spano and Baxter, for example, have developed and implemented a system whereby staff keep daily logs showing the amount of time accorded to standard program functions.[37]

HENNEPIN COUNTY MEDICAL CENTER
MENTAL HEALTH SERVICE

DIRECT CLINICAL TRANSACTION SERVICE RECORD

ORG. UNIT

62	ADULT OPD
63	CRISIS CENTER
64	DAY TRT CENTER
65	MEDICATION CLINIC
66	FAMILY UNIT
67	CIRCLE F CLUB
68	INPATIENT

TO WHOM

1	AN INDIVIDUAL
2	A COUPLE
3	A FAMILY
4	INDIVIDUALS
5	COUPLES
6	FAMILIES

WHAT

1	SCREENING
2	SUITABILITY
3	EVALUATION
4	TESTING
5	TREATMENT
6	REHABILITATION
7	CARE SERVICES

BILLING QUALIFIER

Circle One

0 1 2 3 4 5
6 7 8 9

ORG UNIT SPECIFIC DATA

Write in

WHERE

1	AT HC MH SERVICE
2	AT CLIENT HOME
3	AT RESIDENCE
4	AT AN AGENCY
5	AT SCHOOLS
6	HCMC CONSULT

WHEN

1	8 am to noon
2	noon to 4 pm
3	4 pm to midnight
4	midnight to 8 am

BY WHOM: STAFF ID CODE

Write in

therapist

cotherapist

INTENSITY

1	24 HOUR MILIEU
2	DAY/NITE MILIEU
3	2 HRS. OR LONGER
4	90 MINUTES
5	75 MINUTES
6	60 MINUTES
7	45 MINUTES
8	30 MINUTES
9	15 MINUTES

NUMBER RECIPIENTS SEEN

Write in

Figure 10–2 Part of a clinical transaction record used to monitor client progress and status. (Source: Courtesy of the Hennepin County Mental Health Service, Minneapolis, Minnesota.)

Record keeping One economical way to conduct an effort-oriented evaluation is to analyze the records maintained by a program for administrative and clinical reasons. Rocheleau, for instance, mentions a 1972 Law Enforcement Assistance Administration study in California that stimulated a major change in police department staffing patterns by showing that fully one-half of all burglaries occurred on Fridays.[38]

A potentially significant innovation in the human services has been the development and dissemination of the problem-oriented records system.[39] Abandoning the narrative style of traditional record-keeping schemes, problem-oriented records organize data collection around specific client needs. A problem-oriented record has four components: (1) *data base,* the client's intake data and history; (2) *problem list,* a statement of needs to be addressed; (3) *plans and goals,* an objective to be attained for each need identified, together with a strategy for attainment; and (4) *follow-up,* progress notes on the plan and periodic assessment of goal attainment. This manner of organizing information tends to increase the accountability of service providers by committing them to specific goals, and provides a base for auditing the program's overall quality of care. In the case of medical and certain other sensitive records, the issue of the confidentiality of the records must also be addressed by the prudent administrator, preferably with expert legal advice.

Outcome evaluation This form of evaluation focuses on the results produced by the subject of study. In the human services, outcome evaluation tends to occur at two levels of assessment: the level of the program, and the level of the individual client. Each is capable of further subdivision.

Program-level outcome evaluation: (1) the goal model and goal-free evaluation Currently there are three major programmatic approaches to outcome evaluation in the human services. The most pervasive of these is the "goal model," which includes four main steps in the evaluation process: setting goals to be attained by a program; implementing a program to attain the goals; evaluating the program in relation to level of goal achievement; and using this information to review the goals and make appropriate corrections in the program. Figure 10–3 illustrates the sequence of these steps.

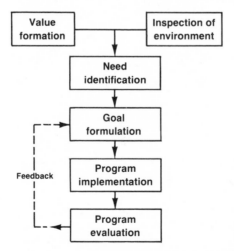

Figure 10–3 Steps in the evaluation process, as defined by the goal model.

Freeman and Sherwood have developed a sophisticated prototype for goal model evaluation.[40] Their approach involves evaluating a program not only in terms of attainment of "intermediate" goals (e.g., completion of a training course in automobile mechanics), but also in terms of attainment of "ultimate" goals (e.g., regular employment as automobile mechanic). Linking the intermediate effects of a program to its long-term objectives creates an "impact model," or theory of the organization, which "posits a sequence of events from input to outcome; in order to reach the desired end, certain sub-goals have to be achieved.[41] Such a model allows analysis of results such that "program failures" (inability to attain intermediate goals) are distinguished from "theory failures" (attained intermediate goals that do not lead to ultimate goals). Program failures can often be rectified through modification of immediate procedures. Theory failures, however, often require abandonment of one approach to a problem in favor of an entirely new idea.

A fundamental criticism of the goal model is that it can be very difficult to determine a program's "real" goals: public goals are often propaganda, and private goals are problematic to determine. Also, since goals are, in a sense, statements of what a particular program would be achieving if all functioned ideally, they tend to be stated optimistically. When attainment is assessed, the program may appear unrealistically ineffective. In a similar vein, Scriven has argued that goal-oriented evaluation is inherently biased because a statement of goals can distract an observer's attention from the effects of the program as a whole.[42]

The goal model has also been criticized because it seems to be associated with a view of formal organizations as rigid, hierarchical arrangements of discrete components. Some organizational theorists, contending that organizations are in a constant state of interaction and change, find the goal model deficient because it fosters isolation among program components and fails to program functions other than goal attainment.

A prominent critic of the goal model has promulgated a "goal-free" approach to evaluation that attempts to avoid the potential biases associated with evaluation based on goal attainment.[43] According to this view, the central question in evaluation should be, Is the program any good?, rather than, Has the program attained its goals? To answer this first question, goal-free evaluation employs an outside evaluator, who is screened from contaminating program influences while conducting a performance analysis. Such analysis involves determination of the needs of the impacted population and application of individualized measures to determine the program's efficacy in meeting needs. Advocates emphasize that goal-free evaluation is intended primarily for situations where a decision must be made regarding the continuation or termination of a new program. It has less relevance when the purpose of evaluation is to generate corrective feedback for a program of accepted utility.

Goal-free evaluation is an innovative addition to the human services armamentarium; however, its applicability may be somewhat restricted. Its reliance on specialized consultants, in particular, may be a limiting factor as may its heavy reliance on isolation to enforce objectivity (although there is often little assurance that mere isolation will necessarily mitigate potential sources of bias). Perhaps an equally effective way to control spurious influences on evaluation results is to select and assess evaluation criteria based upon multiple sources of input.

Program-level outcome evaluation: (2) the systems model   One crucial problem with goal-oriented evaluation is that it tends to lack an empirical basis for interpretation of results. For instance, the goal of an alcohol treatment agency may be to have 75 percent of its clients abstinent six months after termination of services. If it is subsequently determined that only 50 percent actually meet this criterion, the program must be considered a failure under the conditions of the evaluation. If it is also determined, however, that comparable programs with equivalent resources and client populations rarely have a success rate over 30 percent, the "ineffective" program may also be judged the one that merits the greatest degree of outside support. Etzioni has observed in proposing that the goal model be supplanted by the systems model that, "rather than comparing existing organizations to ideals of what they might be, we may assess their performance relative to one another."[44]

Using the systems approach, the focus of evaluation is shifted from a statement of program goals to a formulation of a working model for an organization that is capable of achieving such goals. The systems model emphasizes that goal achievement is only one function of an organization. Equally significant are coordination of subsystems, acquisition of resources, and adaption to environmental conditions. According to Etzioni, the purpose of the systems approach is not to maximize any one of these functions, but to determine, "under a given set of conditions, how close does the organizational allocation of resources approach optimal distribution."[45]

According to Smith, the process of systems analysis involves breaking down the organization into the constituent parts necessary to attain predetermined objectives. The process involves determining the mission of the program, listing the functions that must be performed to meet the mission, and outlining the tasks necessary to perform those functions. This information is usually presented as "a graphical representation of a plan which shows the logical sequence and interdependency of the work from beginning to completion."[46] Such a chart, along with a schedule of dates for completion of tasks, serves to guide the development of the organization and, with constant feedback, is continually redefined in order to find the most effective and efficient interrelationships among organizational components.

Etzioni points to a study by Georgopoulos and Tannenbaum as a good example of how the systems approach can be used in the assessment of organizational effectiveness. Disregarding the public goals of the health care system under study, the researchers developed three measures of important organizational functions: productivity, intraorganizational strain, and flexibility.[47] Thirty-two stations within the system were evaluated with these measures, and it was subsequently determined that these effectiveness ratings significantly correlated with the judgments of various internal and external "experts." If program goals are fabricated without reference to the effectiveness of comparable operations, they may embody a standard of effectiveness divorced from what may be realistically expected of a program.

Although the systems approach is an intriguing method to study formal organizations, it presents some difficulties from the perspective of the evaluator. In the first place, evaluation solely according to comparable performance is problematic if all of the units being compared are functioning poorly. In that situation, holding up the least ineffective unit as a model to the others might actually reinforce poor performance. In the second place, application of the systems model requires more time, resources, and specialized personnel than are available to most human services organizations. Weiss suggests that since the systems model demands "knowing more about the organization than the organization knows itself . . . most evaluators will probably stick with the goal model . . . and give as much attention to the organizational and community systems . . . as the situation seems to warrant."[48]

Program-level outcome evaluation: (3) the eclectic model   Most human services evaluations are hybrids, eclectic manifestations of aspects of diverse evaluation models. Walker, for example, has reported an exemplary evaluation established at a vocational rehabilitation service that displays aspects of goal-oriented, goal-free, and systems-oriented evaluation.[49] The goal model is represented by the construction of specific program objectives that serve as criteria of effectiveness. Goal-free evaluation is represented by having an unbiased consultant construct the objectives, based upon a comprehensive analysis of client needs. Systems-oriented evaluation is represented by the organization of staff into "subsystem" teams and the monitoring of effectiveness according to predetermined base rate data. To these procedures, Walker added explicit accountability mechanisms: each team was allowed absolute control over its own resources, and each team received positive or negative sanctions according to its compliance with program objectives. The result of all this has been an evaluation system associated with a dramatic increase in efficacy of services.

Client-level outcome evaluation: (1) individualized goal attainment measures   Individual client outcome measures are instruments, devices, or techniques that provide an assessment of the effectiveness of services for an individual client, and are much used in the medical treatment component of the human services field. Lund distinguished two kinds of outcomes: systems outcomes, i.e., indicators of effective process (for example, client successfully referred to Alcoholics Anonymous); and client outcomes, i.e., indicators of effective outcome (for example, client stops drinking).[50] A confusion of systems outcomes with client outcomes has been a source of difficulty with many clinical evaluations. Particularly in the case of agencies involved in information and referral, focusing on assessment of successful process may be the only means of getting a measure of effectiveness that is not confounded by the activities of another agency. For the purposes of this chapter, we will confine our discussion to measures of actual client outcomes. As in the case of program-level outcome evaluation, three options are involved: individualized goal attainment measures; standardized outcome assessment devices; and consumer satisfaction surveys.

One means to assess individual client outcomes is to employ what Davis calls individualized goal attainment (IGA) measures, techniques whereby the efficacy of services is measured according to criteria that have been specifically tailored to the needs, capacities, and aspirations of the person(s) receiving services. Existing forms of IGA measurement include concrete goal setting, goal-oriented automatic progress note, and patient progress record.[51]

A prominent approach to IGA measurement is goal attainment scaling which incorporates the following elements in assessing client outcome: "(1) a set of dimensions devised for or by the individual, (2) a system to assign weights among the dimensions, (3) a set of expected outcomes devised for each dimension, (4) a follow-up scoring of these dimensions, and (5) a score summarizing the outcomes across all dimensions." [52] The individualized scales constructed for each client are based on the response to the following question: "Given this patient, with a specific background environment, defined abilities and liabilities, and hopes for the future, and given the capacities of our treatment staff to treat such cases as well as the current state of knowledge, what can we expect this patient to be doing, to be like, at the time of follow-up?" [53]

The flexible and individualized nature of IGA measurement seems to greatly enhance the clinical meaningfulness of evaluation. Clients are no longer rigidly categorized according to diagnostic category. Service providers have targets to shoot for that seem appropriate and realistic in terms of the immediate situation. In addition, there is substantial evidence that client involvement in goal setting is a facilitator of subsequent therapy.[54] However, IGA measurement has been attacked psychometrically because it seems less reliable than standardized forms of assessment, and from a practical point of view because goal setting can be difficult and time-consuming.

Client-level outcome evaluation: (2) standardized outcome assessment devices   A more traditional means of assessing individual client outcome is through measurement devices with standardized content. Examples of such measures include the Minnesota multiphasic personality inventory, the brief psychiatric rating scale, and the self-rating symptom scale. Standardized measures usually take the form of rating scales or checklists: content is linked to one topic or to a broad area of social functioning and the form is filled out by the client, a community informant, a clinician, or a combination of these. An example of a general purpose measurement device is the global assessment scale which has proved useful both in assessing the severity of client distress at intake and the efficacy of services at follow-up.[55]

. According to Nunnally and Wilson, the major advantage of standard measures over subjective assessment is objectivity. "The quantification provided by standardized measures has two advantages. First, numerical indices make it possible to report results in finer detail than would be the case with personal judgments; . . . second, numerical results permit the use of powerful methods of mathematical analysis." [56] In addition, standard measures are cheaper, once developed, and easier to use than individualized techniques and tend to free staff time for other activities. This overall assessment is echoed by Hargreaves and his colleagues who observe "one of the advantages of a standard measuring instrument is that information is available about the psychometric properties it has exhibited in other studies." Since sensitivity to treatment efficacy is central to meaningful outcome evaluation, they have recommended use of instruments that have demonstrated capacity to reflect actual client change.[57] Although there are a great variety of scales and checklists available, it is sometimes necessary to construct a new device. In developing such measures, it is wise whenever possible to take items from proven instruments.

Client-level outcome evaluation: (3) consumer satisfaction surveys   The third, and seemingly most popular, way to determine client outcome is to implement a consumer satisfaction survey to assess clients' opinions, attitudes, and reactions regarding a particular program and the services with which it has provided them. Satisfaction surveys may also be directed toward other community agencies and sometimes toward the "significant other" of clients. Opinions are typically assessed through an interview schedule or questionnaire tailored to the program under evaluation; there are often similarities among surveys and it is generally good practice to borrow questions whenever possible.

Contacting former clients and asking their opinions about the services they received is perhaps the easiest and least expensive approach to outcome evaluation in the human services, and has been used to much good effect. Nevertheless, it must be recognized that some former clients are grateful for any services, effective or not, and some others are unable or unwilling to give negative reports.[58] Assessment of opinion is often an excellent beginning for a comprehensive evaluation system, but should be supplemented by other, more objective, forms of measurement.

Summary   As the preceding discussion has indicated, outcome evaluation can be a complex field, offering a bewildering variety of evaluation methods. The method just adopted has been to divide outcome evaluation into two main subdivisions at the program level and at the client level. Goal model and goal-free evaluation, the systems model, and the eclectic approach have been the three subdivisions examined in the program-level category. Individual goal attainment measures, standardized outcome assessment devices, and consumer satisfaction surveys have provided the corresponding tripartite division at the client level. Each of the methods described has advantages and disadvantages from the management perspective. All, however, are increasingly in use, particularly in the medical components of the human services field, and prudent managers will find it worthwhile to become familiar with at least the outlines of each technique.

Efficiency evaluation   Having discussed effort and outcome evaluation, we now move on to an analysis of efficiency evaluation. This form of evaluation is concerned with the cost in resources of attaining program objectives; specifically, with the ratio of resources extended to results produced. Efficiency evaluation takes three forms: cost accounting; cost-benefit analysis; and cost-outcome analysis. Each will now be introduced and discussed.

Cost accounting   Cost accounting procedures are employed to determine the amount of resources that must be expended to produce specific quantitative program outputs. General accounting principles are used to determine costs, and outputs are determined by counting or measuring specific program actions or events. Examples of human services program outputs might include such units as "number of students graduated," "number of complaints cleared by arrest," or "number of client visits." An extension of cost accounting is program budgeting, wherein cost data are employed as criteria for selection among an array of alternative programs. Planning-programming-budgeting systems (treated in detail in Chapter 9) employ the principles of program budgeting in the development of three kinds of organizational budgets: a "program budget," which organizes resources according to projected attainment of goals and impact on needs; a "performance budget," which concentrates on the relationship of activities inputs to outputs; and an "object budget," which is a line-item presentation of goods and services. All of these are formulated in terms of a program structure, which is an integrated arrangement of goals (major, broad-aim intentions), subgoals (specific programs for attainment of goals), objectives (specific ends for achievement of subgoals), and program elements (activities undertaken to reach objectives).[59]

Cost-benefit analysis   The function of the cost-benefit analysis variety of evaluation is to enable decision makers to assess the relative worth of alternative programs, founding such assessment in data that relate the cost of a program to the financial value of its benefits. If estimates of costs and projections of benefits are used, decisions can be made relevant to proposed programs; if actual data are available, the technique can be used to evaluate operating enterprises. The basic elements of cost-benefit analysis include: *specification of goals* and *transformation* of attainment *into monetary value, assessment* (or projection) of goal attainment, *determination* (or estimation) *of costs,* and *calculation* of the ratio of benefits relative to expenditures. An advantage of this form of evaluation is that it provides a general index of success useful for comparing diverse programs. However, since the meaningfulness of converting "soft" goals into monetary value has been questioned (e.g., how does one determine the dollar value of an art appreciation course?), the technique seems to have its greatest applicability in somewhat "harder" situations, as in the evaluation of water development programs, highway construction projects, or Model Cities programming.

Cost-outcome analysis   Sometimes referred to as cost-effectiveness analysis, this form of efficiency evaluation is a variant of cost-benefit analysis in which outcomes are *not* converted to monetary values. Instead, the goals of a program are held constant, and alternative strategies to achieve them are evaluated according to cost and degree of attainment. Levin has presented the principles of cost-outcome analysis through the evaluation of a hypothetical birth control program.[60] The objective of the program is to reduce the number of unwanted pregnancies each year in a specified population. Since various strategies are potentially available to meet this objective, the problem for the evaluator is to select the one which brings the greatest results at the lowest cost. The use of cost-outcome analysis to solve this problem would involve implementing each of the potential strategies in separate but comparable regions, and then comparing the incidence of unwanted pregnancy in each of the test regions with the incidence in a region that received no attention. The effectiveness of each strategy would be given by the difference between it and the "no attention" group and, when divided into the cost of the strategy, the result would be a cost-effectiveness ratio that could be used to rank potential desirability.

Cost-outcome analysis provides decision makers with a means by which to discriminate among different solutions for the same problem, but it is useless for evaluating programs with dissimilar goals. According to Levin, ". . . the cost-effectiveness approach enables us to rank potential program choices according to the magnitude of their effects relative to their costs, but we cannot ascertain whether a particular program is 'worth it' in the sense that benefits exceed costs because the latter are generally expressed in monetary units while the former are rendered in units of effectiveness for achieving a particular impact." [61] As might be expected, the cost-outcome method has its greatest use in situations where it is problematic to express output in terms of market values. Ironically, the genesis of the technique was the difficulty that military planners experienced converting the extermination of enemy populations into economic terms. Levin speculates that cost-outcome analysis is little employed in the human services because "social planners are less conscious of costs . . . than is the Pentagon." [62]

Impact evaluation　Unlike effectiveness studies, which limit themselves to examination of the consequences of a program for the clients served, impact evaluation—the last of our four main categories of evaluation to be examined—studies the effect of a program on the community as a whole. The purpose of an impact study is to analyze the effect of program outcomes upon the need that created the program, and also to assess the unintended social, political, and clinical consequences of the program. In general, impact studies employ the same research procedures as effectiveness studies, but measures are applied to a larger group of subjects. Very few successful impact studies have been accomplished, owing primarily to their expense and to the difficulty of controlling all sources of spurious variation. Perhaps for these reasons, a frequent "low road" approach to the study of impact is to conduct a comprehensive community opinion survey. The following discussion therefore takes a look at impact evaluation under two categories: social indicators, and social area analysis.

Social indicators　A variety of assessment that seems specially relevant to the study of program impact relates to social indicators. Social indicators are quantitative and qualitative measures of processes and events in a defined community "employed repeatedly and at regular intervals over an extended period of time and which permit one to grasp long term trends as well as sharp variations in rates." [63] The use of the technique requires selection of a set of measures that will provide valid indications of the quality of life in an area. While many feel there is great promise in the technique, Sheldon and Freeman caution against the use of social indicators as evaluation criteria, citing the difficulty of parceling out spurious sources of change. They recommend social experimentation as a superior approach to the study of program impact. [64]

Social area analysis　Social area analysis is an outgrowth of the social indicators method. This technique involves a multivariate analysis, combining cross-sectional and longitudinal assessment, wherein base rates are determined for a host of criterion variables, and groups of variables taken together are used to measure change in various pertinent "domains." The domain of educational quality, for example, might include such variables as percentage of entering sophomores who eventually graduate from high school, incidence of vandalism in the schools, percentage of students participating in extracurricular activities, percentage of citizens involved in parent–teacher groups, student scores on scholastic aptitude and other performance tests, and so on. By developing a detailed and comprehensive picture of a community, the social area analysis technique promises a means to examine the overall impact, both intended and unintended, of a program. Chein, for example, has employed the method to evaluate community programs to reduce juvenile delinquency, anticipating that effective programs will not only reduce the rate of juvenile crime, but will also alter the incidence of such associated social problems as illegitimate pregnancy and youthful unemployment. Struening has proposed social area analysis as a means to "promote the understanding of relationships between health and mental health delivery systems and the residents of . . . catchment areas . . . by explaining the selection of services and evaluating the effects of change as it is introduced into the service system." [65]

Summary   The discussion of impact evaluation concludes our survey of the four main kinds of evaluation, effort, outcome, and efficiency evaluation having been analyzed earlier. At this juncture, it is perhaps helpful to reemphasize the points made when a summary of the complex world of outcome evaluation procedures was offered, that is, that a knowledge of the basics of all these evaluation techniques is becoming increasingly necessary if the prudent local government manager is to make fully informed decisions about significant areas of service delivery in the local jurisdiction. Some evaluation techniques may only be appropriate to those larger entities, especially at the county level, that find themselves funding and assessing major programs in the medical (including mental health) fields. Others may be applicable to a broader range of human services programs and indeed to traditional areas of local government general management. Much will depend on the size of the local community, the political outlook of elected officials, legislative constraints, and the demographic and socioeconomic "givens" of a region. While few managers will need to know everything about all the kinds of evaluation just discussed, it is certain that all managers will need to know something of these kinds of evaluation if they are to make effective decisions in the areas of human services funding and administration. Similar considerations apply to the other potential members of the evaluation "audience"—service providers, consumers, and community representatives.

Evaluation procedures

Having completed an outline of the various kinds of evaluation, our discussion of the mechanics of evaluation continues with a discussion of procedural constraints and designs for evaluation research.

The function of evaluation is to provide information that can be used to make decisions. The quality of such information, the degree of confidence that can be placed in it, is in turn dependent upon the technical integrity of the procedures by which it was derived. Methodological approaches to outcome evaluation are legion. They range from the questionable practice of *ex post facto,* or "after the fact," analysis to the precision of laboratory experimentation. At base, the nature and quality of an evaluation is a compromise between the level of exactitude required by a decision maker and the constraints that may be imposed by the immediate situation.

Procedural constraints   Effective and meaningful evaluation can be prevented by a variety of technical problems. Many such difficulties arise from the differing objectives and perspectives of researchers, administrators, and service providers, and it can be very important that, prior to implementation of evaluation, all concerned parties discuss procedures to head off future conflicts.

Definition   At least in summative evaluation, accurate interpretation of results requires a clear specification of the intentions and procedures of the program. This can be problematic if the aims and methods of the program are not specified before the evaluation study begins.

Control   Related to the problem of definition is the problem of control. To one degree or another, evaluation requires the program under study to be a constant so that it is known to what variable the observed results should be attributed. This can be a severe problem in the human services because operating programs must respond to a variety of stimuli and tend to be in a constant state of change, if not of crisis management.

Cooperation   In the strictly medical field, evaluation often necessitates procedures that are unrelated, that may in fact be contrary, to clinical practice. This sometimes means that clinical staff is reluctant to cooperate in evaluation. Client cooperation can also be a problem, since evaluation can entail filling out forms and participating in interviews that may sometimes appear trivial, time-consuming, and intrusive.

Values   In order to assess efficacy of services, it is sometimes desirable to have a control, or "minimum services," group to compare their outcomes with those who received full services. This can raise ethical considerations, since such a practice can be construed as denial of services. Similar difficulties accrue to such evaluation-related practices as assigning clients randomly to treatment and substituting a placebo for an active form of therapy.

Also of concern to human services personnel is the protection of clients' right to privacy. Collection of sensitive information about service recipients' problems entails a substantial risk to client confidentiality, both because such information is not always protected by clinical privilege and because the manner of obtaining it may be intrusive. Ethical professional practice and governmental regulation both require that potential subjects of an evaluation be fully informed as to the nature and consequences of the study before their participation is requested. The importance of this factor of confidentiality must be stressed.

Measurement   The following list represents a number of potential threats to the validity of social scientific measurement that seem especially appropriate to program evaluation:

1. History—Events outside, and independent of, a program may influence the criteria chosen to assess success. For example, the opening of an abortion clinic in a community during the course of a comprehensive birth control education program may influence the incidence of unwanted pregnancies.
2. Maturation—Subjects may change over time due to personal growth rather than to the effects of the program under study. For example, if a before–after assessment of cognitive skills is used in the evaluation of an educational enrichment program for preschoolers, results might be confounded by the fact that growth is always accompanied in normal children by the appearance of new capacities.
3. Instability—Measurement devices may be unsound and show differences that are trivial or nonexistent. For example, it has been suggested that intelligence tests reflect learning rather than innate ability, and consequently that differences in I.Q. test scores relate to the cultural bias of the test constructor and not the inherent intelligence of the test taker.
4. Testing—The use of a pretest to establish a base rate before a program may sensitize subjects to the content of the test and therefore show spurious change when the test, or one like it, is readministered after the program. This can be a particular problem in tests of cognitive skills, where subjects may figure out the answers to questions during the first application and thus demonstrate artificially high "learning" at the second application.
5. Instrumentation—Alteration of measurement techniques can lead to spurious change. Perhaps the classic case of this is the upward swing in crime rate

figures every time more accurate record-keeping procedures are instituted by police departments.

6. Regression effects—It has been noted in social scientific research that subjects whose scores fall in very low or very high areas of a distribution of scores are likely, on subsequent observations, to move toward the mean of the distribution rather than away from it. This means that if subjects of an evaluation are selected because they score high or low on a pretest, they are in a sense predisposed to demonstrate change because they are likely to move back toward the mean. For example, if it is intended to evaluate a new set of procedures to reduce rape, and precincts are selected as test sites because in the previous year they had the highest incidence of rape, it is probable that a large portion of the change observed in the evaluation will be attributable to regression effects.

7. Selection—If an evaluation involves comparing two or more groups of subjects, differences observed between them may be due to biased selection procedures. For example, if an evaluation is intended to compare group and individual therapies, and young clients tend to be assigned to individual therapy and older people tend to be assigned to group, any differences observed could be attributed to the composition of the samples as well as to the relative efficacy of the treatments.

8. Mortality—Subjects may quit a program differentially, so that their absence gives a distorted picture of the program's actual effects. For example, if half of the participants in a treatment program drop out because the therapy makes them uncomfortable, an assessment based on the outcomes only of those completing the program will provide a slanted impression of effectivness.

Designs for evaluation research   Another significant facet falling under the heading of effective evaluation procedures is the question of designs for evaluation research. There are two general approaches to the development of designs for evaluation research: the experimental approach and the observational approach. In addition, a whole new form of evaluation has been coalescing around a line of thought proposed by Guttentag, and called "decision theoretic." [66] The strengths and weaknesses of these approaches will now be examined. All have managerial implications.

Experimental approach   The classic experimental paradigm is distinguished by two characteristics: the manipulation of the variable(s) under study, and the control of all extraneous sources of variation. Units of study are randomly selected from a target population and randomly assigned to either the condition that receives the treatment under evaluation or to the control condition that does not get the treatment. Measures are taken on specified criterion variables before the program begins and after it ends, and the program is judged a success if the treatment group improves more than the control group. ("Success" is usually determined by analyzing results with an appropriate test of statistical significance to determine how probable it is that the differences observed in the experimental and control groups are due to random variation in the criterion measures.)

The experimental paradigm has two main applications, the laboratory experiment and the field experiment. In addition, the use of quasi-experimental designs may be considered in situations where formal experimentation is not feasible. A laboratory experiment is a research study in which the variance of all possible variables not pertinent to the immediate investigation are kept at a minimum by isolating the research in a physical situation apart from the routine of daily living, and by manipulating one or more of the independent variables under controlled conditions. Research of this sort is admirably precise and reliable; the achievement of absolute control, however, is nearly impossible in actual human services settings. In addition, the artificial conditions under which the data are derived may mean that results are not applicable in the real world where uncontrolled extraneous variation may wash out the main effects.

A field experiment employs the same procedures as laboratory research, but is conducted in a realistic situation. Although the field experiment lacks some of the precision of the laboratory approach, it has superior applicability to program evaluation because it allows investigation of complex social influences, processes, and changes in routine settings. This can mean that the results of field experiments are more useful because they generalize more readily to situations beyond those of the immediate research. Nevertheless, the experimental approach may be inapplicable in most human services settings for two reasons: (1) the necessity that the program remain constant during the experiment, and (2) the absence of feedback until after the experiment is terminated.

Ethical, financial, and administrative considerations frequently preclude the use of fully developed experimental designs in the evaluation of human services programs. Fortunately, however, the technical quality of the experiment can be approached through the use of quasi-experimental designs.[67] A quasi-experimental design involves discarding or approximating some, but not all, of the control mechanisms embodied in the classical experimental model. Although the use of such designs allows some bias into the research, it is known beforehand where the contamination occurs.

Three quasi-experimental designs that have proved useful in the evaluation of human services programs include the "time series design," the "multiple time series design," and the "nonequivalent control group design." The time series design provides for sequential assessment of a program: before, after, and during implementation. In this way, changes over time, and presumably due to the program, can be charted. The weakness of this design is that change resulting from outside events might mistakenly be attributed to the program. Figure 10–4 illustrates the time series design.

The multiple time series design is an extension of the time series, involving staged longitudinal assessment of equivalent programs. Although the design does not provide for randomized assignment of subjects to treatment, by staging the implementation of programs over an extended period of time, it creates a comparison group for each program. This helps control for contamination of results due to outside events. See Figure 10–5 for an illustration of the multiple time series design.

The nonequivalent control group follows the classical experimental paradigm, but uses a control group that has not been randomly selected. A frequent variant of this design in the human services is to use dropouts from the program as compari-

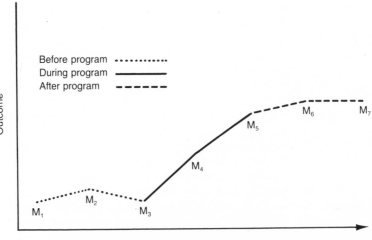

Figure 10–4 Example of the time series design for sequential assessment of a program.

son controls for those who remain in treatment. Since the use of nonequivalent controls involves clear risks to the validity of results (e.g., outcome differences may be due to variation in treatment motivation as well as to treatment efficacy), subjects can be matched on key variables to reduce the possibility of error. Statistical controls, such as analysis of covariance, can also be employed: this procedure involves taking measures on variables thought to be the source of spurious variation (called covariates), and then parceling out variation in the covariates when analyzing the independent variables.

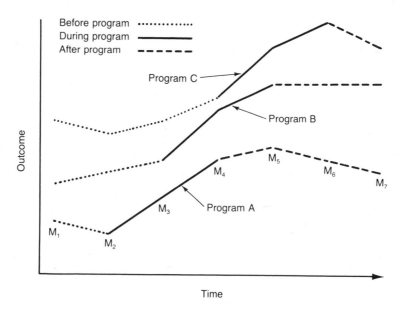

Figure 10–5 Example of the multiple time series design, which allows for comparative assessment of equivalent programs.

Observational approach   As its name implies, the observational approach to evaluation involves systematic observation of a program and its effects without direct manipulation of variables. Pertinent forms of this approach include field studies, case studies, and survey research.

A field study is an *ex post facto* scientific inquiry aimed at discovering the relations and interaction among variables through examination of information collected without manipulation of variables. A distinction may be made between two kinds of field study: exploratory and hypothesis testing. Exploratory studies seek to lay the groundwork for more disciplined research by discovering and clarifying the interrelationships of significant variables. Hypothesis-testing field studies are a somewhat more rigorous form of research, and involve making predictions, or setting goals, and determining how well the predictions have held.

As employed in evaluation research, a case study is an exhaustive description of a program as it develops. Data are accumulated through a variety of methods, qualitative as well as quantitative, including participant observation, surveys, sociometric analysis, and content analysis. Information from case studies can be most useful in describing the nature and quality of program activities. Indirect information can also be supplied on reasons for program performance.

A major component of many program evaluation systems is *survey research,* involving systematic study of populations, or segments of populations, to determine attitudes, opinions, and/or behavior. In evaluation research, the use of surveys typically takes the form of contacting service recipients to determine their assessment of a program's benefit. Procedurally, evaluation surveys have five stages: (1) *designation of target population* (most often the recipients of program services), (2) *selection of a manageable sample* of respondents from the population (employing the principles of probability sampling), (3) *construction of a questionnaire* or interview schedule, (4) *collection and verification of data* (can involve recontacting a subsample of respondents to estimate interviewer and response biases), and (5) *processing, analysis, and reporting* of data.

There are two major ways to conduct a survey: personal interviews and mail questionnaires. As the name implies, a personal interview involves contacting the respondent directly. Sometimes "direct" contact takes the form of a telephone conversation. This form of interview reduces expenses but sacrifices collection of nonverbal information. There are two general varieties of interview schedule: *structured* (i.e., with sequence and wording of questions fixed and with little flexibility allowed to interviewers) and *unstructured* (i.e., with fluid structure, open-ended questions, and flexibility to probe allowed to interviewer). As a rule, structured interview schedules are employed in tightly disciplined research, and unstructured interviews are used in broad-aim exploratory studies. The general *advantages* of the personal interview are that it provides a high level of flexibility and a broad scope of information; it allows establishment of rapport, and the possibility of probing and clarification of problematic questions; it is appropriate for a variety of respondents; and it minimizes nonresponse. The *disadvantages* of the personal interview are that it is expensive and tends to limit the geographic area covered; respondents cannot be assured of complete anonymity; presentation of questions may not be uniform among interviewers; little time is allowed to think about answers; and, with open-ended questions, data analysis may be difficult.

Mail questionnaire survey research follows the same process of development as the personal interview approach, but substitutes mailed questionnaires for direct interviews. The advantages of mail questionnaires are several, and include: their relatively low expense, wide geographical coverage, and ease of distribution; assurance of a large number of responses; maximum anonymity; uniform presentation of questions and absence of middleman bias; ease of tabulation (assuming no open-ended questions); and provision of time to think before answering. The disadvantages of the mail survey are: possible low response rate (percentage responding); lack of personal contact; poor suitability for some respondents (e.g., those who cannot read); inability to probe responses and clarify questions; and inability to evaluate conditions under which the questions were answered (e.g., cannot be certain who did the actual answering).

Other approaches to evaluation   As suggested earlier in this chapter, much of what is included in the rubric "evaluation" has been adopted from other fields, primarily management science and the social–behavioral disciplines. Although most of what has been borrowed has been useful, even indispensable, the moment seems to have arrived for a second generation of procedures, specifically developed for the unique needs of the evaluation enterprise. The experiment, for example, long considered the *sine qua non* of disciplined research and regarded by many as the ideal toward which evaluation designs should aspire, has fallen into some disrepute. There are those who have rejected the experiment as the proper means of evaluating educational programs because it does not provide useful feedback for program decision making and because it sacrifices generalizability of results for internal validity. Others, while accepting the controlled experiment as the most precise means of evaluating programs, call attention to the difficulty of implementing this kind of research in the real world and suggest that "soft" techniques be used to screen out patently ineffective programs, reserving the experiment for situations where relative effectiveness must be precisely tested.

One of the most persistent critics of the experiment has been Guttentag, who argues that "attempts to fit evaluation into the experimental model are often unsuccessful because both the goal of the research—a judgment of value—and the conditions under which it takes place are so different from the experimental situation." [68] Guttentag proposes that "evaluation research (avoid being) . . . arbitrarily squeezed into unwitting presumptions derived from the classical experimental model . . . (by adopting) . . . alternative ways of making observations, alternative logical systems, and alternative inferential models which more closely fit the reality of programs in the field.'' [69] Among the alternative research models suggested by Guttentag are a ''legal model'' and the ''decision theoretic approach.''

According to Guttentag, ''the rationale, logic, and method for making inferences in law offer a way out of the dilemmas presented by the experimental paradigm.'' [70] The *legal model* constitutes the formulation of rules governing the derivation, analysis, and presentation of evidence; levels of proofs are specified; opinions are distinguished from direct and circumstantial evidence; provision is made for examination of precedents; and presentation of surrounding social context that is characteristic of the experiment is supplanted by a disciplined organization of argument and counterargument that encompasses a greater amount of relevant data. Historical, anthropological, and anecdotal observation are allowed to enrich evaluation without opening the door to ''subjective chaos.''

Decision theoretic is an approach to evaluation that ''enables the decision maker to choose a course of action which is consistent with . . . personal judgments and preferences.'' [71] The severest deficiencies in the experimental approach, argues Guttentag, are that it isolates values from the conduct of research and does not allow feedback for intermediate decisions during the development of a program. In decision theoretics, the values of decision makers are specified, quantified, and intrinsically linked to data gathering and feedback, permitting modification of program activities anytime someone chooses to analyze the information accumulated by the evaluation. Analysis is conducted using Baysian statistical methods, which allow for optional stopping of data collection at any point; results are presented in terms of the personal beliefs of the decision maker, rather than being based on the chance probabilities of the classical approach. The same set of data can be analyzed from the perspectives of different value systems.

Stages in evaluation

Having discussed the kinds of evaluation and the procedures for evaluation, it is now possible to consider the last topic under the heading of the mechanics of evaluation, that is, the essential stages involved in the evaluation process: a basic checklist for managers, in fact. Rocheleau has presented an evaluation model that summarizes the steps essential to successful program evaluation. [72] This model is outlined below, and has been modified to reflect the thought of other noted experts in the evaluation field.

Step one: clarifying the background of the program   Suchman considers that ''evaluation always begins with some value'' or system of values, and argues that it is premature to set goals for a program before it is clear what larger good the program intends to serve. A 1976 NIMH publication has carried this suggestion to the point of recommending that organizations to be evaluated prepare ''a written statement of program philosophy'' for public review. A practical application of this recommendation has been reported by Spano and Lund who, in adopting management by objectives to fit a human services milieu, have also determined that a candid statement of the values and beliefs supporting an organization is an essential aspect of comprehensive evaluation. Hargreaves argues that the foundation for a program should be an analysis of the needs of the population the program is intended to serve. [73]

Step two: determining the aims of the program   There is general agreement in the field that a crucial step in the development of an evaluation protocol is formulation or determination of program goals and objectives. It should be noted, however, that a sizable minority do, in fact, dissent from this position, arguing that goal-oriented evaluation is inferior to either the systems approach or to goal-free evaluation (see the discussion on this topic earlier in this chapter).

Derivation of goal statements can be the single most difficult and time-consuming aspect of program evaluation. In order to be useful, goals must be clear, realistic, specific, and measurable. Unfortunately, there is rarely immediate consensus on what a program is, or should be, trying to accomplish. In such cases, four strategies are open to the evaluator. First, program staff may be left to come up with goal statements on their own. Second, the evaluator may conduct an analysis of the program and generate the goals without staff input. Third, the evaluator can present staff with successive approximations of goal statements, modifying each according to staff recommendations, until consensus is reached. Fourth, goals may be set aside for a time, and an exploratory study or needs analysis is implemented. Suchman contends that very early in the development of an evaluation, the program should be clearly defined so that the validity links between the program and the solution of the problem it attacks are specific.[74]

Step three: linking evaluation procedures to decision making   Rocheleau argues that four steps are necessary in order to firmly link evaluation procedures with administrative decision making: determination of the questions to be addressed by the evaluation; decision regarding the kind of information necessary to answer the questions; determination of whether such information is available and, if not, decision as to how best to collect it; clarification with decision makers of how the data will be used.

Step four: determining evaluation design   In this step, a research design is created that incorporates the purposes of the investigation and accommodates the idiosyncracies of the program and its goals. A critical aspect of this process is development of measures that assess relative progress of the program toward its objectives.

Step five: administering evaluation   Objectives should be set for evaluation as well as for the program, and it has been suggested that the evaluation be staged, with target dates set for completion of each stage. A number of those in the field have also called attention to the need for evaluation procedures to develop along with the organization under study since neither endeavor is static.[75] Once an evaluation is implemented, it requires continuous monitoring to assure both that predetermined data collection procedures are followed and that the program is adhering to its agreed plan of development.

Step six: analyzing results   After data is collected, it must be analyzed. Selection of analysis techniques is tied directly to the process of determining outcome measures, and it should be remembered that methods of analysis cannot extend beyond the nature and quality of the data collected. The level of statistical sophistication of the evaluation audience should be kept in mind when analyzing and reporting results.

Step seven: drawing conclusions and making recommendations   Just as evaluations are sometimes implemented without direct reference to the basic values that created a program, they are sometimes concluded without an attempt to see that the information collected will be used. The purpose of evaluation is creation of feedback information that can be used by decision makers to further some social goal. Since results are rarely so compelling as to force immediate action, it can be the responsibility of the evaluation itself to put data into a form that can be understood and used.

Implementation of evaluation

The preceding section has discussed in detail the mechanics of evaluation. It followed sections analyzing the growth of evaluation and exploring how the concepts of evaluation were defined. In other words, these three sections provided, respectively, answers to the questions: How has evaluation come about?, What is evaluation?, and How does evaluation work? If this chapter were to end here, however, it would be of only marginal educational use for local government decision makers. The remaining two sections deal with the all-important answers to two additional, severely practical questions: How is evaluation to be implemented? and How can the results of evaluation best be utilized? The following discussion takes a look at the political and administrative aspects of evaluation before considering specific approaches to its implementation. It is important to note at the outset the questions raised by Wildavsky set out in the opening paragraphs of this chapter. Essentially, Wildavsky suggests that, in a rational world, a rational process such as evaluation would be painless and automatic. Alas, in the imperfect world of all of us, however (and local government is certainly not exempt), implementation of evaluation can be dangerous, difficult, and sometimes meaningless. The political and nonrational aspects of evaluation require that it be undertaken only after careful thought and preparation.

Political aspects of evaluation

Programs as political creatures Human services programs are products of the political process within which all local government managers are inextricably enmeshed. For survival, such programs must serve unspoken as well as manifest objectives. In this regard, Campbell has pointed out that securing funds for needed reforms requires that programs be "advocated as though they are certain to be successful . . . (which in turn) . . . means the political and administrative system has committed itself in advance to the correctness and efficiency of its reforms, and . . . cannot tolerate learning of failure." [76] What makes this situation even more volatile is that, since certain soluble social problems have been resolved, only the more intransigent needs remain. Consequently, the payoff of reformist programs is approaching the point of diminishing returns, and outcomes will always fail to meet prior expectations. In a milieu where survival demands success and failure is almost guaranteed, it is not surprising that program managers operate in a decision matrix that includes considerations other than the "mere" effectiveness and efficiency of a program. It is this circumstance that largely accounts for evaluation results being ignored or put to peculiar uses, and that illuminates one reason that some human services professionals are rather uneasy about evaluation.

A second reason for this uneasiness is that evaluation is often based on goal attainment, and profound pressure can be put on a program to keep its public goals vague and unrealistic. Explicit goals can be dangerous (e.g., a program to assist homosexuals in becoming comfortable with their sexual orientation might well run into trouble in a conservative community) and realistic goals can be embarrassing (e.g., a program to treat alcoholics might sacrifice its reputation by openly anticipating a high rate of remission). Goal ambiguity, on the other hand, can provide a program with room for growth and development. Nonspecific goals, however, render meaningful program evaluation problematic. If the public goals of a program are taken at face value, the results of a fully developed evaluation system can be disclaimed by the simple contention that the "real" intentions of the program were not measured. Such a statement may be a rationalization, but it may also be a subtle indication that the goals of the program cannot by spoken. A governmental decision maker, for example, may not be disappointed at the failure of a job training program to improve vocational skills if the real hope had been that it would keep a minority population quiet. Weiss has observed that "a considerable amount of ineffectiveness will be tolerated if a program fits well with the prevailing values, satisfies voters, or pays off political debts." [77] In such cases, evaluation can be seen as a hindrance.

A third source of uncertainty regarding evaluation among human services professionals, and the managers and elected officials to whom they report, are the demands that research makes upon the operation of a program. Sound research practice, for example, frequently requires a clearly defined program and consistently applied procedures. In the absence of such stability and clarity, it can be difficult to make sense of observed outcomes. Program managers, however, tend to be less interested in the purity of the research design than they are in ensuring that the organization is responsive to its environment: a program nailed down by research controls cannot adapt itself to changing conditions. Other methodological encumberances can also cause complaint. Much paperwork can be demanded by the evaluation, and, in medical areas, alterations are sometimes made in clinical practice. In addition, there is the simple discomfort that goes with being under observation, little of which is mitigated by the fact that the payoff for participating in evaluation is indirect, delayed, or nonexistent.

A fourth, very basic, reason for suspicion regarding evaluation is that results, when there are results, often take the form of bad news. Managers and service providers may ignore such news, attack the evaluation procedures, or put pressure on the evaluator to reinterpret the findings. The consistency with which evaluations turn up ambiguous or negative findings is taken to mean that the very fact of an evaluation being performed is a omen of trouble. In addition, evaluation is far too often a "lose–no win" situation: if results are positive, the program is left alone; if results are negative, it may be destroyed. Evaluations are very often implemented and maintained at the expense of the program to be evaluated; the tendency for evaluations to produce negative findings could cause this source of support to cease. In a somewhat different context, Weiss has suggested that the autonomy typically accorded to evaluators is due more to lack of awareness or concern regarding an evaluation's potential effects than to a respect for research.

Evaluation as a political creature   As gatekeepers for a fund of specialized knowledge, evaluators themselves (that is, quite apart from the department heads or chief administrative officers above them) are potentially influential individuals, and are at the focus of a variety of political forces. For instance, simple agreement to conduct an evaluation accords implicit legitimacy to a program, and an agreement to evaluate according to goal attainment implies acceptance of program goals as meaningful and appropriate. Similarly, by focusing on specific experimental variables in the program, the evaluation can communicate to outsiders that other aspects of the situation are trivial or unalterable. The predilection on the part of evaluators for the controlled experiment has been said by some to have an unhealthy compatibility with the apparent preference in the human services for single-purpose ameliorative programs which occasion a fragmented approach to social problems. In a larger context, the process of selecting programs to be evaluated may itself have political implications. Typically, only new undertakings are required to demonstrate their worth; established programs are generally allowed to go unexamined.

The tendency for evaluation to be shaped by political processes should not obscure the fact that evaluation is itself a political vector, with its own set of assumptions, beliefs, and values. Caro has observed that "interest in evaluation is likely to be greatest among groups predisposed toward gradual and moderate change." [78] This predisposition, together with the assumptions implicit in evaluation that things can be changed by knowledge and that things should be changed, puts the typical evaluator between the extremes represented by the reactionary, who wants nothing changed, and the radical, who wants everything changed immediately. Perception of evaluation's political implications can predispose decision makers to be suspicious of results. Lynn, for example, takes the position that "evaluation is much more of an art than a science, and the artist's soul may be as influential as his mind. To the extent that this is true, the evaluator becomes another special interest or advocate rather than a purveyor of objectively developed evidence and insights, and the credibility of his work can be challenged." [79] The belief that evaluators allow too much of their own values into their work is counterposed by a conviction among some that evaluators are too passive regarding the obligations of their role. The frequency with which evaluations tend to be commissioned by program administrators rather than by service recipients has led to the belief by some that evaluators have been co-opted into the establishment power structure, abandoning their natural role as advocates for the disadvantaged. Indeed, one of the ironic twists of recent years has been the identification of evaluation with the destruction of some many attractive social programs.

Covert uses of evaluation   Like most—if not all—human constructions, evaluation is often put to uses other than those for which it was originally intended. Suchman has developed a typology describing some of the nonrational uses of evaluation. One strategy, called "postponement," involves using evaluation as a means to put off making a difficult or dangerous decision. A second strategy, called "eyewash," occurs when evaluation is used to prop up a failing program by focusing attention only on its positive aspects. "Submarine" is the name given to the use of evaluation to destroy an unpopular program. A fourth use, "public relations," signifies the use of evaluation as a means of program self-glorification. Using evaluation to legitimatize a difficult and unpopular decision is called "ducking responsibility." Covering up program weaknesses by using such evaluation devices as testimony from grateful clients is called "whitewash." Suchman's typology was intended both to be humorous and to illustrate that an endeavor like evaluation, intended at least nominally to clarify and rationalize human activities, can sometimes be employed to the opposite effect.[80]

Administration of evaluation

As is suggested above, the implementation and maintenance of a meaningful and technically sound program evaluation system is not easy. The principal parties in an evaluation tend to have different goals, values, and reference points, and the success of a particular system often depends on an ability to mediate among diverse opinions.

Conflicting perspectives of evaluation objectives   Administrators, clinical staff (where involved), and evaluators often have dissonant notions regarding the purposes of evaluation. Weiss has reported, in a systematic study of ten research grants, that "some program administrators and staff saw evaluation as a ritual to secure funding, others viewed it as a potential guide to adaptations that would strengthen the program during its course, still others expected evaluation to provide 'program vindication' . . . to help obtain further funding. Evaluators . . . tended to see their role as assessing the effectiveness of the program . . . so that NIMH . . . could decide whether to continue, adopt, or advocate it elsewhere. A few evaluators also expected to make contributions to basic knowledge." [81] These disagreements broke into open warfare when it came time to write the final reports: "administrators wanted to put the rosiest interpretation on evaluation findings; evaluators fought for the integrity of the data." [82] Gurel argues that such conflict can be prevented, or at least mitigated, if the evaluator and program manager can agree before the evaluation begins on "specific and detailed answers to a list of questions not unlike those that newspaper reporters are taught to ask: who?, what?, when?, where?, how?, and how much? What are the program objectives, both immediate and ultimate? For what target population? What changes are anticipated as indication that the objectives have been met? When and how will the changes be manifested? What kinds of activities are supposed to produce these changes? How much change? How are the program activities intended to produce change to be conducted? Where and for what length of time? With how much and what kind of resource inputs?'' [83] Gurel also strongly urges that the motivations for the evaluation be explored, and that steps be taken to ensure that the evaluation actually addresses topics of concern. ''The evaluator, the manager, and the sponsoring authorities may have different reasons for haste, but they all want to see something get started. Too often, the something that gets started is different from the kind of effort that would be wanted by all the concerned parties if the evaluation were adequately planned.'' [84] Gurel particularly cautions against the situation where the program manager allows the evaluator too much latitude in developing the evaluation. In such cases, the immediate data needs of the program may be sacrificed in favor of a ''broader inquiry (that the evaluator) would prefer to pursue . . . (for) general professional interest.'' [85]

Conflicts between evaluators and practitioners   Potential sources of conflict between evaluators and clinical staff have been the subject of much investigation. Some writers have suggested that researchers and evaluators are simply different types of people, with different types of personalities. Others contend that role differences are the key source of conflict. Practitioners tend to be committed to their programs and to have particularistic viewpoints, while evaluators tend to be skeptical about a program and have universalistic perspectives. Related to this problem are differences in the rewards accorded the two groups: evaluators are paid on different scales from clinicians; they get ''glory'' in the form of publications and conference presentations; the nature of their work tends to make them look less busy; and they sometimes have authority over clinical staff owing to the nature of the research design. Perhaps the most serious source of difficulty, however, is that evaluation can cause, indeed is intended to cause, change in the way things are done. Clinical staff may sometimes feel as if they are at the bottom of a well, with evaluators throwing things at them from above, forcing them to change accustomed practices without adequate preparation or explanation. According to Kiresuk, such staff feel that they are:

involved in a dismal, annual festival of numbers presentation and budget reclassification and realignment. There are no folk heroes in this celebration, only anonymous workers pushing an ever-increasing mass of data and words upwards through administrative ecological levels leading to an icy, snow-capped top. There, the festival reaches its own climax when the mental health staff find themselves unbelieved, untrusted, second-guessed, unrewarded, and facing a demand for more and different data. Their recommendations go ignored or are replaced by decisions of other individuals (''who know best''). On their way back down the administrative mountain, they can hear that year's juggernaut rumbling behind them, while all about them lie the dust and debris of memos, worksheets, and revised or abandoned reports.'' [86]

Weiss concludes that the problems outlined above can be mitigated through ''. . . clarity of structure and function, avoidance of incursions on others' domains, mutual respect and negotiation, and, above all, consensus on the purposes the study is to serve.'' [87] Beaulieu, an experienced clinician as well as a program manager and evaluator, has proposed a series of commonsense guidelines for reducing staff resistance to evaluation. Included in these guidelines are: (1) give clinicians the respect they are due, (2) do not too early and too glibly label the clinician's fear of program evaluation as basically irrational, (3) do not promise more than you can deliver, (4) avoid all loose talk about preliminary findings within earshot of clinicians, (5) develop a list of potential audiences for conclusions (clinicians want to know who is looking over their shoulders), (6) issue regular progress reports, (7) observe all laws and ethical standards, and (8) learn to tolerate staff resistance as one habituates to background noise.[88]

Personnel problems with evaluation Not all problems in the implementation of evaluation have to do with human relations. Some are simply the result of the structural side effects of evaluation. One source of difficulty can be staffing. Perhaps owing to the ambiguity and conflict accruing to evaluation, there tends to be a high rate of turnover in evaluation projects. Another source of difficulty is the timing of evaluation results. Sometimes an evaluator's desire for technical purity can delay presentation of results beyond the point at which they might be useful. Also, particularly in summative evaluation, final reports may not be turned in because the evaluation staff—in an apt personal application of management by objectives—have all dispersed to find other jobs.

Whether evaluation should be a staff responsibility or should be turned over to an outside consultant is a perennial concern. Staff members usually know more about the organization than a consultant, find it easier to mitigate resistance among other staff, have more time, and cost the organization less. Unfortunately, their status as paid employees tends to compromise their objectivity. Consultants, on the other hand, have greater credibility and technical expertise, and tend to be more objective and innovative. As a general rule, use of internal staff seems most appropriate in formative evaluation (where the paramount need is for "knowledge of results" feedback); use of outside consultants seems best in summative evaluation (where the need is for a disinterested judgment regarding the program's continuance).

Approaches to implementation of evaluation

One aspect of evaluation, only recently receiving serious attention by human services professionals, is the necessity for careful groundwork prior to implementation. Evaluation is a form of change, as well as a stimulus to change, and the probability that an evaluation will be meaningful and successful is increased by adequate preparation.

Provisional analysis One approach to the implementation of evaluation is called provisional analysis. Prior to initiation of procedures, the following action steps are taken: first, program decision makers are consulted to determine what consequences and recommendations should emerge from the evaluation; second, the amount and quality of information necessary to select one of these alternatives is determined; and third, the evaluator generates some artificial data to help decision makers determine if the proposed evaluation will actually meet their needs.

A-VICTORY measurement Drawing upon the evolving literature on planned organizational change, an eight-factor model for guiding implementation of program evaluation has been proposed. According to Davis and Salasin, the A-VICTORY model is composed of "a logical clustering of information . . . derived from learning theory . . . considered to encompass the necessary and sufficient determinants of program attainment." [89] The eight salient factors in the A-VICTORY model are:

1. Ability. Does the organization possess, or have access to, the material and financial resources necessary to implement and maintain the innovation (in this case, program evaluation, although the model can be applied to any form of planned organization change)?
2. Values. Is the change consonant with the personal beliefs of service recipients, the policies of the program, the professional philosophies of staff, and the overall value system of the community?

3. Information. Is clear, relevant, and useful information available on the procedures involved in the change?
4. Circumstances. Is the present situation conducive to successful initiation of the change?
5. Timing. Is this a good time to implement the change? Are other events occurring that increase the probability that the innovation will be a success?
6. Obligation. To what degree is the proposed change mandatory? Has the need for the change been clearly demonstrated?
7. Resistances. Are there any major sources of opposition to the change? If so, from whom and for what reasons?
8. Yield. What will be the positive and negative consequences of the innovation? Have side effects been examined?

One of the earliest applications of A-VICTORY principles involved the use of the model to develop a checklist rating scale for monitoring the implementation of management by objectives at a hospital social services department.[90] Subsequent to this, a questionnaire was constructed to determine organizational readiness to adopt program evaluation.

Utilization of evaluation results

Finally, we address the question: What should be done with the results of evaluation? A perennial difficulty with evaluation in the human services is that, with rare exceptions, findings are not transformed into action. One reason for this, of course, is that some evaluation studies are poorly conceived or badly executed. An additional factor in the nonutilization of evaluation results is a basic and pervasive resistance to change. Every major technical innovation in recorded history (e.g., the automobile, penicillin, nuclear generation of electricity, fluoridation of drinking water) seems to have stirred some serious opposition. Such resistance is often desirable, of course, since some change requires opposition. Nevertheless, even taking the effects of this natural conservatism into account, the record of the impact of evaluation is generally dismal.

Barriers to utilization of evaluation results

There are various explanations, specific to program evaluation, for the nonutilization of evaluation results. These fall under three general rubrics: the evaluators' self-perception of role; methods by which findings are disseminated; and organizational resistance to evaluation and to the change implied by evaluation results.

Evaluators' role   One factor contributing to underutilization of results may be the way in which the evaluators perceive their professional responsibilities. Some evaluators adhere to the traditional canon of science that proscribes personal involvement, equating it with bias, advocacy, and a compromise of objectivity. Thinking it unwise to make recommendations or become entangled in political issues, many traditional evaluators are therefore unlikely to follow up on evaluation to ensure that results are utilized.

There is also a more pragmatic reason why an evaluator may not push for utilization of findings. Some outside consultants, for example, consider their job concluded with the publication of a final report. To negotiate for correct use of their findings would be to waste time that could be used for fulfilling other contracts, and might gain them the unwelcome reputation of being contentious. Similarly, some internal evaluators may be reluctant to stray beyond the boundaries of their technical competence. Public advocacy of an unpopular idea might undermine their credibility and bring them into conflict with powerful and relentless organizational forces.

Dissemination of results Even if evaluators perceive the stimulation of utilization as a professional obligation, impact will be minimal unless findings are disseminated effectively. For maximum effect, information must reach the appropriate decision maker in a form that lends itself to use. Evaluation reports casually circulated through the interoffice mails will probably not even be read. There is ample evidence that absence of a systematic dissemination strategy almost certainly condemns evaluation results to nonutilization.

The root causes of nonutilization vary according to the purposes of evaluation. In formative evaluation, where the intention is to use feedback to improve program performance, nonutilization typically relates to faulty intraprogram communication, to a general distaste for evaluation, or to a failure of the evaluation to provide information of true utility. In summative evaluation, where the objective is to make a decision regarding the success and generalizability of a program, the utilization problems of formative evaluation are compounded with the difficulties involved in transferring findings from the immediate research situation to other appropriate settings. Unlike most research, evaluation tends to be program-specific and, as such, is less relevant to policy-level decision making. This also means that findings are unlikely to be disseminated through formal professional organs of communication. A 1972 NIMH study determined that major innovations stimulated by applied research took hold in only 20 percent of the host organizations after funding was ended. Mort and Cornell estimated in 1941 that, under ordinary circumstances, a latency of up to fifteen years can exist between a research finding and general utilization.[91]

Resistance A pervasive aspect of nonutilization of evaluation results is organizational resistance to change. The magnitude of such resistance tends to be related to the degree to which the change is seen as threatening job security, prestige, or deeply held beliefs. Opposition can also be stirred if its purposes are not understood or if it is perceived as a means of coercion. The probability of serious resistance to change in a program relates to four variables: the program leader, the program staff, the characteristics of the program itself, and the nature of the change.

The characteristics of the program leader can be critical to the successful utilization of evaluation results. According to an NIMH manual on research utilization, "no other factor has been reported as correlating so highly with innovativeness as the attitude of the top man [sic] in a program." [92] Five attributes are characteristic of innovative program leaders. First, they are goal-oriented and encourage staff to be so, too. Second, they are self-renewing, seeking out opportunities to broaden the depth and diversity of their experience. Third, such leaders accept risks and do not shrink from accepting responsibility for failure. Fourth, they reward effectiveness in subordinates and are not distracted by their status or personal characteristics. Fifth, they are personally innovative, not only supporting creativity in others, but developing and initiating new approaches to problems on their own.

As might be expected, organizations that are responsive to change tend to be staffed by individuals who are innovative. A leader can facilitate change by recruiting and rewarding staff who have the characteristics of the "early adopter." Among the attributes of such individuals are: personal intelligence; high levels of respect from other staff; comfort in presenting themselves as they really are; a consistent ability to deviate constructively from group norms; interests which reach beyond the immediate situation; aloofness from personality cliques; positive experiences with change in the past; either a relatively young or old age in comparison with the balance of the staff; a level of personal success that has left room to achieve more; and real security with the organization. By focusing change on those most responsive, the program leader can break ground for the innovation in a way likely to lead to ultimate success.

Highly associated with innovativeness is the openness of an organization. An open system may be defined as one which is democratic, flexible, promotes extensive participation among all levels of employees, fosters mutual trust among organizational members, and allows for three-way communication (that is, workers at subordinate levels do not simply receive orders from above). Innovative organizations tend to be those that allow time for problem solving; have clear, staff-accepted goals and provide feedback on attainment; tend to search internally for solutions to problems; are in competition with similar organizations; have a wide distribution of power and responsibility; and are composed of subsystems that are autonomous.

Systematic research has identified characteristics of an innovation that affect the probability of its successful adoption. Included are the relevance of the innovation to a problem of general concern; the relative advantage of the innovation over the practices it replaces; the degree to which the benefits accruing from the innovation are observable; the ease with which the innovation can be implemented; the extent to which the innovation can be reversed; the extent to which the innovation can be implemented in stages; and the credibility of the information used to justify the innovation.[93]

Mechanisms for improving utilization of evaluation results

There are four strategies for improving the utilization rates of evaluation findings. The first and most important is to *take the time necessary to plan* the evaluation so that it meets real needs. The second is to *communicate findings in a fashion calculated to facilitate utilization*. The third is to *use a middleman, or "change agent,"* to smooth the way for change. The fourth is to *attach rewards to the evaluation* in order to provide incentives for utilization.

Adequate preparation   A pervasive theme of this chapter has been that evaluation is best implemented only after careful and systematic planning. Early involvement of staff in negotiations between the program evaluator and program manager, for example, will not only defuse some of the tensions and anxieties of evaluation, but will often improve the technical quality of the design and open valuable channels of communication for dissemination of results. Meaningful utilization of results often hinges on prior identification of those who will use the information, selection of issues of concern to them, participation of program staff in planning and implementing the study, and involvement of influential outsiders who can disseminate findings and exert pressure on the organization. In addition, a wise course is to prepare a dummy final report before the evaluation is implemented in order to assess the relevance of the information to be collected. An alternative procedure is to specify beforehand the courses of action contingent upon differing levels of evaluation outcome.

Dissemination   As outlined in a previous section, underutilization of evaluation results is often the product of ineffective communication. The targeting of findings to predetermined audiences is a sound beginning to improved dissemination, particularly if results are presented in a style and language that is compatible with the needs and capacities of those who will use it. One approach is preparation of special summaries for particular decision makers. Also, since evaluation data rarely contain self-evident principles for action, a conscientious evaluator will often use the final report to outline guidelines for alternative program strategies.

Various additional aids have been proposed to strengthen the link between evaluators and other human services personnel. A frequent proposal has been to improve the quality of written materials. While the printed report is the main communication medium of the researcher, there is little evidence of its utility for practitioners. Specific recommendations for improving written materials include: (1) make them brief, practical, and readable, and avoid use of specialized vocabulary; (2) put major points up front and do not clutter the document with minor recommendations; (3) avoid sounding negative and analyze past successes as well as past failures; and (4) focus the document on the decision that must be made.[94] It has been found that human services personnel tend to learn best through interpersonal communication.[95] This can be taken advantage of by presenting evaluation findings through a conference or workshop: personal interaction during knowledge transfer does facilitate subsequent utilization. Another personalized means to induce utilization is the demonstration project: some innovations are most convincing when shown in actual operation and are likely to have maximum impact when the demonstration setting is comparable to the proposed one.[96] The personal approach in the form of T-groups, sensitivity training sessions, peer group discussions, etc., is also a possible means to mitigate nonrational resistance to evaluation and change.

Change agents   The intransigeance of the barriers between evaluation and practice has been so severe that many have proposed creation of a middleman, or "change agent," role to facilitate innovation. Such persons may be internal employees or outside consultants, but operate in either case in a way which encompasses the following functions: "*conveyor*—transfers knowledge from producers to users; *consultant*—assists users in identification of problems and resources, provides linkage to appropriate resources, assists in adaptation to use, and serves as facilitator, objective observer, process analyzer; *trainer*—instills in the user an understanding of the entire area of knowledge or practice; *leader*—effects linkages through user system; *defender*—sensitizes the user to the pitfalls of innovation, and mobilizes public opinion, public sensitivity, and public demand for adequate applications of scientific knowledge." [97]

Enlarging the concept of the change agent's role to include program-level activities, there has been a call for the creation of "institutes for change"—permanent resource centers that would serve as clearinghouses for change information and would provide skilled change agents to programs wishing to stimulate innovation. Rothman analyzed three case studies of the development of such institutes, which he calls "organizations for innovation," and concluded that they should possess three attributes: low centralization of decision making (to maximize staff flexibility and responsiveness); emphasis on inducing innovation through demonstration projects (to ensure that the principles disseminated are workable); and a staff congruent with the staff of the potential recipients of change (for improved communication).[98]

Incentives   Another means to increase the probability that findings will be utilized is to attach sanctions to level of performance, rewarding staff for attainment of goals or achievement of a certain standard of success. A related procedure is to create a sense of competition among human services agencies by allowing clients to purchase services through the use of vouchers. Through freedom of choice, clients will presumably seek services at the most effective agency, stimulating competitors to improve their operations.

Conclusion

This chapter has discussed the extremely broad subject of program evaluation—from its development and basic concept through the mechanics and implementation of the evaluation process to the utilization of results. The first section of the chapter traced the historical roots of evaluation and described its status, and the primary issues affecting it, as of the later 1970s. The overall concept of evaluation was reviewed in the second part: definition and purpose were treated as well as the various audiences of evaluation and their needs. The third section detailed four kinds of evaluation—effort, outcome, efficiency, and impact—and their subcomponents, and went on to look at certain procedural constraints and approaches to evaluation research design. The section concluded with an outline of the seven basic stages of the evaluation process. Implementation was covered in the fourth part, with a realistic look at evaluation's sometimes unstated political aspects, at its administrative challenges, and at certain specific approaches. The chapter concluded with a discussion of results utilization, including the barriers to utilization that exist at all levels and, of particular interest to the local government manager, some mechanisms for surmounting those barriers.

Unlike some of the older human services disciplines, evaluation lacks a coherent theoretical base and consequently seems to present a rich and deep confusion to the casual outsider. In conducting the research for this chapter, the authors were frequently bemused to find respected authorities flatly contradicting each other in the same, very few, pages. We do not regard this turmoil despairingly, however, but take it as evidence of continual self-renewal. As Weiss has observed, "old ideas and old ways are working in many critical areas. Social intervention is plagued with a series of important shortcomings. Programs based on intuitive wisdom and extrapolations from past experience are not good enough." [99] The movement toward evaluation is not a narrow-minded repudiation of the quest for social progress, but rather a resurgence, by a new route, toward the fundamental goal of the human services: the mitigation of human suffering and the enhancement of the quality of life.

1   Aaron Wildavsky, "The Self-Evaluating Organization," *Public Administration Review* 32 (September/October 1972): 509.

2   Charles Osgood, George Succi, and Percy Tannenbaum, *The Measurement of Meaning* (Urbana, Ill.: University of Illinois Press, 1957).

3   E. A. Suchman, *Evaluative Research* (New York: Russell Sage Foundation, 1967).

4   Lester Ward, *Applied Sociology* (Boston: Ginn & Co., 1906); and Stuart F. Chapin, "The Experimental Method and Sociology," *Scientific Monthly* 4 (1917).

5   Stephan A. Stephan, "Prospects and Possibilities: The New Deal and Social Research," *Social Forces* 13 (1935): 515–21; F. Stuart Chapin, *Experimental Designs in Sociological Research* (New York: Harper & Bros., 1947); Ralph Tyler, "Evaluation: A Challenge to Progressive Education," *Educational Research Bulletin* 14 (1935); Kurt Lewin, *Resolving Social Conflicts* (New York: Harper & Bros., 1948); and Edwin Powers and Helen Witmer, *An Experiment in the Prevention of Juvenile Delinquency: The Cambridge–Somerville Youth Study* (New York: Columbia University Press, 1951).

6   Frederick Winslow Taylor, *Scientific Management* (New York: Harper & Row, 1911).

7   Elton Mayo, *The Human Problems of an Industrial Civilization* (New York: Macmillan Co., 1933).

8   Peter Drucker, *The Practice of Management* (New York: Harper & Bros., 1954); and Rodney Brady, "MBO Goes to Work in the Public Sector," *Harvard Business Review* 51 (March/April 1973).

9   Daniel D. Roman, "The PERT System: An Appraisal of Program Evaluation Review Technique," in *Program Evaluation in the Health Fields,* ed. Herbert C. Schulberg, Alan Sheldon, and Frank Baker (New York: Behavioral Pubns., 1969); and Allen Schick, "The Road to PPB: The Stages of Budget Reform," *Public Administration Review* 26 (December 1966).

10 Charles Windle and Frank M. Ochberg, "Enhancing Program Evaluation in the Community Mental Health Centers Program," *Evaluation* 2:2 (1975); and Mark Lincoln Chadwin, "The Nature of Legislative Program Evaluation, *Evaluation* 2:2 (1975): 45–49.

11 W. Williams and J. Evans, "The Politics of Evaluation: The Case of Head Start," *Annals* 385 (1969); and Jack Elinson, "Effectiveness of Social Action Programs in Health and Welfare," in *Assessing the Effectiveness of Child Care Services, Report of the Fifth-Sixth Ross Congress on Pediatric Research* (Columbus, Ohio: Ross Laboratories, 1967).

12 Laurence E. Lynn and Susan Salasin, "Human Services: Should We, Can We Make Them Available to Everyone?", *Evaluation* Special Issue (Spring 1974): 4–6.

13 Franklin D. Chu and Sharland Trotter, *The Madness Establishment: Ralph Nader's Study Group Report on the National Institute of Mental Health* (New York: Grossman Pubs., 1974).

14 E. J. Webb et al., *Unobtrusive Measures: Non-reactive Research in the Social Sciences* (Chicago: Rand-McNally, 1966); and Donald T. Campbell and Julian C. Stanley, *Experimental and Quasi-experimental Designs for Research* (Chicago: Rand McNally, 1966).

15 Suchman, *Evaluative Research*, pp. 31–32.

16 Carol Weiss, *Evaluation Research: Methods of Assessing Program Effectiveness* (Englewood Cliffs, N.J.: Prentice-Hall, 1972), pp. 1–2.

17 Marvin C. Alkin, "Evaluation Theory Development," in *Evaluating Social Action Programs: Readings in Social Action and Education,* ed. Carol H. Weiss (Boston: Allyn & Bacon, 1972), p. 107.

18 Don Trantow, "An Introduction to Evaluation," *Rehabilitation Literature* 31 (1970).

19 Henry W. Riecken, "Memorandum on Program Evaluation," in *Evaluating Social Action Programs,* ed. Weiss, p. 86.

20 National Institute of Mental Health, *Program Evaluation in the State Mental Health Agency* (Washington, D.C.: Government Printing Office, 1976), p. 53.

21 Marcia Guttentag, "Subjectivity and Its Use in Evaluation Research," *Evaluation* 1:2 (1973).

22 Edward M. Glaser and Thomas E. Backer, "A Clinical Approach to Program Evaluation," *Evaluation* 1:1 (1972); and Malcolm Parlett and David Hamilton, "Evaluation as Illumination: A New Approach to the Study of Innovatory Programs," in *Evaluation Studies Annual Review*, ed. Gene Glass (Beverly Hills, Calif.: Sage Pubns., 1976).

23 National Institute of Mental Health, *Planning for Creative Change in Mental Health Services: A Manual on Research Utilization* (Washington, D.C.: Government Printing Office, 1972).

24 Jean-Marie Joly, "Research and Innovation: Two Solitudes?," *Canadian Education and Research Digest* 2 (1967).

25 Michael Scriven, "The Methodology of Evaluation," in *Evaluating Social Action Programs*, ed. Weiss, pp. 123–24.

26 Peter H. Rossi, "Boobytraps and Pitfalls in the Evaluation of Social Action Programs," in *Evaluating Social Action Programs*, ed. Weiss, p. 230.

27 Robert Walker and James Baxter, "Effects of Clinical Feedback," report for program evaluation project, Minneapolis, Minnesota, 1972.

28 David Bolin and Laurence Kivens, "Evaluation in a Community Mental Health Center: Hennepin County Mental Health Service," *Evaluation* 2:2 (1975).

29 Zigfrids Stelmachers, "Goal Attainment Scaling and the Crisis Intervention Center," *Proceedings of the Second Goal Attainment Scaling Conference* (Minneapolis, Minn.: Program Evaluation Resource Center, 1974).

30 Walter F. Mondale, "Social Accounting, Evaluation, and the Future of the Human Services," *Evaluation* 1:1 (1972).

31 Robert H. Haveman and Harold Watts, "Social Experiments as Policy Research," *Evaluation Studies Annual Review*, ed. Glass.

32 Suchman, *Evaluative Research*.

33 National Institute of Mental Health, *Program Evaluation in the State Mental Health Agency*.

34 Bolin and Kivens, "Evaluation: Hennepin County Mental Health Service."

35 Southern Regional Educational Board, *Definition of Terms in Mental Health, Alcohol Abuse, and Mental Retardation* (Rockville, Md.: National Institute of Mental Health, 1973).

36 Tony Tripoldi, Phillip Fellin, and Irwin Epstein, *Social Program Evaluation* (Itasca, Ill.: F. E. Peacock Pubs., 1971); John G. Hill, "Cost Analysis of Social Work Service," in *Social Work Research*, ed. Norman A. Polansky (Chicago: University of Chicago Press, 1960); and H. K. Schonfeld et al., "The Development of Standards for the Audit and Planning of Medical Care," *American Journal of Public Health* 88 (November 1968).

37 K. A. Williams and R. Sherman, "The Random Moment Study: An Innovative Technique for Reporting Staff Activities," paper presented at the National Conference on Mental Health Statistics, New Orleans, 1971; and Robert Spano and James Baxter, "An Automated Staff Accountability Review System," University of Minnesota, Minneapolis, 1974.

38 Bruce A. Rocheleau, *Without Tears or Bombast: A Guide to Program Evaluation* (DeKalb, Ill.: Northern Illinois University, Center for Governmental Studies, 1975); and U.S., Department of Justice, Law Enforcement Assistance Administration, *Burglary in San Jose* (Washington, D.C.: Government Printing Office, 1972).

39 Lawrence L. Weed, Medical Records, *Medical Education and Patient Care: The Problem-Oriented Record as a Basic Tool* (Cleveland: Case Western Reserve University Press, 1969).

40 Howard E. Freeman and Clarence C. Sherwood, "Research in Large-Scale Social Intervention Programs," *Journal of Social Issues* 21 (January 1965).

41 Weiss, *Evaluation Research*, p. 48.

42 Amitai Etzioni, *Modern Organizations* (Englewood Cliffs, N.J.: Prentice-Hall, 1964); and Michael Scriven, "Exploring Goal Free Evaluation: An Interview with Michael Scriven," *Evaluation* 2:1 (1974).

43 Scriven, "Exploring Goal Free Evaluation."

44 Etzioni, *Modern Organizations*, p. 17.

45 Ibid., p. 262.

46 Bryan C. Smith, "Process Control: A Guide to Planning," in *Evaluation of Behavioral Programs*, ed. Park O. Davidson, Frank W. Clark, and Leo A. Hamerlynck (Champaign, Ill.: Research Press, 1974).

47 B. S. Georgopoulos and A. S. Tannenbaum, "A Study of Organizational Effectiveness," *American Sociological Review* 22 (1957).

48 Weiss, *Evaluation Research*, p. 30.

49 Robert A. Walker, "The Ninth Panacea: Program Evaluation," *Evaluation* 1:1 (1972): 45–54.

50 Sander H. Lund, "Crisis Intervention Center: A Clinical Evaluation," paper prepared for a program evaluation project, Minneapolis, Minnesota, 1972.

51 Howard R. Davis, "Four Ways to Goal Attainment: An Overview," *Evaluation* 1 (1973); Theodore Bonstedt, "Concrete Goal-setting for Patients in a Day Hospital," *Evaluation* 1 (1973); Richard Ellis and Nancy Wilson, "Evaluating Treatment Effectiveness Using a Goal-Oriented Automated Progress Note," *Evaluation* 1 (1973); and Gilbert Honigfeld and Donald F. Klein, "The Hillside Hospital Patient Progress Record: Explorations in Clinical Management by Objective and Exception," *Evaluation* 1 (1973).

52 Thomas J. Kiresuk, "Goal Attainment Scaling at a County Mental Health Service," in *Trends in Mental Health Evaluation*, ed. Elizabeth Warren Markson and David Franklin Allen (Lexington, Mass.: D. C. Heath & Co., 1976), p. 104.

53 Ibid., p. 105.

54 Susan Y. Jones and Geoffrey Garwick, "Guide to Goals Study: Goal Attainment Scaling as Therapy Adjunct?," *P.E.P. Newsletter*, July–August 1973, pp. 1–3; Lorraine LaFerriere and Robert Calsyn, "Goal Attainment Scaling: An Effective Treatment Technique in Short Term Therapy," Michigan State University, East Lansing, Michigan, 1975; and David L. Smith, "Goal Attainment Scaling as an Adjunct to Counseling," *Journal of Counseling Psychology* 23 (January 1976).

55 R. L. Spitzer, M. Gibbon, and J. Endicott, "Global Assessment Scale (GAS)," 1973.

56 Jum C. Nunnally and William H. Wilson, "Method and Theory for Developing Measures in Evaluation Research," in *Handbook of Evaluation Research*, ed. Elmer L. Stuening and Marcia Guttentag (Beverly Hills, Calif.: Sage Pubns., 1975), p. 234.

57 W. A. Hargreaves et al., "Outcome Measurement Instruments for Use in Mental Health Programs," in *Resource Materials for Community Mental Health Program Evaluation: Part IV—Evaluating the Effectiveness of Services*, National Institute of Mental Health, 1975.

58 Gerald S. Landsberg, "Problems in Review—Consumers Appraise Storefront Mental Health Services," *Evaluation* 1:3 (1973): 67–77; Donna M. Audette, "Activities of the Follow-up Unit," prepared for the Program Evaluation Resource Center, Minneapolis, Minnesota, 1972; and Donald T. Campbell, "Reforms as Experiments," in *Evaluating Social Action Programs,* ed. Weiss.

59 Fremont J. Lyden and Ernest G. Miller, "An Introduction to the Second Edition," in *Planning, Programming, and Budgeting: A Systems Approach Management,* ed. Fremont J. Lyden and Ernest G. Miller (Chicago: Rand McNally College Publishing Co., 1972).

60 Henry M. Levin, "Cost Effectiveness Analysis in Evaluation Research," in *Handbook of Evaluation Research,* ed. Struening and Guttentag.

61 Ibid., p. 93.

62 Ibid.

63 Eleanor Bernert Sheldon and Howard R. Freeman, "Notes of Social Indicators: Promises and Potential," *Policy Sciences* 1 (April 1970): 166.

64 Ibid.

65 I. Chein, "Some Epidemiological Vectors of Delinquency and Its Control: Outline of a Project," New York University, Research Center for Human Relations, New York, 1967; and Elmer L. Struening, "Social Area Analysis as a Method of Evaluation," in *Handbook of Evaluation Research,* ed. Struening and Guttentag, p. 520.

66 Marcia Guttentag, "Models and Methods in Evaluation Research," *Journal for the Theory of Social Behavior* 1 (January 1971).

67 Campbell and Stanley, *Experimental and Quasi-experimental Designs.*

68 Guttentag, "Models and Methods," p. 77.

69 Ibid., p. 92.

70 Ibid., p. 85.

71 Ibid., p. 86.

72 Rocheleau, *Without Tears or Bombast.*

73 Suchman, *Evaluative Research;* National Institute of Mental Health, *Program Evaluation in the State Mental Health Agency;* Robert M. Spano and Sander H. Lund, "Management By Objectives in a Hospital Social Service Unit," *Social Work in Health Care* 1 (March 1976); and William A. Hargreaves, Clifford C. Attkisson, and Frank M. Ochberg, "Outcome Studies in Mental Health Program Evaluation," University of California, Langley Porter Neuropsychiatric Institute, San Francisco, 1974.

74 Suchman, *Evaluative Research.*

75 David G. Hawkridge, "Designs for Evaluative Studies," in *Evaluative Research: Strategies and Methods* (Pittsburgh: American Institues for Research, 1970); and Tripoldi, Fellin, and Epstein, *Social Program Evaluation.*

76 Campbell, "Reforms as Experiments," p. 189.

77 Carol H. Weiss, "Evaluation Research in the Political Context," in *Handbook of Evaluation Research,* ed. Struening and Guttentag, p. 17.

78 Francis G. Caro, "Evaluation Research: An Overview," in *Readings in Evaluation Research,* ed. Francis G. Caro (New York: Russell Sage Foundation, 1971), p. 7.

79 Laurence E. Lynn, Jr., "A Federal Evaluation Office?," *Evaluation* 1:2 (1973): 22.

80 Suchman, *Evaluative Research.*

81 Carol H. Weiss, "Where Politics and Evaluation Research Meet," *Evaluation* 1:3 (1973): 50.

82 Ibid.

83 Lee Gurel, "The Human Side of Evaluating Human Service Programs: Problems and Prospects," in *Handbook of Evaluation Research,* ed. Struening and Guttentag, p. 22.

84 Ibid., p. 24.

85 Ibid.

86 Thomas J. Kiresuk, "Sisyphus Revisited," in *Program Evaluation Forum: Position Papers* (Minneapolis, Minn.: Program Evaluation Project, 1972), p. 109.

87 Weiss, "Where Politics and Evaluation Research Meet," p. 52.

88 Dean E. Beaulieu, "How to Cope With Staff Resistance to Program Evaluation, or If Gridding Is So Damn Much Fun, Let Kiresuk Do It," *Goal Attainment Scaling Workshop Compendium* (Minneapolis, Minn.: Program Evaluation Resource Center, 1973).

89 Howard R. Davis and Susan E. Salasin, "The Utilization of Evaluation," in *Handbook of Evaluation Research,* ed. Struening and Guttentag, p. 648. See also Howard R. David, "Change and Innovation," in *Administration in Mental Health Services,* ed. Saul Feldman (Springfield, Ill.: Charles C. Thomas, 1973).

90 Robert M. Spano and Sander Lund, "Management By Objectives in a Hospital Social Service Department: Phase I," prepared for program evaluation project, Minneapolis, Minnesota, 1972.

91 National Institute of Mental Health, *Planning for Creative Change: Manual on Research Utilization;* and P. Mort and P. G. Cornell, *American Schools in Transition: How Our Schools Adapt Their Practices to Changing Needs* (New York: Columbia University, Teachers College, Bureau of Publications, 1941).

92 National Institute of Mental Health, *Planning for Creative Change: Manual on Research Utilization,* p. 21.

93 Homer G. Barnett, *Innovation: The Basis for Cultural Change* (New York: McGraw-Hill Book Co., 1953); Edwin Mansfield, "Speed of response of Firms to New Techniques," *Quarterly Journal of Economics* (1963): 77; Everett M. Rogers, *Bibliography on the Diffusion of Innovations* (East Lansing, Mich.: Michigan State University, Department of Communication, 1967); Matthew B. Miles, "On Temporary Systems," in *Innovation in Education,* ed. M. S. Miles (New York: Columbia University, Teachers College, Bureau of Publications, 1964); F. C. Fliegel and J. E. Kivlin, "Attributes of Innovations as Factors in Diffusion," *American Journal of Sociology* 72 (March 1966).

94 Edward M. Glaser, "Utilization of Applicable Research and Demonstration Results," report prepared for the Department of Health, Education, and Welfare, Vocational Rehabilitation Administration, Washington, D.C., 1966; Elmo C. Wilson, "The Application of Social Research Findings," in *Case Studies in Bringing Behavioral Science into Use,* Studies in the Utilization of Behavioral Sciences, vol. 1 (Stanford, Calif.: Stanford University, Institute for Communication Research, 1961); R. Likert and R. Lippitt, "The Utilization of Social Science," in *Research Methods in the Behavioral Sciences,* ed. L. Festinger and D. Katz (New York: Dryden Press, 1963); and Aaron Rosenblatt, "The Practioner's Use and Evaluation of Research," *Social Work* 13 (1968).

95 A. O. H. Roberts and J. K. Larsen, *Effective Use of Mental Health Information* (Palo Alto, Calif.: American Institutes for Research, 1971).

96 A. H. Niehoff, "The Process of Innovation," in

Handbook of Social Change, ed. A. H. Niehoff (Chicago: Alpine, 1966); and R. R. Mackie and P. R. Christensen, *Translation and Application of Psychological Research,* Technical Report no. 716-1 (Goleta, Calif.: Human Factors Research, Inc., 1967).

97 National Institute of Mental Health, *Planning for Creative Change in Mental Health Services: A Dis-* *tillation of Principles on Research Utilization* (Washington, D.C.: Government Printing Office, 1972), p. 22.

98 Jack Rothman, *Planning and Organizing for Social Change: Action Principles from Social Sciences Research* (New York: Columbia University Press, 1974).

99 Weiss, *Evaluation Research,* p. 128.

Part four:
Illustrative
programs

Introduction

The purpose of Part Four of this book is to take a close look, from the perspective of a number of differing authors, at some illustrative programs in the human services delivery system. It is clearly impossible within the covers of one book to provide a coverage of human services programs that is fully comprehensive. Neither could such a coverage, even if feasible, begin to keep up-to-date with the ongoing changes in legislation at all levels of government. Some idea of the range of programs involved can be gained by glancing at the 13-page, double-column, alphabetical list of titles to be found in *UWASIS II*, the taxonomy of social goals and human services programs developed by the United Way of America. The programmatic variety is indicated by a random sampling of the alphabetical juxtapositions: adoption, advocacy for animal protection and welfare, alcohol and drug abuse research and information, assistance for claims against foreign governments; babysitting, bonding of exoffenders; car pooling, child protection advocacy, chore assistance; and so on through the alphabet to weather warnings, weight watching and diet control, well-baby clinics, workers import-caused trade adjustment assistance, and work study.[1]

It was felt appropriate, therefore, to introduce the illustrative programs described in Part Four by a short overview chapter assessing the full range of human services programs administered by local governments, and this is the function of Chapter 11. This chapter describes the complexity and variety of local government human services programs and the systems used to classify them. It then provides a brief outline survey of the main service areas, and goes on to present information on the most common types of programs and their financing. The author concludes by emphasizing the theme of program variety but managerial commonality, and introduces the reader to the chapters that follow.

Chapter 12 takes a look at three areas broadly grouped under the heading of social services programs. The three topics are addressed from separate perspectives and experiences by different authors. The first topic is the perennial question of public welfare. The discussion analyzes the major components of public welfare programs, assesses the various prospects for welfare reform, and emphasizes that, in spite of the federal dominance in this area, local governments are still directly or indirectly involved in the welfare function. The second portion of the chapter takes a close look at counseling services. It provides answers to such questions as: What is counseling and who can counsel?; What traditional roles are assigned to counseling services?; and What is the role of the counselor in an age of accountability? Reference is then made to the actual experience of counseling services in an urban area. The final portion of Chapter 12 takes a look at local government roles and responsibilities in the provision of day care services, with an emphasis on the range of options available.

Chapter 13 similarly addresses three topics grouped under the broad heading of health programs. Again, each portion has separate authors writing from different experiences and perspectives. The first topic addressed is that of health services management, an area of fast-rising costs and associated managerial concern. After a discussion of the cost and other issues (including national priorities and intergovernmental aspects), the author addresses a series of managerial issues that must be faced in this field, and then goes on to examine the managerial approaches—from identification of needs and resources to contingency planning—appropriate to those issues. The second portion of Chapter 13 takes a realistic look at the management of mental health services. After discussing the crucial change in emphasis to community (as opposed to state hospital) care, the author illustrates her broad discussion by a detailed examination of the specific experiences of three counties in Illinois as they attempted to come to terms with their programs in this area. The final portion of Chapter 13 presents the views of two experienced California managers on the roles that local governments can (and, increasingly, must) play in the provision of services to the handicapped. The emphasis throughout is, first, on the crucial importance of attitudes in this area and, second, on specific areas of concern where local governments can act.

Chapter 14 groups four programmatic issues under the broad heading of "other target areas." The areas chosen for discussion by the individual authors are services for the elderly; human rights and minorities; housing for low income citizens; and mobilizing community resources for youth. The author of the section on the needs of the elderly presents an overview of problems of definition—Who are the elderly?—and realistically assesses the existing "nonsystem of services." He then offers specific analyses of three service areas: income maintenance for the elderly; health programs; and housing services. The author of the second portion of Chapter 14 takes a close look at the controversial subject of minorities and human rights programs. In addition to a frank assessment of the underlying moral—and pragmatic—issues involved, she also discusses practical steps for setting up, maintaining, and evaluating a human rights program. The author of the third portion of Chapter 14 takes a look at the managerial implications of low income housing programs. After an overview of changing government policies in this area, she addresses such pertinent questions as: Why bother with low income housing?; Where should it be located?; and What are the various programmatic approaches? The final portion of Chapter 14 takes a close look at a systematic approach to the mobilization of local government resources for youth. The emphasis is on planning and management functions and a developing strategy that has been tested in a number of communities across the nation. Specific examples are given throughout.

The two final chapters in Part Four draw back a little from specific program areas. The author of Chapter 15 takes a look at the critical importance of the human services factor in such traditional local government functions as the police department, the annual budgetary process, local government employment practices, and public information activities and programs. Written by an experienced professional manager, the chapter will be of special interest to the managers of smaller communities where human services functions may not find separate organizational expression. The author of Chapter 16, on the other hand, takes a look at the increasing emphasis placed on services integration. The author discusses the various approaches to services integration, with examples of each.

The thrust of Part Four, therefore, is to bring out the essential managerial issues in a selected group of illustrative programs. Some of the writers address the topic from a broad perspective; others use their own experience to present case studies in which the broader issues are given practical expression. Given the wealth of experience developing in the human services field in communities across the nation, it is to be hoped that the years ahead will indeed bring added significance to the statement of Alexander Hamilton made almost two centuries ago, namely, that "posterity will be indebted for the possession, and the world for the example, of the numerous innovations displayed on the American theater in favor of private rights and public happiness." [2]

1   *UWASIS II: A Taxonomy of Social Goals & Human Service Programs,* 2nd ed. (Alexandria, Va.: United Way of America, 1976), pp. 307–19.

2   Alexander Hamilton, James Madison, and John Jay, *The Federalist Papers* (New York: New American Library, 1961), p. 104.

Human services programs administered by local governments: an overview

An enormous number of human services programs are offered by the cities and counties of the United States, but the programs vary tremendously among cities and counties within a state, and among cities and counties in different states. Current information is scarce and historical data on which to base trend analyses are even more difficult to come by. Probably all general purpose local governments offer at least a few human services programs, whether they call them by that name or not. Among American cities, however, probably none offer more than the thirty-nine independent cities of Virginia, plus Baltimore, St. Louis, and Washington, D.C., or the twenty-five consolidated city/counties, such as New York, Philadelphia, Boston, Anchorage, and San Francisco. An independent city in Virginia, for example, runs all the social services generally operated by a typical county in California. In certain states, counties have few social functions and the human services programs are operated by either the state or the cities. Connecticut and Rhode Island do not have county governments as they are known in the other forty-eight states.

The purpose of this brief overview chapter, therefore, is to try to bring some sense of order into this very complex situation so that the illustrative programs described (from a variety of individual experience and perspective) by the authors of Part Four can be seen to fit into the broader discussions in the first three parts of this book. The discussion that follows is quite informal. For the purposes of this chapter, human services programs are given a very broad definition and include, in addition to the traditional health and welfare group, transportation, certain criminal justice services, and housing and advocacy programs. Not all the human services mentioned will be covered in Part Four—nor could they be, given the illustrative nature of the selection. But it is hoped that the following discussion will help to place them in the wider context of a constantly changing field.

The discussion begins with an outline of the complexity and variety of local human services programs, with a brief listing of certain of the services following some preliminary remarks on classification systems. The following section discusses the most common types of program. There are concluding outlines of methods of program financing, a brief discussion of the theme of program variety but managerial commonality, and a look at developing trends.

The complexity and variety of local human services programs

The manager seeking an overview of the human services field in local government should watch out for labels. As has been pointed out repeatedly in this book, such programs are found in many places besides departments called the "Department of Human Services." Job training programs may be found in independent or single-purpose departments, in personnel agencies or human services superagencies, but wherever they are, they are in fact human services programs. Work release programs and halfway houses may be considered part of the criminal justice system, but they can with equal justification be considered part of the human services system. The same can be said for juvenile and family courts. Some human services programs—by accident, by tradition, or by intent to disguise—have ended up under different labels. Senior citizen programs, for example, may exist in the recreation department even though they may offer a good deal more than recreation services. Placing them in recreation departments, however, may arouse less opposition—or so the reasoning goes.

Classification systems

Programs can be classified in many ways. The division between internal and external programs makes one basis for classification. That between maintenance and opportunity programs forms another. Maintenance in this usage stands for those types of services designed to sustain a person or family, such as income maintenance, food stamps, and health services. Opportunity programs include services offering a chance to improve the human condition, such as job training and education.

Maintenance programs have traditionally been provided for the preservation of human life and the provision of the basic necessities for its support. As it became apparent that support by maintenance alone did not assure that persons would be self-sufficient, it was deemed necessary to provide other human services. The elements of ''dignity'' and ''right'' served as strong influences for cities and other governmental units to begin opportunity programs. Because of these beginnings, services continue to be classified into two distinct categories of ''assistance'' (or maintenance) and ''services'' (or opportunity).

In 1972, the United Way developed *UWASIS*—the United Way of America Services Identification System—a classification system for human services.[1] It identified 6 basic goals, 22 service systems, 57 services, and 171 programs. It was updated and reissued in 1976 as *UWASIS II,*[2] and is probably the best general classification system available to local government practitioners.

IRMA—the Information and Referral Manual—was developed by the mayor's office in New York City. This manual identifies 15 major service subject areas, 47 second-level subject areas, and 25 third-level subject areas. Los Angeles County has developed SEARCH, a computerized classification system which features a key word index to enable its users to locate specific problem statements or services quickly and easily.

Services in brief

Human services programs are so numerous and so varied that only a much more extensive discussion could fully examine each type of offering. In the following outline, therefore, only the major types of activities will be highlighted. The reader is referred to the classification systems mentioned above for full details.

Employment Job training has had its ups and downs, but is still an important part of the inventory of human resources programs. Many of the hard-core unemployed lack basic job skills or need retraining. Some are worse off, and need remedial education in reading and writing. Prejob counseling is offered to coach people in the basic techniques of getting and holding jobs.

Many cities have played their most significant employment roles through the fields of job development, job finding, and placement—either within the city government itself or out in the community. In the area of job development, the city works with its own departments or the private sector to create new or trial jobs, such as paraprofessional positions.

Special employment services may be operated for a wide variety of groups with disadvantages or special needs: the physically and mentally handicapped, the elderly (including distinct programs for the semiretired), women, youth, and exoffenders. Homebound employment may be arranged for persons with severe physical handicaps. Sheltered workshops can provide useful job training and employment for the mentally retarded. Some are able to graduate from such workshops to regular employment in private industry on a completely self-supporting basis; others achieve private sector employment, but with continued supervision.

Health Communicable disease prevention, environmental sanitation and safety, public health nursing, maternal and child health clinics, crippled children's clinics, and community education are six of the more prominent of the traditional public health activities. Drug abuse control, methadone maintenance, family planning, nutritional programs for mothers and infants, and alcoholism prevention and treatment programs are some of the more recent additions.

The clinic is still the basic public health facility. Some communities also

Figure 11–1   Services for children are at the heart of many local government programs. (Source: Courtesy of California Office of Economic Opportunity, Sacramento, California.)

operate public hospitals. Medical care will normally include inpatient and outpatient care. A member of health-related programs may well be located outside of health departments. In this category would be, in many cases, emergency medical services and individualized clinics for special health problems, including drug and alcohol programs.

Rehabilitation   Rehabilitation services are designed to restore a handicapped individual or medically disabled person to independent living status. Services may be provided on an inpatient or outpatient basis, depending on the degree of disability. Vocational rehabilitation is directed toward the end of economic self sufficiency for the handicapped individual.

Mental health and mental retardation   Under the mental health category are normally grouped education; consultation; day care services; and inpatient, outpatient, and emergency psychiatric services. Although few cities provide the service themselves, residential care should also be considered part of the package of community mental health services as an alternative to complete institutionalization. Mental retardation services include diagnostic and evaluation centers, schools, sheltered workshops, day care centers, short-term and long-term residential care, recreation, legal rights, and transportation.

Housing   Housing assistance has typically been provided through a variety of federal subvention programs. Because the names and numbers change frequently, they will not be used here. Generally, however, they have included assistance in the purchase or renting of private housing or the direct provision of public housing.

Many cities which have never been into other housing programs have been actively and even aggressively involved in urban renewal or redevelopment programs. Still more have been involved in neighborhood preservation and housing rehabilitation programs. Housing relocation has probably touched more cities than all of the above programs simply as a by-product of public works construction programs. Housing counseling is a service that cities can provide to new low income residents who have not heretofore had houses of their own and may not know how to manage them. Housing is likely to play a much more important role in the activities of cities in the future. Although the major housing subsidies are still handled as categorical aid programs, minor federal housing funds have appeared in community development block grants and are being made directly to cities, rather than to housing authorities or other specialized agencies.

Advocacy   Consumer education and protection programs may seem a relatively new dimension to the list of city offerings, but, in actuality, some of them have been a fundamental part of effective local government for a long time. Building, plumbing, and electrical regulations are an example. Drainage, grading, and subdivision regulations protect the home buyer or business person. Franchises for taxi cabs, private bus lines, and utility companies are other examples. Finally, there are the various consumer facets of public health and safety, such as weights and measures, meat and dairy inspections, and regulation of public eating places. There can be no doubt that a long record exists in this area.

Today's local government consumer programs often involve small staffs and citizen boards of consumer and business representatives who, among other things, hear complaints by consumers and generally see that the interest of the buyer is protected. Landlord–tenant programs are often organized in a fashion similar to consumer programs. A staff investigates complaints and a citizen board composed of tenants, landlords, and perhaps a representative of the general public attempts to resolve disputes and advise the city council. Some localities take their programs a major policy step farther and become involved in setting rent guidelines or even enacting rent controls.

Human rights commissions began to be quite visible on the local government landscape in the 1950s. Some have enforcement powers; others do not. Generally they are charged with work in the civil rights areas, including education, housing, and, in the later 1970s especially, equal employment opportunity. Women's rights are often part of the charge of a human rights unit in a city or county; in other cases, they are in the domain of a special unit or task force. In addition to employment matters, these units may deal with credit, housing problems, education, and rape.

Poverty programs are advocates for the poor, and their scope may be as broad as human imagination and financial resources permit. Most are related to or grew out of the federal community action programs or Model Cities efforts of the 1960s. While they may offer a wide variety of programs, their common feature is representation for the poor and disadvantaged before government agencies and legislative bodies.

Citizen assistance offices and ombudsmen represent organized efforts—usually in larger cities and counties—to give the citizen a special friend and a helping hand in dealing with the bureaucracy. The citizen assistance officer generally serves the needs of citizens and tries to help them obtain desired services. The ombudsman, on the other hand, focuses on the impartial resolution of disputes between staff and citizens.

Transportation   Here we are not speaking of the hardware side of transportation—the freeways, buses, subway stations, or light rail systems. In the human services context, we are speaking of the software—the *transportation programs* designed to help particular groups. Many metropolitan transit systems, for example, offer special fare reductions for senior citizens. Sometimes low income citizens may purchase passes at a discount rate. In other cities, as a matter of public policy, the entire fare structure is kept at an unusually low level to benefit the population and to give clear encouragement to the use of one form of transit over another. This was the long-held philosophy and practice in New York City before the financial disasters of the mid-1970s in that city forced fare increases.

A city does not have to be large to engage in transportation programs for human services purposes. Communities under 25,000 population, for example, have engaged in subsidized taxi programs. The beneficiaries may be the elderly, the poor, the handicapped, or the entire population.

Income maintenance   Income maintenance programs are the basic income redistribution mechanisms in the United States. Included are cash payment programs such as aid to the blind, aid to the permanently and totally disabled, Aid to Familes with Dependent Children, old age assistance, and general relief. With the exception of general relief, these programs are either totally or substantially financed with federal funds; the amounts of money involved are so large, however, that even the local share for participating communities can be a major budgetary concern.

Programs with more state or local initiative are those for tax and rent relief. Called ''circuit breakers,'' these efforts to provide relief to low income persons, specifically property tax rebates for the elderly, gained widespread approval in the early 1970s. Normally they provide limits to certain local taxes based on a diminishing scale, at the upper end of which taxes almost equal those of persons without the relief program.

Social insurance programs differ from the financial aid programs in that they are contributory. Medicare, unemployment insurance, workmen's compensation, and social security are the major examples of social insurance services. Historically, local governmental involvement in social insurance has primarily been in the role of employer, that is, through the contribution it makes for its own employees to workmen's compensation and social security funds. By the mid-1970s, Congress had mandated unemployment insurance as well.

Nutrition   Nutrition programs are, as the name implies, designed to ensure that the target group gets a basic level of nutrition. The federal food stamp program is the core program in this area. Beyond this general low income support program, there are the more specialized programs, such as breakfasts and lunches for school children; a supplemental food program for infants, children, and lactating women; and meals-on-wheels programs provided to reduce the isolation of shut-ins as well as to provide one hot meal per day in the individuals' homes. Variations of the above programs exist. Congregate feeding of elderly persons, often in a school site, is a newer effort geared to both the nutrition and socialization needs of older adults.

Human resources aspects of the criminal justice system   Juvenile and family courts are found frequently at the county or city level around the United States. Community-based group residences serve as a transition point on the way back into society for certain former convicts, or offer an alternative to institutionalization for some members of the offender population. Most city and county law enforcement agencies operate some type of delinquency prevention programs. Probation and parole programs are other major human resources activities within the criminal justice system. Legal aid offices, while strictly private, nonprofit ventures without governmental support in some communities, receive substantial financial assistance from other local governments. The public defender system is the governmental counterpart of legal aid societies. Public defenders have a long and well-established history in some states and are nonexistent in others.

Support and socialization services   Protective services are among the most common in the support and socialization group and are important in the history of human services development generally. They include adoption, foster home, and child abuse programs. States usually regulate these activities to a fairly high degree. In recent years, concerns about child abuse (and wife abuse) have surfaced much more in public discussions.

Counseling services generally involve advice or other assistance in problem solving, given to individuals or groups by professionals such as psychiatrists, psychologists, social workers, ministers, teachers, or paraprofessionals from a peer group. The subject matters covered by counseling are as varied as are human problems. One of the most common is family counseling. Other types include drug, alcohol, youth, career, housing management for first-time home owners, crisis (as in suicide prevention centers), and planned parenthood (discussed below). A large number of private organizations, including churches, and public agencies, including schools, engage in counseling services.

Family planning programs may be offered through health departments or private organizations such as Planned Parenthood. To increase their effectiveness, a strong outreach program—particularly among low income and minority women— is often necessary and helpful. Family planning programs involve education, counseling, and the dissemination of contraceptive devices. Public health departments may also perform minor operations such as vasectomies. Some, but not all, publicly run hospitals and clinics offer abortion services.

Day care services burgeoned with the women's rights movement and are offered by a considerable variety of public and private organizations. Very small as well as large local jurisdictions have become involved. Designed to permit women to enter the work force, day care services have had somewhat mixed results, but are still very popular. Not limited to low income children, day care services are frequently provided at a fee that is based on ability to pay. Nor are day care services limited to daytime; some centers provide night care for children of parents working "swing" or "graveyard" shifts.

Visiting nurse and other services for the isolated or dependent are provided for the specialized group of people unable to leave home to obtain certain health care or other services that they need or desire. Outside the health care field, for example, are the special book programs operated by many public libraries. Group homes are community-based residences for various special groups. Examples of group homes include preinstitution placement for offenders, homes for unwed mothers, and residences for the mentally ill or retarded. Provision of communication links to police departments for the deaf is one of the newer services. Through relatively inexpensive teletype systems, deaf persons may communicate with the police and the police may send messages to the deaf.

Recreation and culture programs have been part of the portfolio of municipal services for decades, and there is little need to elaborate on them here. Suffice it to say that many recreation departments now offer a relatively sophisticated set of programs directed to the expressed needs of many age groups—particularly senior citizens and youth.

Education A broad definition of human services would almost certainly include education. Even though most local government managers do not have the legal responsibility for the management of the public school system, so many of the other human services require strong coordination with the schools that it behooves the manager not to ignore the schools or take a formalistic, ''hands off'' approach. Public health, nutrition, drug and alcohol education, job training, counseling, delinquency prevention, and recreation are some of the human services programs which will benefit from close ties to public school programs.

A special word about services for older and younger Americans The above section has been organized along programmatic lines and has not emphasized the

Figure 11–2 The thoughtfulness of individuals can do much to enhance the overall human services efforts of a local government. (Source: Courtesy of the Cities of Brea and La Habra, California.)

target groups of clients, although this would have been another valid method of classification and description. Services to senior citizens and youth are two of the most common offered by local governments in the United States. Their threads are intertwined through the vast network of human services programs and, in fact, there are specific elderly and/or youth components of the great majority of the categorical services described above.

Internal programs   Although mentioned briefly elsewhere, internal programs are covered again here to focus attention on this low-cost, example-setting, and—sometimes—high-yield approach.

Internal programs are those human services efforts within the city or county government. They cover such areas as hiring, training, purchasing, service delivery policies, tax- and fee-setting policies, social impact analysis, and, perhaps most importantly, the leadership role that the city or county government can play for the community, especially for other employers. The key here is a sensitivity to social issues on the part of local government in the way it goes about conducting its business.

Hiring policies should include major affirmative action considerations. Training efforts for employees can be consumer-oriented—that is, designed with the viewpoint and needs of the target groups in mind. The equitable delivery of services—according to need—should start with training programs so that employees will have the understanding and commitment necessary to make this approach successful. Awareness training programs are specially designed efforts to train employees in the understanding and acceptance of cultural and racial differences.

The above programs and others, such as affirmative action purchasing programs and investment programs designed to break redlining, are relatively low-cost efforts. Municipal semiregulatory programs in areas such as fair housing, consumer protection, and equal employment opportunity cost little compared with most programs in the human services field, but have high visibility. Most costly, but effective and fairly easy to administer, are rate reduction programs for low income citizens for charges for sanitation services or city-run water or electrical utilities. Tax and rent relief programs for elderly citizens are becoming more common each year. A frame of mind at city hall which considers the social impact of major municipal decisions and programs is indispensible. This is as true for the city council and planning commission as it is for the city manager, the planning director, the director of public works, and the chief of police.

A final point—just so that managers don't feel alone or at the edge of an unexplored continent—the important thing to remember is that each of the above programs is operated by some American cities; in fact, some cities run virtually all of them. No matter what the problem, other managers have experienced it, so help is available in getting started. The simplest rule is "just ask."

Most common types

Human services data for cities on a national basis are hard to find. For counties, however, some answers are provided by a 1975 survey of county government services sponsored by the Joint Data Center of the National Association of Counties (NaCo) and the International City Management Association (ICMA).[3]

The most common human service reported was juvenile/family court (81.4 percent), followed by mental health outpatient counseling (79.3 percent) and communicable disease control (79 percent). Others in the top ten were: child welfare (77.2 percent), visiting nurse (76.8 percent), indigent defense (76.3 percent), public service employment (76.2 percent), maternal and child health (74 percent), food stamps (72.9 percent), and alcoholism/drug programs (67.3 percent).

Not in the top ten of the NaCo/ICMA survey, but listed as a responsibility in 50 percent or more of the reporting counties were: coordinated services to the aging

(67.4 percent), emergency medical services (66 percent), family social services (64.7 percent), emergency financial assistance (64.3 percent), work experience programs (59.7 percent), training for the mentally retarded (56.8 percent), individual social services (55.8 percent), and job training (53.2 percent). Interestingly, all but the job training were named as a county responsibility more frequently than was fire protection at 54.5 percent.[4]

Although current national information on municipal human services programs is scarce, a 1976 survey done by the Association of Bay Area (San Francisco) Governments and the League of California Cities is revealing.[5] While in California the principal role in the human services arena is played by county governments, as the discussion earlier in this book has indicated, many city governments have been developing active human services programs during the past ten years. The League of California Cities has been in the vanguard of this effort, beginning with its 1969 *Report and Recommendations on Poverty and Race* [6] and followed by its "Action Plan," adopted in 1973.[7]

The 1976 survey examined the human services activities of 166 cities. Leading the list were the expected, established recreation programs with 134 cities responding; but following very closely behind were programs for older adults. Other activities participated in by 50 or more of the cities included special programs for children and youth (105); employment/economic development (90); housing (88); criminal justice (70); drug abuse (61); and health, handicapped, and education (54 each).[8]

A 1975 report by the Maine Municipal Association covering 359 municipalities indicated that the human services functions most heavily financed by the cities in that state were education, recreation, general assistance, health services, libraries, ambulance, and a group of senior citizen services including meals and transportation. General assistance was the most frequently provided human service—it was provided by 332 of the municipalities.[9]

How the programs are financed

According to the 1975 NaCo/ICMA survey of U.S. counties, most of the human services programs tended to have higher percentages of nonlocal funding than such programs as law enforcement, parks, fire protection, and judicial programs.[10] Food stamps, day care services, manpower programs, public housing, probation programs, health services, income maintenance, child welfare services, and services to the aging—all these receive heavy injections of state or federal funding, or both. In the matter of food stamps, 71.1 percent of the counties received state aid and 61.2 percent received federal aid. Manpower, rural housing, and social services programs operated by counties are heavily dependent on federal funding. State financial backing is usually large for county-operated programs in health, social services, probation, and education. User fees are an important source of funding for county programs like homes for the aged, hospital care, day care, emergency medical services, mental retardation facilities, and development disabilities programs, all of which were reported by more than 10 percent of the responding counties to be receiving funding from private funds or user fees.[11]

The city experience is much like that of the counties—up to a point. Where cities operate them, manpower, health, mental health, housing, most income maintenance programs, and probation programs generally are heavily underwritten by the federal and/or state governments. Emergency medical services, on the other hand, are largely a matter of local finance combined with user fees in many cities. Redevelopment programs, while sometimes tied to federal programs, are increasingly locally financed under tax increment programs such as those in widespread use in California. (Tax increment financing involves the issuing of bonds: the security for the bonds is the tax on the increase in assessed valuation of the properties within the redevelopment project over a base point at the start of the project, such increase being referred to as the "increment." The tax increments thus earned by the project are used to retire the bonds for the project.)

Advocacy programs—with the exception of poverty programs—tend to be financed from local sources. Fare subsidy programs for municipally owned transportation systems are generally a matter of revenues forgone from the local treasury and "charged" to social policy. For general, tax, and rent relief, the financial burden normally falls on the municipal government with perhaps some state participation. Day care programs may be funded totally from local sources, including user fees, or they may utilize federal and state funds. Recreation programs are normally financed by a combination of local tax sources and user fees.

Program variety but managerial commonality

Beyond the questions of funding sources lie the basic questions of which services to fund and at what service levels, and the methodology for policy analysis, needs assessment, and priority setting as has been discussed in Part Two. Some general remarks will, however, be offered here.

Although the number of possible human services programs is large and of great variety, the management functions—planning, needs assessments, priority setting, control, coordination, and evaluation—are common to all the programs. While the chapters which follow focus on various categorical programs, the reader should consider them as illustrative and seek to recognize the shared management techniques and needs.

The question of "Who provides?" will differ from city to city depending on many factors, including needs, existing resources in the community and region, local traditions, state laws, and the fiscal and management capacities of the particular locality. No one right way exists. No city should feel an obligation to operate all programs or to fund them through contract with other government or private agencies. The important requirement is for each city to determine the prime needs of its citizens and then to see that they are met. If a city (or group of adjacent cities) identifies a need for a convenient health clinic and is able to convince the county or state government to erect and operate such a facility in the area, it has performed an important function—an advocacy role on behalf of the citizenry—and may not need to do anything more with regard to the clinic question other than to monitor its progress. In a few states, the legislature, sometimes at the request of financially pressed local governments, has taken over the responsibility for the provision of certain services.

Youth programs and senior citizens services are the two human services categories most frequently managed directly by local governments. Cities commonly depend on their counties, states, or charitable agencies to operate certain other types of services. A city, for example, may contract with the local Salvation Army branch to operate a general aid program for indigents, and with its family service association branch for family counseling services. In the last decade or so, many charitable agencies have turned to municipalities for direct financial support. Cities becoming involved in such aid or in purchase of service arrangements need to develop priority-setting and evaluation mechanisms, or they will not know how to deal fairly with the many worthy groups competing for financial aid.

Coordination—between human services programs in the same city, between categorical programs in adjacent jurisdictions, between public and voluntary agencies, and between programs at different levels of government—is a frequently stressed theme, but one where success is much more rare than managers would like to admit. Integrated service systems, which are supposed to look at the needs of the total person or total family, are also rather hard to achieve in practice.

The city of Dallas' Martin Luther King Center (formerly the Crossroads Center) began operations by providing integrated intake service for all persons using this large neighborhood facility which houses city, county, state, and federal human services programs. After a few years, it modified this approach because it found that more than half the clients wanted only a single service and knew exactly which service it was they wanted. When cities do not have the advantage of a multiservice center, they must develop information and referral systems to match clients with the proper programs, in geographically dispersed facilities operated by different levels of government and private organizations.

Trends

A constant shifting of functions—upwards and downwards—among city, county, and state governments goes on in this country. In 1975, the U.S. Advisory Commission on Intergovernmental Relations (ACIR), the International City Management Association, and the State University of New York (SUNY) at Albany surveyed all cities in the United States of over 2,500 population in order to document the numbers, types of, and reasons for transfers of functions.[12]

Most of the functional shifts have been upward, although shifts from higher levels of government to cities, and from the private sector to cities, also occurred. Public health tied with law enforcement for the second most frequently transferred function from cities between 1965 and 1975: each represented 11 percent of all transfers (solid waste collection and disposal being first).[13] Most frequently, the public health function was transferred to counties (74 percent, or 137), but transfers to state (10 percent, or 19) and special district (11 percent, or 20) also occurred. The survey indicated that states were most frequently the destination of transfer for a package the survey termed "social services" (61 percent, or 82); often, such transfers were state mandated.[14] The survey reported that, in 1966, Rhode Island abolished city and town health departments, transferring their functions to the state health department. By 1970, Vermont, Massachusetts, and Delaware had transferred the provision of public welfare from cities, towns, and villages to the states. Another 34 percent, or 46, of the city respondents transferred social services to counties. Altogether, transfers of social services were the sixth most common type of transfers in the decade, representing 8 percent of all transfers. Among fifteen cases of transfers of the housing and community development function, nine went from cities to counties, one to a state, three to special districts, and two to councils of governments.[15] Between 1965 and 1975, Minnesota and New York shifted welfare from cities to counties, and Mississippi provided for the automatic abolition of city health departments when a county creates a health department. California was reported to have established the counties of over 100,000 population, instead of the state, as the basic providers of mental health services.[16] The survey also projected a continuation of the trend for transfers of functions. Responding cities indicated that additional transfers of public health functions were expected in the two years following the survey.

The reasons cities cited most frequently for transfers in the case of social services were state mandate, achievement of economies of scale, elimination of duplication, and fiscal restraints—each named by over 25 percent of all respondents. In the area of public health, the most frequently cited reasons for transfers were achieving economies of scale, eliminating duplication, lack of facilities, lack of personnel, and fiscal restraints—again, each mentioned by over 25 percent of all responding cities.[17]

While some cities were transferring their health departments and various social services to counties and states, other cities assumed these same functions. In fact, public health was the function second most frequently assumed by cities (with solid waste collection and disposal being first). All told, 137 cities reported assuming public health functions, compared to 185 which transferred them. Forty-five cities in the survey group reported assuming various social services functions, while 134 transferred them.[18]

The same ten-year period covered by the ACIR/ICMA/SUNY study, that is, 1965–75, saw expanded city interest in the human services area. In 1969, ICMA adopted its policy statement, "Managing for Social and Economic Opportunity;" [19] established a human resources task force in 1972; published several reports and articles on various aspects of human services; [20] and included a booklet on human resources programs in its Small Cities Management Training Program in 1975. [21] In its "Action Plan" of 1973, the League of California Cities said, "Each city should prepare and adopt a social services element in its general plan." [22]

Various federal initiatives led cities further into the human services field. Federally funded community action programs sprang up in cities beginning in the mid-1960s, followed by the Model Cities program. Decentralization trends ran strong in the middle and late 1960s with calls for neighborhood government and the breakup of big city school systems. The New York legislature established a federated school system with a certain amount of community control, and the Michigan legislature made provisions for a similar system in Detroit.

Certainly the New Federalism of the Nixon years, with its general and special revenue sharing, gave cities some funding and flexibility they had lacked previously. Although only a small share of general revenue sharing funds seems to have gone into human services programs during the first five years of that program, special revenue sharing funds have been of major importance in the human services field.

About the following chapters

Since Part Four of this book is intended to illustrate current programs and directions, this chapter has been a brief overview of the whole field of operational programs, financing, and trends. In the next three chapters, the text will go into more depth in specific program areas including: public welfare, counseling, day care, health, mental health, programs for the handicapped, elderly services, minorities and human rights protection, housing for low income people, and youth programs. These have been selected somewhat arbitrarily, but on the general assumption that these are a fair sample of the human services functions with which local governments are most frequently involved. Each chapter will consider substantive policy issues and a suggested managerial approach containing the "how to" aspects. Also included will be examples and implementation checklists. Following the chapter on specific programs will be the final two chapters, one dealing with human services aspects of traditional local government programs such as police, fire, and sanitation, and the other addressing the question of services integration.

Conclusion

Human services programs are not new to all city governments in the United States. Some American cities have been major providers of a broad array of such services for decades. For many other cities, however, the attention to the human services field is a relatively recent phenomenon, starting slowly with programs for youth and the aging after World War II, gaining major momentum following federal categorical program leads in the poverty and civil rights fields in the early 1960s and the urban riots of the mid-1960s, and continuing in the 1970s with special emphasis on certain of the advocacy programs such as consumers', tenants', and women's rights.

Funding for programs in the human services tends to be much more of a federal–state–local partnership than in the more traditional city program areas of police, fire, parks, libraries, etc. Similarly, since, in the former cases, the city is often an agent for another level of government, the federal administrative rules and/or state regulations tend to be considerably greater than in the more traditional city programs. The city or county manager must learn to live with this condition and must also become proficient at drawing together the particular resources needed from a most complex array of federal, state, county, and private possibilities. While many of the management problems in the human services area are similar to those that the city or county manager has experienced in implementing other local government programs, human services programs are generally characterized by more intense levels of citizen involvement than are customary in such areas as public works, fire, or police. Research focused on municipal human resources efforts is needed. A comprehensive data base on city-operated programs in this area would be particularly helpful.

The attitude and approach of the city and the city manager are as important as any particular human service. A sensitivity to the needs of the community, and an approach to problems which considers the social impact of municipal decisions and programs, are fundamental to success in the human services area.

1 United Way of America, *UWASIS: United Way of America Services Identification System* (Alexandria, Va.: United Way of America, 1972).

2 United Way of America, *UWASIS II: A Taxonomy of Social Goals & Human Service Programs* (Alexandria, Va.: United Way of America, 1976).

3 Carolyn B. Lawrence and John M. DeGrove, "County Government Services," in *The 1976 County Year Book* (Washington, D.C.: National Association of Counties and International City Management Association, 1976), pp. 91–99. The article cites the survey on which the article is based as "County Functions/Services: 1975 (CSRV/75) by the Joint Data Center of the National Association of Counties and the International City Management Association."

4 Ibid., p. 92.

5 Association of Bay Area Governments and League of California Cities, "Survey of Human Resources Activities in California Cities," Sacramento, 1977.

6 League of California Cities, *Report and Recommendations on Poverty and Race* (Los Angeles: League of California Cities, 1969).

7 League of California Cities, "Action Plan," Berkeley, October 1973.

8 Association of Bay Area Governments and League of California Cities, "Survey of Human Resources Activities."

9 John G. Melrose and Virginia H. Norman, *Municipal Perspectives Study on Human Resources* (Augusta, Me.: Maine Municipal Association, 1975).

10 Lawrence and DeGrove, "County Government Services," p. 93.

11 Ibid.

12 U.S., Advisory Commission on Intergovernmental Relations, *Pragmatic Federalism: The Reassignment of Functional Responsibility* (Washington, D.C.: Advisory Commission on Intergovernmental Relations, 1976); and Joseph F. Zimmerman, *Muni-cipal Transfers of Functional Responsibilities*, Urban Data Service Reports, vol. 7, no. 9 (Washington, D.C.: International City Management Association, September 1975).

13 Advisory Commission on Intergovernmental Relations, *Pragmatic Federalism*, p. 37.

14 Ibid., p. 42.

15 Ibid., p. 37.

16 Ibid., p. 57.

17 Ibid., p. 42.

18 Ibid., pp. 37, 58.

19 International City Management Association, "Managing for Social and Economic Opportunity," statement adopted by the International City Management Association at annual business meeting, New York, 15 October 1969.

20 See J. Robert Havlick and Mary K. Wade, *The American City and Civil Disorders*, Urban Data Service Reports, vol. 1, no. 1 (Washington, D.C.: International City Managers' Association, January 1969); Keith F. Mulrooney, *A Guide to Human Resources Development in Small Cities*, Management Information Service Reports, vol. 5, no. 10 (Washington, D.C.: International City Management Association, October 1973); International City Management Association, "The New Public Administration," *Public Management*, November 1971; ICMA Committee on Human Resource Development, "Managing Human Resources," *Public Management*, September 1973, pp. 12–18; International City Management Association, "Managing Human Resources," *Public Management*, September 1974; and International City Management Association, "Equity in Services," *Public Management*, August 1976.

21 "Human Services," in *Small Cities Management Training Program* (Washington, D.C.: International City Management Association, 1975).

22 League of California Cities, "Action Plan," p. 2.

12

Social services programs

In this chapter, the discussion of illustrative human services focuses, from the managerial viewpoint, on some of the programs falling under the broad heading of social services. The first section of the chapter takes a look at the all-important public welfare function. This area of activity is often at the forefront of public attention when human services are discussed, even though the direct involvement of city governments in providing welfare services may be less than those at the state, county, or federal level. The second portion of the chapter focuses more sharply on the operational problems associated with the management of counseling services in one metropolitan area. The third portion of the chapter analyzes the challenges presented by the provision of day care facilities. In each of the three sections, an attempt is made by the separate authors to bring out the basic policy issues and, most pertinently, the key managerial options rather than to provide the current reference data and the exhaustive case studies that are readily available elsewhere.

Public welfare

What exactly is meant by "public welfare"? How is responsibility for provision of services in this area shared between the levels of jurisdiction in our federal system? What are the main policy issues involved? What are the main outlines of the current welfare programs? And last, but certainly not least, what implications do the answers to such questions have for the local government manager and other key decision makers?

The following discussion is organized so as to address the questions noted above. It begins with a brief overview of the public welfare function from the management viewpoint. The specific components of welfare programs as they have operated up to the later 1970s are then identified and characterized. Next, some attention is given to the question of issues in welfare reform and alternative programs. Finally, patterns of state and local government responsibility are characterized and discussed, and the main points of the discussion are summed up in a brief conclusion.

The public welfare function: an overview

The portion of the total spectrum of human services falling within the definition of public welfare is complex, fragmentary, and none-too-clearly characterized. Individual programs are many and interlocking. They range from the massive fiscal impact of Aid to Families with Dependent Children (AFDC) through such familiar acronyms as the Supplemental Security Income program (SSI), Medicaid, Medicare, the Community Mental Health Centers program (CMHC), the Work Incentive program (WIN), food stamps, and many more. Some programs fall clearly within the purview of public welfare alone; conversely, some components of other, nonwelfare, programs may have a direct impact on welfare—for example, when monies from the Law Enforcement Assistance Administration (LEAA) are used for halfway houses or other rehabilitation functions. These programs will be discussed later in this chapter. The purpose of this overview, however, is to take a look at the welfare function as a whole and to bring out some points of significance to local government managers. What, then, is public welfare?

A basic definition In a 1970 "Statement of Principles" the American Public Welfare Association (APWA) defined public welfare as those "federal, state and local governmental programs which are designed, within a framework of related governmental and voluntary resources, to provide for individuals and families an ultimate guarantee against poverty and social deprivation and the assurance of the recognized basic essentials of living." [1] The APWA statement goes on to state that "by assuring basic social and economic protection to individuals and families, public welfare serves the interests of all people in the community and gives practical expression to the democratic principle that individual well-being is the source of community strength." [2] Public welfare programs are thus a principal instrument of the people, acting through their government, to facilitate more equitable opportunity for participation by all in the social and economic benefits now enjoyed by the majority.

The historical context: a summary The basic moral imperative underlying these public welfare programs has its roots in the feelings of compassion for the less fortunate that have shaped our Judeo–Christian heritage. As the discussion in Chapter 1 of this book indicated, the forerunners of these programs can be traced to medieval society, with the most direct antecedents leading back to the English Poor Law system. The earliest American programs were locally administered, and religious groups or private entrepreneurs under public contract provided minimum care to destitute individuals in public institutions or facilities. As the numbers of persons deserving such aid grew, institutions became impractical and the provision of "outdoor" relief became common. This relief was mostly "in kind" through the provision of groceries, clothing, or fuel, and some form of public work was required by able-bodied recipients. Institutional care continued, however, in the cases of the aged and the physically and mentally handicapped.

As our industrial society developed, changing economic, social, and political conditions led to the belief that all Americans were entitled to at least a minimum standard of living. This, in turn, brought changes in financial assistance programs and in related social and rehabilitative programs. As was noted in Chapter 1, public responsibility that was once limited to custodial care for the mentally and physically ill has broadened to include preventive and rehabilitative services.

Finally, it may be noted that public provision of a human service with public welfare connotations is often the result of pressure groups or advocacy groups focusing on a specific need, as in the cases of the retarded, the blind, or the physically handicapped. The administrative concomitant of this process is often the establishment of a categorical appropriation and a program that is at best illcoordinated with other human services. As knowledge and public awareness increase, they tend to be applied unevenly in a spectrum of programs, creating islands of specialized services and imbalances in the levels and interdependency of programs.

The managerial key: minimum local responsibility, maximum local impact What has all this meant for the local government manager? Two points can be made by way of answer. The first key fact as far as managers in urban communities are concerned is that cities, except in those cases where a city and a county are contiguous, have historically had limited service responsibilities and powers relating to public welfare programs. The states (and, to a lesser extent, the counties) carry the major fiscal and program management responsibilities for the public welfare segment of human services programs. The responsibility of local governments for both financial contributions and management is usually limited to that assigned by the state. And, of course, the federal government, too, plays a major role. The second key fact is that the public welfare programs do, however, have an enormous impact on the residents of municipal jurisdictions. The funds represented by these programs are a major contributor to the economic and social well-being of a community, and many local officials will agree that they ignore this fact only at their peril. These two factors—lack of local responsibility, strong local impact—help set the framework within which urban managers must deal with public welfare programs. Some basic statistics may perhaps help to emphasize the situation.

Some basic facts As of the mid-1970s, for example, in the case of the largest dollar program—AFDC—local governments (cities and counties) paid *none* of the costs of the program in thirty-five states, plus Puerto Rico, the Virgin Islands, and the District of Columbia. Excluding the federal share, there was some local expenditure for AFDC in fourteen states, with varying provisions for the division of both assistance payments and administrative costs between state and local jurisdictions. In California, for example, the state had responsibility for 67.5 percent of the assistance payments and 50 percent of the administrative costs, with local governments assuming responsibility for the remaining 32.5 percent and 50 percent, respectively. In New Jersey, on the other hand, the state was responsible for 75 percent of assistance payments, the localities for 25 percent; administrative costs, however, were assumed 100 percent by the localities. In Virginia, the state assumed 100 percent of assistance payment responsibility, and 80 percent of the administrative costs. Similar variations were found in the other states involved in the AFDC program.[3]

The effect of the AFDC program on local governments, however, is massive. For example, one in five of the recipients of this kind of assistance live in either New York, Los Angeles, Chicago, Philadelphia, or Detroit, and some 41 percent of AFDC families live in central cities with populations of over 250,000.[4] Such cities clearly have a major stake in the welfare program.

These figures merely serve to underline the point that local government officials, while not controlling many programs, are in the position of having citizens look to them for help and intervention on their behalf. The decentralization moves implied in programs of the 1960s and 1970s, such as those in housing, Model Cities, community action, revenue sharing, and community development, may be regarded as representing attempts to strengthen perceived weaknesses in our intergovernmental system. They have not, however, changed the basic fact that the major human services programs with a welfare connotation are mainly combinations of federal, state, and county administration and dollars. The basic thrust of the discussion in this chapter, therefore, is not to instruct the managers of municipalities on how to operate these clusterings of massive programs. Rather, it is to alert city managers and others to their responsibilities in learning what programs are available for meeting the needs of their communities' residents, and how they work. Its mission is to alert such local decision makers to what they must learn about federal, state, and county programs in order to exploit them to the maximum for the benefit of their vociferous constituencies. Many of the observations made, however, will also have relevance to the needs of county and state officials.

This overview concludes with some basic overall facts regarding the size of the major transfer programs (exclusive of Social Security programs, which are paid directly by the federal government) and the distribution of government costs. These facts are set out in Table 12–1. In addition, it may be noted that there are other cash transfer programs which benefit municipal residents. State-administered unemployment compensation, for example, ran to a total of $14 billion in fiscal 1975; the federally administered veterans' benefits program ran to $17 billion; and social insurance, including Medicare—also federally administered—ran to nearly $100 billion.[5]

Table 12–1 Financing
of welfare programs
for fiscal year 1975,
by program area and
level of government.

| Program | Financing costs ($ billions) | | | | |
	FY 1975	% increase FY 1973 to June 1975 [1]	Federal	State	Local
Total	31.8	N/A	19.6	10.2	2.0
Aid to Families with Dependent Children (AFDC)	9.0 [2]	28	5.0	3.4	0.6
Medicaid	12.2	67	6.5	4.6	1.1
General assistance	1.0	57 [3]	0.0	0.7 [4]	0.3 [4]
Supplemental Security Income (SSI)	5.4	N/A	4.1	1.3	0.0
Food stamps	4.2 [5]	186	4.0	0.2	0.0

Source: Extracted from William Gorham and Nathan Glazer, eds., *The Urban Predicament,* Washington, D.C., Urban Institute, 1976, p. 94.
1 Annual rate as of June 1975.
2 Includes $900 million of administrative costs.
3 FY 1974 to June 1975.
4 Estimated.
5 Includes $400 million of administrative costs.

Local governments are involved   Most federal social services funds flow through the states. However, the role of local government is somewhat greater here than in the area of income maintenance, Medicaid, and food stamps. Most social services programs—child welfare (including foster care and day care); programs for the aged; mental health and mental retardation programs—are essentially administered at the state and county levels, but it is important to stress that local governments do, in fact, get involved. There are two main reasons.

First, many of these programs (including Title XX, the social services arm of the Social Security Act) call for a great deal of citizen involvement and planning at the local level. Thus the opportunity to influence the shape and priorities of these programs is available both through the political process and through contacts with various local groups. Citizen participation in planning is one of the more recent methods used to ensure local input into programs.

Second, some of these programs require a nonfederal share (Title XX, for instance, requires 25 percent). While some of this is provided by the states, frequently it is provided by school districts, housing authorities, or voluntary nonprofit agencies who are vendors under contract with states or counties. Sometimes this is done at the city level, sometimes at the regional level. The 1976 Revenue Sharing Act made this potential for local governments even more attractive financially since these federal funds could be used to match other federal funds, thus enabling a local government to purchase services for its citizens using 100 percent federal money.

Regarding services actually provided at the local level, as discussion elsewhere in this book makes clear, these include child and adult day care centers, community living facilities for the mentally and physically impaired, legal services, homemaker services, youth services, family planning, and the like. Many of these programs have a welfare component. Further, it is important to note the role of the private sector in providing monies for welfare social services. In 1975, for example, voluntary contributions to the social welfare field were $2.46 billion. About $1 billion of this amount came from United Way campaigns; the remainder came from a variety of campaigns mounted by or for various sectarian and nonsectarian organizations, and other miscellaneous sources including foundations. These, too, have an impact at the local community level and are thus of significance to the local government official.[6]

The remainder of this chapter will describe the major programs whose existence has been touched on in this overview, and will provide information about their financing and methods of administration. The key point to emphasize again is that, while local governments do not manage or finance most of these programs, they do touch heavily on the lives of city residents in particular, and enter into the complex decision-making process regarding the provision of services to the community that animates much of local government managerial life.

Major components of public welfare programs

The following discussion takes a look at the major components of public welfare programs as they have operated in the 1970s up to the beginning of the Carter administration in 1977. After an introduction which places those programs in historical perspective, the main scope and function of each of the various programs is outlined and discussed.

Money payments: the historical framework   The current system of public assistance money payments began in the 1930s when the Depression produced enormous numbers of dependent people. Work relief was provided through federal programs, and the Social Security Act, passed in 1935, contained social insurance and public assistance provisions.

The Social Security Act provided for grants to states for the care of the aged, the blind, and families with dependent children (now AFDC), that is, to those persons generally outside the labor market. Aid to the disabled is also now included. Federal work relief ended shortly after the Depression and was not provided again until the 1960s. The process included allowing assistance to AFDC families with an unemployed or underemployed father. As of the mid-1970s, the federal government provided roughly 50 to 78 percent of the cost of the AFDC program. Programs for the aged, the blind, and the disabled, formerly shared in part by state funding, are now fully funded and administered by the federal government.

The most significant changes in the Social Security Act since 1935 are:

1. The provisions for aid to the aged, the blind, and the disabled are now covered by the Supplemental Security Income program (SSI), administered and financed by the federal government with optional state supplementation.
2. Medical payments are now provided for those over sixty-five years of age and those covered by SSI's Medicare program.
3. Medical assistance for the poor has been instituted under the Medicaid program; eligibility is determined by the states.
4. A broad social services program has been established, with a $2.5 billion federal expenditure ceiling (Title XX).
5. The Work Incentive program (WIN) has been strengthened including provision for penalties for the refusal of training or work. This has been administered nationally by the U.S. Department of Labor through state and county offices.

Originally, cash assistance under the Social Security Act was conceived as complementary to the Social Security insurance programs included in the original act. It was confidently expected that, as the Social Security programs matured, the assistance programs would be able to diminish; reality, however, dictated otherwise. The insurance aspects materialized very slowly over the years, and many major dependency-creating risks grew rather than diminished.

Further, because of the recent rapid growth of social insurance programs (such as Social Security disability insurance and unemployment insurance), the public assistance programs are not now considered the primary source of income maintenance transfer programs in the United States. To take an illustrative year, for fiscal 1975, social insurance programs, including Medicare, cost $109 billion; unemployment benefits cost $14.4 billion; and public aid for the poor, including Medicaid, cost $50 billion.[7]

Public assistance, as used in the following discussion, includes those cash transfer governmental programs that aid and assist needy individuals. Other programs that are part of the broad public welfare panoply—such as Medicare, Medicaid, social services, child welfare, mental health and retardation programs, and programs for the aged—will be discussed separately.

The general principles of the public assistance program are:

1. Aid should be in the form of money payments, rather than "in kind" (food stamps are an exception).
2. There should be objective criteria for eligibility determination.
3. The cost should be shared among the federal and other levels of government.
4. The basic decisions on eligibility and payment levels should be made by the states within broad limits set by federal law. (Thus, the considerable variation among states.)
5. As a component of state responsibility, the state must prepare a plan indicating commitments and the level of care to be provided.
6. In order to protect the individual against capricious acts, states must provide a fair hearing in all cases, and recipients' records must be kept confidential.
7. A merit system should cover employees administering the program.

There is no consistent organizational, administrative, and financial pattern among the states. As of the mid-1970s, in 30 states, the state government pays 100 percent of the state administrative costs of the AFDC program; in 35 states, the state government pays 100 percent of the state costs for cash payments. In other states, local governments share some costs.[8] Some states administer cash assistance programs directly. In some, local governments take care of the direct administration. Only 28 states provide for the Aid to Families of Dependent Children of the Unemployed program (AFDC-U). State public welfare departments almost all administer the AFDC, AFDC-U, social services, child welfare, Medicaid, and food stamp programs. Some states have umbrella agencies that also administer other programs in such areas as mental health, mental retardation, and aging; other states have established separate agencies for each. These and other patterns of administrative responsibility are analyzed in detail later in the discussion.

Aid to Families with Dependent Children (AFDC) This major endeavor is a federal–state matching public assistance program. The matching formula is based on criteria using each state's per capita income. In the mid-1970s, this resulted in federal government contributions which ranged from 50 percent of the funding for industrialized states to over 80 percent for nonindustrial states: in Mississippi, the federal share amounted to almost 80 percent; in New York, it was about 50 percent. Assistance grant standards are determined either locally or by the states, based on overall standards of health and decency. Of the 11.4 million recipients of AFDC in January, 1976, 8.1 million were children. Nationally, payments per family averaged $229.00 per month. New York had the highest average payment of $367.00 per month, and Mississippi the lowest, at $48.00 per month.[9] A comparison of these figures with the federally determined "poverty level" ($5,500 per year for a family of four, or $458.33 per month) indicates the extent of our failure to provide even a minimum standard of living for these 11.4 million Americans (almost two-thirds of whom are children) who must rely on this program.

In addition to income level, the principle determinant of eligibility is the condition of absence of the father from the home. An exception is the AFDC-U program where a recently unemployed or a partially employed father is eligible. Desertion and unmarried parenthood represent the largest distinguishing elements in this context.

In recent years, the numbers of AFDC and AFDC-U recipients have increased due to the action of a number of variables, including the growth in child population and movement from rural to urban settings; unemployment; and the activities of organized advocacy groups and others to acquaint people with their rights. The length of stay on the AFDC rolls varies greatly. Most people drop off because of new employment opportunities and return when a change in economic conditions results in unemployment.

General assistance   This program is financed (where it exists at all) entirely with state and/or local funds. It is aimed at those needy persons who are not eligible for any of the federally subsidized, categorical programs, that is, usually those able-bodied people who are childless and too young for any SSI program. Eligibility requirements and payment levels vary widely among states, and programs are often limited to short-term emergency cases. The average monthly payment per recipient was $104.00 in 1976.[10]

Supplemental Security Income (SSI)   Title XVI of the Social Security Act established the SSI program by combining the previously separate categorical programs for Aid to the Aged, Aid to the Blind, and Aid to the Permanently and Totally Disabled. It establishes a national means-tested program for those low income individuals who have attained age 65, or are blind or disabled. The program is administered by the federal government through local offices of the Social Security Administration, and the funds appropriated for both the administration of the program and the grants made to the individuals are 100 percent federal money. As of July 1, 1976, an individual may receive up to $167.80 and a couple $251.80. The states may exercise the option of supplementing these funds to whatever level they may so choose. In 1975 over 4 million people received benefits, of which 103,000 were children.[11]

Child welfare   Title IV-B of the Social Security Act authorizes the states to establish services for all needy children in each political subdivision. The aims are essentially to:

1. Prevent or remedy problems that may result in the neglect, abuse, exploitation, or delinquency of children.
2. Protect and care for homeless, dependent, or neglected children.
3. Protect and promote the welfare of children in general, including strengthening their own home environments and, if needed, providing adequate care in foster family homes, day care centers, or other child care facilities.

The child welfare program is not a cash assistance program. It assists states with their own child welfare services. There must be an identifiable single organizational unit in state and local agencies responsible for furnishing these services. The intent of this requirement is to ensure a unified program of services—for children covered under AFDC and all others not eligible for that aid—without any differences in the quality of service.

How has this money been spent? One illustrative national study of fiscal 1972 child welfare expenditures showed that, of the total of $532 million, only $46 million came from federal sources. Services included adoptions, foster care (including institutional care), programs for unmarried mothers, child protection, child care, and delinquency prevention.[12] Recently there is a trend toward use of small, community-based group care. By the later 1970s, every county in the United States had a public child welfare service. Most child welfare services are administered by county governments and are carried out through direct public service, or by public purchase from private, mostly nonprofit organizations.

Food stamps   Excluding Medicare and Medicaid, the largest and most controversial deviation from the money payment principle is the food stamp program. Begun as a demonstration program in 1971, it has grown rapidly to reach every county in the United States, and is the only program that supplements the income of all groups of the needy. By the later 1970s, it was estimated that 9 percent of the population (approximately 18.8 million people) was receiving food stamps.

More significant, perhaps, is the estimate that almost 20 percent of the population is eligible for food stamps at one time or another during the year. By the mid-1970s, the program was costing close to $5 billion annually.[13]

The basic purpose of the food stamp program is to provide nutritionally adequate diets for people who otherwise could not afford to pay for such food. The amount of food stamps given to families depends on family size and the "thrifty food plan" developed by the Department of Agriculture. Families with little or no income are given the appropriate value in food stamps; others are required to spend about 30 percent of their net income (that is, after deducting a variety of set expenses). As of 1976, the "thrifty food plan" allowed for $2,000 for a family of four. The Department of Agriculture pays each state 50 percent of the administrative costs including, but not limited to, costs related to eligibility determination, storage and protection of the coupons, and accounting procedures for the distribution of the food stamps. The value of the stamps themselves is paid for 100 percent by the federal government. Like the cash assistance program, the locus of administration is a state decision; some states have elected to administer themselves, and others have vested this in the local governments.

Social services amendments of 1974 (Title XX) Title XX replaced provisions formerly tied to cash assistance titles of the Social Security Act. It established five goals for social services which may be summarized as follows:

1. Achieving and maintaining economic self-support to prevent, reduce, and eliminate dependency;
2. Achieving and maintaining self-sufficiency to prevent, reduce, and eliminate dependency;
3. Preventing and remedying neglect, abuse, and exploitation of all people—children and adults—unable to protect their own interests, and preserving, rehabilitating, and reuniting families;
4. Preventing and reducing inappropriate institutional care by providing for community-based, home-based, and other less intensive forms of care; and
5. Securing referral and admission to institutional care when other forms of care are not appropriate, and providing services to individuals in institutions.

This title directs the U.S. Department of Health, Education, and Welfare (HEW) to pay to each state, according to a formula based on population, a sum not to exceed $2.5 billion for the nation. The secretary of the department is authorized to pay 90 percent of a state's total expenditures for family planning, and 75 percent of its total expenditures for the provision of other services related to the previously mentioned goals. In providing these services throughout the state, the designated state agency is permitted to enter into contracts with local community agencies for the actual delivery of the services.

Title XX did break new ground in two important ways. First, eligibility was tied to state residents' median income rather than to their eligibility for public assistance. Second, it required both public hearings and publication of the state's official plan in advance of actual service provision. Even though this law considerably eased former eligibility requirements, there has been considerable agitation among senior citizens' groups who favor the elimination of all eligibility criteria besides age and support aid only to those over sixty. This would be similar to existing provisions in the Older Americans Act (see below). Of course, as with any program with a limited budget, there must be some form of eligibility rule, even if it is only "first come, first served."

Although Title XX separated eligibility for services from eligibility for cash assistance, it was clearly the intent of the Congress that low income people have first priority for services.

While Title XX theoretically provides an opportunity for a coordinated approach to social services delivery, the managerial reality is that it is largely used as a "pass-through" device and funding mechanism by which to deliver categorical services to the clients of specialized agencies. As in the cases of cash assistance and food stamps, state-level decision making regarding administration results in both state and local administration.

Older Americans Act   First enacted in 1965, the Older Americans Act has since been revised several times. Since the original act was passed, almost all of the states have established state offices for the aged, and over 400 local "area agencies" have been funded to provide a focal point for planning and organization.[14] In addition, there are hot meal programs, some part-time employment opportunities, and a number of social services and recreational programs, providing homemaker services, counseling assistance, residential repairs and renovations, and transportation, among others. There are no eligibility criteria other than age (anyone sixty or over). The money allocated to each state is based on a per capita formula of those people over sixty years of age, and states vary in the degree of autonomy given to local administrators.

Medicaid   Title XIX of the Social Security Act, Medicaid, is a federal–state medical assistance program jointly financed by the federal and state governments. The federal share ranges from 50 to 78 percent depending on the state's income. The eligibility requirements and the benefits are determined by each state. As a general rule, those who are eligible for cash assistance are also covered by Medicaid; some states have a "medically indigent" category which covers those who are poor, but not receiving public assistance. While the benefits are not uniform among the states, most states cover inpatient and outpatient hospital care, laboratory and X-ray services, nursing facilities, physicians' services, and family planning services. Some states also cover dental care, eyeglasses, various rehabilitative services, intermediate services, and prescribed drugs.

Although the aged and many of the blind and disabled are covered by Medicare (see below), the more restrictive Medicare program has led many of these persons who are in the low income category to have their Medicare supplemented by Medicaid. In the illustrative fiscal year 1975, there were 24 million recipients of Medicaid benefits. Of these, 11 million were on welfare; 7 million were poor, but not on assistance; and 5 million were aged, blind, or disabled. Medicaid costs quadrupled from $4 million in the late 1960s to some $16 billion in 1977.[15]

Medicaid is the responsibility of a designated state agency (usually the public welfare department) which operates the program along federal guidelines. State or local administration follows cash assistance and food stamp patterns in each state.

Medicare   The Medicare program was established by Title XVIII of the 1965 amendments to the Social Security Act. Medicare may be characterized as an "insurance" program to which individuals contribute, as distinguished from Medicaid, which is an "assistance" program. Medicare is administered directly by the federal government through the Bureau of Health Insurance of the Social Security Administration. The Medicare program provides services to everyone 65 years of age or older. It also protects those disabled persons who have been entitled to Social Security payments for at least two years.

Medicare consists of two parts which may be described as follows:

1. "Part A" provides protection against hospital and related institutional costs. In the illustrative fiscal year 1975, nearly 5.5 million (of the 23.7 million people covered under "Part B") received services. The total payment for these services amounted to nearly $10.4 billion. Ninety-five percent of the elderly population in the United States is covered by this part of the Medicare program.

2. "Part B" covers physicians' and other nonhospital medical services. Again in fiscal 1975, 12.6 million (of the total 23.3 million covered by "Part B") received benefits. The total payment for services under this part amounted to nearly $3.8 billion. Over 94 percent of the aged population in the United States is covered under this section.

Hospital insurance pays inpatient hospital bills, except for the first $92 in each benefit period. Under medical insurance, the program pays $4 of every $5 of reasonable medical costs, except for the first $60 in each calendar year. Medicare costs are rising: it was projected that Medicare will cost an estimated $22 billion in fiscal 1977, a 23.5 percent increase over the $17.8 billion estimated for 1976.[16]

Law Enforcement Assistance Administration (LEAA) The Law Enforcement Assistance Administration is designed to assist states and local communities in strengthening their law enforcement operations. It has, however, some human services connections. Although it is not technically a public welfare program, monies spent for drug abuse and alcoholism services and for delinquency prevention clearly have an impact on the total public welfare environment in a community.

The law maintains six separate block grant and categorical grant programs for the states. While allowing wide discretion for expenditure, the law says states should focus specifically on a number of programs, including juvenile justice and treatment for drug and alcohol abuse. The federal share of this legislation was authorized at $3.2 billion. These funds were to be matched by 10 percent state money. Projects eligible for funding include planning grants for state and local governments; training, education, research, demonstration, and special grants; grants for correctional institutions and facilities; and grants for law enforcement purposes. Each state has a central authority appointed by the governor, and a group of regional committees, each of which makes grants in a designated area. The central group may also make direct grants.

Community Mental Health Centers (CMHC) The Community Mental Health Centers program is the major federal program in the development and delivery of community-based mental health services. From the inception of the program in 1963, the federal government has assisted in the development of nearly 600 community mental health centers under public (state and local) and voluntary auspices. These centers are located throughout the United States and serve areas in which some 86 million people reside.[17] In many communities, CMHCs represent the only accessible, locally based mental health services. In others, they have helped to coordinate a variety of existing resources, thus helping to reduce fragmentation and duplication of services. In most communities, however, federal support has served as the catalyst to develop needed services and programs. Without such support, the availability of community-based mental health services would, in many cases, be quite limited. A combination of state, local, and "third party" funds generally support these centers. Despite its progress, however, much remains to be accomplished. Of approximately 1,500 service or "catchment" areas in the United States, 60 percent still do not have federally funded CMHCs.

CMHCs are usually administered by either private or public nonprofit community organizations under the auspices of a local government. The federal monies available for the CMHCs are direct grants for an eight-year period, with an annually descending percentage of federal participation—from 90 percent in the first year to 30 percent in the eighth, and final, year.

Programs offered include comprehensive treatment and prevention programs for all ages; alcohol and drug abuse programs; crisis intervention and suicide prevention teams; rape treatment programs; and the provision of community-based care for individuals who would otherwise be institutionalized.

Child abuse   The Child Abuse and Prevention Act of 1974 established a National Center on Child Abuse in the HEW Office of Child Development. The center makes demonstration grants to public and voluntary agencies for training, creation of regional centers to provide multidisciplinary services, provision of consultants, and the establishment of innovative projects. In order to receive funds, states must have adequate laws in effect and sufficient personnel to carry out the intent of the law. In addition to the 1974 act, there are federal, state, and local programs to meet the costs of protective services mandated under Title IV-A (AFDC), Title IV-B (child welfare), and Title XX (social services).

Work Incentive Program (WIN)   The Work Incentive Program was created in 1968 to prepare AFDC recipients for paid employment through a combination of education, training, and work experience, plus supportive social services such as counseling and day care. Day care under the WIN program is funded 90 percent by the federal government. In 1967, the program was amended to require that a plan be developed for each appropriate AFDC family member, taking into account the goal of strengthening family life, fostering child development, and fulfilling the individual's potential for self-support. Nonexempt AFDC recipients (the ''exempt'' are defined as those who are ill or aged, or who must care for an ill or aged member of the household, or who are under 6 years of age) were required to register with manpower and employment services.

The program has had limited success, reaching only a million or so individuals by the mid-1970s. This situation has been due, at least in part, to the generally weak national employment situation throughout much of the 1970s.[18] The success in placing WIN ''graduates'' in the general job market has not been outstanding. It has been said that the training participants received was of minimal value. The federal strategy in recent years has therefore shifted to earlier job placement and less formal training and education. Administration usually follows the state–local patterns used in a given state for cash assistance, food stamps, and Medicaid.

Housing and community development   While they are not in the purview of a public welfare department, a large number of welfare and SSI recipients are residents of public housing, and many community development programs serve this population. Welfare recipients living in public housing projects may only be charged a certain amount of rent, that is, either 5 percent of their income or that portion of their welfare payment specified to meet housing costs. Many housing benefit programs are available to low income populations and are administered by local housing authorities.

In the Housing and Community Development Act of 1974, Title I specified as eligible for assistance those programs and services directed toward improving the community's public services and facilities, including those concerned with employment, economic development, crime prevention, child care, health, drug abuse, education, welfare, and recreation.

Summary   As the preceding brief discussion of more than a dozen programs has indicated, there is great complexity in the legislative and funding constraints placed on local government managers and their colleagues at the state level in the public welfare area. Further, programs emanating from the federal level of government have been in a state of flux for more than a decade, reflecting the wider public debate about the proper role of government in this area. Finally, it may be noted that a further complication is introduced by the fact that nonwelfare programs in such fields as law enforcement can and do have a welfare connotation. These complexities present severe challenges to government managers at all levels; however, one unifying theme is that all of these programs, by their presence or their absence, do have an impact on the well-being of the citizens of specific communities. For this reason alone, they are a necessary component of the decision-making environment in the public sector.

Welfare reform: issues and alternatives

The following discussion serves to place the programmatic elements of public welfare in wider context by noting some of the basic features of the ongoing national debate on this subject and identifying some of the major alternatives that have been proposed. The discussion is in three parts: first, an outline of the broad debate; second, an attempt to answer the question of "Whither welfare reform?"; and, third, a look at specific welfare reform proposals.

Welfare reform: the broad debate Over the past two decades or so, there has been growing dissatisfaction and debate over our current system—many observers would say nonsystem—of assistance support payments. The desire for change is found among liberals and conservatives alike and, while there is a divergence of opinion on what the ideal solution might be, it is generally agreed that the inadequacies and variety of programs (which often work against each other); the differing interpretations of the means tests; the status of the working poor; and the different state eligibility requirements all combine to render the program rife with inequities and contradictions. The net result is a costly administrative nightmare.

In the last few decades, Congress has enacted separate pieces of welfare-related legislation costing the taxpayers billions of dollars. Unfortunately, the nature of the congressional legislation and appropriations systems and of federal programs has resulted in a very fragmented system of planning, delivery, and administration. The result as of the later 1970s is often unnecessary duplication of certain services, gaps in other needed services, confusion among service deliverers and recipients, and, frequently, wasteful allocation of resources.

As a result of the fragmentation, uneven distribution of service, varying eligibility requirements, and lack of systematic relationships between the components of the welfare "system," the recipient is faced with a maze of services, and cash and "in kind" assistance programs, with little direction as to which is most appropriate to advantageously resolve his or her problem.

It is estimated that, as of the late 1970s, some 23 million people in the United States live in families that are below the poverty level.[19] There are more than 100 federally funded programs to help them, with both cash and "in kind" benefits. Yet all of these programs together have been successful in raising only about one-half of these families above the poverty level.

Probably the most comprehensive national study of the entire system currently available is that completed in 1975 by the Joint Economic Committee's Subcommittee on Fiscal Policy. Some of the most significant findings of this study are:

1. The law now provides substantial cash benefits to female-headed families in high income states while categorically excluding most male-headed families trapped in poverty by low wages, poor health, or frequent unemployment. The system thereby discriminates against the working poor, and encourages husbands to desert their families in order to enable them to get on welfare. The report recommends an end to categorical eligibility rules.
2. The existing multiplicity of welfare programs tends to smother work incentives for multibeneficiaries by reducing the net gain from work to as low as 25 or 15 cents on the dollar, or sometimes to zero. "Notches" in some programs produce situations where an extra dollar earned costs the family hundreds of dollars in benefits.
3. In fiscal 1975 federal expenditures on income security programs were projected to total $142 billion—triple the amount spent on these programs in 1968.

4. There are 11 committees of the House of Representatives, 10 of the Senate, and 9 Executive Department agencies that have jurisdiction over income security programs.
5. Because of the role of the states and localities in deciding whether to offer programs, to whom, and at what level, poorer states have tended to offer fewer programs to fewer people, at lower rates. Thus, federal funds are unevenly distributed.
6. The administration of the AFDC program is inefficient and error-ridden. A recent HEW survey of the program found that almost half of all cases were getting either too much or too little; some were totally ineligible. Since eligibility for food stamps and Medicaid are based on eligibility for AFDC, errors are compounded.
7. Errors abound for several reasons—benefits such as AFDC are based on a detailed examination of family circumstances and needs and, in most states, by family size and income, by the amount of rent and utilities paid, by need for a telephone or special diet, by amount and type of work expenses, and by many other factors that must be verified. Simple arithmetic errors and errors in judgment are inevitable. In the food stamp program, the price that a family must pay for its stamp allotment is related to income, but there is a long list of expenditures that can be deducted from income, and some income is ignored altogether.
8. Another problem is that several agencies at the local level dealing with the same family often do not share information or administrative costs. This has implications for recipients too, when they must shuttle back and forth from agency to agency and find their way through a maze of disparate rules and procedures.

What is the "bottom line" of this dismal situation? The issue in the United States, simply stated, is how to eliminate poverty in what is a generally affluent society; how to use government transfers of resources (primarily money) equitably, that is, in ways that will leave no one in want and will not create a disincentive to work. Many hold that incentives for work must exist in order to sustain our ongoing ability to produce. The present vast system of benefits and transfer programs suffers from the absence of strong income maintenance programs and cohesive social services policies. Social insurance, income "in kind," public assistance, and other transfer programs are created over time without any consideration of the policy relations between one and the other. The result is a crazy quilt of overlapping benefits and inequitable treatment of program beneficiaries.

The Subcommittee on Fiscal Policy study already noted raised a number of basic policy issues.

1. Work incentives—any disincentives for recipients to work which are caused by the design of one program are almost always worsened when additional benefits are available to those same recipients under other programs.
2. Family stability—other financial incentives, which may prompt such behavior as family splitting and which grow out of program design, are sometimes magnified by benefit combinations available to only certain types of families.
3. Administrative error—the costs of inefficiency and error in one program may be multiplied through the link in eligibility rules and other administrative procedures among different programs.
4. Differential treatment based on personal characteristics—the differential provisions of individual programs with respect to such eligibility factors as age, sex of family head, place and type of employment, and family size may be intensified by other programs with similar provisions.
5. Program inefficiency—program interrelationships often serve to undo the intent of Congress in passing legislation for a single program; for example, benefits

to one program may be increased only to result in a dollar-for-dollar substitution for other benefits, thus resulting in no net gain for some of the intended beneficiaries.

6. Administrative complexity—multiple benefit eligibility requires the maintenance of similar beneficiary records by many different agencies, increases the workload involved in agency auditing procedures, and often causes recipients to have to deal regularly with several physically separate bureaucracies.

The subcommittee further pointed out that the interrelationships among programs can undermine their efficiency as tools to alleviate poverty. For example, low income, aged persons who are eligible for Old Age Assistance may not be better off by having entitlement to veterans' pensions or Social Security benefits and may, in fact, be worse off if they are eligible for both. Benefit increases for either of these two programs can cause the public assistance recipient to suffer a loss in real income.

A male receiving unemployment insurance may have a total income that is less than the benefits he would have received from the unemployed father segment of the AFDC program, but, by law, he is not eligible for AFDC funds while he is eligible for unemployment compensation. Suggested by some is a change that would permit eligible individuals to supplement their unemployment insurance with AFDC up to the AFDC level.

Although the SSI program (Title XVI) is far from problem-free, it represents the first step ever taken by the United States toward a guaranteed income policy, albeit a limited and categorical one. Had the political, social, and emotional conflicts of opinion been resolved, the ill-fated Family Assistance Plan (FAP) forwarded by the Nixon administration might have been another fundamental step in this direction. Be that as it may, in the later 1970s, the work incentives that are so much a part of any income transfer plan were insufficiently represented in the existing set of arrangements. For example, in the case of one-tenth of all families on public assistance, the employment (or reemployment) of the head of the household would cause the family's total benefits to be reduced by 85 cents for every additional dollar earned. Leaving the assistance rolls also often automatically makes families ineligible for medical assistance and food benefits.

Testing for eligibility, often referred to as "means testing," is controversial. The real issue is often the method of application of the test. Means testing of some sort, however, seems inevitable as a way to determine the level of income needed to maintain people with predictable resources at a certain standard of living and to fix charges for other services not related to income support.

Whither welfare reform?   Given the situation just described, it is perhaps understandable that, although for the past several years there has been considerable interest in "welfare reform" in Washington, in state capitals, and among the general public, the basic problems have not been solved and nothing like a consensus has developed as to what the preferable mechanism for such a solution might be. The Brookings Institution's budget studies for 1972 stated cogently the basic questions about U.S. programs that purport to provide a decent living standard for those not otherwise able to achieve it:

Is it necessary to have so many diverse programs to accomplish this objective? Is the present emphasis on categorical status instead of need appropriate as a condition of eligibility? To what extent should benefits be tied to prior contributions, and how should these contributions be levied? What is the rationale for providing benefits in-kind, instead of paying cash and letting beneficiaries decide how to spend it? Finally, how should benefits be set—how much variation from state to state or community is appropriate, and how should benefits be changed over time to reflect inflation and general increases in living standards? [20]

An additional question is how to treat the "working poor"—those who are working but whose earnings, based on family size, provide an income below that which they would receive if they stopped work and went on public assistance.

The 1976 task force of the National Conference on Social Welfare, in "Principles for an Income Security System for the United States," established a number of goals to be used as measures against which to assess our future achievements in income security. A basic premise underlying these goals is that "consideration of reform must take place in the context of an approach that recognizes the tax, transfer, and employment systems all as instruments of income security policy." [21] For far too long these independent systems have been viewed separately with the result that they often conflict, contradict, and even negate one another.

The task force established the following goals as measures against which to assess our future efforts in income security:

1. The provision of insurance against loss of earnings due to temporary unemployment, disability, retirement, or death, and to cushion the hardship that would otherwise be incurred. The instruments for accomplishing this include private savings pensions and private insurance, as well as such public programs as unemployment insurance (UI), Social Security, and workers' compensation. Eligibility and benefit levels in the public program depend primarily upon a worker's prior and current earnings.

2. The alleviation of poverty. The means-tested cash programs (Aid to Families with Dependent Children, serving primarily single-parent families, and Supplemental Security Income, serving the elderly, blind, and disabled) are designed to guarantee large segments of the population that income losses will never plunge them below some minimum level. In addition, the social insurance programs prevent large numbers of people from ever falling into poverty by replacing lost earnings.

3. The equalization of opportunity and access to some minimum amount of highly valued goods and services. Programs to achieve this goal include food stamps, Medicaid, low income housing programs, and others that provide specific purchasing power to low income people. Other programs in this category, such as Medicare, involve public sharing in extraordinary family expenditures without regard to family income.

4. The current inadequacies in the level of benefits and in their distribution must be corrected with priority being given to increasing the level for the lowest income groups.

5. Comparable needs should be comparably met. Demographic characteristics that are irrelevant to a determination of need should not be considered.

6. Primary reliance should be placed upon direct cash payments to meet the minimum basic consumption needs of the lower income population.

7. The federal government should finance, administer, and set standards for the basic set of transfer programs (both means-tested and insurance).

8. Criteria for program eligibility and benefits should be simple, objective, and clearly stated to achieve equal treatment for those with equal needs.

While the issues listed above represent what many believe would make an ideal program and, as the melancholy Dane observed, a "consummation devoutly to be wished," it is not likely that they will be implemented in the foreseeable future. In working toward more economically, politically, and socially realistic changes, certain fundamental issues must be addressed. If they are not resolved, then at least an acceptable compromise can be sought. There are two such main issues.

Universal and means test supports   Universal programs have the advantage of no stigma—they represent rights. The primary argument against them is that they provide benefits to those not in economic need.

Contributory and noncontributory programs The old argument that contributory and noncontributory programs are incompatible in one system is eroding. The advent of SSI has produced a situation in which former categorical, noncontributory programs are administered by the federal contributory Social Security program agency. SSI, like public assistance, is means-tested, based on a national standard. Social Security, an insurance program, is also means-tested, but individual earnings are used as the basis for payment levels. Other income besides earnings generally reduces the SSI benefit, but not the contributory Social Security benefit.

Welfare reform proposals As a new national administration came to power in 1977, there was no shortage of welfare reform proposals, each receiving varying degrees of public consideration. Probably none of those before us at time of writing will be adopted in their present form, but certain aspects of several may be adopted incrementally. An attempt at a full outline of each—even an undetailed one—is beyond the scope (and space) of this chapter. However, since the issue will be a major one for Congress and the Carter administration, this section will list the basic principles advanced by various advocates. There are eight main options, and each will be discussed in turn.

Option one State and local governments are pressing for a larger federal share of the cost of cash assistance payments and Medicaid. Some would also like to see full federal administration of these programs. Others favor full federal fiscal responsibility with state–local administration. Federal administration (as experience has demonstrated with SSI) must have the backing of local resources to deal with those emergency situations and changing conditions that require prompt attention. Certainly no one has proposed that the federal government administer social services that require close personal contact. Some place cash assistance recipients in the category of those who also need this type of personal relationship with the service provider.

Option two A tax credit or form of negative income tax has been proposed. Former Congresswoman Martha Griffiths in 1975 introduced a program that would replace the personal tax exemption ($750 in 1975) with a rebatable tax credit of $225. The credit would be deducted from tax liabilities, with any excess credits paid to the filer. Subsistence allowances would be paid to poor families and individuals and reduced by fifty cents for every dollar earned by recipients net of social security taxes. The total value of grants and tax credits would be $3,600 for a penniless two-adult family of four, and $3,000 for a penniless one-adult family of four. The federal government would fund and operate this program. This option provides a work incentive, since benefits are not designed to provide adequate levels of living.

Option three The National Urban League has proposed that the welfare and tax systems be merged to create a Credit Income Tax (CIT) that would provide each person with either a basic annual grant or a tax credit from the government.[22] Everyone—with and without income—would file a tax return. A single rate would be applied to all income for the initial calculation of tax. The actual tax to be paid would be figured as the difference between the amount of the tax credit to which the individual is entitled and the amount of the initial "single vote" calculation (the primary tax). Thus, if a person had no income, the primary tax would be zero, and he or she would receive the total amount of the tax credit in cash. As income rose, the amount of taxes to be paid would increase and the net amount of the tax credit would decline until at some level, as yet undetermined, the personal primary tax would equal the tax credit and the person would pay no tax and receive no credit. As income rose above that level, he or she would pay an income tax. This would be a universal program: therefore, there would be no means test, except for a declaration of income on the tax return; no work requirement; and no criteria for eligibility, except an economic one. There would be no stigma, and the tremendous size and inefficency of the current system of uncoordinated programs would be eliminated.

Option four　The National Governors' Conference urges that there be a national unified income maintenance program for all eligible persons below an established minimum level of income.[23] A national payment level (adjusted for regional differences) would be established by the Congress with full federal financing at 75 percent of all costs. Consideration would be given to a full range of administrative options, and the federal program would be developed so as to give full consideration to all existing social insurance programs. Work requirements would be established for the able-bodied, and existing disincentives for work and self-sufficiency would be eliminated.

Option five　The National Council of State Public Welfare Administrators has proposed that income maintenance be made available through a single payment mechanism for food, clothing, and shelter to all persons (single adults, childless couples, intact and single-headed families) with incomes below an established minimum income level. Eligibility should be conditioned upon compliance with a resources test.

In place of the current AFDC, AFDC-U, food stamp, and SSI programs, the federal government should establish an income maintenance program with a minimum standard of cash assistance paid by the federal government based upon the current SSI allowance for eligible individuals. As an example, this payment would equal $157.70 per month for the first eligible adult in a payment unit and $78.90 for each additional eligible member of the payment unit. Additional federal benefits could be provided to the "working poor." Work or training would be required for those not exempt for reasons of health or responsibility for dependents.

Option six　The National Association of Counties advocates a more national and simplified welfare system, accomplished by the gradual replacement of AFDC and general assistance programs with three discrete programs covering employment security, income security, and social services.[24] Eligibility for benefits would be based solely on need.

Option seven　Another proposal with some support is to replace all categorical systems with a negative income tax (NIT). While intriguing for its simplicity of administration (it would make use of the already existing tax system), it does present some programmatic difficulties that run afoul of the nonpoverty objectives of certain income assistance programs. The three major objections are: (1) unemployment compensation provides temporary relief between jobs and protects an employer's work force; (2) Social Security is based on prior earnings and provides benefits to those with other income; (3) civil and military service retirement benefits and most private pensions are not reduced by other earnings.

Public assistance, if based on national standards and low wage employment could, in part, respond easily to an NIT type of system. There would be a benefit automatically paid when a family income falls below a defined standard of need. There are, however, four main drawbacks:

1. A high minimum guarantee and a high marginal tax rate would provide generous income support for the very poor, but work incentives would suffer since every dollar of earnings would result in a large reduction in benefits.
2. Conversely, a low minimum guarantee and a low marginal tax rate would be conducive to a work effort, but would not provide a decent income for those who cannot work.

3. Deciding who should work is a key question, making such a system difficult to agree upon and administer.
4. The guarantee and tax rate could be differentiated according to categories. This could lead to the same notches and incentive problems in the present public assistance system.

Option eight One approach receiving attention in the later 1970s is to separate cash assistance for people in the labor force (and those only temporarily outside of it) from that for people who are not expected to be in the labor force at all. Such proposals would administer together, for instance, unemployment compensation, employment services, work training, rehabilitation, and cash assistance for working people.

Summary: the outlook Irrespective of which particular programs may be adopted in final legislative form over the later 1970s and the 1980s, certain basic policy and methodological issues seem certain to remain. Local government managers dealing directly or indirectly with the public welfare function as it helps shape their communities will doubtless find themselves considering these matters as well as the minutiae of welfare administration.

For example, one of the first questions that Congress and the administration will have to answer, regardless of what plan is agreed upon, is the method of finance. Funds for all kinds of public social needs must come either from reduced expenditure on other programs or from increased taxation. More than $137 billion (35 percent) of the total fiscal 1977 federal budget, for example, was being used for income security assistance.[25] Payroll taxes alone amounted to $113 billion; Social Security, our largest income security program, was in fiscal stress; and voters clearly want lower, not higher, taxes. It is doubtful that any aspect of welfare reform carrying an increased price tag will make much progress in the near future.

Some who object to "in-kind programs" hold that ability to purchase outright presently subsidized food, housing, medical care, and education services would tend to improve these programs. Others hold that reforming the programs is the key issue. "In-kind" benefits have been increasing tremendously and it is fair to speculate that, with few exceptions, they will continue and perhaps expand—particularly in the field of health and education. From 1960–73, in fact, federal "in-kind" support expenditures grew from $400 million per year to an estimated $19 billion.[26]

Underlying all of the debate on methodology, the basic policy question to be answered is: Should eligibility and benefits be based on need, regardless of family composition and the past or present work status of the individual? Or should there be a different and more generous system that rewards those low income people who are part of the labor market—"the working poor"—or who were part of the labor market and can no longer work—e.g., the aged and disabled?

There is no guarantee that any proposed new system or possible improvements in present programs will reduce public assistance rolls. Errors and abuses can certainly be reduced by applying good management techniques. In the long run, only the fullest possible employment can significantly minimize the numbers receiving assistance. Advanced technological societies, by their very nature, produce people who, temporarily or permanently, cannot cope with society's demands on them. Government—federal, state, and local—has responsibility to help them not only to survive, but to function at the highest possible level.

Patterns of state and local government organization for public welfare

Earlier portions of this discussion—an overview of the public welfare function; an outline of the major components of welfare programs; and an analysis of welfare reform issues and proposals—have taken a look at public welfare at a rather general level, an approach made necessary, as has been indicated, by the complexity and fluid nature of the subject matter. The discussion now concludes, however, with a brief survey of the patterns of actual state and local organization for public welfare, and of some of the managerial aspects stemming from this distribution.

Earlier in the discussion, aspects of federal, state, and local funding were described. It is important to note, however, that the administrative responsibility and structures for operating programs are not always related to the location of fiscal responsibility. Practically all federally legislated and funded public welfare programs flow from the federal government to the state. Each generally requires that either the governor or the legislature (sometimes both) designate a state agency as the authority to administer the program and the funds. Federal law and regulation in most instances allows the state agency, while continuing to maintain overall responsibility, to delegate the administration of the program to a local government, to a combination of local governments or, in some cases, to private or quasi-public bodies.

Basic patterns For purposes of administration of the traditional public welfare programs (public assistance, Medicaid, food stamps, and child welfare), thirty-five of the states (including Puerto Rico, the Virgin Islands, and the District of Columbia) have state administration as of 1976 and eighteen have local.

In thirty-six of the states the traditional public welfare programs are joined in an "umbrella" agency. Of the states with umbrella agencies, twenty-seven have state administration, and nine have local. These figures, of course, change over the course of time, but the main lines of the division of responsibility are clear.[27]

While umbrella agencies have existed in some states for many years, there has been a recent expansion of this type of state and local organization. The concept of the umbrella agency has to do with the desire for administrative efficiency and services integration. This movement arose from the recognition that human services often deal with individuals in the same families and there are many multi-problem families who receive services from a variety of sources. The most consistent element in umbrella agencies is that they contain the traditional public welfare programs—public assistance, child welfare, Medicaid, and food stamps. Beyond these the pattern varies. Some states combine public welfare programs with health or vocational rehabilitation; a limited number even include unemployment compensation and employment services. The best current reference for understanding these structures is contained in the *Public Welfare Directory,* published annually by the American Public Welfare Association.[28]

The administrative considerations outlined above do not apply to general assistance, which has no federal funds at all. Some idea of state agency responsibility and local unit of administration may be shown by the following illustrative figures for the 1970s. As far as state agency responsibility was concerned, general assistance was *administered* by the state public assistance agency through its local offices in twenty-one states; general assistance was *supervised* by the state public assistance agency through local offices which were branches of county or municipal government (usually also serving federally aided programs) in nine states. Further, general assistance was administered by local political jurisdictions in twenty-four states: in seven of those states there was specifically limited responsibility exercised by the state public assistance agency, and in seventeen there was no responsibility exercised by a state agency.

As far as the local unit of administration is concerned, the *county* was the most common unit (geographical area or political subdivision of government) for administration of general assistance (some offices servicing more than one county) in thirty-eight states; townships, towns, municipalities, or combinations of such local units were the most common administrative units in nine states; and a *defined area unit* of the state public assistance agency was the unit of administration in seven states.[29]

Administrative characteristics of public welfare organizations Generally, the umbrella agencies are called departments of "human resources" or "human services," though some are still departments of "public welfare." The nonumbrella agencies—those with only the traditional functions—are usually departments of "public welfare" or "social services." What administrative characteristics of interest to the manager do these entities possess? Whether state- or locally administered, the structure of the public welfare agency is usually the same for purposes of cash assistance, Medicaid, and food stamps. If the programs are state administered, they are carried out through local district offices, which usually follow local, county, or multicounty lines. If a county is large, the state-administered agencies may have subdistricts within the jurisdiction. County-administered programs use the same general structure and, depending on size, may also have district offices. Both state- and county-administered programs have a director and several bureaus or divisions. One bureau usually administers income maintenance programs and determines eligibility for cash assistance, food stamps, and Medicaid; another handles social services; and, in most instances, child welfare functions are in a separate bureau.

There are some few instances in the case of counties which vary from this pattern because the child welfare function is separated from cash assistance, food stamps, Medicaid, and general social services functions. Federal regulations require that cash assistance and social services be administered through separate operating units although they can be part of the same overall structure.

There are also some states where the eligibility for Medicaid is determined by the same agency that determines cash assistance eligibility, but the policies are determined by a health authority. Sometimes this function is within an umbrella agency, other times in a separate department.

Some county governments have created umbrella agencies. There are some cities which also have put their human services functions into one overall department. While small in number, the concept is broadening at the local level with increasing recognition that there is value in putting programs together for better administration and easier access for clients.

Recent developments Among the most popular and promising recent developments are those which package a variety of services and put them together in one-stop service centers so that citizens are able to avoid both the transportation difficulties presented by geographically separated facilities and the bureaucratic complexities involved in making application to a variety of categorical programs. The categorical programs themselves do not necessarily need to be generalized in such arrangements any more than do medical specialties in a hospital. There is, however, controversy over whether coordination and integration, in fact, take away from the quality of specialties.

Another interesting development has been the delivery of public assistance checks through banks to avoid losses in the mail and to diminish the possibility of fraudulent claims for lost checks which often result in duplicate payments. Supported by strong federal legislation, considerable attention is being given to collecting support from absent fathers. Local counties, judicial authorities, and spouses are given financial incentives to assist in location and collection.

The difficulties and complexities of administering massive money grant and payment entitlement programs, including Medicaid and food stamps, have resulted in a wide variety of abuses by a relatively small number of recipients and vendors. While fraud is a small percentage of the total, it adds up to a considerable number of dollars; federal, state, and county governments have applied rigid auditing and investigative techniques as well as sophisticated automated devices to assist in controlling the program and in minimizing abuses and error. A great deal of emphasis is placed on staff training, legal services, and hearings to insure that people get their entitlements and that abuses are minimized. State and federal courts have given strong support to public welfare programs as entitlements, and a great deal of emphasis is placed on providing services to clients who believe they have been treated unfairly and the public welfare agencies must have a sophisticated hearing process in place.

In the administration of the public assistance, cash assistance, and food stamp programs, there is very little involvement of nonpublic personnel (except for the use of banks, for instance, in distributing checks and food stamps). Eligibility determination and delivery of benefits is done by county and state personnel directly.

It is in the Medicaid and the social services programs that other public and voluntary agencies of all types are involved. Both the state- and county-administered agencies buy services from all types of health service suppliers for Medicaid or from a variety of public and voluntary agencies for such activities as day care, family planning, legal services, counseling, homemaker services, etc. It is in these programs that the local governments are often very much involved. Sometimes school districts provide day care services under contract with state or county public welfare authorities. Housing agencies, and a wide range of philanthropic organizations and city departments which engage in personal services to people, contract with county or state governments to sell services to eligible people.

Conclusion: the outlook for local governments

This section began with a discussion of the public welfare function, placing it in its historical and managerial context. A number of brief outlines of some of the primary components of existing welfare programs followed—including, to name a few, Supplementary Security Income, Medicaid, food stamps, the Work Incentive Program, and Community Mental Health Centers. The section went on to treat, first, the issue of welfare reform—both the ongoing debate and a number of specific proposals for reform—and, then, the organizational patterns of public welfare programs in state and local governments.

Efforts at increasing and improving the participation of local governments in the programs described throughout this discussion will continue. The effort will not be to decentralize in giving and furnishing responsibility to local governments. There will be continued attempts to bring citizens and local governments to more participation with respect to the establishment of policy for improving the administration of services, particularly with a view to ensuring that people get their entitlements and that access to service is less difficult. While administrative differences will increasingly become more sophisticated, the size of the programs and the numbers of people involved make it impossible to reduce their complexity.

Specifically for the city manager, the task in this particular set of programs is to understand state and county agencies and the manner in which they function for the citizens of the city. Participation with state and county agencies is, in the long run, the most effective way for a city manager to deal with these programs.

Counseling services

What is counseling? What should the city manager and county administrator and other interested local government decision makers know about this area of human services? How do such services operate in practice?

A good working definition of contemporary counseling is that it is an interventive method used by professionally trained persons for the purpose of enabling individuals and groups to resolve problems that are internal and/or external in origin, thus "freeing them up" to achieve goals that they have established for themselves. From the viewpoint of the city manager and county administrator, counseling is an element of direct service delivery which is, of course, the essence of a given human services operation. Most human services programs either provide counseling directly or refer their clients to other agencies for counseling. A considerable portion of agency budgets may be allocated for the provision of counseling. The contemporary local government official is increasingly charged with developing and implementing such programs from scratch, in addition to operating programs that represent federal and state policies. Counseling services can therefore no longer be approached by using the limited managerial perspective that measures them solely in terms of simplistic staff-to-clients-served ratios. Many public administrators have therefore come to realize that, if they are realistically to hold themselves and their agencies accountable for the efficiency and effectiveness of service delivery, they must acquire more of an in-depth understanding of counseling services and how they operate.

This section of Chapter 12 therefore takes a look at four critical issues which must be explored and acted upon by public administrators if sound judgments and evaluations are to be made where the funding and operation of counseling services are concerned. The issues can be expressed in the form of questions. What is counseling and who can counsel? What traditional roles are assigned to counseling services? What is the role of the counselor in an age of accountability? And, last but not least, what mechanisms exist for providing counseling services?

In the following discussion, some brief answers are offered to the first three questions. The answer to the fourth question is provided by taking an illustrative look at the selection and availability of counseling services in one metropolitan area familiar to the writer.

What is counseling and who can counsel?

The average public administrator, as the average layman, has a generalized concept of the definition of the term "counseling." In general, it is understood to be a process which involves a professional person helping a "client" to resolve some problem. This understanding is consistent with one definition which describes it as ". . . advice; opinion or instruction given in directing the judgement or conduct of another." [30] Can this generalized concept universally be translated to mean a given parameter of specific competencies on the part of all counselors who utilize a common process in helping people? If it could, then the decision-making process of the public administrator would be relatively simple. In reality, such consensus is farthest from the truth. The distinction between counseling and psychotherapy, for example, can have considerable budgetary, as well as conceptual, significance for local administrators.

Counseling is provided by parents, priests, ministers, teachers, faculty advisors, social workers, marriage counselors, vocational counselors, psychologists, and others. These persons are referred to by Galdston as ". . . lay psychotherapists [who] have been such for centuries past and are bound to continue as such for a long time to come." [31] This distinction suggests that a difference does exist between the competencies and counseling processes employed by clinically trained medical psychotherapists and lay psychotherapists. In practice, a similar schism exists among lay psychotherapists. Clinical psychologists and caseworkers are much more apt to identify themselves as psychotherapists than as counselors. Ministerial, educational, and vocational personnel tend to identify themselves as counselors. Psychotherapists are perceived by themselves and many others as representing a higher level of professional competence and status. A public administrator who has to make administrative decisions relative to the funding of counseling services must be cognizant of the fact that programs that plan to employ psychotherapists will cost considerably more than those using counselors. A specialized curriculum content has been developed to train psychiatrists, who traditionally represent the highest level of psychotherapeutic competency. Other professional disciplines representative of the human services industry have similar content in their professional education programs.

Despite the fact that the curriculum content of these disciplines is duplicated to a great degree in professional practice, there exists a hierarchical "pecking order" characterized, in part, by the belief that psychiatry is the only discipline capable of dealing with individual functional problems that are internal in origin. It is suggested that the nonmedical therapists have had to ". . . evolve ways of handling people in distress, largely oriented around advice giving and active interference in manifest environmental disorders." [32] Clinical psychologists, on the other hand, view themselves as psychotherapists and tend to see caseworkers as professionals who should limit their activities to environmental manipulation in relation to a given client's problem. Clinically trained caseworkers manifest similar attitudes toward other helping professions, often underestimating the abilities of psychiatrists and clinical psychologists.

It is interesting to note that:

There is a . . . paucity of research that supports the present, more traditional occupational structure in the human service fields and their related requirements that staff members must have certain levels of education and experiences. These requirements have largely grown out of conviction and judgment rather than research-based knowledge. For example, the little research that is available indicates a general lack of close relationship between education and test scores, on the one hand, and job performance, on the other. [33]

Throughout the human services structure, ". . . there is a marked lack of consensus concerning the appropriate roles for personnel." [34] This lack of clarity exists among as well as within professional disciplines. In the latter case, the greatest conflict exists between staff persons with professional training in a given discipline and those without such training. This continuing conflict has existed since the early 1960s.

There are difficulties, therefore, regarding the definition of counseling, the training of counselors, and the "pecking order" within this field. These are mentioned here solely because they have important managerial implications. Different levels of competence come with different price tags. There may be a trade-off between the budgetary savings associated with the use of paraprofessionals and the nonbudgetary "costs" of bad feeling between groups of personnel. Public administrators wishing to have all the facts at their disposal when making funding or staffing recommendations regarding counseling services are increasingly finding it helpful to take all the above factors into consideration. The current fiscal crises in local government lend urgency to any decisions regarding the disposition of scarce resources, and counseling services—which can be expensive—are no exception.

What traditional roles are assigned to counseling services?

Public administrators assessing proposals for direct service programs also need information as to the goals and objectives implicit in the use of counseling services as an interventive method or process. Although counseling has been understood historically to relate to the resolution of individual problems, it has been understood in broader context in the human services "industry" as a resource potentially capable of helping resolve a range of social problems external to the individual.

The theoretical development of counseling need not concern us in the present discussion. [35] Essentially, there has been an interplay between treatment of the individual (often with heavy debts to Freudian psychotherapy); treatment of individual and familial problems in a group setting (witness the rise of many forms of group therapy, some of them esoteric, from the 1960s on); and, most pertinently for present purposes, treatment as a viable process for addressing social reforms (again, in ascendancy since the 1960s). This last approach has had its critics:

There is a recurrent view that somehow the poor, if only they applied themselves better, would be poor no longer. It is postulated that the poor, through lack of diligence and maladaptive life styles, squander job opportunities. The solution thus lies in counseling them to do better.[36]

The assumption that counseling would resolve the external problem of poverty, has been particularly prevalent in the area of direct services as an element of the overall public welfare system discussed in the preceding section of this chapter. Prior to the separation of the assistance payment from the counseling function, all public assistance recipients were assigned to a caseworker. In addition to an exhaustive needs assessment regarding financial need, applicants were routinely subjected to an in-depth social history inquiry which sought to identify what it was, in their backgrounds or environments, that led to a dependency on public assistance. There was considerable emphasis placed on recruiting professional staff and on securing professional training for existing staff. These policies were predicated upon the assumption (now generally regarded as fallacious) that the more competent the staff, the greater the reduction in the number of dependent persons.

It was also during the 1960s, however, that numerous human services planners and public policy makers returned to the pioneering formulations of the 1920s, relating activities more appropriately to the causes of problems:

There are very few things which are crystal clear in the poverty picture, but the aspect of the problem which comes closest to being self-evident is that there are simply not enough jobs, as jobs are currently defined, for the poor. No amount of counseling will alter this situation. And, no amount of counseling will, given the current prerequisites for employment, create jobs for the poor.[37]

The basic managerial conclusion that can perhaps be drawn from this ongoing debate as to the role of counseling services is that public administrators must view poverty as a social condition rather than a personal trait.[38] Given this framework, they must then be clear as to the specific areas within which counseling may be an appropriate resource for problem resolution.

Figure 12–1   Counseling—in a broad variety of formats and settings—may be viewed simply as a tool for dealing with some area of individual concern. (Source: Courtesy of the City of La Habra, California.)

What is the role of the counselor
in an age of accountability?

"Accountability" is a word much used in discussions of the role of government in the post-Watergate era. As one observer has put it:

A fundamental tenet of a democratic society holds that agencies and organizations, public or voluntary, entrusted with public resources and the authority for applying them have a responsibility to render a full accounting of their activities. This accountability is inherent in our governmental process and is carried over into the field of human services, particularly, among social welfare agencies supported by public funds.[39]

Although this concept of accountability is generally understood and accepted by our total society, local government managers will be aware that it tends to provoke responses of suspicion and hostility on the part of human services professionals. It is because of these responses that some local public administrators encounter difficulty in communicating with human services planners. The latter group sometimes operates under the implicit assumption that, because of their professional identity, they know what is right and their judgments should not be questioned. They thus view requests for accountability as expressions of hostility toward social programs generally and toward them as professionals specifically. From the managerial standpoint, it is unfortunate that they do not view evaluative measures and procedures as positive contributors to human services program planning and implementation.

Scott Briar, in his preface to *Social Work in the New Age of Accountability,* states that:

. . . Many of the questions asked under the accountability rubric are legitimate questions, not readily interpreted as a mask for other motives. "Is that program effective?" is a fair and reasonable question which does not necessarily imply that the questioner dislikes the program. It is, however, not an easy question to answer or, more accurately, more difficult to answer than it was in simpler times, when scientific sophistication was less developed and less widespread.[40]

In order to make objective nonpolitical decisions, the public administrator should utilize some specific criteria for assessing proposals which seek fiscal support for counseling services. With the increased emphasis on accountability, numerous guidelines for evaluating such proposals have been developed. The major themes which run through such guidelines are:

1. Counseling should provide appropriate services to address given clients' problem situations and should not be represented as a "grab bag" activity that will resolve a wide range of community problems.
2. Appropriate concern should be given to organization, program inputs, and effective management; however, these should not be viewed as ends in and of themselves.
3. Emphasis should be placed on output: it should be determined at the beginning how the counseling activity will further the objectives that the clients have established for themselves.

In addition to addressing these basic areas, the public administrator should require that sound evaluative procedures be developed, of the type discussed in Chapter 10. Such a design should, at a minimum, ensure the establishment of procedures which have the capacity to determine the extent to which quantifiable objectives were or were not achieved.

Selected counseling services:
availability in a metropolitan area

The policy questions concerning the role and nature of counseling services in today's local government environment which have just been discussed will be fa-

miliar to many local government managers, and will touch on concerns emphasized throughout the earlier portions of this book. But how do counseling services
operate in practice? The following discussion takes a look at the nature and extent
of counseling services available for alcoholics, drug abusers, families, and youth
in the greater Atlanta area. In addition to its familiarity to the writer, Atlanta has
numerous demographic features similar to those of other cities throughout the nation. Its human services delivery system likewise has characteristics that are repli-
cated elsewhere. Managers will, of course, wish to assess the following discussion
in the light of the size and socioeconomic traits of their own communities.

By way of a brief introduction, it may be noted that Atlanta is the capital of the
state of Georgia and is the commercial, industrial, and financial "capital" of the
southeastern portion of the United States. Greater Atlanta encompasses five counties and has a population of nearly half a million. As with other communities of
similar size, poor citizens reside within the inner city and middle income
citizens—blacks and white—have tended to migrate to the suburbs.

Counseling services for alcoholics   The Metropolitan Atlanta Council on Alcohol and Drugs, Inc., estimates that there are approximately 60,000 alcoholics and
alcohol abusers in the community. When one thinks in terms of the "significant
others" directly affected by the victims' problems, the potential target group for
treatment is massive.

The *Directory of Community Services* of the United Way of Metropolitan Atlanta, Inc., lists twenty-six public and private agencies that provide some level of
counseling services for alcoholics and/or their families. There is a fifty–fifty split
between publicly and privately supported agencies.[41]

The least complex group of agencies are those that are privately supported. Out
of a total of thirteen, only three receive funds from the United Way, and counseling services for the alcoholic are incidental to other service areas. The ten
remaining privately supported agencies are either church-related or dependent
on independent, and aggressive, "scrounging" efforts. The agencies funded by
United Way generally are staffed by professionally trained clinicians; the others,
more often than not, by untrained, but dedicated volunteers. For the most part, the
clientele of such agencies are the inveterate, "skid row" alcoholics.

What's that case of Scotch doing in the filing cabinet?   The village of
Skokie, Illinois, established the first local government employee alcoholism
program in that state. As part of the pro-gram, all supervisors have received
training in how to assist employees who have alcohol or drug-related problems.
Where there is unsatisfactory job per-formance resulting from such problems,
it is the supervisor's responsibility to refer the employee for diagnosis and
treatment. Great care is taken to ensure that the rights of the employee are
respected. A public health nurse has been assigned the responsibility for
coordinating referrals between village departments and the various therapeutic agencies. Every effort is made to encourage employees who suspect that
they may have an alcoholism problem to seek help. The response has been
excellent.

Six county-administered community mental health centers provide the most
comprehensive counseling arrangement. It has been found that the more distant
the facility is from the central city, the more likely the clientele is to be white and
in the lower middle class socioeconomic bracket. It is interesting to note also that
county and city facilities located in geographic areas with the highest concentration of black residents do not have a predominantly black client group or staff.

The primary counseling resources available to and used by black alcoholics and
their families are furnished by two comprehensive community mental health

centers and nine divisional units of the Alcoholism Treatment Program of Economic Opportunity Atlanta, Inc. (EOA). The mental health centers are supported by federal, state, and county funds and, because the level of funding is relatively high, they have been in a position to hire a professionally trained, experienced staff. The EOA programs generally have employed more paraprofessional than professional staff.

A study of the needs of the black alcoholic in the greater Atlanta area found ". . . that an average of 80 percent of the black alcoholics needing service are not being reached." [42] No study has been conducted to establish the service needs of the total population or the capacity of the community to respond to those needs.

Counseling services for drug addicts Agencies which provide counseling services to drug addicts and their famiies in the greater Atlanta area are characterized by a fifty–fifty split between the public and private sector as with alcoholism counseling services. Catholic Social Services and the Jewish Family Service are the only United Way-supported private agencies providing services to this target group.

The community has nine storefront and residential facilities that are technically classified as private agencies. These agencies tend to design their programs with an eye to responding to the needs of the "street people" who congregate in the inner-city neighborhoods. The staffs of these agencies are often comprised of both nonusers and ex-addicts. Members of this latter group sometimes take the position that addiction has to have been experienced before someone can effectively counsel a present addict. The truth in this, and the potential effectiveness of such an approach, can be compared with the counseling format used by Alcoholics Annomyous. Most of these programs in Atlanta operate under a "contract for services" with the Georgia Department of Human Resources.

EOA, after assessing the success and failures of numerous programs supposedly serving the young addict, decided to take a different approach when staffing a new program designed to divert addicts from the criminal justice system. They were successful in creating a staff which combined professionally trained clinicians who were nonusers with some ex-addicts who had acquired professional training during periods of incarceration.

The older heroin street addict is generally provided with counseling and medical services by the comprehensive community mental health centers. In most instances, the programs are administered by physicians and require professional training of all staff.

Counseling for families The question of counseling for families raises issues that are less clearly defined than in the case of the needs of the addict to alcohol or to drugs. The historical starting point is, however, clear:

> In a broad and general way, 1882 to 1920 was a period of transition from the acceptance of the English Poor Law system to the development of the private charity organization. The recipient of help was literally the poor family. It was the "friendly visitor" of the early [1900s] who preceded the social caseworker of later decades. [43]

The "friendly visitor" was one of the earliest family counselors in America. The focus of counseling was primarily related to resource development and money management. Counseling as a process evolved and expanded its parameters based upon theory generated from these early experiences.

Family counseling as we know it today had its origins in the case work practice of private family agencies. In Atlanta today, as with many other American cities, there exist three long-established family agencies: Family and Children Services (under the auspices of the Family Service of America), Catholic Social Services, and the Jewish Family and Children's Bureau. Although many of these and similar agencies initially had "charities" included in their names, poor families have long been viewed as their primary treatment target.

The principal family counseling resource for poor and otherwise dependent persons is the social service unit of the local "welfare" department. The separation of the assistance payment function from social services provision has meant that family counseling has become a service which a recipient may elect if desired. It is generally agreed that many dependent persons are in need of family counseling, but resist requesting it because of past traumatic experiences associated with its previous imposition on them because of their dependent status.

In Atlanta, family counseling is available from the various community mental health centers. However, it is not generally used by blue-collar and lower middle class persons who are much more likely to turn to their clergymen for help instead of to an agency. Families in the higher socioeconomic brackets tend to seek counseling on a private basis with a professional from one of the clinical disciplines, usually a psychiatrist.

Counseling for youth   As the discussion in Chapter 14 indicates, the demand for counseling services for youth is probably greater than that for any other target group in a community. The large range of available counseling services may be classified according to two broad categories: preventive and remedial. Numerous agencies are concerned primarily with helping youth to establish constructive life goals and to assist them in developing a plan that will help in working to achieve those goals.

Counseling services found within the framework of the public school system represent the kind of program that probably affects more youth than any other. School counseling services are an integral part of pupil personnel services and are felt to be as significant in the total educational process as is classroom instruction. The U.S. Office of Education (of the Department of Health, Education, and Welfare) develops and influences the implementation of educational policies. That office made the following statement regarding the significance of pupil personnel services in the public school system:

Pupil personnel services, together with other school services, help the school achieve its educational objectives by providing a coordinated program of services designed to make it possible for each student to gain the optimum growth and development from his experiences. They aid in, but show differentiated characteristics from, educational processes whose chief purpose is mastering of subject matter or skills. Since there is close relationship between knowledge about the child and his [sic] learning, there is need for assisting teachers, parents, and others to understand the individuality of each child. Pupil personnel services, therefore, include the coordinated efforts of all those persons within the school and community whose primary functions are to assist pupils in becoming self-directive and socially minded individuals.[44]

Although the primary focus of counseling in the public school system is preventive, it also assumes a remedial role. The school environment, generally, is the first one within which the psychological and social problems of youth become evident. School systems provide and make referrals for counseling more than any other institution in a given community.

Preventive counseling is an integral part of the "character building" programs of the Boy Scouts of America, the Girl Scout Council, Boys' Clubs, the Big Brothers Association, Girls' Clubs, etc. One or more of these organizations exit within most urban and rural communities throughout the nation. In addition to these programs which are available to youth on an "open participation" basis, numerous organizations—both national and local in scope—exist to serve the interests of specific ethnic, religious, and socioeconomic groups.

Numerous agencies provide remedial as well as preventive counseling services for youth. The organizational unit of the public school system that deals with truancy problems is often the first to become involved in the remedial counseling process. Counselors associated with these programs attempt to intervene at the point of initial "acting out" on the part of the individual.

The continuing "acting out" of youth in many instances leads them into conflict with the law. Although the legal infractions may be minor ones, many communities try to provide services that have as their goal the prevention of further psychological problems and socially maladaptive behavior. In addition to the ongoing program structures that exist in many communities, one sometimes finds also a number of separate "impact" programs designed to respond to the needs of special target groups.

A major counseling resource for youth in every city and county is that provided by agencies involved with foster home care. Children who are deprived of care by their own parents are traumatized to some degree. Although the basic thrust of counseling within the framework of foster care programs is to increase the ability of parents to assume their expected parental roles, a considerable portion of the counseling effort may be devoted to support of the children who find themselves in circumstances which involve the loss of their normal sources of support.

Counseling within the framework of the foster care program, as in numerous other agency programs, provides preventive and remedial services. These dual focuses exist for both long-term and special "impact" programs.

Conclusion: some managerial checkpoints

What points can the manager in city or county government derive from the preceding discussion? The following checklist appears germane to the specific world of the public administrator:

1. Counseling is concerned with the most sensitive and traumatic events in the lives of individuals and their families. In this area, therefore, particular care should be exercised in seeing that the personnel selected are suited to the tasks they will perform. Counseling services may well be the last place to initiate ill-planned experiments or to try out untested administrative ideas. Proper attention must be paid to training programs and to recognition of differing perceptions of the role of professional training.
2. The question of who can or should do counseling is a complex one. Before the local government gets into the act, it is necessary to pay close attention to the roles played by peer groups, families, voluntary agencies, and other social institutions—from schools to churches, social clubs to labor unions—in helping persons in distress.
3. It is necessary to pay full attention to matching available services to the actual needs of different groups of potential clients. The varying use of private psychotherapy between socioeconomic groups is an example: the middle class professional may be more receptive to the offer of therapy from the public sector than either the upper income individual (who can seek and afford a private psychiatrist) or the lower income person (who may seek counseling from a minister of religion).
4. Because of the complexity of the counseling situation, public administrators are faced with a complex task as they seek to ensure equity in the allocation of available funds to meet the needs of a given community. The factor is compounded by the availability of funds from several levels of government and by the possibility of working with many agencies in the private sector.

In dealing with these competing factors, the basic managerial challenge facing the city or county administrator is to look at the broad picture and make some kind of overall determination of the roles that the local government can and cannot play in counseling services provision. Failure to do so will result in an incremental approach and a proliferation of programs which may well duplicate each other, to the detriment both of the government concerned and the potential clients for counseling services in the community.

Day care:
municipal roles and responsibilities

It began over a century ago. Its primary aim was to provide an alternative to institutionalization for poor and unsupervised children, and to enable poor mothers to gain employment—until they could be restored to their "rightful" places in the home. Since that time, through a series of fits and starts, it has reached its current status as a subject of passionate debate. On the one hand, there are those who feel that it is a governmental responsibility and demand it as a right. On the other, there are those who perceive it as the ultimate destroyer of home and family.

It, of course, is *day care,* a human services program that has evolved from innocuous beginnings in the mid-nineteenth century into both a billion-dollar business and a hotbed of controversy.

The following discussion will analyze the delivery of day care services from the perspective of the local government decision maker, with particular emphasis on the municipal role in this field. It begins by briefly tracing the history of day care in this country and by outlining the social and economic forces which have thrust it forward as a fundamental social service that local governments increasingly are asked to support or provide. Four key public policy questions surrounding day care at the federal, state, and local levels will then be explored: the eligibility question; alternative delivery mechanisms; the management question of control and money; and the quality question. Municipal planners and other local government decision makers will appreciate the critical importance attached to an understanding of the historical evolution of day care and of the key policy considerations at the various levels of government. The very nature of the local need and demand for day care and of a given municipality's role in providing it will be shaped by that municipality's assessment of and response to these historical and policy considerations.

The third portion of the discussion analyzes the municipal role in providing day care by outlining the options available; the essential program elements; the experience of one city—New Haven, Connecticut (population 140,000); and related services as exemplified by a child care resource center. The focus throughout is on the provision of public day care services, though it is recognized that private not-for-profit and private for-profit day care operations are also sizable and may be dominant in some communities. It is also recognized that the scope of public day care operations will vary widely according to the policy decisions and fiscal realities impinging on the presence (or absence) of the operation of local day care centers in particular communities. The discussion ends with an evaluative conclusion.

Historical perspective

It is a truism that much has happened in the United States since the first day nursery opened in Boston, Massachusetts, in 1828 to provide care to the children of seamen's wives and widows.[45] A mere listing of some of the potent socioeconomic forces which have generated both the need and the demand for day care would include such major topics as: the industrial revolution; urbanization; two world wars; poverty; the progressive education movement; the growth of the life sciences; and suburbanization. This is not the place for a detailed historical analysis.[46] Essentially, however, it may be noted that the industrial revolution, in the United States as—earlier—in Europe, brought people into the cities, out of the homes, and into the factories. This process opened the doors to employment for millions of previously homebound women. The pernicious working conditions associated with the industrial revolution also brought a public response in the rise of protective child labor laws. These resulted in children being kept at home and being made their parents' responsibility for a longer period of time.

The move to the cities which the industrial revolution spurred contributed to a gradual decline in the extended family. Grandparents, uncles, and aunts might well be left behind in small towns (in the case of immigrants, in the ''Old Country''), and young men and women moved to the apartments, tenements, and railroad flats that sprang up to house the new factory workers in the central cities of the nation. Inevitably, this meant that the new urban, working mothers had fewer persons to care for their children if they wanted or needed to work. Continued urbanization, suburbanization, and the decline of old urban neighborhoods has accelerated the process. A recent study, for example, showed that at the turn of the century, 50 percent of the homes in Boston contained parents, their children, and at least one other adult—a grandparent, aunt, or other relative. Today that figure is 4 percent.[47] With the abolition of slavery and the twentieth century movement to the cities, the black family, too, with its unique historical roots, was also faced with the challenges of urban living.

Further, two world wars helped legitimize the concept of the working woman and made it patriotically acceptable for mothers of young children to hold jobs. As is often the case in times of war, women were charged with those tasks which men formerly performed. Especially in World War II, women took their places in the factories, in the assembly lines, in the offices, and in the mills. As a result, in 1945 more than a one-and-a-half million children were being cared for in some 2,800 day care centers nationwide.[48]

Many assumed that, at war's end, women would return to the home to resume their ''traditional'' roles of wife and mother. The trend toward working mothers continued to grow, however. In 1950, there were 1.6 million working mothers with children under the age of six; in 1960, this figure was 3.3 million; and by the 1970s, it numbered over 6 million. One out of every three mothers with preschool children was working in the 1970s, compared to one out of eight in 1948.

More importantly, however, as of the 1970s, there are over 3 million preschool children whose families have incomes below the poverty level, and probably an equal number of families living near poverty. Statistics also reveal that 13 percent (some 8.3 million) of *all* children in the United States are in single-parent families, and 65 percent of these single parents are working.[49]

The progressive education movement and the rise of an interest in the life sciences are closely allied, and also contributed, to the rise of day care. In the 1960s and 1970s, educators and social scientists became more concerned about the needs of the family, particularly those who were economically and/or socially ''disadvantaged.'' Increasingly they argued that ''early intervention,'' specifically in the form of day care and Head Start programs, could provide the intellectual, emotional, and social stimulation that might be missing from the family. It was hoped that these programs could serve to ensure that the child learns and develops properly so as to assume a productive social, vocational, and economic place in society. Citizens groups, too, made their views felt in this area.

Day care was seen by some professionals as an opportunity to ensure that children would inculcate the normative standards of American life and positive concepts of self in relation to society. Interestingly, day care was also viewed as a means of democratizing society—a way of seeing to it that every child, no matter how disadvantaged or discriminated against, would be equally equipped for an economically and psychologically secure adulthood. In the process it was expected that their families, also disadvantaged, would become involved in the political and institutional lives of their communities. A reinvigorated feminism, too, has left its mark on the ongoing debate.

Advancements in the life sciences—specifically, child psychology—also focused much research on the questions of whether ''children living under conditions of disadvantage may suffer serious environmental deprivations or deficits in their early years . . .'' and whether ''these early circumstances may be critical for the child's development because it may be difficult or impossible to correct for them in later life." [50]

The theory that the first five years of life are critical and may inexorably mold one's psychosocial development, is not new. It is a theory which runs parallel to that which holds that the IQ is "plastic" in the early years—taking its shape from an environment which may either be stimulating and enriching; or else stifling and routine; or, even worse, oppressive. There are, of course, countertheories which hold that one's IQ is largely determined by heredity and there is little that "early intervention" programs can do to improve it. Many social scientists and child psychologists continue to adhere to the former premise, nevertheless, and maintain their belief in the positive potential of high quality early childhood programs.

As the rise of urbanization initially helped trigger the need for day care programs, so the decline of the cities and the growth of the suburbs has helped to sustain that need. The increase in suburban living, particularly since the 1950s, has resulted in a relatively low density of children in the suburbs, necessitating planned, structured play groups such as those offered in formalized day care centers. Similarly, the declining birth rate has resulted in smaller families and fewer agemates within families for children to play with and learn from.

All of the socioeconomic factors touched on in briefest outline above have contributed to the more widespread need, demand, use, and acceptance of day care than ever before. But however far formalized day care has come since its inception, and however much it may be championed as a vital and beneficial aspect of our culture, society (and its constituent groupings) remains ambivalent about the public sector's responsibility to provide day care. That ambivalence is manifested, most blatantly, in the relatively limited financial support which federal, state, and local governments have generally given to day care programs.

As one observer has bluntly stated: "In the midst of fragmentation, competition, and a nonsystematic approach to distribution of resources, any coordinated federal–state–local commitment to comprehensive child care services exists almost by accident." [51]

It was not until the challenges of the Depression and of World War II that the federal government funded any day care programs. As these crises abated, however, federal day care support declined. It was not until the Social Security Act amendments of 1967 and President Nixon's Family Assistance Plan of 1969 that day care regained prominence as a subject of national debate and concern. In the United States of the late 1970s, however, there are still only about one million spaces in licensed day care centers to serve the six million preschoolers whose mothers work.

The ambivalence about public support for day care is partially the result of the coexistence of two rather conflicting social traditions in formalized child care—the tradition of nursery schools and that of day care centers. Although the nursery school and day care movements began simultaneously about a century ago, they served vastly different sections of the populace. Nursery schools, which were intended for the children of the middle and upper classes, served as a sign of family affluence and were viewed as a way of providing "pleasant" social and educational experiences for the children of those classes during their early formative years. On the other hand, day care, which was a service primarily for lower income groups, was established for strictly utilitarian reasons—to enable mothers to get jobs and thus decrease the numbers on public assistance.

Since they served such vastly differing clientele, the nursery school and day care movements established different goals. The former institution, something of a luxury at the time, served a social and educational role, while the latter was seen as serving a custodial one. "Whereas nursery school was developed supposedly for educational purposes, day care was classified as a health and welfare function and thereby considered a charitable program, largely custodial in approach." [52]

Indeed, there has always been a subtle, and sometimes not so subtle, stigma attached to day care, a stigma which it cannot seem to shake. "The association of day care with social pathology and with employment, rather than with childrearing generally, has become an important tradition, and has given day care a welfare image, distasteful to a large portion of the population." [53]

The presently conflicting perceptions of day care, then, seem to have developed from the obvious economic justification for it, combined, however, with the views of some that the families who needed day care are somehow "inadequate;" with the fears of some components of our society of governmental interference in what is regarded as the sacred province of the family; and with the continuing belief that childrearing should take place in the home.

For local government decision makers of the 1970s, however, the issue is no longer, "Shall we have day care?," but rather, "What kind of day care shall we have?" This is the question that will be explored and analyzed in the remainder of this discussion.

Key public policy issues

The eligibility question   At the center of the day care controversy has always been the question of who should be eligible for day care services. Should publicly funded day care be offered exclusively to low income or poverty-level families, or should it be offered to other income groups who need it? What are the legal and constitutional ramifications of such political decisions? How is the term "need" to be defined in this instance? Are women with young children in "need" of day care if their reason is a desire to return to school or take a job to further their personal development? An even more fundamental question is: To what extent will day care become an established institution like public education, and hence an accepted and expected public service in American life, available to middle income as well as low income families?

The federal government appears, as of the 1970s, to be moving in the direction of more widely available day care services. However, the wheels of change turn very gradually. The historical relationship between day care and welfare continues to be reflected in the day care legislation of the late 1960s and 1970s. This process was illustrated by President Nixon's 1969 introduction to Congress of the Manpower and Training Act. The president linked the success of training and employing mothers with the availability of day care services under the proposed legislation.

These would be day care centers with a difference. There is no single ideal to which this administration is more firmly committed than to the enriching of a child's first five years of life, and thus helping lift the poor out of misery at a time when a lift can help the most . . . And as a further dividend, the day care centers would offer employment to many welfare mothers themselves. [54]

At the time, the federal Office of Management and Budget—which wanted day care only for those of low income—and the Department of Health, Education and Welfare's Office of Child Development—which sought to allow access to the day care system to a broader clientele—clashed openly over this bill. This dispute, and the absence of a well-defined administration policy on day care, led to the introduction of a number of other day care bills.

The Comprehensive Child Development Act of 1971 concentrated on a comprehensive system of child care services available *free* to welfare recipients and the "working" poor and, on a graduated scale, to middle income families. The bill provided a "legislative framework for eventual universally available child development programs for all families who need and want them, and offered a variety of medical, nutritional, and educational services for children from infancy—from preinfancy, to be exact, since the bill included prenatal programs—to 14 years of age.'' [55]

President Nixon vetoed this bill in December of 1971, arguing that its passage would too radically usurp the family's role in, and responsibility for, the rearing of its own children. At this point, the federal government seemed willing to go no farther than minimal day care for children of mothers in work training programs.

However, by 1974, after years of haggling and compromising, the 93rd Congress passed the Social Security Act Amendment of 1974, more commonly referred to as Title XX of the Social Security Act. This piece of legislation, which provides for 75 percent matching federal funds for child care, was also designed ostensibly to increase the eligibility and payment standards for child care services.

In reality, however, Title XX has not worked out that way. It provides no more money for social services, retaining the overall $2.5 billion federal ceiling on Title XX. It prohibits the reallocation of unused funds and only changes the eligibility criteria from welfare linkage to actual income, while retaining poverty level income limits for free participation. Additionally, the federal regulations mandated in 1975 for receipt of Title XX funds were extremely stringent and involved, among other things, detailed application forms which some feel discourage program participation and violate personal privacy. In fact, as of 1976, several states had filed suit to contest the necessity of filing the application forms in order to receive Title XX funds.

The year 1974 also saw the introduction of a revised, but equally broad, version of the unsuccessful Comprehensive Child Development Act—the Child and Family Services Act. Its key elements were still the provision of health, child developmental day care, education, nutrition, and other services to a socioeconomically diverse group of Americans. But the Child and Family Services Act went down to defeat in 1975, just as its predecessor had.

Clearly then the federal government's commitment to day care has been diffuse and limited to date, that is, as of the late 1970s. This has been due in part to fragmented congressional support, to the large number of separate funding sources, and to continuing disagreement among child care advocates themselves on exactly how open child care should be in terms of eligibility and range of services.

Toddler expeditions   The recreation department in Arlington County, Virginia, is offering a recreational program for a group who really appreciates it—housebound mothers and their preschool children. Four times a month, a bus picks them up and goes on free expeditions to such fascinating places as a chicken farm, dog show, fire station, puppet show, or bakery. Rides are kept to less than half an hour. Activities are planned for no more than one hour, after which mothers and tots adjourn to a nearby park or playground, then home in time for lunch.

Many critics see universally available day care services for all families who need and want them as threatening to the healthy and necessarily intimate mother–child relationship, to the family, and, in fact, to the whole social order. They fear the notion that the ''State'' may continue to intrude to an intolerable degree in the private lives of Americans, beyond the limits desirable in a democratic and individualistic society. These observers contend that day care services should simply serve children from so-called ''negligent'' and ''inadequate'' families.

Day care advocates, however, argue that the sole purpose of day care should *not* be to remove people from the welfare roles. They stress that day care should serve higher aims; specifically, that it should, as declared by the Department of Health, Education, and Welfare in its *Statement of Principles,* ''meet the needs of children for experiences which will foster their development as human beings.'' [56]

Advocates argue that children of working mothers are not the only ones in need of child care, but that there are many mothers who are students or who are in job training programs. They may be preparing to make their families self-sufficient, but few can find or afford the kind of care they want for their children when they must be away from home. Other parents simply desire day care and feel that it would benefit their children by providing them with the opportunity to be with a variety of other youngsters in a child-centered environment. Day care proponents also argue that the best kind of extensive day care will pay off in later years by eliminating a variety of social ills and educational deficiencies.

How universal should the eligibility for publicly supported day care be? The answer depends on perceptions of the role of women in the world; the effects of day care on young children; the concept of the family; and the long term fiscal and social costs of providing that service. These are basic issues that each local government confronted with the demand for day care must address and resolve before determining the nature and extent of its involvement.

Alternative delivery mechanisms   As problematic as the dilemma of who should *receive* publicly supported day care services is the equally important question of who should *deliver* such services. Historically, this issue has pitted the public provider (the main focus of the present discussion) against the private provider. However, the question is even more complex, as public sector supporters disagree as to exactly *which* public sector agency should be the prime deliverer of services to preschool children. Others advocate the delivery of child care services by a variety of systems, both public and private, which can accommodate diverse family needs.

The argument for the public sector delivery of child care services often focuses on the public school system. To many, the inclusion of child care services within the public education system represents a natural extension of its present function and a method of ensuring that day care be more educational and developmental in nature than may presently be the case.

One prominent (and perhaps not entirely dispassionate) advocate of public-school-based child care services has been Albert Shanker, president of the United Federation of Teachers. Mr. Shanker has contended that the public school system is the best place for day care programs for a variety of reasons, including the system's capacity to set standards for high quality programs with a bona fide educational component; its cost-free and universal availability; its broad federal, state and local fiscal base; its existing buildings and facilities, and its capacity for financing remodeling or new construction; the continuity it could offer by providing early-to-late childhood programs; and its ability to set specific staff qualification requirements and to certify professional employees.[57]

However, the very characteristics which proponents of the school system consider most persuasive, have—not unexpectedly—been found wanting by others. Theodore Taylor, executive director of the Day Care and Child Development Council of America, Inc., sees a variety of drawbacks to delivery of child care services by the public schools. These include the inflexible public school curriculum; the difficulty which teachers may have in communicating with children who (because of their age) are largely nonverbal; the need for closer parental involvement than the school system generally encourages; relatively inflexible hours of operation; and others.[58]

Since this issue has not been resolved as a matter of policy at the federal level, it must, it seems, be settled as part of the local political process. The answer will lie in the degree of local confidence in the school system, the system's willingness and capacity to take on major new responsibilities, and other political, social, and fiscal considerations.

One positive feature claimed for the free enterprise system is that it allows for diversity and options. A pressing need in child care, obviously, is the availability of a multiplicity of day care options to meet the variety of day care needs. If anything is fairly certain, it is that confining day care delivery to the province of any one agency—public or private—would severely restrict its flexibility to respond to the differing needs and preferences of individual parents and children.

Jule Sugarman, former chief administrative officer of Atlanta, Georgia, argues persuasively that:

> There is so much to do that we really need the involvement of everybody. We need the social agencies, we need the health agencies, we need the private, nonprofit organizations, and I would even argue that we need the for-profit organizations, although I do that with some caveats about how they get used. I believe that the job out there (child care) is so tremendous that there is room for everybody (including schools) to be actively involved in it.[59]

In the absence of federal policy and restrictions, it is probable that day care delivery at the local level will continue to be the responsibility of a mix of public and private providers—schools, centers, and family day care homes. The politics of day care, the multiplicity of funding sources, and the concern for organizational survival, will continue to foster the pluralistic mode of service delivery.

The management question: control and money The question of who should control day care programs has been debated on all levels. Which federal agency should have primary responsibility for child care programs? The Department of Health, Education, and Welfare's Office of Child Development would appear to have this responsibility. However, as of the mid-1970s, federally funded programs touching all areas of early childhood development number some two hundred, and were funded through no less than eighteen different federal agencies.[60]

Beyond the question of federal involvement is the issue of where local control of child care programs should be lodged. If child care programs are operated by a local governmental body, by the public school system, or even by private sponsors, should those agencies have the ultimate decision-making power with regard to standards, staffing, policy, programs, fees, objectives, hours, and eligible clientele? Or should those decisions more properly rest with consumers, namely parents speaking for their children?

President Nixon and other federal officials were adamantly opposed to community-controlled day care centers, believing that funds should be channeled through state "prime sponsors." By contrast, the Comprehensive Child Development Act proposed to bypass states altogether, giving funds directly to localities (although not necessarily to the municipalities), thus making other groups eligible for direct federal funding.

The question of control arises as well in the matter of citizen participation in day care programming. Theoretically, public sector day care centers must, in order to receive federal funds, meet certain criteria with respect to parental and community involvement. This is mandated by the Title XX legislation, federal interagency day care requirements, and other regulations; it is not clear, however, that these mandates are effectively enforced.

Another "control" question relates to the staffing of day care centers. Should professionally trained persons—teachers, social workers, child psychologists—necessarily be the primary care providers? Or should that role go to paraprofessionals—mothers, unemployed persons on welfare, or those in on-the-job training programs?

Supporters of parents and community-based paraprofessionals as principal staff stress the "warm and loving" relationship they could offer, claiming that dispassionate, overeducated professionals, particularly those of a differing ethnic background from that of the children in their care, would be miscast in this role. Others would hold that this argument fails in two key respects, however. First, professionals obviously have the potential to be "warm and loving" and indeed may be parents or community people as well. Second, adherents of the counterviewpoint hold that since the early childhood years may be *the* most important period in a child's development, care for children should not be left to "just anyone."

A relatively unexplored question related to control is the degree to which publicly subsidized day care recipients should be given the freedom to choose their own day care providers. Should parents be given vouchers or vendor payments which allow them to select their own day care arrangements, whether in public centers or private centers or family day care homes, rather than being forced to utilize public day care centers exclusively? This option would allow recipients an attractive freedom of choice heretofore unavailable. It could also have the effect of exerting pressure on the public day care system to provide competent staff and quality programs in order to attract clients no longer mandated to attend. If the costs of such a program were roughly comparable to the per capita cost of public centers, then this concept might have much to offer and should be further explored by local government managers and elected officials.

The quality question   In addressing the question of quality in day care programs, we must first define what is meant by quality. After doing so, it must then be recognized that, until radical changes occur in the willingness of the federal and state governments to require and effectively monitor quality, the question is largely academic.

First, the definition; then, the problems. The *Connecticut Child Care Center Guidelines* state: "The daily program shall provide specific experiences which promote learning and health adjustment, such as appropriate physical activity, problem-solving experiences, creative activities, language learning experiences, and opportunities to develop self-reliance." [61] Other attributes of a quality child care program might include:

1. Staff training, including knowledge of child development;
2. Comprehensive services, including elements tailored to the intellectual, emotional, and social development of the child;
3. Parental involvement in policy making, program planning, and even daily activities;
4. Health care, including information on nutrition, physical and mental health, homemaker services, and provision for the handicapped;
5. Coordination with supportive community resources;
6. Development of cognitive skills;
7. Structure which allows flexibility and freedom; and
8. A mechanism for identification of children with special potential or problems.

A long-standing concern of persons interested in the quality of day care has been the provision of an educational component as an essential element of any day care program. The Head Start program was initiated, in large part, to intervene at an early age in the emotional and educational development of disadvantaged, often nonwhite, children in the hope that the devastating impacts of poverty and racism could be overcome or at least neutralized so that youngsters would have a chance for normal emotional and intellectual growth. "The whole promise of early childhood education had been tied to a general belief that an improvement in educational services at all levels—preschool, primary, and secondary—would not only improve educational performance but would also begin to equalize the quality of adult life by preparing people to take good jobs, by equipping people to compete for higher paying jobs." [62]

This issue of the value of intensive educational programming in day care centers is not clear-cut, however. The impact of Head Start participation on youngsters' educational achievement levels has never been verified. Christopher Jencks' exhaustive study, *Inequality,* concluded that "after a thorough review of available data relating to access to education, distribution of educational resources, heritability, and environmental factors in IQ scores and family backgrounds, none of the evidence we have reviewed suggests that school reform can be expected to bring about significant social changes outside the school.'' [63]

However, if child development specialists, child psychologists, and others agree that the preschool years are vital in laying the intellectual, psychological, and emotional foundations for life, then perhaps the concern should be not so much with a formal educational component for day care programs, but rather with the kind of education that is already taking place in day care centers. Until the quality and relevance of curricula are increased, it cannot even be hoped that they will produce positive results or make any substantial impact. Therefore, in order to guarantee the quality of day care programs, it seems that we must look to federal and state regulations with the power of funding and enforcement behind them; specific articulated day care standards, goals and objectives; unified (or, at least, coordinated) funding sources; program monitoring and evaluation; staff training; and ongoing parent involvement.

The municipal role in day care provision

The options Cities and towns have increasingly been called upon to offer day care services directly or else to fund the delivery of such services. This is a complex, sensitive task, with many factors to be carefully considered before a municipality, through its elected officials and professional managers, determines its role. The options in day care services range from custodial home care to comprehensive child development programs.

Custodial home care Custodial home care frequently amounts to little more than babysitting, and is usually based on informal arrangements made between families, friends, and neighbors. Dr. D. J. Cohen has said of this kind of arrangement:

Only the immediate needs of the child are considered—health and safety, something to eat, and some sort of activity to pass the time. There is no planning to meet developmental needs, either immediate or long range. There is no attempt to plan for the child's need for personal responsive human relationships; for intellectual stimulation; for health or nutrition beyond immediate needs; or for parent involvement in the care being given.[64]

This is the most widely used form of child care because of convenience, accessibility, and cost. However, it does not meet all the needs, especially those of low and moderate income families or young, mobile, working parents who are apart from trusted family and friends and living in a large, impersonal urban setting.

Family day care homes A slightly more formalized method of child care involves "family day care homes" licensed by the state or local welfare departments. Once certain sanitation, fire, and safety standards are met, day care can be provided in private homes. Usually no more than six children, including those of the care giver, can be legally enrolled at any given time. Parents of infants and toddlers usually prefer this type of arrangement; and it is also convenient for after school care of older children, keeping siblings together and providing close family relationships for those youngsters who, for one reason or another, have trouble adjusting to large groups of children.

Since providers of family day care homes are not required to possess formal training as a condition of licensing, the services they offer may be no more than custodial care. However, some states, municipalities, and universities have offered low cost voluntary training and incentive programs for providers in order to upgrade the quality of care given in these homes. Also, federal legislation passed in 1975 (Public Law 94105) has made it possible for the day care homes to receive monetary reimbursement for meals served to the children, provided they meet certain nutritional standards and are sponsored by a public or nonprofit organization.

Family group day care providers   Another form of care is represented by "family group day care providers." Group providers care for up to 12 children in a homelike setting that may have been remodeled to meet licensing requirements which are more stringent than those for family day care homes. More than one care giver is required because of the larger number of children; this also assures backup in case of emergency.

Day care centers   The formal day care center, although much more costly, provides a full range of services which might not otherwise be available to both the child and family. These services are aimed at providing support for the development of strong cohesive family units as well as at helping the child to develop social, emotional, and cognitive skills which prepare him or her for learning in elementary school. The center has trained staff to guide the children with a curriculum that includes activities in the areas of prereading skills, arts and crafts, science and nature discovery, music, and field trips.

Health and nutrition services are provided as well as a variety of social services depending upon individual need. Some centers have paid staff members, such as social workers, pediatricians, and nurses to perform certain services; others contract out for such specialized services; and still others maintain a mechanism for referral to other agencies that can provide the services at little or no cost. The typical center has a full-day program, usually operating from 8 to 12 hours per day to allow parents to work or pursue other interests. Day care centers are run by public, private nonprofit, and private for-profit agencies.

Nursery schools and Head Start   Nursery schools and Head Start programs provide educational curricula on a part-day basis, usually three to four hours a day, for children from three to five years of age. Nursery schools do not usually provide health and social services, assuming that the parents can afford to take care of these needs. The typical Head Start program, like the day care center, does provide these adjunct services, since it is designed to meet the needs of poor and disadvantaged children and to give them the necessary support to benefit from their future school experiences. Head Start also seeks to identify and correct any deficiencies that might hinder the child's progress, such as a learning disability, poor hearing or eyesight, lead poisoning, etc. Mandated by federal law, Head Start programs are also required to fill at least 10 percent of their enrollment with physically or emotionally handicapped children.

Considerations for local involvement   In determining whether (and how to) become involved in actually delivering day care, the appropriate decision makers in local governments will probably decide to give careful consideration to the following factors: legal constraints; number, type, and quality of existing programs; availability of space in existing centers or of nonmunicipal funds to expand existing programs; existing locus of control over existing programs and degree of municipal input; socioeconomic group(s) served; percentage of children of working, unemployed, and welfare mothers; public demand for additional services and related political climate; incidence of child neglect and abuse; ability of municipality to support day care over the long term; and impact of expanded day care on local economy and on level of public assistance payments.

These factors are critically important and may vary markedly from community to community. The population of a small suburban town of middle and upper income families will not need or necessarily want the same type of services desired in a more urban or industrialized community.

Needs assessment and funding   A needs assessment survey or public hearing should be conducted to find out how families presently arrange for child care, if this is not already known. This process might reveal how many are satisfied with their existing informal arrangements and how many would enroll their children in a licensed, publicly supported facility if it were available. The study might also show that the existing programs are adequate in number, but the quality of care is poor, or that those who most need child care are unable to afford the services currently offered. There may be vacancies in some programs because parents are wary of enrolling their children in centers where they have no voice in program operation and no control over the day-to-day activities in which their children will be involved. If space were available and parents felt comfortable with the services, how many unemployed and welfare mothers would be willing to join the labor force, knowing their children will be cared for properly? Conversely, can the local job market absorb them if day care could be arranged? Prudent managers will be aware, however, that the mere making of a survey can lead to a rise in citizen expectations about service delivery or stimulate the demand for existing—and perhaps already overburdened—programs.

The level, source, and stability of funding are also vital considerations. There will never be enough funding—whether originating from the Community Development Act, from Title XX, from state aid, from a local general fund, or from private foundation grants—to satisfy the total demand for services. Child care is rarely accorded top priority for funding among the social services. Pay scales for staff are frequently low, even for positions requiring specialized college degrees. This causes high turnover among staff which, in turn, makes it difficult to sustain quality care. When coupled with the fact—discussed earlier—that there is no genuine national policy or commitment to quality child care, the child care "industry" is often perceived of and treated as a stepchild of social services or public education. To reverse this trend—and particularly so in times of urban fiscal crisis—it is imperative that human services planners, responsible for shaping local child care policy and programs, proceed with a seriousness of purpose and thoroughness of approach. Failure to do so only rekindles the debate over the social utility of formalized child care, an issue seemingly resolved and which need not be resurrected.

After completing a needs assessment, it is likely that the responsible officials will find that the results show that no one type of program will adequately meet the requirements of a given population. Parents need alternatives and, most pertinently, so do their children. Care of an infant child might best be handled in the intimacy of a family day care home. A foster child who may have been neglected or abused might also fare better in this environment. The poor and disadvantaged child may need the support of a Head Start program. But the child's mother might want to enroll in the federal government's Work Incentive Program or take a job to get off welfare; she will therefore need the additional coverage of an all-day child care program. An only child can learn how to get along with others at the day care center. Children with handicaps need to be placed in accordance with the degree of their disability. The mother of such a child may not be working, but may feel the need for some free time, away from the full-time demands of a handicapped child. Also, through association with a day care program, the parents of such a child can learn to cope with the stresses they may be feeling and to make the child's life, as well as their own, more satisfying and rewarding.

Given the inevitability of limited public resources, it is impossible to meet all of the child care needs in a community. Consequently, resources must be used most efficiently through careful plannning and full utilization of "in-kind services," private grants and donations, volunteer programs like Foster Grandparents, and the full panoply of free and partially subsidized services available from public or nonprofit health, counseling, and other social services agencies.

Once the municipality determines that it will indeed become a day care provider, the process of establishing a day care center proceeds essentially along the lines suggested in Figure 12–2, which shows an implementation checklist for a municipal day care center. Of all the steps, site selection (no. 7) and licensing (no. 8) may prove to be the most mystifying, frustrating, and protracted, although all may present difficulties.

Implementation Checklist

1. Determine need for center. This will entail a child care needs assessment which might include a survey of existing city child care facilities; census data on numbers of preschool children by neighborhood; neighborhood concentrations of preschool children; income levels by neighborhood; patterns of neighborhood movement; demand for services exceeding supply; and other considerations.

2. Develop program proposal, including statement of need, program outline, target neighborhood, size of center, number of children served, preliminary budget, and scope of services.

3. Determine steps necessary to secure local governmental approval for proposed center. Depending on various factors, including funding source, a determination of the requirement for public hearings and citizen input will also be needed.

4. Determine funding. Municipal day care centers targeted on a population meeting specific economic criteria are eligible for state and federal funding, when available.

5. Secure funding. This involves submission of detailed program proposal to funding source.

6. Establish bookkeeping and financial management mechanism. This can be done once funding has been awarded.

7. Select site. Once a target neighborhood has been identified, a specific site must be determined based on existing state and local health, fire, and zoning regulations for day care centers, as well as on specific designs of the proposed center. If renovations or modifications are required on site, secure cost estimates, time frame, architectural plans, contractor, etc.

8. Secure license for center. The state health department (or similar appropriate agency) issues the day care center license, contingent on fulfillment of specific facility, staffing, program content, health services, and food services requirements.

9. Develop staff. Establish criteria for staff selection; advertise for, interview, and hire staff.

10. Develop curriculum. With regard for federal and state guidelines, a curriculum designed to meet the educational, social, and emotional needs of the children it serves should be developed. Curriculum development also involves purchase of learning tools, toys, equipment, and other items.

11. Link up with appropriate supportive services, including health screening, nutrition, staff training and development, etc.

12. Include and encourage parental and community involvement in as many phases of program planning and implementation as possible. Form advisory council.

13. Admit children and start program.

Figure 12–2   Implementation checklist for a municipal day care center.

Essential program elements   In order for a municipal day care center to meet the minimum standards of the federal interagency day care requirements, its managers must make provisions for health, psychological, and social services either by direct purchase of services or through the use of an existing network of agencies in the community. Health services should include procedures for the screening of all children before they are enrolled: if parents are unable to afford this screening, the center should provide for this service or refer the parent to a facility that will do so, such as a neighborhood health clinic. Care givers should be trained to observe the children with an eye to noting any changes in behavior that might warrant further investigation. Urinalyses and hemoglobin or hematocrit analyses should be routinely performed, as should tests for tuberculosis, lead poisoning, and sickle cell anemia. Provision should also be made for dental, hearing, and eye screening.

Should the child appear to need further attention, the parents should be made aware of the options available to them. The same holds true, of course, for psychological and social services. Follow-up procedures should be instituted to make sure the child is receiving the services needed, and all staff should be informed of specific procedures for emergency medical care. At least one staff person trained in first aid should be present at all times. (If feasible, all staff should be so trained.)

Nutrition and feeding are also essential program elements in day care. The objectives are to provide meals that will help meet the child's total nutritional needs by developing good eating habits, taking into consideration individual and cultural differences. Sound nutrition helps promote good physical, emotional, and social growth. This element of the program should involve parents as much as possible so that meals and habits provided at the center can be complemented by those provided in the home. Strict standards of food purchase, preparation, and sanitation must be maintained in accordance with federal and state standards. (A list of these can be obtained through local health departments.) A full-day program usually serves breakfast, a midmorning snack, lunch, and an afternoon snack. Attractively served, the nutritional service provided through day care can help to develop good habits and attitudes in the children.

Parental involvement is also essential in providing quality care, although this is sometimes difficult to achieve, especially with working parents. Every opportunity should be utilized to inform parents of the goals and objectives of the center. These goals themselves should strive to maintain an environment that is consistent with the child's background and with the values held by his or her parents. The home environment and that of the center should not be so totally different that it confuses the child and forces him or her to live with two different value systems. On this subject, it has been said:

Day care [centers] can become a place where children learn to deal with differences—provided the parents are sufficiently involved to understand the situation, know what the child is experiencing, and help him deal with it to the best of their ability. Parental involvement, then, is not an extra attraction for the parents. It is a basic part of the philosophy that good day care supplements, never supplants a child's own family. Parental involvement is necessary for the social and emotional development of the child.[65]

The following list enumerates some of the ways in which parents can become involved with the activities of the day care program:

1. Parents should be given the opportunity to observe the program in operation;
2. They should be used as teacher's aides, volunteers, or paid substitutes wherever possible;
3. They should be accorded membership on decision-making bodies;
4. They should be encouraged to participate in field trips with children and staff;
5. Staff members should have daily informal contact with parents who drop off and pick up their children at the center;
6. Staff members should make home visits when appropriate to help establish confidence and trust;
7. Conferences should be scheduled periodically to discuss the child's progress and/or other concerns of either parents or staff;
8. Parents should participate in "Parents' Night" or similar social activities.

Conflicts and problems are bound to surface, especially when nonprofessional parents, who may not fully understand the details and complexities of the administration of the program, emerge as leaders and try to gain control of the program for their own purposes.

Some may feel that they are being compelled to compete with the staff for affection from their own child. On the other hand, some professionals may lack appropriate sensitivities to community or ethnic backgrounds differing from their own. Since distrust and misunderstanding are most often the cause of parent–staff conflicts, parent involvement must be developed to the fullest extent in order to build confidence on both sides and promote the total well-being of the child.

There are many models that can be used in developing a daily program or curriculum to be used in the day care center depending upon its goals and objectives. Methods and styles of teaching should reflect, to the degree possible, the ethnic makeup of the children involved. For example, a bilingual center for Puerto Rican children will concentrate on teaching children English to help make their early school years more successful. At the same time, it will gear its activities to preserve some of the rich cultural traditions that are a part of Puerto Rican life. Day care schedules should also be flexible. A weekly evaluation of lessons, often most convenient during staff meetings, should be made to determine whether they were well-received by the children and, if not, what can be done to improve them.

In-service training should be mandatory for all staff and should be conducted on an ongoing basis. Topics for training sessions might include day care curriculum, health and nutrition, social services, leadership training, and parent involvement.

The New Haven experience: a taste of reality   The city of New Haven, Connecticut—a case study discussed in the following section—assumed a direct role in day care delivery only as recently as 1975. In fact, the city got into the day care business more by default than by design. Prior to January, 1976, all but one publicly funded day care center were operated by the Inner City Day Care Council, Inc., an independent nonprofit agency funded by the State of Connecticut's Department of Community Affairs (DCA).

The one other publicly supported center was funded by the city with Model Cities money. The center was constructed in the midst of a low and moderate income housing complex. Originally the center operated as an independent, nonprofit corporation with its own board of directors (primarily comprised of parents) which was responsible for the administration of the center. Beginning in 1974, the center faced the threat of funding termination with the phase-out of the Model Cities program in favor of the new Community Development Block Grant (CDBG) program. Attempts to secure alternate funding from DCA were futile as that state agency had suffered its own appropriations cut. In order not to lose the center, the city's redevelopment agency gave up some of its CDBG contingency funds in February, 1975, hoping that Title XX or other funding would come through later. It did, and at a level which far exceeded expectations. This unexpected windfall caught the city by surprise, with no thoughtfully articulated justification for why the city was involved in direct day care provision, no analysis of what its options were, and no rational plan for the use of its newfound resources. To make matters worse, the local Model Cities agency had just been superseded by an Office of Human Services (OHS). Staff vacancies, turnover, or limitations at every level prevented OHS from undertaking a rigorous assessment of the city government's role and responsibilities in this field. Then, after months of virtually no activity, the city moved precipitously to establish several new day care centers which, in anticipation of the impending municipal elections, were considered high visibility services which would appeal to voters.

Although the incumbent mayor was defeated in the municipal elections, the new mayor inherited the commitments to establish additional city-operated day care centers. The new mayor and his administration (of which the authors are a part) decided immediately to establish new priorities and a fresh image for the city's human services programs. Top priority was given to expanding services for youth (preteens and teenagers) and for the elderly.

While the commitment to day care continued, the city devoted relatively little time or resources during the early months of the new administration to an objective, thorough assessment of its role in day care. As of this writing in early 1977, plans were underway to undertake a study of that role. Through its Human Resources Administration, the city will seek to determine:

1. Whether it should spend any CDBG or other funds at all for day care;
2. Whether it should fund private, nonprofit or for-profit, centers rather than operating its own;
3. Whether it should experiment with voucher payments as an alternative to formal day care centers;
4. Whether, if it elects to continue its centers, city should upgrade the educational quality of service offered and perhaps, with the parents' permission, use them as sites for more innovative research and demonstration projects which explore new techniques of early childhood development.

The outcome of this analysis will undoubtedly be influenced by the fact that the city's program has already built up a clientele of children, parents, and center employees and landlords (usually inner-city minority churches) who are drawing some form of service or sustenance from the existence of the centers. This may make it difficult politically for the city to alter radically its established patterns of service and programs.

Nevertheless, the analysis will have to go forward and be rigorous and pragmatic. The city will be faced in 1978 with the start of a drastic curtailment in CDBG allocations from the Department of Housing and Urban Development (HUD). After three years at a stratospheric level of $18 million per year in CDBG entitlements (New Haven ranked among the top 10 cities in the country in total CDBG allotments despite ranking only 118th in total population), the city's CDBG entitlements will drop precipitously to an annual level of $2 million by 1981.

Unless other human services funds should be forthcoming from as yet nonexistent sources to replace the CDBG losses, the city will have to curtail its entire human services program, including day care. Many cities were, as of 1976, in the same funding predicament because of anticipated extraordinarily high CDBG entitlements mandated by the "hold harmless" provisions of the Housing and Community Development Act of 1974, which established CDBG allotments for the first three years on the basis of most recent pre-CDBG levels of HUD funding. In its 1975–78 CDBG funding, New Haven benefited from the halcyon days of aggressive grantsmanship which, for two decades from the mid-1950s to mid-1970s, saw the city receive more federal funds per capita than virtually any other city in the country. By sustaining a 90 percent cut in CDBG funds between 1978 and 1981, New Haven will finally pay the price for its success. New Haven's plight would evoke little sympathy from other cities, but it will undoubtedly precipitate a crisis in local human services politics and planning a few years hence.

Related services: municipal child care resource center   In addition to operating day care centers directly, there are other roles which municipalities can play in serving parents and children. A Child Care Resource Center, which the city of New Haven was establishing in the late 1970s, is one such program. The Resource Center is to act as a clearinghouse to provide a wide range of information and services to care providers, parents, and others interested in child care. The center is designed to perform the following major functions:

1. Provide information on child care to parents. This would include complete and up-to-date listings of local child care providers.
2. Maintain more detailed information on child care providers, including hours of operation, availability of space, applicable economic criteria for enrollment, ages and types of children served, etc.
3. Establish and disseminate guidelines helpful in choosing a child care provider. This function would concern providing parents with information on which to

base their selection of a child care provider, and is predicated on the belief that if parents possess accurate, detailed information they will be better able to make more informed decisions about the most suitable day care placements for their children.

4. Offer information and limited technical assistance to child care providers, including funding and grants information, available training courses, and workshops.
5. Establish a job bank which would monitor employment openings in the child care field and make this information available to persons seeking employment in day care.
6. Establish a volunteer placement component which would actively seek to match volunteers interested in day care to available volunteer slots.
7. Develop a lending library on child care, designed to help both parents and child care providers become more informed on child care. The library would be filled with pertinent books, articles, slides, and filmstrips on the varied aspects of child care, and would be made available on a loan basis to interested groups, agencies, and individuals.

Direct child care and informational services, as described in the resource center model, address the varied needs of parents, child care providers, and others interested in child care in a comprehensive and vital way.

Conclusion

Why should local governments be involved in the direct delivery of day care services? The answer is not altogether obvious. If the experience of New Haven, Connecticut, is any indication, many municipalities enter the day care business "through the back door." Cities have become operators of day care centers by default or for reasons of political expediency, and often *not* for compelling programmatic reasons.

Clearly the demand for day care from parents of all socioeconomic groups is very legitimate and, given recent historical trends, likely to continue and escalate. In light of the limited federal, state, and municipal resources for day care, that demand (at least from municipal officials' perspectives) may seem to be unmeetable, particularly where budgetary problems and limited grantsmanship capability are involved. Decision makers in cities cannot hope to satisfy the demand; they can only aspire to achieve a modest, incremental reduction in it.

Responsible officials in cities will realize that by committing public resources to a direct role in day care delivery, they will be assuming additional administrative burdens and creating new consumer—and voter—expectations for such services. Given the variety of other essential services which only a municipal government can provide, one might ask why municipal leaders would willingly take on added administrative and financial burdens in a social services area which is somewhat peripheral to the basic functions of government. In most cities of any size, there are numerous other day care providers already in existence. These would eagerly grasp the opportunity to expand their services if municipal funding were provided.

Why then should city governments bother? Perhaps the most compelling and intriguing reason is the exciting opportunity which exists for developing innovative techniques for nurturing the early emotional and intellectual development of children. Public school systems remain frustrated in their ability adequately to serve their student clientele, particularly those from disadvantaged backgrounds. Yet child psychologists and early childhood development specialists place increasing importance on the quality of the formative years of a child's life. Direct municipal involvement in day care provides a unique opportunity to offer vitally needed services while developing new techniques, in a controlled environment, which seek to increase children's prospects and capacity for learning and normal development. When a municipal government elects to subcontract the child care function to third-party agencies or to adopt a voucher system, it relinquishes its ability to establish a continuum of learning and development from early childhood through public school.

On balance, then, local governments may wish to consider opting for a direct role in day care delivery if they have sufficient funds and capable enough administrators to ensure a stable day care operation, and if they have sufficiently imaginative planners and committed parents to explore the potential of day care centers as challenging environments for learning and personal development. In the absence of these strictly programmatic considerations, the compelling rationale for direct municipal involvement may continue to be partisan or community politics. If that is the case, the interests of many disparate groups will continue to be served, but it is not unequivocally clear that those of the children involved will necessarily be among them.

1 "Essentials of Public Welfare—A Statement of Principles," statement issued by the American Public Welfare Association, Washington, D.C., 8 December 1970, p. 3.

2 Ibid.

3 The fourteen states involved were: California, Colorado, Indiana, Maryland, Minnesota, Montana, New Jersey, New York, North Carolina, North Dakota, Ohio, Virginia, Wisconsin, and Wyoming. U.S., Department of Health, Education, and Welfare, Social and Rehabilitation Services, *Characteristics of State Plans for Aid to Families with Dependent Children* (Washington, D.C.: Social and Rehabilitation Services, Department of Health, Education, and Welfare, 1974).

4 U.S., Department of Health, Education, and Welfare, Social and Rehabilitation Services, National Center for Social Statistics, *The AFDC Family in the 1960s,* NCSS Report no. AFDC-2 (Washington, D.C.: National Center for Social Statistics, Social and Rehabilitation Services, Department of Health, Education, and Welfare, n.d.).

5 Data compiled from a number of Department of Health, Education, and Welfare reports.

6 American Association of Fund Raising Councils, Inc., *Giving USA,* 1976 Annual Report (New York: American Association of Fund Raising Councils, Inc., 1976).

7 Data compiled from 1976 federal budget proposals, various issues of the *Social Security Bulletin,* and various publications of the National Center for Social Statistics, Social and Rehabilitation Services, Department of Health, Education, and Welfare.

8 U.S., Department of Health, Education, and Welfare, *Characteristics of State Public Assistance Plans under the Social Security Act,* Public Assistance Report no. 50 (Washington, D.C.: Department of Health, Education, and Welfare, n.d.).

9 U.S., Department of Health, Education, and Welfare, Social and Rehabilitation Services, *The AFDC Family in the 1960s.*

10 Figure obtained from the National Center on Social Statistics, Social and Rehabilitation Services, Department of Health, Education, and Welfare.

11 National League of Cities / U.S. Conference of Mayors, "Income Security Issues," *Income Security Studies Newsletter,* February 1976, p. 7.

12 Data obtained from the Public Services Administration, Department of Health, Education, and Welfare.

13 Press release from office of Congresswoman Martha Griffiths, April 1974.

14 Information obtained from the Administration on Aging, Department of Health, Education, and Welfare.

15 Data obtained from the Medical Services Administration, Department of Health, Education, and Welfare.

16 Information compiled from *Social Security Bulletin,* January 1976 and February 1976, and from the federal budget.

17 Information obtained from the National Institute of Mental Health, Public Health Service, Department of Health, Education, and Welfare.

18 Information secured from National Center for Social Statistics, Department of Health, Education, and Welfare.

19 *Principles for an Income Security System for the United States* (Washington, D.C.: National Conference on Social Welfare, 1976), p. 62.

20 *Setting National Priorities: 1972* (Washington, D.C.: Brookings Institution, 1972).

21 *Principles for an Income Security System for the United States,* pp. 1–7.

22 "Income Maintenance," position paper of the National Urban League, New York, n.d.

23 "National Welfare Reform—A Bicentennial Priority," National Governors' Conference, Washington, D.C., 1976.

24 "Welfare Reform—A Proposal for Change," National Association of Counties, Washington, D.C., 24 February 1976.

25 Figures compiled from FY 1977 federal budget documents.

26 Figures compiled from FY 1977 federal budget documents.

27 The eighteen states with local responsibility for public welfare programs are: Alabama; California; Colorado; Indiana; Maryland; Minnesota; Mississippi; Montana; Nebraska; New Jersey; New York; North Carolina; North Dakota; Ohio; South Carolina; Virginia; Wisconsin; and Wyoming. Of the remaining 32 states, state responsibility appertains in every case and "umbrella" responsibility appertains in every case except Connecticut, Illinois, and Michigan. "Umbrella" responsibility also appertains in some of the 18 states listed above: Maryland; North Carolina; North Dakota; Wisconsin; and Wyoming. In the District of Columbia and Puerto Rico, state and "umbrella" responsibilities are found; "state" responsibility is found in the Virgin Islands. Source: Data supplied by the American Public Welfare Association, October 1976.

28 American Public Welfare Association, *1975 Public*

Welfare Directory (Washington, D.C.: American Public Welfare Association, 1975).

29 U.S., Department of Health, Education, and Welfare, Social and Rehabilitation Services, *Characteristics of General Assistance in the U.S.,* Public Assistance Report no. 39 (Washington D.C.: Department of Health, Education, and Welfare, 1970).

30 The Random House Dictionary of the English Language, unab. ed. (1971), s.v. "Counsel."

31 I. Galdston, "The Problem of Medical and Lay Psychotherapy: The Medical View," *American Journal of Psychotherapy* 4 (October 1950): 421.

32 Lewis R. Wolberg, *The Technique of Psychotherapy* (New York: Grune and Stratton, 1954), p. 111.

33 U.S., Department of Health, Education, and Welfare, Social and Rehabilitation Services, *Poor People at Work: An Annotated Bibliography on Semi-Professionals in Education, Health, and Welfare Services,* by Linda I. Millman and Catherine S. Chilman (Washington, D.C.: Government Printing Office, n.d.), p. iii.

34 U.S., Department of Health, Education, and Welfare, Social and Rehabilitation Services, *National Study of Social Welfare and Rehabilitation Workers, Work, and Organizational Contexts,* by Joseph A. Olmstead (Washington, D.C.: Government Printing Office, 1973), p. 56.

35 Two books which treat the theoretical evolution and implications of the counseling field are: Mary E. Richmond, *What Is Social Case Work?* (New York: Russell Sage Foundation, 1922); and Howard J. Parad, ed., *Ego Psychology and Dynamic Casework* (New York: Family Services Association of America, 1958).

36 Arthur Pearl and Frank Riessman, *New Careers for the Poor* (New York: The Free Press, 1965), p. 27.

37 Ibid.

38 Alexander Thomas and Samuel Sillen, *Racism and Psychiatry* (New York: Brunner/Mazel, Inc., 1972), p. 67.

39 R. O. Washington, *Program Evaluation In the Human Services* (Madison, Wisc.: Center for Advanced Studies in Human Services, University of Wisconsin, [1975]), p. 1.

40 Scott Briar, Preface to "Social Work In the New Age of Accountability," papers presented at an institute sponsored by the School of Social Work, University of Washington, Seattle, June 1973, p. iv.

41 *Directory of Community Services, 1975–76* (Atlanta: United Way of Metropolitan Atlanta, Inc., 1975).

42 Ricardo A. Millett, "A Survey: Service Delivery Systems and Black Alcoholism Needs In Metropolitan Atlanta," *Alcoholism and Blacks,* Alton M. Childs Series (Atlanta: Atlanta University School of Social Work, 1975), p. 56.

43 Nina R. Garton and Herbert A. Otto, *The Development of Theory and Practice in Social Casework* (Springfield: Charles C. Thomas, 1964), p. vii.

44 U.S., Department of Health, Education, and Welfare, Office of Education, *Pupil Personnel Services in Elementary and Secondary Schools,* Circular no. 325 (Washington, D.C.: Government Printing Office, 1951), p. 4.

45 Margaret O'Brien Steinfels, *Who's Minding the Children? The History and Politics of Day Care in America* (New York: Simon and Schuster, 1973), p. 36.

46 Basic works on the social history of child care include: Steinfels, *Who's Minding the Children?;* and Greta G. Fein and Alison Clarke Stewart, *Day Care in Context* (New York: John Wiley & Sons, 1973). For a discussion of British child care laws, see Pamela Roby, ed., *Child Care—Who Cares? Foreign and Domestic Infant and Early Childhood Development Policies* (New York: Basic Books, 1973).

47 Walter F. Mondale, "The Need for Child and Family Services," *Day Care and Early Education,* September–October 1975, p. 14

48 Steinfels, *Who's Minding the Children?,* p. 67.

49 Mondale, "The Need for Child and Family Services," p. 14.

50 Karla Shepard Goldman and Michael Lewis, *Child Care and Public Policy: A Case Study* (Princeton: Educational Testing Service, 1976), p. 32.

51 Tom Keating, *Child Care and Public Policy: A Dilemma at All Levels* (Claremont, California: Claremont Graduate School, 1975), p. 1.

52 Karla Shepard Goldman and Michael Lewis, *Child Care and Public Policy: A Case Study,* p. 12.

53 Day Care Consultation Service, *Toward Comprehensive Child Care* (Washington, D.C.: Day Care and Child Development Council of America, Inc., 1974), p. 18.

54 Richard M. Nixon, *New York Times,* 6 August 1969, quoted in Steinfels, *Who's Minding the Children?,* p. 188.

55 Steinfels, *Who's Minding the Children?,* p. 187.

56 U.S., Department of Health, Education, and Welfare, Office of Child Development, *Day Care I: A Statement of Principles* (Washington, D.C.: Office of Child Development, 1970), p. 2.

57 Albert Shanker, "Child Care and the Public Schools," *Day Care and Early Education,* September–October 1975, pp. 18–19, 53–55.

58 Theodore Taylor, "Let Us Reason Together," *Day Care and Early Education,* September–October 1975, p. 16.

59 Jule Sugarman, cited in Keating, *Child Care and Public Policy,* p. 9.

60 Ibid.

61 Connecticut State Department of Health, "Connecticut Child Care Center Guidelines," Hartford, Conn., 1974, p. 41.

62 Steinfels, *Who's Minding the Children?,* p. 199.

63 Ibid., p. 199.

64 D. J. Cohen, *Serving Pre-School Children* (Washington: Department of Health, Education, and Welfare, 1974), p. 1.

65 Cohen, *Serving Pre-School Children,* p. 63.

13

Health programs

The condition of being sound in body, mind, or spirit, or a state of freedom from physical disease or pain—these and other connotations of the word "health" as set forth in the anonymous print of the dictionary underlie concerns that lie at the very core of our lives as individuals and as members of our communities.[1] And thus programs to preserve the fortunate condition of the healthy, and to assist the members of the community rendered less than healthy through circumstances not of their own making, must be on the agenda of every local government, though their scope will, of course, vary from community to community in accordance with prevailing community sentiments and legislative expression. In the present chapter, three areas of health program management are described and analyzed from the perspective and experience of the separate authors. In the first section, a broad view is taken of the managerial issues underlying the provision of health services, supplemented by pertinent examples from the author's experience in Dade County, Florida.[2] The second portion of the chapter presents a similar analysis from the perspective of an experienced manager in the mental health field, using, in this case, examples from three contiguous counties in central Illinois. In the third section of the chapter, two authors with experience in local government management in California present their perspective on how local governments can approach the special problems of the handicapped—a field where attitudes of mind are equally as important as the minutiae of specific legislation. As in the case of the preceding chapter, the emphasis throughout is on bringing out the basic policy issues and managerial options, rather than to provide current reference data and case studies readily available elsewhere.

Health services management

The health services delivery area in local government is a broad one, ranging from the provision of emergency medical services to massive investments in public hospitals, with many variations in between. The spectrum ranges from traditional public health programs, public hospitals, and ambulatory health clinics through mental health programs and homemaker services to environmental health and occupational safety considerations. The precise range and the degree of local government commitment will, as with all human services, vary from locality to locality. The following discussion, therefore does not even pretend to provide a comprehensive survey of all facets of health services delivery systems or management, nor could it in the space available. Instead, a broad overview will be presented of the policy environment within which all local governments (and the private sector, too) must operate. This will be followed by a discussion of the basic managerial issues involved. Finally, some managerial approaches, based on the author's experience in Dade County, will be outlined.

An overview

Escalating costs In recent years, rapidly escalating costs have been the dominant feature of the health services delivery system. Health care increasingly has come to be looked upon as a basic right for all people, and citizens are demanding that health services be available to them regardless of their ability to pay for them. Not only are citizens demanding more and better health services, but they are demanding more convenient access to health facilities. No longer are those persons who cannot afford the services of a private physician or a private hospital willing to be herded into the central city charity hospital, often many miles from where they live. The impact of these trends, along with the possibility of some form of national health insurance, has enormous implications for local government managers in the near future.

Intergovernmental aspects Unlike traditional municipal services over which the manager and other local officials exercise virtually all policy control, health services have become the responsibility of the federal government and, to a lesser extent, of state governments. Policy direction and funding have traditionally been federally directed, in part due to a recognition by the federal government of its responsibility for the nation's health and, in large measure, as a result of the tremendously high costs involved. The federal government has preempted the major taxing mechanism and is distributing these dollars to state and local governments to help finance those services that are beyond the ability of local taxing authorities to fund. Recognizing that the cost of health services and facilities generally fall into this category, the federal government has provided money for the construction of hospitals and clinics and for services as well, particularly for identified populations. Rising costs of health services, particularly during the past two to three decades, are partly the result of an increasingly high level of personnel specialization and equipment specialization caused in turn by a burgeoning technology. The health services field is dominated by a profession which is characterized by a limited membership, a high level of reimbursement for services, and the absence of public policy control over the time spent in the profession. Oversight of the profession is accomplished only by a peer review system. Although only an estimated 20 percent of the cost of medical care can be attributed to physicians' fees,[3] it is the sole province of the physician to admit a person to a hospital or nursing home, or to order X rays, blood tests, and other medical procedures which escalate costs. As physicians increasingly have moved away from general medicine toward practicing increasingly narrow specialty fields, they have tended to use increasingly sophisticated (and costly) techniques and to serve more selected populations.

The attitude of the American people toward life itself is a major cause of high rate of health care services used by them and of the resulting costs. Through modern technology, it is possible to detect and prescribe cures for a vast array of illnesses. Lives are certainly saved as a result of modern technology and the discoveries of new drugs, but it is difficult to apply a cost–benefit ratio to the saving of a life—particularly when the life saved is one's own.

The dominance of the federal government in the health field has caused local managers to respond in almost a yo-yo fashion, as priorities have emanated from Washington and as dollars have flowed down the governmental ladder. Health dollars traditionally have been funneled to state governments and through the states to the county government level. In some states, federal and state funding has also flowed down to municipal public health departments. Cities frequently have responsibility for public hospitals. Generally, however, there have been in the past few federal or state legislative mandates to city governments in the health services field. County government officials, on the other hand, traditionally have been more concerned with the "soft" services; the growing awareness of city government officials to the human services needs of their constituents may in the future strengthen the city's role in hierarchical health systems.

National priorities For the rest of the 1970s and probably into the 1980s, national health programs will be governed by the priorities established in the National Health Planning and Resources Development Act of 1974. Through this act,

Congress set certain priorities to be applied through health planning and resources development programs. Because of their importance to local government managers, they are summarized herewith:

1. Provision of primary care services for medically underserved populations.
2. Development of multi-institutional systems for coordination or consolidation of institutional health services.
3. Development of medical group practices (especially those whose services are appropriately coordinated or integrated with institutional health services), health maintenance organizations (HMOs), and other organized systems for the provision of health care.
4. Training and increased utilization of physician assistants, and especially nurse clinicians.
5. Development of multi-institutional arrangements for the sharing of support services necessary to all health services institutions.
6. Promotion of activities to achieve needed improvements in the quality of health services.
7. Development by health services institutions of the capacity to provide various levels of care (including intensive care unit, acute general care, and extended care) on a geographically integrated basis.
8. Promotion of activities for the prevention of disease, including studies of nutritional and environmental factors affecting health and the provision of preventive health care service.
9. Adoption of uniform cost accounting, simplified reimbursement, and utilization reporting systems and improved management procedures for health services institutions.
10. Development of effective methods of educating the general public concerning proper personal (including preventive) health care and methods for effective use of available health services.

National priorities such as those just set out clearly emphasize the need to view health services from the *systems* standpoint. Integration within the health services system implies a spectrum of services consciously developed and related to other support systems. National emphasis has been placed on, and local communities are exploring, new configurations of primary health care services and HMOs. Local officials speculate on the implications of various proposals for national health insurance which have undergone congressional debate during the seventies. What changes would a health insurance program make in the relationship between private and public health systems? Local managers making decisions on capital programs and changing roles in health services need to keep an ear cocked to Washington for clues on appropriate responses.

Other distinguishing characteristics As the 1980s approach, municipal and county managers have become aware of other characteristics of the health services field that distinguishes it both from other human services and most other municipal functions as well. There is the overwhelming complexity of the health services field. Aside from the private sector, which provides the major part of the country's health care, there are the traditional public health programs, public hospitals, ambulatory health clinics, and extended care facilities. (Figure 13–1 sets out the complex situation in Dade County.) Increasingly, government has become involved in environmental health programs, including the increased attention to the control of air and water pollution. Mental health programs, drug and alcohol treatment programs, emergency medical services, home health programs, and homemaker programs are but a few of the health-related responsibilities that local officials have had to assume during the past decade. Organizationally, health services are often fragmented and frequently uncoordinated.

It is difficult to think of any other municipal service, or group of services, which has been subjected to so many changes in approach and practice as have been the health services. The categorical approach of the 1960s to the funding of specific health programs gave way in the 1970s to the integrative approach to both funding and organization. As Chapter 7 has pointed out, at the state and county level of government, health services frequently have been integrated into umbrella agencies housing other human services: departments of human resources, human services, or, as in Florida, health and rehabilitative services. The Dade County Department of Human Resources includes nursing home care, primary health care, some mental health programs, drug and alcohol treatment programs, noninstitutional elderly programs, child care, manpower, veterans services, and other miscellaneous programs.

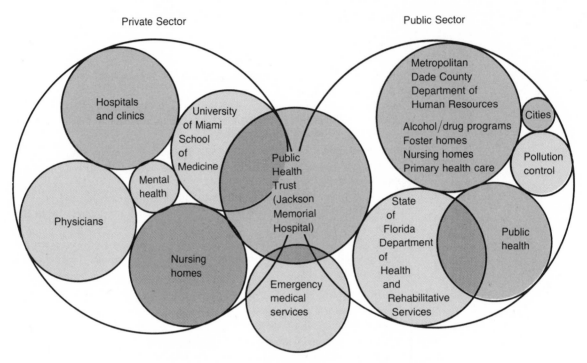

Figure 13–1   Health services administration in Dade County, Florida. The Public Health Trust (Jackson Memorial Hospital) and the emergency medical services system represent the link that connects the county's public and private sectors.

The necessity for managers to utilize advances in technology in order to improve the quality of other local government services is equally essential in bringing about the required changes that advanced technology can provide in the health field. Electronic data processing is fast becoming an integral part of providing quality medical services. Video telemetry, commonly referred to as "telemedicine," is being used to provide high quality medical care, particularly to patients who are at long distances from medical facilities and medical specialists. This technology may provide both an alternative in future years to the construction of expensive facilities and increased access to specialized medical help for persons distant from the locus of medical expertise. Telemedicine, accompanied by the use of nurse practitioners, has been used in Dade County in an experimental program linking several penal institutions with Jackson Memorial Hospital (see Figure 13–2).

Finally, managers are cognizant of pervasive constraints to the development of health policy, because health services (unlike most services for which local governments have monopolistic, or near monopolistic, control) is to date essentially dominated by the private sector over which government at any level has little control; in fact, realism dictates the recognition that the reverse is often true.

Managerial issues

Every city and county government has a piece of the health services system, even if it is no more than the disposal of waste products or the control of rabid dogs. For the local government manager seeking a new or a changed role within the health services system, a number of policy issues must be faced. First and foremost is the high cost of virtually all parts of the health system. The high cost of health services and the large cash investment needed for the building of modern health facilities may lead to a reluctance to take on new health services responsibilities. In the design of a highway system, the engineer recognizes a predictable and steady ''clientele'' and a twice-daily peak demand. Highways serving urban population are rarely designed to meet those peak demands: the cost would be prohibitive and even the motorist creeping along the expressway during a rush hour would be unwilling to pay for such overdesign. For most services provided by government, we can establish a level beyond which we are unwilling to be taxed. The frequent defeat of bond issues is evidence of such public policy setting.

Establishing the proper level of services: some questions to ask
Establishing an appropriate level in the health field is more difficult. For the most part, there is no steady and regular demand. Citizens of a community do not need a doctor or a hospital until they are sick; then they want the best possible medical care with the least possible delay. The community wants the best in medical services and equipment because lives are at stake and we find it difficult, if not impossible, to place a dollar value on saving a life. We want a health system designed for the peak load, for the epidemic or the emergency.

As the manager faces decision points regarding an expanded or changed role in the provision of health services, a number of basic questions need to be answered. Should *this* city get into the provision of health services? At what level will this city enter the health services system? Will this city be in competition with other governments, or is some new health service needed to complement services provided by other levels of governments or the private sector? Will a new health service compete with the private sector? To whom will health services be provided? All citizens? Poor people? Special risk populations? Would it be in the best interest of the city or county to provide the service directly or to contract with another unit of government or a private organization? Are there alternative approaches to the building of a clinic or a hospital? What should be the role of consumers in the planning and administration of health services?

Town doctored Faced with a threatening shortage of doctors, and after several unsuccessful efforts to attract new doctors into the community, the town manager of Enfield, Connecticut, took a more direct approach. He arranged for a grant from HEW to cover the services of two doctors from the National Health Service Corps to come to the city for a period of two years. The city rented a doctor's office, engaged nurses, equipped the office, and set the doctors up in practice. Fees are charged on the same scale as other doctors in town, and are used to repay the city and HEW for their proportional shares of program costs.

Analyzing alternatives
The high cost of providing almost any health service makes it imperative that alternative approaches be analyzed carefully. Among these alternatives are various levels of home care provided by paraprofessionals. A return to midwifery, utilizing neighborhood clinics, may be an alternative approach to the building of a new hospital obstetrical ward. Nurse–midwives are also being used increasingly to provide high quality care, under the direction of a

physician, at a lower cost than if an obstetrician provided the equivalent level of care. Nurse practitioners are increasingly being used for similar reasons. The development of a transportation system which will take a patient to a distant clinic or hospital providing a wide range of professional services may be a less expensive and more practical alternative than building a new facility.

Mobile health units are used by some communities as partial alternatives to health facility construction. The training of physician assistants, nurse practitioners, and paraprofessionals—and even the training of "people to help people" and to help themselves—is an approach that must be taken to make even a bare beginning in the containment of costs for medical services. A further discussion of alternatives is included in the next section.

The role of community pressures   Decisions regarding health services responsibilities are not made in a vacuum, of course. Most managers are acutely aware of political realities and community attitudes. Managers' decisions cannot help but be affected by the relative power of vocal pressure groups: in large cities, it could,

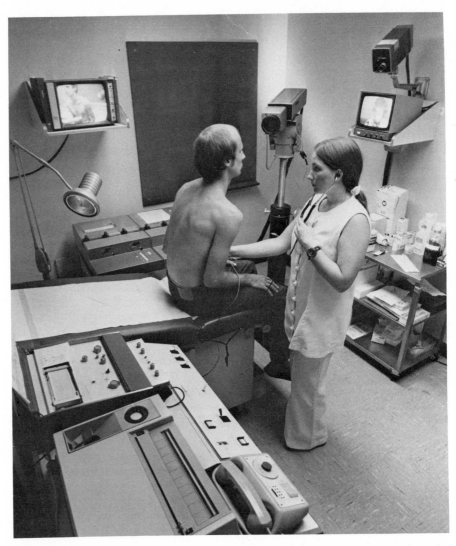

Figure 13–2   An experimental program in Dade County, Florida, has employed a telemedicine system. A nurse practitioner examines an inmate in the county jail medical clinic (left), while a doctor at Jackson Memorial Hospital views the scene (right). [Note: The persons in the photographs are professional models.]

for instance, be the medical school that will really be "calling the shots" for the local government in the health services field. Private physicians' groups or hospital associations may influence decisions. Minority groups may be effective in making their demands for better health services heard in the council chambers. Community crises may move managers in unanticipated directions. If a patient dies in the hospital emergency room because of overcrowded conditions or understaffing, the community's emotional response may dictate the purchase of some new facility to relieve the overcrowding. National publicity about overcrowding in the emergency room of Jackson Memorial Hospital in Dade County and the death of an elderly patient waiting to be seen, led to the decision by the Dade County Commission to purchase a nursing home. Overnight, the county government was in the nursing home business.

The decentralization issue   Another consideration facing local government decision makers is the decentralization issue. Would it be better to concentrate the available medical talent and equipment in a central location capable of handling the whole range of medical services than to develop a system of neighborhood health clinics providing greater access, but a more limited array of services? Cost as well as convenience must be taken into consideration. Major community controversies may rage over this issue, and decisions relating to it may well be among

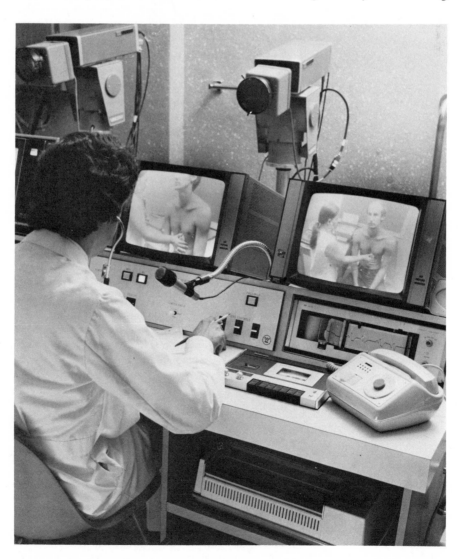

the most important and far-reaching of any the manager is called upon to make. On the one hand, there may be the medical establishment and perhaps a powerful medical school arguing for a bigger and better central facility. On the other, there will be community-based groups demanding better health services closer to home. In the umpire's role on this as well as other issues will be the health systems agency (HSA) provided for in the National Health Planning and Resource Development Act. Perhaps in no other local government area has so much authority and responsibility been placed in a body not appointed by, or responsible to, the electorate. Local government managers are directly affected in their health planning and policy-making roles by the existence of the HSA mandate, whether the local government itself becomes the HSA or whether it is an independent organization. The legislation provides that the governing body of the HSA shall be 60 percent consumers of health care and 40 percent providers of health care. Because of the influence which the local HSA will exert on managers dealing with health care issues, the defined functions are identified here. According to the act, the functions of health systems agencies include that it:

1. Shall assemble and analyze data pertaining to the health systems area.
2. Establish, annually review, and amend as necessary a health systems plan (HSP).
3. Establish, annually review, and amend as necessary an annual implementation plan (AIP) which describes objectives that will achieve the goals of the HSP and set priorities among the objectives.
4. Provide copies annually of the agency's HSP to the state agency and statewide health coordinating council (SHCC).
5. Shall provide the SHCC with a copy of the HSA's AIP.
6. Shall develop and publish specific plans and projects for achieving the objectives established in the AIP, including strategies for the development and implementation of programs and the priority assigned to the plans and projects developed.
7. Shall seek, to the extent practicable, to implement its HSP and AIP with the assistance of individuals, and public and private entities, in its health service area.
8. May provide, in accordance with the priorities established in the AIP, technical assistance to individuals, and public and private entities, for the development of projects and programs which the HSA determines are necessary to achieve the health system described in the HSP
9. Shall, in accordance with the priorities established in the AIP, make grants to public and nonprofit private entities and enter into contracts with individuals, and public and private nonprofit entities, to assist them in planning and developing projects and programs which the agency determines are necessary for the achievement of the health system described in the HSP. (No grants or contract under this subsection may be used to pay either the costs incurred by an entity or individual in the delivery of health services or the cost of construction or modernization of medical facilities.)
10. Shall seek to enter into written agreements with both the Professional Services Review Organization and the A-95 agency in the health services area for the purpose of achieving coordination of their respective activities.
11. Shall coordinate its activities with appropriate entities in the health services area. Where appropriate, the HSA shall secure data from such entities for use in its planning and development activities, provide technical assistance to such entities, and enter into agreements with such entities that will assure that actions taken by such entities which alter the area's health system will be taken in a manner which is consistent with the area's HSP and AIP.
12. Shall review the need for new institutional health services proposed or developed in the health services area of such HSA, and make *recommendations* to the appropriate state agency respecting such services.

13. Shall review on a periodic basis (but at least every 5 years) all institutional health services offered in the health services area of the HSA and shall make *recommendations* to the state agency respecting the appropriateness in the area of such service. (An initial review of existing institutional health services to be completed within 3 years after full designation as a HSA.)
14. Shall annually recommend to the state agency projects for the modernization, construction, and conversion of medical facilities in the health services area which will achieve the HSP and AIP of the HSA, and priorities among such projects.
15. Shall review and *approve* and *disapprove* each specified proposed use of federal funds within its health services area.

The centralization/decentralization issue also needs to be viewed in a regional perspective, particularly by managers of small communities. The range of medical facilities and services available on a regional basis will affect decisions on the nature of services to be provided. For example, the availability of a major metropolitan medical center at some distance from a small community may suggest the desirability of providing a primary health care clinic rather than construction of a small hospital.

To contract or not to contract Another vital issue with which managers are concerned is the question of whether to provide or to contract. Can the city or county government provide a particular health service efficiently and effectively? Or is service best provided, through a contract, by some private organization? Questions of managerial control, accountability, and quality control need to be raised. The HSA may espouse a philosophy of operation which may or may not be consistent with a manager's philosophy, but which may in fact influence the decision-making process.

Sometimes health issues must be viewed against a socioenvironmental background relating to the cultural and social mores of the community's population. Cultural minorities and the poor, which are the prime populations in need, often perceive the health system as an alien bureaucratic organization oriented toward maintaining its own good jobs and high pay. Such groups suggest solutions that would require "establishment" health care personnel to change their patterns of behavior to agree with those groups' own life styles.

Professionals and clients: contrasting moves Health professionals, in contrast, perceive health problems as consequences of poverty—overcrowding, educational limitations, disorganized family structure, etc. Most professionals suggest a major education program for the community, with emphasis on teaching individuals how to enter the health system and how to utilize resources once in it. Essentially, they contend that recipients of service should change their patterns of behavior to agree with standard professional operating procedures.

Cultural minorities and individuals of low socioeconomic status see the same problems in health care that professionals do; however, they resist attempts to be reshaped or resocialized into a middle class mold in order to use the system "correctly." The sensitive manager is aware of this shortfall and makes an attempt to determine what these various groups want, and is willing to try to solve their problems on their terms. "Their" terms may be community-based planning efforts and community control over neighborhood health institutions. Migrant workers, as an example, may put emphasis on the presence of public health nurses in the labor camps (for a variety of good and valid reasons) rather than on the transporting of the migrants to the antiseptic, and perhaps intimidating, clinic.

Consumer participation in the planning and administration of a health service is likely to be an increasingly important issue. Citizen groups, particularly among minorities, have perceptions of their needs which may be quite different from those held by the professional health planner or clinic administrator. (See Chapter

5 for discussion of "perceived need.") Citizens may demand a strong role in the planning process and may, in fact, organize themselves with the intention of receiving funds to operate a facility. Local government managers often struggle to define the appropriate role for citizens to play. In an evaluation of the nature of the delivery of primary health care in Dade County, Florida, a panel of health professionals agreed on a statement of responsibilities which a citizen board might have, whether it was an advisory group to a health service provided by the local government or a nonprofit corporation board established to operate a health facility. This statement might serve to guide others:

1. Report personal impressions of health services and the opinions of others.
2. Review and comment on health program assessment reports.
3. Name and rank health problems.
4. Review and recommend relative to the goals statements from planners.
5. Review facts presented by planners and program operators.
6. Review health service problem definition statements about facts and problems.
7. Review capital expenditure problem definition statements.
8. Review and tentatively approve alternative feasible plans for health service projects.
9. Rank health service project plans.
10. The citizen's advisory committee to a public agency or the board of directors of a corporation, as appropriate, endorses the implementation of the most preferred project plan.[4]

Managerial approaches

Whether or not a local government is providing direct health services, local officials do have a responsibility for the health needs of their constituency. The city or county manager, the director of a department of human resources, a public health director, is responsible for establishing a perspective against which decision-makers can formulate policy. Basic to this is the identification of the role a particular governmental entity will play in the health services field; what it is at the present, what it may be in the future.

Identifying needs and resources Identification of needs and of resources to meet those needs is crucial. Before making any changes, it is important to identify the role and influence of other agencies. Alternative organizational approaches and the role of consumers must be identified. The importance assigned to identifying the role of a particular local government in the health field is based on recognition of the fact that elected local government officials are voted into office by the citizens to provide for their health, welfare, and safety. Even though a particular local government may decide against providing a particular health service, or any service at all, there is a responsibility at the local government level to ensure that the citizens do have access to needed health services. That responsibility may be exercised through the monitoring of services provided by other agencies, public or private, or the referral of persons to other agencies.

City and county roles Certainly all local officials have an obligation to serve in an advocacy role and to ensure that other systems treat citizens equitably. The city may provide fiscal coordination through the management and distribution of funds derived from multiple sources, and may participate in joint planning efforts with other governmental agencies. The county's role in direct health services delivery will, in most states, be stronger and more varied than the city's, although lead responsibility will vary from state to state. Whether the city manager is weighing the advantages and disadvantages of getting into the health services field at all, or the county manager is developing priorities for meeting new needs or restructuring the current system, similar approaches will be used.

Assessing health needs   City or county planning processes will include an assessment of the health needs of the community (a process outlined in Chapters 5 and 6). Local government planners should work closely with the health systems agency staff on needs identification; the extent of cooperation in the process will vary from community to community. Demographic information will be used to identify needs of particular populations. Taking the elderly as an example, longer life expectancies dictate increasing attention to all the needs, and particularly the health needs, of this population subgroup. It is the role of the manager to identify population trends in order to make plans for meeting as many predictable needs as possible. As needs for new services or changes in services are identified, the manager will recommend how that service should be provided and by which agency, in accordance with established policy on the appropriate role of the city or county government.

Facilities: the "bottom line"   Medical facilities are expensive to build and even more expensive to operate. Periods of tight budgets may cause managers to doubt the feasibility of financing certain services in the future—services to be provided in facilities mandated by the voters when, during a more expansionist period, they approved a bond issue. Careful cost analysis must be done before such decisions are made. The glamor of a beautiful hospital or clinic equipped with the latest technologically advanced equipment must be weighed against projections of ever-increasing costs of staffing and operating such facility. How elaborate a facility is really needed for the provision of primary care, or secondary care? A costly plant may only be justified for the provision of tertiary care. The possible location of primary health care services in storefronts, in a portion of a multiservice facility, or in prefab or mobile units needs to be considered. Are there existing services already in place that can be tapped and perhaps expanded? Can the fire department, for example, be used in the provision of an emergency medical service system?

In the consideration of alternatives, managers should view the entire service picture to best determine the appropriate facilities for their particular communities. This service picture ranges from a variety of institutional settings to various home care arrangements, including visiting nurses, home health aides, homemakers, and "night watchers" (who sit with ill patients so that their families can get some sleep).

Nursing reduces disbursing

Gainesville, Florida, began an occupational health nurse program through which a nurse was hired to serve municipal employees in much the same manner as a school nurse serves pupils. The nurse serves as liaison between physicians, management, and employees in areas such as medical leaves of absence and temporary or permanent job transfers due to illness or injury. Through this program, the city has achieved substantial cost reductions in workmen's compensation plans since much of the primary care and treatment are provided by the nurse in a clinic. Moreover, through follow-up care, there has been a significant reduction in time lost due to employees being away from their jobs owing to injury or illness. The city also has reduced its emergency medical services cost.

When consideration is being given to building a health facility or to establishment of a health service, the manager will identify the resources available to meet the defined need. Availability of staff with the required professional training is, of course, the most basic resource. Because of the high costs associated with the use of the services of doctors and nurses, increasing attention is being given to the training and utilization of paraprofessionals and paramedics. Paraprofessional positions in the medical profession include for example, nurses aides and laboratory technicians. A paramedic is trained to provide some level of medical assistance beyond first-aid treatment, particularly of an emergency nature.

Sometimes, of course, there will be a need for staff with specialized training. If required skills are not presently available, the manager will need to determine whether the local medical school, university, community college, or hospital can provide necessary training. For example, when Dade County was ready to establish a kidney dialysis unit to serve an area of the county that was distant from the county's hospital, it was necessary to develop a program at the hospital to train additional nurses in the use of the specialized equipment. In connection with this, decisions will be made on whether the local government needs to cover the cost of such training. One possible method is to provide scholarships in return for the recipient's agreement to work for the local government for a period of time.

Because of particularly high costs, funding considerations are more important in health services than in many other governmental services. Are federal or state dollars available? At what level will local tax dollars be committed? If the local government is contracting with another agency for services, will there be a flat fee or a fee-for-service contract? Will patient fees be charged and at what level?

Roles of other agencies   In addition to a thorough analysis of resources available, it is important that the manager identify the roles and influences of other agencies (a matter discussed in detail in Chapter 8). Chief among these other agencies will be the HSA, which will have a strong influence and will be in a position to exercise veto power over the use of federal dollars for health programs. The public health department and the local medical association may well influence decisions regarding the provision of a new service or facility. Agencies established by the state or federal government for planning or funding purposes may need to be consulted. Voluntary agencies may, depending on the community, have a role to play. The relationship between private hospitals and clinics to a new health service will need to be identified. It is also important to take into account the regulatory agencies whose approval is needed before a new service or facility can become operative. As one local official put it, "You add up all of the people who can say no."

Selecting the right organizational structure: a case study   A further managerial responsibility is to identify and recommend the appropriate organizational structure for the delivery of a particular service along the lines developed in Chapter 7. Organizational approaches include direct provision of the service by the city or county using government personnel; contracting for the service with another unit of government or a private organization; and the establishment of a public "authority" or a consumer-based corporation. Many local government officials have had experience with direct operation and with utilization of public authorities for provision of health or other services. The utilization of consumer-based corporations may not be as common. The experience of Dade County, Florida, in the establishment of Community Health Incorporated (CHI) for the purpose of operating a major medical facility in the far south end of the county, may be illustrative of some of the issues to be considered.

Having become acutely aware of the enormous community demand for an expanded health program—which resulted from the county's decision to close an old, small hospital serving the indigent population—county officials explored alternatives. Of particular concern to county officials and to their advisers, the staff of the independent health planning council (now the local HSA), was the role of physicians in the determination of what health services should be provided. Recognizing the strength of physician influence, the planners opted for an organizational structure which placed consumer–citizens in an intermediary position between the medical establishment and the public administration. The reasoning behind this was based on the fact that citizens can often exert pressures for particular health services which public officials cannot. In order to assure a strong role for the consumer–citizens, a nonprofit cooperative CHI—was formed, composed of citizens representative of the various groups in the surrounding area. Unclear from the beginning was a definition of the organization's role, a problem which plagued CHI and the county government in subsequent years. Some thought the organization should be the voice of the vast South Dade community in pressuring public and private resources to better serve the community; others saw it as a governing body for operation of primary health care services (to be provided ultimately in a shiny new clinic facility).

The need for citizen–consumer concern for the total health concerns of a large area of the community fell by the wayside as organizational problems relating to the operation of a particular health facility took precedence. Whether a consumer-based organization, rather than a governmental body, should *operate* rather than *advise* and express satisfaction or dissatisfaction with services rendered, is an issue not easily resolved, but one with which the manager must grapple. From the experience with CHI, county staff concluded (a decision not approved by the professional health planners) that the advisory role was the preferable one.

Aside from the rationale behind the selection of a particular organizational structure, Dade County's experience in providing a new health service is illustrative of a number of other issues which faced the county manager. In spite of great public insistence on construction of a new hospital to replace the old one (which was ultimately demolished), the county manager chose to accept the recommendation of the health planning council which had taken a careful look at the demographic characteristics of the area. An increase in the upper income population in the area indicated to the planners a need for a new private hospital. The needs assessment indicated, however, that the low income black and migrant population was almost totally unserved by existing primary health care facilities. At the time, ambulatory care facilities were ineligible for third-party payments and the planners accordingly recommended a new county-supported primary health care facility to serve the population unable to purchase health care from private providers.

The design of the facility illustrated another problem often faced by managers: the glamor of architectural design elements. Too often, planners and administrators are carried away by design considerations and end up adapting service programs to design, rather than the reverse. When physicians are the designers, their inclination is to design the ''biggest and best.'' Some control must be exerted by the funding entity. In reflecting on the overdesign of the Dade County health clinic under discussion, one local official suggested the desirability of utilizing the advice and judgment of the publically oriented physicians on the local payroll to evaluate the recommendations concerning health services and facilities made by the physicians who are outside of the public policy makers' control.

Contingency planning   In health services, as in other municipal services affecting the health, welfare, and safety of citizens, it is important to undertake some contingency planning. Local officials are ''on the spot'' when an emergency occurs. Plans are made for the mobilization of health services to meet natural disasters and mass tragedies, such as an accident involving a bus load of school children or an airplane crash. Labor problems assume particular gravity when nurses go on strike. When nursing home operators refuse to accept patients during a rate dispute, hospitals will become overcrowded, and life and death situations are more likely to arise.

Major community events may also have implications for health services. In 1972, both political conventions were held in Miami Beach, a major city in Dade

County. Because of the potentially explosive emotions related to the war in Viet Nam of many of the people who converged upon Dade County, extraordinary protective measures were taken, ranging from extra protection of the public water supply to street drug therapy and the utilization of "street medics."

Multiservice facilities   The emphasis of human services integration in the late 1970s has led in the health field to greater attention to medically based, multiservice facilities. In Minneapolis, primary health care for senior citizens is provided as an adjunct service by a local hospital. Geriatric "day hospitals" are in use in England to provide hospital-based evaluation and treatment without having to admit patients as residents. In Dade County, two county-operated nursing homes serve as the base for multiservice facilities. One, a geriatric nursing home, includes a kidney dialysis unit and physical therapy treatment program serving residents of the surrounding area, plus an adult day care center for the frail elderly.

Dade County Standards: Primary Care or General Health and Medical Care

1. A public ambulatory health care center takes part in a person's health and medical care when the person cannot do it adequately and desires health services, or when the well-being of the larger community is jeopardized by the person's problem.

2. The objectives of the center, as well as the objectives of the services which it offers, are clearly stated in writing.

3. The organizational structure of the center is designed to implement the objectives effectively and efficiently, and this structure is established by the governing authority and appropriately documented.

4. A private nonprofit or public center is operating under the direction of an identified governing authority which is responsible for the center and for the services rendered in it.

5. The governing authority for a public center has established an advisory body responsible for review and comment on policies and activities as they pertain to the center.

6. The governing authority or advisory body composition is a cross-section of consumers and providers of health services, with consumers comprising the majority of the membership.

7. The authority for administration of the center is delegated by the center's governing authority to a chief executive officer.

8. Policy and procedure manuals are

developed for effectively implementing the objectives of the center so that the benefits which people derive from being served at the center are clearly those authorized by the governing authority.

9. The center has in effect a program, based on written policies and procedures, to review and evaluate systematically the administrative and professional services it provides, and to determine the extent to which its stated objectives are being met.

10. The administrative organization of the center is so structured as to facilitate its management by isolating costs within those categories useful to cost containment, by fostering incentives to reduce costs, and by contributing to the ease, convenience, and accuracy of monitoring.

11. The center has policies that require financial accountability, compliance with all laws, controls and agreements, economy in operations, efficiency in the use of resources, and success in achieving the results expected of the program.

12. The center has a sufficient number of qualified personnel to meet the needs, including those of cultural uniqueness, of the patients it serves in accordance with its stated objectives, and priority is given to the hiring of qualified individuals from the community served.

13. Space, facilities, and equipment

necessary for effective patient care are in accordance with the personnel authorized and the stated objectives of the center.

14. The center has an organized professional staff responsible for creating and maintaining an optimal level of professional performance, and for the continuing review and evaluation of patient care in a manner that helps achieve the objectives of the center.

15. The center objectives provide for general health and medical care activities, which identify, diagnose, and treat relatively uncomplicated illnesses and injuries, including referral to and consultation with specialized professionals when necessary and the professional supervision of continuing care. The center objectives also provide for activities which enable individuals to care more effectively for their own health, to care for their own problems and the problems of their families, and to participate constructively in the health institutions of the community.

16. Each person who comes to the center is served promptly and appropriately within the center's scope of service and by the personnel appropriate to the health and medical assessment needed. The problems identified are made known to the person served, and a jointly made plan to alleviate the problem is developed by the person and the center personnel in such form that subsequent judgments can be readily made as to whether or not the services rendered have assisted in solving the problem.

17. The center provides health education only in relation to specific identified personal health care issues which are judged necessary by the person served, by the health professional serving that person, or by the public health agency which has the duty to protect the community.

18. The center informs all persons it serves of the services which they should expect from the health professionals serving them, including the kinds of information with which health professionals should provide them.

19. Radiology services consistent with the center's objectives are provided by arrangement with an accredited or certified hospital or other qualified provider, or by the center itself.

20. Laboratory services consistent with the center's objectives are provided by an outside laboratory which is part of an accredited or certified hospital, or by an outside laboratory which is approved to provide services as an independent laboratory, or directly by the center itself.

21. The center has a unit to care for minor problems for which immediate medical attention is desirable. The unit has the same hours as the center.

22. The center does not provide an emergency room.

23. The center maintains written agreements with medical and surgical institutions for the referral, diagnosis, and treatment of center patients.

24. Pharmaceutical services are consistent with the objectives of the center. If pharmaceutical services are offered directly by the center, they are provided in accordance with accepted professional principles and appropriate federal, state, and local laws.

25. A reporting system to carry out program evaluation and to meet all applicable professional, administrative, and legal requirements is established and maintained.

26. A patient health and medical record system is established, currently maintained, and evaluated periodically in relation to center objectives.

Figure 13–3 Standards established by Dade County, Florida, for primary or general health and medical care. See text for further discussion. (Source: Administrative Review Panel, "Review of Family Health Center Program and Facility Plan," County Manager's Office, Dade County, Florida, 30 June 1976, pp. 13–15.)

The other county-operated nursing home provides care for hard-to-place nursing home patients and also serves as a detoxification center for both drug and alcohol abusers. Health clinics are included in human resources service centers in Chattanooga, Tennessee, and other cities. Prudent budgeting demands the maximization of existing facilities. Often the location of health services facilities in close proximity to other human services facilities and the combining of health-related services is mutually enhancing.

Enunciating objectives and guidelines Any new program in which government participates should have clearly enunciated objectives and guidelines; health care programs are no exception. Figure 13–3 reproduces a set of guidelines to be applied to the provision of primary care, and developed for Dade County by a panel of health professionals. With some modification, the principles contained in the guidelines could be applied to other kinds of health services. The Dade County guidelines for primary care or general health and medical care, developed after months of attention from a multidisciplinary group of health professionals, may be useful to local government managers and health services directors in the development of new programs or in the evaluation of existing programs.

Summary

The preceding discussion has presented some of the thoughts of one group of professionals in one department on the broad aspects of health services management that often get overlooked in the pressure of day-to-day budgetary and other crises. Some of the national trends shaping health services management have been noted, with rising costs being a prime concern. The discussion has continued by ranging through some of the basic managerial issues regarding the level of services; alternative approaches to providing those services; community pressures; centralization and decentralization; the role of contracting; and the different mindsets of clients and professionals. Finally, a look has been taken at some of the practical managerial approaches using examples from the Dade County experiences: the question of identifying needs and resources; the roles of other agencies; organizational structure; contingency planning; multiservice facilities; and the all-important enunciation of objectives and guidelines.

But what of the future? It seems highly probable that cost containment of health services will in the future be a major concern to local government managers. More careful consideration will need to be given to providing a spectrum of services and to assigning a patient to the least expensive appropriate health services alternative. Local government managers will be giving increasing attention to the training and employment of "physician extenders" and paraprofessionals.

The National Health Planning and Resources Development Act of 1974 emphasizes the interrelationship of health services and other support services. Health services do need to be related to other human services and many local managers will seek ways of colocating health services with related social services and of viewing "person care" as a total system. Alternatives to institutionalization through the provision of a variety of social services will be explored not only as cost containment measures, but as means of preserving and enhancing human dignity.

City and county managers trained in the broad field of public administration may find that this most significant role in improving the quality of health care will be in the integration of services into a system of health care which will reflect the wide range of intensity of needs for health and supporting social services.

Managing mental health services

The psychologically distressed exist in every community and at every level of society. If their distress reaches beyond their capacity to handle it, they may well need help. The help may come from family, from friends, from private agencies, or—most pertinently in the present context—from the local government in whose jurisdiction they live. The following discussion therefore first takes a broad look at the profound changes that have occurred in recent years in perceptions and policies regarding public sector provision of health services for the mentally ill. These changes underlie all major managerial options in this area. Secondly, the discussion analyzes the specific managerial experience and challenges encountered in the operation of mental health delivery services in three continuous counties in central Illinois.

The change to community care

Since the 1960s, changes in the delivery of mental health services have indeed been both numerous and profound. The most dramatic change has been from institutional to community-based care for the mentally ill, a change that has broad implications for political and legislative action and whose long-term repercussions for local government managers and others have not yet begun to surface.

Four critical factors   The departure from treatment in institutions to treatment in the community came about primarily from four factors: changes in treatment philosophy; exposure of the horrors of the state hospital back wards; the cost of residential care; and legislation supporting the development of treatment alternatives.

Changes in treatment philosophy   The impetus for change in treatment philosophy originated during and following World War II when the need for expediency forced a new treatment model. It became apparent that wartime psychiatric casualties treated briefly and returned to duty fared as well or better than their counterparts who were hospitalized for lengthier periods. The latter group not only required longer treatment, but the initial hospitalization seemed to establish the chronicity of their illness and, with unfortunate frequency, to guarantee subsequent rehospitalization.

A further treatment change of critical significance to the institutional exodus was the development of psychotropic drugs. When chemical management of disturbed behavior became possible, community management of "troublesome" people became a reality.

Deficiencies in the state hospital system   Overcrowded, understaffed, and desperately underfinanced, the state institutions of the 1950s and early 1960s were parodies of the rural retreats envisioned as healing agents by the humanitarians of the preceding century. As the public media exposed the deprivation and degradation of citizens warehoused in state hospital back wards, the public climate not only heated up considerably, but became somewhat more receptive to community care of its citizen rejects.

Mushrooming costs   As a result of the exposés of the institutional system, state hospital costs skyrocketed as these institutions provided some approximation of reasonable care. Improved staff–patient ratios, capital improvements, salary upgrading, active treatment—all came with a high price tag attached. In at least one state, by the mid-1970s, the mental health department employed more persons than any other department. As costs and demands for services accelerated and the scope of the problem mushroomed, state government increasingly encouraged local participation in the planning, provision, and financing of mental health care.

Legislative intervention   Meanwhile in 1963, the federal government passed the historic Community Mental Health Centers Act and, subsequently, amendments to this act. Later, by override, Congress effected the Community Mental Health Centers Act of 1975. Basically the acts encompass grant mechanisms whereby public and private not-for-profit entities may secure federal dollars to engage in an extensive set of mental health activities. Like many federal funding mechanisms, the mental health grants provide federal funds on a declining scale and require proportionate nonfederal funding on an increasing scale. Many observers have felt that the fine print on the grant applications invites communities to perjure their souls in guaranteeing financial, treatment, and personnel resources to be, if not all things to all people, a reasonable facsimile thereof.

As part of the financial plan which theoretically assures continuation of comprehensive mental health services, applicants must prognosticate substantial increases in nonfederal dollars. A local tax base supporting mental health services is surely one of the more attractive funding possibilities and appears with some frequency as part of the creative writing on grant applications.

Problems of definition   For therapeutic, humane, financial, and legislative reasons, therefore, the local community has become increasingly involved in the care of the mentally ill. There remain unanswered, however, the questions that have consistently defied resolution. What is mental illness? What causes mental illness? What is effective therapeutic intervention? And, finally, who is responsible for providing uncertain treatment to an undefined population?

These knowledge gaps pose particular problems for governmental units trained to do their homework prior to the planning and decision-making process. The planning process assumes definition of a problem, rational solution, and resources available whose application would solve the problem. It simply is not like that in mental health.

Changing popular perceptions   Most citizens are generally aware that an amorphous thing defined as "mental illness" exists. The state of their knowledge may range from the individual's own personal encounter with a mental health professional to gossip-level repetition of a horror story whose central character is one of those afflicted citizens who probably ought to be safely stashed away behind bars—indefinitely. But second-hand knowledge of emotional problems is decreasing. A significant proportion of our citizens, as well as their elected or appointed officials, have themselves or within their families experienced and sought help for some recognized form of emotional distress. However, recipients of mental health services do not as a by-product develop expertise in semantics.

Changing professional viewpoints   Not only is the general public hard-pressed to define mental illness or mental health; there is nothing approaching consensus among the professionals. One of the problems of definition is elaborated by Franklyn Arnhoff in an article in which he summarized developments germane to current thinking: "The term mental health which had at first served primarily as a euphemism for 'mental illness' now expanded to aggregate all behavior ranging from the everyday thoughts and feelings and inner life of everyman to the extreme psychosocial disturbances of the florid psychoses." [5]

Dr. Arnhoff is representative of persons who subscribe to the theory that mental illness is a disease entity, separate from the disturbances in feelings and functions which to some degree and in varying schedules of frequency are universally experienced. He postulates that proponents of the continuum theory (that there is no distinct malaise, mental illness per se, but rather a pathological progression of the thoughts, feelings and actions common to all human beings) are ignoring the evidence of psychobiologic findings.

At the other end of the spectrum are proponents of the sick society as opposed to the sick individual hypothesis. Advocates of the community-as-patient theory cite sociological studies and community demonstration projects as prima facie evidence. Their point of view is expressed by Dr. Leo Levy as follows:

What we call mental health is a problem of major proportion which is related to and is a part of the spectrum of social problems which include slums and urban congestion, rural health and welfare, alcoholism and drug addiction, ethnic and racial conflict, poverty, dependence, unemployment, illness, and education.

Mental health is part of the total set of problems which fall under the rubric of health, education and welfare. Their boundaries overlap and it is doubtful if one can be solved without simultaneously working with the others. There is also serious question as to how much of what we now call mental illness is, in effect, social incompetence in which psychotherapeutic treatment is of little or no effect.[6]

David E. Bazelon, chief judge of the United States Court of Appeals for the District of Columbia, further supported this point of view in discussing the plight of the mentally and emotionally handicapped children, primarily the children of the urban poor who wind up in juvenile courts and institutions. "For these children, society's promise of treatment and rehabilitation are illusory deceptions. For child psychiatrists, the greatest contribution to help such children is to be totally honest in loudly proclaiming that you do not have either the knowledge or the tools or wizardry to wipe out the afflictions of children in our communities or institutions. It's time for all of us caretakers to stop hiding the smell of society's outhouses." [7]

Changing financial and legislative attitudes   The confusion of terminology and etiology extends into the financial and legislative components of the mental health service delivery system. In practice, most state governments act as though they recognize a particularly vulnerable, high-risk population (Dr. Arnhoff's "floridly psychotic") for whom they continue to bear financial and treatment responsibility. Almost without exception state governments continue, for instance, to operate the institutional system.

The change is that such institutional treatment is now as brief as possible, perhaps only long enough to stabilize medication prior to returning the patient to the community. Comprehensive mental health services assume that as part of the continuum of services, postdischarge care is available in the community. How much responsibility the state assumes for community care and how much local sources are expected to provide is subject to wide fluctuation across the country. In Massachusetts local mental health outpatient clinics, as well as public hospitals, are part of the mental health service delivery system. In California, the Short–Doyle Act defines the shared responsibility of governmental units in providing comprehensive mental health services, specifying 90 percent state, 10 percent local governmental support. In Illinois passage of similar mandatory legislation has, as of the later 1970s, been effectively blocked. Permissive legislation—whereby, following a successful referendum, local taxes for mental health services are levied—has been partially effective, most frequently in the smaller communities.

The 1969 Progress Report of Illinois' Department of Mental Health clarifies the dilemma to some extent in the following statement, "A mental illness condition does not become a public mental health problem until it is first recognized and defined as a social problem. It is not so much the existence of a psychiatric problem itself, but rather its social consequences that cause it to be labeled as problematic or mental illness." [8]

Social consequences of mental illness   The social consequences of the problem defined as mental illness are both immediate and long-range.

Impact on differing size communities   For the large city the consequences of the institutional exodus are more immediately evident. The massive reduction in the institutional population resulted first of all in a shift of bodies. The most severely and chronically impaired were transferred to nursing homes, some of excellent quality, some of which effortlessly qualify as the new community back wards. Insofar as local governments are involved in the enforcement of building, fire and safety codes for these nursing homes, they are at least peripherally in the mental health business. As the nursing homes multiply, the need for inspection and enforcement escalates. The record for either inspection or enforcement is not impressive.

Statutory responsibility for licensing is often confused and contradictory. The mentally ill, formerly institutionalized patient is not an attractive one, either in terms of behavior or financial recompense. To impose sanction by removing the patient is at best an empty gesture. No one is really in competition for a public aid recipient who presents severe management problems.

A second tier of the formerly institutionalized has collected, sometimes literally by the thousands, in the deteriorating hotels of the large cities. These former patients are generally victims of impaired judgment. They may act directly upon their impulses with unfortunate consequences. The combination of high-risk housing and high-risk individuals constitutes a time bomb. These mentally ill persons are a present and potential hazard to themselves and to their fellow citizens. As agents responsible to some degree for the welfare of all its citizens, it would appear logical that urban government will sooner or later be involved in the care of this particular population of the mentally ill.

Wherever there are either urban or rural slums, the formerly institutionalized population will usually exceed the normal proportionate distribution. They are poor. They have virtually no housing options. They tend to settle in the vicinity of their institutional home where readmission is more readily accomplished.

The smaller cities and the rural communities have usually experienced less immediate impact, but they are not exempt from the long-term consequences of the current policy of treatment of the mentally ill.

Without question the former institutional system was one of widespread abuse. Institutions were dumping grounds for the aging and the unwanted. However, institutionalization also meant that a subset of the population confined within the four walls was, by anyone's definition, mentally ill, and that as a by-product, the institutional system restricted the reproduction rate of the defined mentally ill population. It is a matter of fact that the change to community based treatment has virtually eliminated this control, although this of course raises questions of policy—controversial questions—beyond the scope of the present discussion.[9]

Although research relative to the most common and perplexing psychosis, schizophrenia, has yielded uncertain results, there is increasingly respectable evidence of a genetic factor as significant to this disease and other mental illnesses. Whether there is a genetic factor or whether schizophrenic or mentally ill adults provide the environment conducive to the development of mental illness in their offspring is not, however, the immediate problem for social planning. It is a fact that an identified malfunctioning population is, for whatever cause, increasing in members.

Impact on community institutions   Future school systems, legal systems and financial support systems are among the government functions that will most assuredly be affected by our current infatuation with community based treatment. Although both elected and appointed officials, as well as their constituencies, still debate the basic question of whether involvement in the mental health delivery system is a legitimate function of local government, the decision has already been made.

It is also true that the private pain which traditionally motivated the bulk of our citizens to seek help at a mental health facility was rarely related to population density, to substandard housing, or to poverty. But this too has changed. Not only are the urban and rural poor seeking and demanding treatment resources and treatment accessibility, but across the economic spectrum, families of patients, as well as the patients themselves, are using the courts to assess the quality of that treatment which is available and accessible. Dr. Milton Greenblatt, defendant in a class action suit when he was commissioner of mental health in Massachusetts, makes the following assertion: "Throughout this country we are engaged in a long and historical struggle for acceptance of the principle of universal rights of citizens to adequate care and treatment. The era of use of judicial procedures on behalf of the disenfranchised in our health system has just begun." [10]

Mental help   Grandview, Missouri, is using trained professional mental health specialists for training its own personnel. Human relations classes have been conducted for several departments and, in addition, crisis intervention training has been provided for members of the police and fire departments. The police department also is using the mental health staff on an "on call" basis to assist the police in such problem areas as suicide and neighborhood feuds.

Those communities that have so far avoided looking at the adequacy of human resources including mental health care are only postponing a date with destiny. Exclusion of pupils from a school system concomitant with failure to provide recommended treatment is no longer acceptable. Limits on incarceration of juveniles for any purpose without proof that the least restrictive environment and treatment, i.e., community treatment, are not adequate—these are some of the citizens' rights being tested through the process of litigation.

The managerial experience: an Illinois example

Despite the confusion about this pervasive mental health problem, and, although in most localities the professionals, the private and public sectors, the courts, and the schools are trying to sort out some of the current chaos, there are some communities where units of local government are working effectively and compatibly with mental health systems. Illustrative of the variety of local government involvement in the mental health field are the disparate mechanisms functioning in three contiguous counties—Peoria, Tazewell, and Woodford—in central Illinois.

The counties jointly support certain tricounty agencies, primarily planning groups related to population, economic, and transportation assessment and projections. However, not only is the Illinois River a barrier between the largest county, Peoria, and the two smaller counties, but there is a strong emotional county identity barrier that militates against combining legal, governmental, and service functions. Each county has distinct sociodemographic characteristics. Each county exercises unique selectivity in which problems it will address and how it will address them.

The experience in Peoria   The largest county is Peoria with a population of

about 200,000. Within the county, the city of Peoria has a council-manager form of government, whereas Peoria County management is vested in a board of supervisors. Both the city and the county are in some small measure involved in the delivery of mental health services. One aspect of county involvement takes place primarily through the mechanism of state legislation which by back door referendum permits local levies of up to one mill for the "care and treatment of mentally deficient persons." As locally interpreted, any agency which can document that its services or any portion thereof are provided to a mentally deficient population may be eligible for indirect support.

Role of the multiagency building   Utilizing income generated by this legislative

mechanism and a smorgasbord of other funding mechanisms ranging from federal legislative to local philanthropic, citizens planned, and saw to completion in 1968, a multiagency building generally recognized as unique in the country. The time lag between the concept and the building completion was five years. Probably the greatest anxiety for the agencies through the years of negotiation was the feared loss of autonomy. As they have lived within the agency complex, agency autonomy is still a prevailing and constant irritant and major issue.

The intent was to improve service delivery for families who, needing multiple social services, were bouncing around the community like so many ping-pong balls. The qualifying factors for tenancy in the building were service to persons with any handicapping condition and commitment to coordinated and cooperative service delivery. The actual implementation of the service delivery concept falls somewhere between the ideal envisioned and the reality of human and agency frailty. Among the lessees in the allied agencies complex is the Tri-County Mental Health Clinic.

The literature has a paucity of information evaluating the service integration concept (a topic discussed in more detail in Chapter 16). There is certainly a great deal of enthusiasm for and sublime faith in the presumed magic of coordination, cooperation, mergers, consolidations, multi-service agencies and all those other good sounding words. There are, however, limited outcome studies of such concepts put into operation. Peoria's allied agencies complex illustrates some of the positive and negative consequences of shared space and services.

Although the Board for the Care and Treatment of Mentally Deficient Persons provides token direct program support to agencies serving a mentally deficient population, budgetary items are primarily for expenditures benefiting all agencies, some of which are enumerated below.

Housing   The building itself is extremely well designed, adapted for use by handicapped individuals with adjustments ranging from ramps to Braille push buttons in the elevators. A less than tangible benefit is the fact that bricks and mortar do make a difference to staff morale, and inasmuch as staff morale and the quality of client service are closely interrelated, living in an attractive, well maintained building does contribute to agency effectiveness.

A more concrete benefit comes from the fact that agencies experience cost reduction by sharing common facilities such as meeting rooms, gymnasiums and libraries. Because there is a local tax subsidy, the per square footage outlay for housing is significantly less than for equivalent commercial footage. Such subsidy has benefited the mental health clinic by releasing funds to provide more effective programming for a greater number of persons.

It should be noted, however, that despite original space projections, all major agencies in the allied agencies' building are now out of space and are operating in one or several annex operations. Multiple locations engender their own set of problems, among them reduced administrative efficiency and productivity.

Equipment   Expensive equipment shared by several agencies is also a cost-effective procedure. For instance, the allied agencies complex provides paper reproduction facilities, mimeographing equipment, postage meter, and microfilming so that each of the eleven agencies utilizing these aids to efficient operation can do so without assuming the total cost factor. Bulk purchase of supplies and the combined quantity of paper reproduction further reduce operational costs.

Videotape equipment and biofeedback equipment are further examples of capital expenditures for equipment which have increased the mental health clinic's effectiveness and made possible in some instances treatment methods whose cost would otherwise have been prohibitive.

Services   Shared medical resources, management and consultative services, and dial dictation and maintenance services have resulted in better quality and lower cost operations than would have been possible without the complex.

Leverage   The actual amount of tax dollars invested in the allied agencies complex is minimal, about one-third mill per assessed valuation. However, this small amount provides disproportionate leverage in grantsmanship when soft match is acceptable. This is of particular value to a mental health agency whose costs far exceed the capacity of the voluntary sector for support and whose services are not uniformly covered for third-party payments.

Problems   When several service organizations live under one roof, interagency cooperation and coordination may not only fail to improve, but may very well deteriorate. On a personal level, cooperation may be much easier when the agency directors see each other occasionally for a specific purpose rather than more frequently as pseudofamily members who may still be smarting from yesterday's battle over parking space one-upmanship. Sometimes the personality that is tolerable at well spaced intervals becomes intolerable with increased togetherness.

Characteristically, individuals who become executives in government, business, or in not-for-profit organization have substantial power drives. They could not be effective managers without this characteristic. This fact of life has implications for the happy team work illusion. The agency executive is paid to do a good job for his or her agency. Cooperation with another agency depends on where the payoff is. All theory to the contrary, reasonable executive paranoia may be more constructive than destructive as a factor in accomplishing the individual agency's mission.

Shared benefits   Some interesting joint projects have, however, evolved from the agency mix. The mental health clinic and the Arthritis Foundation have been involved in original research in arthritic pain control. The mental health clinic, community workshop, United Cerebral Palsy, Association for Retarded Citizens, the vocational assessment and training agency have collaborated in joint planning for adult clients to provide improved sheltered work experiences. All agencies have some clients in common; all relate in some aspects of their work to the Division of Vocational Rehabilitation. Improved adult rehabilitative services as well as reduced duplication are predictable by combining the unique resources of each of these agencies.

Living under one roof provides no guarantee of cooperative, coordinated, shared, or any other kind of multi-agency effort. Conversely, common tenancy in the Allied Agencies building has been a catalyst for the specified and other cooperative projects.

Role of the police department   The city of Peoria is linked to the mental health service delivery system in a totally different partnership. Recipient of a Violent Crime Reduction grant under LEAA, the police department subcontracts with the mental health clinic for intervention, assessment and follow-up in a subset of family trouble calls originating in the police dispatch system. The basis for this component of the grant was the conviction of both the city manager and the chief of police that social agencies could be used more effectively and could work in partnership with the police. A further hypothesis was that the incidence of some categories of violent crimes such as aggravated assault and battery could be reduced if the offender were linked into the social service stream. The decision to contract with the mental health clinic was more fortuitous than anyone realized as subsequent statistical analysis indicates that 27 percent of the calls handled jointly by police and mental health clinic staff involve formerly institutionalized patients.

The project was well designed and, as part of its preoperational phase, police officers and emergency response system staff of the mental health clinic participated together in crisis intervention training. One of the most important accomplishments was seen in the breakdown, prior to operation, of the traditional hostility, suspicion, and distrust between the law enforcement and the mental health agencies. The quality of the training and the environment itself contributed to the working relationship between the two staffs which has been integral to the success of the project. The training package was developed in conjunction with the local junior college. A faculty member of the psychology department spent several weeks prior to the formal training sessions in the police station and riding with the police, acquiring necessary information and establishing credibility. Administrative staff from the mental health clinic participated in the planning sessions relative to the total "violent crimes reduction" project. This participation increased understanding of the total conceptual framework and laid the groundwork for subsequent contract and budget negotiations and evaluation procedures. ·

The project was financed by a three-year grant (LEAA) and an Illinois Department of Mental Health grant-in-aid. As the LEAA grant terminated, preliminary indications were that, at its then level of success, a portion of the funding would be picked up as a component of the police department's budget.

Role of the emergency response staff   The mental health clinic's emergency response staff consists of a coordinator, who also fulfills a regular field counselor assignment, seven field counselors, and an administrative assistant. The staff is generally young and energetic with a background in the behavioral sciences and/or experience in a public agency, the criminal justice system or the like. Equipment consists of a leased vehicle, a two-way radio, scanner, and leased beepers.

The Emergency Response System staff is on duty 24 hours per day, seven days per week. Although it responds to any community crisis call, 67 percent of its activity is police-generated. The police officer responds to family trouble calls as usual and makes a decision about using the ERS counselor. If the decision is affirmative, the officer defuses the situation and waits for the counselor to arrive.

The field counselor is then responsible for any combination of activities which may include on-the-spot counseling, providing a temporary and expedient solution, and connecting the individual to a referral source. By contract, making an immediate, as well as a 30 day follow-up and disposition report, is mandatory. In responding to other community mental health emergency calls, the emergency response system counselor may, by reciprocal agreement, call on the police for help in a volatile situation.

Evaluation data are in the process of being accumulated and analyzed as of this writing. Preliminary subjective analysis from the point of view of the police is that among the benefits are that the police officer's time is spent less in doing "mental health" work and in serving as a taxi driver for psychotic patients. This is an appropriate component of a violent crimes reduction project inasmuch as time realized from diverting such calls into the social service system can be more effectively and appropriately used. More attention can be given to that subset of the population which generates a major proportion of criminal offenses.

A further benefit is that the social service resources of the city are used appropriately and with a high percentage of completed linkage by virtue of the 24-hour emergency response system capability.

As an unexpected benefit, the state's attorney's office reports less Monday morning paper work; the usual husband-wife complaints filed on Monday morning and dismissed later in the week when reconciliation is effected are down substantially as a result of the family crisis intervention work over the weekend.

Role of revenue sharing funds   A second involvement of local government with the mental health delivery service system is related to federal revenue sharing funds. The passage of the federal Revenue Sharing Act sparked unrealistic hopes in the breasts of impoverished mental health executives. Although the only mandate was that there should be public statements of planned and actual revenue sharing expenditures in the local news media before and after the entitlement period and that revenue sharing funds should be spent in accordance with the laws and procedures applicable to the expenditures of the local government's own revenues, the rhetoric accompanying the federal Revenue Sharing Act was impressive and did offer the possibility for local governments to expand their scope and capacity.

The reality is that nationally, as of the mid-1970s, less than three percent of federal revenue sharing funds have actually been allocated into the human services delivery system.

In Peoria, the percentage of federal revenue sharing funds allocated to the delivery of human services is below the national average.

A restructured Department of Human Resources was enriched with $125,000 of federal revenue sharing funds. As a result of public testimony, meetings among citizens and public officials and boards of directors, the decision was made to launch a demonstration project to increase social services to residents living in that area of the city characterized by poverty, high density, high unemployment, below average educational and job achievement.

The agencies involved were the city's department of human resources, which would provide coordinating functions and secretarial support; the housing authority, which donated office space in the housing project; and the United Way, which paid communications expenses, some travel expenses, and agreed to fund one additional professional staff position on a match basis to each social service agency which allocated a full-time existing position to outreach work in the neighborhood.

An OSS for the handicapped   The city of Bloomington, Minnesota, is using community development funds to establish an office of special services for physically and mentally handicapped persons. Planned services include counseling, information and referral, parent education, consumer education, leisure time activities, and a resource library. The project is starting out with a citywide effort to identify disabled persons of all ages, and to pinpoint their needs for services.

Negotiations were completed. Three agencies entered into contract with the United Way and the human resources department: the Urban League, Counseling and Family Service, a private social agency, and the mental health clinic. The plan was that there would be three neighborhood service locations in census tracks 1 through 15, each one staffed by two professionals and with a receptionist–secretary who would also provide semiprofessional services in the area of information and referral.

The first concrete task was to hire a team leader who would coordinate the activities of the three centers. Immediately some of the problems relative to combining the agencies in the coordinated effort became evident. The selection process for team leader took place with a committee composed of representatives from the cooperating agencies. Membership included paid executives from the service agencies and board members from the United Way, as well as commission members from the human resources component.

As the candidates began to be assessed and the committee began its deliberations, two opposing groups quickly formed—the volunteers versus the paid executives. The executives were looking for some dimension of administrative experience and training, as well as some indication of a successful track record in community organization. The volunteers seemed to have an agenda that was not necessarily congruent with that of the paid staff nor that usually expected of a personnel committee. Among the agendas that surfaced during the meeting was the need to placate an angry black constituency, to demonstrate the volunteers' own liberal and tolerant philosophy, possibly assuaging a troublesome conscience or two, and the desire to use the position to provide career advancement for an un-qualified minority candidate.

The executives were outnumbered and acknowledged defeat when a team leader was selected who had no formal training nor demonstrated interest or expertise in management skills. The failure of the committee's assignment can be judged by the summation of one volunteer who stated that the important thing about the selected candidate was that he "cared about people and anyone can pick up ad-ministration." A second volunteer who supported the choice stated rather omi-nously that perhaps it was time that the social service agencies had a new kind of administration but did not care to elaborate on this point.

A year later when the team leader and the neighborhood service centers parted company, neither the city council, the United Way, the human resources commis-sion, nor any of the participating agencies could speak coherently about where they had been, nor could they speak with much greater clarity about where they were going. They had all attended an awful lot of meetings.

The combined neighborhood service operation is a demonstration project. It is funded for another year. It is not a tale of dismal or total failure. If specific problem areas of an urban setting have a legitimate claim to social services beyond those provided the total population, local governments need to get acquainted with the citizen groups and agencies who have long had community sanction for social planning and implementation. Both groups will in all likelihood not only survive the culture shock but will profit from the experience.

Strengths and weaknesses of a demonstration project Out of the initial year of operation has come confirmation of the hypothesis that regardless of proscribed identity, agency functions are blurred and resistant to categorical definition. In the Peoria neighborhood service centers project, the mental health clinic staff, more than that of any other agency, assumed a strong advocacy role. Such staff opera-tion may seem incongruent with the traditional role of a mental health clinic. Ac-tually it is a most appropriate role in keeping with current precepts of community psychiatry that addressing environmental and community problems as they con-tribute to mental illness is equally and probably more important than addressing individual problems. Further, it is commonly observed that neurotic behavior yields magically when the individual begins to feel that he or she has some control over his or her own destiny. Encouraging residents to organize and act on their own behalf is a most positive step toward mental health.

However, some staff of the other cooperating agencies and at least some of the community volunteers were less than appreciative of the mental health clinic staff's failure to confine itself to dealing with the intrapsychic phenomena of public aid mothers.

The question of ultimate control of the neighborhood service center project has not been resolved. The human resources commission envisioned an agency with an identity all its own, a one-stop-shopping service, if you will, where the needs of any individual could be met by an entity called the "neighborhood service cen-ters."

The participating service agencies were equally firm in holding the line, insist-ing that any personnel employed by the individual agency is first of all an em-ployee of that agency and that personnel policies, for instance, supersede any policies operating in the neighborhood service centers. Problems have centered around authority and control. The United Way has experienced the pain of provid-ing funds but having little control; the human resources council has experienced this same problem.

Ownership of client records has been a thorny issue. Are they sacrosanct to the individual agency? How is confidentiality assured? How is accountability to the multiple funding bodies implemented without violating the individual's right to privacy?

A stronger team leader would probably have forced resolution of some of these issues during the first year of operation. That they must be confronted and solved is a healthy situation. The public and private planners and providers have an excellent opportunity to use one year's experience constructively, learning some of the pitfalls, and hopefully some of the benefits of pooled resources and coordinated functions.

The experience in Tazewell County   Across the river in Tazewell County a different kind of local government involvement in the mental health service delivery system has experienced both success and failure.

Tazewell County is essentially a rural county, with a population of about 90,000. For more than thirty years mental health services for both Tazewell and Woodford Counties were provided by the Tri-County Clinic located in Peoria. The need for a separate operation to more adequately serve the distant populations had long been evident. However, by the 1970s, the importance of establishing a strong local financial base prior to establishing services was also increasingly evident.

In one of Illinois' attempts to establish local tax bases for mental health services through legislative action, SB-553, a somewhat less than crystal clear law, attempts a shotgun marriage between mental health and public health. The legislation provides that where there are public health departments established by referendum, they shall levy for mental health services; the levy ceiling for public health is increased by one-half mill to meet the increased cost of providing mental health services. The method of provision, direct or contracted out, is optional.

When Tazewell County passed a referendum establishing a public health department, the time seemed opportune to utilize the 553 legislation to establish the local tax base for mental health services and to realize the plan for a geographically accessible clinic for Tazewell County residents.

Establishing a clinic   A representative community citizens' advisory group was formed, and the necessary planning activities ensued, among them a projected service load, staff complement, proposed budget and necessary contracts. Among the contracts were agreements that the Tri-County Clinic and the state institutional system would lend professional staff and that the Tri-County Clinic would also allocate funds to help establish the Tazewell Clinic. The County Health Department committed itself to financial support of about 25 percent of the projected first year's budget.

Communication was good. Community support was assured. Professional staff were enthusiastic. The public and private systems were actively and voluntarily participating in the formation of the Tazewell Clinic. The traditional paranoia toward Peoria was yielding to open and honest communication. The clinic opened its doors in a promising aura of good feeling.

From the beginning, the Tazewell Clinic has experienced a healthy and growing utilization rate, gained community acceptance and attracted a competent staff. However, three years later, no local tax dollars are part of its financial base. At the end of its first year, the clinic's board of directors failed to comply with a public health department ultimatum that the clinic be absorbed into the public health department as one of its program components or have its public health funds cut off.

Problems   The precipitating issue was power and control symbolized by the allocation of funds without direct control over their expenditure. Whether greater efficiency would result from a merged mental health/public health operation was also an issue.

Proponents of the consolidation cited financial and manpower savings possible by elimination of duplicate functions in both administrative and service areas. They proposed that by bringing the mental health clinic under the public health department and its director, duplicate funding of top administrative positions would be avoided. Savings in space requirements, equipment and support personnel would also be ordinary and expected benefits of a combined operation.

A further argument was that consumers of public health services have mental health needs, and conversely many individuals served in mental health agencies have unmet physical health needs. With a merged operation a more adequate and comprehensive set of broadly based health services should theoretically be available.

Opponents of the consolidation were convinced of the folly of the proposal on the basis of equally convincing arguments.

Public health functions such as sanitation services, restaurant inspection, and nursing home licensing operate under legal mandates and enforceable standards. The community mental health system is a voluntary noncoercive operation. The voluntary aspect of the mental health service delivery system is essential to the therapeutic process as well as a guarantee of the rights of individual citizens.

The nonstatutory activities of the public health department are generally concrete and measurable. Services such as immunization are based on epidemiological data and have clear-cut cause and effect relationships. Other specific activities engender certain and predictable results.

The uncertain nostrums of the mental health field are in sharp contrast to the above certainties of the public health field.

In some communities where mental health services are part of the public health department's function and where there have been irreconcilable conflicts, the ultimate compatibility of the two services is open to question. The rational public statements touch on the surface issues only. The less definable problems are conflict implicit in the fabric of the two agencies. Staff autonomy, individual responsibility and self motivation are congruent with the desired product of the mental health clinic's endeavors. They are what the therapeutic process is all about. Therefore, the work environment of a thriving mental health agency tends to be nonhierarchal, open and democratic. It is probable that this factor is the sticky one that makes it very difficult for mental health agencies to be co-opted by more typically structured organizations.

Results In Tazewell, a majority of the citizens' advisory committee, and the mental health clinic staff strongly resisted becoming a division of the public health department. Therefore, following two fiscal year appropriations, the presumed stable source of local tax funds came to an end.

The subsequent steady growth of mental health services has perhaps unwittingly benefited from the early decision to go it alone. In contrast to Peoria County, the Tazewell clinic is not pursuing federal dollars, a decision most compatible with the temperament of this particular community. It has, however, evolved some limited partnerships with local governmental systems. In the judicial system when a citizen appears in court on a driving while intoxicated charge, the judge may offer him the option of an educational/treatment program at the mental health clinic in lieu of sentencing. If the offender agrees to this alternative, he is assigned to a probation officer and signs a release of information waiver so that clinic personnel may inform the probation officer of failure to complete the prescribed course, failure to actively participate, or failure to pay for the treatment.

A further contract with the Tazewell County court is for diagnosis/assessment in selected felony cases. The court pays for the evaluation and uses it as part of the documentation in the pre-sentencing procedure.

Current economic developments and the public health controversy have reinforced the conservative philosophy of this community, some of whose citizens are now presenting petitions to recall the referendum which established the public health department.

The experience in Woodford County   Woodford County, the smallest of the three counties, has a population of about 28,000 and is governed by a county board of supervisors. Among the county board committees is the health committee whose chairman, a few years ago, was the target of citizens interested in providing mental health services. Of the three counties Woodford has probably experienced the closest and most direct citizen involvement. It is also the county whose only visible social services prior to the development of mental health services were public welfare and probation.

Establishing a human services center   As a result of community meetings with representatives of churches, schools, the county sheriff, and the county board's health committee, the county board agreed with the health committee's recommendation that if the citizens raised $5,000 of voluntary funds, $5,000 of federal revenue sharing funds would be appropriated as match to establish mental health services. Thereupon, the citizens organized the community, recruiting chairmen for business, churches, political subdivisions and door-to-door solicitations as well as a speakers' bureau. Within a month, they raised $7,000 to establish the Human Services Center. From the beginning the citizens and the county board have insisted on coordination and unification wherever possible and chose this name as expressing their philosophy. They have aspired to housing not only this private not-for-profit agency, but public aid and the state children's protective agency under the same roof and sought community development funds to build a multiservice building for this purpose.

Organizational and financial patterns   What has developed under the mental health umbrella is a social agency that is tailored to the needs of this particular community. The parent agency is the mental health clinic (the Human Services Center). It now administers the senior citizens' transportation grant and provides senior citizen information and referral services. It employs social workers and as a vendor contracts with the school district within the county for school social work services. It is a subcontractor for drug abuse services under a tricounty comprehensive drug abuse grant. Drug charges are processed in the judicial system, but sentencing frequently involves education and treatment at the Human Services Center. In these instances costs are assessed the violator, and the court enforces payment of the costs.

The mix of financial support currently comes from federal revenue sharing, general revenue, federal funds for the aging, state Department of Mental Health, Illinois Dangerous Drugs Commission, fees for service, and third-party payments.

The results   The next service expansion will be hiring of a community nurse, primarily to respond to the home health needs of the elderly. This health service will be integrated into and responsible to the Human Services Agency. Characteristically, growth occurs in response to a concrete need and services are added only after a thorough airing by the county board.

Although Woodford County has maintained its separate agency status, the Human Services board of directors and the Tazewell County board of directors have merged. One executive director supervises both operations. Specialized professional staff serve both counties. Economies in fiscal and statistical systems operations are a by-product and ongoing staff training in alcohol, drug abuse, and mental health methods are delivered more economically.

Mechanisms to maintain communication have been established. Members of the Woodford County board's health committee attend the board meetings of the human services agency, and the human services board members and staff attend the Woodford County board meetings.

Summary: the lessons for local government managers   The involvement of local government in mental health services in all three counties share certain common elements: (1) demonstrated interest from the citizens, local government, and the mental health agency; (2) establishment from the beginning of the mechanisms for on-going communication between the unit of local government and the service agency; (3) the local government's contracting out for services rather than operating services directly; (4) leadership/liaison activities by one or more persons as central to the successful operations.

Be specific and be successful?   In general, it would seem that services have been most successful when they have been most specific. Peoria's neighborhood service centers project experienced normal difficulties in identifying the problem, crystalizing the objectives and in outlining activities to accomplish necessary tasks. The gross disparity, however, between problem sets in a high density, low economic, inner-city neighborhood and a rural community invalidate any comparison. In the urban setting, a service specific contract such as that between the Peoria police department and the Peoria mental health clinic seems to augur more hopefully for success. The performance contract has certain merits as an instrument for local governments to utilize in agency negotiations.

On the surface it would appear that in the smaller rural communities problems are more manageable. Perhaps rather than aspiring to large multilayered, multicoordinated organizations, the cities might do better by dividing into small, manageable, autonomous neighborhood units, utilizing only the hardware and other proven cost efficiencies of large systems. The alternative would seem to be creation of one more massive governmental division that is most costly, least responsive and least effective.

Human services departments created by fiat as sops to political pressure will probably be not only wasteful and ineffective but will reinforce the sorry conviction that management of human service is hopeless, and that in any case its products will not stand up to careful scrutiny. Evidence will rapidly accumulate to reinforce all the negative concepts about the human services field as chaotic, mismanaged and ineffective.

Needs assessment: its uses and abuses   As a necessary preliminary to any action, the serious manager may determine to undertake his or her own community needs assessment along the lines indicated in Chapters 5 and 6. He or she should first inquire whether there is not a fairly recent and costly community analysis gathering dust somewhere on the closet shelf. These assessments are generally outdated by the time they are published, so resurrection of a reasonably well done study completed within the last ten years is probably not a bad idea. It should still be sufficiently reliable and valid and have enough unrealized and unmet virginal recommendations to keep any five agencies busy for the foreseeable future.

Needs assessments should be recognized as providing evidence of symptomatology, not of basic causes. In theory the manager's concern should not be to create one more agency to address the symptoms of community dysfunction, but for local government to address community dysfunction itself. For example, if the rate of juvenile arrest is cause for concern, it is at least questionable whether government should either operate or contract for a youth counseling service. As an option it might more profitably continue to address the recreation, education and employment needs of young people, increase the allocation of tax dollars for these services and establish a new list of priorities, recognizing that such action will not win a popularity contest and will be more difficult to sell to numerous vested pressure groups and their elected officials.

There are no panaceas   Creation of a new department or a new position is more visible and generally makes everyone, including the manager, temporarily feel better. Also, a not inconsiderable benefit is that down the road it creates a scape-goat for lack of measurable progress.

The less dramatic approach would have the virtue of paying attention to our long history of disenchantment with mental health's rosy promises. In the 1930s, the child guidance clinic was guaranteed to assure the trouble-free generation of the 1950s. In the 1950s sensitivity training was a most marketable commodity, and in the 1970s community psychiatry is hailed as the panacea. There are, of course, no panaceas, but somewhere between the extremes of viewing mental health services as coddling and destructive to the fibre of the American character and the unexamined laying on of many hands to exorcise human suffering, there can be and needs to be a useful and effective partnership between local government and the mental health service delivery system.

Managing programs for the handicapped

Discrimination, whether blatant or subtle, is not a pleasant concept. For whatever reasons, the historical record shows that the basic rights of human beings, individually or in groups, have often been denied by power, ignorance, or even benevolent paternalism. In the 1960s, local governments and indeed the entire nation were swept by currents of social, legal, and political change stemming from the fact that a significant minority population had, amongst other inequities, to sit at the back of the bus. More recently—and, sadly, partly as a result of outspoken efforts by young men crippled in the Vietnamese war—it has been realized that there is a significant minority, the handicapped, some of whom cannot even get on the bus.

The present brief discussion does not pretend to give an exhaustive survey of the needs and problems of the handicapped in our society. It does, however, attempt to outline some of the challenges presented to local government managers by the needs of the handicapped amongst the citizens of their communities, needs that are increasingly finding legislative expression. After an introductory overview, the discussion is divided into two parts. The first takes a look at areas of concern where local governments can act: architectural barriers; attendant care; education; employment; health services; housing; recreation and socialization; and transportation. The second section discusses planning for the handicapped, under such topics as needs assessment; the resource inventory; the action plan; and implementation and evaluation. A checklist for managers is also provided, and the emphasis throughout is on practical steps that, it is hoped, will be useful to the authors' colleagues in local government practice. The emphasis throughout is also on the importance of the human relations aspect of providing care for the handicapped.

An overview

It is difficult to know how many handicapped persons are affected by discrimination. Society's attitude of "out of sight, out of mind" may contribute substantially to this exclusionary tactic. To put the problem in perspective, it should be noted that about 10 percent of the nation's population can be classified as physically disabled. But numbers can only give a partial view of the picture.

The moral imperatives   Handicapped persons have a right to live independently. Middle class, sighted, ambulatory America does not have an exclusive claim to goals, aspirations, success, happiness, and self-esteem. But, before a person can change the world, mount a revolution, or even proceed with daily tasks, relative certainty is needed that he or she can get up in the morning and get dressed (with help, if necessary), and that adequate transportation is available for getting to and from a job or school.

Legislation is no panacea, but it is necessary. The removal of architectural barriers is basic. Perhaps the single most important obstacle to be overcome is attitude. It should be history to hear of handicapped persons having to use a freight elevator because of their being in a wheelchair, to use a garbage ramp to get into a restaurant, to pay two or three times normal auto insurance premiums, or to bring along an adult companion or a doctor's certificate in order to travel by plane.

It should not be a revolutionary concept to ensure that handicapped persons have the opportunity to choose among alternative ways of living. It should go without saying that handicapped persons have a right to have a say about their lives. They have been heard and will continue to expect their rights.

The role of government   As of 1976, the federal government, all fifty states, and the District of Columbia had passed architectural barrier laws which require that various types of new 'and existing buildings be made accessible to the handicapped. Many states have passed antidiscrimination and civil rights statutes to ensure the rights of the disabled. The federal government has also passed an antidiscrimination statute to apply to federal grants.

Cities and counties, too, have dealt with the question of how they can serve the handicapped to help ensure independent living. Starting in-house, some local governments' affirmative action programs have sought to include the handicapped in their work forces, and the enforcement of state and local codes relating to architectural barriers is generally a government responsibility.

Perhaps the foremost response cities and counties have made to serve the handicapped is through recreation programs. Many cities, large and small, have some city-sponsored activities, or coordinate with private groups, to serve the handicapped. In addition, institutional therapeutic recreation has emerged with the goal of preparing persons to return to their communities. This has brought with it increased needs for communication between institutions and the community and for programs that assist the individual in the transition to community life.

Areas of concern where local governments can act

Architectural barriers   Social planners are constantly faced with the question of latent results of various decisions. The lack of access to the handicapped of buildings, streets, schools, and other facilities is a good example of this. It is fine to offer employment opportunities, but if a person cannot negotiate steps, how does that person get to the job? A park facility can be refreshing, but if rest room doors are too narrow, some will find them impossible to use. To encourage citizen participation is admirable, but if some are left at the bottom of the stairs, it is incomplete.

Barriers and wheelchairs   The city of Palo Alto, California, is eliminating architectural barriers to the physically handicapped throughout the community. To launch this effort, a special awareness and training day was held in which the city manager, key staff, building inspectors, engineers, council members, and all city advisory commissioners as well as experts from associations for the physically handicapped, spent the day in wheelchairs encountering typical barriers in municipal and commercial areas. Projects under way include curb ramps at intersections, special training for building and code inspectors, and outreach to architects and other key private sector individuals.

As mentioned earlier, architectural barrier laws have been passed by all fifty states, the federal government, and the District of Columbia. In various forms, these laws require that certain new and existing buildings be made accessible to the disabled. At the construction stage, it costs very little to make buildings accessible to the disabled. Yet the effects of habit, and possibly attitude, often have more impact than cost. As an example, rest room doors are often designed so that they are too narrow for wheelchairs—simply because they have always been narrow. (Narrow-width specifications are something of a legacy of Victorian thinking, the general rule being that bathrooms should be as inconspicuous as possible.)

Architectural barrier laws often affect the elderly as well as the disabled, providing two-fold reason for vigorously enforcing laws which mandate adequate access. It seems, in any case, that sound logic—regardless of the law—would show that physical planning to eliminate architectural barriers would be beneficial for many. Ramps would aid the parent with a stroller as well as the person in a wheelchair. Foot-operated rest room facilities are usable by all persons.

Local government planning officials can do much to encourage nonenforceable access, particularly for various leisure-oriented facilities, restaurants, theaters, and other establishments which are part of independent living.

Attendant care   Perhaps the most frustrating experience imaginable is to live with the inability to care for one's basic needs—to require assistance with the simplest tasks: dressing, bathing, or using the toilet. This demands almost limitless endurance by the handicapped person and unusual understanding and sensitivity by the helping person. Difficult as it may appear, this is the situation faced by many with severe physical impairments. Yet, most of these citizens prefer to maintain an independent life-style outside of an institution.

The role of the attendant requires a close intimacy with the daily life of the handicapped person. It is important that they share common interests and philosophies. However, bringing together this smoothly functioning team of handicapped and helper often presents a problem for the handicapped person. The government may provide some financial assistance for compensating attendants, but locating qualified persons in the free market through normal methods of recruiting has limited success.

One response has been for the handicapped to join together to deal with the issue as a group, a trend particularly noteworthy at the university level. In this manner they have been able to share information about their individual needs and to bring about a better mechanism for locating and training attendants.

Local governments can provide assistance in this area. In addition to providing the financing necessary to compensate attendants adequately, they can help to bring about a better system for attendants to learn about and become trained in this field. While developing a career corps of attendants may not be feasible or necessary, there are, nevertheless, large numbers of qualified candidates for these jobs who could gain a great deal from the experience. University students, in particular, could greatly benefit by the free housing and small salary provided by these jobs and could offer their sensitivity in return.

A principal thrust of local government in the field of attendant care may be to become an advocate for the handicapped; to support legislation liberalizing financial aid for the payment of attendants; to urge university, college, and government employment offices to aid in the search for attendants; to make the local information and referral operations of welfare offices and other human services agencies aware of this need. Homemaker services and other nontechnical services can be provided through various programs. Cities and counties can act as advocates in this matter as well.

Education   The handicapped person's ability to adapt to our complex society and attain an independent lifestyle is greatly influenced by that person's ability to gain a meaningful education. Recent legislation at the federal level (including especially the Developmentally Disabled Assistance and Bill of Rights Act) now guarantees equal educational opportunities to the handicapped. Many traditional problems of the disabled make the opportunity difficult to seize, however.

Transportation (discussed below) is a major obstacle. Specially equipped buses are now commonly used by primary and secondary schools to transport handicapped children, but transportation to college or university, vocational schools, adult education classes, or other specialized schools is generally nonexistent. Some of the more fortunate handicapped adults are able to drive specially adapted cars or vans, but most cannot. For this latter group, unequal mobility may mean unequal education. Most modern schools are being constructed in a fashion which makes them totally accessible to the handicapped. Many older schools, however, still have areas inaccessible to those in wheelchairs. Still others among the handicapped encounter mobility difficulty with curbs, stairs, narrow doorways, heavy doors, and steep slopes.

Physical education for the handicapped is not a new concept, but it is a relatively recent phenomenon in public schools. School districts are now required by law to provide specialized physical education experiences for handicapped children. Because of the need for a relatively low ratio of students to teacher, this instruction is more costly than traditional physical education classes. This cost factor and the lack of specially trained physical education instructors have inhibited compliance with the law, particularly in smaller school districts.

The California experience is probably similar to that of many states where New Federalism has meant a shift in emphasis from state institutionalization to care and treatment at the community level. Most of those concerned with the welfare of the handicapped acknowledge that the community generally provides a healthier environment than do state institutions. Yet the state has not provided sufficient funding to adequately cover local programs.

Vocational training for the handicapped is lacking in many communities. The capacity to become employed, to pay all or most living expenses, is vitally important to the handicapped. Vocational schools and workshops span the scope of education from highly technical training to on-the-job, rudimentary, repetitive work experience. Our college and university system must be made completely open to the handicapped. The number of handicapped students has risen markedly during the past few years. Even multihandicapped persons are now gaining acceptance and success at university levels. One reason for this increasing level of success at some universities may be the realization by enlightened university administrators and governing boards that opening their campuses to the handicapped is both a moral responsibility and practical in a long-term economic sense. The moral responsibility comes from the belief that a portion of our society should not be denied an education or a means of earning a living simply because they cannot get up the school steps. The practical advantage is based on the assumption that educating the handicapped can be seen as a long-term economic investment, that is, the educated person—handicapped or not—will likely become a taxpayer rather than a tax burden someday.

This section has dealt primarily with educating the physically handicapped. Providing skills for the mentally handicapped, particularly the retarded, is equally challenging. Great strides have been made in providing education programs and special schools for educable and trainable mentally retarded children. What is lacking in many communities, however, are programs to teach basic work skills to the adult retarded. Workshops exist in some communities and have had varying degrees of success, but they are often located in larger cities and are frequently unavailable or inaccessible to those living in small towns or suburbs. If these among the handicapped are going to live independent lives, they need to be sufficiently educated to earn a living and to function in society.

Employment   Self esteem is derived from many sources. A person's job plays a large part. Besides the obvious impact that a regular earned income has, the relationship between the satisfaction of job accomplishment and self-image is almost immeasurable. The job market is a tough place for anyone. When one's entry is compounded by prejudices, fears, and other barriers—both architectural and social—it can be a nearly impossible task. Few employment agencies exist to place the handicapped in jobs, and even government rehabilitation programs give no guarantee of jobs. Often the only alternative for the disabled who cannot compete in the job market is a sheltered workshop, many of which do not offer even minimum wages.

Hiring handicapped is good business An extensive study has been completed by the Burbank, California, research and budget office on hiring the handicapped. The study concludes after extensive research that there is absolutely no basis for discriminatory employment practices. The handicapped have proven themselves to be superior employees in every way. An implementation plan is outlined in the report which covers, among others things, actions that should be taken to eliminate architectural barriers limiting public access, personnel policies as they apply to the physically limited, and a job checklist.

Many major corporations are making an effort, as of the later 1970s, to hire the handicapped, but there is a long way to go. Employers often fear insurance rate hikes, reduced productivity, and other potential problems. Ironically, handicapped persons generally have a better than average attendance record and perform as high quality work as their nonhandicapped counterparts.

Many states have included the disabled under their fair employment practice laws, civil rights statutes, or other specific statues. Cities and counties can look closely at their hiring practices to see if opportunities are being equitably provided. They can also ensure that manpower employment and training programs include meaningful and realistic plans for the handicapped.

Health services Fortunately, health care for the handicapped has long been recognized by government officials and private organizations as a vitally needed support service. (California's Crippled Children Services, for example, has helped families with physically handicapped children since 1927.) The federal government, in particular, provides hundreds of programs, and funding for organizations involved in medical testing, evaluation, and treatment; case management; mental health services; physical restoration (prosthetic appliances); medical research; and special equipment for and retraining to aid the handicapped (specially equipped vehicles, etc.).

In addition, major funding and direct services are provided by private nonprofit organizations. Particularly active in this regard are organizations assisting those afflicted with cerebral palsy; epilepsy; cystic fibrosis; speech, perception, or hearing disabilities; heart disease; mental health problems; muscular dystrophy; asthma; and cancer. Fraternal organizations also provide services—usually indirectly through donations and other contributions—including counseling and guidance services; programs in the areas of transportation, recreation, and child care; day camps and other camping experiences; rehabilitation centers; workshops; scholarships; professional training; and research.

While critical medical and mental health services are available to most handicapped persons, there are, nevertheless, many difficulties often associated with receiving these services. The traditional problems of accessibility and high cost, for example, may inhibit the delivery of services, particularly to the handicapped who do not live in large metropolitan areas. This situation has sometimes forced families of handicapped persons to move closer to treatment centers in areas where they may be subject to higher costs of living and reduced employment opportunities. Fees are charged for some services, the amount determined in many cases by the individual or family's ability to pay. For the very poor, the services are free; for those with a modest income, the fees may represent a major expense.

Historically, the role in support of health care services for the handicapped in cities and counties has varied a great deal. In California, for example, county governments and a few large cities are responsible for providing direct health care to needy handicapped children with funds provided by the state; most cities, however, have had little or no involvement in servicing the health needs of the handicapped.

Phone without words   The deaf live in a difficult world. Many are nonverbal, and even those who can verbalize and lip-read are still stymied when they want to use the telephone. In an emergency, how can they call for help? The police department of High Point, North Carolina, has installed a TTY unit in its communications center. The TTY uses a coupler to connect a teletype in the communications room at the police department with a like unit in the home of a deaf person, utilizing the normal telephone wires and instruments.

It is encouraging to note a trend of increased municipal interest in ensuring the fulfillment of the health care and other social services needs of the handicapped. Some of the supportive actions being taken by cities are purely philosophical or informational in nature, such as including questions in the census which will give social planners better data on the nature of impairments, numbers, and location of handicapped persons. Other more substantial measures—particularly in light of increased funding through the Housing and Community Development Act—have included the construction of facilities which serve the health care and other needs of the handicapped. Increasing numbers of multiservice centers, of the type mentioned in the preceding section of this chapter, being constructed by cities are including the handicapped among their target clients. The multiservice concept is one which should have a significant impact on the handicapped, poor, and aged. A large number of services (or at least the point of intake for them) can be clustered in one location, thereby reducing the need for clients to travel long distances between agencies providing services. Having a number of agencies occupying the same facility also tends to improve coordination and encourage better referral procedures.

The emerging role of cities and counties in the public health field, including services for the handicapped, may be one of taking an advocacy position and working to see that health services are affectively delivered to all local residents. Rather than take on the responsibility of directly offering health services, cities and counties are providing facilities and offering technical support and funding to other public and private agencies so that they may better serve the handicapped and the general public.

Housing   Independent living includes the right to choose alternative forms of housing. Housing represents a major problem for the handicapped. There is little low and moderate cost accessible housing, and specialized housing for the severely disabled is almost nonexistent. The highest priority lies with low cost, accessible housing, where the greatest need in numbers exists. However, few proposals for low cost housing for the handicapped have ever been submitted.

The handicapped person must be provided with a full range of choices in housing—what section of the community; what kind of residence, i.e., private home or apartment; etc. Segregated communities for the handicapped have no place in today's society. In this respect, the State of Iowa can be considered in the forefront of the integration of the handicapped with the rest of the community since it requires that all apartments, no matter what size, be accessible. For the severely disabled, a community-based housing system may be the more viable solution. However, existing zoning regulations, building codes and standards may be impediments. Deinstitutionalization is the goal, and if these standards simply recapitulate an institutional atmosphere creating, in effect, mini-institutions, then the goal is lost.

The big red "I"   The Walnut Ridge, Arkansas, volunteer fire department has initiated a campaign which should be helpful to invalids when there is an emergency, especially in the event of fire. The firemen have cards on which is printed a big red "I," five inches high.

The cards are placed on the front of each home in which an invalid resides. In event of a fire, a team will go directly into the house to attempt to rescue the invalid while other firemen concentrate on the fire.

As with other services, attitude may well be the major barrier to overcome regarding housing. A well-planned housing element can help. So can education of the nondisabled. More than anything, it takes leadership on the part of the local officials to ensure that housing is available to all citizens in the community.

Recreation and socialization   Our society has eagerly strived for, and is enjoying, an ever-increasing opportunity to engage in leisure activities. For most citizens, the increase in discretionary time indicates a rise in standard of living. For the severely handicapped, elderly, and poor, an increase in the amount of idle time, because of their inability to fully utilize it, can be a frustrating and demoralizing experience. Many of the handicapped have a great deal of time, but no way to enjoy it. The severely physically and mentally handicapped, some mentally retarded, and others who are homebound or institutionalized have limited or no formal leisure opportunities at all.

The importance of recreation in aiding the social, physical, intellectual, and emotional development of individuals and families has long been recognized. Because the handicapped have been denied equal access to these experiences, their chances for full development of social, physical, intellectual, and emotional skills have been reduced. Recreation, and learning how to utilize leisure time, can be more important to the handicapped person than to others. While active recreation can be a positive form of maintaining our physical and mental well-being, it can often become a method of physical or mental therapy for the handicapped. For example, a visit to the swimming pool can be physical therapy for the arthritic or stroke victim; a camping experience can build confidence for the blind or deaf child; or a sewing class might be a form of reentry into community life for a mental patient.

Most local government recreation administrators are well aware of the physical and mental benefits of recreation and can readily accept the need to provide programs for the handicapped. Most are unaware, however, of the large number of people—as many as one out of seven [11]—who are excluded from most recreation services due to disabilities. In addition, with about 1 percent of the municipal recreation work force assigned to programs for the handicapped—who make up about 10 percent of the population—there is an imbalance in the use of tax dollars. [12]

Adapting existing programs   There is growing agreement by many administrators that local funding for specialized programs for the handicapped is difficult to generate. Yet much can be done to adapt existing programs and assist other public and private organizations which provide supportive services for the handicapped. One method of assistance is to take a proactive approach in showing concern for clients. For example, recreation agencies should contact public and private agencies, such as county mental health departments or Easter Seal societies, and let these groups know that the handicapped are welcome to utilize existing programs and facilities. Recreation professionals thus become recreation consultants and advocates without significantly increasing their costs of operation. The results of an outreach, or client-centered, philosophy can increase services to the handicapped, create better relations between agencies, and be a personally rewarding experience for recreation administrators and staff.

Beach for handicapped   A wheel chair ramp at the beach? Fort Lauderdale, Florida, has one leading all the way into the water from a parking lot reserved for handicapped persons.

Full-time lifeguards at the beach stand ready to give assistance in using the ramp, which has a specially roughened surface for traction.

Many recreation administrators have been reluctant to undertake activities aimed at the handicapped. Lack of funds is a prime reason. Unfamiliarity with the kinds of recreation programs which could be offered, and the belief that social services programs should be offered by some other agency, also pose barriers.

Overcoming the lack of funds   While lack of local funds is certainly an obstacle, it can be overcome. A traditional playground program could be modified, for instance, to provide one site for playground recreation for trainable mentally retarded or hyperactive children. The regular staff could be used. They would need some training and orientation as to which playground activities are best suited for these children. Volunteers could be utilized to improve the ratio of staff to participants. In addition, grant funds from public and private agencies are becoming more available to local government agencies. Further, an approach to reducing agency costs is to jointly offer programs with other organizations.

Recreation administrators should learn about the types of programs offered for

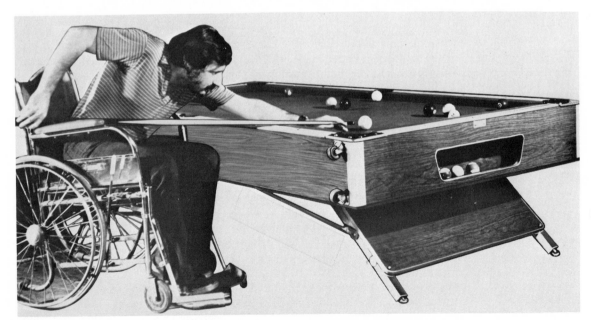

Figure 13–4   The height of this pool table can be adjusted to allow use by those unable to play from a standing position. (Source: Courtesy of North American Recreation Convertibles, Inc., Bridgeport, Connecticut.)

the handicapped. This education process must be given greater emphasis by the handicapped themselves and by those who are their advocates if an increase in programming is going to occur. The process starts with the development of a greater consciousness of the recreation needs of the handicapped. It then involves research into the techniques of programming, types of facilities and equipment needed, and staffing requirements.

Most administrators feel programs for the handicapped require a large staff of highly specialized, expensive personnel. This may be true in some cases; in most situations, existing staff can be assigned to many activities for the handicapped. It is often forgotten that the recreational desires of the handicapped differ very little from those of people who do not have physical or mental impairments. It does not take a highly trained therapist to order a pool table that adjusts to various heights so that those confined to wheelchairs can use it; or to offer pool time and provide lifeguards for a school for the mentally retarded; or to organize a local theatrical group to visit convalescent hospitals. These are all "pure" recreation skills which have long been part and parcel of the work of recreation administrators. They should be utilized so that all clients can benefit equally from them.

Addressing the overall issues Each city or county must address the issue of its role in social services, and services for the handicapped are no exception. For the large public recreation agency operating in a metropolitan area, the need for programming may be reduced by the probable existence of private agencies dealing with the handicapped. The need for cooperation and funding assistance for handicapped programs will still need to continue. For the small city or county, there is a good possibility that few local private agencies for the handicapped exist. It may be necessary for local government agencies to attempt to fill this gap. Meeting the local need should not be restricted to cities and counties. School districts, recreation and park districts, and others share the responsibility.

Transportation Mobility is the key to social integration and job flexibility, and a vital ingredient to a productive and useful life. However, without either a private car or a very expensive van, a mobility-impaired person may be deprived of the opportunity to attend school, to recreate, or to explore job opportunities. The 1964 Mass Transit Act stated that efforts should be made to provide transportation for the disabled. Adequate urban mass transit is lacking in most metropolitan areas. This is certainly an inconvenience to the general public and a disaster to many disabled people, who simply cannot function without it.

Inadequate transportation ranks high as a factor in the unemployment of the handicapped. Of those who are employed, fewer than one-half are able to get to their jobs by walking or using their wheel chairs; more than one-quarter must be driven to work by others. When job choices are limited to those who can be reached without using mass transportation, opportunities for employment are drastically reduced.

Even if a disabled person is able to drive an automobile, he or she is often charged up to three times the rate for a normal driver for insurance. This is so, despite information that trained handicapped persons are no less competent behind the wheel than a normal driver.

Summary The above discussion has done no more than skim the surface of the options available to local government managers who are seeking ways to respond to the needs of the handicapped. Readers are referred to the specifics of legislation in their state or community to obtain a full picture of the measures that they may now be required or eligible to adopt. Perhaps more important, however, is the need to approach the problems of the handicapped with a humane attitude and sensitivity, and an imaginative approach to using existing programs and facilities.

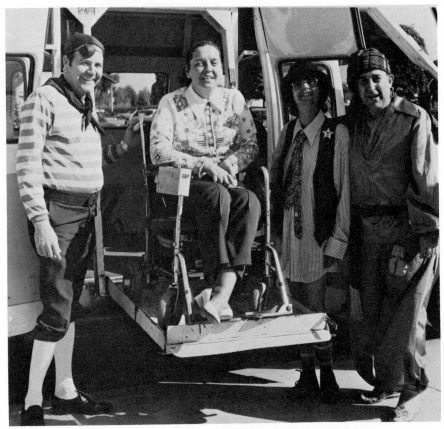

Figure 13–5   The "hustle bus" of Norwalk, California, operates for use by any of the city's residents. Handicapped residents' needs are met by a special unit equipped with a power lift gate and by telephone-response, door-to-door service. (Source: Courtesy of the City of Norwalk, California.)

Planning for the handicapped

The planning process for developing a strategy to help the handicapped lead useful and personally fulfilling lives offers many of the same challenges encountered in attempting to enhance the quality of life for other disadvantaged groups. As Chapters 5 and 6 have indicated, there are several steps commonly being used by human services planners which may generate the data needed to devise programs or policies in response to needs. Simply stated, these steps are: development of a statement of the principal unmet needs; compilation of a listing of available resources (agencies servicing the handicapped, funding, scholarships, etc.); development of an action plan to respond to unmet needs; implementation of the plan; and evaluation of the plan. The accompanying checklist (Figure 13–6) sets out some of the items local government managers will wish to take into account when they consider the needs of the handicapped in their communities.

Needs assessment   Developing an action plan to respond to the human needs of the handicapped requires a clear understanding of the size and nature of the client group to be served. Research must be undertaken to collect gross statistical data, such as number of clients, their age, geographic distribution, kinds of disabilities, and other indicators. Most communities, however, lack complete and reliable data. As a result, researchers must improvise. The collection of these data will generally involve a systematic search of the records of public and private agencies, and interviews with individuals, client advocacy groups, and others. The

Implementation Checklist

1. Are your public works, planning, and building and safety staffs familiar with the latest building code and other regulations dealing with the removal of architectural barriers to the handicapped?

2. Is there someone on your staff who is knowledgeable about local programs for the handicapped and who can advise the public?

3. Do you have a citizens' advisory board which counsels the staff and elected officials on the needs of the handicapped?

4. Do you have handicapped persons appointed to citizens' advisory boards which consider personnel, architectural, or planning matters?

5. Does your transit system make provisions for transporting the handicapped?

6. Do city parking lots have parking stalls reserved for the handicapped?

7. Does your recreation program include activities for the handicapped?

8. Are all city programs, including meetings of elected officials, located in buildings which are accessible to those with limited mobility?

9. Does your city provide public information and education regarding the needs of the handicapped, and do you have an "awareness day" or other activities demonstrating support for the handicapped?

10. Does your public housing program have units specially designed or equipped for the handicapped?

11. Does your affirmative action plan include the handicapped?

12. Do you send recruitment materials to agencies providing services to the handicapped?

13. Do you hire handicapped persons in proportion to their numbers in the community?

Figure 13–6   Implementation checklist for program to remove barriers to the handicapped.

search for data is further complicated by the general lack of communication among agencies serving the handicapped. School districts, for example, will often offer special classes for the physically handicapped and some of the mentally retarded, but may have little contact with state vocational rehabilitation agencies, city recreation departments, or local colleges' handicapped aid offices.

Most private and public agencies are very cooperative and pleased that local government officials are interested in gaining a better knowledge of their clients' needs. These agencies are invaluable sources of detailed information on the needs of the handicapped. However, local regulations or state laws on the confidentiality of data about the handicapped, particularly minors, often inhibit the collection of usable data. This problem of indirect contact between client and researcher can often be overcome, however, by such means as having the serving agency establish a procedure by which interested clients can contact the researcher directly. For example, a school district may send to the parents of handicapped students a survey seeking information on the need for a city recreation program for the handicapped.

The resource inventory   Upon completion of the needs assessment, the next stage of planning involves the compilation of a listing of resources potentially available to help meet needs. Inasmuch as contact with service agencies was a part of the needs assessment process, research into the services offered by these agencies can often be accomplished at the same time. This research should include public agencies which directly provide services, such as school districts; state rehabilitation agencies; local public health, welfare and transit offices; veteran affairs agencies; college aid offices; and others.

Private agencies are also very active in providing services. Agencies such as the Easter Seal Association, the Cancer Society, the Heart Association, mental health associations, and organizations concerned with specific conditions such as cerebral palsy, epilepsy, cystic fibrosis, muscular dystrophy, and asthma, should be contacted and their services fully considered in the resources inventory.

There is also a third group of agencies providing indirect services for the handicapped which should be included in the inventory. This group includes service clubs, churches, fraternal and philanthropic organizations, and private individuals. The services provided by these organizations include scholarships, transportation, home visits or phone calls, support of camping and athletic events, and much more. These organizations also play an important role in educating the community on the needs of the handicapped. They often provide the spark which is needed to get programs under way. In addition, they are a vital source of volunteer help and can almost always be relied upon to provide some amount of funding for special equipment or materials for handicapped programs.

The action plan   The plan which evolves from analysis of the needs of the handicapped and an evaluation of resources may or may not suggest the establishment of local programs. It should, however, suggest a policy for assisting the handicapped in overcoming architectural barriers and should clearly establish the city or county's position in support of the handicapped in other areas. This support may take the form of a commitment for the jurisdiction to become an advocate, including the establishment of public services for the handicapped, or it may simply be a policy statement acknowledging that there are unmet needs.

Implementation and evaluation   The nature of activity required for implementation will vary greatly, depending upon the policies outlined in the plan itself. If the city or county envisions a modest involvement in direct support of the handicapped, the implementation will accordingly involve less activity and fewer staff. Regardless of the level of support, a contact person, preferably within a department offering human services, should be established as liaison with handicapped individuals and groups. The individual assigned to act as liaison should use the plan as an operating guide and should endeavor to keep the policy current. Finally, the plan should have an evaluation process of the type described in Chapter 10 as a basic component. In addition, there should be a mechanism so that evaluation can regularly take place.

1   Webster's New Collegiate Dictionary, 1974 ed., s.v. "Health."

2   This paper was based in part on a staff conference which included the following persons: Gerald T. O'Neil, Dade County Department of Human Services (DHR), Health Services Division; Frances Greer, Assistant Director, DHR Health Services Division; Michael Gruber, DHR Program Services Unit Director; and Beverly Mirman, DHR Health Planner.

3   Victor R. Fuchs, *Who Shall Live? Health, Economics, and Social Choice* (New York: Basic Books, 1974), p. 58.

4   Administrative Review Panel, *Review of Family Health Center Program and Facility Plan* (County Manager's Office, Dade County, Florida, 30 June 1976), pp. 9–10.

5   Franklyn Arnhoff, "Social Consequences of Policy Toward Mental Illness," *Science*, 27 June 1975, p. 1277.

6   Leo Levy, *1969 Progress Report: State of Illinois Department of Mental Health* (Springfield, Ill.: Department of Mental Health, State of Illinois, 1969), p. 110.

7   David E. Bazelon, "Issues and Approaches in Child Psychiatry," *Hospital and Community Psychiatry*, February 1974, p. 97.

8   Levy, *1969 Progress Report*, p. 62.

9   This issue is discussed in detail in Arnhoff, "Social Consequences of Policy."

10 Milton Greenblatt, "Class Action and the Right to Treatment," *Hospital and Community Psychiatry*, July 1974, p. 452.

11 Figure from the President's Committee on Employment of the Handicapped.

12 Committee on Recreation and Leisure, *Newsletter*, February 1974.

14

Other target areas

The present chapter continues the discussion of illustrative programs that is the main focus of Part Four of this book. The four target areas chosen for discussion are: services for the elderly; minorities and human rights; housing for low income citizens; and mobilizing community resources for youth. As local government managers will be aware, each subject area, in its own way, presents significant challenges for both community and top decision makers in the public sector. The separate authors of the four sections that follow their present their individual perspectives on their areas of expertise. Throughout the discussion, however, an attempt is made to focus on the key managerial issues involved rather than provide an exhaustive coverage of four constantly-changing human services functions. That is, particular examples are used to bring out managerial principles that transcend a specific legislative or geographical environment.

Services for the elderly

Over the past two hundred years the status of older Americans has changed dramatically: attitudes toward the elderly have shifted from veneration to contempt to modest concern. Among major factors contributing to this change have been immigration policies, industrialization, increased mobility, declining fertility rates, and the erosion of family networks.

As the status and influence of the elderly waned in the post-Civil-War era, they began to lose visibility. By the turn of the century, older people were viewed with a great deal of negativism, and they were receiving very little attention from the increasing number of public and private social institutions. Even though the twentieth century brought a knowledge boom in many fields, we continued—for reasons perhaps best left to psychologists to explore—to rely on ignorance and mythology when it came to the aged. Very few research projects were focused on the elderly. Even as human services programs were first developed, older people were largely ignored, and this situation continued until the 1930s. Although a variety of programs have been developed for the aged since the decade of the New Deal, these have often been ill-conceived because of the lack of reliable information about the target population. Realism dictates that we recognize that, today, programs for the aged, like most other human services programs, are "organized" into an incoherent maze that defies description and impedes utilization.

In spite of these difficulties, increased understanding of the elderly and their problems, and the imaginative utilization of resources, can improve service programs and benefit local economics—factors of no small concern to local government decision makers. There is a growing body of knowledge and experience available. This presents a managerial "fund" on which local government managers developing services for the elderly can draw with profit. It is not limited to the North American experience. To take just one example, in the western European and Scandinavian countries (to say nothing of Eastern Europe and the Soviet Union), where many have observed a greater respect and concern for the elderly, a number of novel "case finding" tactics have been developed. In several of these countries, mailmen, milkmen, neighbors, and others are utilized to check out the status of older citizens and to run errands and perform other minor tasks. Some of these countries subsidize telephone service for those unable to afford it, in recognition of the important link to the community that the phone represents. Most of these countries have a system of integrated services that the case finders plug into. For example, the flow chart in Figure 14–1 outlines the health and social services system in England as described by Michael J. Austin. This chart reflects Austin's conclusions that England has a more comprehensive set of services, and that they are more highly integrated and more accessible.[1] The burden on local officials in the United States is to fully utilize the expanding resources for services to the elderly in a more imaginative way in order to produce comprehensive service programs in the community. This will require not only imagination, but also the reordering of priorities, organizational changes, and personnel training programs. Only by taking what may be viewed as drastic action can we meet the needs of our elderly population and thus improve our local communities.

It is the goal of the following discussion, given the space restraints involved, to present information about the elderly, outline the range of program resources, and suggest how resources may be employed by local public officials. It is divided into five portions. The first presents an introductory overview attempting to address the question: Who are the elderly? It also offers some observations on the ''nonsystem'' of services in this area. The three following sections deal, respectively, with income maintenance of the elderly; health services for the elderly; and housing services for the elderly. Each of these three sections is divided into three parts, which state the problem; indicate program resources; and offer program illustrations.

This discussion should not be considered exhaustive in any sense. It seeks to illustrate the problems inherent in developing service programs for the aged and to help local officials gain a ''mind set'' that should result in more effective and efficient service programs. The discussion of three problem areas is intended to help local officials design an appropriate strategy to cope with the problems of their respective older populations and to negotiate functionally organized state and federal agencies.

An overview

Who are the elderly?   Since 1900, both the numbers and percentage of persons sixty-five years of age or older in the United States have risen dramatically. In the ensuing discussion, these persons will be referred to as the elderly. In 1900, the elderly represented only 4.1 percent of the total U.S. population, or 3.1 million persons. By 1975, one out of every ten Americans was sixty-five years of age or older; in that year, older Americans numbered 22.4 million. Moreover, the Census Bureau predicts that by the year 2000, 11.7 percent of the total population, that is, a total of 30.6 million persons, will be elderly.[2]

Too old to cut the mussed turf   The Action Center of the city of Dallas, Texas, is lending a hand to elderly citizens cited by the city for code violations such as high weeds, litter, and minor building code offenses. The Action Center has compiled a list of 600 volunteers who are willing to contribute a Saturday morning to mowing and clearing a lot or applying a coat of paint to a house. The cases are referred to the Action Center by the municipal courts. The volunteers are given sixty days to complete their work. When the violation is brought into compliance, the case can be dismissed.

Changing composition   The twentieth century has seen major shifts not only in the size of the elderly population vis-à-vis other age groups, but also in the composition of the older population itself. For example, the ratio of males to females among the elderly population has changed substantially. As recently as 1930, the numbers of American men and women sixty-five years of age or older were about equal. By 1975, however, there were only 69.3 elderly men for every 100 elderly women in our society. This trend is expected to continue; census projections indicate that by the year 2000 there will be only 64.9 men to every 100 women among those sixty-five years or older.

Another significant change is that the elderly population is becoming increasingly aged. The greatest increase since 1900 has been in the proportion of persons sixty-five years of age or older (from 29.0 percent to 38.1 percent of the elderly), while the proportion of the aged population from sixty-five to sixty-nine years old has actually decreased (from 42.3 percent to 36.2 percent).

It should be noted that, in many instances, the status of the minority aged differs somewhat from that of elderly whites, primarily because of varying socioeconomic circumstances. While 11.0 percent of the white population is sixty-five and over, only 7.4 percent of blacks and 3.6 percent of the Spanish-surnamed are elderly. In 1974, the life expectancy at birth was 72.7 years for whites, well above the 65 years predicted for minorities. However, the gap in relative life expectancy closes as the majority and minority groups age. The sex ratios of the older popula-

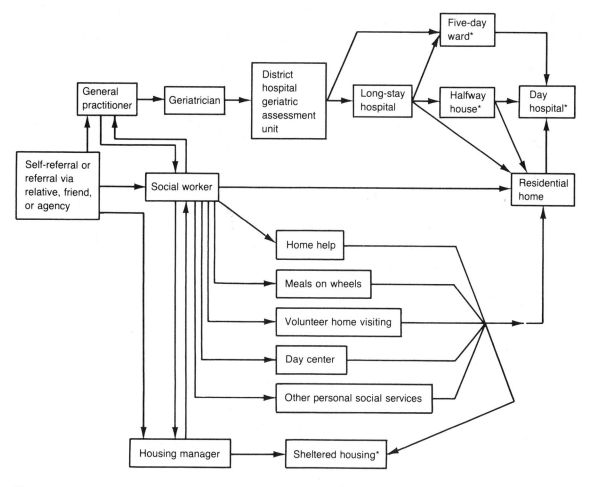

*People using these facilities might also be receiving services organized by a social worker.

Figure 14–1 Public health and social services pathways for the elderly in England. (Source: Michael J. Austin, "A Network of Help for England's Elderly," *Social Work* 21 [March 1976]: 114–19.)

tion also vary with racial/ethnic background; while there were 68.7 white men for every 100 white women in 1974, there were 73 black men per 100 black women and 87 men per 100 women among the Spanish-surnamed.

Distribution and mobility   Seven states—New York, California, Pennsylvania, Florida, Illinois, Texas, and Ohio—have older populations of more than one million people, accounting for about 45 percent of the total elderly population of the United States. In 1975, the proportion of persons sixty-five and over varied from a low of 2.4 percent in Alaska to a high of 16.1 percent in Florida. States of the midwestern farm belt also had a high proportion (12 percent or more) of older persons living within their borders, according to the Census Bureau. The older population moves less frequently than do younger age groups and when they do move, they are most likely to move to a different location within the same county.

The Census Bureau reports that "the highest proportion of elderly persons (13.6 percent) is found in small towns, i.e., rural places of 1,000 to 2,500 inhabitants. The next highest proportion is found in urban places of 2,500 to 10,000, followed in order by urbanized places of 10,000 to 50,000; central cities of urbanized areas; 'other rural' areas; and the urban fringe." [3] In 1970, about 34 percent of the total elderly population lived in the central cities of our urban areas. Once again, sharp differences can be noted between the majority and minority groups. Over half of both the black aged (52 percent) and the Hispanic aged (51 percent) lived in central cities in 1970.

Educational attainment   Historically, the elderly have usually been less educated than the succeeding generations. In recent times, a contributing factor has been the high number of foreign-born elderly, who demonstrate a higher proportion of illiteracy and lower educational attainment than is found among the native population. In 1970, the foreign-born constituted 15 percent of the total elderly population. The percentage of foreign-born increases steadily for higher age groupings within the older population.

It is expected, however, that the difference in educational attainment between those twenty-five years and over and those sixty-five years and over will be significantly reduced by 1990. By that time, it is predicted that about half the elderly population will be high school graduates, while the traditional rise in educational attainment among adults less than sixty-five years of age is expected to decrease.

Institutionalization: a myth   In spite of widely held stereotypes, the fact is that, in 1975, slightly less than 5 percent of the elderly resided in institutions. This proportion is beginning to rise concomitantly with the increasing numbers of widowed females and the extremely elderly. The nature of the institutionalization has also been changing. Since the 1960s, there has been a decreasing use of mental hospitals for the elderly, and as of the later 1970s, the majority of institutionalized elderly live in homes for the aged. Thus the vast majority, about 95 percent, of the elderly are living in noninstitutional settings and must be served by local units of government.

The shorter life span of men results in different living arrangements for them than for older women. The vast majority of older men are married and living with their wives. Only one out of seven older men lives alone. On the other hand, over half of the women over age sixty-five are widowed, and over one-third live alone or with nonrelatives. These facts must be taken into consideration as local services for the aged are being planned.

Sensory impairment   Another general characteristic of the aged that has broad implications for public planners is the sensory impairment experienced as one grows older. Of particular importance are age-related decrements, that is, gradual decreases, in vision, hearing, and touch. These sensory losses result in a special set of needs in areas like housing, transportation, and public safety. The photograph shown in Figure 14–2 illustrates the effects of the normal loss in vision experienced by older drivers in their late seventies or early eighties.[4]

Figure 14–2   The left half of this photograph has been specially treated to show how an elderly person with a normal loss of vision would perceive the traffic signs.

Summary   The forgoing data are meant to convey the general circumstances of the elderly in America. Conditions vary drastically from one part of the country to another as demonstrated by the data presented. Officials responsible for planning services will need to obtain specific data for their communities. Each state is required by the Federal Older Americans Act to have a state agency to plan and coordinate services for the aged. One of the responsibilities of these state agencies is the submission of an annual plan that describes the conditions of the aged and the relevant service needs and programs. These agencies are often valuable sources of information about the particular circumstances of the elderly within each state and its subregions. And, of course, state and local agencies responsible for handling census data, and other socioeconomic data, possess a wealth of information available to local officials who are planning service programs for the elderly.

The nonsystem of services   As our understanding and concern about the plight of the elderly has increased in recent decades, a wide variety of disparate services have been developed. The cornerstone of the federal programs is the Social Security Act, first enacted in 1935 and since then amended more than a dozen times. Other federal programs have been established in a rather sporadic manner—to put it kindly. Thus, currently we have what can only be described as a nonsystem of partial and uncoordinated federal programs that tend to engender similar incoherence at the state and local level.

Three national conferences   This condition has been confirmed and reported in the proceedings of the three national conferences on aging sponsored by the federal government. The first of these conferences was sponsored in 1950 by the Federal Security Agency. In 1961 and 1971, the first and second White House Conferences on Aging were held. In 1965, the Older Americans Act (OAA) was passed in an effort to centralize leadership and services on behalf of the nation's elderly. The act provided for the creation of the Administration on Aging (AoA), within the Department of Health, Education, and Welfare (HEW), and established ten service objectives which cut across several federal departments. Those ten service objectives which continue to have a high program priority, covering such matters as income, health, housing, social services, transportation, recreation, and personal freedom.

Role of the Administration on Aging (AoA)   The mission of the Administration on Aging is to analyze the needs of the elderly, to plan and advocate needed service programs, and to optimize the coordination of operating programs. As of the later 1970s, AoA has a tier of agencies with which local units of government must negotiate in order to acquire AoA-controlled funds for service programs. At the federal level, AoA and its regional offices operate as a part of HEW. At the state level, there must be an agency with specific responsibility for statewide planning, coordination, and evaluation of programs. These state agencies take on a variety of forms, ranging from strong agencies with a great deal of independence to "paper organizations" housed within a state department. At a substate or regional level, there are Area Agencies on Aging (AAAs), each of which usually covers an area large enough to embrace many local units of government.

The stated intent of this hierarchical arrangement was to decentralize policy-making and planning activities and to maximize the participation of officials and citizens at the state and local levels. Unfortunately, the consequence (with few notable exceptions) has been the creation of hundreds of agencies with limited authority, competence, and resources, and virtually guaranteeing the mediocrity of programs. In many instances, the AAAs are staffed by personnel who lack training and experience in gerontology and/or planning.

It is extremely important that local government managers obtain information about the purposes, organization, and programs of the state and area agencies on aging within their respective states. And it should be understood that, frankly, these agencies may sometimes prove to be a liability rather than an asset.

Role of other federal departments   Although AoA, with its subsidiary agencies at the state and local level, was created as a federal focal point with respect to the needs of the aged, as has been mentioned before, this intent has not been realized. In reality, the majority of programs benefiting the aged are operated by other federal departments or other units within HEW. Programs are organized along functional lines (housing, transportation, crime, health, income maintenance, etc.) and, for the most part, are managed independently. Figure 14–3 identifies the major federal programs that provide resources to state and local agencies to assist the aged, and the federal agencies that sponsor these programs. Illustrations of how these resources can be used are discussed later.

Summary   The significant point for local officials is that, to utilize resources available to assist the aged in a local community, one must be familiar with the operation of the federal bureaucracy and in many cases must seek multiple financing for the multifunctional service programs required by older persons. In conclusion, it can be noted that the situation at the state and local levels is too diverse to be described here. Suffice it to say that any local unit of government seeking to establish a comprehensive or multifunctional program for the elderly will need to establish an interdepartmental mechanism to include relevant local agencies and to cope with the appropriate regional, state, and federal agencies. Area agencies and state agencies on aging may be able to assist local officials to identify and utilize available resources.

Income maintenance of the elderly

The problem   Multiple factors combine to sharply reduce the income of today's elderly. Among those factors are poor health, compulsory retirement, age discrimination, and inflation. Irrespective of cause, the net result is that the vast majority of the elderly are not employed and must live on inadequate income. The elderly

Figure 14–3   Matrix showing the variety of federal programs that benefit the elderly. (Source: U.S., Congress, House of Representatives, Select Committee on Aging, *Funding of Federal Programs for Older Americans,* 94th Cong., 2nd sess., September 1976.)

MAJOR FEDERAL PROGRAMS BENEFITING THE ELDERLY

By Category and by Agency

Column key (Executive Departments and Independent Agencies):

AGRICULTURE — 1. Farmers Home Administration; 2. Food and Nutrition Service
HEALTH, EDUCATION, AND WELFARE — 3. Health Services Administration; 4. Social Security Administration; 5. Office of Education; 6. Administration on Aging; 7. Social and Rehabilitation Service; 8. Office of Nursing Home Affairs; 9. National Institute on Aging
H.U.D. — 10. Housing Production and Mortgage Credit; 11. Housing Management; 12. Community Planning and Development
LABOR — 13. Office of Fair Labor Standards; 14. Employment and Training Administration*
D.O.T. — 15. Urban Mass Transportation Administration; 16. Federal Highway Administration
17. Treasury; 18. Office of Revenue Sharing
INDEPENDENT AGENCIES — 19. ACTION; 20. Community Services Administration; 21. Legal Services Corporation; 22. Railroad Retirement Board; 23. Small Business Administration; 24. U.S. Civil Service Commission; 25. Veterans Administration

Program	1	2	3	4	5	6	7	8	9	10	11	12	13	14	15	16	17	18	19	20	21	22	23	24	25
EMPLOYMENT																									
AGE DISCRIMINATION IN EMPLOYMENT													●												
EMPLOYMENT PROGRAMS FOR SPECIAL GROUPS														●											
FOSTER GRANDPARENT PROGRAM																			●						
OLDER AMERICANS COMMUNITY SERVICE EMPLOYMENT PROGRAM														●											
RETIRED SENIOR VOLUNTEER PROGRAM (RSVP)																			●						
SERVICE CORPS OF RETIRED EXECUTIVES (SCORE)																							●		
VOLUNTEERS IN SERVICE TO AMERICA (VISTA)																			●						
HEALTH CARE																									
HEALTH RESOURCES DEVELOPMENT, CONSTRUCTION AND MODERNIZATION OF FACILITIES (Hill-Burton Prog)			●																						
CONSTRUCTION OF NURSING HOMES AND INTERMEDIATE CARE FACILITIES									●																
GRANTS TO STATES FOR MEDICAL ASSISTANCE PROGRAMS (MEDICAID)							●																		
PROGRAM OF HEALTH INSURANCE FOR THE AGED AND DISABLED (MEDICARE)				●																					
VETERANS DOMICILIARY CARE PROGRAM																									●
VETERANS NURSING HOME CARE PROGRAM																									●
HOUSING																									
HOUSING FOR THE ELDERLY (sec. 202)										●	●														
LOW AND MODERATE INCOME HOUSING (sec. 8)										●	●														
MORTGAGE INSURANCE ON RENTAL HOUSING FOR THE ELDERLY (sec. 231)										●	●														
RURAL RENTAL HOUSING LOANS	●																								
COMMUNITY DEVELOPMENT												●													
RENTAL AND CO-OPERATIVE HOUSING FOR LOWER AND MODERATE INCOME FAMILIES (sec. 236)										●	●														
LOW RENT PUBLIC HOUSING										●	●														
INCOME MAINTENANCE																									
CIVIL SERVICE RETIREMENT																								●	
OLD-AGE, SURVIVORS INSURANCE PROGRAM (Social Security)				●																					
RAILROAD RETIREMENT PROGRAM																						●			
SUPPLEMENTAL SECURITY INCOME PROGRAM				●																					
VETERANS PENSION PROGRAM																									●
SOCIAL SERVICE PROGRAMS																									
EDUCATION PROGRAMS FOR NON-ENGLISH SPEAKING ELDERLY					●																				
FOOD STAMP PROGRAM		●																							
LEGAL SERVICES CORPORATION																					●				
MODEL PROJECTS						●																			
MULTIPURPOSE SENIOR CENTERS						●																			
NUTRITION PROGRAM FOR THE ELDERLY						●																			
OLDER READER SERVICES					●																				
REVENUE SHARING																		●							
SENIOR OPPORTUNITIES AND SERVICES																				●					
SOCIAL SERVICES FOR LOW-INCOME PERSONS AND PUBLIC ASSISTANCE RECIPIENTS							●																		
STATE AND COMMUNITY PROGRAMS						●																			
TRAINING AND RESEARCH PROGRAMS																									
MULTI-DISCIPLINARY CENTERS OF GERONTOLOGY						●																			
NURSING HOME CARE, TRAINING AND RESEARCH PROGRAMS								●																	
PERSONNEL TRAINING						●																			
RESEARCH AND DEMONSTRATION PROGRAM						●																			
RESEARCH ON AGING PROCESS AND HEALTH PROBLEMS									●																
RESEARCH ON PROBLEMS OF THE ELDERLY						●																			
TRANSPORTATION																									
CAPITAL ASSISTANCE GRANTS FOR USE BY PUBLIC AGENCIES															●										
CAPITAL ASSISTANCE GRANTS FOR USE BY PRIVATE NON-PROFIT GROUPS															●										
REDUCED FARES															●										
RURAL HIGHWAY PUBLIC TRANSPORTATION DEMONSTRATION PROJECT															●	●									

*Formerly Federal Housing Administration   ** Formerly Manpower Administration

who are employed, with the exception of professional personnel, are usually found in the lowest paying service and agricultural jobs. Those who have limited or no financial resources and qualify for some form of public assistance find themselves among the poorest members of our society.

Most Americans can expect a 50 percent reduction in income upon their retirement. In 1974—to take an illustrative year—the median income of families with heads sixty-five and over was approximately 57 percent of the median income for all families ($7,298 versus $12,836). Unrelated older individuals (those not living with relatives) have a median income of $2,956, two-fifths that of older families. Few elderly persons are reasonably secure in economic terms: only 23 percent of the families headed by a person over sixty-five have incomes over $10,000 per year. Many more are either below the poverty line or hovering just above it. In 1974, 9.5 percent of all elderly families and 31.8 percent of unrelated individuals fell below the poverty level, based on a nonfarm income of $2,364 or less for unrelated individuals and $2,982 or less for a couple. In numbers, this amounts to 760,000 older families and 2,065,00 individuals. Moreover, a startling number of elderly are near poor: in 1973, 39 percent of older couples had incomes under $5,000 per year; 57 percent of elderly unrelated individuals had yearly incomes of less than $3,000.

Minority elderly men and women often face situations of double and triple jeopardy. To be old, black, and female in this country generally means extreme poverty. In 1974, the median income of black families headed by men sixty-five years of age or older was $4,909, while black families headed by women had an annual income of $4,602. Unrelated older blacks fare even worse: 1974 median income figures for unrelated black men and women were $2,385 and $1,998, respectively.

Another important factor to consider when analyzing age and its relationship to income in our society is this: *Many elderly poor become poor only after reaching old age.* According to Dr. Robert Butler, director of the National Institute on Aging:

. . . the elderly are the fastest growing poverty group. This is new poverty, not simply the poverty transmitted from generation to generation within the same family. Independently of previous means and previous socioeconomic status, one may be thrown into poverty for the first time in old age. Catastrophic diseases, or the sheer cutback of income in retirement, may create instant poverty where none previously existed.[5]

For the total population over sixty-five years of age, the primary sources for 46 percent of their income are retirement benefits from Social Security at 34 percent; public pensions, 7 percent; and private pensions, 5 percent. Social Security is the only means of support or over two million of the American elderly. Of the aggregate income of the elderly, 29 percent is derived from employment.[6] Fourteen percent of older people were in the labor force in 1974, most of these in low paying positions.

To fully appreciate the dire economic circumstances of the elderly as Dr. Butler suggests, one must look beyond income data. The elderly have extraordinary expenses as a result of declining health, inadequate housing, and decreased mobility. Their income is not only low, but usually fixed. Thus, inflationary periods like that of the early 1970s can have a devastating impact on the purchasing power of the elderly.

When the elderly are socially and economically stranded by poverty, it is the local community that must, in the final analysis, be responsive. To ease what can become an insurmountable burden, local officials must devise ways to improve state and federal programs and to increase the utilization of these programs.

Program resources Decision makers in local units of government can move in a number of ways to raise the income level of the elderly and consequently to improve local economic conditions. One step that can be taken is to establish an "advocacy service" to help the elderly apply for and receive benefits to which they are entitled. Since income maintenance programs, with very few exceptions, are financed by the federal and state governments, optimal utilization will work to the advantage of local units of government. The major federal programs are identified in Figure 14–3 under the heading "Income Maintenance." The food stamp program and the nutrition program listed under "Social Services" in the figure are very effective tools to stretch the limited "food dollars" of our older citizens.

In many instances, a combination of benefits from income maintenance programs may be secured to raise the income of aged local residents above the poverty level. The key to optimal use is the delegation of responsibility to expedite claims and the employment of trained personnel to carry out the assignment. In an organized advocacy service, such personnel may be drawn from the ranks of the elderly, serving as volunteers or part-time employees.

There are other programs that can be used to increase the income of the elderly and to finance the operation of a variety of local services. These are employment programs that have not been widely or imaginatively used by local governments. Such programs include: the Comprehensive Employment and Training Act (CETA), the Older Americans Community Service Employment Program, and the Foster Grandparent–Senior Companion Program.

There are, additionally, some volunteer programs designed specifically for the elderly. While these programs do not serve to increase the income of the elderly, they can be used by local governmental bodies to expand community services that alleviate the financial problems of the elderly while providing socially productive service opportunities for other elderly persons. They are: the Retired Senior Volunteer Program (RSVP), the Volunteers in Service to America (VISTA), and the Service Corps of Retired Executives (SCORE).

It should be noted that several states, counties, and cities have established programs to complement these federal programs. An inquiry to the state agency on aging should produce specific information about additional resources that can be utilized in particular states and localities. In this connection, it should also be emphasized that private nonprofit community service agencies often support and/or operate a variety of emergency assistance and other programs that can be used to assist the elderly to conserve their resources. Local government officials should become familiar with the entire range of voluntary community services offered in their respective localities.

Program illustrations   Many local units of government have developed a dual approach to improving the economic status of their elderly residents. First, they have created employment opportunities designed specifically for older people. Second, they have devised ways to reduce the expenditures of the elderly.

Let us first look at a few examples of employment opportunities that have been developed. Under the Foster Grandparent Program, a number of municipalities and school districts have employed older adults to work as aides to professional personnel in a wide variety of educational and recreational settings. In this capacity, the older participants may be serving children, or perhaps other persons. There is a possible side effect to the use of the elderly in such programs that public officials should appreciate: it has been suggested that when the elderly are employed in a program related to education or recreation, they are likely to become advocates of millage and bonding campaigns to support the program of the sponsoring institution. This would seem to be unusual behavior for older persons living on very limited incomes.

Many communities have used the CETA programs to employ the elderly and as a means of expanding and developing municipal services. Libraries, hospitals, and counseling agencies are illustrative of the kinds of settings in which older CETA personnel are located. RSVP has been used by a number of communities to establish services for the elderly such as tax counseling, consumer education, and home repairs. While RSVP does not provide income for other than out-of-pocket expenses of the volunteers, it can be used to develop services that stretch the income of older citizens.

Elderly can hack it, too   In Richland, Washington, the city manager was asked by representatives of senior citizen groups to provide a transportation service that could get the elderly to the doctor, market, church, etc., at a cost they could afford. To be effective, the system had to be door-to-door. After finding that any kind of bus system in a city of this size was uneconomical, the city contacted a local cab company and started an experimental program. Seniors buy tickets for thirty cents which provide them a one-way taxi ride anywhere in the city. The cab company presents its tickets to the city, which pays sixty cents per ride. Tickets and eligibility are administered by the city, with the cab company providing information on origin, destination, and number of riders. Riders are encouraged to "double up," since single rides would mean a deficit. The project has proved attractive for several reasons—no capital expenditure was required; an existing resource having radio control and 24-hour capability was utilized; data on actual demand–response experience could be gathered; and private enterprise was helped to provide a service needed in the community, but otherwise economically infeasible.

The other major action that can be taken by government at all levels to assist the elderly with their income problems is to reduce their expenditures. Many municipalities offer reduced transportation charges for older citizens, and reduce or abolish admission fees to public institutions such as art institutes, parks, zoos, and so on. Several municipalities and states have developed "tax relief" programs to benefit persons over sixty-five years of age. In a number of communities, public and private groups have worked in cooperation with local business firms to arrange special discounts for the elderly on such items as foods, drugs, clothing, prosthetics, and home repair services. A few experimental programs have been undertaken to reduce the charges for the use of public utilities by the elderly.

The above illustrations are simply a few samples of how some local officials and community organizations have been able to improve the economic circumstances of the elderly and the larger community, while simultaneously enriching community service programs.

Health services for the elderly

The problem   In general, older people are a reasonably healthy and active group. In 1972, approximately 18 percent of the elderly reported limitations on their mobility due to chronic conditions; and among those having limitations, only 5 percent are homebound.[7] As mentioned earlier, only 5 percent are institutionalized.

It is clear, however, that health problems do increase with age. Chronic diseases, such as heart disease and arthritis, are reported to become far more prevalent with age, as do various orthopedic, visual, and hearing impairments.[8] Older people have a one-in-six likelihood of being hospitalized during a given year, as opposed to one in ten for persons under sixty-five. The average hospital stay for an older person is five days longer than that for younger people (12.2 as opposed to 7.2 days). Elderly people also see physicians more often than do younger persons (an average of 6.5 as opposed to 4.8 visits per year). Almost all older people have vision loss, and about 92 percent wear eyeglasses.[9] Nearly 30 percent report hearing impairments,[10] and 5 percent use hearing aids.[11]

The health care needs of older people differ substantially from those of other segments of the population. The treatment and management of chronic illness are the major medical care needs of the elderly. Moreover, older people's greatest needs occur in the areas where our medical care system is weakest: the treatment of chronic disease, rehabilitation, health maintenance, long-term care, and home health care.

It appears that one of the most pervasive health problems encumbering the aged is that of malnutrition—and this is one of the most affluent societies known to humanity. Many older adults, as a result of inadequate income, inadequate housing facilities, decreased mobility, or a lack of interest in food, do not prepare or purchase well-balanced and nutritious meals. Such behavior, for whatever reasons, produces and intensifies health problems.

Serious dental problems are very common among the elderly and frequently lead to other health problems. These dental problems, as painful and common as they are, are not generally attended to because dental care is not included in many public or private health insurance programs. The AoA reports that "half of the older population had either not seen a dentist for 5 or more years or had never visited a dentist." [12] The cosmetic importance that we attach to the teeth often results in the social isolation of the elderly who are embarrassed about their appearance. The loss or poor condition of teeth also affects food intake for older persons.

One little-recognized problem relating to the health status of elderly persons is substance abuse, particularly alcoholism. American society is increasingly concerned about problem drinking and although social drinking generally drops off for persons fifty and over, there is evidence that some older men and women turn to alcohol as an antidote for depression and loneliness. Older men living alone seem to be a particularly vulnerable group.

There is also the question of abuse of medication, including both prescribed and over-the-counter drugs. Many older persons seeking relief from pain and general debilitation shop around for medications. When they reach a physician, counselor, or social worker, they are rarely asked—nor do they volunteer the information—about the contents of their medicine cabinets. Yet the interactive effects of different medications are often counterproductive and occasionally fatal.

Door-to-door service Although several communities in the United States and Canada have a dial-a-bus program, Haddonfield, New Jersey, claims to have the only complete door-to-door service. After calling for a ride, a bus will arrive within twenty minutes at your door to take you anywhere within an eight-square-mile service area for sixty cents (special rates for senior citizens and groups). Commuters also can arrange to be picked up every day. This project, funded by DOT's Urban Mass Transit Administration from the New York–New Jersey Department of Transportation, is a 24-hour operation.

As mentioned earlier, a common problem of the elderly is the depreciation of such senses as sight, hearing, touch, and smell. The loss of these senses is normally gradual, often almost imperceptible, and consequently the problems often go untreated. These conditions impact on every aspect of the lives of older adults, and a number of accommodations must be taken into consideration. As an example, vision and hearing losses influence mobility. The same losses may require special housing, transportation, and other services.

Another general health problem of the elderly relates to the accessibility of services—accessibility in terms of cost, distance, and dignified treatment. It was mentioned earlier that significant numbers of older adults live in small communities and rural settings. These settings often lack comprehensive and conveniently located health services. Similarly, most of the elderly residing in urbanized areas are located in the older parts of the central cities. Physicians and most health facilities are located elsewhere. Getting to and from health service facilities is thus a major problem for the aged.

The high cost of health services has, of course, impacted on nearly the entire population. For the elderly, it is a particularly serious problem. Medicaid payments do cover most of the costs for the very poorest, but the coverage of medicare and private insurance programs is grossly inadequate in view of the chronicity of the health problems that the elderly frequently experience. A major consequence of the patchwork set of health insurance programs for the elderly is that local public and private hospitals often are forced to absorb the losses incurred by serving older patients.

The problem in securing dignified treatment for the elderly is pervasive and relates back to the lack of reliable information about them. Only two aspects of the problem will be mentioned here. First, health professionals, sad to say, appear to be less interested in older patients because they perceive a bleak and brief future for them. Second, the general tendency is to treat the elderly in an offhand and patronizing manner and not to take the time for a careful and thorough examination of problems. Such attitudes and behaviors on the part of health professionals, coupled with or rooted in the mythology about the elderly, frequently result in low quality care.

Program resources   In Figure 14–3, six health programs are identified. Three of these are operated by HEW, two by the Veterans Administration, and one by the Department of Housing and Urban Development (HUD).

Of these six programs, the two most important are Titles XVIII (Medicare) and XIX (Medicaid) of the Social Security Act. A crucial point for local officials to keep in mind with respect to these two programs is that if persons are ineligible or they exhaust their benefits, the responsibility to provide essential services falls on local units of government or private health agencies.

Other federal resources include two programs to combat the malnutrition suffered by so many older adults. The food stamp program operated by the Department of Agriculture permits low income persons, including the elderly, to purchase food stamps that have a greater value than the purchase price. Of particular importance to the elderly is the feature that permits persons over sixty years of age who are homebound to exchange food stamps for home-delivered meals. A weak aspect of the program is that it does not recognize the propensity of older persons to require special diets. Many of the items required in special diets are not covered by the program. Also, the complicated process of certification of eligible clients tends to discourage many elderly persons from participating.

The second program is the Nutrition Program for the Elderly (Title VII, OAA), which is operated by AoA and provides formula grants to state agencies on aging to establish and support low cost group meals and home-delivered meals for persons over sixty years of age. A common difficulty associated with the nutrition program is the need for supportive transportation services. On the other hand, many agencies have successfully used the nutrition program as a vehicle to introduce older persons to a variety of health maintenance concepts and services.

A wide range of federal health programs which concentrate on particular problems or fields of service of significance to the aged are sponsored by HEW. Illustrative of these are the programs in such areas as arthritis and rheumatism, heart, cancer, stroke, hypertension, diabetes, and long-term care. These many programs provide funds for research, teaching, and service. They should be of particular interest to local communities that operate sophisticated health care systems or in which institutions of higher education are located.

Program illustrations   There are key roles that local communities can play in improving health care services for the elderly and increasing the utilization of such services. It is important to note that health care services in America by and large have been developed and organized with the provider, rather than the consumer, in mind. The consequences of this approach, a complex system of highly bureaucratized services, often located in facilities that are at once socially and physically formidable, are of particular significance to older patients. Frequently older people are unable to locate or reach a needed service, or are bewildered by the physical setting and the maze of barely visible forms that they are required to sign. And, as mentioned earlier, they are generally turned off by the insensitivity of health care personnel.

The question confronting local communities, then, is what kinds of services are required to keep the elderly healthy and enable them to negotiate the "system."

Many communities have established programs with a health maintenance orientation, such as health education classes, exercise groups, health screening clinics, outreach consultation services, and so on. These also become important "case finding" services. When problems are detected, the all-important referral process can be initiated. Because such programs are often sponsored by churches, trade unions, service clubs, or service agencies—groups perceived positively by the elderly—a successful referral can be made more readily than by someone unfamiliar to the patient. These types of "threshold" health services can often be funded in part by local communities through the employment programs mentioned earlier, e.g., CETA, RSVP, etc. Service clubs such as Rotary or Kiwanis, or professional associations, may sponsor such projects in their communities. Revenue sharing funds can be assigned to underwrite the cost of such projects.

Seals on wheels The city of Berkley, Michigan, issues free parking stickers to senior citizens excusing them from paying into city parking meters. The rationale is that many seniors take longer shopping or running errands. They used to be penalized by parking tickets when they came back to an expired meter. Under the new program, retired people obtain stickers from the city recreation department, and now can have a fineless time shopping.

Because health problems and services are inextricably interwoven with other problems and services of the elderly, many communities have seen fit to construct multipurpose centers that serve as a focal point for their older citizens. Two funding sources not mentioned earlier are the Local Public Works and Capital Development and Investment Act of 1976, and Title V of the Older Americans Act. The former Act provides funds to local communities with unemployment in excess of 6.5 percent. The latter does not permit construction but does not allow acquisition or renovation of facilities.

Another approach taken by some communities has been to purchase specially designed vehicles to serve as mobile dental and/or medical clinics. These mobile units serve the elderly in housing developments, churches, shopping centers, or other convenient locations.

In addition to providing services that will link the elderly to the health care system, local units of government can take an active role in supporting other phases of health care and guaranteeing the quality of care. It should be noted again that, at very little cost to local government, programs like CETA can be used to provide personnel to nursing homes, hospitals, and day care programs. Or Title XX of the Social Security Act can be used to provide many services that can assist an older person to maintian an independent living arrangement. Local communities can play a protective role for the elderly by using their powers to license, zone, and enact local ordinances. In addition, associations of local government can work with state authorities to plan more efficient health care services for the elderly.

Housing services for the elderly

The problem As noted earlier, 95 percent of the elderly live in non-institutional settings. The housing needs of these older persons are markedly different from those of other sectors of the population.

Elderly Americans are disproportionately represented among those who are in need of federally assisted housing. More of them are poor and thus unable to afford suitable private housing. Elderly poor are often in worse economic straits than the nonelderly poor, partly because they are less able to find work to augment their inadequate incomes. Further, the elderly are more likely to have health problems. Their mobility is often curtailed. If they live in a high crime area, age and accompanying infirmities make them more vulnerable to robbery or assault. Even those who own their homes may require medical or nursing services, or assistance in homemaking or shopping, if they are to remain in the community. Because of their special needs, the elderly require special assistance.[13]

The 34 percent of persons 65 and over who live in our central cities have a number of particular problems. Their housing is likely to be older and in a greater state of disrepair. Their resources for having repairs made are likely to be fewer. Loneliness is often a more serious problem given the high rates of mobility within central cities on the part of younger persons, including relatives of the elderly. Property taxes are very likely to be higher than in smaller communities and services are declining with the declining resources of central cities. The fear of crime is pervasive and compounds the problems associated with social isolation.

The approximately 20 percent of the elderly who live in the urban fringe (suburbs) are likely to live in newer housing that is in better condition but may be more expensive to maintain. They are likely to be closer to relatives if not contemporaries. Property values and taxes are usually high and services may be geared to younger families. A major disadvantage of suburban residence for the elderly is the near total dependence on personal transportation by automobile.

The better than 20 percent of aged persons living in small and medium sized cities and rural towns are likely to live in older housing in need of repairs. As compared to their central city counterparts, their costs of purchasing and maintaining a home are likely to be more modest. They are likely to have better access to shopping and other services. Local taxes are likely to be lower, but fewer public services may be available. Also, as noted earlier, some of the specialized services required by the elderly, such as sophisticated health care, may be located at a greater distance.

The slightly more than 20 percent who live in other rural areas have special problems. Their housing is quite likely to be older, too large, and in a state of disrepair. Resources—capital and personnel—are less likely to be available for repair and maintenance purposes. The flight of the young from the most rural areas has created problems of loneliness and dangers of isolation. Dependence on personal transportation is absolute.

The importance of adequate housing for the elderly cannot be overstated. It impinges on all other aspects of their lives. Unless it is subsidized, housing consumes a disproportionate share of their income. If it is poorly designed, or in a state of disrepair, it poses health hazards. If it is not strategically located, it creates serious transportation problems and contributes to social isolation. If the neighborhood is in a state of social decline, it creates a number of public safety problems.

Let us consider the issue of design in greater detail. Sensory impairments require special lighting and color cuing. Similarly, special acoustical treatment is needed. Safety features such as guard rails, tub rails, warning signals, and high traction flooring are highly important. These are but a few of the design problems that must be considered in planning or evaluating housing for the elderly.

In view of the wide range of special housing needs of the elderly, and the centrality of housing to the well-being of the aged, one might expect a far-reaching set of programs to provide such an essential service. Unfortunately the response of both the public and private sectors has been niggardly.

Program resources Resources that may be tapped by local officials to improve and expand housing for the elderly are, like other resources for serving older citizens, often difficult to identify. In Figure 14–3, seven housing-specific federal programs are identified. Six of these programs are administered by agencies within the HUD, and one program is administered by the Department of Agriculture. These housing-specific programs present a number of options to local officials in promoting the development of public or private housing programs for the elderly.

Additionally, it should be noted that there are several housing related programs that can be used to assist the elderly. The major housing subsidy program for the elderly is not generally recognized as such. Over the years public assistance programs have provided the primary funding to meet the housing costs of low income elderly in publicly and privately owned facilities. As of the later 1970s, the Supplemental Security Income (SSI) program is serving that purpose. The SSI program is managed by the states and varies somewhat from state to state. Some states are required to supplement the federal grants. State grants may be directly influenced by fixed costs, such as housing, experienced by SSI beneficiaries. Thus local authorities should investigate the possibility of negotiating grant levels that will permit residents of public housing to pay legitimately established rental rates. Additionally, local authorities should intercede with state officials to guarantee elderly home owners grants high enough to permit them to maintain their properties and pay their taxes.

Job opportunities Newburg, Oregon, has approved a plan to employ senior citizens and handicapped persons on parking meter patrols. This plan calls for hiring elderly and handicapped persons to work twenty to twenty-four hours a month checking meters and making collections. Regular police personnel will continue to handle the associated paperwork and mail the notices of violation. The city currently is working with the state employment division to encourage applicants for the job.

There are very few resources available for the millions of elderly home owners. The major housing assistance program for home owners is the federal tax deduction based on interest paid on mortgages and the payment of property taxes. These provisions of the federal income tax are of limited value to the elderly because, with few exceptions, their income is not high enough to benefit substantially from itemized deductions. Programs designed to assist homeowners to secure loans for the rehabilitation and improvement of homes are not widely used by the elderly because of their limited incomes. Lenders are not eager to provide them with funds, even when loans are insured. The elderly are not able to take on debts to finance improvements that may result in higher taxes as well as principal and interest payments.

Other federal programs listed in Figure 14–3, including revenue sharing. Title XX (Social Security Act), and the Legal Services Corporation Act, can be utilized to fund services that are essential to adequate housing programs for the aged. The organization of an effective housing development team, as mentioned later in this chapter, will help to guarantee the comprehensiveness of the program and the input of persons familiar with the maze of federal and state programs that provide resources.

Program illustrations The near complete lack of high quality housing programs for the elderly reflects a widespread indifference to this problem and a lack of knowledge about how to solve it. Although there are serious constraints to the development or improvement of housing facilities for the elderly, there are a number of actions that local communities can take to alleviate the current deplorable conditions.

There is every indication that throughout the foreseeable future the majority of older adults will continue to reside in privately owned units. A large proportion of these units, as noted earlier, are in a serious state of disrepair. This situation has been brought about, in part, by the economic inability of elderly homeowners to afford repairs and improvements. The problem has been compounded by the disincentive of higher taxes once repairs or improvements are completed. Therefore, local units of government should consider the feasibility of a tax relief program for the owners of units occupied by persons sixty-five years of age or over. Any such tax relief program should be based on a set of rigidly enforced standards that reflect the special housing requirements of this age group.

As noted earlier, there are a number of employment, health, and social service programs that can be implemented at little or no local cost to provide a wide array of supportive services to help the elderly maintain independent living arrangements. Possible services include home repairs, mobile or neighborhood health facilities, and home-delivered nutritious meals. These types of services are absolutely essential to sustain a community's older persons whether they are in congregate or private housing situations.

For communities interested in constructing new housing for the elderly, the revitalized Section 202 loan program and Section 8 subsidy program offer considerable promise. However, a word of caution is in order. Building inadequate housing for the elderly is not particularly useful. Building adequate housing for the elderly is complicated and expensive. It is complicated because of the special physical and social needs of the elderly and the maze of bureaucratic policies and procedures that must be followed. It is expensive if appropriate standards are developed and followed. A manual has been developed by the Michigan State Housing Development Authority that should prove most useful to local officials and nonprofit sponsors interested in housing for the elderly. It is called *Housing for the Elderly Development Process.*[14]

Whether communities wish to undertake new housing or develop improvement programs, they must focus their attention on neighborhood conditions as well as housing structures. The elderly need a wide range of supportive facilities located in their own neighborhoods. They should have easy access to recreational, health, transportation, and shopping facilities. They require a safe, private neighborhood environment. Sensory impairments and physical disabilities make them particularly vulnerable to fire, crime, and traffic hazards. Many such problems can be corrected or alleviated at the local level by using ordinances, zoning restrictions and specially trained personnel to create a positive environment.

If a community desires to provide housing for elderly persons who are significantly incapacitated, the special needs become more numerous and demanding. In turn the design process and required amenities take on greater complexity.

Any community contemplating a housing program for the aged should begin by establishing a multidisciplinary planning team of experts from such fields as architecture, law, gerontology, urban planning, finance, health sciences, public safety, and social services. Some communities have also found it most useful to include representatives of the elderly on planning groups.

Conclusion

The forgoing discussion has outlined some of the special problems of the elderly, and has suggested ways in which they can be assisted to continue as functioning members of the community. Similar sketches could have been drafted regarding crime, transportation, education, and recreation. Under present circumstances there are two major barriers to developing an efficient and effective network of services for the elderly. One, our attitude in the United States continues to be ''out of sight, out of mind''; and two, the maze of partial resources at the federal and state levels of government makes it most difficult to operationalize the kind of comprehensive service programs required at the local level. Consequently, our elderly population finds it almost impossible to enjoy a healthy and secure way of life as contributing members of the community.

There are indications that the situation is changing. In recent years a flurry of action has taken place at the federal level of government to expand the resources required to meet the needs of the aged. This action probably reflects increased concern for our elders, and the increased political influence of this growing segment of the population. It must be emphasized, however, that more resources alone will not permit us to get the job done. A barrier to the development of an effective system of services at the local level is the organization of federal and state programs along functional lines. The lack of joint planning or program coordination on the part of our federal agencies is abundantly apparent. This fact is particularly important with respect to the elderly population because of their multiple problems and need for an integrated and complete set of services.

Community Checklist

How does your community rate? Which of the following does it have?

_____ A senior ombudsman or advocacy program.
_____ A citywide or areawide information and referral center.
_____ An area agency or local council on aging.
_____ Transportation and escort services for the elderly.
_____ A senior center or centers, offering social activities, recreation, education, and a setting for community services.
_____ Health care services, including:

    _____ health clinic.
    _____ health maintenance organization.
    _____ health screening program.

_____ In-home services, including:

    _____ visiting nurse service.
    _____ home health service.
    _____ homemaker service.
    _____ handyman service.
    _____ telephone reassurance.
    _____ friendly visiting.
    _____ meals on wheels.

_____ Nursing homes with high standards and a wide range of fees.
_____ Group meals program, providing a social setting for improved nutrition for older persons.
_____ Recreation activities for seniors.
_____ Library, museum, art gallery, and performing arts programs for older people.
_____ Adult education opportunities.
_____ Job opportunities.
_____ Volunteer opportunities.
_____ Senior talent pool.
_____ Consumer education and protection program.
_____ Legal aid and tax counseling.
_____ Low rent public housing for the elderly.
_____ A range of moderate income housing—for sale and rent.
_____ Repair and renovation program for existing elderly housing.
_____ Property tax relief for older Americans.
_____ Discount programs for utilities, drugs, food, and clothing.
_____ Senior citizens employment service or job registry.

Figure 14–4 Community checklist for inventorying services for the elderly. (Source: Adapted from U.S., Department of Health, Education, and Welfare, Administration on Aging, Office of Human Development, *To Find the Way: To Opportunities and Services for Older Americans,* Department of Health, Education, and Welfare, Washington, D.C., 1975.)

There are no easy answers to the above dilemma. Local government managers and others interested in the efficient—and compassionate—provision of services for the elderly can perhaps learn from the experience of other countries. In the interim, it is hoped that the above discussion has assisted local officials by providing a broad sample of the managerial options open to them, not only in providing human services to the elderly, but also in grappling with state and federal bureaucracies and other entities who occasionally may seem to put their own organizational interests ahead of those of citizens who have given a lifetime of probably unheralded service to their country and to their community.

Minorities and human rights

A special focus on minority populations and on the protection of human rights is fundamental not only to the effective delivery of human services but also to the management of the entire range of local government involvement in our community life. The impetus for such a focus stems from ethical, pragmatic, and legal currents in contemporary society—currents that in recent decades have swept through local governments large and small as well as the federal and state systems.

The present discussion therefore begins with a brief recapitulation of these ethical, pragmatic, and legal considerations since these have helped shape the contemporary managerial environment in these vitally important areas—just as they have also helped shape that of the provision of services to the elderly discussed above. The specific relationship between human rights and human services is then analyzed, and an overview of human rights programs—a brief managerial checklist of the options available—provided. Four basic elements of human rights programs—questions of multiple targets; of history and roles; of diversity and range; and of basic structural considerations—are then reviewed from a managerial perspective, as are the scope of human rights functions. Implementation guidelines for establishing a program, and the practical question of maintaining a program once it is set up, are then considered. The discussion ends with a summary and outlook touching on some of the changing issues in human rights.

Some general points need to be made explicit at the outset, however. First, it may be noted that as women are in a slight majority in the population it might be argued that they are thereby excluded by definition from any discussion under the heading of minorities. Be that as it may, it is clear that the whole question of women's rights, though intertwined with that of minorities, is sufficiently significant to warrant separate treatment beyond that which can be given in this chapter. References to discrimination by sex (and also by age—a subject germane to the treatment in the preceding section of this chapter) will therefore be passing only. Second, it must be pointed out that the whole human rights area in local government (and in our society generally) is an extremely sensitive one. This is in no way surprising, since the topic has its roots in issues that go to the heart of our national heritage (as in the conflict between slavery and the democratic ideal) on the one hand, and to sensitive areas of personal and interpersonal psychology (as in stereotyped behavior between races and sexes) on the other. The intent of the following discussion, however, is to provide some helpful managerial insights and not, hopefully, to exacerbate the controversy: this does not mean that sensitive areas will be ignored. Third, the writer—like several others for this book—has chosen to focus on the managerial experience that she has participated in at first hand, while at the same time attempting to at least outline the broad range of managerial options in this many-faceted area.

Human rights and local governments: basic considerations

Ethical considerations   A writer in *Public Management* has summarized the ethical considerations underlying much of the managerial environment in this area:

The denial of opportunity for equal participation in our social economy is one of those intractable and threatening problems. The persistence in our society of inequities based on race, color, national origin, and sex today appear to be due more to systems failure than to policy orientation.

It is clear that equal opportunity is the law of the land, but the institutions and social processes of the country, more through inadvertence than through conscious intent, work to deny execution of that policy. It is therefore a management issue of the purest order, and if for no other reason should offer a singular challenge to those of us who are managers of the public business.[15]

Far more than the pragmatic and legal considerations, ethical considerations for a government administrator who accepts this "singular challenge" are highly personal as well as professional. On a personal level, matters of vested interest cannot easily be separated from ethical responsibilities. The author has been a staff member of a human relations department as well as an assistant to the city manager in two cities, and can thus claim a vested interest in the effectiveness of local government administration and human rights programs in furthering the transformation of systems such that characteristics of equality and justice are enhanced. In the roles that the author has played, she typically found herself observing both community and governmental dynamics, often acting as a catalyst for action alternately in the two sectors. The following observations emerge from such a perspective, and are offered in that context.

It is a scarcely refutable proposition that, historically and systematically, minorities have been excluded from equal participation in governmental processes (including the administration of government) and from equal receipt of government goods and services. That the pattern of exclusion is no exception at the level of local government as attested to by the fact that as of the mid-1970s, there were only six black city managers, eight Chicano managers, and fifteen women managers,[16] and only 1,705 members of county and municipal governing bodies were black.[17] But many would also hold that the most effective redress of the grievances of minority citizens is at the local level, for it is here that the day-to-day living of local residents is most directly affected.

That is not to say that white government administrators are necessarily "guilty" for the fact that institutional racism exists, though they, like all citizens, cannot be entirely absolved from guilt. City governments were structured long before widespread consciousness about minority problems and perceptions was raised; managers often inherit systems which tend to perpetuate themselves and the status quo.

Disavowing guilt, however, does not eliminate the question of responsibility. Given the relative power of the top administrator and given the multitude of dilemmas faced in the form of inadequate funds, personality conflicts, deteriorating facilities, legal obligations, labor strikes, competing interest groups, and political dynamics—given all that—what is the ethical responsibility of the administrator to protect the human rights of all citizens?

In considering that question, it is appropriate for local government decision makers to review the definition of racism offered by the U.S. Commission on Civil Rights:

Racism may be viewed as *any attitude, action, or institutional structure which subordinates a person or group because of his or their color.* . . . Racism is not just a matter of attitudes: actions and institutional structures, especially, can also be forms of racism. An "institutional structure" is any well-established, habitual, or widely accepted pattern of action or organizational arrangement, whether formal or informal. Racism can occur even if the people causing it have no intention of subordinating others because of color, or are totally unaware of doing so. . . . Racism can be a matter of *result* rather than *intention* because many institutional structures in America that most whites do not recognize as subordinating others because of color actually injure minority group members far more than deliberate racism. . . . *Overt racism* is the use of color *per se* (or other visible characteristics related to color) as a subordinating factor. *Institutional subordination* is placing or keeping persons in a position or status of inferiority by means of attitudes, actions, or institutional structures which do not use color itself as the subordinating mechanism, but instead use other mechanisms indirectly related to color.[18]

The question of responsibility raised here addresses not so much the individual overt acts of bigotry and discrimination based on race or sex, but rather the often subtle day-to-day manifestations of racism and sexism. Much as city or county facilities may present physical barriers to handicapped persons, psychic barriers exist for minorities and often for women as well. Any practice in an organizational structure that acts to exclude is unacceptable. The top administrator, by virtue of power, has the ultimate responsibility for eliminating such barriers and preventing such exclusions.[19]

Exercising this responsibility—as with any other action managers take—inevitably invites certain reactions. Fear may be aroused on the part of white employees. Staff members may charge that "incompetent" persons are being hired, or that a certain constituency is not "deserving." There may be legal complications. The already sizable burden of management may be increased. In short, exercising the responsibility with the necessary values, commitment, determination, and resource allocation requires a considerable degree of risk taking. As practicing managers are well aware, the process of "taking risks" involves maintaining a high degree of openness. Further, it requires a shifting of managerial priorities so that a concern for the community as a collective human entity, and for the social well-being of individuals, truly takes precedence over the traditional local government priorities of physical maintenance and development. The personal, managerial, and local community rewards, however, may well be considerable.[20]

Pragmatic considerations   Experience has time and again verified that unless the perceptual and value shifts discussed above are internalized and acted out, neither the provision of human services nor aggressive affirmative action programs will necessarily lead to any significant changes in the institution of local government. It has also become evident that the presence of minorities in the system, in itself, provides no assurance of transformation. It is entirely possible for the potential influence of minorities merely to be channeled in establishment-determined directions that maintain and benefit the status quo rather than providing for the genuine exercise of power to bring about change.[21] A realistic analysis must note similar tendencies towards "tokenism" in the case of women in local government.

The involvement of minorities, however, is a necessary starting point. A major consequence of the exclusion of minorities from the local government process—aside from the obvious deleterious impact on minorities themselves—has been the loss to the municipality or county as a whole of the talent, support, and contributions of large segments of the population. As an example of such pragmatic considerations, it may be noted that enforcement functions—that is, those relating to police, fire, and health services, and to building codes—are carried out more effectively if minorities are a part of the local government concerned because their presence increases the enforcers' understanding of the minority community and improves the minority citizens' perceptions of the enforcers. Voluntary compliance is more likely as a result. As minorities alter the way of doing business that has proved inadequate in human terms, the response of minority citizens to the system is often altered, resulting in less hostility and conflict, and thus less expenditure of resources on problem solving. Similarly, a multiethnic approach to planning, public works, and recreation functions will enrich and improve the resulting policies and programs to the benefit not only of minorities, but whites as well.

If the perceptions, assessments, and values of minorities (and, for that matter, of women) are excluded from local government, then a biased managerial mind set, oriented toward the conservative white middle class life-style, can and often does evolve. Such mind sets obviously alienate minority groups and thus perpetuate the pattern of exclusion. It is increasingly recognized that the breaking of this cycle can come about only through full commitment and action on the part of local governments to serve minority populations and to guarantee protection of the human rights of all citizens.

Legal considerations   Quite aside from such powerful ethical and pragmatic considerations, action concerning minorities and human rights at the local government level is also clearly mandated by law. As the U.S. Commission on Civil Rights has stated:

Municipalities are generally not constitutionally required to provide [basic municipal] services to their residents. Once services are provided, however, the services cannot be provided to some citizens and not to others. For example, if a municipality paves streets in white neighborhoods, it must do the same in black neighborhoods.

In other words, counties, cities, towns, villages, and special districts cannot discriminate against blacks, Chicanos, Puerto Ricans, Indians, or any other racial or ethnic group in the provision of municipal services. This is because the 14th amendment to the United States Constitution, as well as the new revenue sharing law, forbids such discrimination. Many State constitutions and laws also forbid it.

The law in this area may be summarized in three general statements:
1. *Great* gaps or differences in the provision of municipal services on the basis of race establish a presumption (strong suspicion) or racial discrimination, at least where there is a long history of past discrimination. Once such a history is shown, recent change of policy by the locality is not a defense.
2. The fact that these gaps or differences may not have been intentional doesn't matter; actual intent or discriminatory motive need not be proved directly.
3. A locality found to have discriminated against its residents on the basis of race in providing municipal services must cure the gaps or differences.[22]

From the managerial perspective, therefore, the basic conclusion to be drawn from this brief discussion of ethical, pragmatic, and legal considerations is that the protection of human rights is an issue not only in the human services area, but rather one that permeates the administration and delivery of all local government services (a subject taken up again in Chapter 15).

Human rights and human services

The question of human rights is nevertheless an issue of particular significance in the human services area. This is because of the obvious fact that the greatest need for human services remains in low income populations, and because minorities continue to be disproportionately represented among those of low income.

Although the human rights imperative of social services is self-evident, it is also important not to overestimate the extent to which such services constitute the solutions to the problems addressed. Social services delivery—whether by the public sector or a private agency—is often characterized as a remedy to the consequences of racism and even as proof of the absence of racism. That it is not necessarily such a remedy is attested to by the frequent paradox of a refusal by minorities to utilize the services offered, and by the exclusion of those poorest citizens for whom the services presumably were intended. It has increasingly become recognized that, too often, policies and practices related to publicity, applications, screening, admissions, and continuing eligibility requirements reflect standards and values other than the values and preferences of poor and minority groups and consequently act to reject large portions of potential service recipients.[23]

Even the avoidance of such pitfalls does not necessarily attest to the absence of racism. A realistic evaluation must recognize that, while the provision of social services may be a tool to combat racism, it may also be inherently racist in itself. A number of local government managers and their staff members have come, through experience, to the realization that social services delivery too often addresses the symptoms, rather than the causes, of disparate needs among different groups and communities. A primary explanation of this failure to address root causes may be the lack of opportunity on the part of the recipients of services to participate in decision making. Administrators themselves often decide for recipients what they need and what they receive. The recipients may well perceive such approaches as paternalistic and patronizing, constituting a perpetuation of oppression and powerlessness. Indeed, the very provision of social services may create a sense of helplessness and psychological impotence by creating dependence on institutional care.[24]

In sum, both the disparate needs for human services, and the shortcomings of such services, make a concern for human rights a central integrative element in the delivery of human services. At the same time, the field of human rights is in itself a distinct area of the human services.

Human rights programs: an overview

The preceding discussion has touched on some general considerations in the ongoing assessment of human rights and minority participation as they relate to local governments and their operation. As this area is fraught with strong emotions, such an outline and recapitulation is perhaps more necessary than might seem the case at first glance. It may be helpful to bear in mind the points made above during the following discussion, which is more practical in focus.

Points of entry for human rights programs   While the concern for human rights ought to permeate the entire local government organization, the points of entry for specific human rights programs in municipal and other local governments as of the later 1970s are many and varied.

Federal programs   In the 1960s, the federal programs directed at poverty—Model Cities and the Office of Economic Opportunity being the salient examples—were primary locations of human rights activity by virtue of the economic, political, and cultural awarenesses developed. As of the later 1970s, however, many of these programs have disintegrated, although other programs may have evolved into more comprehensive approaches to integrated human services delivery. Under the direction of administrators and their staff members oriented toward human rights, such programs may provide a positive thrust for minorities and nonminorities alike. Alternatively, such programs may represent a dilution of an earlier focus on the needs of minority groups.

Separate organizational units   Further, in the 1960s—largely, it seems in retrospect, in response to the rise of militancy and eruptions of civil disorders, youth rebellions, and the cultural shock of integration—many local governments created separate organizational units variously labeled "human relations commission," "human rights department," "community relations committee," and so forth—all having the purpose of addressing escalating tension and conflict. (Hereafter, for convenience, the term "human rights" is used to include the commissions, departments, and programs labeled "human relations" or "community relations.")

Affirmative action programs   In the 1970s, a primary thrust in human rights has been in the area of affirmative action programs. Many communities have adopted affirmative action plans to increase minority and female representation in local government employment. A number have established contract compliance programs that require vendors to improve minority employment. In some instances, affirmative action has been broadly defined to include achieving equitable service delivery in the entire city work program, including in such traditional services as public works, law enforcement, transportation, and fire protection.

Broader concepts In some few instances, municipalities have claimed the responsibility for eradicating racism in the entire system. In Berkeley, California, for example, the city manager issued a memo to city staff saying that the spirit of affirmative action included such things as avoiding all-white or all-male meetings since no item of business that the city conducted was devoid of impact on minority communities.[25] Similarly, checks on racism can be initiated by such actions as scrutinizing the city's investment practices, reviewing negotiations with unions, and simply considering the image of the organization projected through bulletin boards and paintings in offices.

Moving to an even more expansive connotation, the concept of affirmative action has been enlarged to incorporate the concept of "humanization," in which maximizing opportunities for individual growth and development as well as revising the entire process and procedures by which government relates to its constituency is viewed as a necessary and legitimate corollary to removing barriers based on race, ethnicity, and sex.[26]

Managerial options What should the role of managers be in the human rights area? Much will depend on the organizational structures available in particular communities. In some cases, the manager may not have a direct organizational role to play, particularly if a human rights commission is ancillary to, rather than an integral part of, the local government structure for which the manager has responsibility. Human rights commissions themselves may have declined in both numbers and influence since the 1960s. A "no commission situation" may, in fact, be today's most important organizational variant. The following managerial checklist of available organizational options brings together points discussed in greater detail under subsequent headings.

1. Strong commission form. Human rights commission is established with adequate funding and strong enforcement powers. Its executive staff may be appointed through procedures beyond the purview of the chief administrative officer, or as part of a process in which such officers play a major role. Commission plays major role in local government functions.
2. Weak commission form. Human rights commission is established with inadequate budget, and functions in an advisory or educational capacity only.
3. Noncommission situation. Some of the managerial options here include:
   3.1. sensitizing local government staff to the fact that virtually every function has a human rights dimension;
   3.2. making full use of existing laws and ordinances on matters ranging from equality in housing to consumer protection or pressing of new or amending laws or ordinances;
   3.3. providing or contracting for legal service programs; and
   3.4. special emphasis on affirmative action and contract compliance either through a special unit or within existing agency structures.

The balance of this discussion will focus on the roles of human rights commissions and departments as the most visible and concentrated community-related human rights activity of local governments, but the remarks made will have appropriate application to less visible organizational forms.

Managerial viewpoints: multiple targets

It follows from the earlier discussion of ethics and vested interests that the target of human rights programs is as much whites as it is racial minorities. There are two reasons for this emphasis. First, it is necessary to point out that the fact that there is a need for human rights programs is the responsibility not of minorities, but of whites. The historical record clearly indicates that this responsibility is that of those individuals and institutions who collectively have exercised their economic and political power so as to create and perpetuate inequality based on race, sex, ethnicity, and national origin. In a most fundamental sense, the target of human rights programs is that same power bloc. Second—and especially significant in a governmental system that purports to be democratic—it is necessary to emphasize the truism that the freedom of all is diminished to the extent that any among the governed are less than free. To the extent that bias, prejudice, discrimination, and racism are diminished, the humanity of whites is enhanced, and the freedom of whites made more secure.

Managerial viewpoints: history and roles

It is also important from the managerial viewpoint to emphasize that the rationale for human rights programs has varied from time to time, and certainly has not always incorporated the objectives just stated. A few human rights commissions were established in the 1950s, primarily for the purpose of improving intergroup relations. These commissions were typically composed of middle class professionals and homemakers. The bulk of their efforts focused on education, employing such techniques as interracial fellowship programs and home exchange visits. The primary objective was to change attitudes regarding race and stereotypes associated with race.

In the 1960s, as already noted, the growth of human rights programs mushroomed. Hundreds of cities and counties established commissions and, in many instances, departments as well. The enabling ordinances of these groups typically stipulated these functions:

1. The promotion of mutual understanding and respect among groups.
2. Research into human relations problems and tested solutions in order to offer recommendations for the local situation.
3. The investigation of discrimination complaints and referral to appropriate agencies.
4. The preparation and dissemination of civil and human rights material.
5. Cooperation with, and assistance to, other groups dealing with discrimination and human relations problems.
6. The preparation and submittal of annual reports outlining the year's achievements and tasks still to be completed.[27]

These programs were ostensibly created out of a new consciousness and concern for the welfare of minority communities. Many minorities and human rights workers nevertheless have come to believe that the real impetus for the sudden growth of local human rights programs was one of fear; in other words, that the establishment of such programs was at least in part an act of desperation on the part of local elected officials and administrators to appease minority communities and to dilute the growing tide of militancy and violence. Such sentiment is given credence by the fact that with the lessening of overt civil rights activity and the passing of riots, the support for such programs has also diminished. Indeed, as more and more communities experience budget crises, human rights programs are often the first to be cut (if not entirely eliminated) or, alternatively, to be merged with other social-services-oriented departments.

The decrease in support for human rights programs may have come about, in part, not because a need is no longer perceived, but because such programs proved to be more effective than desired.

Almost by definition, human rights workers are change agents. They ought not to be operating maintenance programs; they cannot have the preservation of the status quo as their objective. They instead act as advocates of the powerless—of those excluded from the governmental machinery—and as mediators in conflicts between the powerless and the powerful. Accordingly, the focus has shifted from changing attitudes to changing behavior.

The role of a human rights program is potentially two-edged, however; the other side of the sword is the danger of being used to coopt efforts for social change on the part of the community; that is, the department may end up having the effect of diverting the community from access to sources of power in the larger governmental system. This has typically been the case, for example, with the appointment of a high-ranking minority to serve as the race relations officer in police departments. Such developments are prone to result in loss of supporters, both from within and without the system, who feel the department or program is less effective than anticipated and desired.

But to the extent that the role of advocacy finds expression, human rights programs come to be of considerable symbolic value to minority groups. The human rights office is seen by many as the primary, if not exclusive, point of entry into city hall, and is perceived as being responsive to the needs and concerns of poor people and minorities. In some instances, these benefits undoubtedly extend to the institution of local government as a whole. Some governments become more responsive—in the council chambers, the manager's office, and various departments. Minorities, in turn, begin to claim city or county government as *their* government.

With such a support base, many human rights programs evolved from the approach of education and conciliation in intergroup relations to addressing discrimination through legislation and enforcement powers. In both areas, human rights workers developed considerable expertise as the range of involvements expanded and professional specialization became more and more necessary. This expertise—and the continuing need for it—has expanded generally at a greater rate than acknowledgement of its legitimate presence in local government. As of the later 1970s, professional human rights workers are too often either excluded from the newer thrust toward integrated human services delivery, or cast in a role of service deliverer void of the priority concern for human rights implications.

Clearly, a key managerial issue is the recognition that the need for such specialization has not dissipated. Racism and discrimination are no less a specter in American society—and in city hall—than ten or twenty years ago. Whether or not local governments and their managers will show the commitment and the courage necessary to accord the proper priority to this concern will undoubtedly be revealed in the decade to come. Given the commitment, however, the modes of expression are many and varied. A number of these will now be examined.

Managerial viewpoints: diversity and range

The structure and functions of a local human rights program will, of course, vary in accordance with the characteristics of the jurisdiction, particularly with regard to size, composition, and density of population.

A rural town or county may have a five-member advisory commission with no staff. A town of 30,000 may have an executive secretary staffing the commission. A city of 200,000 may have a seven-member commission with a three-member staff, composed of an executive director, secretary, and field worker. A large metropolitan area may have an advisory commission of fifteen or more, and a staff of twenty or more.

Similarly, the diversity and scope of activity will vary. A small commission with no budget will be primarily concerned with intergroup and government–community relations. A major city department will be addressing a multitude of issues with a great array of programs and techniques, including administering antidiscrimination ordinances, affirmative action plans, and contract compliance programs. Municipalities of intermediate sizes may fall at various points on that continuum. What is important is the recognition that, irrespective of size, staffs and commissions will undoubtedly find themselves not only carrying out the formally recognized mandate of their enabling legislation, but also operating in an informal, behind-the-scenes manner in the effort to eradicate discriminatory policies and practices.

Managerial viewpoints: structural considerations

The discussion that follows is within the illustrative framework of a city of approximately 500,000 population, and draws in large measure on the experience of the Kansas City, Missouri, human relations commission and department from 1970 to 1973.[28] It depicts program options from which municipalities or counties of comparable or lesser size might draw according to need. The Selected Bibliography suggests additional resources that can be consulted for designing and managing a program that addresses the unique characteristics of any given municipality or county.

Principal considerations in determining the structure of a human rights program include process and criteria for selecting commissioners; staff positions and qualifications; relations between the commission and staff; and relations of the commission and staff to the city or county organization as a whole. A consideration cutting across all of these is that of value orientation. Then, unavoidably, there is the matter of budgets.

Appointed and advisory members Undoubtedly, the most common pattern with regard to city commissions is for the mayor to make the appointments. Frequently, the human rights staff, as well as the manager, if there is one, make recommendations to the mayor on appointments. The advantage of this procedure—as compared, for example, to making arbitrary appointments from applications submitted to the city clerk by individual citizens—is that more assurance is obtained that appointees are in fact committed to the objectives of the human rights program and have some background in the field. Whatever the procedure, a screening process and set of criteria should be established to provide for a commission as representative as possible of the entire community. These criteria would include geographic distribution (a system of appointment by district is used in some cities); race, ethnicity, age, sex, religion, and income; affiliation with private business, public education, higher education, religious organizations, and other governmental agencies. "Grassroots" representation might come from community organizations such as welfare rights, youth groups, or from individual interested citizens.

Some commissions, in addition to regular appointed members, provide for advisory members as well. These generally include representatives from other human rights agencies such as the regional office of the U.S. Civil Rights Commission, the State or county human rights commission, or other groups concerned with civil rights such as Jewish community relations organizations. They may also include representatives from the board of education or from other city offices such as police, health, or recreation departments.

The role of committees and task forces Typically, commissions conduct their business through committees and task forces. Officers, at a minimum, include the chairperson, vice chairpersons, and secretary. These, along with chairpersons of the standing committees, constitute the executive committee. Standing committees traditionally include at least Education, Employment, Housing, and Police Community Relations. Task forces are generally organized for a limited period of time to address a specific project such as preparing a report on media harassment or investigating an allegation of police brutality. Citizens who are not members of the Commission itself may also be invited to serve on the committees and task forces to increase the extent of community involvement.

The terms of commissioners may vary from one to four or more years, with some limit established on the number of consecutive terms that may be served. Terms of too short duration are not advisable, since it requires a period of time to become involved and develop the expertise to be effective. Te investment that commissioners make in terms of volunteer time and energy is often considerable, and they should be retained long enough for the jurisdiction to gain the full benefit of that investment, as well as for the commissioner to achieve some sense of satisfaction and progress from their efforts. On the other hand, they should not be retained so long that their interest—and the commission as a whole—begins to stagnate.

The director: a key position   The executive secretary or staff director is in some instances selected and appointed by the commission itself, and in others by the chief administrative officer or city manager. Chief among the considerations in selecting the director is the philosophy toward social change. Who does the director serve? Is she or he community oriented? Will he or she represent the interests of the disenfranchised? Or will he or she be a "flunky" for the "establishment?" The director should be politically sensitive, skilled in intergroup relations, knowledgable of prevailing civil rights legislation and court decisions, genuinely understanding of the needs and dynamics of poor and minority populations, and sophisticated in the way the "system" operates. This is of course in addition to basic management and supervisorial skills.

Staff functions   Similar considerations will apply to the staff below the position of director. Perhaps more than in any other public agency, human rights staff members—from the receptionist to the accountant—ought to be alert to the subtle messages of vocal inflections and facial expressions; must be able to respond effectively to tension, conflict, pressure and pain; and must be supportive of the program goals and objectives. It is therefore of utmost importance that the director be intimately involved in the selection of staff members. In a civil service system, this means obtaining the full cooperation of the personnel and budget departments.

Where do loyalties lie?   Of even greater importance, the director requires the support of and accessibility to the city or county manager (if that form of local government appertains). Managers typically place a high premium on the loyalty of their department heads. Human rights directors typically place a high premium on loyalty to the community. The two need not be mutually exclusive. Ideally, the director should be treated as a full and complete member of the manager's "team." And it is incumbent on the manager to not only project this to all other department heads, but to assure their full cooperation. If this observation seems a statement of the obvious, it should be pointed out that human rights staff members are often treated like the "step-children" of the management family. But the task of a human rights program lies as much within the system as without. The expertise and the resource that a human rights director represents should be fully utilized. Care must be taken however, not to over-burden the person who occupies one of the most demanding and pressure-ridden positions in government.

In the case of directors appointed by the commission, the position is even more ambiguous. Regardless of the appointing authority, the relationship between the staff and the commission needs to be carefully delineated.

At a minimum, the staff will be expected to provide clerical support in the form of typing minutes and maintaining files on records of activity. Beyond that, the question of who works for whom can be a source of much dissension. Probably the more common pattern is for the commission to establish a policy framework within which the staff carries out programs. In Kansas City, for example, the commission and department exist as separate entities, with neither being charged with the responsibility for directing the other. As the relationship has evolved, the commission more often looks to the staff for guidance on priorities and positions. On the other hand, the Missouri State Human Rights Commission was once involved in the most detailed tasks of administration, including firing staff and deciding on budget expenditures—an arrangement which most of those involved agreed led to absolute chaos, and one which obviously does not recommend itself to professional managers.

Justifying the budget   The matter of budget, as always, both follows from and dictates the overall staffing pattern, inasmuch as personnel costs constitute by far the largest expense item. As with other local government programs, the easiest way to sabotage a human rights program is through underfunding. Unlike many other programs, the human rights budget is rather more difficult to justify on a clearly quantifiable cost-benefit basis. This point is taken up again later in the discussion.

Staffing patterns will be largely dictated by the functions a particular agency elects to carry out (discussed below). Program staff might include various supervisory levels and line workers. The line staff might be community workers assigned to particular geographic areas or minority communities; human relations generalists; or specialists in subject areas such as education and training, employment, housing or police community relations. And within these areas, or transcending them, there might be specialists in research, investigation, conciliation, or communications. The administrative unit would at a minimum consist, in addition to the director, of one or more assistant directors, administrative officers or administrative assistants; the department secretary and a clerical staff; the accounting staff; and may include public information staff as well.

While personnel will constitute the bulk of the budget, it is important to consider that factors such as mobility and information dissemination are particularly crucial to an effective human rights program. Sufficient allowances should thus be made for such items as subscriptions, printing, phones, postage, and car usage. In addition, conferences and training programs serve an invaluable function both in developing professional competence and in providing an essential source of support for those engaged in a profession replete with occupational hazards in the form of anxiety, anger and frustration.

Scope of functions

The areas addressed by commissioners and staff members may overlap considerably, though the techniques and strategies employed by each will often differ. As a generalization, commissioners tend to function more at the policy level, interacting with the decisionmakers and powerholders of the local government, law enforcement agencies, board of education, business sector, and media. Staff members, on the other hand, are somewhat more likely to interact with other staff members in those same institutions and, in addition, have far more community contact at the grassroots level.

The "big four" social problems   The range of involvement resulting, at least in part, from this dual approach to social change was suggested in a survey of human rights agencies across the country conducted in the mid-1970s by Fred Cloud, director of the Nashville, Tennessee, Human Relations Commission.[29] According to this survey, "the 'big four' social problems that most human relations agencies deal with on a daily basis," in the order of their ranking, are education, police/community relations, employment, and housing.[30]

Some of the dimensions of these problems, and strategies employed to address them, are suggested, though not exhaustively identified, in extracts from the survey presented in Figure 14–5.

A second way of classifying local human rights work has been suggested by

Jack Bullard, director of the Charlotte, North Carolina, Community Relations Committee:

An analysis of the materials and interviews gathered from human relations agencies in North Carolina indicated that theere were three general areas included in descriptions of human relations work: *problems, clients,* and *processes* used to solve problems. *Problems* were defined as unsettled community issues, as unwarranted actions or inadequate services of community agencies or businesses, and as difficulties experienced by individuals living in communities. *Clients* were defined as individuals or groups seeking human relations help in solving problems. Clients included respondents as well as complainants. *Processes* were defined in three ways: (1) *types* of actions taken by human relations staff to solve problems; (2) *results* of these actions; and (3) *measurements* used to evaluate the actions performed. . . . Cases will refer to requests, complaints, or projects sponsored by human relations agencies.[31]

Still another way of delineating the breadth of human rights programs is by a review of common organizational and functional arrangements of activities. Again, the following categories only suggest a model, and are not necessarily comprehensive or exhaustive.

Education and training　This type of unit has evolved from earlier interpersonal and intergroup relations programs to become quite diverse and sophisticated programs designed to facilitate improvements in human relations at a variety of levels. Objectives of such programs include becoming better informed about the intricacies of social problems, increasing cultural awareness, developing skills in implementing civil rights legislation, and enlarging the potential for social change.

Various techniques in the area of education and training include lectures, seminars, workshops, retreats, tours, urban exposures, school exchange programs, drama, simulated games, portable displays, audiovisual effects, and supervised field assignments or internships. Topics may be as diverse as minority history and culture, interaction skills, citizen participation, equal opportunity laws, violence, invasion of privacy, health services, drugs, and affirmative action. Participants in these programs are drawn from a wide variety of groups and organizations, including elementary school students; business management and labor; private social service agencies; churches; and civic organizations.

Community relations　The range of activities in this category might include: attending community and institution meetings to foster an awareness of developing concerns, and acting as an integrative force toward problem prevention and resolution; field involvement by community workers to promote neighborhood harmony and provide technical assistance to community groups and organizations; facilitating community observances of special events by drafting resolutions or proclamations for issuance by city officials, arranging for press coverage, assisting in obtaining meeting space, and typing and printing programs and agendas; facilitating citizen participation and community social action by organizing neighborhood councils to participate in solving problems specific to a particular geographical area; facilitating the formation of coalitions around common interests to address such issues as changing neighborhoods and school integration; sponsoring conferences to address an emerging issue of concern to the community, such as revenue sharing; acting as consultants to other departments or agencies in program planning, service delivery, or human rights problem resolution.

Conflict resolution　While overt demonstrations of violence are not as dramatic as in the 1960s, conflict and tension are ongoing characteristics of most communities wherever and whenever unfair treatment is experienced or perceived. The efforts of human rights workers in this area serve the two-fold purpose of protecting the rights of the individual unfairly treated, while working to eliminate the initial cause of conflict.

Education

Dimensions
  School desegregation
  School busing
  Educational neglect of minorities
  Student suspensions and expulsions
  Sex discrimination
  Need for bilingual education

Strategies
  Participation in school board policy making.
  Preparation of guidelines for drafting and implementing desegregation proposals.
  Formation of alliances for quality education.
  Work with teacher-training institutions.
  Work with individual principals on specific problems that arise and on preventive measures.
  Investigative analyses and reports.
  Conferences with and presentations to school officials and PTAs.
  Conducting training workshops.

Police–community relations

Dimensions
  Need for reform of the criminal justice system
  Employment of women and minorities by police departments
  Special efforts to assist victims of rape
  Conflict between police and minority citizens

Strategies
  Organization of joint committees of police and human relations commission members to deal with any complaints of police misconduct in the area of discrimination.
  Monitoring and review of investigations of police cases alleging the use of excessive force.
  Holding meetings in various locations for citizens to express their grievances regarding treatment received from police.
  Compiling and publishing reports of findings regarding grievances.
  Workshops on equal employment opportunity regulations for police (and fire) departments to promote hiring of minorities and women.
  Initiating programs for rape victims.
  Obtaining policy commitments of police chiefs toward such ends as de-escalating the use of deadly force by police officers.

Employment

Dimensions
  Discrimination in employment
  Affirmative action plans
  Contract compliance

Strategies
  Drafting plans and ordinances and "presenting the case" for such legislation to municipal officials.
  Working with department heads to determine the best methods for implementing the ordinances.
  Making referrals of minority persons to municipal contractors.
  Persuading management, labor, and minority groups to work together to develop voluntary compliance agreements and structures.
  Facilitating accessibility to suburban jobs.

Housing

Dimensions
- Stabilization of racially changing communities
- Countering reaction against public housing
- Discrimination in rentals and sales to minorities
- Problems of access to jobs
- Inadequate supply of housing for low and moderate income families
- Racial steering
- Exclusionary zoning
- Federal housing policies

Strategies
- Investigation and conciliation of complaints of housing discrimination.
- Cooperation with HUD in the enforcement of the Fair Housing Law of 1968.
- Development of proposals for housing programs under the Community Development Act of 1974.
- Workshops on fair housing.
- Creating special coordination committees to deal with abuses, such as unscrupulous real estate and mortgage company practices.
- Stabilizing communities in which public housing is located by creating advisory groups of community agencies and organizations; planning community activities that facilitate interaction between persons of different backgrounds and work toward the achievement of mutual goals; and creating resident advisory councils composed of representatives elected by tenants.

Figure 14–5   Selected dimensions of human rights problems and programs, and related strategies for action. (Source: Based on Fred Cloud and Gerald Donaldson, "Human Relations Commissions as Social Change Agents," paper presented at the annual conference of the National Association of Human Rights Workers, Portland, Oregon, October 1975.)

Typical incidents calling for intervention and mediation range from conflict between police and minority residents, to confrontations between radical youth and conservative adults, to tension between white groups of differing socioeconomic backgrounds. Others might include tenant dissension in public housing, school disturbances, rivalry between youth groups, mass demonstrations, labor-management disputes, and confrontations with local officials over policies and proposed programs. Short of intervention, observing and reporting on developments of tension can in itself play a significant role in conflict prevention.

Complaints and antidiscrimination ordinances   Human rights programs are focused increasingly in the 1970s on the administration of antidiscrimination ordinances. This is particularly the case in Northern states and less so in Southern states. Commissions that do not have enforcement powers are nevertheless engaged in receiving complaints of discrimination, relying on persuasion and conciliation to effect resolution of the discriminatory acts.

The extent of the powers of a local jurisdiction is frequently defined by existing state and federal legislation. In many such instances, however, complaints are deferred for handling to the local jurisdiction.

Changing trends   The most common antidiscrimination ordinances relate to fair public accommodations, to fair housing, and to equal employment opportunity. As of the later 1970s, the trend is toward greater emphasis on equal employment rather than fair housing statutes, with relatively little attention devoted to statutes covering public accommodations. The rationale for this rests on the belief that equal employment opportunity would remedy in large measure other human rights problems.

The earliest anti-discrimination ordinances typically prohibited discrimination based on race, color, religion, and national origin. Nearly all housing and employment ordinances now include prohibiting discrimination based on sex and many ordinances also prohibit discrimination based on age (usually specifying a range such as from 40 to 62). In the mid-1970s, there was a movement to greatly expand coverage to include such groups as homosexuals, the handicapped, and various others.

Of the ordinances mentioned, equal employment ordinances generally have the most comprehensive legal powers, in many instances providing for subpoena power, issuance of cease and desist orders, and imposition of penalties of fines and incarceration.

Administrative aspects   Technically, most ordinances are administered by an ordinance committee established via the anti-discrimination legislation. The ordinance committees are usually appointed by the mayor, and are separate and distinct from the committees of the human relations commission. Some overlap in membership is not unusual, however; for example, two out of five ordinance committee members may also be members of the human relations commission, the other three members being appointed from the private sector.

The procedure for responding to complaints typically involves the following steps: investigation of the facts by staff members; efforts to gain conciliation between the complainant and employer or landlord; referral to the ordinance committee upon failure to reach conciliation; the holding of a public hearing on the matter by the committee; and finding of cause or dismissal.

Considerable expertise is required, particularly in the areas of investigation and conciliation. Often, departments will have complete units specializing in one or the other of these aspects of handling complaints. The rapidly evolving body of law in this area requires continuous training and education if the responsible individuals are to keep abreast of developments and operate an effective program.

Central to this effectiveness is a complete and comprehensive record keeping system. Such a system entails designing forms, preparing periodic reports, and maintaining detailed files on all cases received.

Inasmuch as antidiscrimination ordinances—unlike much other human rights activity—may result in legal charges against the administering jurisdiction, a note here on the question of conflict of interest is appropriate. The human rights staff members, as well as ordinance committee members, clearly are an arm of the government. At the same time, they are charged legislatively to thoroughly and fairly respond to complaints of discrimination—including against the local government. While this dual role may appear awkward on the face of it, the relationship of the human rights unit to the government officials is not unlike that of a state public defender. As such, there should be no impediment to aggressively pursuing enforcement of the law.

Affirmative action and contract compliance   The process of receiving individual cases of discrimination depends on isolated instances of unfair treatment. While this does provide an essential avenue of redress for the particular citizen, it has limited impact on general patterns of discrimination and institutionalized racism. This shortcoming has been remedied somewhat by legislation providing for the expansion of individual complaints to class action suits.

Proceeding from the assumption, however, that discrimination is due more to illegal or unethical ways of doing business than to the isolated acts of individuals, new approaches have been developed in an attempt to bring about changes in the policies and practices of social systems. Included among these are affirmative action plans and contract compliance programs. Whereas antidiscrimination ordinances essentially operate on a basis of refraining from breaking the law, these new programs stress taking affirmative steps to create equal opportunities. The objective is to institutionalize change, rather than having to repeat the change process with the filing of each individual complaint.

Human rights staffs may plan, implement and/or monitor the local government's plan and program, and probably do so more effectively than other units of government, e.g., a separate compliance office or a unit in the manager's office. They typically design seminars and workshops for management personnel in private industry to assist in increasing their sensitivity to minority employees; provide technical assistance to employers in designing recruitment, hiring, and promotion programs to provide fair opportunities for minority persons; and develop programs to encourage utilization by businesses and industries of minority recruiting services and employment agencies. A further objective, in addition to increasing the number of minorities, is to create understanding and acceptance of a new concept of ''best qualified''; that is, a recognition that minorities and women, by virtue of their experiences, often bring qualities that tend to be undervalued and excluded in traditional criteria for assessing the best qualified job applicants.

In many jurisdictions, the efforts of local departments have been supplemented by grants from the federal Equal Employment Opportunity Commission (EEOC) that support the development of affirmative action programs in private industry.

The area of affirmative action is also one of considerable specialization and requires extensive technical skills as well as expertise in handling interpersonal dynamics and system change.

Ombudsperson Although the title of Ombudsperson is not frequently attached to a human rights office in any formal way, it does convey in some degree the great variety of miscellaneous, but important, tasks that a human rights commission and staff are invariably called upon to perform, but which do not always fall into any of the preceding categories discussed. The term as used here depicts a role that differs from that of a citizen's assistant or complaint officer found increasingly in local jurisdictions in that it is focused on human rights issues and therefore is less concerned with responding to typical complaints of a white middle class constituency.

Of all the human rights functions, those that fall in this category may do the most to create a sense on the part of the community that the human rights office is their advocate.

Many citizens will contact a human rights office out of desperation, not knowing where else to go, or out of distrust of, or frustration with, another office or agency. The problems raised may not be related to an issue of direct discrimination, but they are invariably related to issues of dignity and a sense of personal control and well-being. Supportive efforts by the human rights staff may entail providing factual information, making referrals, following up to make sure appropriate services are obtained, intervening to secure the waiver of an unnecessary or irrelevant regulation, and documenting the need for changes, followed by making policy recommendations designed to accomplish the change.

Areas of involvement may be as diverse as obtaining emergency food; assisting in having utility services restored; securing bail bonds, making court appearances, facilitating release on recognizance, and obtaining legal resources; facilitating release of welfare, veteran, or social security payments; making referrals to drug and alcohol abuse or hypertension or sickle cell anemia detection programs; obtaining temporary lodging; providing socioeconomic data for research and papers; accepting police referrals for mediation of domestic disputes; advising on education and employment opportunities and many more.

On a broader scale, a human rights commission may, in its function as ombudsperson, address those conditions of living that, in isolation, are small sources of irritation, but can accumulate to a point where they become sources of despair and helplessness. The form of address may be through comprehensive analyses, reports, and recommendations to policy makers in such areas as the media, health services, and education; through public hearings on volatile subjects such as police brutality or the establishment of an office of citizen complaints; through conferences with key personnel and community leaders in such groups as the United Way, the Chamber of Commerce, and ministerial alliances.

At still another level, commissions, in particular, may provide human rights leadership through position papers and resolutions taking stands on issues of current concern and controversy such as, for example, a United Farm Workers boycott, and by supporting or opposing local, state, and federal legislation having an impact on social welfare and human rights.

Research and information   A key unit in any effective program is one that is supportive through research and information dissemination of all other human rights efforts. Such a unit provides a foundation for the planning and design of operational programs, develops resources for justifying proposed legislation and budgets, and facilitates the development of a support base by telling the human rights "story" effectively to the public. This unit may also be responsible for internal program evaluation.

The tasks of the research and information unit may include preparing regular newsletters and annual reports; publishing special pamphlets, brochures, and flyers; assuring mass media coverage of activities; airing public service spots on radio and television; maintaining an information resource center; developing reading lists and bibliographies; and drafting in-depth reports on social conditions, intergroup relations, changing trends, emerging issues, and other areas of particular concern.[32]

Beyond providing information on specific issues in an effort to increase informed opinion, if not influence policy decisions, such a unit assumed responsibility as well for attempting to devise ways of coping with and managing the voluminous quantities of information that we are all subject to in these times. Information is clearly a major source of power; how to harness information in a way useful to the impoverished and disenfranchised is not among the lesser challenges of human rights workers.

Establishing a program: implementation guidelines

It seems realistic to observe that the single most important factor in the success of a human rights program is community-based support. A new program may, in fact, have its origins in the efforts of concerned community residents. Whether the impetus comes from representatives of the community or from the manager's office, the initial and continuing guideline that shoud prevail above all others is the development and maintenance of broad-based community support. Figure 14–6 identifies some of the additional guidelines to be considered in the planning process once a decision has been made to establish a human rights program. The suggested guidelines may be useful as well for revitalizing existing programs.

A planning process of course, is not realistically fulfilled merely by adhering to a series of linear steps. Some of the guidelines may be observed in a different phase than that indicated, or may be repeated, as for example, when the need to amend legislation becomes apparent. Similarly, the definition of an "adequate" budget will change with experience. Anchoring of the program with both sufficient proximity and distance to all sectors involved—including local government—is a key factor in effectiveness, and an ongoing as well as an initial task. Related to this, structuring of the program in such a manner that the system is opened up, rather than the community being coopted, is a critical consideration from the very beginning, but also one that requires constant diligent monitoring. "Educating" of power holders and officials in order to cultivate their support with

Implementation Checklist

1. Demonstrate the need for a program through documentation of discrimination, compilation of statistics on social needs and problems, and surveys of opinions of other agencies and community organizations and individuals.

2. Organize a coalition of public and private agencies and groups concerned with human rights to develop the proposal and obtain support.

3. Designate a committee to approach the mayor and/or council members and obtain support for the program.

4. Establish a legal basis for the program which spells out specific responsibilities, powers, and location of authority.

5. Obtain an adequate budget, preferably from general fund allocations or, if necessary, from other sources.

6. Appoint a commission representative of the community, taking particular care to provide representation of low income and minority populations.

7. Set clear goals and objectives, and design the organizational structure of the commission for carrying out the work program.

8. Involve as many citizens as possible in the planning and implementation of programs.

9. Build a competent staff unit of sufficient size to address the scope of human problems prevailing in the community.

10. Establish the program as an authority in human rights through thorough research and documentation, sound and reasoned recommendations, and a track record of successes in addressing issues and problems.

11. Establish constructive relations with the media.

12. Demonstrate identification with low income and minority groups, and facilitate their participation in decision-making processes.

13. Retain a position of leadership by defining issues and initiating action as well as mediating disputes and responding to community-expressed concerns.

14. Maintain an atmosphere of openness and fairness that encourages genuine communication, understanding, and improved intergroup relations.

15. Establish working relationships with private community and civic organizations; other civil rights groups; and federal, state, and local governmental agencies.

Figure 14-6 Implementation guidelines for establishing a human rights program. (Source: Based on U.S., Department of Justice, Community Relations Service, *Guidelines for Effective Human Relations Commissions,* Department of Justice, Washington, D.C., 1970, pp. 3–13.)

regard to new and progressive concepts and practices in the human rights field is almost a daily task. And while attention is paid to managerial, technical and political considerations, the overriding concern must be to *be more human,* without which any other efforts will remain ineffective in altering the social structures, and thus fail to fulfill the very purpose for coming into existence in the first place.

Retaining the program

Contrary to some prevailing notions regarding governmental entities, not all continue indefinitely on their own inertia. Human rights programs, as noted earlier, are particularly subject to frequent review and questioning, or worse, arbitrary cuts or elimination without thoughtful evaluation. Admittedly, human rights programs themselves are sometimes the source of their own vulnerability. Self-criticism with regard to actual effectiveness, to the caliber of training and performance of the commission and staff, and to whether the role being played is one of advocacy and social change, or cooptation and system maintenance, is therefore perpetually in order.

Under attack?   In many instances, however, criticism of programs is initiated for reasons neither rational nor deserved. Such attacks may take many forms and have various origins.

As noted earlier, many programs were originally established and supported for the "wrong" reasons—the threat of violence, fear of militancy, or need for votes of minority constituencies. Since civil disorder, which provided the initial impetus for many of these programs, has subsided, some persons now find it easier to oppose such programs. In addition, as programs become more effective, they represent a "threat" to some officials who wish to maintain the *status quo* and are fearful of power shifts in the economic and political arenas.

Some critics may be threatened as a result of their own personal racism and resulting insecurity of their sense of identity. Such fears may be manifested in the assertion that "the problem no longer exists" or that minorities are receiving preferential treatment at the expense of whites, i.e., reverse discrimination.

Changing attitudes   Many persons have recently shifted their concern and efforts to newer issues such as pollution, energy, and conservation. Rather than seeing the relationship between these issues and human rights, opponents assert the greater importance of these issues over human rights. As the public sentiment shifts accordingly, it is not surprising that elected officials do likewise in the interests of staying in office.

The impact of inflation and/or recession figures prominently in the tenuous status of human rights programs—a paradox in that human rights problems are clearly aggravated as unemployment increases and competition is sharply heightened. Still, human services are often the first to be cut, and human rights programs are often the first of these services to be eliminated.

Vulnerabilities   An inherent vulnerability of human rights programs, given prevailing criteria for decision making, is its characteristic of being a "soft" program. Even more so than many other human services programs, the impact, efficiency, and effectiveness of a human rights program is difficult to measure in objective, quantifiable terms.

Another vulnerability has to do with the qualities that tend to be rewarded in the profession of administration. Minority administrators and staff, who are apt to be represented in greater proportions in human rights programs than in traditional services, may challenge the stereotyped "desirable" attributes of administrators. They tend to have far more demands placed on them, including "flack-catching" by community residents, peers and superiors, than white administrators. They must not only perform their duties at a level of competence at least equal to whites, but they must be constantly scrutinizing the actions of whites for indications of deliberate or unconscious racism. They expend considerable energy providing support to one another in order to sustain their faith and maintain their sanity in an environment that is fundamentally hostile to what they are trying to accomplish. They are often more sensitive—and expected to be so—in responding to community requests in order to maintain a credible reputation and to fulfill their commitment to improving the life conditions of poor and minority people. They frequently insist on injecting a human element into an otherwise mechanistic plan or prodecure, with seemingly inadequate concern for efficiency.

Countering the opposition   Any of these characteristics may become a source of dissension and grounds for criticism, a development that provides ammunition for attacking the entire human rights effort.

Managers and directors who wish to counter the opposition may take several approaches. They can, of course, always appeal to the moral and ethical imperative of supporting a human rights program. They can appeal to existing legislation and legal precedents, pointing out potential liability with regard to violation of federal guidelines and requirements.

They can develop criteria, and some have, for evaluating department heads and staff that take into account skills in community relations and commitment to eliminating racism.

They can improve basic management skills in areas that human rights programs have perhaps placed too little emphasis on in the past—or that minority administrators have not had as much opportunity to acquire. These include increasing financial knowledge and skills; developing a comprehensive work program with clearly specified goals and objectives; developing measurement criteria to assess progress in those areas where it is possible to quantify; and documenting and justifying the budget on the basis of needs assessments. Evaluation—an exceedingly difficult task due to the invariable lack of substantive baseline data—is being increasingly demanded of human rights programs, and is an area accordingly receiving greater attention in the field.[33]

And once again, managers and human rights staffs and commissions can build support through community groups who will themselves make the case for retaining or expanding the program.

What they cannot afford to do is to acquiesce in the face of charges that the program is no longer needed. The line between principle and practicality can be thin indeed. So, too, is the line, for many citizens, between bare survival and a life of dignity and opportunity.

Summary and outlook

The preceding discussion has intended to place emphasis on the social and psychological environment within which human rights programs operate, or fail to operate, as well as to point out some of the practical decision-making issues involved. Some basic ethical, pragmatic, and legal considerations underlying such programs have been outlined, the distinction between human rights programs and human services clarified, and a number of important programmatic elements outlined. Practical guidelines for establishing and retaining human rights programs, have also been discussed.

An in-depth analysis of the many issues that have recently emerged in the field of human rights exceeds the scope of the present discussion. The mention of a few examples, however, will serve to demonstrate that human rights is by no means a static area of involvement.

One issue is the debate over the relative emphasis that should be placed on intergroup relations versus enforcement versus affirmative action. All approaches have merit; none in itself holds forth a total solution. A combination of approaches seems to be most fruitful in tackling the many dimensions of discrimination.

A related issue is the increasing trend toward combining human rights programs with social services departments. If the entire range of human relations activity is not organized as a separate unit, the compliance section is probably most critical to retain separately from the social services department. Short of that, the compliance activities, as well as other human rights activities, must be highly publicized. Otherwise, minorities generally will tend not to identify with a social services department—particularly for the purpose of addressing human rights grievances.

With regard to affirmative action programs, two volatile issues have arisen: first, the distinction between "goals" and "quotas" and, second, the concept of "reverse discrimination." A legitimate concern related to the question of goals versus quotas is that the setting of goals will become, at some point in the future, a basis for minimizing minority involvement—as was the case with Jews in the past—rather than maximizing it. In order to avoid this potential negative effect, goal setting should be understood to provide only an initial benchmark; it should not represent a restrictive covenant.

As for the notion of "reverse discrimination," which argues that the implementation of affirmative action programs has the effect of discriminating against white males, an historical perspective must be invoked and programs designed in that context. And, of course, one of the most emotionally charged human rights issues continues to be that of the use of busing to achieve racial integration in schools.

A philosophical and practical debate continues among human rights workers with regard to the system of priorities for responding to complaints of discrimination. Some argue that complaints should be handled on a first-come, first-served basis: to the individual complainant, his or her case is of foremost concern, and equitable treatment requires taking each case in the order received. Others take the position that the reality of limited staff and resources combined with unavoidable backlogs mandates careful selection of cases, electing to act on those which are most likely to set precedents, that is, those which have the greatest potential for accomplishing the greatest good for the greatest number of people. Another rationale for priority setting relates to the relative urgency of certain types of cases. For example, a complaint of termination may be established as high priority, within the priority of employment, on the grounds that such a case has the most basic and most immediate impact on the individual complainant.

Another issue revolves around the extension of coverage by anti-discrimination ordinances. Many state laws and local ordinances have been amended to provide protection against discrimination based on age, sexual orientation, physical handicaps, mental handicaps, marital status, and prior criminal record. Some have added coverage for such things as political affiliation, draft status, receipt of public assistance, and refusal to participate in performing an abortion. Some commissions have supported such revisions on the grounds that added coverage increases the range and degree of community support for human rights programs. On the other hand, there are those who oppose expansion, arguing that it will only further dilute already strained resources and drastically decrease the effectiveness of efforts to erase discrimination against minorities. Further, the question is often raised as to whether such expansions of coverage are not in fact deliberate racist attempts to render human rights programs impotent. It seems clear that discrimination against minorities remains systemic to an extent not felt by other identifiable groups. If human rights programs are to adequately address these problems, they need to be afforded resources commensurate with the extent of their responsibilities.[34]

The issues discussed only hint at the dynamic and evolving nature of the field of human rights. That there is controversy should not act as a deterrent to the continuance, expansion, or establishment of human rights programs. The protection of human rights is undoubtedly one of the most complex and challenging endeavors; few would argue that any area is of greater importance.

Two points can usefully be made by way of conclusion. The first point is that human rights issues are "on the agenda" for managers and their staffs as they consider every single perspective on human services delivery discussed in this book. The second point relates to the future. In the words of the editors of a companion volume to this book: "In general, overall economic factors would appear to indicate that, during the coming decade, the major tasks of mayors, councils, and city managers will be to allocate a relatively *fixed* amount of resources among the competing and shifting demands of their constituencies."[35]

The local government environment is thus one in which human rights programs will probably continue to find themselves under fiscal and political pressure. Abandoning or diminishing such programs, however, may exact a formidable toll in later years from the fabric of our society and the life of our local communities.

Housing low income people

The problem of obtaining suitable housing is known to most Americans. While decent housing may mean different things to different people, it clearly means more than a sound physical structure. The composition of the neighborhood, the type of educational, recreational, and commercial facilities, the availability of public transportation, the proximity of employment, and the quality of the government services are all important components of a suitable living environment. And the National Housing Policy as expressed in the Housing Act of 1949 makes the attainment of a decent home and a suitable living environment for every American family a national goal. As Frieden has observed:

Housing patterns are related to a nation's social and economic well-being in many important ways. Such factors as life-style, family size, migration patterns, and social mobility influence the decisions people make about housing. In turn, the kinds of houses people live in affect many of their other choices. Where people live determines to a large extent the public services they receive, influences their access to jobs, and shapes their social relationships. The location of new housing also has important consequences for municipal finance and local politics, for demands made on energy resources, and for the quality of the urban environment.[36]

Yet the price of decent housing is high. Too high, in fact, for many Americans. In today's housing market, the average family cannot afford the median price of a new house. Every $2,500 increment in housing costs eliminates about one-half million families from the housing market. The result is a nation which is substantially underhoused. The problems are as much the result of straightforward economic pressures as they are attributable to a physically inadequate housing supply. Frieden quotes some striking figures to this effect:

Although the quality of American housing has steadily improved, its cost has risen beyond the means of much of the population. . . . In 1960, 15.3 million households were classified as housing deprived. Of these, more than 70 percent were living in physically inadequate shelters, 24 percent carried an excessive rent burden, and 5 percent were overcrowded. By 1970, the number of housing-deprived families fell to 13.1 million. Slightly more than half these families occupied physically inadequate units, and the proportion paying excessive rent had risen to 42 percent. The households classified as overcrowded remained at 5 percent. Since 1970 . . . it is likely that this trend has continued. Homeownership costs and operating expenses for rental property have risen sharply—more rapidly than incomes— largely because of higher fuel prices, interest rates, and repair costs. There is little prospect of major reductions of these costs in the near future. In all likelihood, the housing problems of the poor will increasingly take the form of excessive cost burdens rather than shelter inadequacy.[37]

The supportive services which figure so highly in one's choice of housing likewise carry substantial price tags. These costs are traditionally shared by community residents and their representative governments. But what happens when those residents are without sufficient income to afford either the cost of housing or the desirable support services?

This portion of Chapter 14 will therefore focus on the responses of government to the housing needs of low income people—a group that has traditionally presented administrators at all levels of government with major challenges in the housing field. It seems that these challenges will be no less in the future. As the generations produced by the high birth rates from the 1940s to the 1960s begin to raise their own children, and as the number of nonfamily households (i.e., unmarried young people, the divorced, and old people living alone) continues to increase, then, as Frieden concludes, "during the decade beginning in the mid-1970s, changes in the American population will lead to a substantial increase in the demand for housing." [38] The poor will be the least equipped to come out ahead in this environment.

The discussion that follows is divided into three parts. The first gives an overview of the historical role of government in housing the poor, emphasizing the federal role as this has, indeed, been the primary one, but also indicating the role of the wide spectrum of options open to local governments wishing to make a direct or indirect impact on the low income housing situation in their communities. The second section analyzes some of the basic policy questions involved in dealing with low income housing, ranging from the "why bother?" question to target populations, location of housing, and available programs and financing options. The third section addresses the managerial problems associated with making low income housing work.

The historical role of government in housing: an overview

The main thrust of public sector involvement in the housing of Americans has been at the federal level. As Frieden states: "state and local governments are the main regulators of the homebuilding industry, but in most other respects the federal government is dominant." [39] Low income housing is no exception. Substantial governmental involvement with low income housing has occurred only since the 1930s.

Legacy of the 1930s   The federal government's first major attempt to construct housing for the poor through the Public Works Administration in 1934 proved unsuccessful. A federal Court of Appeals examined the provisions on eminent domain of the National Industrial Recovery Act which authorized condemnation of private property for low cost housing and slum clearance, and held that benefits of employment and aid to a limited group of low income people did not constitute a "public use" as required for eminent domain and were thus unconstitutional. [40]

Urban homesteading   More than 100 years after the Homestead Act, Philadelphia, Pennsylvania, has passed an urban homesteading ordinance encouraging families to buy one of the city's thousands of abandoned brick row houses, rehabilitate it, and live in it. A homesteader must be twenty-one, a citizen (or about to become one), have proven financial ability or building trade skills, agree to begin rehabilitating within sixty days after taking title, submit an acceptable plan and a winning bid of at least one dollar, and pledge to occupy the house for at least five years.

The Congress came back with the Housing Act of 1937 which provided financial assistance to local public bodies for the construction of low income housing and the clearance of slums. This program was to be administered on the local level by local housing authorities—semiautonomous public bodies created by the states to avoid the constitutional debt limitation imposed on most general purpose governments. The act also recognized the need for rural housing assistance; however, the assistance provided was only for farms. But despite these apparent housing goals, the intent of the 1937 act was to provide employment. This use of housing as a means of countercyclical assistance to achieve economic stability would later become a fundamental part of the government's housing policy—although it is also important to note that since the late 1960s the fear of uncontrollable inflation has also led to an emphasis on turning the housing flow "off" as well as "on."

From the 1940s to the 1960s   The Housing Act of 1949 was a milestone. To fulfil the commitment of "a decent home and a suitable living environment for every

American family'' proposed by the act, Congress created the Urban Redevelopment (later called Urban Renewal) Program (Title I); made additional funds available for public housing (Title II); and established new programs to meet rural housing needs (Title V). Over the next twenty years, these basic programs were expanded and augmented as the role of the federal government in housing continued to grow.

Ever since the New Deal programs of the 1930s, federal policy has been concerned in varying degrees with certain basic objectives: maintaining a high level of housing production, helping middle income families to become homeowners, and providing special assistance for the poor. Policies aimed at stimulating the housing industry and creating a mass market for home ownership have received the highest priority and have been the most successful. High levels of housing production and the ready availability of home mortgages have made it possible for most American families to find good housing that is within their means. Subsidy programs for the poor have been more difficult to implement and to maintain. With the new housing system working reasonably well for the majority, a series of new federal programs undertaken in the 1960s attempted to encourage the industry to do for the poor what it was already doing for the middle class.[41]

The Housing and Urban Development Act of 1968, incorporating production goals (new construction or renovation of an annual average of 600,000 housing units for low and moderate income families over the next decade) of President Johnson's 1967–68 Committee on Urban Housing, was a significant milestone in this process, as was, of course, the entire gamut of Great Society programs.

Developments in the 1970s   The place of the Great Society programs in history is still being assessed.[42] In any event, they have been well and truly overtaken by the events of the 1970s. By the early 1970s, there were 40 subsidized and 20 nonsubsidized programs for housing assistance operated by a dozen federal agencies.[43] Yet, at the same time, the housing needs of the nation were not being met. Housing construction had fallen substantially behind the target goals established in the Housing and Urban Development Act of 1968. Moreover, the bulk of federal housing assistance had flowed to middle and upper income families. Only the public housing, rent supplement, Farmers Home Administration Section 503 and 504, and Section 8 programs have served primarily the lower income groups.

Further, federal policies made a rapid change of direction in the early 1970s. Inflation became an element in the picture. ''Between 1970 and 1972, when private starts were at peak levels, federal programs also reached record volumes, adding to inflationary pressures and soon becoming costly themselves.''[44] Early in 1973, President Nixon impounded congressional appropriations destined for new housing starts and placed a moratorium on all major federal subsidy programs. Thus, even as the economy took a sharp downturn, federal housing programs fell back to the lower levels of the mid-1960s. In 1974, Congress authorized a new low income rental program and, in 1975, the Ford administration reactivated the homeownership program suspended earlier, in 1973. And of course the prospect of a new administration in 1977 cast further uncertainty over federal housing efforts. Virtually every federal housing program was up for renewal during 1977.[45] And the future, as already indicated, may also bring fresh problems because of demographic and economic changes.

Summary: policy trends and the implications for local governments   Clearly the federal response to low income housing needs has not been exceptional. But it has provided a pattern of assistance which has been a model to state and local governments. The National Housing Policy Review has suggested that three broad areas of concern have guided federal government actions in the housing field: (1) the recognition that the federal government has a responsibility to maintain and promote economic stability; (2) a social obligation to help provide for those in need; and (3) an emerging interest in how the country's communities develop. Each of these concerns have directly affected the production of housing for the nation's low income population.[46]

In its efforts to promote a stable economy, the federal government has often used housing as an important element in its countercyclical economic strategy. It is also unfortunately true that when the Federal Reserve Board has restricted the money supply and raised interest rates, the result has been a movement of funds out of savings and loan associations and mutual savings banks to more lucrative short-term investments, and to the detriment of funds available for mortgage lending and hence for new housing starts.

Frieden summarizes the role of the housing sector of the economy as follows:

The housing sector, by serving as a balance wheel, helps stabilize the economy. However, the frequent housing slumps that result also involve large social costs, such as substantial unemployment in construction and related fields, underutilization of plants and equipment, and expenses for inventory maintenance. Subsequent start-ups are also costly, often involving new hiring and a period of retraining. The cost of construction materials fluctuates substantially over the course of the housing cycle. Because most housing is built during the peak of the cycle when prices are at their highest, consumers pay much of the cost of instability in the form of high housing prices.[47]

And high prices, of course, are an even greater obstacle for poorer people than others. However, before the changed circumstances of the national economy in the 1970s, the historical record indicates a more positive role for federal intervention in the housing field. Indeed, the federal government's entry into low rent public housing construction came as a byproduct of a post-Depression program to stimulate employment. In times of economic recession, the government has devised special measures—such as mortgage insurance, extension of credit, and technical research—to stimulate the production of housing. In times of economic prosperity, the federal government's intervention has worked to stabilize the housing economy at levels of sustained high production and to encourage, among other things, the replacement of slums and substandard housing with new structures. In any event it is clear that the federal policies of housing the poor are intricately intertwined with the nation's economic strategies. It may well be that, as Frieden states, "political support for [federal housing] plans has weakened since the late 1960s. Because of the inevitable delays in making new programs operational, it now appears unlikely that federal programs will make substantial contributions to the nation's housing stock by the end of the seventies." [48] However, the fact remains that the federal role in housing has shaped many policies and attitudes, positive or negative, at the local government level.

In sum, therefore, the federal government has been actively involved with housing the poor since the 1930s and has instituted, with varying success, programs ranging from public rental housing and rent supplements to assistance in obtaining home ownership. Further, the nature of the federal involvement has taken a major change since the passage of the Civil Rights Act of 1968 and the concurrent Supreme Court decision of Jones v. Mayer.[49] Prior to these events, the federal government which had taken an active role in housing the poor had maintained a position of noninvolvement in the often related task of assuring equal housing opportunities to members of all races. The federal housing legislation which emerged after 1968 required compliance with federal antidiscrimination laws as well as a commitment to house low and moderate income people.

Additionally, concerns about wasteful and irrational patterns of development, especially within the nation's urban areas, aroused the federal government's interest in how communities and the nation were developing. This interest generated Title VII of the Housing and Urban Development Act of 1970. While the biennial reports on national growth and development required under this act may be little more than pious expressions of goals, it is a matter of political fact that the federal government, in conjunction with state and local governments and the private sector, has taken a new interest in the broader issues of community development.

A final element in the picture has been added by the Housing and Community Development Act of 1974. As Frieden and Kaplan have realistically noted:

Initiation of Community Development Revenue Sharing represents more than a reform of managerial practices and a retreat from the unrealistically ambitious objectives of the Model Cities Program. Early evidence suggests that local governments have used their freedom to shift funds quickly from poverty neighborhoods to other parts of the city, with at least tacit federal approval. And despite the rhetoric of local control, national policy is once more encouraging the use of federal money for public works projects and discouraging its use for public services.[50]

And so the debate goes on. What, however, do these ongoing policy changes at the broad level mean for the local government manager approaching the low housing problems in a specific community? What range of options are there available for those active in this controversial field?

The range of local options   Because there are a number of different approaches to housing low income people and a number of actors involved in housing programs, a local government manager must develop an understanding of the wide spectrum of options which are available in order to determine which ones are best suited to the particular jurisdiction to be managed. Central to this understanding is an appreciation of the roles which are played by the federal government versus state and local governments.

As has been indicated, the federal government has traditionally played the major role in housing the poor. It has set down operational parameters for state and local governments which choose to participate in federally sponsored programs; provided financial incentives to encourage the involvement of reluctant governments; and established federal constitutional minimums for state and local governmental actions. For these reasons, managers should stay apprised of the changing federal trends in low income housing programs.

More bang than books   The city of Cohoes, New York, operates a municipal "tool library" for residents. Its purpose is to help home owners and tenants make home improvements. It started as a Model Cities project five years ago with a handful of members, and gradually increased to 1,500 members. Two staff members control and maintain the inventory of hammers, saws, and power tools of various kinds. The program was first administered by the Cohoes Library, and later taken over by the planning and development agency.

Attempts to combine federal fiscal assistance to housing and housing programs into a broad block grant to state and local governments have been unsuccessful thus far. Consequently, federal housing assistance must be applied for in a piecemeal fashion. There are numerous categorical housing programs. To effectively utilize these federal programs, managers need to familiarize themselves with the following kinds of information: the definition of low income; the eligible program applicant; the requirements for location of the housing; the applicable federal laws and procedures governing the use of the funds; and the types of financing mechanisms.

Many state and local administrators find their own systems of housing assistance to be preferable to that of the federal government. It is common to find local jurisdictions using their own programs in addition to, or in place of, federally sponsored ones. One reason is that state and local programs are sometimes simpler. They may even require less paperwork. Some are better tailored to the needs of the jurisdiction. There is less interference by outside authorities.

Other reasons can also be found for concentrating heavily on state and local projects. In some states, the programs are more progressive and more effective than federally sponsored ones. For example, urban homesteading and neighborhood preservation techniques had their origins in state and local programs. The federal government followed their lead. In such a situation, a manager may find greater flexibility to experiment with new program ideas by working on a subnational level. Similarly, some state housing finance agencies have been found to be more willing and better able to experiment with new methods of financing low income housing. These can be important factors for innovative managers.

An equally important reason for a manager to develop close working relationships with the governing officials on the state and local levels is the fact that all programs will be automatically subjected to the laws of the jurisdictions. Code enforcement, land use, energy conservation standards, rent controls, and building requirements are usually governed by local and state laws, for example. Even federally sponsored projects will be required to meet these standards.

Sweat equity   Cambridge, Massachusetts, is taking some unusual approaches to housing rehabilitation with the aid of its community development block grant. Under one program, the city purchases at a low cost older buildings that are somewhat run down, and contracts with a nonprofit agency to rehabilitate them. They then are offered for sale to low and moderate income purchasers on a condominium basis, with an apartment unit selling for approximately $15,000 to $17,000. The new owners do the work of painting and other improvement chores ("sweat equity") as a down payment toward condominium ownership.

Under another program, specially trained crews of young people from the city's youth employment program are made available to assist in rehabilitating homes where owners cannot afford market prices of the rehab. The young workers will reshingle a house, repair a roof, and make other such improvements; the owner has to pay only the cost of materials. There are several other programs as well in this multifaceted approach to rehabilitation.

The challenge which faces the housing program manager is to mesh the various program possibilities into a cohesive and effective package which meets the approval of the sponsoring agents, the low income clientele, and the constituents of the jurisdiction where the housing is to be located. In some cases, that will mean combining existing program options. In other situations, a manager might find that none of the existing program options fit the characteristic of the jurisdiction in question, and a new and innovative program is necessary. The remainder of this discussion will focus on some of the more significant policy options and program considerations in greater detail.

The basic policy questions

Why bother with low income housing?   With all the problems which low income housing programs present, a threshold question for some administrators is: Why bother with these programs at all? In some cases, the answer is simple. Their communities contain a substantial number of low income people who cannot, and often will not, be ignored. Or their communities are faced with imminent court action which threatens a substitution of judicial housing policy for an illegal administrative policy. But for those communities with less immediate problems, different reasons can be suggested.

First, housing is a problem which never ceases. As communities and houses grow older, they are generally occupied by persons of increasingly lower income households. This is the natural result of the filtration process in housing. Neighborhoods are rezoned. Large houses are subdivided. New buildings grow old and fall into disrepair. Eventually some housing problems will arise. And more than likely, low income persons will be involved.

Added to this is the fact that the housing needs of the nation's low income people have not diminished over the years. As has been noted, housing production, which had increased prior to 1970, fell behind the minimum national target goals for housing (established in 1968) during the years after 1970. The higher cost of operation pushed the price of new housing which was built beyond the

Figure 14–7 Abandoned housing presents severe problems for local governments. (Source: Jon A. Blubaugh et al., *Human Resources Development: Capacity Building for Local Government,* Lawrence, Kansas, Division of Continuing Education, University of Kansas, June 1974, unnumbered page.)

reach of most low income persons—even those who were eligible for federal housing assistance. At the same time, the cost of decent older housing began to rise as the new housing shortage was felt in the housing market. Although it is true that the level of income of the nation's poor has also been rising during this time, inflationary housing costs have made the rise meaningless. Among the hardest hit in this inflationary spiral have been the nation's elderly who are joining the ranks of low income groups in ever increasing numbers. Further, as an outgrowth of the civil rights movement of the 1960s, considerable attention has been called to the practices and policies in suburbia which have resulted in the exclusion of minority and poor people.

For these reasons, it has become increasingly unrealistic for any administrator with foresight to ignore the needs of the nation's poor. Rather than have a housing plan for low income people imposed on them as a result of judicial intervention, more and more communities are voluntarily examining alternative means for providing for the housing needs of the poor.

Who is the target group for low income housing programs?   Once the decision has been made to plan for low income housing, the initial question may be who is the target group for the proposed program. The answer is not a simple one. The definition of a low income person can vary from state to state, region to region, and program to program. Although it would seem that some national uniformity would be provided by the definition supplied for federal housing programs, the truth is that even these programs have eligibility requirements which can differ one from another. The end result is to leave a rather confused picture of the intended beneficiaries of these programs.

Pad for senior citizens   Eugene, Oregon, has made a direct grant to a local nonprofit corporation named PAD (Presbyterian Action for Development). The funds are being applied to the mortgage of a 24-unit apartment complex being built for senior citizens. The city's contribution will reduce the rental on these apartments, and additional financing under the state's low interest loan program will further keep costs down. The PAD program is one of three housing projects for the elderly that were made possible by a $150,000 allocation of general revenus sharing funds which the city council approved last summer for housing assistance to the elderly.

Generally, low income housing programs are targeted to families, elderly persons on fixed incomes, the handicapped, and persons displaced by public improvement projects who meet some established definition of need. Consideration is currently being given to include some single nonelderly persons in this category. These persons can live in urban as well as rural areas. Generally, the urban poor are serviced by the Department of Housing and Urban Development (HUD) while the rural poor are serviced most frequently by the Farmers' Home Administration (FmHA).

Role of minorities   The large percentage of minority people served by low income housing programs has caused some people to think that housing low income people is synonymous with housing nonwhites. This misconception often makes the placement of such housing more difficult. But it is true that minorities comprise a disproportionate share of the low income population. While the number of whites below the low income level actually fell from 11.5 million in 1960 to 8 million in 1970, 31 percent of all minorities continued to remain in this category.[51] This fact partially explains their presence in public housing programs.

A second factor also explains the presence of minorities in these programs. Housing discrimination practices—many of which have continued long after federal and state legislative and judicial policies have declared them illegal—have limited the potential housing markets for this group more so than for white low income people, and subsequently force a greater percentage of minorities to look to public housing programs. Discriminatory housing practices have often combined with other discriminatory practices (e.g., in employment or in the receipt of governmental services) to produce a highly unsatisfactory environment in low income neighborhoods. All too often, the neighborhood which results from this combination of factors is deemed to be a byproduct of the low income housing alone. This misconception generates unnecessary apprehension about and opposition to the creation and placement of low income housing programs.

How low are the incomes?   How low are the incomes of the program participants is a second common question. Again the specific answer will differ depending upon the type of program which is selected. For instance, federal programs often establish eligibility for housing assistance in terms of the median income of the particular area where the program is operating. A low income family's income must be less than a set percentage of the area median income. In the Housing and Community Development Act of 1974 (HCDA), for example, very low income families have income less than 50 percent of the area median income.

In more concrete terms, the range of incomes in low rent public housing programs goes from $1000 to over $10,000 annually.[52] The majority of the persons serviced by the FmHA Section 504 rural home loan program fall in the income range from $1,000 to $4,000. A new trend in federal legislation is to lump together the low and moderate income family, so it is also possible to have a higher annual income figure entering into certain programs. There have, for instance, been charges that Section 312 rehabilitation loans for homeowners were given to persons with annual incomes in excess of $15,000. But such cases are generally the exception to the rule and the bulk of the housing assistance can be found to go to families with annual adjusted incomes of between $4,000 and $9,000.

State and local governments are certainly free to establish their own income limits for their own low income housing programs. In the recent New Jersey case of the Urban League of Greater New Brunswick v. the Borough of Carteret, the Superior Court of Middlesex County went so far as to establish its own income levels for the purpose of dispering low and moderate income housing throughout the county.[53]

Anomalies   An anomaly of most low income housing programs is the fact that no income or too little income can disqualify a person from many of the programs. Most of these programs balance two basic considerations: the need to provide decent housing at a low and affordable cost to poor people versus the need for the housing programs to remain financially solvent. Housing assistance in the form of a loan or a rent subsidy usually requires the recipient to have a minimum income to pay the lowest rent or interest payment possible under the particular program. Nonpayment can result in eviction or default. In this sense, there is no "free housing" available.

Nor do federal programs give a preference to the needs of the lowest income persons in all programs. Critics of the Section 8 subsidized rent program note that the inclusion of moderate income persons in the eligible category raised the number of potential persons to be serviced by 16 percent over the predecessor programs which served only low income people, but gave no preference to the needs of the poorer people.[54] In the program's first year of operation, however, the bulk of the money has gone to low as opposed to moderate income families. Section 8 is nevertheless *the* major federal subsidized housing program, and a full review of its progress, or lack of it, will be an ongoing matter. Named after its placement in the Housing and Community Development Act of 1974, Section 8 was intended to replace public housing programs and the more popular Section 236 program. The program subsidizes the rents of low and moderate income families in existing and new privately owned housing units. The goals of the program are to reduce the cost of housing the poor and allow for a fairer distribution of housing funds.

The federal government did recognize that a housing payment which uses up a major portion of a family's income is counterproductive and has placed a ceiling on the percentage of a low income family's income which can be required in payment for public housing. The Brooke Amendment supplies extra subsidies so that the poor will need to pay no more than 25 percent of their total income in rent. These subsidies, however, have not been forthcoming at any great speed.[55] This provision has been criticized for its effect on the financing of public housing programs. Since the amount of total rent contribution by tenants is limited, operating increases and other excess costs must be absorbed by the local housing authority. For these authorities, it is a losing proposition economically.

Where should low income housing be located?   Poor people have generally moved from rural areas to the cities, with an eye on a move to the suburbs when they have finally "made it." Therefore, low income housing programs have primarily focused on urban and rural areas. Thus, to even pose the question of where to locate new housing programs for poor people seems unnecessary unless a change in this pattern were in order.

The change is inevitable. Federal legislation has already begun to espouse—at least in theory—a policy of spatial deconcentration of the poor. Similar policies are beginning to appear on the state level, often under the title of "fair share" housing. These policies are an attempt to reverse long-term housing practices which have resulted in high concentrations of low income people in certain central city areas and their virtual exclusion from many of the surrounding suburban areas.

What this policy means for local and regional administrators is that special consideration should be given to the placement of any new low income housing development in areas with low numbers of low income families. The Supreme Court's landmark decision, Hills v. Gautreaux, reinforced this policy by finding that HUD had an obligation to approve public housing sites on a metropolitan basis to prevent further racially segregated housing patterns in the city of Chicago.[56]

In most areas, this is not an easy or popular task. It often requires a change in land use and zoning ordinances in the selected site area. Such changes generally require community approval or acquiescence. Sometimes—and this is putting it kindly—such requests for change are met with hostility, generally stemming from misconceptions and fears about the effects of low income housing on community property values and general life-styles. These situations require special political skills if they are to survive major crises.

Other programs, however, have little flexibility in choosing a target area. Once a decision is made to conserve existing housing stock or to concentrate on upgrading neighborhoods or existing programs, the target area is automatically designated. But decisions about locating low income persons within a rehabilitated neighborhood must still be made. Should some portions of the houses to be rehabilitated be set aside for middle and upper income families to increase the tax base? If doing this requires displacing some low income families, where will they go? Federal legislation mandates certain guidelines for relocation assistance for displaced persons in neighborhood improvement programs.[57] Experience showed that it was not fair to assume that these people could find decent and affordable homes in the general area from which they were displaced. A keen sense of the political environment, and careful and coordinated planning, are crucial.

What are the various program approaches for housing low income people?
The success of a low income housing program is partly a function of choosing

the program which best fits the needs of the occupants and the community. This selection has become even more important as the range of available programs and possible site locations increase. No longer is low rent, no service public housing the primary means for assisting low income families. Communities are constantly devising creative ways of meeting the housing needs of this target group. Public administrators now have a range of housing assistance programs from which to choose. These programs are variations of three basic program approaches to housing: housing production subsidies; income assistance for housing; and housing management services.

Subsidies The basic strategy for providing housing for the poor since the 1930s has entailed subsidizing the cost of new or rehabilitated housing with the intent of increasing the supply while lowering the price. This strategy underlies a number of the current housing programs, including low rent public housing projects, the popular Section 235 homeownership and Section 236 rent supplements, FHA insured mortgage loans to limited profit builders, tax incentives for investment in residential rental and subsidized properties, tax exemptions of interest income on public housing bonds, urban homesteading, and rehabilitation loan programs.

Housing allowances A second strategy for low income housing assistance is housing allowances. The housing allowance programs seek to influence the demand for housing by adding to the income of those persons looking to buy or rent housing. Basically, these programs would give low income families cash to spend for housing in the private housing market and would allow them a certain amount of freedom to select suitable housing. Proponents of this type of housing assistance argue that it is a more flexible system which involves less interference with an individual's choice of residence and lifestyle. They also argue that it will bring housing assistance to more of the nation's poor households in a quicker and more efficient manner.

Classy urban renewal Two deserted and rundown duplexes are getting a new lease on life, and several classes of high school vocational students are getting valuable training in a joint city/school program in University City, Missouri. The city bought six old and decrepit properties from HUD earlier this year for one dollar each, and turned two of them over to the students. One class each day works on the buildings for regular vocational arts credit— doing rewiring, carpentry, plastering, plumbing, painting, and everything else that is needed to make a comfortable home. Each house is being renovated on a budget of $3,500, split between the city and the state education department. When completed at the end of the semester, each will sell for $22,000 to $25,000, and funds will be pumped into expanding the program.

Housing allowance programs are entirely in the experimental stage. HUD has been operating an Experimental Housing Allowance Program in a dozen locations across the country since 1974. No final conclusions have been drawn from these experiments to date and there are no local options in this program. The new Section 8 rent subsidy program could be described as a hybrid of the housing allowance and housing production subsidy programs. As the newest federal approach to housing, it attempts to combine the best of the two basic low income housing approaches.

Maintenance and management A final basic program approach to housing needs addresses not the provision of housing so much as its maintenance once it is provided. Housing management has only recently been recognized as a vital component of a housing approach. In 1972, a National Center for Housing Management was established to highlight the importance of this function in the area of housing. Prior to this time, housing management had been approached in a piecemeal fashion on the national level.

Housing management addresses the people side of the housing challenge. It recognizes that the test of a sound housing program is its ability to maintain its high standards over time. To do this effectively requires the joint efforts of all the participants in the housing process. Good housing management instructs tenants about housekeeping, maintenance and budgeting—often with an eye towards the ultimate goal of preparing them for homeownership. It recognizes the value of using professional housing managers and seeks to assure that these persons are trained to meet the demand. Managers can assess the range of supportive social services needed to insure a suitable living environment and translate these needs to the proper administrators and lawmakers. Their knowledge of housing needs can assist developers in planning housing developments which fit that particular community. In fact, the range of possible housing management activities are limited only by the imagination and skills of the involved parties.

How are low income programs financed? Assuming that the commitment to go ahead with some type of low income program has been made, two fundamental questions still remain unanswered: How much will it cost? and Where will the funds come from? Depending on the severity of the housing needs, these programs can be an expensive proposition. Financially hard pressed communities, particularly those which are not enthusiastic about accepting low income housing to begin with, are apt to view low income housing as an expendable item on the budget. But several factors which mitigate the cost of housing ought to be pointed out to reluctant administrators and decision makers.

Housing and the economy First, the housing market for years has been used as a regulator of the nation's economy, at least until the 1970s. Since the passage of the first federal public housing program, there are times when the federal government has used the production of housing, and particularly low income housing, as a countercyclical measure. A decision to spend money on housing—either directly or through tax incentives—can be a decision to stimulate the community's economy. Furthermore, it is possible that good housing and good neighborhoods with healthy economies can attract new businesses, or at least stem a decline. The community then has the opportunity to recoup much of it original housing outlay.

Federal assistance Second, federal assistance programs offer funds for low income housing programs to help defray the costs. General purpose governments as well as state and local housing authorities are eligible for the funds as sponsoring agencies for these programs. But federal assistance comes with strings attached. Most programs condition receipt of funds on compliance with a host of national goals and laws. These include minimum wage protection and labor provisions of the Davis–Bacon Act; environmental impact information under the National Environmental Protection Act; the antidiscrimination provisions of Title VI of the 1964 Civil Rights Act and Title VIII of the 1968 Civil Rights Act; provision for displaced persons and acquisition of property as required by the Uniform Relocation Assistance and Real Property Acquisition Policy Act; and various Office of Management and Budget circulars, such as A-95. Many of these federal mandates carry additional financial costs as well as social obligations to participating communities. The implications of these various federal program "strings" should be assessed and understood.

State programs Third, communities can look for housing development funds through state programs and state housing and finance development authorities.

State governments are increasingly moving into the area of housing. More than thirty states have created housing finance authorities, although it is true that only a few are spending money to build housing. Their activity in the bond market, in control of lending practices and in influencing tax policy have helped to make necessary funds available to interested jurisdictions for housing assistance. Some state governments also provide technical assistance to those communities which have difficulty fettering out the complicated and often confusing regulations of federal housing programs.

Other state and local options   Fourth, a range of local and state activities can be investigated to lower the cost of low income housing. These include encouraging the involvement of the private sector in financing the development and rehabilitation efforts; land banking; establishing uniform building and code requirements.

Making low income housing work

There is no cookbook approach to low income housing programs. Just as meals are tailored to the tastes and availability of foods in a given region, so are individual housing programs tailored to the needs and resources of a given community. But a skilled administrator—like a skilled cook—can take the basics and improvise. This section looks at some different types of programs and approaches which have worked in various areas of the country to meet identified housing needs of low income people.

Assessing the needs   Because a range of programs for low income housing exists and because all programs do not address the needs of all communities, the first and probably most important step in planning a program is to obtain a clear definition of problems and objectives. For this task to be done effectively, however, a detailed assessment of the target groups and their short- and long-term needs is essential.

As the discussion in Chapters 5 and 6 has indicated, a number of questions need to be answered. First, who are the area low income people? Are they small families? large families? elderly on fixed incomes? Second, where are they presently housed? Are they there by choice or is their location the result of legal barriers in other areas? Third, in what kinds of housing are they presently living and what is the condition of that housing currently? Fourth, what is the residential trend in the area, i.e. are people moving in or moving out? What is the expected rate of growth or decline for the target group and the community as a whole?

From this information, a community can develop a local housing assistance plan for meeting the needs of the low income population. A formal housing assistance plan (HAP) is a prerequisite to entitlement and discretionary HUD funding under the Title I Community Development Block Grant Program of the 1974 Housing and Community Development Act.[58] The purpose of these HAPs is to give HUD as well as the applicant community an assessment of the housing stock and needs and to get communities to define short and long term objectives for housing and community development. Although the process has been criticized by smaller communities as being time consuming and expensive, it has proved to be a good planning exercise in many cases. Furthermore, state and regional planning authorities are now gearing up to provide assistance to these smaller communities in many areas.

Included in the formal HUD HAP is another requirement which could be used by some localities. Communities are asked to make an estimate of the number of low and moderate income persons who could be ''expected to reside'' in their area if there was available housing. The actual mechanics of determining the number have undergone revisions at HUD after many communities had an initial problem with the instructions. These figures can prove especially helpful to communities involved in regional planning for housing.

With the move to disperse low income housing, some communities are developing plans to allocate subsidized housing on a regional basis. The Dayton Plan of the Miami Valley Regional Planning Commission in Dayton, Ohio, was adopted in 1970 to promote housing opportunities for all income levels in the five-county area surrounding Dayton.[59] As a result of the plan, the area has increased its assisted housing production by 1,600 percent and has tried to spread low income housing throughout the region in a planned and acceptable manner. Similar regional cooperation has resulted in progressive zoning and land use revisions to accommodate regional housing growth and to make it easier to place low income housing. Such progressive planning avoids the kind of situation which occurred in Middlesex County, New Jersey. A state court has ordered eleven Middlesex municipalities to accept 18,700 low and moderate income housing units by 1985.[60] Clearly, where states have embraced the federal policy of dispsered low income housing, the choice is to act . . . or react.

A warm and snuggly building code   Saginaw, Michigan, is taking pioneering steps to include requirements for thermal insulation, vapor barriers, and storm glass in its building code. These standards are based on the performance of the materials and design, and not on requirements for specified materials, thus avoiding any charges of favoritism. The consumer will be assured of a home that is easy to heat and cool and that will keep the family dry and comfortable at minimum cost in energy.

As a final suggestion, some assessment might be made of the attitudes of the residents in the affected communities. This factor is particularly crucial when low income housing is being introduced into an area for the first time. Misinformation and misapprehensions about the effect of low income housing on communities are common and potentially detrimental to the success of a program. A well orchestrated information campaign which explains the housing program and gives administrators a chance to learn about the community's views can make the difference between community acceptance and community rejection.

Advisory neighborhood councils, task forces on housing, regional councils or other established citizen participation mechanisms can be especially useful as channels of communication. The Community Development Block Grant program requires public meetings for citizen input prior to the submission of an application for community development assistance. As more jurisdictions participate in this or other programs with citizen participation components, the communication mechanism may become more firmly established and prove to be a most effective tool for promoting better understanding of housing problems and community solutions. Unfortunately, experience to date indicates that the whole process can also be little more than a force.

Choosing the program   Even after all the necessary data is gathered and analyzed, the task of tailoring the general programs to meet the particular identified needs of the jurisdiction still remains. What works in one area does not necessarily work in another. The following program examples have been grouped under the areas where they work best.

Central and older cities   New national emphasis has been placed on neighborhood preservation. City officials are being challenged to find ways to use existing housing stock. These programs have taken a variety of forms.

The wisdom of public housing projects which concentrate large numbers of low income people in poorly serviced complexes in low income neighborhoods has increasingly been questioned. Substitutes for the public housing programs are continually being tried. The result of rethinking the role of public housing projects has been twofold. First, there has been less emphasis on old style housing projects. Where new projects are built, they tend to be less congested. More attention is given to their architectural design and their location. Better arrangements are made to integrate the social services with housing. These arrangements have been particularly beneficial to the low income elderly.

Second, where old public housing exists, some administrators are striving to make it viable. In the Bronx, for example, the New York City Housing Authority has turned a housing project located in former munitions workers' barracks into a modern, model program.[61] With architectural assistance from the Institute for Community Design Analysis, Clason Point Houses was redesigned and modified to create a more acceptable living environment. At the same time, 85 percent of the ground area was turned over to residents for their own maintenance and control. The project has succeeded in creating a spirit of community and pride. Clason Point Houses was selected by HUD as a model public housing project in its bicentennial salute to outstanding community achievement in community development.

Urban homesteading is a program approach which is receiving increased support in the nation's older cities. This program is directed towards declining neighborhoods with a supply of blighted, abandoned city houses owned by HUD or VA (often acquired as a result of tax delinquency or default). The houses are sold for a minimal fee (generally $1) to a resident who is willing to put in time, work and money to rehabilitate the house and bring it up to code standards. There is usually a requirement that the family then occupy the home for a set period of years.

The real advantage of this program is that it makes home ownership a reality for some persons who have been priced out of the housing market. But it has one real drawback as a low income housing program. It is premised on the new owner's ability to finance the cost of rehabilitation. In Baltimore, Maryland, where one of the most successful urban homesteading programs has operated, the median rehabilitation cost was $17,400 at 7½ percent interest. Unless some special arrangements are made to assist low income persons in obtaining the proper financing for the rehabilitation loan, the program may be beyond the means of most low income families.[62]

Rehabilitation loans can be made separate from the urban homesteading type of program. One of HUD's most popular programs was its Section 312 rehabilitation loan program which can supply low interest loans directly to interested occupants of deteriorating housing. But these programs are subject to a similar criticism as the urban homesteading program. They require that the loan recipient demonstrate a certain degree of economic stability to insure the loan's repayment. This requirement tends to benefit the moderate to middle income families. Indeed reports have been made that families with incomes in excess of $20,000 have utilized the program. New regulations are now more restrictive.

On the other hand, it has been argued that low income neighborhoods, and thus low income people indirectly, are benefited when middle income families return to declining areas to rehabilitate the deteriorating housing. The increase in the city's tax base which results from the return of financially more stable persons helps to finance better city services for everyone, attracts new business to the area and generally improves low income neighborhoods. This could be a part of a housing assistance plan, provided, of course, that the low income families which are displaced are suitably relocated elsewhere. Consideration could also be given to a mixture of rehabilitation loans for moderate income families and rehabilitation grants for those of lesser means.

As already indicated, Section 8 Housing is the newest housing program for the poor. While the program is reported to be working well with existing houses in some areas, it has numerous critics. Some complain that not enough new housing is being built under the current HUD policy. The more serious criticism, however, charges that Section 8 apartment units cost the government up to 14 percent more than comparable units would cost under the old public housing programs. This cost differential has been attributed to the government's ability to obtain lower interest rates to finance its own housing projects and its immunity from local property taxes. Neither condition exists under the Section 8 program in which federal subsidies are paid to private developers.

Housing allowances, which were called "the most promising approach" for subsidized decent housing for the poor by the Nixon administration, are still in the experimental stage. Details of how the program has worked are sketchy.[63] In areas where there is poor housing stock or a pattern of segregated housing to begin with (such as in the experimental site in Jacksonville, Florida), no significant increase in housing opportunities has been noted for the minority participants. An assessment—not necessarily definitive—of the Kansas City experience indicates that certain supportive services such as housing counseling, inspections, and referrals to nondeclining neighborhoods may be required to guarantee the success of the program. However, the cost of such services may have the effect of increasing the amount of subsidy per family to a price beyond acceptable financial limits, although this seems unlikely as the cost is very small.

Suburban metropolitan areas   The low income housing concerns of the urban counties and their included municipalities often differ from those of central cities, although those which have deteriorating housing stock may find some of the programs applicable. But for the most part, the suburban areas tend to be newer. Many are grappling with growth related problems. There is also a greater likelihood that the officials of the counties and their included jurisdictions have established some type of working relationship to meet regional problems, particularly when the problem is low income housing.

A major suburban housing question has been the efforts of suburban governments to balance growth policies with the requirement of "fair share" allocations of low income housing. The use of "controlled growth" and "no growth" plans to prevent the entry of new housing developments, particularly in bedroom communities, has received mixed reactions in the courts. While blatant actions to exclude minority and low income people will not be sanctioned, courts are recognizing the right of communities to plan their growth rates. These plans which often involve zoning and land use restrictions can present major barriers to low income housing. Efforts to affect changes on the regional level in this area were mentioned earlier in this article. While sometime difficult to achieve, these changes are crucial to opening up these areas to low income people.

Urban counties are moving into a more active role in the area of community development and housing planning. More than eighty urban counties became eligible for entitlement funding under HUD's Community Development Block Grant program. These counties entered into cooperative agreements with close to 1,900 jurisdictions within their boundaries. Under the terms of these agreements, county officials agree to cooperate with their included jurisdictions in the provision of housing services for low income people. This cooperation also entails the development of a countywide housing assistance plan, with short and long range developmental goals. This program portends a new era of intracounty cooperation in meeting the housing needs of the poor.

New Communities emerged from the Housing and Urban Development Act of 1970 as a potential source of housing for low income people. Although New Communities were established four years earlier under the Demonstration Cities and Metropolitan Development Act of 1966, there was not an official federal policy at that time which required that these communities serve low income people. This important policy change was not made until Congress made its statement on national urban growth policy in 1970. In any event, such new communities ran into severe economic problems in the 1970s.

A New Community is a housing development of such size and scope as to make a substantial contribution to the economic growth of the area in which it is located. Its location must provide maximum accessibility to a major city as well as to employment, commercial and recreational centers.

Reston, Virginia, located in the Washington, D.C., metropolitan area, is one of the first and best known New Communities. After enjoying a five-year period of successful operations, it has recently undergone a period of turmoil between some of its lower income residents and the residents of the remainder of the development. The low income residents have complained of poor housing management and maintenance. The housing managers have noted that a failure to effectively screen new residents had resulted in a higher rate of defaults on rent payments and eviction. There were, as a result, fewer funds for maintenance. Recognition of the problem has resulted in more efficient management techniques, underscoring the key role which housing management can play.

Rural areas   Most of the country's poorest people live in rural areas. These areas have the nation's highest percentage of people living in substandard housing. Social services are poor to nonexistent. The overall housing needs are substantial.

The low level of housing service afforded these areas in real need is a commentary on the nation's general policy concerning the needs of rural America. The bulk of the housing assistance for rural areas comes not from HUD but from the Farmers Home Administration (FmHA), a subagency of the Department of Agriculture which has been under continual attack for operating its housing program well below its apparent capacity, especially in light of the housing requirements in this area.

There are two major FmHA programs servicing the poor in rural areas. Section 502 is a homeownership loan program for lower income families (generally between $4,000 and $7,000, adjusted annual income in fiscal year 1972) who cannot obtain credit from conventional sources to build new homes or to buy or improve existing homes. This program provides interest credits to the recipients at a rate determined by the income of the family. A Section 502 noninterest credit loan is available to persons in the next higher income range ($7,000 to $9,000).

The second major program is the Section 504 Loan Program which lends money to owner–occupants to make minor home repairs in order to remove hazardous living conditions. These loans are for "below standard" housing and tend to serve persons in the $1,000 to $4,000 income group.

Under the 1974 HUD act, nonmetropolitan areas and rural areas within SMSAs can now apply for block grant funds for community development and housing assistance from HUD. This assistance is distributed on a discretionary basis; but 20 percent of the program allocation is specifically reserved for nonmetropolitan communities. During the first year of the program, the largest increase in program participation came from these smaller, often rural, communities.

Self-help programs for building and repairing houses have been a crucial tool for housing assistance in these rural areas. These programs have operated with the assistance of rural interest groups, in particular the National Rural Housing Alliance. But rural housing, maybe even more so than urban housing, is an area which needs innovation, direction, and assistance.

Conclusion

The preceding discussion has taken what can only be an overview of a vast and complex area. It has taken a look at the historical role of government in housing and given an indication of the range of options open to the local government manager. Four basic policy questions have then been addressed: why bother with low income housing?; where would low income housing be located?; what are the various program approaches for housing low income people?; and how are low income programs financed? A final section has taken a look at some of the problems encountered in making low income housing work.

By way of summary, and because of the constantly changing nature of the field, managers are referred to the accompanying managerial checklist (Figure 14–8) for those grappling with the challenge of low income housing. It should be noted that the examples given of approaches to low income housing needs barely tap the surface. New thinking in the area of housing occurs constantly. Talk of reviving the housing block grant concept has begun in Congress. The discussions will go on, endlessly, for one thing is clear to most policy makers. The search for new housing programs must continue until the national housing policy of a decent home and a suitable living environment for every American family—whether rich or poor—is realized.

Implementation Checklist

1. Develop a housing assistance plan. Assess the existing housing stock which is used by low income persons and which could be used by these persons. Determine the needs of the low income persons residing in the area (both for housing and supportive services). Where possible and appropriate, include in this plan those low income persons who might be expected to reside in the area if low income housing were available.

2. Coordinate local housing plans with regional and statewide planning agencies. Give consideration to fair share housing allocations to ensure the dispersal of low income housing on a regional basis. Resolve any inconsistencies between local plans and regional and statewide plans.

3. Involve the community in the planning process. If the housing program places low income housing in new neighborhoods, consider the possible use of information campaigns to ensure maximum community cooperation. In all programs, use citizen participation mechanisms wherever possible.

4. Select a housing program which is tailored to the jurisdiction. Investigate the field of federal, state, and local program options. Feel free to experiment with innovative programs if existing ones do not serve the needs of the community.

5. Encourage private investment. Include state and local financial institutions in the planning process. Work with them to develop a financial feasibility test for the development and operation of the project. Investigate responsible tax incentives which would encourage investment.

6. Develop housing management skills. Establish a program which trains managers in the special needs of low income housing projects. Involve tenants in the management process.

7. Identify and promote legislation favorable to low income housing. Concentrate on legislation which lowers the cost of housing (e.g., uniform statewide building codes) and which amends zoning and land use regulations that bar the construction of low income housing.

Figure 14–8   Implementation checklist for establishment of housing for low income people.

Mobilizing community resources for youth

Young people are in many ways the most precious of all our human resources and one of the most significant areas of human service delivery by the local, state, or federal government. If the resources inherent in youth are underutilized, alienated, or neglected, the costs today and tomorrow in all aspects of our community life, from educational attainment and economic productivity to criminal justice system costs, can be immense—and not measured in dollars alone. And young people, too, by their very status as growing members of the community, are recognized as being a particular focus of community services.

The following discussion, in line with others in this section of this book, presents the perspective of one author who has extensive familiarity with the field. The focus of the discussion is on a major, systematic, federally initiated project that has had an impact on some 10,000 young people in seventeen local communities across the nation. An attempt is made, however, to point to the wider managerial implications of this experience in the hope that this will assist local government managers as they contemplate the most viable approach to mobilizing community resources for youth in their own local environments.

The discussion begins with an introductory overview of the three major changes that have been shaping the mobilizations of resources for youth. Four main sections follow. The first analyzes changing federal roles in this area. The second discusses how local government capacities can be increased by effective planning and management. The third, and major, section looks at the basic steps for systematizing community approaches to youth development and delinquency prevention. The fourth looks at pertinent examples of community implementation. There is a brief concluding summary.

An overview: the threefold thrust for change

In recent years, the managers of state and local efforts in managing community resources have been affected—if not confounded—by three major changes: the changing relationships between local agencies and federal funding sources; a disinclination to accept traditional answers to basic questions about the "need" of youth; and the emergence of the new approach to the planning and management of community youth services that will be analyzed in the present discussion.

Changing federal–state–local relationships   The first and perhaps the most visible of the three changes has been in the relationships between state and local units of government and the federal departments which fund public and private agencies to provide community youth services. Since the late 1960s, more and more of the responsibility for improving human services has been thrown into the laps of state and local elected officials. Whether the national policy is referred to as the New Federalism, devolution, subfederal centralization, or capacity building, the effect has been the same. Human service programs which were once administered directly by federal authorities through direct grants to local private and public agencies have been transferred to local general purpose government.

Being put into the driver's seat has given community leaders added opportunity to analyze community youth problems and solve them. As chances for getting things done locally have grown so have responsibilities and demands for expertise. Local governments have greater opportunity than ever before for determining needs, for setting priorities and adopting goals, and for determining how resources will be used. They also have greater demands on them for building coordination; for providing opportunities for citizen participation; for organizing, managing, and evaluating youth development programs; and for documenting effectiveness and efficiency of their efforts. They also find themselves short of money.

State legislatures, county commissions, city councils, chief appointed administrators, and others, all have new issues to ponder and both policy and technical questions to answer. What, for example, constitutes "need"? What are the sources of delinquency and other youth problems? What should be done about them? How do we avoid waste? What can we do to find out if our programs succeed?

Changing answers to traditional questions   The second change is that at present traditional answers to these questions are being contested. The prevailing view in the youth services field has been that youth problems and needs inhere in individual young persons. If there is delinquency it is because there is something wrong with delinquents. If there is truancy it is because there is something wrong with truants. If the unemployment rate of youth is high it is because youth have no marketable skills. Programs based on this conception seek to *treat* individual youth—fix them up somehow so the problem will be diminished.

However, mounting evidence from social science research calls the effectiveness of these treatment programs into question. Recent evaluation research raises new management considerations as well.[64] The new perspective goes so far as to suggest that community agencies which serve youth are organized so as to unintentionally produce the very problems they think they are solving. From the new viewpoint, education, youth employment, and the juvenile justice system become the prime targets for change, rather than the youth these social institutions affect.

Changing planning and management strategies   The third change is the emergence of a new approach to the planning and management of community youth services. In 1970, the Office of Youth Development (OYD),[65] Department of Health, Education, and Welfare, began a research effort to establish a youth policy which was responsive to the changing federal role and to new research findings mentioned above.[66] Under OYD auspices, experts constructed an integrated theory which could serve to guide the design of comprehensive planning for community youth services. The product of the policy research effort was a validated theory described as the "national strategy for youth development and delinquency prevention." While the testing of the strategy was underway in seventeen cities, the agency expanded its research efforts to determine the kinds of community structures which would be needed by local general purpose governments to implement the strategy. The model for providing comprehensive service to community youth became known as the "youth service system." [67]

By 1974, the strategy had received sufficient verification and the Youth Service System approach appeared to be practicable enough to attract the interest of other federal agencies. The American Public Welfare Association sought and received funds from the Law Enforcement Assistance Administration (LEAA) to pilot test the approach in five communities.[68] Also in 1974, the Department of Labor funded the National Office for Social Responsibility (NOSR) to apply the Strategy and the Youth Service System approach in two sites involving a number of communities.[69] In these sites, NOSR sought to integrate community youth services around the Department of Labor's Youth Manpower Training Programs.

By 1976, more than a score of communities, under state, county, and municipal sponsorships, were engaged in implementing the approach now known as capacity building for youth development and delinquency prevention.[70] In most cases, the only support supplied by federal agencies was in the form of technical assistance and consultation. Funds already available to state and local governments for comprehensive planning are sufficient to implement the new approach.

In the following pages, the elements of the emerging approach to the planning and management of community resources for youth are described. It is important to remember, however, that the role of the public (or private) sector in helping or working with young people is effective only to the extent that it harmonizes with positive influences in the church, the neighborhood peer group, the family, and, above all, in the hearts and minds of the youngsters themselves as they grow up in a fast-changing world of seeming endless crises at all levels from the international to the domestic. Many managers active in the youth area have come to realize that a coldness, a clinical tone, an overemphasis on overall bureaucratic procedures or sweeping principles at the expense of getting close (both literally and figuratively) to the kids and the people who work with them, can wrack havoc in the best program.

The new federal role

In the early spring of 1973, a forty-page memorandum was developed in one federal agency which described the rethinking that has been going on for several years regarding human services programs.[71] These ideas, paraphrased in this section, were reflected in the State and Local Assistance Act of 1972 (General Revenue Sharing) and the Comprehensive Employment and Training Act of 1973 (Special Revenue Sharing) and in later legislation. It is important to note, however, that the same kind of reasoning appears in amendments to much of the categorical human services legislation, including Title XX of the Social Security Act, the Elementary and Secondary Education Act, and the Juvenile Delinquency Act of 1974—to name only three pieces of legislation that are important to the youth population.

In general, human development programs have not held up well under critical evaluation because: (1) program objectives are given vague and shifting definitions; (2) program objectives cannot be achieved because they are directed at problems on which the program has a limited impact; (3) program objectives may not or cannot be assessed well by the available measures; and (4) responsibility for the management of programs has been diffuse.

Objectives   The federal government ought to attempt only those objectives in human services, including youth services, which can be judged appropriate and practicable on three grounds.

1. Equity: the federal government has responsibilities to protect groups suffering discrimmination, poverty, or other forms of deprivation.
2. Externalities: the federal government may perform some services more efficiently than the states because some problems are beyond the interest or scope of state governments.
3. Practicability: the federal government should not attempt to reach objectives, no matter how laudable, which experience has shown it cannot achieve. Large scale policy shifts, enforcement of federal legal guarantees, and strengthening of state and local responsibilities may be the most effective federal roles.

Means   If a program serves a legitimate and practicable end, the next question is how best to organize it. The basic choices concern the form of service—the federal government can provide service directly to those who need it, provide cash with which to buy the service, or provide vouchers or insurance—and the form of organization—the federal government can administer the program directly or can transfer the resources to intermediary levels such as the states and localities.

Options for reform   The above choices generate several options for the reform of human services. The most important option for present purposes is that whereby the federal government concerns itself less with the direct provision of services and more with the development of institutions to provide the services through state and local governments.

The advantages of this option are that the states and local institutions are strengthened through attention to capacity building; federal involvement in the details of service provision is decreased; federal protection of specified national interests is enhanced; and responsiveness of programs to individual needs is improved. The major disadvanlage of this option is that it requires an orchestrated set of changes simultaneously at the federal, state, and local levels.

Increasing capacity: the planning and management capability of local government

In every community, large or small, there are a variety of public agencies, private organizations, and individuals who are operating or trying to develop sound youth programming. As is often the case in human services, their efforts are seldom co-ordinated, and their approaches anything but integrated. They are frustrated and blocked continuously. They compose the citizen groups that appear time and time again before government budget committees seeking resources to pursue their program goals. They are persons and organizations who care deeply about community youth and their problems. A process which mobilizes their joint energies through participation in youth development planning and program implementation can build an important capability for general purpose government in a community.

Planning model   In such a situation a model for community planning is needed as one method for bringing some order into what many managers perceive (or experience) as chaos. A linear planning scheme familiar to all administrators and planners as applied to youth programming is shown in Figure 14–9. The steps in implementing such a model are also familiar to community planners.

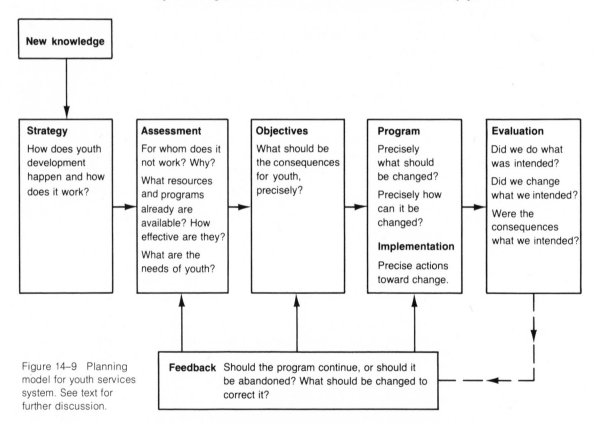

Figure 14–9 Planning model for youth services system. See text for further discussion.

Step one   The first step begins with an analysis of the state of knowledge—particularly theory—which is necessary for the selection of a direction and a content that will become the focus of the planning process. Upon selection of the direction, hypotheses or propositions which can be tested during the course of the planning and implementation process are formulated. Using these propositions as a base, instrumentation can be created for assessing youth needs and counting the real and potential resources for meeting those needs.

Step two   A communitywide assessment of youth needs must be undertaken as the second step in the process. Overlapping the youth needs assessment should be a survey and analysis of the quantity and geographic distribution of service resources for youth provided by public and private agencies. One then proceeds to an analysis and interpretation which balances needs against resources, and leads to value judgments about the magnitude and seriousness of problems and priority setting.

Steps three, four, and five   This second stage is logically followed by goal formulation, which is followed by step four: program development and design, allocation of resources, objective setting, and program implementation. These steps are followed in turn by monitoring to see that the program is following action steps that can be expected to achieve objectives and goals. An impact evaluation should then be done to measure the effects of the overall program on the client population being served.

Step six   The final step of evaluation consolidates all information collected and makes recommendations to policy makers for improving the program in successive years. In addition, the feedback process enables corrections and adjustments to be made to the ongoing operation.

Difficulty in applying linear planning   Local general purpose governments, as their responsible officers are only too well aware, have seldom found it possible to follow this kind of linear design. There are too many contingencies and constraints in such planning. First and foremost, planning staff is limited in size if not in experience. Staff must administer a variety of programs to meet community needs besides those for youth. Economic resources are not unlimited. Public pressure for services is great. The process of following the planning scheme may well appear too expensive and uncertain in terms of payoff, and may not fit into the harsh realities of the local political environment. Months of expensive staff time can be spent in searching through abstract descriptions of programs and their evaluation reports without discovering any information applicable to the community's particular problems. If sound guiding propositions can be uncovered, the time involved in implementing the propositions with measureable indices; constructing survey instruments; pretesting, evaluating, and correcting instrumentation—all part of step one of the process—could easily take a year. Policy research, necessary as it is to increasing the managerial capability of general purpose government, requires more investment of time and capital than is available to most communities.

A basic economic assumption   Be this as it may, it is also true that the bulk of resources which ever will be available for youth development and delinquency prevention already is available and being used in local communities. These resources are reflected in the budgets of schools and of main permanent service agencies as well as in the temporary sources of state and federal funding. It is unlikely that any additional resources will be of a magnitude large enough to have any substantial effect on youth problems. Further, preoccupation with supplemental funds distracts attention from examining effectiveness of programs already in place. Therefore, *any substantial progress in youth development and delinquency prevention must come from improvement in the use of resources already in place.* This can be accomplished only by systematic reallocation of funds and by realignment of programs in accordance with need and with appropriate goals. The managerial aspects of this process will now be analyzed.

Increasing capacity: a community approach to youth development and delinquency prevention

A major activity of the federal government in the new role just discussed is that of conducting research and demonstration efforts, evaluating results, and transferring findings and technology to general purpose government.

A promising approach to youth development and delinquency prevention, geared to the needs and practical possibilities of state and local general purpose government—known by the phrase, "capacity building for youth development"—was begun during the early 1970s under the auspices of the Department of Health, Education, and Welfare's Office of Youth Development.[72] The approach has four main elements: a tested strategy for youth development; a social institutional change perspective; a developing theory of coordination; and a transferable applied technology. Each of these elements will now be described and analyzed.

A tested strategy for youth development   This strategy sets forth a set of theoretical propositions which has been verified and validated through field testing in more than seventeen different communities using a population of more than ten thousand youth.[73] Based on this research, it is now possible to specify criteria, guidelines, and objectives which communities may use in planning for the implementation and administration of their efforts in the areas of youth development and delinquency prevention. There are three basic propositions involved. They concern access to roles; negative labeling; and alienation and commitment.

Access to roles   Many youths develop satisfactorily to assume productive places as adults (they don't get into trouble) because the society provides them an opportunity to perform tasks and to enter situations in which they are regarded by others, and regard themselves, as being useful, competent, belonging, and with some power over their immediate futures. This is known as having access to desirable social roles. It is having a stake in society, a reason to conform to society's laws.

Negative labeling   There are negative labeling processes in community institutions which systematically (and frequently for no very good reason) define some youth as undesirable, dangerous, deviant, unworthy, or crippled. Being black (or an Appalachian white), scoring low on an I.Q. test, being seen being put into a police car, going to court, and being nearsighted (and hence being bored at the back of the class) are all ways to get a negative label. Youth who get negative labels tend not to be regarded by others as useful, competent, or belonging. They come to regard themselves as useless, incompetent, and outside.

Alienation or commitment   The consequence of being negatively labeled and of having no access to desirable social roles is *alienation,* a state in which youth may perceive that they have to break rules in order to get ahead, that they are neither cared for nor supported by others, or that they are powerless (nothing they can do will change the situation). Such youth feel they have no stake in their community, no bonds. Delinquency, school dropout, truancy, and running away are some observable consequences. The reverse situation, perceived access to roles and positive labels, leads to a stake, or *commitment,* to some segment of the social order and conforming or prosocial behavior.

Validation of the strategy's propositions   The validity of these propositions has been tested in the course of developing the strategy. Considerable energy has been devoted to assuring that the propositions are more than nice-sounding claims, that they do, in fact, describe what happens to youth. The variables of the strategy—access to roles, labeling, and alienation—have been operationalized, and instruments have been developed to measure them. Data have been collected since 1973 in a number of locations. Analysis provides persuasive evidence of the validity of the strategy's propositions.[74] The results confirm the expected relationships: when access to roles, labeling, and alienation changed in favorable directions, the commission of delinquent acts was reduced. Even if the impact of this program has only touched the lives of a small fraction of the nation's youth, it is of sufficient managerial interest to warrant further discussion.

A social institutional change perspective A social institutional change perspective shifts the decision-making focus of attention from a sole concern with treatment of young persons who are troubled (or about to be in trouble) to a balanced concern for *intentionally guiding and directing change in social institutions*—particularly the social institutional contexts surrounding the world of work, traditional and alternative education processes, and the justice system (police, court intake, adjudicatory procedures, probation) as they influence the healthy development of *all* youth in the community. The following discussion breaks down like concern into an analysis of the significance of social institutions; of goals; and of programs.

Significance of social institutions Lack of access to desirable roles, negative labeling, and alienation are three obstacles to youth development. They have something important in common: each kind of trouble can hit youth who have done nothing to bring it upon themselves. This is because processes which produce the trouble are institutional; they are built into customary policies and practices of organizations with which youth come into contact regularly.

Youth may be able to hustle occasional jobs, but they cannot control most of the forces which make desirable work roles available to them. Nor do young people exercise much control over the processes which produce negative labeling. Access to desirable social roles and negative labeling are characteristics or attributes of social institutions, notably schools, work, the family, and the juvenile justice system. For many youth problems, the appropriate response is to change those institutions so as to increase access to desirable roles and to reduce negative labeling. This is not the only response which can help young people, but it is one which is often overlooked despite its promise of producing extraordinarily widespread benefit for modest additional expenditure of resources. It is this institutional response which should be attempted.

The game "In a certain high school in Chicago things start out at 7:15 in the morning. Students come to the old building always drowsey when they get their and sleepy when they leave. The drug problem is probably one of the worst in any school. The students have become so bold with marijuana they smoke it right in the school building. They also drop pills, gamble, and smoke cigarettes right in the assembly hall or the lunch room. You can go outside in the lunch hour, but then you risking your life because you in a dangerous neighbourhood, from the gangs that surround the school. You go home at the end of the classes. You feel tired, depressed, like you just going to school because your people wanted you out of the house in the morning. They start off teaching you something useful but as you stay around there for any length of time you find out that you don't learn nothing in school that you can learn more on the outside. The best thing about going to school is talking to all the girls that go there. It's pretty tuff when you're a black teenager trying to get out of high school. But for me that's life and I have to play the game . . ." (Source: Quoted in Richard Herbert and Erwin Pollack, "Inner-city education, a humanistic alternative," *Humanist*, March/April 1972, p. 22.)

Goals Knowing what it takes for young people to "turn out right"—a characterization fraught with difficulties, but nevertheless a useful one—and identifying prevalent obstacles in their paths are first steps in deciding what a youth development program should accomplish. The core propositions direct attention to likely problem areas in any community; they help answer the question, "What do young people need most?" Understanding the institutional processes which create obstacles helps planners to decide now to address those needs most effectively. The greater this kind of know-how is, the more useful the answer to the question, "How many young people will be helped and for how long?" The questions tell the planners and managers what areas to consider dealing with; institutional understanding tells how to deal with them. As in other human services areas, however, the danger of raising community expectations simply by asking questions about possible solutions must constantly be borne in mind.

Certain program outcomes may be judged as critically important. In order of their priority, they are:

1. A program of youth development should secure the general well-being of *all* youth as reflected in educational attainments, employment, access to leisure pursuits, good health, and participation in family and community life.
2. A program of youth development should help youth who are disabled or disadvantaged to resume (or assume) a satisfactory course of development. This goal covers efforts to help young persons get over drug and alcohol dependencies, recover from illness or malnutrition, and successfully adjust to physical handicaps.

As program goals go, the emphasis built into this set is far from typical. Currently, rehabilitation activity (that is, the second category just mentioned) receives the most attention in public programming for youth. It is clear that rehabilitative efforts are needed, but they should be planned and implemented within the context of a broader effort. Some young people need treatment and can benefit from it; a much larger number can benefit from changes in policies and practices which affect *all* youth.

3. A program of youth development should increase prosocial behavior and prevent juvenile delinquency, producing measurable change on at least three levels:
   a. Young people should commit fewer delinquent acts. This is primary prevention of delinquency. Typically, the actual number of delinquent acts committed will be several times greater than official delinquency rates. Looking first at self-reported delinquency rates gives a truer picture both of the condition of youth and of the cost of delinquency to the community.
   b. Rates of youth contact with law enforcement authorities and subsequent processing through the juvenile justice system should be reduced. This is secondary prevention of delinquency. It requires efforts over and above those aimed at cutting down the number of delinquent acts committed. Occasionally severe enforcement of the law is necessary. More often, resorting to the law is for sheer convenience; it is a quick, routine way to avoid dealing with a problem by turning a youth over to someone else. However, it always has some negative consequences. For many kinds of behavior now classified as juvenile offenses, resorting to the law may be an inappropriate response. This is especially true of status offenses, that is, acts which would not be offenses if committed by adults (truancy, possession of liquor, and runaways, for example).
   c. The rates at which youth who have had contact with the justice system repeat that contact should be reduced. Reduction of repeat contact—recidivism—is tertiary prevention of delinquency.

Programs   Programs designed to handle the emphasis just outlined are as uncommon as the emphasis itself. A program is simply any intervention intended to produce a particular desired outcome. Consider the several examples that follow. The first two are directed at changing individuals; the second two, services; the last two, institutions.

1. Some programs are intended to change the knowledge, skills, attitudes, perceptions, or physical and mental states of individual *youth*. Counseling, teaching, and therapy are examples.
2. Some programs are intended to change the knowledge, skills, attitudes, perceptions, or physical and mental states of individual *adults* who affect youth. Parent effectiveness training, sensitivity training, and teacher education are examples.
3. Some programs are intended to change the organization or operation of a service in order to make it more effective. Organizational development, introduction of new management techniques, and introduction of new service techniques are examples.
4. Some programs are intended to change the organization and operation of services in order to eliminate or limit their negative effects.
5. Some programs are intended to change community institutions such as education, juvenile justice, work, or recreation in order to eliminate their negative effects.
6. Some programs are intended to change community institutions in order to increase their capacity to promote positive youth development.

Most existing programs aim to change individual youth or adults or to increase the effectiveness of services. Programs intended to reduce the negative consequences of services are rare: it seldom occurs to well-intentioned persons that their programs could produce negative effects. Unfortunately, and frequently enough to warrant attention, some programs can and do have undesirable, albeit unintentional, poor outcomes.

Programs intended to change community institutions—such as education, work, or the juvenile justice system—are equally rare. Proposals to undertake such programs usually are dismissed with the statement, "We can't change the whole society." This statement misses the point; to improve youth development, no radical upheaval of society is needed or desired. With the use of proper tools to identify what actually needs to be altered, modest changes in community institutions will produce substantial gains.

Moreover, an institutional change approach creates lasting benefit for large numbers of youth. Most of the flaws in existing policies and practices which produce problems for youth are not isolated flukes. They are the consequences of integrated pieces of systems which process young people. As such, these flaws affect and are affected by other parts of the system. Trying to "rehabilitate" a selected group of teachers, policemen, or other service providers makes no more sense than trying to rehabilitate delinquents if the environment which produced their undesirable behavior in the first place is left unchanged.

Permanently changing their practices is impossible if outside pressures on them are left unchanged. No matter how much it might help youth, if behaving in a different way means going beyond the range of actions defined by their organization as permissible, hardly anyone will keep it up for long. And the organization itself is constrained also by forces in the environment in which it operates. Getting a school superintendent or welfare director to agree to an official policy change may temporarily support the workers in those organizations in new, more desirable behavior toward youth, but if heat from other parts of the system is too great, the change will be shortlived.

A developing theory of coordination A developing theory of coordination is no more than a set of propositions which may be used to make a "systems perspective" practical and useful to locally elected government officials and their appointed administrators. As of the later 1970s, that set of propositions is being tested. Currently, the theory can be used to describe and examine the elements of a community youth services system (including elements which should be, but are not, included). When fully operationalized and tested, the set of propositions may provide methods and procedures for prescribing changes in agency-agency relations which will permit improved management of interorganizational activities and resources in pursuit of community youth development objectives.

If there is one thing about any community that makes it different from all others it is the peculiar accidents in its historical development that have determined its unique political organization and structure. The composition of its citizenry, the geographic distribution of constituencies within its boundaries, the overlapping of various governmental entities which were established to solve certain kinds of problems (school districts, fire districts, water districts, etc.), what voters believe to be appropriate areas of concern, and a thousand other factors join to make a community unique.

If one believes this to be true of every American community, one cannot propose a specific organizational structure which will define the desirable relationships of all community agencies and organizations whose efforts are needed in the development of sound programming for youth development and delinquency prevention.

Having acknowledged that no two communities are the same, one can also notice that, in order to meet the needs of its citizens, various structures have evolved to provide support in solving various human problems. A number of elements can be identified which should be taken into consideration if one wishes to enchance opportunities for youth development. Each unit has an important stake in the effort. The following discussion touches on eight such elements: general purpose government; statutory agencies; the private sector; community youth programs; the policy advisory group; the technical support unit; the technical unit administration; and the technical unit manager. Methods of coordination are then outlined and discussed.

1. General purpose government   It is not possible to create a sound youth development-delinquency prevention program without the fullest involvement of the elected officials and appointed managers of local government.

Assuming that current trends continue, the responsibility of local officials—elected and appointed—for social policy and resource allocation will increase. Organizations seeking public funds will have to obtain them from the city councils, county commissioners, or state legislatures. The accounting for programming will be made to the general purpose government and the electorate.

2. Statutory agencies   The vast majority of public funds to support youth development flow to the community through programs conducted by public agencies legally required to provide services. Each agency has some kind of planning capability to analyze needs, set priorities, and evaluate its programs. Each agency also has distinctive purposes defined in laws or ordinances. Although there is much discussion about interagency cooperation or coordination, as has been pointed out in Chapter 8, little joint planning occurs.

One of the major problems inherent in building an interagency effort is that the policy-making authority frequently resides at different governmental levels for different agencies: the police are municipal, the welfare department and courts are either county or state. Schools are governed by local boards, but their accountability to any other local government official is, to put it kindly, problematic. Lack of a single authority to whom all agencies are accountable means that no one in the community can command coordination of all agencies; therefore, building a coordinated, integrated service delivery system must be a voluntary activity on the part of the agencies. Recognizing that the demands for efficiency and accountability will govern the distribution of revenue-sharing monies, these agencies appear to be increasingly more willing to cooperate, to subordinate their traditional desire for independence through agreements with policies decided by a policy board which can be fully supportive of the budgetary request that is submitted to the revenue sharing allocator.

One may handle the difference in authority and in policy making by the creation of formal and informal agreements signed by the mayor, county commissioners, or governor in which they agree to perform in a particular way, to coordinate and integrate planning and policy decisions.

Teens run center The North Suburban Youth Service Center in Coon Rapids, Minnesota, is directed principally by the young people involved in the program. The center serves youth from junior high school through college age in Coon Rapids and surrounding areas. Services include a bureau which finds jobs for teens, a free medical clinic, crisis intervention telephone line, and counseling on youth problems, drugs, etc. Although it is a city operation, it has no "establishment" connotation; the young people provide leadership in designing the programs. The city has entrusted the operation to a management board composed of young people and representatives of related agencies.

The family, too, might be included as a statutory social institution. The family is usually classified as a basic but informal social institution. Although the family is a private social institution, the duties of parents to their children and of children to parents are defined by statute. In the context of the present discussion, family is clearly the largest service provider to young children in the community. The statutory agencies usually serve young children through supporting the family unit. And without the stimulus of a normal, healthy, intra-family environment, many efforts at helping youth may well be doomed before they even begin.

3. Private sector The remaining input of resources to youth development and delinquency prevention efforts in any community are produced directly and indirectly by the private sector. Religious groups and United Fund agencies raise money and recruit volunteers to conduct youth programs and supporting services.

Business, industry, and labor unions donate dollars, encourage volunteerism, and as voters or representatives of advisory boards influence community social policy with respect to youth. Another key element is made up of representatives of business, industry, and labor who, as a part of the community economy, make policy decisions which influence the job-employment opportunities for young people.

The purposes of the private sector with respect to youth are governed by bylaws and personal or religious commitment rather than by statute, but its stake in youth development and delinquency prevention is no less real. The future employees, businessmen and businesswomen and members of congregations come from today's youth and are influenced on a daily basis by private sector decisions.

The youth peer group, another informal social institution, may well be placed above the private sector. The peer group relationships of youth can be problematic. Support for prosocial behavior and insulation from negative influences can be a consequence. Peer groups can also be a major influence in permitting and even demanding antisocial behavior as well. There are no bylaws or legal statutes for this informal institution which becomes more significant as family influence decreases during adolescence.

4. Community youth programs Every community has programs for its young people. Some programs, such as the welfare department's Aid to Dependent Children program are legal, public sector responsibilities. Others such as the Boy/Girl Scouts, YMCA, and Girls'/Boys' Clubs are supported by private donations. Some programs for youth are jointly funded by both public and private funds. The professional staffs, the volunteer workers, and the youth who participate or are served represent an additional element of importance. These programs are contact points where service and treatment programs connect with youth. Programs are the focal point for analysis and evaluation; they are the major source of accountability as an element of general purpose government's managerial capacity.

5. Policy advisory group In most communities, a general purpose government or its agencies has established advisory groups composed of appointed citizens as representatives of interested groups to provide citizen input to the governmental decision-making process. Federal legislation invariably requires the presence of client populations on advisory boards as well. Such groups may serve as a barometer of public opinion for elected officials. As such, they can play a critical role in strengthening the capacity of youth development and delinquency prevention programs if they are informed. Unfortunately, advisory groups may not have staff to provide basic information essential to give sound policy advice. If policy advisory group lacks staff or time to study issues themselves, their activities tend to rubber-stamp the suggestions of various public or private agency interest groups, thus providing only the illusion of democratic participation.

6. Technical support unit In every community's private and public sector agencies there are technical specialists who do research, plan and evaluate programs, prepare budgets, and advise policy makers. These expert personnel seldom are encouraged or provided the opportunity to work with technicians in other agencies on joint efforts in need and resource analysis, monitoring, or program evaluation.

Such information as they may offer to policy advisory groups can seldom be integrated with data from other agencies to provide a comprehensive view of problems or impact of programs in solving problems. The crux of capacity building for general purpose government may well be the creation of mechanisms which can facilitate joint activity on the part of these specialists so that a comprehensive approach can be undertaken.

7. Technical unit administration The primary purpose of composing the technical unit from the cadre of operating agency specialists in planning, budgeting, and evaluation is to avoid the creation of an additional bureaucratic layer in city, county, or state government. In most cases, these specialists will be well acquainted with each other. The performance of their day-to-day tasks requires them to engage in continuous informal consultation. For the welfare department to prepare its annual plan, information has to be solicited and assembled from the knowledgeable persons in the school system, the United Fund agencies, the police and health departments, and so on. Perhaps for reasons of bureaucratic politics, it is seldom the practice of such an agency to assemble all the experts from other agencies whose assistance is required in one place at one time. The information is gathered in a series of informal one-to-one personal meetings and phone calls. With proper structuring and support, the technical unit will provide a forum in which the experts can form a team around a comprehensive planning effort based on a common perspective. Experience suggests that this is more effective and satisfying than a planning processes based on a series of ad hoc informal connections, however viable the latter might be politically.

The cementing of the informal relationships among these technical experts accomplishes two major purposes. First, each agency's information about community needs and processes is best understood when interpreted by the technician who collected and assembled the data. Thus, the process of analyzing needs and resources is enhanced. Second, the ten to fifteen days per year required for the joint planning process for youth services broadens the knowledge base of each individual agency planner. Attendance at technical unit meetings provides the technicians with opportunities to exchange ideas and information which support their individual agency efforts in many areas only peripherally related to youth as a target group. Participation in the process is seen as supportive of rather than detracting from work efforts in the home agency.

8. Technical unit manager   Given the cooperation of public and private agency technical personnel, a small staff, usually a manager (coordinator, director) and a secretary, are required to facilitate the unit. The manager, in addition to having a good working knowledge of community organizations and local politics, should have a background in social research/program analysis and evaluation. No single educational background guarantees success in this complex managerial task. Teachers, probation caseworkers, social workers, public administration graduates, and sociologists all appear to have done a good job in the manager role. Those not specifically trained in planning have learned how to support the efforts of the unit. Those without a knowledge of social science research, sampling, automated data processing, and statistical analysis have found those skills available either among the experts in the technical unit or at nearby educational institutions.

In addition, the manager needs those organizational skills which permit the use of volunteers (e.g., League of Women Voters, Junior Chamber of Commerce) for survey efforts. This means the person must have the ability to communicate the ideas associated with the strategy for youth development and the youth service system approach to the lay public as well as to political officials and youth-serving agency personnel.

Methods of coordination   In most communities in recent years, there have been calls for coordination by the public, by lawmakers, by administrators, and by service providers and receivers (general aspects of this process have been discussed in Chapter 8). They all recognize that the network of organizations which already serve youth have a large untapped potential, that those organizations could be more effective, more efficient in their use of resources, more accessible, more capable of mounting combined programs, and more responsive to changing needs if they could be organized properly—if they could be "coordinated."

At the same time, there has been considerable confusion about what coordination is or what it means. For some, coordination means that organizations refer clients to each other for services. For others, it means that they share information and plan together. For still others, it means that the organizations work under some overall coherent policy which sets the main goals and assigns priorities to the various needs. There is equal confusion about the methods for obtaining coordination. For some, the method is to adopt uniform procedures for referring or budgeting or planning. To others, "If we could just get together and talk about it, we could work it out." There are numerous "models" for coordination which promise that, if everybody does it this way, it will all work out for the best.

It appears that—to put it kindly—the matter of relationships between organizations is quite complex. The policy level, the administration level, and the service level must all be considered. Procedural change may be needed. Organizations will have to plan together. Coordination is a continuous business for adjusting relationships so that they will do the work needed. Experimentation will be needed, but it should be more sophisticated than mere trial and error.

Professor Eugene Litwak of Columbia University has developed an approach which permits human services agencies to analyze the way in which they relate to each other.[75] A set of propositions about coordination of human services organizations has been derived from Litwak's research. Using these propositions, different aspects of the coordination problem can be measured and change over time can be measured. When the propositions are applied to a set of interorganizational relationships to describe the existing situation, analysis permits a researcher to suggest appropriate changes. Out of this comes a procedure which allows decision makers to be deliberately experimental in adjusting relationships, measuring, adjusting again—each time gaining more experience with the propositions and more knowledge about what works and what does not. No ''model'' is presented on a take-it-or-leave-it basis. Rather, the method lets decision makers take charge of coordination, know what the current situation is, how they have changed it, and how they can proceed from where they are at any given time.

The coordination propositions cover several main aspects of the setting in which organizations work and of their manner of relating with each other. The first consideration in the setting is *interdependence*—the degree to which organizations must take each other into account in order to accomplish their goals. Some cases of interdependence are crystal clear, as when there is a strong public demand for a program which will require two organizations to work together. They must take each other into account in order to satisfy their goals of satisfying the public. Other cases are not so clear, as when there is a group of youth who need a joint program which could be, but is not, provided by two organizations. Unless there is some way to notice that those youth are worse off for lack of the program, the interdependence between the organizations may never be noticed. Noticed or not, it still has consequences.

Listening to youth   In Bowie, Maryland a group of young people concerned about problems such as job opportunities for teens, bike paths, and recreational opportunities asked the city to establish an election process whereby teenagers could select their own representatives and have a clear channel into city council. City officials agreed. For six months, the young people worked on an organizational structure and drafted a council resolution to establish the system. The council passed the resolution. Nine young people were elected to a new youth advisory committee in an active election with thirty candidates in the running. The chairman of this committee occupies the nonvoting seat and is the teen advocate on the city council.

Organizations can be competitively or facilitatively interdependent. They are competitive if, to accomplish one organization's goals, another organization must be prevented from achieving its goals. They are facilitatively interdependent if neither organization can attain its goals without helping the other. Organizations which get funds from the same source, for example, are competitively interdependent with respect to the funds needed to attain the goal of preservation and growth of the organization. They may be competitive even though their announced service goals are in accord, and that competitiveness may be a barrier to the cooperation.

Interdependence is one aspect of the setting in which organizations operate. Other aspects are: (1) the degree to which they officially recognize their interdependence by taking steps, such as appointing liaison personnel or providing policies for coordination; (2) the degree to which the exchange between the organizations is standard, predictable, or routine, as opposed to nonroutine and unpredictable; (3) the volume of exchanges between them; and (4) the type of internal structure each of the organizations has (some are more formal and bureaucratic, some are more informal). Each of these characteristics of the setting makes a difference in how the organizations relate to each other. For example, one proposition says that the more standard, routine, and predictable the services being exchanged, the more formal rules and procedures there should be in order to make the exchange more efficient and to minimize dependence on the memory of the person who has the job but may leave. If the exchange is nonroutine, complex, and unpredictable, there should be fewer rules and the exchange should be handled by persons who can set precedents and commit the organization. This proposition may explain why many attempts at procedural coordination fail: standard forms and procedures don't work when matters are nonroutine and unpredictable.

Concerning the ways in which organizations relate to each other, the propositions deal with: (1) the degree to which the rules and formal procedures are used; (2) the level (rank) of the person who handles the exchange; (3) the type of occasion at which exchanges take place (board room or bar, for example); and (4) the type of communication which takes place (open, free exchange of information as opposed to guarded communication or communication used to win over the other organization). Different kinds of settings require different kinds of relations with respect to clients, money, planning, information, and staff exchanges.

A transferable applied technology Since 1973, a set of community-oriented research instruments and methods, based on the verified theory contained in the strategy for youth development, has been tested, modified, and made available for use. This technology, when combined with the three elements already described, may be used by communities to begin a process of planning, implementation, and evaluation which will permit a guided experimental approach of planned improvement in community youth development programs.[76] The following analysis outlines six elements of such a technology: the system description instrument; the youth needs survey; the community resources survey; impact scales; flow analysis; and social area analysis.

System description instrument [77] The theory of interorganizational relationships indicates that the atmosphere or setting in which organizations deal with one another determines the ideal ways of handling their relationships. The theory contains guidelines which look in turn at several dimensions of the setting. A high, average, or low rating on any dimension carries with it at least one recommendation for the most suitable manner of relating in that situation.

Items on the system description instrument are designed to describe relationships between organizations in enough detail to permit applying the theory. Responses yield information on several elements or dimensions of both setting and manner of relating. This situation permits comparing recommended ways of handling any given relationship with existing ways of relating and allows pinpointing specific areas where change appears desirable for greater effectiveness. This instrument is administered by interview to at least two representatives each of from ten to fifteen organizations with responsibility for serving youth (including schools, courts, police, welfare, and local government). The interviews last from one to one-and-one-half hours apiece.

Youth needs survey This instrument is designed to find out about youth's own perceptions of their needs. The core items are questions about potential needs and problems relating to school, employment, juvenile justice, recreation, and health. For a series of items about each sector, respondents are asked to indicate which ones are or are not problems. For those items which are seen as problems, respondents are asked to note their perceived seriousness and frequency. The instrument includes a section covering youth's perceptions of and experience with selected local services available to them. In addition, there are scales which measure perceived access to desirable roles, negative labeling, alienation, and self-reported delinquency. Demographic information is collected to permit assigning priorities to various needs by age, sex, ethnicity, and neighborhood. The instrument takes about an hour to administer. Ordinarily, it is given to an appropriately representative sample of about one thousand youth and administered in the schools. By using a representative sample, an accurate measurement of the perceptions of all youth in the area can be projected. Once again, the specter of unduly aroused expectations must be borne in mind.

Community resources survey The purpose of this instrument is to obtain information from major service providers on their budget allocations, policies, regulations, eligibility requirements, and habitual practices. Analyzing data collected with this instrument provides knowledge of what kinds of youth are receiving which services and under what conditions. In addition, one section deals with the question of how agency personnel perceive the needs of youth, using the same checklist as that in the youth needs survey described above. This permits comparison of agency and youth perceptions. The community resources survey is administered by mail with intensive follow-up. In a small community, every agency may be included; in a large city, a sample of fifty or so agencies may be used in the survey.

Impact sales   This instrument is specifically intended for evaluating youth-serving programs to determine whether being in a program results in increased access to desirable roles, in reduced negative labeling, in reduced alienation, and in reduced delinquent behavior. The instrument contains scales which measure each of these dimensions. It should be administered to both experimental and matched control groups at two or more points in time. By comparing changes in the youth in a program with changes in a similar group who receive no special attention, the effects of the program can be sorted out from changes experienced by others in the community. The instrument may be presented in either interview or questionnaire form, so long as every administration on a particular site is handled in the same manner. Each experimental and control group should consist of thirty subjects, at the very minimum.

Flow analysis   Intervention in a network of organizations that deal with young people should aim at points where decisions are made which have substantial impact on youth. Effective intervention requires examining the forces which govern decisions, and it requires knowing where in the system the crucial decision-making points are. Flow analysis is a means of keeping many such points in mind simultaneously and is especially useful when applied to more complex parts of the network. It is recommended particularly for the juvenile justice system. Inserting actual numbers of youth at each step in a diagram such as that illustrated in Figure 14–10 can help in deciding exactly where in the system a change can benefit the greatest number. Once a few high priority decision-making points are identified, the reasons for existing decisions at those points can be studied in depth. Knowing the extent to which they are following formal or informal local policy or are merely conforming to habitual practice is a first step in developing an effective intervention strategy.

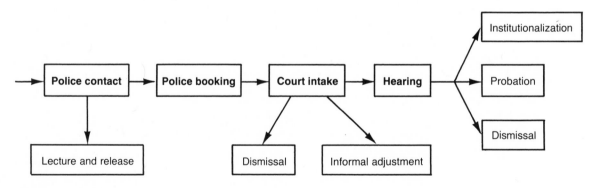

Figure 14–10 Flow diagram of the juvenile justice system. See text for further discussion.

Repeating the same kind of flow analysis at intervals following invention provides an ongoing measure of success. It is important to note that the interpretation of subsequent figures for evaluation purposes requires uncommon care—a matter touched on in Chapter 10.

Social area analysis   The information on youth needs and resources for meeting those needs becomes most meaningful when plotted on a map which characterizes the community in terms of various kinds of population characteristics as they are geographically distributed. A variety of techniques are available for classifying areas of a community through the analysis of census track data (see Chapter 5 for a full analysis of this topic). While indications are that changes occur slowly in communities, permitting us to use the decennial census data without fear of drastic error, it is clear that over a thirty-year period sufficient change can occur to generate dramatic disallocation of physical facilities for human services with respect to the location of the population at risk or in need of the service. A social mapping of population characteristics is essential for sound planning for youth development and delinquency prevention efforts.

Community implementation   Implementation of the National Strategy/Youth Service System management approach has been undertaken by cities, counties, and states with extremely different population sizes, geographic areas covered, and resource bases. While in most cases the sponsor or initiator of the effort has been a unit of general purpose government (mayor, city council, county board of supervisors, or state agency), there have been examples of private sector agencies (YMCA for example) or service programs which have taken the lead. No two communities have followed the same steps in implementation. However, all have sought to engage all of the elements described as essential components of a Youth Service System.

A case study: Burlington, Vermont   Burlington, Vermont, has a population of almost 40,000. When delinquency became a public issue in the summer of 1975, Mayor Gordon Paquette called a committee into being. After several months of discussion and a preliminary report to the city, the committee reformed itself as the Burlington Youth Council.[78] Its tasks were to look carefully at the full range of problems affecting youth and to begin a coordinated planning process. In order to do that, however, the council felt it was important to identify its long-term missions. As a result, four general purposes concerning youth development were agreed upon: increased access to desirable social roles among youth; reduced negative labeling by institutions and others; reduced alienation among youth; and reduced delinquent behavior.

In addition, the council developed a workable structure. A policy-making body also emerged, that is, decision makers and a technical resources group combining to provide technical help. Policy makers represent the following groups: school system, police, division of social services, United Community Services (UCS), Youth Opportunities Federation, city departments, board of aldermen, youth, and adult citizens.

Since early in 1976, the council's strategy has been to conduct systematic research in order to develop a comprehensive picture of youth needs and available resources. Although specific problems (such as vandalism, use of school facilities, housing problems, availability of recreation, and problems of access to jobs and social services) spurred the work, the council tried to develop a broad outlook. To do this, the council has:

1. Conducted a survey of youth in public and parochial junior and senior high schools;
2. Interviewed agency managers and workers to create a description of the system serving youth;
3. Requested information from the juvenile justice system concerning complaints and processes; and
4. Met with community groups to find out what resources are available to solve problems.

The council has also attempted to solicit the participation and cooperation of many groups interested in youth as a basis for future work and the sharing of resources.

The council views this research and this report as a beginning, a first concrete step toward citywide coordinated human services planning. The council believes that it can be a vital instrument which brings many independent systems together, building communication and joint action. Their rationale is: only together can we avoid duplication of services, misallocation of funds, and wasted effort; only together can we improve existing services and begin to deal with the social problems facing us.

The mayor's youth council made recommendations to the Burlington Board of Aldermen which fall into seven different categories: neighborhood development, family involvement, intervention with 14-to-16-year-olds, legal education, isolation of the court, recreation and jobs, and the role of the mayor's youth council. The final recommendation requested $1,000 for the continuation of the work of the council. The request was granted.

A case study: the Commonwealth of Pennsylvania   The Commonwealth of Pennsylvania, an early innovator in developing different approaches to the delivery of youth services, represents an example of state sponsorship of capacity building for youth development and delinquency prevention. In the early 1970s, as information on the national strategy and the youth service system approach became available, the Office of Children and Youth of the Department of Public Welfare—the state agency responsible for delinquency control—designed and implemented its own policy research effort to test the approach. In 1974, the Office of Children and Youth sought and received $800,000 from the state legislature to provide grants-in-aid to counties to initiate countywide youth service systems.

By the end of 1975, the office had established its own technical assistance capability to provide consultation and transfer of new knowledge and technology to counties that wished to experiment with new modes of youth services' organization. As part of the state technical assistance capability a contract for computer and automated data processing was let to the Educational Development Center. The center is affiliated with the Pennsylvania State Department of Education and Wilkes College, Wilkes-Barre. This contract provides counties with services to support the processing of data from the youth needs survey and other community planning and feedback instruments.

The problem orientation of the youth service system grant-in-aid programs clearly illustrates the extent to which traditional solutions to community youth problems are being questioned.

There are thus two specific problems on which the youth service system grant program requires that applicants place their primary focus:

1. *Fragmentation of services to youth.* There is general agreement among social scientists and those working in the field that a number of factors correlate highly with the occurrence of delinquency—factors such as low socioeconomic status, poor school record of achievement, high rates of joblessness, learning disabilities, multiple health problems, etc. These are all factors that decrease the capacity of normal social agents within our communities to help youngsters in need—and it is this community breakdown that has lead to an over-representation of youngsters from these backgrounds within the juvenile justice system.

The manner in which youngsters in need are (or are not) served by communities' agencies has a significant impact on their futures. It is also held that a youth service system established at the local level can have a significant impact toward developing the needed community services and strengths, by mobilizing the various youth-serving agencies to eliminate the duplication of their efforts and their unhealthy competition.

2. *Excessive reliance on the juvenile justice system.* Nearly all youngsters engage in certain kinds of behavior that is illegal at some time during their youth, especially in their teenage years. Only about 3 percent of these youngsters actually come before the juvenile court each year, although twice as many youth come to the attention of the police.[79]

The juvenile justice system in Pennsylvania is thus much more than a passive recipient of delinquent children. It is focused to make thousands of decisions each week regarding who will and who will not be processed through that system.

At the same time, studies clearly indicate that the more seriously involved the justice system becomes with a youngster, the better are that youngster's chances of becoming an adult offender.

The youth service system project proposes, therefore, that local communities become involved in systematic efforts to divert youngsters in trouble *to* appropriate services in their communities and *away* from the juvenile justice system (whose efforts should be reserved for cases involving direct and serious danger to that community). The standards applying to the grants-in-aid program include:

1. Willingness of a community to establish legislation creating a youth service system.
2. Willingness to provide a minimum 10 percent matching funds the first year and an increasing percentage thereafter to a maximum of 50 percent after three years. Of course, refunding will be based on program effectiveness, continued need, and availability of funds and expenditures from local funds shall not be decreased by reason of the grant.
3. Programs must provide linkages to appropriate community resources such as legal services, police, schools, child welfare, juvenile court, juvenile probation, MH/MR, private child caring agencies, government officials, LEAA, etc.

At the local level, the youth service system is an effort to coordinate and integrate the youth service functions of (at a minimum) the thirteen following groups and agencies: county commissioners; county juvenile court; county child welfare agencies; county juvenile detention home; county juvenile probation officer; mental health/mental retardation program (at both community and base service unit levels); county board of public assistance; local school districts within the county; local police jurisdictions within the county; public and private human services agencies within the county; leaders of other political subdivisions within the county (mayors, borough managers, township supervisors, city counselors, etc.); regional offices of the public welfare department and the governor's Justice Commission that service the county; and local citizen groups involved in issues affecting children and youth.

It should be clearly stated in the proposal introduction, then, the extent to which the applicant can (and cannot) speak for the agencies and group leaders above. Since the youth service system is an effort at service integration for children and youth at the local level, the major task of any proposed program will be to develop communication, coordination, and integration among these agencies and groups. A major criterion for funding consideration of the department, therefore, is the extent to which the applicant is judged to be in a position to successfully reach toward the service integration objectives of the department's grant-in-aid program.

Counties supported by the youth service system grant-in-aid program have included Erie, Beaver, Clearfield, Lycoming, Centre, Bucks, and Lehigh/Northampton.

Other states A similar approach at the state level is underway in the state of Iowa under joint sponsorship of the governor's Office for Programming and Planning and the Iowa Crime Commission. It involves capacity building in four communities and a statewide youth needs survey in sixty schools. The state of New

York, under sponsorship of the New York State Division for Youth (five counties, including Rochester, New York), and Montana, under a joint cooperative agreement between the department of social and rehabilitation services and the Montana State Board of Crime Control, are also undertaking similar approaches.

A case study: Oakland, California Oakland, California, has a population of about 340,000. The capacity-building process in Oakland demonstrates a different approach for the development of a youth service system. Oakland's effort began in 1974 with a special youth manpower project—the Oakland Youth Work Experience Program.[80] This program was designed to provide six months of special vocational counseling, educational remediation skill training, and on-the-job work experience for two hundred youth between the ages of 16 and 18 years. During the initial stages of program development, the sponsor proposed that the elements of the national strategy for youth development and delinquency prevention be accepted as the criteria for guiding the program and the evaluation of its impact. Because of the large minority population in Oakland and the desire of sponsors to have a proportionally representative group of youth in the program, it was necessary to involve all of the private sector organizations which represented neighborhood groups in the recruitment process. The organizations became a special kind of youth service system policy advisory board. The board advised the program director on all aspects of the program from recruitment to program evaluation.

In order to mobilize and integrate the resources necessary to support the youth manpower training, full involvement of the city and county public agencies was needed. Representatives from the school district, the probation and police departments, public health, welfare, and the state department of employment formed a technical resources council to advise the policy advisory group.

Both committees determined that the application of the community planning and feedback instruments would enhance their ability to strengthen the data base for comprehensive planning for all organizations and agencies involved. When the special demonstration effort for the two hundred youth was completed in the spring of 1976, the group continued its activities by expanding the membership of the technical advisory group.

When funds became available to develop a series of neighborhood centers for Oakland youth, the technical unit changed its name to the Technical Advisory Council Interagency Group. The unit then divided into a CETA program task force and a coordinated youth services task force and expanded its responsibility to advise both the Manpower Advisory Board and the Oakland City Council.

Staffed by personnel from the city of Oakland's Department of Manpower Development, the technical advisory council has full responsibility for comprehensive planning of youth services (including manpower programs), monitors and evaluates youth services delivered by both public and private agencies, and approves allocations for youth service agencies in Oakland.

It is important to note that Oakland has clearly delineated the functions of planning and management of youth services from implementation and service delivery functions. The youth service system approach calls for a separation of responsibility for these two different important functions. The Youth Service Bureau model approach to the management of community youth services, the only model available since the late 1960s and early 1970s, failed to make this differentiation. Lacking a theory as well as a structure, YSBs consistently became engaged in the direct delivery of services to the detriment of their planning and management functions.[81]

Conclusion

The national strategy–youth service system approach to the management of community youth resources is being used by enough political jurisdictions and different levels of local government to suggest that it is no longer simply a pilot or demon-onstration model. Good comprehensive planning is always experimental. It is always based on designing and implementing/evaluating and correcting. The approach described here is no exception. Elected officials of city, county, and state government will recognize that the approach is complex and difficult. They will also recognize that simple solutions to youth problems proposed and implemented in the past have not been able to keep up with rapid changes in community conditions. It is doubtful that simple solutions will work in the future.

The theories which compose the national strategy are inadequate and cannot fully explain all youth problems. More research is required to fill out our understanding of cause and effect relationships. The elementary propositions of a theory of coordination require addition of new insights from research in the rapidly developing field of complex organizational behavior.

The major advances in our knowledge and skill in managing community resources for youth are most likely to be achieved by continuing to strengthen and expand the capability of local general purpose government. The answers will be found in our local communities.

1 Michael J. Austin, "A Network of Help for England's Elderly," *Social Work* 21, (March 1976): 114–19.

2 Unless otherwise noted, statistical material is drawn from: U.S., Department of Commerce, Bureau of the Census, *Demographic Aspects of Aging and the Older Population in the United States,* by Jacob S. Siegel, Special Studies, Series P-23, Number 59, May 1976, 68 pp.

3 Ibid., p. 23.

4 Leon A. Pastalan, Robert K. Mautz II, and John Merrill, "The Simulation of Age-Related Sensory Losses: A New Approach to the Study of Environmental Barriers," in *Environmental Design Research,* ed. Wolfgang F. E. Preiser, Community Development Series, vol. 1 (Stroudsburg, Pa.: Dowden, Hutchinson and Ross, 1973), p. 383–92.

5 Robert N. Butler, *Why Survive? Being Old in America,* (New York: Harper & Row, 1975), p. 24.

6 Ibid.

7 U.S., Department of Health, Education, and Welfare, Office of Human Development, Administration on Aging, National Clearing House on Aging, *Older Americans 1975,* DHEW Publication Number (OHD) 75-20006.

8 U.S., Congress, House, Subcommittee on Health and Long-Term Care, Select Committee on Aging, *Elderly Health Needs and Services in Tennessee,* 94th Cong., 2nd Sess. 1976, p. 154.

9 DHEW Publication Number (OHD) 75-20006.

10 U.S., Congress, House, Subcommittee on Health and Long-Term Care, *Health Needs,* p. 155.

11 DHEW Publication Number (OHD) 75-20006.

12 Ibid.

13 U.S., Congress, House, Committee on Government Operations, *Housing for the Elderly: The Federal Response,* House Report Number 94-376, 94th Cong., 1st Sess., 1975, p. 3.

14 Michigan State Housing Development Authority, "Housing for the Elderly Development Process," 1976.

15 Philip J. Rutledge, "Can Local Government Afford Not to Pay the Price?," *Public Management,* November 1975, p. 4.

16 International City Management Association, *The 1975 Municipal Year Book* (Washington, D.C.: International City Management Association, 1975), pp. 154–55.

17 Joint Center for Political Studies, "Black Political Participation: A Look at the Numbers," Washington, D.C., December 1975, Figures III and IV.

18 U.S., Commission on Civil Rights, *Racism in America and How To Combat It* (Washington, D.C.: Government Printing Office, 1970), pp. 5–6.

19 For a provocative discussion of the relationship between power and responsibility, see Rollo May, *Power and Innocence* (New York: W. W. Norton Co., 1972).

20 White as well as black administrators may feel a sense of "liberation" in combating oppression and actively discouraging racism. For an elaboration of the concept of "white consciousness," see Robert W. Terry, *For Whites Only* (Grand Rapids, Mich.: Wm. B. Eerdmans Publishing Co., 1970).

21 For an excellent discussion of the roles and problems encountered by minority administrators, see Adam W. Herbert, "The Minority Administrator: Prospects and Challenges," *Public Administration Review* 34 (November/December 1974): 556–63.

22 U.S., Commission on Civil Rights, "The Other Side of the Tracks: A Handbook on Nondiscrimination in Municipal Services," Clearinghouse Publication 49, Washington, D.C., September 1974, pp. 3–4. The summary of the law is drawn from the holdings in two cases: Hawkins v. Town of Shaw, 437 F. 2d 1286 (5th Cir. 1971) *aff'd en banc,* 461 F. 2d 1171 (1972); and Beal v. Lindsay, 468 F. 2d 287 (2d Cir. 1972), commented on in 51 Texas L. Rev. 1247 (1973).

23 S. M. Miller, Pamela Roby, and Alwine A. de Vos van Steenwijk, "Creaming the Poor," *Transaction,* June 1970, pp. 38–45.

24 For analyses of the consequences of exclusion from participation in decision making, see William H. Grier and Price M. Cobbs, *Black Rape* (New York: Bantam Books, 1968); Paulo Freire, *Pedagogy of the Oppressed* (New York: Seabury Press, 1974); and Frantz Fanon, *The Wretched of the Earth* (New York: Grove Press, 1968).

25 "Affirmative Action—What It Is," memorandum from John L. Taylor, City Manager, city of Berkeley, California, to all city employees, 18 September 1974.

26 For an elaboration of this concept, see Erich Fromm, *The Revolution of Hope: Toward a Humanized Technology* (New York: Harper & Row, 1968).

27 Extracted and summarized from "Human Relations: A Function Definition for Local Government," paper prepared by the Southern California Association of Human Relations Directors, March 1975.

28 For further details, see the following monograph and reports, prepared by the Kansas City, Missouri, Department of Human Relations: "Human Relations Monograph No. 1: Overview," 1971; "Three Year Report: The Quality of Urban Life," 1971; and "Annual Report, 1971–1972."

29 Fred Cloud and Gerald Donaldson, "Human Relations Commissions as Social Change Agents," paper presented at the annual conference of the National Association of Human Rights Workers, Portland, Oregon, October 1975.

30 Ibid., p. 3.

31 Jack Bullard, "Classification For Local Human Relations Work," paper presented at a meeting of the North Carolina Association of Human Relations Officials, July 1976, p. i.

32 For further general discussion, see William H. Gilbert, ed., *Public Relations in Local Government* (Washington, D.C.: International City Management Association, 1975).

33 Bullard, "Classification for Local Human Relations Work." The classification scheme developed further posits "the use of various measurements to evaluate the processes used by human relations agencies." These measurements include quantity of time expended, effectiveness rankings according to an established scale, efficiency assessments, results obtained, and clients served.

34 Galen Martin, "New Civil Rights Act Coverages—Progress or Racism?," *The Journal of Intergroup Relations* 4 (April 1976): 14–37.

35 J. Richard Aronson and Eli Schwartz, "The Outlook," in *Management Policies in Local Government Finance* (Washington, D.C.: International City Management Association, 1975), p. 331.

36 Bernard J. Frieden, *Housing in America: 1976,* Working Paper no. 274 (Berkeley, Calif.: University of California, Institute of Urban and Regional Development, December 1976), p. 1.

37 Ibid., p. 12.

38 Ibid., p. 2.

39 Ibid., p. 17.

40 United States v. Certain Land in the City of Louisville, Jefferson County, Kentucky, 78 F. 2d 648, cert. granted 269 U.S. 567, appeal dismissed 297 U.S. 726 (1935).

41 Frieden, *Housing in America: 1976,* p. 1.

42 For further discussion of the programs of the 1960s, see Bernard J. Frieden and Marshall Kaplan, *The Politics of Neglect: Urban Aid from Model Cities to Revenue Sharing* (Cambridge, Mass.: M.I.T. Press, 1975).

43 U.S., Department of Housing and Urban Development, *Housing in the Seventies: A Report of the National Housing Policy Review.* Washington, D.C., 1974. This report, though it will inevitably become dated with the passage of time, is a comprehensive review of housing policies. It provides an excellent summary of the federal role in housing.

44 Frieden, *Housing in America: 1976,* p. 10.

45 International City Management Association, "Supplement no. 1: update," *Newsletter,* 17 January 1977.

46 Department of Health, Education, and Welfare, *Housing in the Seventies,* p. 5.

47 Frieden, *Housing in America: 1976,* p. 9.

48 Ibid., p. 11.

49 Jones v. Mayer, 392 U.S. 409 (1968).

50 Bernard J. Frieden and Marshall Kaplan, *Community Development and the Model Cities Legacy,* Working Paper no. 42 (Cambridge, Mass.: Joint Center for Urban Studies of the Massachusetts Institute of Technology and Harvard University, November 1976), p. 4.

51 Department of Health, Education, and Welfare, *Housing in the Seventies,* p. 167.

52 Ibid., p. 124.

53 Urban League of Greater New Brunswick v. the Borough of Carteret, Superior Court, Middlesex County, New Jersey, Chan. Div. No. C-4122-73, 4 May 1976.

54 "New Housing Program Found Costlier," *Washington Post,* 13 June 1976.

55 Housing and Urban Development Act of 1969, Sec. 213(a).

56 Hills v. Gautreaux, No. 74-1047, 20 April 1976.

57 Uniform Relocation Assistance and Real Property Acquisition Policy Act (PL 91-646).

58 For more detailed information on the Housing Assistance Plan, see 24 C.F.R. 570.303(c).

59 National Association of Regional Councils, *Straight Talk About Housing Your Region* (Washington, D.C.: National Association of Regional Councils, August 1973), p. 18.

60 Urban League of Greater New Brunswick v. Carteret.

61 U.S., Department of Housing and Urban Development, *Horizons on Display A Catalogue of Community Achievement* (Washington, D.C.: Government Printing Office, 1976), p. 29.

62 Ibid., p. 25.

63 Some preliminary reports can be found in the "1976 Report on National Growth and Development: The Changing Issues for National Growth," Washington, D.C., February 1976, pp. 111–12; and James A. Kushner and W. Dennis Keating, "The Kansas City Housing Allowance Experience: Subsidies for the Real Estate Industry and Palliative for the Poor," *Urban Lawyer* 7 (Spring 1975).

64 Michael C. Dixon and William E. Wright, *Juvenile Delinquency Prevention Programs: Report on the Findings of an Evaluation of the Literature* (Washington, D.C.: National Science Foundation, n.d.), pp. 11–37; and Comptroller General of the United States, *How Federal Efforts to Coordinate Programs to Mitigate Juvenile Delinquency Proved Ineffective,* Document No. GGD-75-76, 21 April 1975.

65 In 1970, the Office of Youth Development was called the Youth Development and Delinquency Prevention Administration.

66 *Delinquency Prevention Reporter,* Youth Development and Delinquency Prevention Administration, Social and Rehabilitation Service, Department of Health, Education, and Welfare, Washington, D.C.: "National Strategy to Prevent Delinquency," January 1971, pp. 1–2; and "Youth Services Systems," July–August 1972, pp. 1–7.

67 *National Evaluation of Youth Service Systems—FY74,* Behavioral Research and Evaluation Corporation, Boulder, Colorado, for the Office of Youth Development, Department of Health, Education, and Welfare, July 1974; and *Community Planning and Feedback Research,* Vols. 2–11, Behavioral Research and Evaluation Corporation, Boulder, Colorado, for the Office of Youth Development, Department of Health, Education, and Welfare, September 1975.

68 Charleston, South Carolina; Jefferson County, Colorado; Providence, Rhode Island; Savannah, Georgia; and Tacoma, Washington.

69 Oakland, California; Dubuque and Emmetsburg, Iowa.

70 Spokane, Washington; Jamestown, North Dakota; Jefferson County, Adair County, and Wayne County, Kentucky; Delaware County, Pennsylvania; Rochester, New York; Burlington and Winooski, Vermont; Orlando, Florida; Council Bluffs, Iowa City, Fort Dodge, and Mason City, Iowa; and a statewide needs survey of sixty schools in Iowa.

71 "Human Development/Social Service Program Memorandum: I. General Considerations," Department of Health, Education, and Welfare, n.d., pp. 2–8 (mimeographed).

72 *Delinquency Prevention Reporter*.

73 Behavioral Research and Evaluation Corporation, July 1974 and September 1975.

74 Delbert S. Elliott and Fletcher Blanchard, "An Impact Study of Two Diversion Projects," paper presented at the American Psychological Association Convention, Chicago, 1975; and Delbert S. Elliott et al., "The Long and Short Term Impact of Diversion Programs," Behavioral Research and Evaluation Corporation, Boulder, Colorado, April 1976.

75 Eugene Litwak, "Towards the Multi-Factor Theory and Practice of Linkages Between Formal Organizations," Final Report, for the Department of Health, Education, and Welfare, Social and Rehabilitation Services, June 1970. The propositions have been developed into a survey instrument for use by youth service agencies: Grant Johnson, "System Description: Analyzing Interorganizational Relationships," Bureau of Sociological Research, University of Colorado, Boulder, Colorado, 1974.

76 These materials were developed by the Behavioral Research and Evaluation Corporation (BREC), Boulder, Colorado, under contract with the Office of Youth Development (OYD), Department of Health, Education, and Welfare. More detailed descriptions (scale characteristics, reliability, homogeneity ratios, etc.) can be obtained frmm BREC or OYD.

77 Ibid.

78 Excerpted from "What About Kids? Youth Development in the City of Burlington," report of the Mayor's Youth Council Youth Development Project, Burlington, Vt., 26 July 1976.

79 Excerpted from "Policies and Procedures for Grants-in-Aid, Delinquency Control Programs for Juveniles," Office of Children and Youth, Department of Public Welfare Harrisburg, Penn., March 1975.

80 The program was sponsored by the city of Oakland's Department of Manpower Development, and utilized U.S. Department of Labor funds under contract to the National Office for Social Responsibility, Arlington, Virginia.

81 See "The Challenge of Youth Service Bureaus," a national study of 195 youth service bureaus, Department of the California Youth Authority, Social and Rehabilitation Services, Department of Health, Education, and Welfare, Washington, D.C., November 1972. For more information, see Sherwood Norman, *The Youth Service Bureau: A Key to Delinquency Prevention* (National Council on Crime and Delinquency: Paramus, N.J., 1972).

The human services dimension in traditional local government functions

The specific programs in the human services field discussed in the previous three chapters have naturally focused attention on individual currents within the stream of goods and services provided by local governments to their citizens. Although the management of such programs may well have involved complex working relationships with other levels of government and with the private sector, the express intention has been to flesh out the specifics of planning, operation, and evaluation from the managerial perspective. The remaining chapters in this book, however, aim at rounding off that discussion by analyzing human services functions in the context of the mainstream of local government activity. The chapter immediately following will take up the theme of services integration in the human services field. The present chapter will take a close look at the human services dimension in traditional local government functions.

The chapter is divided into three portions. The first section considers the important human services element in some illustrative areas of the policy-making and managerial process that cut across operating department lines. It touches on some of the human services aspects of discussions regarding the services package provided for citizens and also on the deployment of resources. Topics outlined include the question of equity in service delivery; the annual budget process; local government employment; and public information activities and programs.

The second, and core, section of the chapter attempts to identify some of the key areas of human services activity in operating departments, as in such areas as the police function, community development, recreation, and code enforcement. The third and final section discusses some aspects of the training function insofar as it impinges on human services activities of the type described. The chapter ends with a brief evaluative conclusion.

It is hoped that the examination carried out in this chapter will be useful to the writer's colleagues in professional local government management in two ways. First, it is generally recognized that, with the continuing fiscal difficulties of the 1970s, more efficient use of existing resources may well prove a basic managerial imperative. For those concerned with human services functions, it is important to recognize that traditional activities of local government can indeed have a vital and productive human services dimension. Secondly, it may be noted that local government human services functions are often viewed as requiring some kind of separate administrative personality or expression. Managers will be aware that it is always difficult to give organizational expression to newer service areas within an established system, the more so in times of fiscal stringency. It is hoped that this chapter's emphasis on the best use of existing resources may help, in appropriate cases, to smooth the path for the varying new forms of human services departmental organization.

The role of human services in the policy-making and managerial process

The human services element has a role to play in the deliberations of the local government legislative body as its members decide what services are to be provided, what service levels are to be maintained, and how human services "input" is related to "achievement." Managers and their staffs, too, need to be aware of this human services dimension. The following discussion outlines some of these topics in terms of two decisions that have to be made regarding the services package, the first relating to service delivery and the second to the role of the budgetary process in the deployment of resources.

Decisions regarding the services package: delivery of services

Input and equity   Traditionally, the delivery of municipal services has been organized and evaluated on an "input" basis. Over and above legal requirements, administrators and policy makers have long been most comfortable with a system which was based on the provision of similar amounts of any service to each citizen or group of citizens. A great deal of care has been taken to ensure equal treatment to all, particularly in the delivery of the traditional—and basically physical—services. Equal treatment has most often been defined in terms of equal expenditures for the same service in all neighborhoods or areas of the community. Service activities such as refuse collection and road maintenance traditionally have been designed, staffed, and performed with the assumption that each taxpayer is entitled to the same level of service as every other.

Years of experience has shown that this approach was relatively uncontroversial for two reasons. First, the physical nature of the services provided was such that they could be easily quantified and distributed accordingly. Data could be accumulated showing the number of dollars spent per mile of road or the number of park areas per 1,000 population. Justifications for existing service patterns so developed are generally easy to understand and accept for policy makers and citizens alike.

Second, the concept of equality of services—based on the "equal input per unit" definition—has been generally acceptable to the majority of citizens. *Perceived* inequality in service provision among the various members of the community has historically roused citizens to a greater extent than *actual* low, but equal, levels of service.

The example of education   This approach has been particularly noticeable in the area of public education. Until recently, the prime concern of policy makers, educators, and taxpayers alike was in equalizing input, and considerable efforts were made to quantify the value of the input. As part of this, school districts compared costs per pupil, pupil/teacher ratios, ages of buildings, etc. The parents of students attending the oldest school building have then sometimes felt that their children's education has suffered because of the age of the facility. The underlying assumption of a direct relationship between dollars expended and quality of education has undoubtedly caused some of the all too frequent and expensive competition between towns and school districts to have the newest buildings or largest budgets.

Since the 1960s, however, increasing emphasis has also been placed on the recognition that the ability of children to learn varies considerably from child to child. It is generally accepted that an educational program which is perfect for one child may be completely wrong for another. The trend among educators is, as a result, to spend more time evaluating the individual abilities of different children and designing different educational programs to match those abilities. Local government decision makers are therefore beginning to judge school systems on their effectiveness in meeting this variety of needs, that is, the equity of output—in this case, the maximization of skill development—rather than the equity of input.

The example of the police patrol   Another municipal service which serves as an excellent example of the difference between equal and equitable delivery of service is the police patrol. At one time, some municipalities operated on the basis of designing the patrol system so that cruisers covered each area of town with equal frequency. However, as more emphasis has been placed on police patrol as a crime prevention rather than an enforcement or apprehension activity, different criteria for judging the effectiveness of service delivery evolved. The modern police administrator analyzes the incidence of crime in relation to such items as time of day, day of the week, and section or area of town. Based on this information, the patrol input is varied to control crime during the hours and location of greatest incidence in hopes of reducing the overall rate. Thus, measuring the effectiveness of patrol involves measuring its output i.e., reduction of crime incidence rather than measuring input (i.e., hours, frequency, and/or miles of patrol). If the objective of the service delivery system is to achieve an equitable delivery of police patrol services, input must be adjusted to achieve the desired output.

Lessons for human services If a local government is to respond to human services needs, understanding the ''equitable delivery of service'' concept is crucial. The very nature of such programs means that they are designed to meet the particular needs of different individuals.

Most governments today, for example, are providing programs specifically designed to meet the needs of older citizens. In doing so, we have recognized that there are certain specific factors—increased leisure time, declining health, limited income, loneliness, etc.—which require special attention to this group of citizens. Whether these programs involve tax relief, more intensive health services, transportation, or social activities, they should be specifically designed to meet the unique needs of the participants. Few, if any, would argue that the goal of equitable service delivery demands that we put the same hours or dollars into providing the same services for each identifiable group in the community.

Matchmaker Haverford Township, Pennsylvania, has started a temporary help bureau to match teenagers and senior citizens with available jobs, both full- and part-time. The service is staffed by twenty-five volunteers operating from an office provided for them in the municipal building. The township also picks up overhead expenses, such as stationery, telephones, and the like. During one year, the service placed almost 900 job seekers.

The programs described earlier in this book are designed to meet the needs of select groups of people who have been identified as having needs which are different from those of others. Meeting those needs obviously will require a different level of input for each. Further, the delivery of human services is often done in a decentralized manner. Such services may well be concentrated in the more densely populated neighborhoods where we often find concentrations of poorer citizens. Historically, we can find many instances where the level of municipal services was considerably *lower* in poorer neighborhoods than in more affluent areas within the same municipality. A combination of factors—a more transient population with less political influence, a lack of understanding of the services available, and so on—produced this situation. In any human services delivery system, however, an opposite orientation is required: the design must specifically include recognition of the need for maximum impact in the poorer neighborhoods.

There are two reasons for this. First of all, the well-known stresses placed on families and individuals who live in crowded lower income areas must be considered. They are often reflected in a broad group of unmet human services needs. Better housing is needed to combat overcrowding and unsanitary conditions. Better health care is needed to combat inadequate diets and medical attention. More intensive education programs are needed to combat illiteracy and low motivation. More youth activities are needed to occupy children from single-parent families with a great deal of leisure time. More recreational programs are needed where crowded conditions do not provide space for informal activities as in less crowded areas. More help is needed for those who succumb to alcoholism or drug addiction. Let us hasten to recognize that any of these problems may exist in any neighborhood or income group. Certainly symptoms such as alcoholism, drug addiction, and low educational motivation are found in all geographic areas and at all income levels. However, many more families with a combination of unmet needs are found in lower income areas. They, and their communities, have become much more activist in seeking to resolve those needs (often perceived as a result of historical injustices) in recent decades.

Secondly, residents of higher income areas, of course, can better afford private services or treatment of such problems. Coupled with a much greater reluctance to publicly acknowledge the need for such remedial measures, this results in lower utilization of such services among the middle and upper income population.

Summary   The impact of all of this on local government decision makers is that, as human service programs are initiated and provided, a commitment to the concept of equitable delivery of service means that more service input will be required to meet the same standards in the more crowded, lower income neighborhoods. The implications of this on the development of public policy should not be underestimated.

Decisions regarding the services package: annual budget process

The annual budget process is another broad policy area which will be substantially affected as a municipality or other local government becomes more and more involved in meeting human services needs. This will be felt in two ways. First, in order for the process to be responsive to the human services needs of the community, more citizen participation will be necessary. Second, assuming that few jurisdictions will find themselves able to fund the programs necessary to meet all the needs of the community, the budget process will be fraught with competition between interest groups advocating one program over another.

Group advocacy and the budget process   It is, of course, true that the budget process has always been subject to competition—even before human services programs were involved. Nevertheless, the addition of the human services dimension makes the competition more intense. One reason for this is that, as has been noted, over the years certain accepted measures for evaluating traditional local government services delivery have developed. Therefore, the budgetary competition has, by and large, occurred between tacit limits which were generally accepted by the competitors. One could argue over how much road resurfacing should be undertaken or which roads should be resurfaced first, but certain factors such as the cost per mile and personnel and equipment requirements were well-established. Once the political compromises were made regarding areas to be covered and amount of money to be expended, the rest of the discussion was relatively routine. In addition, most people—taxpayers and policy makers included—had a good understanding of the needs and benefits under discussion.

The lack of agreed measures   In the human services area, however, the discussion is not usually limited to commonly accepted physical needs and programs. Many such programs are relatively new and, to a large extent, somewhat experimental. Methods to achieve certain results are not standardized nor do the programs lend themselves to any accepted statistical quantification. In the example of road resurfacing, the debate centered around "how much?" and "where?". In the human services arena, "how?" and "by whom?" become just as much at issue, thus increasing the strain on the usual methods of political compromise.

We have all seen examples of this in the budget process of the public education system in recent years. Here, the annual budget process recently has been subjected to competition between various interest groups with virtually no common ground that could serve as the basis for compromise. Most important, the average taxpayer could not understand what the participants were competing for, what the benefits of a particular program would be, or what the effect of not providing the program would be. As a result, numerous education budgets with even relatively small increases (less than the rate of inflation) have been rejected by the voters.

Summary The more local governments venture into human services programs, the more such budgetary experiences will occur unless reliable and accepted ways to evaluate program results are established. There must be developed some measures which can serve as a basis for the political compromises necessary to the completion of the budget process. The budget and evaluation processes are discussed in detail in Chapters 9 and 10 of this book.

There is no question, therefore, that attempts to respond to human services needs in a jurisdiction will have a significant effect on the annual budget process. Whether this effect is one of generating more controversy or of responding to the human services needs will depend to a great extent on the ability of managers to develop understandable and accepted measures of both human services needs and program benefits. The competition for budgeted funds can then take place within limits that are understood by all of the participants in the process.

Local government employment policies

Employment is another traditional function of local government which will be substantially affected by attempts to respond to human services needs. Much has been written in this book and elsewhere about the need to open up municipal, county, and other local government employment to women and minorities in order to counteract past discrimination. Many state and federal laws and regulations prescribe specific plans for recruitment, selection, training, and promotion of minorities designed to make local government employees as a group representative of the population they serve.

In addition to reversing the effects of past discrimination, if a government is to command a position of understanding and responsiveness to a broad cross section of human services needs, the recruitment of people who can relate to these needs is crucial. The impact of any particular human services program on an individual or family is usually determined by three elements: confidence in dealing with the case worker or other officials; perceptions of the employees themselves; and knowledge of resources and programs available. These three elements are now discussed.

Relating to officials with confidence First, the potential recipients must be able to explain in some depth the nature of the problem, its immediate causes and the results for themselves or their family. To do so requires dealing with a person to whom they should be able to relate with confidence. Certainly this does not necessarily require someone of the same race or sex or possessing the same handicap in all cases. However, in many cases, it can be a definite help to create a situation where potential recipients perceive that the persons with whom they are dealing really do understand what the problems are. An elderly widow with limited income is much more likely to feel that an older person who also lives alone can understand her problems better than a 25-year-old social worker just out of college, regardless of the fact that the latter may have all the necessary educational credentials. Credibility is an extremely important ingredient in relations between a person in need and a government representative assigned to help satisfy that need. Many times, this credibility depends more on a feeling that the person is listening and can understand than on any academic considerations.

Affirmative action   Santa Fe Springs, California, has developed a two-tiered eligibility list for city jobs, consisting of candidates who "satisfactorily" and "outstandingly" complete the examination process. Numerical scores and rankings are not assigned to candidates because testing mechanisms cannot finely distinguish between candidates, i.e., a candidate with a 90 percent score is probably no better qualified than a candidate with 89 percent. But, in a competitive exam, this may make a difference of 4 or 5 ranks on an eligibility list. When the department head makes appointment decisions, he or she reviews all the "outstanding" candidates and perhaps the "satisfactories." This means a larger number of qualified candidates than the "rule of two or three" permits, thus increasing the likelihood of target group appointment. (At no time are unqualified candidates placed on the eligibility list; they are rated "unsatisfactory.") This approach is part of an unusually comprehensive affirmative action program developed for this city of 16,000 population aimed at "target group" persons in racial minority groups, the physically handicapped, women, and persons with arrest and conviction records.

Perceptions of the local government employee   A second element which affects the impact of human services programs is the extent to which the employee actually does understand the circumstances in which potential recipients find themselves. Whereas in the previous paragraph the discussion forcused on the perception of the recipient of the service, here the focus is the perception of the employee providing the service. People in need of government services may make their initial request for services with a feeling of shame or inferiority because they must ask for help. When this is the case, they will typically limit the amount of information they provide in the interest of getting the whole interview or application process over with as quickly as possible. This type of situation can be handled successfully only if the potential recipients are met by employees who can put the recipient at ease and, from experience, can ask the right questions in an appropriate manner to elicit the necessary information. For example, a black social worker who has had to cope with discrimination in school and employment may be more likely to understand the frustrations of the black worker who has been laid off and seems unable to get a job, but needs help in supporting a family.

Knowledge of available resources   The third element affecting the impact of services is knowledge of the available resources and programs. In some larger communities this may involve direct delivery of services, but in most cases it will involve referral to other agencies who directly deliver services and subsequent coordination of service delivery. This element is the one that depends to the greatest extent on the academic and technical experience of the employee. It should be noted, however, that the first two elements discussed—recipient relations with officials and employee perceptions—are the most important: the benefits to be gained from the third element are dependent on the quality of information and understanding established in the first two.

   For these reasons, therefore, it is essential to have as great a diversity as possible among the employees responsible for human services delivery. With this diversity and the flexibility to adjust assignments as necessary, the impact of such programs can be greatly enhanced.

Using manpower resources outside the normal employment pool   Another way in which employment practices can be beneficial in the delivery of human services is by increasing employment opportunities for special segments of the community. In any local government there are jobs which can be performed extremely well by members of specific groups outside of the normal employment pool, for example, by teenagers or senior citizens. If these jobs are identified and recruitment is designed specifically to reach these groups, the jurisdiction, the groups, and the programs benefit. Examples of such positions can be found in most departments, including those of library assistant, receptionist, cafeteria worker, minibus dispatcher, and recreation supervisor. To make a program of this type more successful, it may be helpful to replace full-time positions with more part-time positions in order to make them available for more people. In cooperation with the local school system, it may be possible to utilize high school students after school performing duties related to their major field of study, thus providing them with additional learning experience and obtaining enthusiastic employees at a reasonable cost. Such a modification can serve as an example to other employers in the community of a way in which economic resources can be used for the benefit of disadvantaged groups while continuing to provide needed services.

Women power planning   Westchester County, New York, has a program that is the first of its kind in the country. In cooperation with the U.S. Department of Labor, it has developed a program to help women enter nontraditional jobs. All on-the-job training and employment is in areas that have previously been closed to women. A women's center has been established to take women through the entire process of obtaining employment. The center includes a resource library and a job-finding workshop that will teach skills such as resume writing and interviewing.

An additional benefit to the community of such a program may well be increased communication with groups who normally consider themselves isolated from the government. Particularly among teenagers and the elderly we often hear the complaint that the government is run by the "establishment" and does not care enough about the problems of the group to help. This potential alienation can be substantially reduced if members of such groups are given responsibilities within the government's service delivery operations. The benefits are twofold. In performing their jobs, these people can better relate to others of their group and, therefore, affect the services performed in a positive way. In addition, working within the government will give them a better understanding of the operations and problems it faces. In this way, they can help others in their group to understand and appreciate them. Even though this may not directly affect human services programs, a better understanding of this type will improve the effectiveness of all programs.

Summary   Employment opportunities should not, of course, be limited to placing members of the community in low skill jobs, or the local government may well be accused of limiting upward mobility and placing minorities and others in low paying, dead-end jobs. Any employment opportunity policy of the type described in this section—employing perceptive persons in human services occupations who can relate well to client groups, as well as tapping manpower resources outside the normal employment pool—must naturally fit into personnel policies that encourage upward mobility for all local government employees. This subject is taken up again later in this chapter in reference to community development programs, but at this point it can be stressed that properly conceived and implemented manpower and personnel programs throughout a local government can, of themselves, enhance the human services function of the public sector in that community.

Public information activites and programs

All local governments are engaged in public information activities to some extent. The degree of involvement may range from active promotion carried out under the auspices of a separate operating department to official responses to inquiries from the media. The role of the public information function in forwarding the success of a community's human services programs is particularly important because two of the greatest handicaps facing these programs stems directly from citizens' lack of information about them.

First, those community members whose need for services is greatest are often the people least likely to be aware of just what their local government can provide for them. Second, many communities can find groups of citizens who are not among the needy, but whose negative impressions and vociferous disapproval of "welfare" programs in general can actually jeopardize valuable and effective human services programs.

A public information program designed to reach groups with insufficient or incorrect information should focus on positive aspects of existing human services efforts. A better "image" for the people involved in various programs can be encouraged by the dissemination of feature stories for use by the local media, developed around the experiences of both program participants and service providers. The availability of accurate information on the costs of existing programs and alternative activities can greatly help to reassure taxpayers that their dollars are not being unwisely or frivolously spent. Dissemination of accurate information regarding the organization and administrative structures involved in the implementation of human services programs can also serve to highlight the government's coordination efforts.

A local public information program should rely on formats besides the most commonly used mass communication methods of television and newspapers, and should include radio programs; flyers posted in commercial establishments, schools, and libraries; neighborhood meetings; and community "bulletin boards." The information presented in any of these formats should, for the reasons discussed above, emphasize the positive aspects of the activities and programs being "sold." Assurances of confidentiality to potential service recipients will be important to many, as well as being a judicial imperative. Efforts should also be made, if possible, to decentralize the application process (avoiding "general registration days" in public halls) and to let potential recipients know that their first contact with the service agency need not necessarily be traumatic.

An additional medium for dissemination of information is a directory of services available within the community, listing programs sponsored by all agencies—local, state, federal, and private—and including pertinent addresses, phone numbers, names of contact persons, and a brief program description. The impact of such a directory is dependent, of course, on its distribution throughout the community. Figure 15–1 shows a sample page from the "Director of Community Services" for the Bloomfield, Connecticut area.

Summary

The preceding discussion has set the scene for the more detailed treatment which follows analyzing human services activities in operating departments. It has taken a look at four areas where discussion of the role of human services can permeate the policy-making and managerial process. The first area concerned decisions regarding the delivery of services, ranging from input and equity through the examples of education and the police patrol. The second area noted some of the human services dimensions of the annual budget process, a matter of pertinent concern to local government managers at a time of continuing fiscal crises. The third topic discussed was the equally sensitive area of local government employment policies, with emphasis on developing appropriate perceptions in local government employees regarding the use of resources both within and without the normal employment pool. The last topic discussed was the role of public information activities and programs—an area wider than that traditionally ascribed to the public relations function.

Human services activities in operating departments

Having completed the discussion of the impact of human services activities on several broad policy areas within local government activity, it is now possible to turn to an examination of the various ways in which a human services dimension can be added to traditional operating department activities. It should be noted at the outset that, while municipal or other local government organizations and structures vary widely from community to community, there remains a common core

---

```
                              EMPLOYMENT


566-5160        CONNECTICUT STATE EMPLOYMENT SERVICE
   or           90 Washington Street
566-5772        Hartford, Connecticut  06106

                PURPOSE:   Employment, retraining and testing services

                PROGRAMS:   Job Bank (566-5400) offering a list of job openings
                in the Hartford area, computerized and printed daily, employ-
                ment counseling, selective placement for handicapped and older
                citizens, special services to veterans.

                NEED:   Social Security number.  Discharge or separation certifi-
                cation from armed services.


242-0720        JOB BANK - YOUTH SERVICES
                73 Rockwell Avenue
                Bloomfield, Connecticut  06002

                PURPOSE:   Help Bloomfield youth find full and part-time employ-
                ment;  help Bloomfield residents and employers find dependable,
                energetic, full-time or part-time workers.

                PROVIDES:   Referral service for regular work and a call-in
                service for odd jobs.


242-6241        SOCIAL SERVICES DEPARTMENT
                Robert Watkins - Director
                Bloomfield Town Hall
                Bloomfield, Connecticut  06002

                PROVIDES:   Supportive Counseling Service offered to the Town's
                welfare recipients, as well as to any individual or family who,
                although ineligible for financial assistance, could benefit
                from this counseling service.  Counseling work done in area
                of employment.


566-5790        UNEMPLOYMENT COMPENSATION DIVISION
                State Labor Department
                Hartford Office
                90 Washington Street
                Hartford, Connecticut  06105

                PURPOSE:   To administer the Unemployment Compensation Act.
```

Figure 15–1 Sample page from the *Directory of Community Services* for Bloomfield, Connecticut. (Source: *Directory of Community Services,* Town of Bloomfield, Connecticut, 1973, p. 16.)

of traditional departments. The following discussion examines the police department, the newer role of community development administration, the parks and recreation department, and code enforcement. The extent of the involvement of such traditional departments in human services activities—explicit or implicit—is often quite extensive. A review of the provision of human services in Merced, California, for instance, revealed that the following activities were being carried out within the indicated departments and agencies:

Transit Department—Provides "dial-a-ride" bus service anywhere within the city limits at very economical rates thus increasing the mobility of senior citizens, youth, or any persons who either do not drive or do not own an automobile.

Police Department—"Community relations program" operates to promote good relations between the Police Department and the community, and to implement various crime prevention programs such as Neighborhood Alert, Operation Identification, Block Parent, Drug Abuse Prevention, etc.

Recreation and Parks Department—In addition to providing the city's parks and recreational facilities, and maintaining these, the department offers over sixty leisure service programs in five broad categories of activity: 1. athletics and sports; 2. adult classes; 3. youth classes; 4. special events; 5. youth recreation. In addition, there is the "Senior Citizens Title III Project" which serves to identify and provide many needs of the elderly. "Youth Employment Service" places approximately fifteen students per week in part-time or temporary employment during the summer months.

Fire Department—Provides diverse and numerous community services a few of which are: periodic free blood pressure check-ups, charity drives, first aid classes, free home inspections, means of entry to persons locked out of their homes/cars, etc.

Building Department—Conducts housing rehabilitation programs to fulfill one of the most important social needs. These programs such as FACE and the present one-year rehabilitation program focus on improvements in areas of primarily low income, retired, or racial minority persons. These programs serve the particular health–housing needs of the persons living in these area, and serve the city overall by eliminating blighted areas.

Farmers' Market—Provides a low-cost retail outlet to private persons in the area who wish to sell a wide variety of items ranging from prepared food and agricultural produce to hand crafted items and used items. This is of special benefit to low income persons, whether they be buyers or sellers, as well as to economy minded persons in the community.

The Bridge—A complex agency providing a wide variety of counseling, values clarification, and crisis intervention–prevention services to the city residents. It provides such programs as "Diversion," an alternative to incarceration for drug offenders; marriage, family, individual, youth, and group counseling programs; counselor training programs and volunteer training programs; etc.

Action Council—Provides a "consumer affairs" office open to any Merced citizen who has a consumer complaint, inquiry, or who wants information on consumer legislation or the reliability of any company. It produces a monthly newsletter, *Caveat Emptor,* as part of consumer education as well as consumer workshops. In addition, it recruits, evaluates, and places volunteers with various service agencies in the city; it also conducts the Big Brothers/Big Sisters of Merced program.

Youth Council—In conjunction with the Recreation and Parks Dept., consists of sixteen youths who "investigate all aspects of activities and advise the city as to the development of programs for the benefit of youth in the city." This serves an important social need by providing legitimate means for young people to have input into the determination of affairs that affect them.

Human Relations Commission—An advisory body whose main purpose is to deal with complaints and problems brought before it by members of the community who cannot obtain satisfactory resolution elsewhere. Examples of problems to be brought before the commission are problems with discrimination, housing, employment, or anything else which is likely to plague minority or otherwise disadvantaged members of the community. The commission operates either to solve the problem at the local level or to direct the complainant to higher agencies for resolution if this is appropriate.[1]

The police department

In many ways, discussion of the human services dimension of police activities is potentially the most frustrating of all. The reason for this is that, on the one hand, police departments tend to be one of the most traditional of all in any municipality because of their commonly "military" organization and appearance and the particular nature of "law and order" operations. On the other hand, it may well be that no department or activity of any municipality has more contact or earlier contact with those people who need human services programs. Because of the round-the-clock nature of police operations and the fact that they are often the first called for help in many situations, it may well be that the human services program potential of this activity is the greatest of any.

Local government police management is treated at length in a companion volume of that title in the Municipal Management Series.[2] The reader is referred to that volume for a fuller account of the increasing awareness among responsible police officials of the human relations and human services dimension of police work, in particular to chapters discussing juvenile programs, community relations, and the outlook for local policing. Some general points can nevertheless be emphasized in the present brief discussion. This focuses, first, on some of the basic human relations aspects of police work; second, on some significant roles that the police can play in the area of youth services; and, third, on the broad importance of police–community relations.

Basic human relations aspects of police work   As has been noted, the round-the-clock nature of police work coupled with the association of a police presence with overt manifestations of personal, family, and communal dysfunctioning (whether or not associated with criminal behavior) often places police officers right on the front line in cases of human services need. By inclination, experience, or training, they may or may not be suited to an appropriate response from the human services viewpoint, and may, of course, be further aided or impeded by the organizational environment within which they move. Any public administrator can cite numerous examples of cases where a police officer has taken a personal interest in the plight of an individual as a result of a police call, perhaps assisting that individual in obtaining other human services assitance above and beyond the call of duty. The same administrators, however, could also cite examples where a police officer, operating under the strict law enforcement concept of his or her job, did not take that simple extra step of referral which might have provided the help necessary to prevent a recurrence of the problem or incident. Sometimes this may be due to the press of other work activities. Sometimes the individual officer may be placed in a difficult situation. For a young male officer, a stressful situation may not in fact be the apprehension of an armed criminal, for which his training will probably have prepared him. Instead, it may be occasioned by a call to a domestic disturbance where he immediately becomes the focus of intramarital or intrafamilial resentment and conflict which he is psychologically ill-prepared to cope with, let alone surmount. Neighborhood or community perceptions of law enforcement agencies may add to the difficulty of effective communication, particularly if contact has to be made across differing categories of age, sex, socioeconomic status, and, most pertinently, racial or ethnic background.

The local government police department, therefore, offers both a challenge and an opportunity to local government managers seeking to maximize the human services potential of exising departments and their staffs. The nature and the extent of the police role offers the human services opportunity; the traditional departmental focus and community perceptions of the police may offer the challenges particularly when jurisdictions are fiscally hard pressed.

The example of youth services   Some aspects of relations between youth and the police in a community serve to emphasize these points. The youth of any community make up a significant portion of the population and their activities throughout the community often bring them into contact with the police department. Unhappily, teenagers and young adults also comprise the largest client group of police departments because of their disproportionate share in criminal activity. Thus, as one observer points out: ". . . the police administrator must balance the competing demands of delinquency prevention, delinquency control, service to young people, protection of the community, protection of basic human rights, and enforcement of the law. It is not a new dilemma for the administrator. Nor are these competing demands necessarily categorical; but they do involve questions of values and priorities for which there are no universally accepted answers." [3]

Within this framework, however, police officers can take positive steps to enhance their human services role. Many people who have observed the dynamics of contacts between youngsters in a community and the police argue that the nature of the first two or three contacts any youth may have with the police can well have a significant effect on that youngster's future. If these contacts are positive and the youngster gains respect for the police and the law, it may influence him or her toward becoming a law abiding, constructive citizen. If, on the other hand, the first contacts are not positive, the youngster may well become defiant of all police officers and law enforcement, thus continually being in conflict with them.

To their credit, many police officers were among the first municipal employees to recognize this situation and, as a result, the history of officers becoming involved in organizing and running constructive programs for youth in many communities is a long one. One of the first of these efforts were the Police Athletic Leagues (PALs), which started as programs sponsored by the large city police departments and spread during the 1940s and 1950s to towns and cities of all sizes across the country. The PALs and other similar programs provided a variety of supervised sports programs for youth through high school age. The purposes were twofold: first, to provide organized activities to occupy the time of the youths as a deterrent to trouble making and, second, to create an atmosphere where youth and police officers could get to know each other in a friendly atmosphere.

Family fuzz The city manager of Union City, California, reports that his city's entire police force has now received special training in domestic crisis intervention. Union City is the second in the state of California (San Jose was the first) to provide such training for all its personnel. The course, provided by the Santa Clara Valley Criminal Justice Training Center in Menlo Park, seeks to reduce the possibility of injury to police officers and citizens and to provide alternatives to arrest in domestic disturbances. Trainees learn how to "defuse" a situation, and how to mediate disputes.

In all but the larger cities such programs have declined in popularity, in part being replaced by the growth of programs organized and run by municipal parks and recreation departments. In recent years, however, police departments have sponsored a whole variety of organized youth activities designed with similar objectives. This includes "explorer scouts;" baseball, basketball, and football teams; camera clubs; rifle clubs; motorcycle groups; and police cadet programs. An interesting aspect of the explorer scout and police cadet programs is that the participants are given training in some police activities and, with supervision, perform nonenforcement activities with department members. With proper supervision, use of youth for parking and traffic activities, vacant house checks, business door checks, and other such functions may provide a supply of enthusiastic help in addition to meeting the primary objective. Police officers can accomplish the same objective by becoming active in the local recreation department as instructors or supervisors during off duty hours. Many police departments have found that the nonofficial, informal contacts which come from such activities are often most productive in gaining the respect and cooperation of a large majority of the young people in a community.

Another way in which police departments have assisted in youth-oriented human services activities is in advocating and cooperating with the establishment of local youth counseling activities. In many communities over the past couple of decades, police officers have become increasingly frustrated with the established systems of dealing with juvenile offenders. This frustration has often been caused by their belief that these established systems are not only ineffective, but in many cases counterproductive. Juvenile courts in many parts of the country have been severely hampered by an acute shortage of properly trained case workers to adequately supervise the tremendously growing case load. As a result, many young people referred to the juvenile court are seen very infrequently and receive little assistance in correcting the problems which exist. A "revolving door" situation may well develop. The result is often complete frustration for the officers who apprehend the youth again and again, refer him at her to juvenile court again and again, and thereby have to deal with the system's failure again and again. In many instances, the officers have repeatedly expressed this frustration until a local counseling or referral system is established as an alternative to the established court system. The specifics of such alternatives differ from place to place, but typically include such common ingredients as a case review board, the use of individual and family counseling, and periodic case reevaluation. Many times the review board will include representatives of the school system, the police department, youth council, and social services department as well as lay people interested in youth. In this way it is hoped that all of the resources of a community can be focused to assist youth in a positive way so as to reduce repeated negative contacts with the police department. With such a system, an officer has the alternative, depending on the seriousness of the offense, of referring the juvenile to the court or into the local system. While it is important that any such system be flexible enough to fit a variety of situations, it is equally important that definite guidelines be established covering elements such as confidentiality, record keeping, and follow-up which may be more difficult in a volunteer effort. It is also important to reassure police officers that such an alternate system is designed to assist and cooperate with them, and not to control or review their activities.

The example of police–community relations programs   There are other important aspects of police work apart from the role of youth services. Other police–community relations programs would include the employment of family dispute specialists, the establishment of community advisory boards and "ride along" programs, a return to foot patrols to reestablish neighborhood contact, team policing, and other related activities. These and other programs reflect a changing society and a changing communal perception of the police role. What is important to the local government manager concerned with human services is the fact that both police and community representatives have been developing new organizational methods to bridge the isolation that many feel separates the police from their communities; and that these mechanisms have a strong human services element. They can therefore also serve as a bridge between the police department's activities and other human services delivery systems, private as well as public, in a particular community. This contemporary thrust in police administration was represented during the 1960s by the emergence of literally thousands of programs, mostly cosmetic in nature, labeled "police–community relations."

These beginnings, however, have become refined into much more sophisticated policy-related programs during the 1970s. Police–community relations are approached in a systematic manner, with emphasis on overall management and approaches at many levels: the manner in which the police function is itself carried out; development of programs that enhance public awareness of police operations and procedures; and levels of involvement by the police officer in a community as a private citizen (e.g., by providing financial incentives for officers who undergo training or participate in volunteer activity). The implementation of such programs is, of course, linked to broader administrative issues concerning minority hiring, affirmative action, modification of military-type organization, and so on. They also relate to such operational matters as firearms policy, discretion granted to the beat officer, training in conflict management, and so on. Community relations units and advisory boards continue to play a role. Methods adopted will naturally vary between particular communities, but the example of community-oriented policing used in San Diego may offer a good indication of the evolving philosophy of police functions in a community.

Patrol officers in the San Diego police department must complete and regularly update a profile of the beats to which they are assigned. That profile defines the socioeconomic makeup of the particular area and the nature and patterns of crime, traffic, and community problems in that area for the shift to which the officer is assigned. Officers have received training in how to use and interpret statistics and how to perform a community analysis. Officers indicate their priorities with regard to those problems, their objectives with regard to each, and the activities they will pursue toward their accomplishment. Officers must subsequently specify reasonable and appropriate measure of accomplishment, so that the department can assess each officer's progress toward stated objectives.[4]

Summary For the manager concerned with human services, therefore, the most significant lessons that may be learned from recent developments in local police administration are: (1) that there is increased awareness of the human relations and human services component in police work; (2) that this awareness is finding stronger and more efficient organizational expression in community relations programs and elsewhere; and (3) that these factors present an opportunity for better mobilization and more efficient use of total community human services resources.

Community development

One department or governmental function which has shown significant changes in terms of increasing emphasis on human services programs over the past two decades is the area of community development which, of course, has its roots in predecessor urban renewal and Model Cities programs.

Main implications of community development for human services This is not the place to enter into a detailed discussion of the political factors involved, but it may be noted that, after several years of debate and numerous attempts to improve various urban programs, Congress, in 1974, abolished urban renewal and several other categorical programs and replaced them with the Housing and Community Development Act, popularly known as Community Development.[5] Essentially, Community Development is a move back in the direction of urban renewal: it does include social concerns, but it is not as generous in those areas as was the Model Cities program.

Two points about Community Development are particularly important for the present discussion: (1) federal legislation requires each community to look at the total needs of the people in the eligible areas and go beyond the simple replacement of physically deteriorating structures, even though this latter goal is at the core of the program, and (2) there is marked emphasis in the controlling legislation, if not in practice, on concentration on a neighborhood program approach. In this sense, therefore, broad areas of human services programming can be linked to specific attempts, using Community Development funds, to physically stabilize or revitalize neighborhoods or areas within the urban community.

Because of the novelty of this approach, it is far too early, as of the later 1970s, to judge whether or not it will be successful. It is certain, however, that attempts are being made in many communities to make it a success. It is even too soon to have a comprehensive list of the individual programs which have been tried. However, some examples are worth mentioning.

Example: a senior citizen facility and program   One community used a portion of their funds to establish and set up a health screening program for senior citizens. This program provided for the necessary professional staff in a clinic. It is typical of many older citizens that there is a reluctance to make periodic visits to private physicians because of concern about cost, transportation, test results, etc. Therefore, this program operates in conjunction with the senior citizen recreation and social program, and provides the opportunity for each senior citizen to have routine tests conducted. No treatment is performed at the clinic, but, if problems are discovered, they are referred to a private physician for treatment. In addition, in accordance with the instructions of a private physician, frequent periodic checks can be made of blood pressure between office visits to the physician to monitor the individual's condition.

One of the early conclusions which has been reached by those involved in the program is that one of the biggest problems for people in this age group is the lack of understanding about the normal health problems to be expected with advancing age. Typically, after completing the routine tests and finding no major problems, further discussion revealed that many of the anxieties which bothered the participants were caused more by fear of what might happen to their health. As a result of the recognition of this phenomenon, the program has been modified to include, along with the diagnostic screening, an intensive educational element. This element utilizes group meetings where topics such as high blood pressure, heart trouble, cancer, and other specific topics which cause anxiety are discussed. This program has been carried out at a community center as well as at elderly housing developments. Thus, the Community Development program can provide both the capital funds for the facility and equipment and the operating funds for the program itself. Prior to development of Community Development programs, the same result might have been achieved, but only after processing two or three different applications through as many different agencies and even then, only if accompanied by vigilant coordination efforts.

Example: facilitating comprehensive approaches   Community Development programs can also be used to include attention to human services needs in neighborhood preservation or rehabilitation programs. Prior to Community Development, many communities attempted to establish comprehensive programs designed to stop the deterioration of older neighborhoods or areas. Typically, a great amount of lead time was consumed, often at considerable expense, to develop an overall plan which included a variety of specific programs such as storm drainage, street reconstruction, sidewalk construction, street tree planting, neighborhood recreation areas and community centers. Plans were also developed in such areas as housing code enforcement and rehabilitation, housing construction, sewer, water, and other utility work, and a variety of other physical construction projects. Two major factors often led to partial, if not total, failure of such plans. The first of these was that they almost always depended on applications being developed and approved by the municipality and then submitted to a variety of different agencies—state and federal—for funds for each of the projects. Even when several of the grant programs were administered by one executive department, there were often separate divisions or offices which tended to operate independently. As a result, it was virtually impossible for a municipality to coordinate the various applications or implement the programs necessary to really follow through on the plans. The history of such plans is replete with examples of blocks of buildings being demolished with nothing built to replace them, simply because subsequent programs were not approved. The eventual result in many cases was not only the inability to implement the plans, but also an increasing bitterness and sense of failure on the part of taxpayers and government officials at all levels.

A second major reason which often led to the failure of such plans was that very few of the available grant programs included funds beyond those needed for physical activities. Funds were available for demolition, construction, reconstruction, or alteration, but not for operation. Thus, the planning process came to pay very little attention to the future operation of the facilities included or to the programs for which they were to be used.

In many cases, this factor particularly affected programs related to human services. When the facilities involved were "items" such as roads, sidewalks, or recreation facilities, they were often replacements of, or improvements on, existing facilities. The standards for these facilities were already accepted as items of local government concern and, importantly, as part of their budgets. As discussed earlier in another context, the lack of transferable standards and existing programs in the human services area often resulted in their being given very little attention during the planning and budgeting processes.

An example of the new multifaceted approach which is made possible by Community Development may be helpful. In Bloomfield, Connecticut, several plans and applications had been developed over a period of about five years for an urban renewal, a neighborhood development housing code enforcement, and other programs which were to be concentrated in the southeastern area of the town. This area, developed during the 1920s, 1930s, and early 1940s, was beginning to show signs of deterioration which town officials and residents wanted to prevent. None of the applications were approved and, therefore, the programs were not implemented. The town became eligible for Community Development funds and decided to concentrate on a comprehensive program designed to accomplish many of the plans prepared for the original applications and also to incorporate other items which had not been previously included. As a result, the following activities and programs were functioning as of early 1977: street reconstruction including a storm drainage system, curbs, and sidewalks; street tree planting; housing code enforcement; housing rehabilitation; neighborhood recreation areas; acquisition of vacant lots and development of green space areas; improved access to industrial land in the area to increase its marketability and create more jobs; and development of a multipurpose community center. In addition, Community Development funds have been used for the town's obligation (under an agreement with the city of Hartford) to correct a long-term, major drainage problem existing along the town–city line.

Two factors are relevant to the discussion here. First, all of these programs could be coordinated because they only required one application to one federal department, that of Housing and Urban Development. Second, human services program employees have been involved throughout the planning and development phases, thus ensuring the integration of their concerns in the final result. An example of this integration is the neighborhood community center. Prior to the Community Development program, the school district closed a forty-year-old elementary school and turned the building over to the town administration. The oldest, most deteriorated portion of the building was demolished and the newer portion was renovated. The building presently houses an early learning center with a capacity for sixty children and a state-operated center for the mentally retarded. In addition, the large gymnasium has been retained and is used for meetings of community organizations. In the first year of Community Development, a substantial amount of funds was used to convert the surrounding fifteen acres of land into a neighborhood recreational facility, including three baseball fields, four lighted tennis courts, a small ice skating rink, and a "tot lot" area. Along with this work, the adjacent streets and parking areas were reconstructed with improved storm drainage. With further funds, the town intends to develop a multipurpose social services center including the municipal health and social service departments, plus offices for state programs in such areas as employment, social services, job training, and family counseling. Thus, the Community Development program has been a vehicle to coordinate a variety of specific projects, including physical and program improvements, to have maximum impact on a particular neighborhood.

Human services needs and programs have been included throughout the planning and development process.

During the development of this program, one problem unfolded which should be noted. Because so many different municipal, state, and regional departments and agencies were involved throughout the effort, overall coordination could not be provided by any one operating department. Consequently, overall coordination and direction has been provided on a day-to-day basis by the town manager's office. Effective coordination was ensured by assigning the assistant town manager with management responsibility for all Community Development concerns. Community size may make this arrangement unfeasible, but this writer believes it essential that overall responsibility be assigned to the chief executive's office and not to any single operating department.

Figure 15–2   This multipurpose community center in Bloomfield, Connecticut, was constructed with the help of community development funds from a forty-year-old elementary school building scheduled for closure. (Source: Courtesy of the Town of Bloomfield, Connecticut.)

Summary   Community Development programs are still relative newcomers on the local government scene. The examples cited in the preceding discussion show that, while such projects continue to have physical rehabilitation as the core of their urban goals, it is entirely possible to utilize the opportunities provided by Community Development to integrate a number of disparate human services projects and to more effectively mobilize total human services commitments in a jurisdiction. Overall, many local government managers would already agree that Community Development represents a more moderate position than did either the urban renewal or Model Cities programs. It gives more weight to social concerns than urban renewal projects did, yet there is less leeway with the use of funds than was the case with Model Cities.

The recreation department

Recreation department programs and activities have seen tremendous changes over recent years, many of which are a result of human services concerns. Traditionally, the recreation department for any community was almost exclusively involved in the operation of athletic programs. These programs were designed to serve the youth of the community who were not involved in school athletic programs, as well as young adults who wished some form of athletic activity. The recreation department typically organized leagues for competitive sports in baseball, softball, basketball, football, soccer, swimming, tennis, etc. In addition, many departments also ran instructional programs aimed at teaching elementary skills in many of these same areas. Until the mid-1950s, most recreation departments were only involved in operating programs to serve young people from about the ages of eight through seventeen. These programs often included supervised summer playgrounds and various group activities for after-school hours and school vacation periods. This latter type of program was primarily designed to give youth something to do when school was not in session.

The roots of expansion   During the later 1950s, this situation began to change because of three changes taking place in society: increased leisure time; increasing income; and increasing interest in varied activities. First of all, the normal work week for many people was gradually being shortened from six to five days, or from forty-eight to forty or fewer hours, thus providing more leisure time for adults to pursue their interests—sports, arts and crafts, camping, and so on. Along with this increase in available time, the rapidly increasing level of family income meant that more money was available to allow families to buy the necessary equipment or whatever was needed to pursue these various activities. In addition, during the next decade, public school systems began to offer a much greater variety of programs to their students because they began to understand that different programs were needed to interest and motivate different students. One result of this change was to expose students to a number of different activities, thereby whetting their appetites for more of these different activities.

Sure, litter cans talk   A park owner in Pennsylvania installed talking litter receptacles in the shape of pigs, hippos, and elephants. When trash is deposited, a tape recording comes on and says: "Thank you, that tastes good, can you find me anything else to eat?" After a busy Sunday, the park is as clean as when it opened. Children fall all over each other searching to find litter to feed the animals.

These three factors combined to encourage recreation departments to greatly expand their areas of activities through the 1960s. The departments' roles changed from merely organizing athletic programs to developing a wide variety of programs designed to satisfy a broad cross section of community interests. As this happened, recreation departments became more and more involved in human services concerns. The traditional athletic and playground activities could be successful with departmental provision of organization, schedules, officials, playing fields, and instruction. When departments began to move into providing programs other than athletics (and thus began dealing with people and groups with significantly different interests), the human services dimension of their work became much more important. In many cases, staff members were not trained or equipped to deal with these concerns, but were expected to move into new areas as needed.

Example: involving senior citizens   Senior citizen activities again offer an excellent example of this phenomenon. Traditionally, recreation departments had virtually no contact with senior citizens in any program operation. The combination of earlier retirements and longer lives resulted in a growing group of older citizens with more leisure time than before. The needs of this group were given greater priority, and increasing pressure was placed on communities to develop programs for them. This concern was often directed first at organizing social activities to combat the loneliness and boredom which many senior citizens faced. Since many were faced with limited, fixed incomes, they were often confined to a life with little outside activity. In most communities, the first response to this need was to organize a senior citizen club which met on a regular basis, sometimes for a meal or to hear a speaker or to participate in a program of interest. Such clubs filled a real need by providing an opportunity for senior citizens to get together on a periodic basis and socialize with each other. In doing so, they were able to share experiences with each other and develop friendships which helped combat their loneliness. Such clubs were often organized with the assistance of the recreation department in the community which was frequently able to provide a meeting place, publicize the meetings, and help arrange the programs. As these organizations became popular, their activities became more varied. Activities came to include group trips, dances, and parties requiring greater organization and assistance, again often provided by the recreation department. Through these groups, an increasingly complex network of needs gradually came to be recognized. Such areas as nutrition, health, exercise, hobbies, and arts and crafts instruction were just a few concerns which were addressed by such groups. Often without a great deal of planning, different activities were added. At budget time, it was very common for senior citizens to campaign for funds for their activities—often comparing the amount of money spent for youth recreation programs with that spent for older citizens, and demanding a more equitable share. The typical recreation department, after several years of expanding such activities, came to the point where the available time and the training and experience of existing staff members were insufficient to properly operate or coordinate the programs. When this point was reached, communities usually reacted in one of two ways. Either a separate operating agency was created to operate senior citizen programs or a new recreation staff position was created to deal solely with senior citizens' activities. In smaller communities, the latter approach was usually more feasible because of the complications likely to arise from creating another operating department.

As senior citizens organized themselves, more attention was devoted to their concerns and those concerns became more complex and far-ranging. A community attempting to address housing, health, and transportation problems, for example, to utilize skills and expertise not generally located in recreation departments.

All of these changes meant that recreation departments began to move away from providing facilities for a limited activity and to move toward dealing with a diverse group of people. A direct result of this was the greatly increased importance of the human services dimension of their activities. The process is often incremental, but the result is a geometric change.

Code enforcement

Code enforcement is another traditional local government activity which has a growing human services dimensions.[6] The present discussion will focus on such areas of code enforcement as housing codes which involve existing structures (as opposed to new buildings under construction). Enforcement of the codes applicable to new construction is less likely to involve human services concerns than those involving existing and inhabited buildings.

Example: housing codes and the community   A housing code has two purposes. First, it is designed to ensure that all dwelling units in a community are maintained in a safe and sanitary manner for the protection of the residents as well as those living in surrounding dwelling units. Second, a housing code enforcement program also serves to preserve a neighborhood's housing stock in good condition so as to maintain property values in the neighborhood.

Keeping these two objectives in mind, we also must recognize that, in most cases, the areas with the greatest need for housing code enforcement are often those areas with the oldest and lower priced housing in the community. To the extent that this is true, this housing is often occupied by people who are most limited in terms of financial ability to do the necessary repairs to achieve code compliance. Consequently, any code enforcement program must cope with the dilemma of requiring repairs by people unable to afford them. In most cases, the ultimate authority provided under a housing code if repairs are not done is that of declaring the unit unfit for occupancy until brought up to standards. Therefore, if the enforcement officer orders repairs which the owner/occupant cannot afford, the officer then has to determine if eviction is a viable course to pursue. Aside from substantial legal questions which an attempted eviction of this type may produce, the question of the effect of such an eviction is paramount. If a family is evicted, will they be able to find a new code-approved residence? If that is accomplished, what will happen to the vacated unit?

The role of rehabilitation programs. Faced with these dilemmas, many communities have realized that a strict code enforcement program alone is not very practical. Quite apart from paying appropriate attention to the human relations aspect of code enforcement, which can range from settling for good faith progress and distinguishing between truly hazardous violations and the less urgent, such communities have also developed rehabilitation assistance programs designed to help the willing owner (who is hampered by limited means) accomplish the necessary repairs. These rehabilitation assistance programs usually have two major ingredients: financial assistance and counciling for the owner.

Some type of financial assistance to fund the required repair costs is obviously a major factor. Sometimes this financial assistance is provided in a "write down" of normal loan interest costs. Sometimes it may involve an arrangement for a longer repayment period than the standard bank loan normally carries. In other cases, it may require an outright grant of part or all of the money necessary to complete the repairs. One type of assistance which is being attempted in some communities is for the municipality to make an arrangement with a local financial institution to establish a guaranty fund on deposit as security to cover the potential default of a greater amount of loans. For example, if the standard rate of default on home repair loans is 20 percent, an arrangement might be made whereby the community would place on deposit with the bank a certain amount, say $100,000, as a security against which the bank will make rehabilitation loans for structures involved in the code enforcement up to five times the security amount, or $500,000. If a loan issued under this program goes in default, the bank, after collection attempts, will deduct the amount of unpaid principal and interest on the loan from the guaranty fund. Through this process, termed "leveraging," the community can multiply funds available for housing rehabilitation several times, thereby accomplishing more rehabilitation. In addition, in order to make such loans available to more people of limited means, a community may also decide to write down the normal interest rate by a one-time payment to the bank in sufficient amount to reduce the standard interest rate to one which can be afforded by the owner.

A second part of such rehabilitation assistance programs is often an extensive amount of counseling for the owner. Often it is found that the owner of a unit needing repairs has little or no experience in doing such work or in dealing with the contractors who do such work. Therefore, it is often necessary to assist the owner with such things as writing specifications for the work to be performed, evaluating proposals from different contractors, inspecting the work in progress, and financial counseling.

The examples discussed above again indicate that it is possible to enhance the human services dimension in what had traditionally been considered a routine local government function. If local government managers aim for a proper balance of human services and enforcement concern, the objectives of the program are more likely to be met than if just the enforcement objectives were involved. Good training in human relations, and an appropriate flexibility of procedures, further facilitate the accomplishment of overall community goals.

Summary

The preceding discussion has touched on some aspects of human services activity in traditional operating departments in local government. We have taken a look at the police department, one of the earliest of local government functions, and also at the growing role of community development programs, an innovation of the 1970s. Finally, the human services aspects of code enforcement have been considered. Throughout the discussion, practical examples as well as general principles have been utilized. Local government managers will agree that an essential prerequisite to initiating any new management activity in these areas is an evaluation of existing programs in the light of community traditions, administrative goals, and current community needs. There will, as always, be wide variation among communities. A rural county will have problems that differ from those of a large metropolitan core, which will differ in turn from those of a growing suburb. Further, whatever the existing administrative structure of local government, changing economic patterns and changing social perceptions may add new emphases that render some operations less relevant than hitherto. Perhaps the key to successful management in this area is an identification of underutilized resources in traditional departments which can be given a sharper human services focus, coupled with a sense of how local government functions interpenetrate.

Training

The preceding sections of this chapter have looked at community-wide policy issues and some operating department opportunities, insofar as potentially enhanced human services activities are involved. Frequent references have been made to the importance of adequately trained personnel who are aware of the human services aspects of their work. The final portion of this chapter will therefore discuss ways in which the various departments can be sensitized to the human services dimension of their work.

Interdepartmental lines

One of the most difficult factors presented in the area of human services is the fact that most human services concerns do not fall clearly within the jurisdiction of just one operating department. To be effective, most programs designed to meet a particular need must cross departmental lines. For example, youth programs often involve the recreation department, the school system, and the police department, as well as the social services department. Programs for the elderly will, in many cases, benefit from participation by the health department, the local commission on aging, the recreation department, the transportation department, as well as the social services department. The interdepartmental nature of these and other programs related to human services requires a concomitant in-service training effort which is interdepartmental in scope. Employees in each department should be aware of the overall program objectives, of the role each department can assume in meeting these objectives, and of each department's capabilities and limitations. Only with this type of understanding can separate departments work together on a single program with a minimum of duplication and maximum effectiveness.

Example: the Small Cities Management Training Program The Small Cities Management Training Program, developed by the International City Management Association, is an example of a training program designed on an interdepartmental basis.[7] The objective of this program is to take department heads (or their equivalent) and give them, in a relatively limited period of time, an understanding of what the activities and programs of the other departments are. This is done by having each participant study and make a presentation to the group on the objectives, functions, and programs of a department other than his or her own. Obviously, the depth of such examination may be somewhat limited by the time available. However, the fact that the leader of the discussion on the finance department is the police chief, rather than the finance director, tends to ensure that the expla-

nation will not be so technical as not to be undertood. In addition, more discussion should result because the other participants will be more likely to question a person who is not the in-house expert on the subject. This program was developed to give each department head a working knowledge of other departments in hopes of generating more cooperation between departments through mutual understanding.

Example: developing programs for senior citizens   Such an approach can be very useful in the human services area. For example, if it were decided that greater attention should be devoted to developing programs for senior citizens, a series of discussions could be organized on the needs of this group. After some general background presented by a specialist in aging, a series of discussions could be scheduled on such topics as health needs, housing needs, recreational needs, transportation needs, etc. These topics could be studied and presented by the participants with the objective of developing programs to meet these needs. Following this format, the recreation director might examine housing; the library director, recreation; etc. This procedure has two benefits. First, someone not directly involved in a specific area may well be able to provide a fresh approach to that area, thereby generating new ideas which might not occur to the person dealing with that area on a day-to-day basis. Second, the person who makes the presentation will, in the future, have a better understanding of the problems in that area and will thus probably be willing to make more efforts at cooperation. Certainly, to the extent that new programs are developed in these discussions, the fact that several departments have participated in developing them will ensure better cooperation in operating them.

Intergovernmental links

In the area of human services program delivery, another factor must be recognized and dealt with. As Chapter 8 has discussed, in any community, there may be numerous agencies which are involved both within and outside the structure of the municipal government in delivery of human services. For example, within the local United Way or Community Chest organization, there are often numerous agencies which may well be involved in one or more human services programs.

The problem of diversity   This phenomenon is not often encountered in other areas of governmental activity such as police protection, fire protection, road construction and maintenance where local and state government usually have exclusive jurisdiction over delivery of such services. In the human services area, however, this is far from true. Probably because local government historically was not involved in human services programs, a multitude of organizations have come into being, all involved in one aspect or another of providing programs. Consequently, any municipal government beginning to develop a human services dimension in its activities is faced with a need for understanding what these organizations are and what programs they can provide, and for coordinating such activities.

Example: an interagency council   One possible way of accomplishing this is to organize an interagency council which has as its objective promoting communication between the various organizations. Membership on such a council should be open to any organization interested in the field. In Bloomfield, Connecticut, this organization (the Bloomfield Interagency Council) was originally formed by the Director of Social Services and the Director of Pupil Services for the school system. Other participants include police and recreation departments, churches, visiting nurses association, the health department, the private family service society, the libraries, the YMCA, YWCA, and several other organizations who deal in "people" programs. Prior to the council's organization, the people in these groups very often did not know one another, let alone have any experience working together. The existence of the council has produced two noticeable benefits. The representatives of the organizations meet on a regular basis and discuss their programs and any problems they may be having. As a result, each organization or agency has a much better understanding of the activities of the others. This sharing of information alone has produced significant benefits. In addition, by having the individuals in the organizations get to know each other, they have, on many occasions, worked together on specific cases. This allows for much greater coordination of effort and potentially greater efficiency in delivery of services. While the details may differ depending on the size of the community, some similar mechanism is invaluable in fostering communication between the myriad of public and private agencies involved in delivery of human services. In organizing such a council, the initial activities may be hampered by mistrust and exaggerated emphasis on confidentiality, but over a relatively short period of time, the benefits of the increased communication become obvious to all the participants.

Conclusion

The preceding discussion on training programs brings us to some concluding remarks which apply to this chapter as a whole. As we have seen, the chapter has discussed the role of human services in the policy-making and managerial process as well as in select operating departments. Of central importance to managers, however, is the general recognition that in any attempt to develop an understanding of human services needs and programs, one of the underlying factors which must be recognized is that most human services do not easily fit into typical governmental functions. Most municipal and other local government activities are organized on a functional basis and, therefore, deal with only one service designed to meet one need, e.g., police protection, recreation, and road maintenance. When physical services are involved, this can be done conveniently. When dealing with human needs and services, however, we find that they cannot be easily separated by function. On the contrary, they normally are very complex and involve an interdisciplinary approach. Therefore, the training required for effective human services programs must involve the ability to cross departmental lines so that those working in each of the disciplines involved can learn from one another. Only if this is done can the resources available be effectively focused to serve human needs, and to help all those involved in the effort realize the goal expressed in the words of Ralph Waldo Emerson, that "The test of civilization is the power of drawing the most benefit out of cities."

1   Linda Cooper, "Merced's Provision of Human Services: A Concise Review," included in letter from Allan R. Schell, City Manager, City of Merced, California, to Mark Keane, Executive Director, International City Management Association, Merced, California, 24 March 1976.

2   See Bernard L. Garmire, ed., *Local Government Police Management* (Washington, D.C.: International City Management Association, 1977).

3   Steven M. Ward, "Juvenile Programs," in *Local Government Police Management,* ed. Bernard L. Garmire (Washington, D.C.: International City Management Association, 1977), p. 267.

4   Thomas J. Sweeney, "What Next for Local Policing?" in *Local Government Police Management,* ed. Bernard L. Garmire (Washington, D.C.: Interna-

tional City Management Association, 1977), p. 505–506.

5   For a thoughtful and detailed discussion of this subject, see Bernard J. Frieden and Marshall Kaplan, *The Politics of Neglect: Urban Aid from Model Cities to Revenue Sharing* (Cambridge: MIT Press, 1975).

6   Detailed discussion of the local government role in code enforcement is included in Chapter 21 of William E. Korbitz, ed., *Urban Public Works Administration* (Washington, D.C.: International City Management Association, 1976).

7   The accompanying publication for this program is Thomas J. Mikulecky, gen. ed., *Small Cities Management Training Program* (Washington, D.C.: International City Management Association, 1975).

16 Services integration

What is "services integration" and what is its significance for the informed local government manager? Services integration is a new name for an old attempt to bring together the many agencies and programs that deliver human services to our citizens. At one time that concern was primarily in the private sector, but the expansion of the public sector as a dominant force in human services has made it a public management issue. In particular, the two decades since the 1950s have been marked by a rapidly expanding role for local, state, and federal governments in the areas of funding and delivery of services to people in need. This, in turn, paved the way for a complex network of public and private funding and operation of human services programs. Since the late 1960s and early 1970s, the very extensiveness of the evolving network of human services has generated a movement to achieve some overall responsiveness and coherence in this public enterprise.

Services integration is the movement which coordinates public and nonpublic agencies and programs, consolidates related public programs, and creates new administrative relationships among the various organizations delivering human services. As of the later 1970s, the services integration movement was still relatively new, and definition of the "traditional" or "best" integration systems was not yet possible. In its broadest sense it includes any attempt by political decision makers, administrators, planners, or service providers to develop and implement coherent policies. This process includes activities such as passing new legislation, creating new organizations, and delivering services that address the needs of human services clients. An integrative approach to human services problems proceeds from the standpoint that the most effective way to meet peoples' needs overall will come from broad concern with the needs of the entire governmental system or the entire set of a client's individual needs rather than from concern based on a single problem or the demands of a single advocacy group or in response to a single categorical agency.

The historical antecedents to public services integration in the United States stem from the voluntary (that is, the private and/or charitable) sector, from local health and welfare councils, and from local unified fund organizations. The earliest attempts at coordination date back to the nineteenth century central case registries and service inventories performed by the charitable organization societies in major cities.[1] In the twentieth century, local health and welfare councils established in many cities were responsible for producing the first plans in the United States outlining broad human needs and developing strategies for fulfilling those needs. Unified funding agencies such as the United Way and United Fund organizations were also established to centralize funding, establish program priorities and disperse priority-determined resources. These organizations, which still exist in many American cities, were made up of representatives of such individual agencies and programs as the Lighthouse for the Blind, the Legal Aid Society, the Jewish Vocational Service, local speech and hearing societies, the Family Service Agency, and dozens of others. Their purposes included the sharing of information, the joint raising of funds, the avoidance of unnecessary duplication, the service of unmet needs, and a general goal of working together.

The voluntary sector has been overshadowed by public sector program growth in recent decades. The federal and state governments enacted legislation funding new programs to be delivered at the local level. They did not, however, always go through city and county decision makers in arranging for the implementation of these programs. Often new units of government were set up or local program directors made directly responsible to their professional peers at the state or federal level. The result was administrative confusion. Local government leaders found themselves faced with a bewildering array of programs. They generally had little or no influence regarding the adoption of the programs, possessed little operational knowledge of them, and, most pertinently, had little capacity for control over them. Subsequently, however, federal money of a more discretionary nature began to come into the picture. The mechanisms have been such programs as the Office for Economic Opportunity, the Model Cities program, general revenue sharing, and block grants for community development. These allowed for local decisions regarding allocation of resources, and engendered a local advocacy process for human services, often focusing attention on previously unserved needs and constituencies. As a result, the provision of human services at the local level became more than just an outlet for state and federal health and welfare programs. Local governments became responsible for assessing needs, making choices, and allocating resources across a broad spectrum of issues. As these programs grew, it became important to local government managers to put together into a functional human services policy the independent and local discretionary programs. The interest in human services integration burgeoned as a result.

How can human services integration specifically be defined? Essentially, services integration includes three major components: (1) *a policy development/policy management capability cutting across independent programs and categories* of human services, such as a comprehensive approach to the rehabilitation of injured persons, meeting their financial, legal, medical, therapeutic and training needs; (2) *a services delivery system designed to meet the needs of clients whose problems go beyond a single agency or program,* such as the tying together of agencies through an information and referral network; and (3) *an organizational structure supportive of the policy management capability or the service delivery system, or both,* such as a consolidated human services department.

Most services integration efforts selectively stress one or two of these three components at the expense of the others. There are those who correctly argue that true, or pure, services integration is not possible without all three. However, many political, constitutional, legal, and technical barriers stand between the present array of human services programs and complete services integration. Therefore, this discussion will encompass all types of movements toward local governments services integration, ranging from voluntary coordination of existing programs to the creation of entirely new human services systems. This inclusive approach is consistent with the definition of human services integration used in a mid-1970s census of local services integration: "An innovative organizational effort to coordinate or consolidate human services activities at the local level in traditional agencies as a means of enhancing the effectiveness, efficiency and/or continuity of comprehensive service delivery." [2]

The approach followed in this chapter is to structure the discussion around four main themes. The first theme is treated in a section which focuses on the need for human services integration and identifies five major factors which, in recent years, have brought the movement to the attention of professionals in this field. The second section places human services integration in its intergovernmental context: it examines integration mechanisms at the local level; federal initiatives; state and county activity; and the related topics of integrated services as a service activity in themselves, and "bottoms up" integration. The third section speaks to the local government focus of this book by itemizing managerial aspects of the search for local services integration systems. The fourth section analyzes some of the problems and issues associated with services integration, and the chapter ends with an evaluative conclusion. Pertinent examples are cited throughout the chapter. An attempt has also been made to focus on those aspects of particular interest and concern to the key decision makers in local government. It is recognized, of course, that local government managers in particular communities will find it most useful to relate the cited experiences to the size, history, and socioeconomic structure of their own jurisdictions.

The need for human services integration

Five major factors can be associated with the movement toward the integration of human services. First, *the expansion of categorical human services programs* in the public sector has made the array of services more striking and the responsibility for their management more difficult to avoid. Second, *the role of government in human services has become multi-faceted;* it now goes beyond the operation of services to funding, to regulation, to the purchase of services, and to other functions. Third, the way these expanded services have generally been organized and operated (that is, categorically and under public, proprietary, and voluntary auspices) has led to *generic problems in service delivery, including fragmentation, discontinuity, inaccessibility, and unaccountability.* Fourth, questions have begun to surface as to *whether the services provided are really meeting the goals* on which their design and implementation was based. It is now felt that programs and clients should be measured against levels of expected attainment. And fifth, there is a desire in local government to develop *a policy management capacity*—to put it all together, to see what it means, to be responsive to needs, and to be efficient and effective. The following discussion will focus on each of these elements in turn.

Getting them all together Portland, Maine, has come forward with the novel approach of combining a neighborhood facility with a new police station to improve the image and public acceptance of the police as well as to promote better police–community relations. The neighborhood facility has a common entrance with the police department, and has a regulation-size gym, large multipurpose meeting room, and small classrooms. A lounge with an adjacent canteen area is available for both the public and police, and further serves to bring the public into closer contact with the police.

The growth of programs

Human services programs, initiated by the social legislation of the 1930s, accelerated in the 1960s and 1970s due to the addition of new programs and the expanded usage of older programs. The chief stimulus for this expansion came from the federal government. Federally funded human services programs were expanded to include, for example, such wide-ranging areas as economic resources development, well-baby clinics, predelinquent youth activities, nutrition for the elderly, job training for welfare recipients, day care for senior citizens and for children of working mothers, family planning, homemaker services, and community mental health programs. The number of programs administered by the U.S. Department of Health, Education, and Welfare (HEW) expanded to over three hundred by the later 1970s. Many human services programs are also associated with other departments—in such areas of concern as employment, veterans, schools, courts, police, industry, and housing—and are operated through other agencies. In addition to these direct services, there have emerged such auxiliary or supportive services as diagnosis, referral, advocacy, transportation, case finding, and follow-up. The "bottom line" of this expansion is that, in the early 1970s, we spent over $200 billion annually on all types of human services. At the time, this amount was approaching one quarter of the gross national product. As of the later 1970s, human services expenditures accounted for about half of all government expenditures, with public sector involvement greatly overshadowing that of the private and voluntary sectors. In fact, excluding health expenditures which are about 58 percent private, 90 percent of all other human services expenditures are public.[3]

The development and implementation of this expansion through independent channels is a crucial factor for understanding the move to services integration. Nearly every program came about in response to the needs of a distinctly identifiable group. Ordinarily, a group of persons in need or their advocates perceiving a failure to meet a specified set of needs petitioned the government to support their program, usually for research, training of professionals, and aid to the states for service provision. Each group wanted its own agency to minister to the perceived needs. This process has been common in many areas of concern, including public health, mental health, criminal justice, developmental disabilities, vocational rehabilitation, public assistance, employment security, and employment and training. Although an extensive public services establishment has been created in each area, the independence of the services further nurtured the idea that had persisted for a century that health and social welfare programs are essentially professional in character and should be isolated from political considerations. A federal system of agencies, professionals, and citizen advocates was created through which policies are established and administered in line with categorical channels of interest. The lines of communication tended to vertically link functional specialists at local, state, and national levels, sometimes excluding a direct role for city halls, state houses, and the White House. There were few expenditures—of money or personnel—geared to the development of general social services approaches.[4] Thus, human services activities have typically been part of a categorical system of agencies and programs that are relatively independent of each other.

The changing role of the public sector

Unlike the defense, postal, or highway systems in the United States, which have always been dominated by the public sector, human services systems evolved out of the proprietary and voluntary sectors. (These historical patterns have been discussed in some detail in Chapter 1 of this book.) In the late nineteenth century, there was considerably more human services activity under private than public auspices. The "for-profit" sector only expanded in areas such as health where there was a widespread demand for services and where delivery of such services was profitable. In the twentieth century, there was a gradual public takeover of many voluntary social programs. This was due to increased demand for a greater number of services as target populations also grew in number and as the need for broader geographic coverage made the cost of service provision beyond the ability of any private entity to handle. Until the 1960s, a "takeover" usually meant public operation of services, sometimes parallel in nature to operations of the voluntary and proprietary sectors but usually financially and administratively independent of them. In general, however, a program was either public, voluntary, or proprietary.

This pattern has since changed: public involvement need no longer be restricted to delivery of services, and the distinction between public and nonpublic activity has become blurred. Governments have become involved in different mechanisms for human services provision in addition to the operational provision of services. A city, for example, can also become involved in the following ways:

1. As a funder—through direct grants to voluntary programs, through purchase of services from voluntary or private agencies, by matching voluntary agency

deficits, or by providing third party matching funds for a formula grant program.

2. As a facilitator/coordinator—by using its influence, management expertise, and staff resources to bring together various organizations for coordination of existing programs and development of new programs.

3. As a capacity builder—by using its skills and knowledge in planning and evaluation in order to improve human services program effectiveness.

4. As a regulator/taxer/employer—through tax and regulatory policies and through its economic influences as a major employer to facilitate resolution of human problems.[5]

Other governments also have these nonoperational options, and they too have chosen to take advantage of them. Therefore, publicly generated human services programs can now include any (or a combination) of these options. When government is granting funds to voluntary agencies, purchasing services from for-profit providers, or helping voluntary and proprietary agencies plan, evaluate and regulate nonpublic programs, it becomes less meaningful to speak of public and nonpublic programs. Instead, it is more suitable for local government managers to think of contemporary human services programs as a continuum, each with some degree of a public–nonpublic relationship. The implications for services integration are obvious. With a greater, almost universal, involvement in programs, many administrators agree that it has become imperative that they, their staffs, and elected officials all think in terms of managing the array of programs from the standpoint of some public purpose.

Generic problems in service delivery

Categorically funded programs administered under various auspices have led to some serious problems in service delivery. As programs were independently established they were usually organized for the purpose of delivering a single service. Such basic program requisites as eligibility determination, physical location of programs, professional staffing, service approaches, and lines of responsibility were established along vertical functional program lines. This categorical system for human services programming has contributed to what many social policy analysts consider to be the four key problems in service delivery:

1. *Fragmentation*—separate organization of services due to location, specialization, duplication, or lack of cooperation;

2. *Inaccessibility*—obstacles for a person trying to make use of the network of local social services, such as restrictive eligibility on the basis of social class, race, success potential, or other exclusionary criteria;

3. *Discontinuity*—obstacles to clients moving from provider to provider, or other gaps in assistance that appear as an agency tries to match resources to needs, such as when communication channels or referral mechanisms are lacking; and

4. *Unaccountability*–a lack of interactive relationships between the individuals being served and the organizations' decision makers, such as inability of clients to influence decisions that affect them or the insensitivity of service providers to clients' needs and interests.[6]

Thus, persons who enter the categorical services system may discover (often to their distress, frustration, or anger) that they must first wend their way through an intricate maze of social services and then, when they have ascertained which service they need, that they are not able to get it because eligibility requirements exclude them from the program for some reason. Finally, if they wish to find some resolution of their problem, they may well have no viable course of redress.

Numerous practical consequences of these problems occur at the local level and may be illustrated by a few choice, even Kafkaesque, examples. By 1971, New York City had about 6,000 public, quasi-public, and voluntary agencies which provided a wide variety of human services to four million clients with no central source of information and no overall coordinative mechanism.[7] Clients in search of services in the Boston area once averaged 330 hours of form processing and delay time from their entry into the system to receipt of services. It is estimated that 15 percent of professional time in Lancaster, Pennsylvania, is spent on duplicative preservice and postservice activities. In Baltimore, as many as eight case monitors from different public agencies were making home visits to the same family. Lancaster County, Pennsylvania found itself with 29 separate recreation programs run by separate agencies. Chattanooga had 40 different transportation systems. These kinds of duplication and lack of coordination have the greatest effect on the multiproblem client, for whom it is often necessary to arrange for the services of more than one agency. Various studies estimate that 40–80 percent of all service clients, nationwide, are in need of multiple services: 80 percent in the Boston area; 75 percent in Contra Costa, California; 68 percent in Jonesboro, Arkansas; 42 percent in Nyssa, Oregon; and 40 percent in Devils Lake, North Dakota.[8] Even these figures may be understated, inasmuch as service workers often have to make considerable effort to determine the existence of multiple problems. In any case, less than half of those referred to another agency ever receive service.

These service delivery problems are not intentional. They are the dismal consequence of the way services have been organized and operated. Services integration mechanisms attempt to reduce such problems or, at least, eliminate their effects.

Achieving goals

One might facetiously conclude at this point that if the clients do not get the services needed, then the implicit aim of human services programs must be to foster the vertical functional system and provide occupational outlets for professionals. Indeed, many observers do feel this way, primarily because professionals have never been held accountable for the services they deliver. Traditionally, funding and accountability systems have been tied to specific programs rather than geared to specific outcomes. Programs were budgeted on the basis of delivery of relatively discrete services to an estimated number of clients. The auditing process then accounted for these previously specified items. It was always vaguely understood that, based on their condition, clients were to be restored to some level of self-sufficiency, but the expected outcomes were never measured.

It also became apparent that clients did not always reach the promised objective. Welfare recipients were not removed from the unemployment rolls; they remained, sometimes for more than one generation, creating a "culture of poverty." Mental hospital patients were not successfully treated before being discharged to communities, only to be readmitted, creating a "revolving door" situation. Vocational rehabilitation clients were said to have a high placement rate, yet it would ultimately emerge that many quickly lost their jobs and were then included in new head counts; only the least handicapped and most skilled actually remained placed in their original jobs. This and similarly misleading methods are known as "creaming." The aged and medically disabled were placed in proprietary nursing homes for care under federal and state payments; the profit motive precluded all but custodial care, creating spurred on by what has sometimes been called "tender loving greed." The prevalence of these conditions has led to considerable cynicism about social programs generally and to greater concern on the part of policy makers asking whether social programs actually accomplish any of what they are supposed to.

In order to prevent "cultures of poverty," "revolving doors," "creaming," and "tender loving greed," programs will have to be measured on the basis of outcomes. At the policy level, the greatest concern has been for measurements of clients' functioning levels—can they hold jobs, stay off welfare, live independently in the community, and so on? On the whole, there has been a shift in interest from the number of clients served to what happens to the clients that are served.

The interest in outcome measures has led to a concern for a "total system intervention" on clients. The measurement of social program interventions against desired future states of affairs tends to be independent of programs. The aim is to look at what happened to clients rather than how many were served and at what cost. The outcome question has, in turn, led to a whole series of related human services questions. Are services cost-effective? Are they equitable? Do they meet reasonable standards of quality? Do they have any impact on community incidence rates (extrusion from the community, divorce, delinquency)? Do programs meet expected goals? It is believed that cross-program questions such as these, focusing on outcomes of individuals and program achievements, can best be answered through an integrated planning and evaluation capacity where there is an overall perspective and a capacity for independent assessment.

The search for a policy management capability

The enormous size and diversity of human services programs, the varied roles of government, the problems generated by the categorically organized system, and the need to measure overall accomplishment all suggest the conclusion that human services policies are in need of some management independent of, and at a higher level than, any individual program. A mid-1970s Study Committee on Policy Management and Assistance of the U.S. Office of Management and Budget defined policy management as "the identification of needs, analysis of options, selection of programs and allocation of resources on a jurisdiction-wide basis." [9] Members of that committee distinguish policy management from program management—the implementation of policy or the daily operation of agencies carrying out policy along functional lines—and resource management—the establishment of basic administrative support systems. [10] While each of the independent agencies has its own planning and policy development staff, they tend to analyze problems and objectives in terms of existing problems and resources, and to establish operational solutions in response to particular concerns within their areas. The need for a policy management capability cuts across all of the functional agencies. It includes consideration of strategies for unified approaches to problems, of comprehensive resource allocation, and of supportive organizational mechanisms.

Although most local human services planning and management has been within programs, there is a growing trend toward the development of policy management within municipal government. [11] The evolutionary expansion of the local government role in many new areas, including human services, has given rise to a need to establish a policy development capability. This has been encouraged by a number of federal initiatives (discussed in the following section of this chapter), coupled with the desire on the part of local executives to understand where they are going and to have a role in developing strategies affecting all policy areas. Indeed, a study by the National League of Cities/U.S. Conference of Mayors examining the roles for cities under any national unified human services legislation concluded that issues regarding city-level participation in policy planning and management were far more important to city administrators than issues appertaining to the question of responsibility for the maintenance of program operations. [12]

The growth of a policy management role is a logical stimulant to services integration. As one assesses needs, analyzes options, selects programs, and allocates resources on a broad scale, it becomes more difficult to justify the existence of independent agencies performing similar services, duplicating programs, generating service gaps, leaving needs unserved, and producing cost-ineffective programs. Given such circumstances, the logical "next step" to coordination, consolidation, and unification becomes more apparent.

Summary

The preceding section has discussed some of the factors that help to explain why growing numbers of local government managers and other decision makers have had the topic of human services integration under consideration in recent years. The five factors cited—growth of programs; changing role of the public sector; generic service delivery problems; goal achievement considerations; and the search for a policy management capability—bring into focus themes that have been touched upon in one way or another throughout the earlier portions of this book.

Services integration in the intergovernmental context

Before proceeding to a discussion of the practices employed in the search for local human services integration systems, it is helpful to outline and discuss the broader questions of services integration, particularly insofar as they relate to the major components of our governmental system. The following discussion first identifies some of the basic activities relating to services integration. Both state and local-level operations, however, have a direct relationship to federal initiatives in this area, so the discussion then proceeds to take a look at the thrust of federal programs. The third section considers the role of state and county activity, particularly as it impinges on local level operations. This portion of the chapter ends with an analysis of some general questions stemming from, or appropriate to, this intergovernmental context.

Services integration mechanisms

Efforts employed to accomplish combined efforts in the human services ordinarily involve an integrating agent. This integrator is charged with coordinating or otherwise jointly operating the services or functions of autonomous units or providers, and integrating linkages, or mechanisms that maintain the joint or unified endeavors. An integrator can be a governmental executive, board, staff, or individual within an agency. Linkages tie together, consolidate or unite various administrative, fiscal and service delivery functions providers ordinarily perform separately.[13]

Thus, the simplest way to explain current practices in services integration is in terms of the integrator tying together the service providers with linkage mechanisms. In Figure 16–1 the "I" at the top is the integrator, who has responsibility for coordinating service providers to give comprehensive services to clients. Strung out below the integrator are a series of service providers, SP1, SP2, . . . SPn, as many as 400–500 in many cities. In the existing human service system integrators are either weak or nonexistent. Service providers, on the other hand, are usually strong. Funding is channeled directly to them, their organizational autonomy is often stipulated in state and federal law, the services they are to offer are regulated in the state capitol and Washington, and even their ability to coordinate with other programs may be hampered by laws and regulations. "I" and "SP" relationships exist at every level of government: at the federal level, the integrator is the president and the service providers are the cabinet members; at the HEW level, the integrator is the secretary and the service providers are the specific agencies; at the local level, the mayor, manager, or some other agent is the integrator and the departments, agencies, and programs are the service providers. The essence of services integration, then, is to strengthen the integrator and the

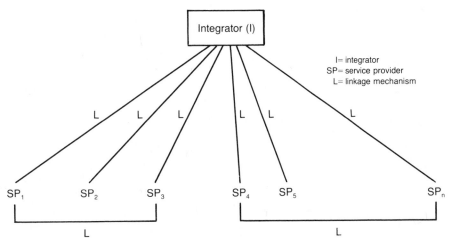

Figure 16–1 Linkages between integrators and service providers. See text for further discussion. (Source: Lyle M. Spencer, "Planning and Organizing Human Services Delivery Systems," paper presented at a seminar on human services integration, sponsored by the Social Welfare Research Institute, University of Denver, Denver, 1973.)

linkage mechanisms (L) that the integrator uses to tie the service providers together.[14]

The more common services integration linkages and their definition would include:

Joint planning—the joint determination of total service delivery system needs and priorities through a structured planning process.

Joint development of operating policies—a structured process in which the policies, procedures, regulations, and guidelines governing the administration of a project are jointly established.

Joint programming—the joint development of programmatic solutions to defined problems in relation to existing resources.

Information-sharing—an exchange of information regarding resources, procedures, and legal requirements (but not individual clients) between the project integrator and various service providers.

Joint evaluation—the joint determination of effectiveness of service in meeting client needs.

Coordinated budgeting/planning—the integrator sits with all service providers together or individually to develop their budgets but without any authority to ensure the budgets are adhered to *or* the traditional service agencies develop their budgets together.

Centralizing budgeting—a centralized authority develops the budgets for the traditional service agencies with the authority to ensure that they are adhered to; may or may not include central point funding.

Joint funding—two or more service providers give funds to support service; most often in a broad programmatic fashion.

Purchase of service—formal agreements that may or may not involve a written contract between the integrated system and some other party or among agencies to obtain or provide service; generally a fee-for-service arrangement.

Transfer of budget authority—funds are shifted from one agency within the integrated system to another agency in that same system.

Consolidated personnel administration—the centralized provision of some or all of the following: hiring, firing, promoting, placing, classifying, training.

Joint use of staff—two different agencies deliver service by using the same staff; both agencies have line authority over staff.

Seconding, cross-agency assignment—one or more employees are on the payroll of one agency but under the administrative control of another.

Organizational change across agencies—service agencies in the integrated system or newly created agencies receive staff or units from another agency in the system *and/or* an umbrella organization is created.

Organizational change within the agency—reorganization of agency staff or organizational units involving changes internal to each organization only (may be similar changes in each agency).

Co-location of central offices—central administrative offices for two or more agencies at the locale are relocated at a single site.

Co-location of branch functions—several agencies co-locate personnel performing branch as opposed to centralized administrative functions at a single site.

Outstationing—placement of a service provider in the facility of another service agency; no transfer of line authority or payroll responsibility takes place.

Record keeping—the gathering, storing, and disseminating of information about clients.

Grants management—the servicing of grants.

Central support services—the consolidated or centralized provision of services such as auditing, purchasing, exchange of material and equipment, and consultative services.

Satellite services—are provided whenever personnel from one service agency are restationed so as to increase the number of site-agencies in the integrated network.

Outreach—the systematic recruitment of clients.

Intake—the process resulting in the admission (including determination of eligibility) of a client to the provision of direct service.

Transportation—provision of transportation to clients.

Referral—the process by which a client is directed or sent for services to another provider by a system that is in some way centralized.

Diagnosis—the assessment of overall service needs of individual clients.

Follow-up—the process used to determine whether clients receive the services to which they have been referred and to shepherd the client through the service delivery system.

Case conference—a meeting between the integrator's staff and staff of agencies who provide service to a given family for the purpose of discussing that family either generally or in terms of a specific problem, possibly determining a course of action and assigning responsibility among the agencies for implementing the solution.

Case consultation—a meeting of staff members of agencies who provide service to a given family for same purposes as specified in ''case conference'' above.

Case coordinator—the designated staff member having prime responsibility to assure the provision of service by multiple autonomous providers to a given client.

Case team—the arrangement in which a number of staff members, either representing different disciplines or working with different members of a given family, work together to relate a range of services of autonomous providers to a given client. The primary difference between case conferences and case teams is that the former may be ad hoc whereas the latter involves continuous and systematic interaction between the members of the team.

Data system—any machine or computerized record keeping system containing at a minimum information regarding patients contacted and clients treated.[15]

These examples of linkages are taken from actual services integration mechanisms undertaken by state and local governments. While improving the local service delivery system is the intent of integration, such efforts have not come without federal influence.

Federal initiatives in services integration

While most of the experiments with creating integrated human services systems have come at the state, substate or local level the movement has not been without federal government influence. Dissatisfaction with increasingly expensive and difficult to manage social programs has led federal government officials—particularly in the Department of Health, Education, and Welfare—to support programs that would aid in the coherent delivery of services. Because these supportive efforts have stemmed from a desire to overcome the effects of the federal government's pattern of categorical programming, each federal initiative shares the common thread of attempting to link together one or more federal program (or previously organized single program) and to facilitate area-based planning for policy development, organization building and development of service delivery systems. Although the more recent attempts to integrate services have been direct research and demonstration efforts, other stimuli have been indirect, such as revenue sharing, and earlier programs such as economic opportunity and Model Cities shared similar linkage goals.

Community Action Agencies   One of the earliest direct coordinative efforts were the Community Action Agencies (CAAs) that grew out of the community action program of the Economic Opportunity Acts of 1964 and 1967. CAAs organized on the local community level were charged with mobilizing public and private community resources for combating poverty, providing supportive type services that would develop employment ability and opportunity, strengthening community capabilities for planning state and federal poverty-related assistance, and encouraging residential participation in these efforts.[16] The CAAs were the first social agencies to systematically use local residents to serve in lieu of professionals. These paraprofessionals brought in by CAA tended to see problems as multiple and interrelated, and were early human services generalists. CAAs were coordinators and advocates working with local housing agencies, welfare departments, state employment agencies, and school boards arranging for services and helping solve problems for persons who had trouble with these agencies. A study of this coordination effort concluded that most CAA's were too far from the power center of their communities to be effective in a comprehensive sense. Where they were successful, it was usually in limited ways, in a neighborhood or in a small component of human services such as coordinating manpower programs.[17] CAA's were, nevertheless, an important early influence on services integration. The paraprofessional generalists introduced the need to manage the case of the multi-problem client. CAA's pointed out the need for coordination, the problems of dealing with independent agencies, and the fact that many persons in need were not obtaining services. In addition, OEO principles demonstrated the need to develop a more comprehensive policy planning and management approach to human services.[18]

The impact of Model Cities   The Model Cities program represented another effort to develop coordinated planning and service delivery. The basic thrust of Model Cities was to rebuild deteriorated neighborhoods in selected cities by coordinating the array of federal, state, local, and private approaches, particularly in housing, education, health, and transportation. In practice, this meant that the Model Cities director had to look to the neighborhood to mobilize and coordinate resident citizen participation, then look laterally to numerous public and private agencies in the community to enlist their resources and coordinate their proposals. Meanwhile, he or she had to reflect the views of city government and maintain liason with the federal government to assure compliance with requirements. Sundquist's study of the process concluded that it worked reasonably well.[19] Most Model Cities programs established co-located one-stop service centers, integrated health service programs, combined child care programs, and cooperative programs linking public and private agencies.

According to one study for the Department of Health, Education, and Welfare (HEW), the problem of Model Cities became not how cities were to relate to the department's hundreds of programs, but how HEW was to fit into an almost completely unfamiliar setting of urban government. The direct involvement of city government through Model Cities in health, educative, and social services programs ran against tradition. First, HEW ordinarily worked within its own boundaries; Model Cities demanded interdepartmental relations. Second, program managers preferred to deal with local agencies on single programs; Model Cities required interprogram and multiprogram communication. Third, HEW agencies saw little need to work across health, education, and social services agency boundaries within the department; the Model Cities review of cities' entire social planning required interagency ties. And fourth, HEW officials in regional and central offices preferred to deal with state or local agencies in separate negotiations;

Model Cities demanded a genuinely intergovernmental involvement of both state and local government with the federal department. "The Model Cities program illuminated in bold relief for the first time that HEW was fundamentally a department organized around a host of overlapping constituencies that were committed to a categorical view of the department's role at state and local levels." [20]

Local review of federal programs Yet another stream that has influenced services integration is the independently administered review and comment procedures and planning mechanisms of categorical programs. Among the more significant programs are: 1) community action checkpoint—a sign-off on categorical HEW applications by the chief elected official, as well as from designated local agencies; 2) law enforcement assistance—review of applications by local governments, central clearance of special purpose agencies through general purpose governments; 3) comprehensive employment and training—comprehensive planning and flexible funding of interagency employment training and supportive services with sponsorship by general purpose government; 4) health resources planning—comprehensive planning for unified private and public health programming on a substate district basis, with elected official participation on boards; 5) community coordinated child care (4-C)—local level coordinating mechanisms for day care and preschool programs; 6) community mental health centers—construction and staffing grants, applications must demonstrate coordination with city, metropolitan area and interstate planning agencies; and 7) elementary and secondary education—Title I planning requires a comprehensive plan for meeting the special education needs of disadvantaged children. The goal of each of these is to involve local government to some degree in the planning by independent categorical agencies for federal grant applications. Local applicants, for example, must inform the general purpose government of their intent to apply for federal monies and secure some form of sign-off.[21] While these mechanisms are only indirect steps in enhancing city or county government policy management capacity and in bringing services together, they have undoubtedly pointed to the logic of services integration.

Other stimuli Somewhat more direct federal mechanisms include revenue sharing, A-95 review, and standardized federal grants. Revenue sharing has added impetus to services integration by offering local governments financial flexibility to accompany any administrative flexibility promoted by other programs. It is an impetus for allocating dollars according to locally determined needs, plans and programs. Special revenue sharing and special revenue sharing type programs work toward decategorization by lumping together many related service programs and giving them directly to units of general purpose government. The federal government is moving in the direction of a standardized grant procedure under the A-102 procedure, allowing for standardized application forms, budgeting and reporting requirements, property management procedures, and so on. The familiar A-95 review procedure, which establishes a series of federal grants clearinghouses in substate districts and at the metropolitan level, is designed to assure that construction, economic development and social programs are consistent and coordinated with area-wide plans.

Each of these mechanisms and the categorical program requirements for review and sign-off represents a step toward mutual policy development. They work to shift the game at city hall from grantsmanship to policy management:

The new management problem is different from the grantsmanship problem mainly in the need for sustained city commitment of skilled staff to achieve objectives through multi-agency planning and negotiation. As more local government staff become involved in various functional areas, the local chief executive must develop a more structured process for staying in touch with strategy development and implementation by his [sic] administration.[22]

This shift in focus makes it more possible to think in terms of services integration, in that it is consistent with the trends in such other policy areas as physical development, environmental protection and transportation.

Research and demonstration efforts   The 1970s has proved to be a decade of experimentation with various forms of services integration. These efforts were spurred by federal efforts to get local communities to try different approaches. Service delivery aspects of integration were developed under the Services Integration Targets of Opportunity (SITO) program, which ended in 1975. SITO was designed to seek demonstration results on components, and for techniques that are critical to the delivery of integrated and comprehensive approaches. This focus was predicated on the assumption that no single uniform model existed and that it is entirely possible that a variety of approaches and models could be applied, with elements applicable in differing environments and situations. In all, nearly fifty projects were funded at different levels of government organization, of different sophistication and technical expertise, and with differing techniques and approaches to services delivery.[23]

The ongoing HEW Partnership Grants program is intended to develop methods of strengthening the capacity of state and local general purpose government chief executive officials in planning and managing the delivery of human services. The Partnership program is aimed at a number of specific objectives, including: assessment of needs, planning and priority setting; technical assistance; and managing, defining and rationalizing the roles of general purpose governments in human services delivery. While the SITO and Partnership programs are different, the latter is supposed to build on the knowledge of the former. They are linked through the goal of improving services delivery through coordinative and integrative means.

These two programs have been shepherded by a relatively new unit in HEW, The Office of Intergovernmental Systems. This office is specifically charged with developing alternative strategies to services integration, with developing means of breaking down the barriers of categorical programming and with fostering cooperation with state and local governments. In addition to administration of the SITO and Partnership projects the office is: evaluating the effectiveness of information systems; studying the technology as applied to services integration planning and evaluation; and studying effectiveness measures to identify how to measure what works in order to assist local governments in determining funding priorities.

HEW has also initiated national legislation that would facilitate state and local planning and management of human services in a more coherent manner. While presented to Congress in various forms, basically the "allied services" concept is to support grants to the states, and through states to localities, for the development of "allied services plans," providing for the coordinated delivery of human services. Included are special implementation grants to states and localities to assist in covering the initial costs of consolidating or allying administrative support services and management functions. Allied services would also permit those states which have approved allied services plans to transfer funds from one HEW program to another for similar uses. At the national level, allied services would empower the secretary to waive administrative and technical barriers applying to categorical programs when they impede the allied or coordinated delivery of services. At an early period in HEW's attempt to secure passage of allied services, entire states were to be divided up into human services planning units and a wide range of HEW programs were to be included. As a result of sustained opposition from categorical groups, professionals, agency administrators, and members of Congress, the program has been modified. Instead of including a wide range of HEW programs on a statewide basis only demonstration areas of states need be selected out, and only two required and three additional optional programs need be covered, apparently reducing allied services to a research and demonstration effort.

Summary   While noteworthy antecedents, none of the federal initiatives discussed has had the effect of transforming the old human services into comprehensive integrated systems. With varying weight, each has had an indirect influence at the local level by demonstrating and encouraging city hall to understand the existing state of services, setting policy goals and mapping out how to get there in a reasonable fashion.

State and county activity

As new federal social programs are enacted, they generally are implemented by state plans, and through states to independent county departments or county level offices of state departments. The states and counties have thus also undertaken services integration. The states and counties, however, are faced with more independent categorical human services than cities, and integration has necessarily been a prime concern at these levels.

Reorganizing the states   As of the late 1970s, over thirty of the states have developed some form of linking activity, ranging from small coordinating offices attached to the governor's staff to completely unified departments, merging administration and service delivery. Most states fall somewhere between, with a comprehensive human resource department which administers public assistance-social service programs and at least three other major human service programs.[24] Each state's organizational form is somewhat different, being a product of its own history, its political environment and its geographical, demographic, and socio-economic characteristics. Each state, in turn, puts a somewhat different emphasis on the dimensions of services integration. Since most of these departments came about as a part of general state reorganization, they tend to emphasize organizational form. Many states have adopted different patterns for organization at the state level and for service delivery at the local level, making it very difficult to categorize them into a particular model. Within these limitations, a study by the Council of State Governments has nevertheless divided the states that have reorganized into three categories: *confederated* agencies, where organizational or legal authority remains in line departments but a new agency, program or function is created to coordinate human resource programs (Virginia, Minnesota); *consolidated* agencies, where all or most administrative and planning/evaluation authority rests in a newly created human services agency but programs are developed and services are delivered along traditional agency or divisional lines (North Carolina, Oklahoma); and *integrated* agencies, where a new vertical structure is created, responsible for both management and operations (Florida, Arizona).[25]

Experimentation at the county level   There is a greater variety of integration approaches at the county level. Indeed, much of the experimentation at the city level to be illustrated in this chapter is similar to county human service innovations. Polk County, Iowa, under the directorship of the manager's office, has placed responsibility for coordinating human services into 12 lead agencies that cover major human services at the county level. In addition, they have developed a case manager system for client tracking, problem diagnosis, service coordination and monitoring. In Lancaster County, Pennsylvania, the county government, Lancaster city government, and a voluntary service agency council have combined, under the leadership of the latter, to encourage citizen participation and engage in needs assessment and planning for human services. Its emphasis, therefore, is primarily on the policy management component.

Dade County, Florida has created a department of human resources out of 12 previously independent departments. This department administers 22 separate programs in 6 divisions, including health, rehabilitation, employment and training, aging, child development, and public assistance. Personnel and financial management have been centralized, but central management provides only assistance to the divisions on program planning. (See Chapter 13 for a detailed treatment of the Dade County case.) Contra Costa County, California has created a human resources agency (HRA), which is responsible for all public health, mental health, social services, public assistance, and inpatient and outpatient medical care. The county HRA employs several methods to coordinate and integrate the services of all providers including purchase of service contracts, inter-agency service contracts, joint planning, and the establishment of community groups to increase citizen participation. The HRA also operates a central service center for persons living in remote areas providing outreach, intake, information and referral, diagnosis and case management on an integrated basis.[26]

Many other county human service organizations have been created as they become absorbed into state and regional structures created under state reorganizations, thereby becoming local administrative units of a state department of human resources. However, the degree of consolidation is usually more minimal than that of the state structures. Few states have actually merged an entire state's county agencies into human resources programs. California, Wisconsin, and Minnesota have encouraged such mergers, however, by passage of permissive legislation. Minnesota, for example, has passed enabling legislation for a limited number of counties to experiment with the adoption of human services boards which have responsibility for the planning, administration, and service delivery on a completely integrated basis.[27] As subunits of the state, the counties will face many of the same barriers to services integration as cities do.

Integrated services as a service

At this point it is helpful to step back from the intergovernmental context and note the important fact that human services is an emergent service strategy employed in many of the categorical services. That is, to many a professional, one approaches the client as a whole individual with multiple needs, all or most of which must be addressed if one is to restore the client to the highest possible level of functioning or self-sufficiency. Indeed, some would argue that this approach to service would be an additional component of services integration, to be added to the three listed at the beginning of this chapter. If a provider adheres to such a service ideology, it implies that one must think in terms of linking the client with the services of others.[28]

The concept of the whole individual with multiple needs   It has been found that persons disabled by injuries more readily adapt to the community if they receive medical, social and psychological services along with their vocational training. It has also been found that the tendency to fractionate services to mentally ill clients mitigates against successful job placement. Mental health and vocational training workers once thought that vocational rehabilitation should come after treatment, whereas the emergent approach is toward simultaneous services. Immediate involvement of the client in the two services results in a higher rate of self-sufficiency than with a two-step procedure. Successful retention of employment by alcoholics is higher when treatment and job finding are combined with counseling and "readiness" training sessions. Successful rehabilitation of inner-city drug addicts has been found to be based on physical restoration of clients—detoxification and basic medical treatment—followed by interpersonal skills development and vocational rehabilitation.[29] Most people who come to a public social service agency are in distress. The subject's distress could be due to a financial, emotional, interpersonal, or physical crisis, a barrier caused by a landlord, another agency, or the city, or any combination of these factors. Often they are interrelated; the financial stress of unemployment can lead to emotional, inter-personal and alcoholic problems. It is difficult to channel this distress within the scope and mission of a single agency.

Implications for services integration   Recognizing this as a common situation with many clients, the service provider sees that the solution to the problem involves going beyond his or her agency or program. One must provide for a range of services: providing linkage on income support, arranging for the rehabilitative service of another agency, informing of the availability of legal services, and/or intervening on behalf of the client. Thus, the service worker becomes more than a direct service provider; he or she links, advocates, expedites and monitors.[30] The approach to the service is to build these additional activities into the client's service plan.

What are the services integration implications of this emergent approach to mental health, vocational rehabilitation, alcohol and drug treatment, children and youth services, corrections, and so on? The essential answer is that the direct service worker must think in terms of a complex human service system rather than narrowly within a particular program or service. One must think in terms of other professional workers and helping agencies in human services. One must bring into one's "field of forces" for successful resolution of client problems all of the supportive organized community resources that are not part of the formal helping system, such as recreation and activity programs, church activities, YMCAs, Boy Scouts, and many others. Also, one must think in terms of persons who are outside of organized programs but whose occupational roles give them special leverage, or put them in touch with people in distress, such as physicians, attorneys, police, teachers, barbers, bartenders, even astrologers and fortune tellers. Finally, one must think in terms of informal helpers, persons who have no recognized or occupational role but are strategically located or have special talents to help people in distress, such as family members, coworkers, friends, associates, volunteers, even local community "Dutch uncles," "Jewish mothers" and "bleeding hearts." [31] Any service worker who brings such a complex set of community forces into his or her approach to service will be aided by a more integrated human service system.

"Bottoms up" integration

The approach to dealing with clients depicted in the previous section should have suggested to local government managers why it is important to incorporate modes of service delivery into human services integration. It is difficult to foster a multi-service concept by focusing attention on organizing administrative structures and building policy management capacities alone. That is why many have concluded that successful integration must therefore deal with questions of service delivery as well. It is important to provide coherent services to the individual as well as reducing fragmentation and duplication of agency activities.[32]

Coherent service delivery: the example of spinal injury patients   In approaching integration at the service delivery level one is allowed to assess individual needs, search for resources across agencies, arrange for service, follow up these services, and monitor the impact of these services. A prime example, related by Perry Levinson, is the spinal cord injury projects sponsored by the Rehabilitation Services Administration of HEW, which attempts to coordinate the sequencing of services from the moment of the accident to re-entry of the patient into an active community existence including a steady job. Many people must be trained, pre-placed, and integrated into a reasonably smooth delivery system. These include police personnel, National Guard helicopter pilots, private physicians, ambulance drivers, architects designing barrier free building and transportation systems, recreation facility leaders, volunteer groups, and vocational rehabilitation counselors. All of their roles and services must be anticipated and properly sequenced if the spinal cord injured are to have any chance of returning to a "normal" life.[33] Creating a working system of services such as this, involving numerous actors and programs, logically begins with clients and their needs.

Organizing around client need sets: the "bottoms up" approach   Approaches such as that just described have led to what is commonly known as the "bottoms up" mode of human services planning. Rather than looking at agencies and agency functions for purposes of linking, one plans by organizing around sets of client needs. For example, the Olympic Center in Bremerton, Washington planned and organized its services around clusters of client needs rather than categorical or program structures. They analyzed the various presenting problems into client types—"individual adults" eligible for a limited number of services, "individual children" eligible for limited services, and "services for families" not made available to the other two—and established the fundamental components of the service delivery system around these three client types.[34] Promoting a multi-service approach at the point where the services meet the clients can eliminate situations where program gaps exist, cases are inadequately evaluated, services offered are inadequate or in conflict, and/or simultaneous services are not meshed.[35] "Bottoms up" planning is as necessary to svoid these problems as top down planning is to promote program coherence.

Summary

The preceding discussion has brought the need for human services integration into closer focus by considering some of the implications, insofar as addressing those needs is concerned, of the existence of varying levels of government in our federal system. The entire discussion took place within a defined conceptual framework relating to the role of an integrator and the linkages tying that person to sets of service providers. The emphasis has been on the local level of activity, but the discussion has indicated that federal initiatives and ties at the regional, state, or county level are all significant components to be considered when integrative mechanisms are contemplated. Pertinent examples have been provided wherever possible. The analysis concluded by emphasizing the managerial and administrative implications of the growing professional concept of servicing whole individuals with multiple needs, and of the associated focus on organizing coherent service delivery around sets of client needs—the "bottoms up" approach.

The search for local service integration systems

The following discussion outlines and analyzes components of what might be termed the search for managerially viable local human service integration systems. The approach taken is to take an introductory overview of the basic managerial approaches involved, and then to consider the role of such elements as informal cooperation; coordination within services; linking independent agencies and programs; creating new departments; developing new systems; a concluding section on pooling the experiences. Examples are again provided throughout, and the discussion attempts to maintain a managerial perspective highlighting appropriate decision making points for local officials involved.

Overview: the search as subsystem of the organized community

The establishment of integrative mechanisms is the development of systems. Each of the services brought together has its own interrelationships of agencies, supporting groups, clientele, and interactions. They tend to be isolated from one another, with a network for the income poor, a network for the mentally disabled, a network for the physically disabled, a network for the blind, and so on. Services integration works toward combining these networks into a functioning system meeting human needs.

The search for a community human services system should be conceived as a subsystem of the organized community. The human services subsystem deals with how human input is received, directed to community goals, transformed into policies, and delivered as services. In this sense it is no different than a community development or land use subsystem. In any of these subsystems the human resources must be used to coordinate the entire process, including: the skills and abilities of people; the community leadership and citizen norms; the formal systems for reward, evaluation, bargaining, influencing, and redressing grievances; and informal and unprogrammed activities and interactions, including people's actions of resistance, social and power coalitions, competition, group norms, feelings, values and status.[36]

In any community the structural components of the human service system go beyond the public helping agencies. They include school districts, voluntary charitable organizations, workshops for the handicapped, resident treatment houses for boys and girls, adoption agencies, family counseling agencies, the Salvation Army, urban coalitions, the Urban League, emergency relief organizations, Big Brothers, halfway houses, hot lines, job counseling services, legal aid groups, alcoholic rehabilitation groups, associations for retarded children, peer group drug treatment programs, rape crisis centers and nursing homes. Also, churches operate welfare and social programs and a number of business organizations and labor unions operate job training programs.[37] All of these agencies deliver human services of some type and ultimately are part of a system.

The voluntary agency councils and unified fund organizations are also elements that must be brought into a system. Depending on the size of the city, one might face a health and welfare council, a United Way type of funding organization and such religious-based councils as Catholic Charities and Lutheran Welfare. In addition, each type of service may have its own coordinating council, such as an alcoholism council, a speech and hearing council, a mental health consortium, or a rehabilitation services steering committee. At one time these councils were parallel structures to the public system, but with growth of government grants and purchases of service, they must now be considered as part of the community human services system. Communities with such coordinative agencies will have to deal with them in creating an integrated human services system. In most cases this will prove to be a challenging but unavoidable situation, given their historical and prestigious position in the community.

Informal cooperation

As a precursor to any formalized human services system one must take note of the thousands of informal cooperative activities that are regularly undertaken between agencies as service workers deal with multiproblem clients. Some of these relationships are formalized but are so regular they can be patterned. Others are formalized to the point where working agreements for certain types of clients have been established between agencies. Many developmental disabilities agencies, for example, have worked out arrangements to have psychological testing and psychotropic ("acting on the mind") medications dispensed at the mental health center or family service agency. Still other arrangements are based on the purchase of services across agencies. A growing number of school systems have opted to purchase social work and speech and hearing services rather than operate them in their own departments. Other cooperative arrangements are required by administrative rule as stipulated by law or a condition of a grant or purchase. The local mental health center in many states is charged with monitoring and coordinating the efforts of public assistance, Social Security (SSI), vocational rehabilitation and other programs to support former mental hospital patients in the community. Federal welfare program recipients must link up with employment services and they are entitled to a range of social and medical services as a condition of their eligibility. These working relationships between agencies are not systematic but they could be used as basic building blocks of more formalized human services networks, particularly if client flow through the system is used as a basis of organizing.

Coordination within services

Not only is there a need to link fragmented categorical programs but many of the categories themselves represent a multiplicity of agencies and programs. In the health field there are the local health department, public and private hospitals, private physicians and group practices, neighborhood health centers and school health programs. In the employment and training field, there are the public employment agencies, private employment agencies, Urban Leagues, job training centers, sheltered workshops, vocational rehabilitation programs, job counseling programs and employer-based on-the-job training programs. In the developmental disabilities field, there are inpatient residential facilities, transitional residential facilities, intermediate care facilities, group living facilities, work readiness programs, sheltered workshops, day activities programs, day-care programs, school special education programs, case-finding programs and other special education and training programs. Similar listings could be generated for practically any category of service. These programs are in the public, voluntary and proprietary sectors. Ordinarily they are connected to each other in a very loose way, further compounding the human services confusion, contributing to gaps in service, unnecessary duplication and discontinuous service.

This situation has made it difficult to speak in terms of a coherent policy in a given category, and makes its administration difficult. It has led to a movement *within* categories to develop "systems" for the coordinated delivery of services.[38] The leadership in this area has come from the public sector. In some cases it has been through law, such as in health (with the Health Resources and Development Act) and in manpower (with the Comprehensive Employment and Training Act [CETA]). In other cases, encouragement to coordinate has been through administrative rules, or as a condition of a grant or contract. The search among administrators of human services programs for networks within the categorical services is an important parallel concern that local government managers should be made aware of. There are some who claim that the creation of such networks is a precondition for integration between services.

The key components of creating and maintaining a comprehensive human services system for a local community need not be complex (although the process of developing and managing it may be). A comprehensive system would bring all of the elements of the community mentioned into an interrelated structure that would perform the necessary policy development, organizational and service delivery functions. One such ideal human services system includes:

1. The identification of community members who have been, who are, or who may be, candidates for service;
2. A governance body, controlled by community members to develop policies related to desired effects on the target population;
3. The enumeration of desired effects on the population, which can be assessed by performing a measurement on individuals;
4. A system manager, to provide interface between governance and the system, providing a single point of accountability;
5. The organized human service system, which acts on the target population by providing services;

6. A system audit, which will measure the actual "delivered" status of target populations, that is, what has actually happened to clients; and
7. System funding, that flows through governance to the system manager, providing energy which enables the system to operate.[39]

This system is graphically illustrated in Figure 16–2. These components describe what one set of observers considers to be the structures and connecting functions of a "true" human services system.[40] As will be demonstrated, few human services integration projects actually approach the creation of new systems patterned after this example.

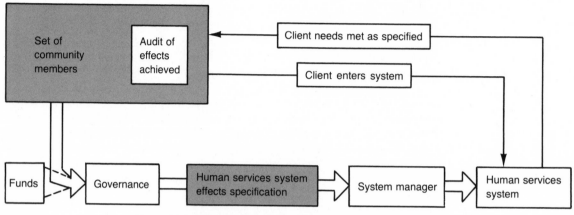

Figure 16–2   Flow diagram for a comprehensive human services system. See text for further discussion. (Source: Stephen D. Mittenthal et al., *Twenty-two Allied Services* [*SITO*] *Projects Described as Human Service Systems,* Wellesley, Massachusetts, Human Ecology Institute, 1974, p. 5.)

The development process for services integration experiments has been found to involve essentially the same four phases of system building, the components of which may be summarized as follows:

1. *Phase one*—capacity building and analysis of the existing system—including integrators organizing their own staffs and developing the political support and strength needed for reform, definition of populations, needs assessment, services inventories, operations analysis associating costs with services, and possible analysis of client through-put, or pathways, through the system.
2. *Phase two*—design and feasibility study for the changed system—including the development of measureable objectives and accountability systems; design and implementation of specific governance changes; actual development of linkages; and estimation of system investment costs and benefits, including such process variables as accessibility of service and continuity of service and such output variables as change in client dependency status.
3. *Phase three*—development and implementation of the integrated system—including similar attention to objectives and accountability, governance, linkage development, and cost-benefit as phase two.
4. *Phase four*—documentation and evaluation, which is an ongoing, feedback cycle—including similar attention to objectives and accountability, governance, linkage development, and cost-benefit as phase two.[41]

Services integration experiments have varied in the quality of performance in these phases, but progress in adhering to these steps has proved to be an important evaluative device for investigating services integration progress. It may be that any community will have to consider this process.

Linking independent agencies and programs

The bringing together of autonomous units need not start with an elaborate structure. In many city governments, such as Dayton, Ohio, the role of "city coordinator of human resources" may be a part-time assignment, allocating a portion of someone's time in the mayor or city manager's office to routinely maintain liason, continuity and consistency with policy. In small cities it may be the manager who takes on this responsibility. For example, in addition to personally coordinating city programs for the elderly, juvenile corrections, and youth activity, the manager of Pasco, Washington maintains regular contact with county agencies, a Bicounty CAA and with a Bicounty Social and Educational Liason Board.

Since, as we have already indicated, most city human service programs are in some way funded by state and federal governments, many programs are coordinated through the intergovernmental relations function. In New Orleans, the mayor has centralized all federal and state funds, human services and others. An assistant to the mayor directs the operation of programs funded through non-municipal sources and another assistant is responsible for coordinating and maximizing grants and contracts. In addition, Model Cities, the Council of Aging, the Community Action Program, Manpower, and the Law Enforcement Assistance Administration (LEAA), all "relate" to the mayor's assistant (traditional departments of health, welfare, and recreation "relate" to an assistant chief administrative officer for administration). The term relate includes: formal authority, as in the case of charter agencies; formal arrangements, such as the Council on Aging which is an independent, private, nonprofit organization to which the city contributes funds and is an official designee of the city to handle matters concerning the elderly; and loose informal arrangements, such as relations with the school board, the LEAA district and the manpower body. In addition, each agency director also has direct access to the mayor and chief administrative officer, and meet with the mayor in an executive staff-like capacity. In a more limited scope, Minneapolis has an assistant city coordinator for human resources, who coordinates Model Cities, employment, and youth programs. The office has engaged in a service inventory, although planning is in a planning department. Richmond, California, conducts both planning and coordinative activities out of the planning department, whose director reports to an assistant city manager for community development. Tuscon, Arizona, has a deputy city manager with responsibility for their community development department, although they have not engaged in much cross-program planning or policy development.

One of the more concerted attempts to coordinate human services may be seen in the overall policy, planning and management functions engaged in by San Jose, California, through its office of intergovernmental affairs, which is a part of the office of the city manager. The three divisions of the intergovernmental unit and their functions are as follows:

1. *Program review and coordination,* which is responsible for maintaining systems for tracking pending and active federal and state programs; coordinating individual grant applications; operating the municipal systems related to the A-95 review process; and routing of project notifications through the city system of review.
2. *Program development and coordination,* with prime responsibility for relating city policy to programs and projects outside of City Hall, development and evaluation of program proposals to carry out city developmental policies, coordination of grant applications by outside agencies with city departments, working with various planning groups and agencies (manpower, CAA, county departments, etc.), and development and maintenance of a community participation structure.

3. *Community planning and management,* which is responsible for developing a body of policy and an overall development strategy by which priorities can be generated and proposed projects measured, including integrating planning and program development activities of all service delivery systems, provide the strategy and framework for new project applications, to explore the impact of the HUD-Annual Arrangement process on health, education, employment and training, transit and criminal justice, and to apply the experiences from the latter to the development of similar systems for defining needs, setting objectives, and developing mutually supportive projects for other service delivery systems.[42]

Each of these functions represents a specific division, having responsibility for human services and non-human services programs. The San Jose plan emanated out of the "planned variations" program of Model Cities. Its structure is one of the most comprehensive approaches to policy planning and coordination.

In some cases, human services coordination has been shifted from city hall to a lead agency. Under this form, a single operating agency is designated to take on certain policy management, planning and coordination activities in addition to their service role. Service delivery remains in the individual agencies. In Monessen, Pennsylvania, fourteen service agencies have formed a Mon Valley Health and Welfare Council and have placed leadership for integrative activities in the Mon Valley Health Center. Among the activities delegated to the lead agency are: a management data system designed to provide agencies and the Council with planning information, including sociodemographic data on users of their services and aggregate data on agency and system users; a centralized intake process, with service resource information; a computerized information system located in the health center, for basic client information; a computerized eligibility matrix and on-line capability for referrals; advocacy–intervention on behalf of the client; and tracking and "follow-along" of clients.[43] The system is coordinated by case managers, called "information specialists," who operate out of the lead agency. In this case the emphasis is on service delivery rather than policy management.

Colocation of human services agencies is another emergent form of coordination. Location of categorical agency field operations in the same place is designed to facilitate coordinated service delivery. The state of Delaware has been covered by a network of fifteen such centers, where service personnel for state departments work through their parent agency for professional and technical direction and center administrators have coordinative responsibilities, such as scheduling, developing record keeping, and office management. One of the largest colocated programs is the Crossroads Center of Dallas, Texas where over fifty state, city, and voluntary agencies are outstationed on a multibuilding campus in south Dallas. The Center is operated by the City of Dallas, and the central staff is responsible for promoting coordinated service delivery and general management. A group of generalist workers perform outreach, intake, referral, follow-up, and evaluation tasks.[44] An even more ambitious project is in the greater Brockton, Massachusetts area, where four state agencies, ten towns and their elected officials and community leaders have formed a governance body to create and operate a series of multi-service centers. In addition to operation of centers by the independent agencies, a Brockton area policy group is working toward the development of an integrated delivery system based on "client pathways" through the service system.[45]

One of the most interesting modes of linkage is the Louisville–Jefferson County nonlocational model, which links city–county public and voluntary human services agencies through an on-line computerized information system. The program, called the Human Services Coordination Alliance, is governed by a policy board, comprised of agency executives, representatives of city and county governments, and a representative from the regional area development district. The operational mechanisms of the system have been developed by a central staff and technical representatives from each agency. It is comprised of: an intake, screening and referral network, containing an agency resource file; a service selection system; a standardized referral system and a client tracking system; and, a human services information system, a software system providing agency and client data for needs assessment, planning and evaluation.[46] The system operates by having each client-contact professional fill out a simple information form, enter it into the system and retrieve any necessary information; all in their own agency.

Local human services councils or consortia have been formed for other purposes as well. The Health and Welfare Planning Council of Memphis and Shelby County is the principal area human services planning agency. It also provides program development assistance to its voluntary member agencies and operates a volunteer service bureau and an information counseling and referral service. The mayor of Memphis is linked to the council through liason between the agencies under the mayor's office (manpower and CAA), through placement of juvenile delinquency planning staff on the council, and through funding and budget review of the Health and Welfare Planning Council. Five city managers in Rockingham County, New Hampshire, formed an interesting human services consortium to develop the ability to assess needs and determine priorities, build municipal capabilities for human services planning and management, and to develop an effective method for the five municipalities to compete for federal funds. The group has combined to perform a needs assessment and services inventory for the five communities as well as developing specific budgeting and evaluating tools for use by municipal officials and agency executives. A number of other "spin-offs" have resulted from these efforts: an internal evaluation of a recreation commission; the creation of a human services advisory board to assist selectmen; the formation of a task group to coordinate resources available to ease the energy-related problems of low-income citizens; and, other management reforms.[47] The previously mentioned city–county–voluntary agency cornsortium, the Council of Planning Affiliates of Lancaster County, Pennsylvania, attempts to achieve coordination through the creation and maintenance of a unified human services data base (resource data, client data, community data, administrative data, central library services, and a standardized terminology) and development of a planning framework which relates the basic components of services (direct service, service-supportive, planning, administration and information) in the county.[48] Another consortium attempt to plan and engage in the development of a coordinated delivery system was undertaken by the Community Life Association of Hartford, Connecticut, a private, nonprofit research organization. Their experimental model had four major elements: (1) a pooling of public (state welfare and aging, city departments) and private (United Way and Robert Wood Johnson Foundation) funds under a central management; (2) the use of these pooled funds to purchase services from community agencies on behalf of individual clients; 3) employment of a case management staff to assess client needs, develop a service plan, purchase the required services and monitor the delivery of service; and (4) conduct of performance measures to evaluate the effectiveness and efficiency of the services purchased.[49]

Reflecting the diversity of city human services programming, the linking of independent agencies and programs has taken a variety of forms. They range from coordination of programs inside and outside city government by a designated executive level coordinator to the actual operation of a delivery system—including public agencies—by a private body. They share the characteristic of leaving existing organizations as they are, focusing on interrelationships.

Creating new departments

Decision makers in a number of governments have decided that coordination does not go far enough in solving human services problems. They have gone on to create departments of human resources or human services out of existing departments and old divisions. The primary motivation for city level consolidation appears to be for planning and policy management, with consolidation of administration as a secondary concern and to a lesser extent, service delivery. Cities usually consolidate around Community Action, Model Cities, revenue sharing funded human services, youth and aging. The federal Housing and Community Development Act has been an added impetus to consolidation, under requirements to define the role of human services as the social services support for community development activities and subsequent allocation of funding. Bringing the activities together in a single unit, with an overall planning and management capacity was a major aim of this legislation.

An Office of Human Development was created in the Dallas city government with broad responsibilities over employment and training, youth, elderly and community assistance. Structurally it contains: an administrative unit, which is responsible for overall planning, evaluation, coordination, technical assistance and administration of city-sponsored contract administration; a direct operations unit, with a division responsible for delivering each program under the city's responsibility; and, an advisory council.

The department of human resources (DHR) in the city of Norfolk, Virginia was created by a merger of the city's department of public welfare and the Norfolk City Demonstration Agency (Model Cities). The welfare department was the state's agent for administration of public assistance and child welfare. The department operates through three divisions: an office of management planning, which is responsible for program planning and development, evaluation of programs, and administrative review of departmental operations; a division of human resources, responsible for operation of a municipal hospital, an employment and training bureau, a juvenile services bureau and a series of neighborhood services centers; and a division of social services, responsible for income maintenance and eligibility certification under public assistance. Policy planning is conducted in the city planning department, whereas the office of management planning in the DHR is responsible for developing implementation programs. Coordination of services or planning activities with providers outside of the city government are not major functions of the office. Linkages between public and non-public services are only informal, and there has not been any division of responsibility between them.[50]

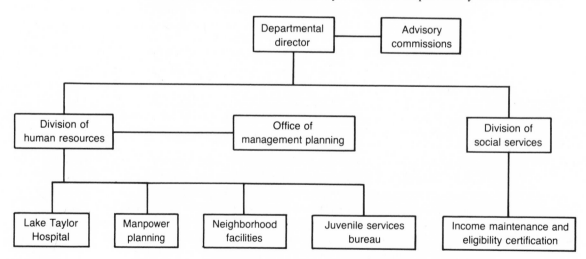

Figure 16–3 Organization chart for the Department of Human Resources of the city of Norfolk, Virginia. See text for further discussion.

One city with a merged department that has attempted to link together public and private providers into a service delivery system is Chattanooga, Tennessee.

The Human Services Department of Chattanooga was created out of that city's Community Action Agency, Model Cities Program and Concentrated Employment Program. There are four major units in the department: Administrative Services (planning, evaluation, budget); Citizen Participation; Manpower Services; and Health, Housing and Social Services. Consolidation was undertaken because of a desire to overcome ineffective and inefficient management of fiscal resources, and the lack of an adequate planning system within the city's management process.[51] The Human Service Department participates in a four-county regional coordinated management information system, Urban Management Information System, which is designed to:

Provide baseline information about the needs of people in a service area; provide for and monitor the sequencing and scheduling of services on an orderly basis; track individuals and families through the service system to ensure that they receive services as planned; and, provide information for management decisions about the amount of services individuals and families received and their progress in breaking out of the cycle of poverty.[52]

The information provided to participating agencies, including the City of Chatanooga Human Services Department, assists them in operating, managing and evaluating their own programs. The City of Chattanooga is attempting to build a service delivery component for the entire region, based on a pathway for data forms and operating procedures affecting clients. That is, the basis of the system is on actions which have to be designed and implemented in order for clients to achieve such desired states as acute medical treatment, emergency housing and income support.[53] A series of neighborhood centers have been established to provide the system's supportive services, including outreach, intake, assessment of client needs, referrals, follow-up and transportation. A report on the project reveals greater success with using management information systems to achieve efficiencies than with voluntary coordination of agencies.[54]

Developing new systems

Few instances exist of a government at any level creating an entirely new human services system. Ordinarily, the political and organizational problems involved with numerous existing agencies present significant obstacles, particularly with the existence of many loci of operation and control. For a city this problem is particularly acute because the bulk of the human services are delivered under the auspices of other governmental units or by quasi-public or voluntary agencies within the city. Also, services integration is in such an experimental phase is of the later 1970s that it is not clear what an appropriate system is. Nevertheless, there have been a few illustrative attempts to approach human services from a more systemic viewpoint.

Several cities have attempted to work toward completely integrated delivery systems on a developmental basis, including San Diego, Washington, D.C., New Haven, Conn., and Seattle. Project 86+ in San Diego is representative of these efforts. It is based on the development of interdisciplinary teams of social service practitioners whose primary function is the utilization of comprehensive social services. This sixteen-member team, which includes public assistance, social services, probation, employment and training, mental health, public health, youth employment, and probation services, is involved in planning and delivering integrated services within a pilot area.[55] Staff have been deployed to the project from the participating departments, and their activities are supported by the planning and management activities of the San Diego County human resources agency, a consolidated department.

One city that has attempted to create a new system is East Cleveland, Ohio, through the East Cleveland community human services center. Under the supervision of the city commissioners and city manager, the city department of research and program development (formerly the division of human services) is responsible for coordinating existing human services and creating new ones if needed. It is a cooperative venture with the Ohio Department of Public Welfare and HEW. After conducting a household survey needs assessment and a services inventory of over 300 agencies, the project began to establish a system which includes: an information/case management system; service delivery contracts, agreements, and cooperative arrangements among service providers; a data control system; a decision-making tool that serves as a means to communicate system failure and to propose changes in project design; and an evaluation model including effectiveness measures and methodologies. The project also contains a service unit providing communitywide resource information and counseling, transportation services for the elderly, ''tele-friend'' reassurance service, and youth job development, in addition to providing other support services, technical assistance and training.[56] Several outputs of the East Cleveland experience—the client control system, the total system feedback mechanism, the client management system, the service resource file of agency capabilities, and state policy change experiments—combine to make it one of the more noteworthy city level system changes.

Conclusion: pooling the experiences

The recency and variety of services integration projects have led to considerable interest in assessing their impact. Thus, HEW has commissioned a series of studies that attempt to develop generalizations out of these experimental efforts. None of the completed studies represent an organizational process or impact study. They merely attempt to pool the experiences into a common framework.[57]

Service integration projects have occurred in all types of communities: almost one-third in major population centers, two-fifths in small and medium-sized cities, and one-fourth in small towns and rural areas. Although considerable support and encouragement for local integration experiments has come from the federal and state governments (most were federally funded), this support is ordinarily not crucial to getting started. Not surprisingly, state encouragement for local services integration was more likely to be found in states with some form of state-unified human services agency.[58] Generally, the impetus for services integration is local.

Few local services integration projects attempted to create new systems of human service delivery. Rather, the dominant strategy was to bring together the existing elements into a more coherent system, adding support or joint administrative services. With a single exception (New York City neighborhood governments), all projects undertook centralization strategies. This is undoubtedly due to the major emphasis of services integration on using organization design to overcome the effects of decentralization.[59] Few projects start new direct service organizations, offer new services, or serve new locales. The extent of ''pure'' integration is quite minimal. Therefore local services integration can best be characterized as system development, rather than creation of entirely new human service systems.[60]

Almost all of the projects have been initiated by local public agencies. The support of local general purpose government is very important for getting a project off the ground, but not absolutely crucial. Few projects precisely followed the comprehensive planning model depicted earlier, including needs assessment, a service resource inventory, interagency planning, preparation of planning documents and evaluation, but most took one or more of these steps along the way.[61]

Although most projects included both service delivery and administrative changes, ordinarily a single objective was dominant. The major reasons for initiating a project are building planning capacity, administrative consolidation, improvement of case services, bringing a variety of services to a neighborhood, and/or the development and planning of coordinative mechanisms. The nature of the objective obviously affects the allocation of resources devoted to and the approach taken in developing linkages, and differentially impacts a new structure accordingly.[62] Continued system growth, that is, the ability to pursue additional linkages beyond initial objectives, is apparently not positively associated with any particular approach. The establishment of coordinated planning and budgeting mechanisms, case management techniques and data systems exhibited a non-significant association with subsequent growth. Projects emphasizing centralized outreach, transportation and support services are even less likely to develop further system growth.[63] The authors presenting these findings suggest that, because these latter three links do not involve agency personnel directly, it could be that the key to the growth of human services systems should require continuing interactions among agency personnel, thereby ensuring continuing dialogue, making each other aware of service gaps and duplications, and of opportunities for further integration.[64]

One very significant shortcoming of the experiments with services integration is that few have undertaken an evaluation strategy that can define outcome changes. Most projects have established general organizational or service objectives rather than specific goals or effects on clients they wish to attain.[65] Thus, one can conclude that new services integration linkages have made new services available to clients, the clientele for existing services has been expanded, the service network has become more continuous, and the services are more efficient, but one cannot, as yet, make definitive statements about whether these innovations have led to higher rates of self-sufficiency, rehabilitation, or adaptability.[66] There are many other unanswered questions about service integration, and some are quite complex. For example, to the extent that centralized core services reduce duplication and result in cost savings, such savings are "traded off" by administrative costs for the implementation and maintenance of complex management systems. Yet these investments can be said to be a protection of a public investment in human resource development, contributing to efficiency. Clearly, many local government managers will agree that a research agenda on services integration is necessary, incorporating such assumptions and trade-offs, and measuring outcomes against goals.

Problems and issues in local government services integration

Services integration at the city level, like that at any other level, operates within a context. A services integration context would include the existing structure of government, the political configuration, the type and extent of services offered, the role and attitudes of service providers and provider agencies, and available technologies. Each setting provides a different configuration of the elements of the context, and thus there has not proved to be a single way to deal with the problems. There are, however, some commonalities and experiences at each level that provide a context of considerations for integration, including those for cities. As with any emergent concern in local government, the problems encountered in generating appropriate managerial, administrative, and operational roles should not be underestimated. The following discussion focuses on three items: the limited role for cities; the importance of government structure; and the all-important role of political factors.

Limited role for cities

The limited role of cities in human services compared to other governments is clearly of primary concern. Federal and state legislation restricts the role of cities in many human resource functions. Most HEW federal–state programs are operated at the local level by counties or state subunit organizations. To the extent that municipalities are involved in such programs, support often comes indirectly through grants or purchase of services. In only a few instances have operational responsibilities for state programs been transferred to the cities. Some cities are involved in joint city–county departments, usually with the county as the lead or operational agency. This means that service delivery "systems" are split between direct state, county and local entities, plus the voluntary agencies. Thus, Gans and Horton conclude that the concept of local human resources agencies in municipal governments has stemmed from the consolidation concepts that give rise to community development departments, but it is a concept far from reality because of the very real jurisdictional limitations on cities in human services.[67]

Nevertheless, as the coverage of this book itself indicates, the emergence of the cities in human services areas, particularly employment and training, aging and the youth/drugs complex of both public safety and social services, blended with the influence of Model Cities, Community Action, Revenue Sharing and Community Development, leads to the inescapable conclusion that local officials are resigned to "the irreversibility of more than a decade of increasing local participation in social programming."[68] Cities now have these programs and feel the need to efficiently manage them and effectively deliver services. The emergent management approach, linked services, however, is largely beyond the means of cities because the bulk of the services lie outside of their hands, at other public levels or in the private sector. Moreover, a number of municipal officials have expressed the feeling that most federal interest in services integration lies primarily within the purview of HEW-administered programs, not all of those covered by cities.[69] Yet, the city is the highly visible entity wherein the most complex human problems are embedded, and is the location where most programs meet people. Any attempt to foster a multi-service concept, whether planning, organization, or delivery, must come to grips with a role for cities.

While recognizing the inevitable role for cities in integration, it is also important to note the ambivalence and confusion of local officials about respective roles in services integration. It has been noted there is presently greater concern at city halls for coherent policy development than there is for assuming responsibility for operating programs. Many city officials are quite comfortable with their role as funders, monitors and coordinators. There is also the understandable confusion of local officials regarding federal intent and levels of funding for social programs, particularly as administrations change at the national level, as in the case of the 1976 elections. The associated uncertainty generated by national debates over income versus service strategies, national health insurance, consolidation of grant programs into special revenue sharing bloc grants, and cutting back on spending for social programs makes it hard to map out a future.

Another category of uncertainty is interlocal in nature. Which level of local government is to play the role of integrator under an allied services strategy, that mandates local coordination? What will the outcomes of interlocal negotiation and bargaining be regarding the issues of required coordination?[70]

Even without legislated coordination between governments, however, issues of interlocal cooperation are preeminent. With cities, counties, councils of governments, substate districts and special districts involved in human services programming, development of new human services systems is particularly problematic. Even coordination is an increasingly difficult task, but somehow the relationships will inevitably have to be forged. There are some who claim that counties are the logical primary coordinating jurisdiction, given their historical prime responsibility for the bulk of local human services. Many city officials would not resist this, if they could have an equal partnership in policy development, and the system was clearly defined with distinct service boundaries, service agreements, purchase of services, and the like.

Whether there is to be a comprehensive interlocal human services system or not, the fact that cities are inextricably engaged in human services programming means that they cannot avoid putting the pieces together for the present. Realism dictates that city elected and administrative leadership *must* engage in policy management. A study on the roles of cities in human services by the U.S. Conference of Mayors/National League of Cities suggested that this function should include: 1) setting of broad goals, ranging across programs; 2) setting priorities among programs explicitly reflected in plans and budgets; 3) establishing a time frame which is more than reactive and extends beyond the next budgetary year; 4) incorporation of effectiveness measures, such as program impact on beneficiaries; 5) operational techniques designed to implement policy, such as management by objectives; and 6) review and approval of policy by final authority levels in local government, i.e., the chief executive and city council.[71]

The importance of government structure

The structure of government is a very important consideration for human services integration. As will be elaborated upon in the discussion of political factors which follows, federal government organization itself stands as a prime example of significant barriers. Many conflicting rules and regulations of categorical programs present road blocks to integrated planning and delivery, which perpetuate the informal vertical–functional system. It is hoped—from the perspective of the later 1970s—that Title XX of the Social Security Act, providing social services to a broad population on a flexible basis, will serve as a catalyst for further unification.[72] At the local level, the ability of a unit of government to effect integration is related to its structure. Generally the human service structure one can create is dependent on the amount of self-determination granted by the state. The greater the amount of self-determination, for example through home rule, the more flexibility a city will have in responding creatively to problems in human services delivery.[73]

Another structural factor is the configuration of human services within a local area. In states that have reorganized, they have rationalized service boundaries of various programs, making it easier to work with programs, if not units of government. Thus, one no longer has to relate to one mental health district, another health planning district, and yet other social services and vocational rehabilitation jurisdictions. States that have a strong county-administered tradition for their welfare, health, children's services and vocational rehabilitation are said to make state level integration more difficult. It could well be that county departments with independent traditions in these same states can hold out against local integration. On the other hand, it would seem logical that these counties would have more freedom to act without concern for state constraints if they so wished. At any rate, the creation of revised human services systems is dependent on the relationship of human services agencies to the governmental structures of an area.

Political factors

Last, but certainly not least, it is vitally important to consider the political dimensions of services integration. The foremost political consideration is that services integration always involves a struggle for power. Its primary effect is to transfer control from the advocates of narrow interests to those with broader interests, from specialists to generalists, and from the managers of programs to the managers of policy. Laurence Lynn's study of the politics of Florida's reorganization to a statewide integrated model illustrates the aspects of power contained in that case:

. . . Proposing reorganization may represent a symbolic declaration of intent to challenge entrenched interests, to take the initiative on behalf of those seeking to change or "shake up" the system. It may represent a more specific political challenge to specific vested interests, a means of putting these interests and their protectors on the defensive and of eroding their power and credibility. It may represent an attempt to gain greater control over an existing organization and its resources by mandating change and then controlling or influencing the steps necessary to carry it out, e.g., the filling of new positions, the reallocation of payroll and budgets, the definition or refocusing of organizational missions. Depending on the form it takes, reorganization may be seen as a way to increase the scope of an agency's responsibilities and enlarge its budget and personnel, as a way to weaken or eliminate competing organizations, or as a way of increasing the visibility and apparent priority of an agency's missions and programs. Reorganization may signal a desire to "do something" about a problem when it is not clear what should be done.[74]

He concludes that viewing reorganization in this context means: that different parties to the issue can be expected to react, in large measure, depending on whether they stand to gain or lose by the change; that the actual resolution of the issue can be expected to depend on the relative political power of the actors involved in the decision; and that the issue of integration itself is unlikely to become a serious issue unless a relatively powerful political actor sees sufficient advantage in it to warrant sustained advocacy.[75]

Many local government managers would agree that another consideration in services integration is that it is not to be understood as a popular movement. Ordinarily, services integration has no constituency to speak of. Indeed, the major constituencies for human services programs generally align with the opposition to integration. The chief proponents are usually a few elected officials, generalist public administrators, professionals with a human service outlook, and some agency board members who have become frustrated by the experience of having to work with a panopoly of programs. Among these groups there is a concern for developing more comprehensive policies, developing clearer lines of responsibility and accountability, making wiser use of scarce dollars, developing organizations and systems that meet policy objectives and human needs, and delivering services that actually help people. These global objectives are pitted against the very real demands to provide dollars for social workers, psychologists, nurses, physicians, special educators, activity therapists, speech therapists, and rehabilitation counselors for clients who are in the waiting rooms of the agencies. The political support is in the independent agencies and programs. Professional employees, their academic professional trainers, and the prestigious citizens that make up the advisory or governing boards have the expertise and the power to protect the interests of specialization. They can easily see the implications of integration—loss of agency and professional autonomy—and are likely to resist it. As for clients, however fruitful the benefits of integration may ultimately be to them, it is commonly known that, in this American context, they are not generally powerful advocates of their own interests within programs,[76] let alone with the complexities of service integration. This often leaves the small core of supporters standing alone.

The mode of agency operation, public or voluntary, mitigates services integration. Local service programs are the embodiment of professional expertise pertaining to specialized problems. The community, either through a voluntary board or elected officials, has indirectly put their trust in these well trained persons to deal with human problems, according to the tenets of their professionalism. These tenets include the freedom to deal with a client according to their professional training, norms and outlook. Often this precludes looking at the complex of needs as expressed by the client, or any concern for those problems which are beyond the expertise of the professional. Prospective clients who did not fit into the mode are deflected away, and of little concern to most professionals. With the exception of non-categorical neighborhood multi-service centers employing indigenous paraprofessionals, the agencies are not structured to handle multi-service needs. They bring specialists together with people who have specialized needs, or to deal with a single need of persons who have more than one.

The key problem, then, is to preserve the special mission and unique contribution of the independent categorical agency, yet meet the concerns that services integration addresses. Specialists and the specialities are obviously needed. Services integration suggests they are needed within a new, coherent framework. It is a significant boundary problem, raising many questions. When is the problem something beyond the agency's expertise? When does the client need other services? When is the agency using public funds for purposes out of tune with public intent? When is the configuration of programs contributing to waste, inefficiency and duplication? These questions are significant "turf" or "public interest" questions, depending on whose ox is gored. What to one side is preserving the professional mission of serving a need is to the other side managing public policy in the public interest.

Funding is another issue connected to specialization. The system of fragmented categorical funding, going directly to service departments and agencies supports the existing system. More than 99 percent of federal project and formula grants administered by HEW are channeled to individual agencies. The integrating agents have to rely on the good will of the service providers, because rarely do they have the fiscal weapons to accompany the organizational ones. There is little discretionary money to speak of; most of the consolidated departments depicted here really combine categorical programs. Title XX is a new tool for cross-category funding, but it is largely in the hands of state planners. If all or most of the money would go through the integrators, service providers would be dependent on them for their budgets, and integrators would have more control, and they could ensure greater cooperation. A series of national–state changes in funding patterns to a more centralized human services function, should result in basic changes in accountability and organization, away from provider organizational and professional loyalties toward client needs.

Categorical funding patterns, however, are only one among several federal barriers placed before managers in general purpose governments as they deal with human services programs. In a survey of planners, budget officers, and program administrators investigating federal–state–local interrelationships in administering HEW programs, it was revealed that, in addition to funding rules, compliance requirements, categorical eligibility and service restrictions, organizational and structural requirements, geographical districting requirements, advisory group requirements, sign-off regulations, out-of-sequence application times, difficulties in anticipating federal resources, and difficulties in locating federal responsibilities also present significant barriers to services integration.[77] The survey was appropriately titled, *Ties That Bind.* Thus, despite the federal encouragement of integration described above, one must conclude with Sidney Gardner that "the policy environment for HEW's efforts to expand general purpose government involvement in human services integration was mixed . . . characterized by both new managerial incentives and some sizeable political *disincentives* to seek such involvement." [78]

Anyone who has concluded that most services integration efforts have thus far relied on voluntary coordination and its attendant administrative weaknesses has arrived at the correct conclusion. Few local experiments have the benefit of mandated linkages or the support of meaningful legislative changes. Independent programs that are linked give the integrator only the modest tools of being at the center of information, operation of the linkage mechanisms, and perhaps the support of the top political leadership. The departments and agencies have the operating resources, the clients, and their own set of political supporters. New departments are constrained by the categorical funding and rule-making patterns which make it necessary to perpetuate "divisions," with their own sets of operating resources and clientele. To be sure, a new department may be able to assess needs, plan, allocate resources, evaluate and perform central administrative services on a more comprehensive and efficient basis, but it almost always is within the context of predetermined operations. As any administrator knows, only a small proportion of the resources are committed to non-operational functions. This reduces the role of the integrator to that of an informer, negotiator, bargainer, and facilitator of cooperation within a system rather than that of a director of a new authority structure.

It appears that more fundamental systems change may be necessary to achieve the aims of services integration. The illustrations of services integration presented here reveal that managing the local human service matrix has been largely within the system as it now exists. It is basically tinkering with the old system, relying on the existing agencies to continue to deliver their services. Whether a series of coordinative linkages between free standing agencies are established or programs are consolidated into a new department, little has been done to alter the basic operations of individual programs. Unified budgeting, joint funding, purchase of services, fund transfers, joint planning, mutual operating policies, joint programming and the like are largely built upon what is there. It is easy for the reader to conclude that few, if any, changes have been made. From the standpoint of the organizational designer, the innovations are weak structural solutions.

From the standpoint of the realities of the American system of administrative organizations, these linkages are, however, a step in the direction of "public" management. The juxtaposition of multiple categorical agency responses to various clientele interests with the need to manage an integrated human service system is a reflection of the ambivalence between a more executive leadership (managerial-centered) philosophy and a more representative, democratic bureaucracy that is part of public administration theory and practice.[79] One can argue that the intent of services integration is to facilitate executive leadership, support policy development, create a semblance of public accountability, move toward rational organization, meet public needs and attempt to match public programs with public goals within a framework of democratic administration. Using these principles as standards of achievement, one can say that we are, indeed, achieving some success with services integration.

Fundamental success will ultimately rest on the adoption of national social policy. Until the myriad of human services programs are turned into coherent policies, reflecting comprehensive approaches to agreed upon goals, service integration will be difficult. Despite problems in inconsistency and lack of coordination of component units, it is much easier to identify a national security policy, an economic policy, a transportation policy or an agricultural policy than it is to think in terms of policies that support human development. Instead of programs, policies are needed that are targeted to maintenance of self-sufficiency, preservation of living in the community, maintenance of given levels of health and retention of employment over time, independent of categorical services. Only linkage mechanisms—coordinative devices, cooperative endeavors, review and sign-off procedures, central clearance—not programs that are based on the primacy of reaching national goals presently exist.[80] If social programs followed policies it would be easier to plan, organize and develop accountability at all levels.

Conclusion

The requisites of establishing a comprehensive human services system are indigenous to the local governmental setting. Each community will have to develop their own, based on its structure and traditions. Frank Carlucci, former Undersecretary of HEW, has testified that a sound system should attempt to: place the needs of people ahead of organizational interests; be community-based and capable of planning, conducting and evaluating the comprehensive delivery of human services across agency lines; be capable of making a comprehensive assessment of a person's multiple needs for services at a single entry point, then take the responsibility for ensuring that appropriate services are provided; and be accountable to the governmental leadership of the community if it is to be fully responsive to the needs of people.[81]

Shifting existing services toward a more integrative system need not be an elaborate undertaking. Alfred Kahn once suggested a very simple service network: an access system, or numerous neighborhood information centers charged with giving people information and options, and allowing for selection and monitoring; generalist social service offices that would offer general counseling and manage the case if specialized services are needed; and specialized programs.[82]

The previous enumeration of weak supports for program unification of services does not necessarily mean that change is impossible. In addition to important national and state level encouragement, a numerically small but influential set of elected officials and public administrators can create a local environment that is responsive to change in human service delivery. In many categorical programs there are some providers and citizen advocates who recognize the need for creating some means to serve the multi-problem client. Moreover, there are some activists in the community whose activities go beyond the interests of a single agency or program and can be united for action. This group would be made up of people who are interested in general community development, either on their own or through such vehicles as neighborhood action groups, community councils or neighborhood development corporations. These important actors in the local structure, are interested in, or have a stake in, improving the public service delivery system In the final analysis, however, the governmental leaders of the community must assert themselves.

1   Walter I. Trattner, *From Poor Law to Welfare State* (New York: Free Press, 1974), p. 84.

2   William A. Lucas, Karen Heald, and Mary Vogel, *The 1975 Census of Local Services Integration,* working note prepared for the Department of Health, Education, and Welfare (Santa Monica, Calif.: Rand Corporation, 1975), p. 2.

3   Alfred J. Kahn, *Social Policy and Social Services* (New York: Random House, 1973), pp. 37–41.

4   Ibid., p. 62.

5   *Opportunities for Municipal Participation in Human Services* (Durham, New Hamp.: New England Municipal Center, 1975), unpaged.

6   Neil Gilbert, "Assessing Service Delivery Methods: Some Unsettled Questions," *Welfare in Review* 10 (May/June 1973): 25.

7   New York State Temporary Commission to Revise the Social Services Law, *New York City and The Social Services: Selected Bronx Communities,* Interim Study Report no. 5 (Albany: New York State Temporary Commission to Revise the Social Services Law, 1973), p. 1.

8   Testimony of Frank Carlucci, Under Secretary of the Department of Health, Education, and Welfare, before the Committee on Education and Labor, U.S. House of Representatives, on the Allied Services Act, 10 July 1974, p. 2.

9   "Strengthening Public Management in the Intergovernmental System," *Public Administration Review* 35 (December 1975): 701.

10 Ibid.

11 U.S., Department of Housing and Urban Development, *The Changing Demand for Local Capacity: An Analysis of Functional Programming and Policy Planning,* Community Development Evaluation Series no. 12 (Washington, D.C.: Government Printing Office, 1972), pp. 17–25.

12 National League of Cities/U.S. Conference of Mayors, *A Study of the Roles For Cities Under the Allied Services Approach of the Department of Health, Education and Welfare* (Washington, D.C.: National League of Cities/U.S. Conference of Mayors, 1974), p. 96.

13 Sheldon P. Gans and Gerald T. Horton, *Integration of Human Services: The State and Municipal Levels* (New York: Praeger Publishers, 1975), p. 36.

14 Lyle M. Spencer, Jr., "Planning and Organizing Human Services Delivery Systems," *Proceedings of a Seminar on Human Services Integration,* sponsored by the Social Welfare Research Institute (Denver: University of Denver, 1973), pp. 14–15.

15 Gans and Horton, *Integration of Human Services,* p. 36; Lucas, Heald, and Vogel, *The 1975 Census,* pp. 70–71.

16 Joseph A. Kershaw, *Government Against Poverty* (Chicago: Markham, 1970), pp. 45–47.

17 James L. Sundquist, *Making Federalism Work: A Study of Program Coordination at the Community Level* (Washington, D.C.: Brookings Institution, 1969), pp. 74–75.

18 Department of Housing and Urban Development, *Changing Demand for Local Capacity,* p. 5.

19 Sundquist, *Making Federalism Work,* p. 103.

20 National League of Cities/U.S. Conference Mayors, *The Cities, the States and the HEW System* (Washington, D.C.: National League of Cities/U.S. Conference of Mayors, 1972), p. 40.

21 For a review and discussion of these mechanisms at the city level, see U.S., Department of Housing and Urban Development, *Coordinating Federal Assistance in the Community: Use of Selected Mechanisms for Planning and Coordinating Federal Programs,* Community Development Evaluation Series no. 8 (Washington, D.C.: Government Printing Office, 1972), pp. 21–34.

22 Ibid., pp. 12–13.

23 Several overviews of SITO projects are referenced in this chapter, including those in notes 2, 13, 24, 26, 39, and 50.

24 Council of State Governments, *Human Services Integration: State Functions in Implementation* (Lexington, Ky.: Council of State Governments, 1974), p. 1.

25 Ibid., pp. 24–25. For a detailed analysis of states representative of these models see Robert Agranoff, ed., *Coping With the Demands for Change within Human Services Administration* (Washington, D.C.: American Society for Public Administration, 1977), chaps. 3–7.

26 National Association of Counties, Research Foundation, *Human Services Integration at the Community Level: A Six County Report* (Washington: National Association of Counties, 1974), p. 8.

27 Minnesota State Planning Agency, *Human Services Integration Planning: A Case Study* (St. Paul: Minnesota State Planning Agency, 1974), unpaged.

560   *Managing Human Services*

28 Frank Baker, "From Community Mental Health to Human Services Ideology," *American Journal of Public Health* 64 (June 1974): 577.

29 For a summary of these findings, see U.S., Department of Health, Education, and Welfare, Rehabilitation Services Administration, "Research and Evaluation Strategy for Fiscal Year 1976."

30 For further details on these activities see Robert Agranoff, "Human Services Administration: Service Delivery, Service Integration and Training," in *Human Services Integration,* ed. Thomas J. Mikulecky (Washington: American Society for Public Administration, 1974), pp. 43–44.

31 Ibid., p. 44.

32 Lucas, Heald, and Vogel, *The 1975 Census,* p. 37.

33 Perry Levinson, "A Management Strategy for Departments of Human Resources: The Indirect Line Authority/Decentralization Principle," in *Human Resource Administration,* ed. Beryl Radin (Washington: Section on Human Resources Administration, American Society for Public Administration, 1975), pp. 3–4.

34 Carsten Lien, *A Design for a Multi-Service Delivery System,* report prepared for the Department of Social and Health Services, State of Washington (Menlo Park, Calif.: Stanford Research Institute, 1973), p. 19.

35 Aflred J. Kahn, "What is Social Planning?" in *Readings on Human Services Planning,* ed. Gerald Horton (Arlington, Va.: Human Services Institute for Children and Families, Inc., 1975), p. 13.

36 Jon A. Blubaugh et al., *Human Resources Development: Capacity Building for Local Government* (Lawrence, Kan.: Division of Continuing Education, University of Kansas, 1974), p. 105.

37 Keith F. Mulrooney, "A Guide to Human Resources Development in Small Cities," Management Information Service Report, International City Management Association. Reprinted and cited in Blubaugh, pp. 14–15.

38 Council of State Governments, *Human Services: A Frankwork for Decision-Making* (Lexington, Ky.: Council of State Governments, 1975), pp. 4–28.

39 Stephen D. Mittenthal et al., *Twenty-Two Allied Services (SITO) Projects Described as Human Service Systems* (Wellesley, Ma.: The Human Ecology Institute, 1974), pp. 6–9.

40 Other systems are outlined in Michael Baker, ed., *The Design of Human Service Systems* (Wellesley, Ma.: The Human Ecology Institute, 1974); Kahn, *Social Policy and Social Services,* pp. 149–53; Social Services Delivery Project, *A Conceptual Framework for the Description and Analysis of Human Service Delivery Systems* (Denver: Social Welfare Research Institute, University of Denver, 1972).

41 Spencer, pp. 21–24.

42 Department of Housing and Urban Development, *Changing Demand for Local Capacity,* pp. 73–74.

43 Robert Pecarchik and Bardin H. Nelson, Jr., "Services Integration in the Mon Valley," Mon Valley Health and Welfare Council, Inc., n.d., pp. 3–8. See also Robert Pecarchik and Bardin H. Nelson, Jr., "The Development and Capabilities of the Mon Valley Management Data System," *Health Services Reports* 88 (November 1973): 844–51.

44 Frank Breedlove, "The Crossroads Community Center Concept and Relationships," in Mikulecky, *Human Services Integration,* pp. 69–70.

45 Mittenthal, pp. C8–12.

46 Human Services Coordination Alliance "An Overview of the Human Services Coordination Alliance" (Louisville, Ky.: Human Services Coordination Alliance, 1975), pp. 4–7.

47 New England Municipal Center, *Human Services Consortium: A Combined Municipal Effort in Human Services Management* (Durham, New Hamp.: New England Municipal Center, 1975), p. 6.

48 Council of Planning Affiliates, *Integrated Human Services Information Systems: Resource Data Operation and Procedures Manual* (Lancaster, Pa.: Council of Planning Affiliates, 1975), pp. 1–3.

49 Community Life Association, "CLA Progress Report," Community Life Association, Hartford, Conn., 1975, pp. 5–6.

50 Gerald T. Horton, *Alternative Approaches to Human Services Planning* (Arlington, Va.: Human Services Institute for Children and Families, 1974), p. 129.

51 National League of Cities, *Roles for Cities Under the Allied Services Approach,* p. 112.

52 Mittenthal, p. D1.

53 Ibid., p. D11.

54 Jean Givens, *Final Report City of Chattanooga Human Resource Development Program* (Chattanooga: City of Chattanooga, 1975), p. ii.

55 Human Resources Agency, "A Report on Proposed Agency Reorganization and Integration of Human Services," Human Resources Agency, County of San Diego, California, 1976, pp. 23–24.

56 Mittenthal, pp. Q1–2.

57 William A. Lucas, *Aggregating Organizational Experience With Services Integration: Feasibility and Design* (Santa Monica, Calif.: Rand Corp., 1975), pp. 16–20.

58 Lucas, *Census of Local Services Integration,* pp. 14–26.

59 Robert Agranoff, "Organizational Design: A Tool for Policy Management," *Policy Studies Journal* 5 (Autumn 1976), p. 15.

60 Gans and Horton, *Integration of Human Services,* p. 11; Lucas, *Census of Local Human Services Integration,* p. 32; Mittenthal, p. 51.

61 Lucas, *Census of Local Services Integration,* p. 30.

62 Gans and Horton, *Integration of Human Services,* p. 14.

63 Lucas, *Census of Local Services Integration,* pp. 42–43.

64 Ibid., p. ix.

65 Mittenthal, p. 53.

66 Gans and Horton, *Integration of Human Services,* p. 10.

67 Department of Housing and Urban Development, *Changing Demand for Local Capacity,* p. 6.

68 National League of Cities, *Roles for Cities Under the Allied Services Approach,* p. 10.

69 Ibid., p. 9.

70 Ibid., p. 10.

71 Ibid., pp. 74–75.

72 Robert Morris, "Public Administration Responsibility for the Evolution of Human Resource Services," in Agranoff, *Coping with the Demands for Change Within Human Services Administration.*

73 National Association of Counties, *Human Services Integration at the Community Level,* p. 15.

74 Laurence E. Linn, Jr., "Organizing Human Services in Florida: A Study of the Policy Process," *Evaluation* 3 (1976): 61–62.

75 Ibid., p. 42.

76 Sherry R. Arnstein, "A Ladder of Citizen Participation," *Journal of the American Institute of Planners,* 35 July 1969): 3–9.

77 U.S., Department of Health, Education, and Welfare, *Ties That Bind: HEW National Management*

Planning Study (Seattle, Wash.: HEW Region X, 1976), passim.

78 Sidney Gardner, *Roles for General Purpose Governments in Services Integration* (Rockville, Md.: Project Share, 1976), p. 18.

79 Herbert Kaufman, "Emerging Conflicts in the Doctrines of Public Administration," *American Political Science Review* 50 (December 1956): 1057; Vincent Ostrom, *The Intellectual Crisis in American Public Administration* (University, Ala.: University of Alabama Press, 1974), pp. 110–11.

80 Melvin Mogulof, "Elements of a Special Revenue-Sharing Proposal for the Social Services: Goal Setting, Decatorization, Planning and Evaluation," *Social Service Review* 47 (December 1973): 599–602.

81 Carlucci. p. 9.

82 Alfred J. Kahn, "What Are Social Services?" in Horton, *A Reader in Human Services Planning*. pp. 7–8.

Part five:
The outlook

17 The outlook

[I]n periods of flux and tumult, the consensus which constitutes "public opinion" is shattered and fragmented. . . .

Something of this sort, it is clear, has been happening in the United States during the past fifteen years. There is no traditional value, no venerable cliche, that has not been challenged or inverted. . . .

In the field of mental health, for instance, Robert Coles' essay shows how, after many decades of development and debate, the psychiatric community is increasingly uncertain that there is even such a thing as "mental health," however hard it may be to define. One now hears it commonly said that people in our mental institutions are not really sick, but that society cruelly defines them as sick. . . . In recent years this chaos has come to encompass, as Sheila Rothman illustrates, the one non-political institution which is the ultimate source of social stability: the family. When people are no longer certain what a family is or should be—and, by extension, what it means to be a man, woman, or child—their uncertainty infects every other institution and every other accepted value. . . .

And how does a democratic statesman cope with such a state of affairs? . . . He [sic] will have to sponsor all sorts of "reforms" which he may not himself have much faith in, which in many cases may be more symbolic than real, and which frequently have no real bearing on the deeper sources of discontent—and which, since they rarely "cure" anything, may even have the effect of aggravating an already inflamed condition. Then, in his heart of hearts, he can only pray that the body politic is basically healthy enough to survive both its maladies and his ministrations.[1]

By this characterization of the last fifteen years, Kristol and Weaver provide one base from which to speculate about the next fifteen. Their quoted words appear in one of the first volumes released by the Commission on Critical Choices for America, a body whose mission is clearly expressed in its name. A further reading of the output produced by the 100 eminent authorities they enlisted sustains that, within human services broadly defined, almost all are being subjected to deep reevaluations, not just as to methods, but beginning with the nature of man and moving from there to realistic societal objectives and means. Certainly welfare, health services, mental health, manpower, and major elements of criminal justice are marked by more doubt and ferment than we have known in our lifetime.

For additional signs bearing on the future, turn to the world of government as President Carter takes office. Financial austerity hems in all of our governmental levels, and it does not appear transitory. "Sunset" and "zero-based" are just two of the terms arising out of a new concentration on governmental accountability. There is, furthermore, reason to believe that progress will be made in reordering and centrally managing our federal aid system to achieve greater consistency in policy and better-coordinated delivery. (That system, of course, heavily finances and determines the form of many of our human services.) And high on the nation's agenda is change in welfare and education financing; and in our health care system, changes that can profoundly affect other human services areas.

So what is the outlook? Could it be that, with the vast expansion of human services in the 1960s and thus far in the 1970s, we are now entering a period of relative stability, consolidation, refining at the edges? Something closer to the opposite—perhaps change as fundamental and sweeping as we witnessed in the 1960s and in the 1930s—would seem to be a more supportable prognostication for the next decade or so. Some new programs, but perhaps more consolidating and shaking out; some new approaches and revisions of what is considered attainable; intergovernmental financing shifts affecting the delivery of perhaps several of the major human services; further thrusts to achieve service equalization; greater stress on management and service integration; and continued experimentation with organizational arrangements in the state–local orbit—all of these are en route or appear likely.

As is always the case, there are problems in generalizing about what the outlook is in any urban services field because the situations of urban managers vary so widely. In the human services realm, some administrators directly manage a hundred services and some, none. But for every one of these urban managers, the new minimum would seem to be full awareness and acceptance of the fact that local governments, irrespective of their own direct servicing role in human services, are now looked to by their citizens to make more sense of the service package, to urge and participate in its improvement, and to assist people in securing services. Knowledge of the service network, effective relations with other governmental providers and private providers, and familiarity with the community processes and analytical tools for deciding on changes—these are increasingly expected of the urban manager. To say this is to do no more than synopsize this new "Green Book" in the ICMA series.

One more thought deserves pointing up even though Chapter 16 covers it. I refer to a management phenomenon that perhaps any urban manager, if queried, would recognize, but many have not come to think of it and use it as a management technique, a power they have, even a responsibility. It is that an urban chief executive, consciously or unconsciously but unavoidably and through many kinds of signals, shapes the "tone" or atmosphere, the service concept, and limits of behavior in the city hall or county courthouse where he serves. Even when his words and actions do not track, his principles and moral values are read, transmitted, and reflected back in the behavior of his fellow employees. This power to change the atmosphere may be the greatest force he has to improve the management of human services and, indeed, the humanity in all services.

1 Irving Kristol and Paul Weaver, "Introduction,"
   The Americans: 1976.

Selected bibliography

This bibliography is highly selective and represents informed judgments about basic materials of managerial interest in the proliferating field of human services publications of all kinds. It is intended to supplement the material footnoted in the individual chapters in this book by a selection of both local government case studies with a managerial flavor and also of basic texts and journal articles which help to set those case studies in a wider discussion of policy issues and theoretical contexts. The bibliography is arranged by chapter for the convenience of the reader, although a number of the items so listed will, of course, have reference to more than one of the many functional divisions in human services management. In order that readers may supplement the materials set out in this bibliography with other basic sources, the following brief outline identifies some of the references available in journals, year books, and the like.

A basic reference source for all human services practitioners is Project Share. Project Share is a national clearinghouse for improving the management of human services. It was established in 1975 as a major component of the Department of Health, Education, and Welfare's capacity-building program. The clearinghouse acquires, evaluates, stores, and makes available a broad range of documentation on subjects of concern, interest, and importance to those responsible for the planning, management, and delivery of human services. Project Share has an active publications program which includes the quarterly *Journal of Human Services Abstracts,* a *Bibliography Series,* a *Monograph Series,* and a newsletter. Project Share also offers a reference service specializing in nontraditional sources, which provides customized annotated bibliographies upon request. This service was utilized in locating local government case studies for incorporation into this bibliography. Further details can be obtained from Project Share, P.O. Box 2309, Rockville, Maryland 20852.

A fundamental reference source for statistics on matters of concern to human services

managers is the *Statistical Abstract of the United States,* published annually by the U.S. Bureau of the Census and obtainable from the U.S. Government Printing Office, Washington, D.C. 20402, or through any U.S. Department of Commerce district office. The annual appendix entitled "Guide to Sources of Statistics" is an invaluable guide to the many specialist statistical reference sources likely to have application to the human services field. The *Municipal Year Book* (annual, published by the International City Management Association, Washington, D.C.) and the *County Year Book* (annual, published by the International City Management Association and the National Association of Counties, Washington, D.C.) are both authoritative reference sources. Each contains detailed guides to further sources of information—organizations as well as bibliographic materials—in the field of local government management.

Two other basic reference sources may be mentioned. The two volumes of the *Policy Analysis Source Book for Social Programs: March, 1976* comprise a report prepared for the Research Applications Directorate of the National Science Foundation by RANN [Research Applied to National Needs], Division of Advanced Productivity, Research, and Technology, under Contract No. C904 (Reference NSF-RA-76-0010). It is a compilation of about 3,750 abstracts of significant books, articles, and reports concerned with policy issues and the analysis of social programs, and a list of about 775 titles recommended by experts as additional sources for policy information. It is extensively cross-referenced and indexed. *City in Print: an Urban Studies Bibliography,* edited by R. Charles Bryfogle (Agincourt, Ontario: General Learning Press, 1974), contains approximately 1,500 annotated entries relating to urban studies in the English language, many of which have significance to the human services administrator seeking to place his or her work in broader context.

Finally, the following journals are recommended for additional reference: *Evaluation,* irregularly issued experimental magazine,

Program Evaluation Resource Center, Minneapolis Medical Research Foundation, Inc.; *Harvard Business Review,* bimonthly, Harvard University Graduate School of Business Administration; *Journal of the American Institute of Planners,* quarterly, American Institute of Planners; *Policy Analysis,* quarterly, University of California Press; *Human Resources Abstracts,* bimonthly, Institute of Labor and Industrial Relations, University of Michigan–Wayne State University; *Public Administration Review,* bimonthly, American Society for Public Administration; *Public Management,* monthly, International City Management Association; *Public Policy,* quarterly, John F. Kennedy School of Government, Harvard University; *Social Casework,* monthly, Family Service Association of America; *Social Science,* quarterly, Social Science Publishing Company; and *Social Work,* four/year, National Association of Social Workers.

Part one: the role of local government in human services

1 The Human Services Function and Local Government

Freeman, Howard E., and Jones, Wyatt C. **Social Problems: Causes and Controls.** Chicago: Rand McNally and Co., 1970.

Frieden, Bernard, and Kaplan, Marshall. **Community Development and the Model Cities Legacy.** Working Paper no. 42. Cambridge, Mass.: Joint Center for Urban Studies of the Massachusetts Institute of Technology and Harvard University, November 1976.

Frieden, Bernard J., and Morris, Robert, eds. **Urban Planning and Social Policy.** New York: Basic Books, Inc., 1968.

Kahn, Alfred J., and Kamerman, Sheila B. **Social Services in the United States.** Philadelphia: Temple University Press, 1976.

National Association of Social Workers. **The Encyclopedia of Social Work,** 16th ed. New York: National Association of Social Workers, 1971.

New England Municipal Center. **Opportunities for Municipal Participation in Human Services.** Durham, New Hampshire: New England Municipal Center, August 1975.

Okun, Arthur M. **Equality and Efficiency: The Big Tradeoff.** Washington, D.C.: Brookings Institution, 1975.

Task Forces on the Organization and Delivery of Human Services. **The Future of Social Services in the United States.** Preliminary Report. Washington, D.C.: National Conference on Social Welfare, June 1976.

U.S., Department of Health, Education, and Welfare. **The Measure of Poverty: A Report to Congress as Mandated by the Education Amendments of 1974.** Washington, D.C.: Department of Health, Education, and Welfare, 1976.

2 Relations with Other Agencies Delivering Human Services

Benson, J. Kenneth, and Kunce, Joseph T. **Coordinating Human Services: A Case Study of an Interagency Network.** Columbia, Missouri: Missouri University Press, 1974.

Center for Action Research, Inc. **Interorganizational Linkages Study.** Des Moines, Iowa: Center for Action Research, Inc., 1975.

Dobmeyer, Thomas W. et al. **Improved Coordination of Human Services.** Final Report, vol. 6. Minneapolis, Minn.: Institute for Interdisciplinary Studies, 1972.

Lane Council of Governments. **Human Service Coordination and Delivery System Plan for Lane County, Oregon.** Eugene, Oregon: Lane Council of Governments, 1976.

League of California Cities. **Action Plan for the Social Responsibilities of Cities.** Berkeley, Calif.: League of California Cities. 1973.

Maryland Department of State Planning. **Present Status and Future Directions of the Human Services Planning and Coordination Project.** Baltimore: Maryland Department of State Planning, 1974.

Massachusetts League of Cities and Towns. **Report on Brockton Human Service Accountability System.** Boston: Massachusetts League of Cities and Towns, 1974.

Multnomah County Department of Human Services. **Handbook of Organization and Decentralization.** Portland, Oregon: Multnomah County Department of Human Services, 1974.

Smith, David H. et.al. **Voluntary Sector Policy Research Needs.** Washington, D.C.: Center for a Voluntary Society, 1974.

Southern Iowa Economic Development Association. **Model for the Operation of Integrated Services in the Rural Setting.** Ottumwa, Iowa: Southern Iowa Economic Development Association, 1973.

3 The Changing Role of Local Governments

Blumstein, James F., and Martin, Eddie J., eds. **The Urban Scene in the Seventies.** Nashville, Tennessee: Vanderbilt University Press, 1974.

Gans, Sheldon, and Horton, Gerald T. **Integration of Human Services: The State and Municipal Levels.** New York: Praeger Publishers, 1975.

Gardner, Sidney. **Roles for General Purpose Government in Services Integration.** Project Share Human Services Monograph Series, no. 2. Washington, D.C.: Department of Health, Education, and Welfare, October 1976.

Moynihan, Daniel P. **Coping: Essays on the Practice of Government.** New York: Random House, 1973.

Ostrom, Elinor, ed. **The Delivery of Urban Services.** Urban Affairs Annual Review, vol. 10. Beverly Hills: Sage Publications, 1976.

Piven, Frances Fox. "The Urban Crisis: Who Got What, and Why." In **The Politics of Turmoil.** Edited by Richard A. Cloward and Frances Fox Piven. New York: Pantheon Books, 1974.

Project Share. **Roles of Cities in Human Services.** Project Share Bibliography Series, no. 3. Washington, D.C.: Department of Health, Education, and Welfare, September 1976.

Sahlein, William J. **A Neighborhood Solution to the Social Services Dilemma.** Lexington, Mass.: D.C. Heath and Company, 1973.

Sarason, Seymour. **The Creation of Settings and the Future Societies.** San Francisco: Jossey-Bass, 1972.

Part two: planning for the human services

4 Social Planning and Policy Development in Local Government

Armentrout, Edmund H., and Horton, Gerald T. **State Experiences in Social Services Planning: Eight Case Studies on Social Services Planning in Response to Title XX of the Social Security Act.** Atlanta, Ga.: The Research Group, Inc., 1976.

————. **Techniques for Needs Assessment in Social Services Planning: State Experiences and Suggested Approaches In Response to Title XX of the Social Security Act.** Atlanta, Ga.: The Research Group, Inc., 1976.

————. **Techniques for Resource Allocation in Social Service Planning: State Experiences and Suggested Approaches In Response to Title XX of the Social Security Act.** Atlanta, Ga.: The Research Group, Inc., 1976.

Brooks, Michael. **Toward a More Effective Social Planning Process.** Chicago: American Society of Planning Officials, 1970.

Erber, Ernest. **Urban Planning in Transition.** New York: Grossman Publishers, 1970.

Kahn, Alfred. **Theory and Practice of Social Planning.** New York: Russell Sage Foundation, 1969.

Mayer, Robert R. **Social Planning and Social Change.** Englewood Cliffs, N.J.: Prentice-Hall, 1972.

Miller, Joan Hutchinson, and Horton, Gerald T. **Alternative Approaches to Human Services Planning. Nine Case Studies on Human Services Planning in State, Regional, and Local Organizations.** Arlington, Va.: Human Services Institute for Children and Families, Inc., 1974.

Puget Sound Governmental Conference. **Comprehensive Human Resource Planning Guide.** Seattle, Wash.: Puget Sound Governmental Conference, 1974.

————. **Guide to Human Resource Planning for Elected Officials.** Seattle, Wash.: Puget Sound Governmental Conference, 1974.

5 Needs Assessment

Bauer, Raymond, ed. **Social Indicators.** Cambridge, Mass.: The MIT Press, 1966.

Bowers and Associates. **Guide to Needs Assessment in Community Education Programs.** Reston, Virginia: Bowers and Associates, 1976.

Florida State Department of Health and Rehabilitative Services. **Annotated Bibliography of Needs Assessment.** Tallahassee, Florida: Florida State Department of Health and Rehabilitative Services, 1975.

Gundersdorf, John. **Human Service Needs Assessment Study.** Durham, New Hampshire: New England Municipal Center, 1975.

Harrington, Michael. **The Other America: Poverty in the United States.** New York: Macmillan, 1962.

League of California Cities. **Assessing Human Needs: Handbook.** Sacramento: League of California Cities, August 1975.

Learning Institute of North Carolina. **Who Cares for Children? A Survey of Needs.** Raleigh, N.C.: North Carolina Department of Human Resources, 1972.

Moroney, Robert. **The Family and the State: Consideration for Social Policy.** London: Longmans, 1976.

Storrs, William G. et al. **Human Resource Indicators.** Arlington, Texas: Institute of Urban Studies, University of Texas, December 1974.

Warheit, George J.; Bell, Roger A.; and John J. Schwab. **Planning for Change: Needs Assessment Approaches.** Gainesville, Florida: Department of Psychiatry, Florida University, 1974.

6 Deciding on Priorities and Specific Programs

Note: see also bibliographic listing for Chapters 4 and 5.

Fukuhara, Rackham A. **Improving Effectiveness: Responsive Public Services.** Municipal Management Innovation Series, no. 10. Washington, D.C.: International City Management Association, June 1976.

Kahn, Alfred J. **Theory and Practice of Social Planning.** New York: Russell Sage Foundation, 1969.

Levine, Robert A. **Public Planning: Failure and Redirection.** New York: Basic Books, 1972.

Mulrooney, Keith F. **A Guide to Human Resources Development in Small Cities.** Management Information Service Report. Washington, D.C.: International City Management Association, October 1973.

New England Municipal Center. **Opportunities for Municipal Participation in Human Services.** Durham, New Hampshire: New England Municipal Center, 1975.

United Way of America. **The Painful Necessity of Choice.** Alexandria, Va.: United Way of America, May 1974.

Urban Management Consultants of San Francisco, Inc. **Title XX and CETA: A Coordination Guide for Title XX Administrators.** San Francisco: Urban Management Consultants, March 1976.

Part three: management of human services programs

7 Organizational Approaches for Human Services Programs

Note: see also bibliographic listings for Chapters 4 and 16.

American Society for Public Administration. **Human Services Integration.** Washington, D.C.: American Society for Public Administration, 1974.

Baker, Michael, ed. **The Design of Human Service Systems.** Wellesley, Mass.: Human Ecology Institute, 1974.

Council of State Governments. **Human Services Integration: State Functions in Implementation.** Lexington, Kentucky: Council of State Governments, 1974.

Human Ecology Institute. **The Design of Human Service Systems: An Overview.** Wellesley, Mass.: Human Ecology Institute, 1975.

Interstudy. **Information and Referral Services: The Resource File.** Minneapolis, Minn.: Interstudy, 1973.

Knight, Fred S. **Human Resources: A Multi-City Approach.** Municipal Management Innovations Series, no. 3. Washington, D.C.: International City Management Association, August 1975.

League of Kansas Municipalities. **A Guide for Human Resources Development in Local Government.** Topeka, Kansas: League of Kansas Municipalities, 1973.

Morris, Robert, et al. **Social Service Delivery Systems: Attempts to Alter Local Patterns 1970–1974: An Exploratory National Survey at Midstream.** Waltham, Mass.: Florence Heller Graduate School for Advanced Studies in Social Welfare, Brandeis University, 1975.

National Association of Counties Research Foundation. **Human Services Integration at the Community Level: A Six County Report.** Washington, D.C.: National Association of Counties Research Foundation, 1973.

8 Coordination with Intergovernmental and Private Agencies

American Institute of Certified Public Accountants. **Audits of Voluntary Health and Welfare Organizations.** New York: American Institute of Certified Public Accountants, 1974.

Board for Fundamental Education, Inc. **Unified Program for Human Services. Putting the Puzzle Together.** Indianapolis, Ind.: Board for Fundamental Education, Inc., 1975.

Commission on Private Philanthropy and Public Needs. **Giving in America: Toward a Stronger Voluntary Sector.** N.p.: Commission on Private Philanthropy and Public Needs, 1975.

Howard, Dick. **Human Resource Agencies: Creating a Regional Structure.** Lexington, Ky.: Council of State Governments, 1975.

Human Ecology Institute. **Twenty-Two Allied Services (SITO) Projects Described as Human Service Systems.** Wellesley, Mass.: Human Ecology Institute, 1974.

Maryland Department of State Planning. **Present Status and Future Directions of the Human Services Planning and Coordination Project.** Baltimore, Md.: Maryland Department of State Planning, 1974.

Michigan Department of Management and Budget, Governor's Human Services Council. **Michigan SITO Project Documentation: Intergovernmental Dimensions of Comprehensive Planning and Evaluation for Human Services in Michigan.** Lansing, Mich.: Department of Management and Budget, 1974.

New England Municipal Center. **Opportunities for Municipal Participation in Human Services.** Durham, New Hampshire: New England Municipal Center, 1975.

United Way of America. **Report on Project Rename. An Enquiry into Local United Way Organization's Role in Linking with Local Government on Human Care Services Delivery Programs.** Alexandria, Va.: United Way of America, 1974.

————. **UWASIS II: A Taxonomy of Social Goals and Human Service Programs.** Alexandria, Va.: United Way of America, 1976.

New York: Family Service Association of America, 1976.

Moak, Lennox L., and Hillhouse, Albert M. **Concepts and Practices in Local Government Finance.** Chicago: Municipal Finance Officers Association, 1975.

National Tax Journal. Vol. 29, No. 3, September 1976. (Special issue on urban fiscal problems.)

United Way of America. **Accounting and Financial Reporting.** Alexandria, Va.: United Way of America, 1974.

————. **A PPBS Approach to Budgeting Human Service Programs for United Ways.** Alexandria, Va.: United Way of America, 1972.

————. **Budgeting.** Alexandria, Va.: United Way of America, 1975.

U.S., Department of Health, Education, and Welfare. **Approaches to Budgeting and Cost Analyses.** Project Share Human Services Bibliography Series, no. 5. Washington, D.C.: Department of Health, Education, and Welfare, December 1976.

9 Management and Financial Controls

American Institute of Certified Public Accountants. **Audits of Voluntary Health and Welfare Organizations.** New York: American Institute of Certified Public Accountants, Inc., 1974.

Aronson, J. Richard, and Schwartz, Eli, eds. **Management Policies in Local Government Finance.** Washington, D.C.: International City Management Association, 1975.

Baker, Michael, and Ramm, Amy. **The Brockton Multi-Service Center Community Audit for 1975.** Brockton, Ma.: Brockton Area Human Resources Group, Inc., 1975.

Henderson, Bill, and Young, Randy. **Program Performance Budgeting: An Effective Public Management System for Evaluating Municipal Services.** Special Bulletin 1976A. Chicago: Municipal Finance Officers Association, 1976.

Manser, Gordon, and Cass, Rosemary Higgins. **Voluntarism at the Crossroads.**

10 Program Evaluation and the Management of Organizations

Guttentag, Marcia. "Models and Methods in Evaluation Research." **Journal for the Theory of Social Behavior** 1(1971).

Haveman, Robert H., and Watts, Harold. "Social Experiments as Policy Research." In **Evaluation Studies Annual Review.** Edited by Gene Glass. Beverly Hills, Calif.: Sage Publications, 1976.

Kiresuk, Thomas J. "Goal Attainment Scaling at a County Mental Health Service." In **Trends in Mental Health Evaluation.** Edited by Elizabeth Warren Markson and David Franklin Allen. Lexington, Mass.: D. C. Heath and Company, 1976.

Rocheleau, Bruce A. **Without Tears or Bombast: A Guide to Program Evaluation.** DeKalb, Ill.: Center for Governmental Studies, Northern Illinois University, 1975.

Rothman, Jack. **Planning and Organizing for Social Change: Action Principles From Social Sciences Research.** New York: Columbia University Press, 1974.

Scriven, Michael. "The Methodology of Evaluation." In **Evaluating Social Action Programs: Readings in Social Action and Education.** Edited by Carol H. Weiss. Boston: Allyn and Bacon, 1972.

Smith, Bryan C. "Process Control: A Guide to Planning." In **Evaluation of Behavioral Programs.** Edited by Park O. Davidson,

Frank W. Clark, and Leo A. Hammerlynck. Champaign, Ill.: Research Press, 1974.

Suchman, E. A. **Evaluative Research.** New York: Russell Sage Foundation, 1967.

Webb, E. J., et al. **Unobtrusive Measures: Non-reactive Research in the Social Sciences.** Chicago: Rand-McNally, 1966.

Weiss, Carol. **Evaluation Research: Methods of Assessing Program Effectiveness.** Englewood Cliffs, N.J.: Prentice-Hall, 1972.

Part four: illustrative programs

11 Human Services Programs Administered by Local Governments: An Overview

United Way of America. **UWASIS: United Way of America Services Identification System.** Alexandria, Va.: United Way of America, 1972.

————. **UWASIS II: Taxonomy of Social Goals and Human Service Programs.** Alexandria, Va.: United Way of America, 1976.

Lawrence, Carolyn B., and DeGrove, John M. "County Government Services." In **1976 County Year Book.** Washington, D.C.: National Association of Counties and International City Management Association, 1976, pp. 91–99.

12 Social Services Programs

Aaron, Henry J. **Why is Welfare So Hard to Reform?** Washington, D.C.: Brookings Institution, 1973.

Baltimore City Department of Planning. **Day Care in Baltimore. A Study of Needs, Available Services and Problems of Day Care for 0–5 Year Olds in Baltimore, Maryland.** Baltimore, Md.: Baltimore City Department of Planning, 1975.

Community Change, Inc. **Study of Consumer Participation in the Administration Process in Various Levels of HSMHA's Service Projects. Final Report.** Sausalito, Calif.: Community Change, Inc., 1972.

Day Care Consultation Service. **Toward Comprehensive Child Care.** Washington, D.C.: Day Care and Child Development Council of America, 1974.

Goldman, Karla Shepard, and Lewis, Michael. **Child Care and Public Policy: A Case Study.** Princeton, N.J.: Princeton University Press, 1976.

Goldman, Joyce, ed. **Improving Children's Services Through Better State Coordination.** Washington, D.C.: Day Care and Child Development Council of America, 1973.

Handler, Joel F. **Reforming the Poor: Welfare Policy, Federalism and Morality.** New York: Basic Books, 1972.

Keating, Tom. **Public Policy Issues in Day Care: A Dilemma on All Levels.** Claremont, Calif.: Claremont Graduate School, 1975.

Komisar, Lucy. **Down and Out in the U.S.A.: A History of Social Welfare.** New York: Grolier, Inc., 1973.

Levitan, Sol A. **Programs in Aid of the Poor for the 1970s.** Policy Studies in Employment and Welfare, no. 1. Baltimore, Md.: Johns Hopkins Press, 1969.

McClellan, Keith. **Considerations in Day Care Cost Analaysis.** Chicago, Ill.: Welfare Council of Metropolitan Chicago, 1971.

Mueller, B. Jeanne. **Systems of Service. Report No. 2: Studies of P.L. 92-603.** Ithaca, N.Y.: Cornell University, 1974.

National Institute on Alcohol Abuse and Alcoholism. **From Program to People. Towards a National Policy on Alcoholism Services and Prevention.** Washington, D.C.: National Institute on Alcohol Abuse and Alcoholism, 1974.

National Institute on Drug Abuse. **Effective Coordination of Drug Abuse Programs: A Guide to Community Action.** Rockville, Md.: National Institute on Drug Abuse, 1972.

Staffierir, J. Robert. **What Do We Believe about Child Rearing?** Washington, D.C.: Day Care and Child Development Council of America, 1973.

Steinfels, Margaret O'Brien. **Who's Minding the Children? The History and Politics of Day Care in America.** New York: Simon and Schuster, 1973.

U.S., Department of Health, Education, and Welfare, Social and Rehabilitation Services. **National Study of Social Welfare and Rehabilitation Workers, Work, and Organizational Context.** Washington, D.C.: Government Printing Office, 1973.

Thomas, Alexander, and Sillen, Samuel. **Racism and Psychiatry.** New York: Brunner and Mazel, 1972.

13 Health Programs

Abt Associates, Inc. **Case Studies of Statewide Comprehensive Health Planning. Final Report.** Cambridge, Mass.: Abt Associates, Inc., 1972.

Baumheier, Edward C.; Derr, Janel Morton; and Gage, Robert W. **Human Services in Rural America: An Assessment of Prob-**

lems, Policies, and Research. Denver, Colorado: Social Welfare Research Institute, Denver University, 1973.

Burling, Edward, et al. **Deinstitutionalization in Oregon. A Review of Services within the Human Resources System.** Salem, Oregon: Oregon Department of Human Resources, 1975.

Butts, Sarah A. **Social Services for Persons Who Are Blind. A Guide for Staff in Departments of Public Social Services.** Washington, D.C.: Community Services Administration, 1975.

Deshaies, John C., and Wallach, Harold C. **Social and Health Indicators System. Atlanta: Part 1.** Washington, D.C.: Bureau of the Census, Department of Commerce, 1974.

Dugger, James G. **New Professional: Introduction for the Human Services/Mental Health Worker.** Denver, Colorado: Metropolitan State College, 1975.

Florida Department of Health and Rehabilitative Services. **Comprehensive Services Delivery System (CSDS) Evaluation. Final Report.** Tallahassee, Florida: Florida Department of Health and Rehabilitative Services, 1974.

Fuchs, Victor R. **Who Shall Live? Health, Economics, and Social Choice.** New York: Basic Books, 1974.

Harris, Amelia. **Handicapped and Impaired in Great Britain.** London: Her Majesty's Stationery Office, Social Survey Division, Office of Population Censuses and Surveys, 1971.

Kugel, Robert B., and Shearer, Ann, eds. **Changing Patterns in Residential Services for the Mentally Retarded.** Washington, D.C.: President's Commission on Mental Retardation, 1976.

Levey, Samuel, and Loomba, Narenha B. **Health Care Administration: A Managerial Perspective.** Philadelphia: Lippincott, 1973.

McLaughlin, Curtis, and Sheldon, Alan. **The Future of Medical Care.** Cambridge, Mass.: Ballinger, 1974.

Morton, William Duke, and Muse, Robert B. **Deinstitutionalization. Initial Report.** Salem, Oregon: Oregon Department of Human Resources, 1975.

New England Municipal Center. **Evaluation of Municipal Government Health Care Roles.** Durham, New Hampshire: New England Municipal Center, 1976.

Reveley, Patricia Massey. **Deinstitutionalization: Problems and Opportunities.** Baltimore, Md.: Maryland Department of State Planning, 1976.

Roemer, Miltin I. **Evaluation of Community Health Centers.** Public Health Paper no. 48. Geneva: World Health Organization, 1972.

Steward, James C., and Crafton, Lottie Lee. **Delivery of Health Care Services to the Poor: Findings from a Review of the Current Periodical Literature.** Austin, Texas: Center for Social Work Research, University of Texas, 1975.

Westchester Community Service Council, Inc. **Community Residences: Some Perspectives and Issues. Community Residence Information Services Program.** White Plains, N.Y.: Westchester Community Service Council, Inc., 1975.

Wisconsin Department of Health and Social Services. **Proposal for Reorganization of the Wisconsin Department of Health and Social Services.** Madison, Wisconsin: Wisconsin Department of Health and Social Services, 1974.

14 Other Target Areas

Baizerman, Michael, et al. **Self-Evaluation Handbook for Hotlines and Youth Crisis Centers.** St. Paul, Minnesota: Center for Youth Development and Research, University of Minnesota, May 1976.

Butler, Robert N. **Why Survive? Being Old In America.** New York: Harper and Row, 1975.

Frieden, Bernard J. **Housing in America: 1976.** University of California, Working Paper no. 274. Berkeley, California: Institute of Urban and Regional Development, December 1976.

———— and Kaplan, Marshall. **Community Development and the Model Cities Legacy.** Working Paper no. 42. Cambridge, Mass.: Joint Center for Urban Studies of the Massachusetts Institute of Technology and Harvard University, November 1976.

———— and Kaplan, Marshall. **The Politics of Neglect: Urban Aid from Model Cities to Revenue Sharing.** Cambridge, Mass.: M.I.T. Press, 1975.

Greenawalt, Kent. **Legal Protection of Privacy: Final Report.** New York: Columbia University, 1975.

Hess, Beth B., ed. **Growing Old in America.** New Brunswick, New Jersey: Transaction Inc., 1976.

Lawton, Mortimer Powell. **Planning and Managing Housing for the Elderly.** New York: John Wiley and Sons, 1975.

Nyman, Nancy B. **Locally Funded Low- and Moderate-Income Housing Programs.** Management Information Service

Report. Washington, D.C.: International City Management Association, April 1974.

Max, Laurence, and Downs, Thomas. **Decentralized Delinquency Services in Michigan. Differential Placement and Its Impact on Program Effectiveness and Cost-Effectiveness.** Lansing, Michigan: State Department of Social Services, March 1975.

Polansky, Norman A., et al. **Profile of Neglect: A Survey of the State of Knowledge of Child Neglect.** Athens, Georgia: School of Social Work, Georgia University, 1975.

Reeb, Donald J., and Kirk, James T. **Housing the Poor.** New York: Praeger, 1973.

Solomon, Arthur P. **Housing the Urban Poor.** Cambridge, Mass.: M.I.T. Press, 1974.

Tobin, Sheldon S.; Davidson, Stephen M.; and Sack, Ann. **Effective Social Services for Older Americans.** Ann Arbor, Michigan: Institute of Gerontology, The University of Michigan–Wayne State University, 1976.

U.S., Commission on Human Rights. **The Other Side of the Tracks: A Handbook on Nondiscrimination in Municipal Services.** Clearinghouse Publication no. 49. Washington, D.C.: U.S. Commission on Human Rights, September 1974.

U.S., Congress. House. Select Committee on Aging. **Funding of Federal Programs for Older Americans.** Report No. 78-435, 94th Congress, 2nd session, September 1976.

U.S., Department of Housing and Urban Development. **Housing in the Seventies.** Washington, D.C.: Government Printing Office, 1974.

15 The Human Services Dimension in Traditional Local Government Functions

Brockton Area Human Resources Group, Inc. **Financing and Budgeting. The Brockton Integrated Human Service Delivery System.** Brockton, Mass.: Brockton Area Human Resources Group, Inc., November 1974.

Crouch, Winston W., ed. **Local Government Personnel Administration.** Washington, D.C.: International City Management Association, 1976.

Garmire, Bernard L., ed. **Local Government Police Management.** Washington, D.C.: International City Management Association, 1977.

Gilbert, William H., ed. **Public Relations in Local Government.** Washington, D.C.: International City Management Association, 1975.

International City Management Association. **Small Cities Management Training Program.** Washington, D.C.: International City Management Association, 1975.

Kroes, William H., and Hurrell, Joseph, eds. **Job Stress and the Police Officer: Identifying Stress Reduction Techniques.** Proceedings of a symposium held in Cincinnati, Ohio, 8–9 May 1975. Washington, D.C.: Department of Health, Education, and Welfare, December 1975.

New England Municipal Center. **Opportunities for Participation in Human Services.** Durham, New Hampshire: New England Municipal Center, August 1975.

Powers, Stanley Piazza; Brown, F. Gerland; and Arnold, David S., eds. **Developing the Municipal Organization.** Washington, D.C.: International City Management Association, 1974.

16 Services Integration

Agranoff, Robert, ed. **Coping with the Demands for Change within Human Services Administration.** Washington, D.C.: American Society for Public Administration, 1977.

American Society for Public Administration. **Human Services Integration: A Report of a Special Project.** Washington, D.C.: American Society for Public Administration, March 1974.

Council of State Governments. **Human Services Integration: State Functions in Implementation.** Lexington, Kentucky: Council of State Governments, 1974.

Gans, Sheldon P., and Horton, Gerald T. **Integration of Human Services: The State and Municipal Levels.** New York: Praeger Publishers, 1975.

Horton, Gerald T. **Alternative Approaches to Human Services Planning.** Arlington, Va.: Human Services Institute for Children and Families, 1974.

Minnesota State Planning Agency. **Human Services Integration Planning: A Case Study.** St. Paul, Minnesota: Human Resources Planning Unit, Minnesota State Planning Agency, February 1974.

National Association of Counties. **Human Services Integration at the Community Level: A Six County Report.** Washington, D.C.: Research Foundation, National Association of Counties, 1974.

Wulff, J. Jepson, and Baker, Michael. **Human Service System Specification.** Wellesley, Mass.: Human Ecology Institute, March 1975.

List of contributors

Persons who have contributed to this book are listed below with the editors first and the authors following in alphabetical order. A brief review of experience, training, and major points of interest in each person's background is presented. Since most of the contributors have published extensively, no attempt is made to list books, monographs, articles, or other publications.

Wayne F. Anderson (Editor, and Chapter 17) is Executive Director of the U.S. Advisory Commission on Intergovernmental Relations. He was formerly City Manager of Alexandria, Virginia, and Evanston, Illinois. He has also served as president of a welfare council and as vice president for administration of a United Fund organization. He holds bachelor's and master's degrees from the University of Wisconsin.

Bernard J. Frieden (Editor) is Professor of Urban Studies and Planning at the Massachusetts Institute of Technology. He served as Director of the Joint Center for Urban Studies of M.I.T. and Harvard University from 1971–75, and continues as a member of the center's Faculty Executive Committee. During the 1975–76 academic year, he was on leave from M.I.T. as a Guggenheim Fellow at the University of California at Berkeley, conducting research on local growth management and national housing needs. He has served as a consultant to government and industry, and has been a member of a number of White House advisory groups in the areas of housing and community development. His published work includes studies of housing policy, social planning, intergovernmental relations, and federal aid to the cities.

Michael J. Murphy (Editor, and Chapter 7) is Deputy Director, Management Development Center, the International City Management Association. He has served as Executive Director of the Model Cities agency in the city of Binghamton, New York, and as Director of Planning for Opportunities for Broome, an antipoverty agency in Broome County, New York. Prior to that, he worked with the Catholic Relief Services, in New York as assistant director for community de-

velopment activities in developing nations and in northeast Brazil as program director of a "food for peace" program. His educational background includes master's degrees from Marquette University and New York University, and doctoral work in sociology at Louvain University, Belgium.

Robert Agranoff (Chapter 16) is Associate Professor of Political Science and Director of the Center for Governmental Studies at Northern Illinois University. He holds a bachelor's degree from the University of Wisconsin at River Falls and a master's degree and doctorate from the University of Pittsburgh. He has served as chairperson of the American Society for Public Administration's Section on Human Resources Administration, and has worked extensively with various human services agencies at the local, state, and national levels.

Paul Akana (Chapter 8, "Coordination with Private Agencies") is Senior Vice President, Research, Development, and Program Evaluation Division, the United Way of America. His professional experience includes positions as Executive Director, Bay Area Social Planning Council (San Francisco); Associate Director, Health and Welfare Association (Pittsburgh); and Planning Director, Health and Welfare Council of Seattle and King County (Washington). He holds a bachelor's degree from New York University and a master's degree from the Columbia University School of Social Work.

Charles S. Berman (Chapter 12, "Public Welfare") is Assistant to the Executive Deputy Secretary for Federal Policy and Programs, Pennsylvania Department of Public Welfare. He has taught on a part-time basis at the University of Pennsylvania's School of Social Work, and has held administrative positions with a number of settlement houses, welfare planning councils, and state governments. He holds a bachelor's degree from Boston University and an M.S.W. in community organization from the Boston College Graduate School of Social Work.

Richard S. Bolan (Chapter 4) is Professor of Community Organization and Social Planning at the Boston College Graduate School of Social Work. He holds a B.E. from Yale University, an M.C.P. from the Massachusetts Institute of Technology, and a Ph.D. from New York University. Prior to his appointment at Boston College, he was associated with the Joint Center for Urban Studies of M.I.T. and Harvard University, and served in various governmental planning posts. He was the Editor of the *Journal of the American Institute of Planners* from 1971–76.

Cynthia J. DiTallo (Chapter 12, "Day Care") is a Research Associate with the Human Resources Administration of the city of New Haven, Connecticut. She worked previously in the administration's youth services unit where she participated in a study of the city's student absenteeism problem and in an evaluation of an experimental middle school program. She has also worked as a newspaper reporter. She holds a bachelor's degree in English from Albertus Magnus College in New Haven.

Joanne Doddy Fort (Chapter 14, "Housing") is Staff Director, Committee on Community and Economic Development, the National Governors' Conference. She worked on the staff of the U.S. Advisory Commission on Intergovernmental Relations, and has conducted research in the areas of housing, community development, and state and local government law. She holds a bachelor's degree in political science from Bryn Mawr College and a law degree from the University of Pennsylvania.

Sidney L. Gardner (Chapter 3) is President of Gardner Associates, a governmental consulting firm in Hartford, Connecticut. He served previously as a Deputy Assistant Secretary in the Department of Health, Education, and Welfare; as Assistant to the Mayor in New York City; and as Chairman of the city of Hartford's Commission on Aging. He holds a bachelor's degree from Occidental College and a master's degree from the Woodrow Wilson School at Princeton University.

Don Gomes (Chapter 13, "Handicapped") is Human Resources Coordinator for the city of San Leandro, California. He serves as part of the consultant network for the National Center for Voluntary Action, and is a member of various local, regional, and statewide advisory bodies, including the League of California Cities' Human Resources Development Committee. He has wide experience in the areas of aging, volunteer services, leisure services, and social planning. His educational background includes a bachelor's degree in psychology from the University of Santa Clara and work toward a master's degree in recreation and leisure studies at California State University at San Jose.

John Gundersdorf (Chapter 9) is a Senior Staff Associate with the New England Municipal Center. He worked previously as Director, Budgeting and Allocations, the Montgomery Area United Way (Alabama). He has managed a variety of human services programs, including a number designed to assist New England municipalities to improve their planning and management capabilities. He holds a bachelor's degree in government from Lehigh University and an M.P.A. from Auburn University.

Richard R. Herbert (Introductions to Parts One, Two, Three, and Four) is Senior Editor, Publications Center, the International City Management Association. His professional experience as a writer and editor includes positions as, respectively, Research Editor, Associate Editor, and Principal Editor with the *Encyclopaedia Britannica*. His educational background includes a bachelor's degree from the University of Wales, and he held a British Government Award for postgraduate research in urban affairs.

Marian R. Higgins (Chapter 13, "Mental Health") is in private practice in Peoria, Illinois, and teaches on a part-time basis at the University of Illinois Graduate School of Social Work. Her professional activities have included both management and clinical assignments in residential and outpatient psychiatric settings. She holds a bachelor's degree from Syracuse University, a master's degree in literature from Bradley University, and a master's degree in social work from the University of Illinois.

Robert M. Hunter (Chapter 14, "Youth") is Associate Professor of Sociology and Director of the Center for Action Research at the University of Colorado at Boulder. Since the late 1960s, he has directed technical assistance and policy research programs for the Department of Health, Education, and Welfare's Office of Youth Development and, in 1972, he headed the department's National Task Force on Youth Development and Delinquency Prevention in Rural America. His professional interests include capacity building for local general purpose government in the planning and management of community resources for youth. He holds a doctorate from the University of Colorado at Boulder.

Carol Jackson (Chapter 12, "Day Care") is Child Care Coordinator with the Human Resources Administration of the city of New Haven, Connecticut. She worked previously with the Education Counseling Program of the Urban League of Greater New Haven and the Youth-Tutoring-Youth Program of the New Haven Board of Education. She holds a bachelor's degree from the Hampton Institute and a master's degree in public administration from the University of New Haven.

Harold Johnson (Chapter 14, "Elderly") is Professor of Social Work at the University of Michigan where he has been a faculty member and administrator since 1969. He holds degrees from the University of Western Ontario and Wayne State University. He heads the Institute of Gerontology on the University of Michigan campus; has directed both public and voluntary social welfare agencies in the United States and Canada; and has served as consultant to local, state, and the federal governments in the areas of social welfare and urban affairs.

Thomas J. Kiresuk (Chapter 10) is Chief Clinical Psychologist and Director of Research and Program Evaluation at the Hennepin County Mental Health Service (Minnesota). He is also Director of the Program Evaluation Resource Center, a research and dissemination project funded by the National Institute of Mental Health, and Chief Editorial Reviewer for *Evaluation* magazine. He holds a doctorate in clinical psychology from the University of Minnesota, and is a Clinical Professor in the university's Graduate School and a Professor in the Medical School's Department of Psychiatry.

Aileen R. Lotz (Chapter 13, "Health") is Director, Department of Human Resources, Metropolitan Dade County (Florida). She has worked previously as Senior Administrative Assistant, County Manager's Office, Metropolitan Dade County, and as Executive Director, Government Research Council, the Miami–Dade County Chamber of Commerce. She has also served as a consultant in the area of urban governmental affairs. She holds a bachelor's degree in government from the University of Miami and has done graduate work at Florida Atlantic University.

Norman V. Lourie (Chapter 12, "Public Welfare") is the Executive Deputy Secretary for Federal Policy and Programs, Pennsylvania Department of Public Welfare. He was previously a Welfare Consultant on the staff of the Fels Institute of Local and State Government. Other professional activities include work with various voluntary child welfare and mental health agencies, university teaching, and consulting for a number of federal agencies. He is the former President of the National Association of Social Workers, the National Conference on Social Welfare, and the American Orthopsychiatric Association; and is a member of the Executive Committee of the American Public Welfare Association. He holds a master's degree in social work from Columbia University and a Doctorate of Humane Letters from Adelphi University.

Sander H. Lund (Chapter 10) is Associate Director of the Program Evaluation Resource Center in Minneapolis, and Director of Research for *Evaluation* magazine. He has also served as an evaluation consultant to a variety of human services organizations. He holds a bachelor's degree from the University of Minnesota, and has done work toward a master's degree in sociology at Mankato State University.

Robert M. Moroney (Chapter 5) is Associate Professor of Social Planning in the Department of City and Regional Planning at the University of North Carolina at Chapel Hill. He holds a bachelor's degree and a master's degree in social work from Boston College, a master's degree in public health from Harvard University, and a doctorate from the Florence Heller Graduate School for Advanced Studies in Social Welfare at Brandeis University. His professional experience includes positions with the U.S. Public Health Service and the states of New York, Pennsylvania, and Massachusetts. He has also served as a consultant in human services to a number of local and state governmental agencies, and has been a visiting scholar at the Centre for Studies in Social Policy, in London, and at the Center for the Study of Families and Children, at Vanderbilt University.

Robert Morris (Chapter 1) is Professor of Planning at the Florence Heller Graduate School for Advanced Studies in Social Welfare at Brandeis University. He holds degrees from Columbia University, Case Western Reserve University, and the University of Akron. He has served as consultant to numerous local, state, and federal human services agencies, including the Massachusetts Department of Public Welfare, the U.S. Department of Health, Education, and Welfare, and the Veterans Administration. He has also conducted research in England and Italy, and has acted as consultant to the International Assistance Agency of the Italian government.

Keith F. Mulrooney (Chapter 11) is Executive Director of the American Society for Public Administration. He was previously City Manager for the cities of Alexandria, Virginia, and Claremont, California. He holds a bachelor's degree from Stanford University and a master's degree in public administration from the University of Southern California.

Joseph B. Murphy (Chapter 12, "Counseling") is Associate Professor of Social Welfare Policy and Director of the Graduate Alcoholism Training Program at the Atlanta University School of Social Work. He holds a bachelor's degree from Fisk University, a master's degree from the University of

Michigan, and an M.S.W. from Our Lady of the Lake University. He has previously served as a Staff Planner and Researcher with the American Public Welfare Association; Interstudy, Inc. (Minneapolis); and Copeland Associates of Minneapolis.

Hugh B. Price (Chapter 12, "Day Care") is Human Resources Administrator for the city of New Haven, Connecticut. His professional experience includes a partnership in Cogen, Holt and Associates, an urban affairs consulting firm, and the position of Executive Director of the Black Coalition of New Haven. He has also been a visiting lecturer at the Yale Law School and the Columbia University Law School. He holds a bachelor's degree from Amherst College and a J.D. from the Yale Law School.

Edward Schoenberger (Chapter 6) is Deputy Director of the Institute for Local Self Government in Berkeley, California, and a Special Assistant for Human Resources with the League of California Cities. Prior to 1971, he held a number of positions in education, manpower training, and curriculum development. He is also an Editor of *Affirmative Action in Progress,* a quarterly publication of the Institute for Local Self Government and the California State Personnel Board. He holds a bachelor's degree from Antioch College and a master's degree from the University of Chicago.

Alvin N. Taylor (Chapter 2) is former Executive Director of the Bay Area Social Planning Council (San Francisco). Prior to that, he was Assistant to the City Manager, city of Oakland, California; Community Relations Consultant to the Oakland Parks and Recreation Department; and Chief of Psychiatric Social Work at the United States Army Disciplinary Barracks in Fort Gordon, Georgia. He is a member of the Planning Advisory Committee of the United Way of America. He holds a bachelor's degree and two master's degrees from the University of California at Berkeley.

Robert B. Taylor (Chapter 13, "Handicapped") is Director of Parks and Recreation for the city of Ventura, California. His professional experience includes positions with three other municipalities and as a consultant in the area of human services administration. He has also been a member of the Board of Directors of the Tri-County Area Agency on Aging in California. He holds a master's degree in international public administration from the University of Southern California.

Clifford R. Vermilya (Chapter 15) has been Town Manager of Bloomfield, Connecticut, since 1970. He was previously Town Manager of Newington, Connecticut, from 1966 to 1970; of Springfield, Vermont, from 1963 to 1966; and of Brandon, Vermont, from 1960 to 1963. He has served as President of both the Vermont and Connecticut Town and City Managers' Associations, and as President of Southeast Vermont Community Action, Inc. He holds a bachelor's degree in political science from Wesleyan University and a master's degree from the University of Connecticut.

Mary B. Warner (Chapter 14, "Minorities and Human Rights") is a free-lance researcher and writer. She holds bachelor's and master's degrees from the University of Missouri, Kansas City. Her professional experience includes positions as Assistant to the City Manager of Berkeley, California, and of Kansas City, Missouri; and as Research Analyst for the Kansas City, Missouri, Human Relations Department. She is a member of the Board of Directors of the National Association of Human Rights Workers.

John Williamson (Chapter 6) is a Technical Assistance Specialist with the Alameda County Training and Employment Board/Associated Community Action Program, based in Hayward, California. He previously served for six months as a Human Resources Research Assistant for the League of California Cities and worked in community organization and neighborhood development with the Neighborhood Services Organization in Oklahoma City, Oklahoma, and with Urban Encounter in Springfield, Ohio. He holds a bachelor's degree from Oklahoma State University in Stillwater and a master's degree in social welfare from the University of California at Berkeley.

Robert W. Wilson (Chapter 8, "Coordination with Public Agencies") is Chief Administrative Officer of Prince George's County, Maryland. He has served previously as Administrative Assistant to the County Manager of Arlington County, Virginia, and as the appointed County Executive of Fairfax County, Virginia. He has also taught political science at the American University. He holds a bachelor's degree from Shepherd State College and a master's degree from the American University.

Index

Page numbers in italics refer to illustrations.

Municipal Management Series

Managing
Human
Services

Text type
Mergenthaler VIP

Composition
Vail-Ballou Press, Inc.
Binghamton, New York

Printing and binding
The Alpine Press Inc.
South Braintree, Massachusetts

Paper
Glatfelter Offset

Production
Ruth Gregory

Design
Herbert Slobin